Teaching British Women Playwrights of the Restoration and Eighteenth Century

Modern Language Association of America
Options for Teaching

For a complete listing of titles,
see the last pages of this book.

Teaching British Women Playwrights of the Restoration and Eighteenth Century

Edited by

Bonnie Nelson and Catherine Burroughs

The Modern Language Association of America
New York 2010

Library of Congress Cataloging-in-Publication Data

Teaching British women playwrights of the Restoration and eighteenth century / edited by Bonnie Nelson and Catherine Burroughs.
p. cm. — (Options for teaching, ISSN 1079-2562 ; 30)
Includes bibliographical references and index.
ISBN 978-1-60329-082-1 (hardcover : alk. paper)
ISBN 978-1-60329-083-8 (pbk. : alk. paper)
1. English drama—Restoration, 1660–1700—History and criticism—Study and teaching. 2. English drama—Women authors—History and criticism—Study and teaching. 3. English drama—18th century—History and criticism—Study and teaching. I. Nelson, Bonnie A. II. Burroughs, Catherine B., 1958–
PR698.W6T43 2010
822'.4099287071—dc22 2010032077

Options for Teaching 30
ISSN 1079-2562

Cover illustration of the paperback edition: Close-up of Heather Robison and Gregory Linington as Letitia and Doricourt at the masquerade in *The Belle's Stratagem*, 2005. Photograph by Jenny Graham. © Oregon Shakespeare Festival

Support for the production of this volume was generously provided by the John Louis Haney Fund.

Published by The Modern Language Association of America
26 Broadway, New York, NY 10004-1789
www.mla.org

To our inspiring teachers and enthusiastic students

Contents

Bonnie Nelson and
Catherine Burroughs

Introduction

In the 1990s, as the scholarship on Restoration, eighteenth-century, and Romantic women playwrights began to increase, it was possible to include some of these playwrights in our courses. More difficult, however, was obtaining a perspective on the ways in which their newly available texts were reshaping theater history. Today, as more scholars engage in editing and analyzing plays that have previously been either unavailable or underexplored, the temptation to try to tell a single story about women and playwriting is giving way to a realization that any narratives we create are multiple and continually unfolding. This acknowledgment has guided our conception of the essays in this volume. Each was commissioned to help undergraduate and graduate teachers and their students gain a clearer sense of the kinds of plays written by Restoration and eighteenth-century women; to explore the historical and cultural issues that contextualize their writing; to bring attention to the growing research in this field; and to offer theoretical and practical suggestions for teaching these writers in the classroom.

Teachers wishing to introduce students to the work by women playwrights between 1660 and 1800 will appreciate the recent anthologies that have made their plays more accessible. Aphra Behn, Mary Pix, Catharine Trotter, Susanna Centlivre, and Hannah Cowley are each represented in *The Broadview Anthology of Restoration and Early Eighteenth-Century Drama*, edited by J. Douglas Canfield. *The Broadview Anthology of Romantic Drama*, edited by Jeffrey N. Cox and Michael Gamer, offers plays by Cowley, Elizabeth Inchbald, and Joanna Baillie. The Oxford English Drama Series has published *Eighteenth-Century Women Dramatists*, edited by Melinda C. Finberg, which features one play each by Pix, Centlivre, Elizabeth Griffith, and Cowley. The English publishers Pickering and Chatto have devoted a six-volume series to the plays of Delarivier Manley and Eliza Haywood, Pix and Trotter, Centlivre, Griffith, Cowley, and Inchbald (Hughes, *Eighteenth-Century Women Playwrights*), and meticulous editions of lesser-known dramatists such as Frances Burney and Frances Sheridan are now available. The forthcoming *Broadview Anthology of British Women Playwrights, 1777–1843*, edited by Thomas C. Crochunis and Michael Eberle-Sinatra, will highlight plays by Hannah More, Cowley, Burney, Inchbald, and Baillie.

Inspired by and spurring on this work by anthologists, scholars have offered valuable assessments of Restoration and eighteenth-century women playwrights, including the following: *Broken Boundaries: Women and Feminism in Restoration Drama*, edited by Katherine M. Quinsey; *Women, Nationalism, and the Romantic Stage: Theatre and Politics in Britain, 1780–1800*, by Betsy Bolton; and *Women in British Romantic Theatre: Drama, Performance, and Society, 1790–1840*, edited by Catherine Burroughs. In addition, *The Cambridge Companion to British Theatre, 1730–1830*, edited by Jane Moody and Daniel O'Quinn, contains a chapter by Misty G. Anderson specifically on women playwrights and one by Laura J. Rosenthal on actresses, including Margaret Woffington, Elizabeth Farren, and Hannah Pritchard. Margarete Rubik's *Early Women Dramatists, 1550–1800*; Susan Staves's *A Literary History of Women's Writing in Britain, 1660–1789*; Ellen Donkin's *Getting into the Act: Women Playwrights in London, 1776–1829*; and Anne Mellor's *Mothers of the Nation: Women's Political Writing in England, 1780–1830* are especially useful in setting the stage for understanding the historical contexts that affected the female dramatist.

Women's drama of the Restoration and eighteenth century has also received attention in critical studies that address specific topics, such as Misty G. Anderson's *Female Playwrights and Eighteenth-Century Comedy: Negotiating Marriage on the London Stage*; Jean I. Marsden's *Fatal Desire:*

Women, Sexuality, and the English Stage, 1660–1720; and Nancy Copeland's *Staging Gender in Behn and Centlivre: Women's Comedy and the Theatre.* Studies on individual playwrights include Janet Todd's *The Secret Life of Aphra Behn*; Derek Hughes's *The Theatre of Aphra Behn*; Patricia Demers's *The World of Hannah More*; Annibel Jenkins's *I'll Tell You What: The Life of Elizabeth Inchbald*; and Judith Bailey Slagle's *Joanna Baillie: A Literary Life.* Online sources have also begun to proliferate. Some of the most useful are *Early English Books Online*, *Eighteenth-Century Collections Online*, and *British Women Playwrights around 1800*, created by Thomas C. Crochunis and Michael Eberle-Sinatra. The *Brown University Women's Writers Project* covers writers from 1400 to 1850, and *The Orlando Project: Women's Writing in the British Isles from the Beginnings to the Present* offers information on women playwrights from the lesser-known Jane Wiseman to the more familiar Behn, Centlivre, Inchbald, and Cowley, among others (for additional sources, see Ziegler 334–44).

Our volume contributes to this field by addressing the long eighteenth century (covering Behn to Baillie) and shedding light on the chronological development of women's drama. It also analyzes theater as an arena for national politics and gender issues; explores stagecraft and modes of performance throughout the long eighteenth century; and compares female playwrights with their male counterparts as well as other female dramatists. The volume's essays bring together historical, critical, theoretical, theatrical, cultural, and pedagogical research that will encourage our colleagues to include these women playwrights in both undergraduate survey classes and upper-level and graduate specialty courses.

To serve a range of students and professors, the volume is divided into five parts: historical contexts, individual playwrights, the playwright-novelist, comparative approaches, and classroom strategies. Part 1, "Historical Contexts," contains background essays on theater, politics, and society. Jane Milling's essay introduces the period with an overview of some early women playwrights and their relationships with critics, theater managers, audiences, and actors. Milling argues that, although the female dramatist did face difficulties, she should be viewed not simply "as a literary figure disconnected from the mechanics of performance and the politics of theatrical industry but [rather] as an active worker within the playhouse economy." To support her view, Milling details the success of benefit nights, as well as the various ways women gained access to the theater: patronage (both literary and political); assistance from theater managers; and inside information and acumen acquired over time, since several of the women playwrights were performers. George E. Haggerty examines the contributions of the emerging female playwrights as well as the effect that the late-seventeenth-century actresses had on male actors—like Edward Kynaston—who had previously played female roles. Jacqueline Pearson adds to Haggerty's exploration and analyzes the impact of women as members of the audience and readers of plays. She also reevaluates the period since the publication of her groundbreaking book, *The Prostituted Muse: Images of Women and Women Dramatists, 1642–1737* (1988). Pearson's and Haggerty's discussions of the celebrity status of early actresses and its effect on the theater as an institution is also taken up by Catherine Burroughs, who describes the climate surrounding actresses after Sarah Siddons made her second London debut in 1782. Burroughs's essay begins where Milling's essay ends, focusing on the second half of the century and the success of particular women playwrights, despite the lingering obstacles of the Stage Licensing Act of 1737.

The heart of the volume is part 2, "Individual Playwrights," which starts appropriately with Aphra Behn, the first professional woman playwright, and ends with Joanna Baillie, whose publication of one comedy and two tragedies first appeared in 1798 in the ambitiously titled *A Series of Plays: In Which It Is Attempted to Delineate the Stronger Passions of the Mind—Each Passion Being the Subject of a Tragedy and a Comedy.* Several contributors to this section explore a playwright's canon of work, as does Victoria Myers, who investigates "how the theme of trial emerges in both Baillie's drama theory and in the rhetoric and dramaturgy of *Count Basil, The Tryal,* and *De Monfort.*" Others focus on works that have recently been anthologized or on those that have received little attention to date, as Betsy Bolton does in her exploration of Hannah Cowley's *A Bold Stroke for a Husband.* Both this play and Cowley's best-known comedy, *The Belle's Stratagem*, allude to earlier works (Susanna Centlivre's *A Bold Stroke for a Wife* and George Farquhar's *The Beaux' Stratagem*) and emphasize disguise and lovers' difficulties. But while both plays "use masks and performance to win or retrieve a beloved's affections, *Belle's Stratagem* contains its potentially transgressive energies strictly within conventional boundaries." Nora Nachumi's essay on Elizabeth Inchbald as drama critic describes the ways in which Inchbald's prefaces to *The British Theatre* "demonstrate how a woman, working in a profession almost exclusively male, can exercise judgment and write with authority." Nancy Copeland's essay focuses on the continuing popularity of Behn. Copeland reviews modern-day stage adaptations of Behn's works, especially *The*

Rover, and helps us appreciate how well these works can still speak to audiences. Misty G. Anderson's essay on Centlivre emphasizes the playwright's consummate skill in producing plays that the greatest actors of the time—such as Robert Wilks, Anne Oldfield, David Garrick, and John Philip Kemble—chose for their revivals and benefits.

Part 2 also highlights three lesser-known playwrights from a neglected but important period of British theater history, 1760 to 1780: Elizabeth Griffith, Frances Sheridan, and Hannah More. Griffith was the author of seven plays, ranging from the never-performed drama *Amana* to commercially successful comedies such as *The Double Mistake* and *The School for Rakes*. As Betty Rizzo, the editor of Griffith's plays, argues, Griffith and her protofeminism helped pave the way for a resurgence of female playwriting in the 1780s, yet she still found herself something of an anomaly during the midpoint of the century—a female playwright whose plays were actually being performed—and the result was a tendency to rein in her more radical dramaturgical impulses. Griffith had begun her theater activities as an actress; her father had been an actor and manager of Smock Alley Theatre in Dublin. This situation is similar to Sheridan's, whose husband, Thomas, was an actor and theater manager as well, even performing "one of the principal roles when her first sentimental comedy, *The Discovery*, premiered at Drury Lane in 1763" (Staves, *Literary History* 330). This play had "a good run of seventeen nights . . . enjoyed repeated revivals throughout the later years of the eighteenth century . . . [and] appeared in published form several times . . . into the nineteenth century" (Hogan and Beasley, Introduction 22). Frances Sheridan's second comedy, *The Dupe*, was not as successful. Cami D. Agan's essay explores reasons for the poor reception of the play and describes how a study of this historical reaction can reveal to students the ways in which plays are "affected initially by cultural conditions" and how "the power of later discourse [can] erase or devalue a theatrical era." The third mid-century dramatist highlighted is More, whose *Percy* not only was a huge success in its opening season but also "remain[ed] in the repertoire for the next ten years" (Newey 83). But More's apology for her theatrical writings in the preface she published with each edition of her *Works* brings into focus the ambivalence of some women who wrote for the stage—a subject that Patricia Demers analyzes in her essay—as well as the complicating factors of More's evangelical convictions.

The scarcity of new plays in the middle years of the century, especially plays by women writers, has been attributed by some to the passing of the Stage Licensing Act of 1737. Although this legislation discouraged risk taking by managers, some women writers were able to create notable dramatic experiments. As Matthew J. Kinservik has argued, "What censorship *produces* is often more important than what it prohibits" (10), and this statement is also true of the eighteenth-century sentimentalism movement, which, rather than cultivating a drama antithetical to social critique or political relevance, allowed certain writers to veil social criticism under the guise of familiar domestic situations. Inchbald, for instance, found sentimentalism to be an effective method for accomplishing her serious purposes. (See O'Quinn's essay in part 5 of this volume.) As Katharine M. Rogers explains:

> While sentimentalism might undermine the cause of women's rights by glorifying female martyrdom or exaggerating female helplessness, the movement as a whole provided an essential impetus towards feminism. . . . In fact, sentimental feeling did more than rational argument to improve the position of women. (*Feminism* 143)

Joanna Baillie, the last dramatist featured in this section, provides a bridge into the next century. Many critics have explored the significance of Baillie's "Introductory Discourse," a document that establishes the thematic and discursive contours of much of the drama, theater history, and theater criticism of the late eighteenth and early nineteenth centuries. Baillie's plan to write plays in both the comic and tragic modes that would provide audiences with opportunities to meditate on different passions—hate, remorse, fear, and love—launched one of the most ambitious projects in drama history and prompted some critics to regard her as a "female Shakespeare" (see Burroughs, *Closet Stages*).

Part 3, "The Playwright-Novelist," draws on the fact that female writers could often find more monetary success and popularity in genres other than drama. Eliza Haywood and Frances Burney are two prime examples. Haywood found the erotic novel "more remunerative than the stage" (Cotton 204), but her most popular novels (more than fifty volumes) owe a great deal to her theatrical experiences. As Catherine Ingrassia argues in this section, these novels establish "a consistent pattern of fictional female characters who are self-consciously actresses, powerfully suggesting the performative nature of social interaction and also revealing Haywood's familiarity with contemporary acting theory." Ingrassia reminds us that, although we are used to studying "genres discretely," eighteenth-century readers and authors "moved rather seamlessly among the then contiguous available genres in a commercial world not yet preoccupied with niche marketing."

We also see this "dynamic continuum" in the work of Burney, better known for her novels, especially the very popular *Evelina; or, The History of a Young Lady's Entrance into the World.* (The only play of Burney's produced on the London stage was her tragedy, *Edwy and Elgiva*, though she was writing plays at the same time as her novels.) Francesca Saggini establishes the dramatic form of *Evelina*—its three-act structure and its two entr'actes—to examine some of the ways that Burney drew on several popular stage genres of the time to construct her novel: comedy of manners, sentimental comedy, domestic tragedy, and farce. Gillian Skinner argues that Burney's plays *A Busy Day* and *The Woman-Hater* rework key plot elements of *Evelina*, each for very different purposes. One reason Burney's comedies deserve attention, explains Skinner, is that they "significantly broaden our understanding of [Burney's] treatment of class, developing concerns well explored in her novels, such as the status of trade (and those who engage in it) and anxieties about lack of breeding." Peter Sabor and Geoffrey Sill's paperback edition of Burney's plays has led to an increased scrutiny of her dramas, especially of *The Witlings.* Although this play was never staged (Burney's father worried that the supposed criticism of the Bluestockings would backfire on her successful writing career and hurt his social and professional reputation), Marjean D. Purinton's essay (in part 5 of this volume) views *The Witlings* as a productive play for encouraging students to reflect on present-day issues central to the promotion of a meaningful liberal arts education.

Elizabeth Inchbald is best known today for her novel *A Simple Story*, but essays in this volume are designed to broaden interest in her playwriting and critical careers as well. Although she was represented in her day as an antagonist to Mary Wollstonecraft, who called Inchbald "Mrs. Perfection" in her correspondences, Inchbald's plays offer impressively progressive challenges to mainstream attitudes toward marriage, divorce, the plight of the poor, and tyrannical policies at home and abroad. This last concern is portrayed in two never-performed plays, *The Massacre* and *A Case of Conscience.* Anna Lott views both plays as part of Inchbald's "revolutionary writings" and indicative of Inchbald's hatred of tyranny. *A Case of Conscience*, she argues, "depicts Inchbald's fear of despotism, encapsulated in a tyrannical father so moved by jealousy that he nearly causes the tragic dissolution of his family," a theme prominent in *A Simple Story* as well.

Because we believe that teaching plays by female playwrights alongside their more frequently studied male counterparts and other women dramatists can result in significant insights, we have designated part 4, "Comparative Approaches," for essays that focus on pairing plays and authors in the classroom. Emily Hodgson Anderson demonstrates the value of teaching Oliver Goldsmith's *She Stoops to Conquer* alongside Cowley's *The Belle's Stratagem.* Drawing on the title of Gail Finney's edited collection of essays on gender and comedy, *Look Who's Laughing*, Anderson uses the phrase to ask us "to think about how laughter, or its absence, can teach us something about audience demographics and, specifically, gender divisions." Pilar Cuder-Domínguez analyzes the ways in which Behn, Pix, and Manley pair tragedy with the concept of the "ethnic other" for their own political purposes. Tassie Gwilliam employs a cross-genre approach to explore how Haywood's novel *Fantomina* and Cowley's play *The Belle's Stratagem* make use of female disguise, as well as to draw students into a contemplation of the links between theatricality and the eighteenth-century novel. And Kathleen Leicht offers a way for students to gain a better sense of the history of the long eighteenth century by comparing Behn's *The Luckey Chance* (1686) with Cowley's *The Belle's Stratagem* (1780).

Although all the essays in this volume have pedagogical implications, those in part 5, "Classroom Strategies," are overtly concerned with some of the theoretical and practical considerations that pertain to teaching in a variety of venues—from introductory courses to graduate seminars. While focusing on how to teach the scholarship that is emerging on a wide range of Restoration and eighteenth-century women playwrights and their historical contexts, the essays also offer suggestions on what to teach. Marie E. McAllister uses Judith Milhous and Robert D. Hume's seminal text, *Producible Interpretation: Eight English Plays, 1675–1707*, to encourage her students to think about how production choices can change the tone of an entire play and how production feasibility can be used "to test the persuasiveness of different interpretations." Laura J. Rosenthal employs a cultural studies approach to historicize libertinism and prostitution in Behn's *The Rover*, and Thomas C. Crochunis emphasizes the importance of women's dramaturgical history by featuring Inchbald's *The Massacre* and Baillie's *Orra* as texts that can connect women's writing from the Romantic period to postrealist feminist drama. With the help of early English newspapers and other primary documents, Daniel O'Quinn leads his students to discover Inchbald's subtle intervention in contemporary politics with her play *Every One Has His Fault.* Ellen MacKay draws on performance theory to illuminate Centlivre's subversiveness, focusing on a moment of stuttering and its implications in the comedy *The Busie Body* (*The Busybody* in editions using modern spelling).

Serving as a segue from the volume that is a precursor to ours—Susanne Woods and Margaret P. Hannay's *Teaching Tudor and Stuart Women Writers*—the essay by Vimala C. Pasupathi gives a detailed analysis of approaches and resources for teaching Margaret Cavendish's *Bell in Campo*, composed during the closing of the London theaters some years before Behn burst on the scene. Jones DeRitter suggests that one way of piquing the interest of undergraduate students in eighteenth-century drama is by pairing Centlivre's *The Wonder: A Woman Keeps a Secret* with Ridley Scott's buddy movie *Thelma and Louise*. The dramaturg Melinda C. Finberg centers her teaching of Centlivre's *The Busybody* on the highly popular and humorous Marplot, a character Finberg sees as "an early-eighteenth-century homosexual stereotype." Cynthia Richards frames the success she has had in teaching Behn's *The Widow Ranter* by raising the question, "To whom does the New World belong?" Does Behn "champion the rebel Nathaniel Bacon . . . the Native Americans . . . the colonial council . . . [or] women like the Widow Ranter"? Also addressing the topic of Behn in the contemporary classroom, Anita Pacheco suggests how much richer *The Rover* can be if one includes an exploration of the physical properties of Restoration theaters, as well as discussions of the original actors. And, lastly, Jean I. Marsden offers her "dream course"—focused entirely on women playwrights of the Restoration and eighteenth century—as well as the rationale for her choice of plays, specific goals for the course, and appropriate assignments for both undergraduate and graduate classes.

Although the volume contains five discrete sections, several issues recur throughout, connecting the essays in ways that are designed to foster further dialogue and inquiry. One can read the sections in their entirety or range across the essays to pursue a particular topic or thematic focus. Several contributors examine the relationship between female playwrights and theater managers to evaluate the degree to which the establishment aided or hindered women writers. In her essay on Frances Brooke's *The Excursion*, Michelle Ruggaber Dougherty describes how the novelist mirrors her own real-life difficulties with David Garrick through the "ill-fated interactions" that her heroine, Maria, has with the famous manager. Rizzo also discusses the impact that Garrick had on the career of Elizabeth Griffith. And Agan addresses the theater manager's considerable power by pointing out that, although Garrick had admired Frances Sheridan's *The Discovery*, which he called "the best comedy of the age," he refused to produce her play *A Journey to Bath* (Hogan and Beasley, Introduction 13).

A fuller sense of the playhouses can be derived from the analyses of audience reception by Pearson, Haggerty, Copeland, Agan, Rizzo, and O'Quinn and from the essays that address the desire of many female playwrights to educate their audiences: Roxanne Kent-Drury's on Trotter; Demers's on More, Lott's on Inchbald, and Myers's on Baillie. Other essays emphasize these dramatists' engagement with national politics and foreign policies, as well as with philosophical, social, and educational questions of their time. Elizabeth Kubek argues that Pix's London comedies justify the political legitimacy of Queen Anne, while demonstrating that Pix was very much involved with the politics of her day. Kent-Drury explains that an examination of Catharine Trotter's plays and philosophical writings can help readers appreciate the ways in which early women writers strove to develop strategies that would enable them to participate more fully in public discourse. Misty G. Anderson offers a view of the ways in which Centlivre extended to women her Whiggish beliefs about contract. Myers places Baillie's plays in the "cultural developments [of] several areas of eighteenth-century thought and practice," such as the sentiment movement, new psychologies, and forensic medicine, and Purinton argues that Burney's *The Witlings* is "about education and learning . . . in its historical moment of late-eighteenth-century London."

The volume's essays also explore both the comedic and serious drama undertaken by women playwrights. In *Getting into the Act*, Donkin states:

> Lack of education may partly explain why women dramatists tended to gravitate towards comedy rather than tragedy, since comedy could utilize contemporary domestic situations with little risk of exposing their ignorance of classical references. (93)

Canfield and Payne offer another possibility—that "the ostensibly mimetic world of comedy may give us greater access to observing power relations that pervade everyday life . . . such power relations as the control of sexuality and gender . . . indecorous behavior, social mobility" (Introduction 11). But comedy's structure can be limiting as well. In *Female Playwrights and Eighteenth-Century Comedy*, Misty G. Anderson writes:

> Comedies end on the same cloying note with few variations: happily ever after, order restored. The security of this repetitive narrative offers

> pleasures of its own, but the laughter comedies generate comes from comic events that tap into cultural anxieties about the problems with happy endings. (3)

Indeed, the discussions in this volume clarify some of the ways "comic drama discourages, accommodates, and/or promotes change" (S. Carlson 2).

Although comedy enabled some women writers to confront directly the issues that affected them socially and although "the tragic pattern seems to have functioned as a kind of straitjacket against which the authors chafed"—as Cuder-Domínguez observes in her essay—the various ways in which Manley, Trotter, Pix, and even More "regendered tragedy" is attended to here as an important development (Merrens 32). Kent-Drury claims that, for Trotter, the theater was "a place where significant cultural conflicts might be resolved." In Trotter's moral and didactic tragedies, her characters face a number of difficult choices; by portraying female characters acting "with honor and restraint," Trotter challenges the accepted belief that men were ruled by reason and women by passion. Cuder-Domínguez observes changes in the later plays of Manley and Pix and argues that, in *The Conquest of Spain*, Pix's use of "pathos" becomes an effective weapon for questioning "both monarchy and patriarchy by showing them as equally abusive and oppressive." Demers, in her essay on More, explains how the tragedy *Percy* demonstrates a "trenchant criticism of patriarchal politics" through the fate of its heroine. The same is true of More's *Moses in the Bulrushes* (published in *Sacred Dramas*), which expresses the poignant feelings of Pharaoh's daughter when, "critical of her own father," she saves the life of the infant Moses and "understands immediately the dilemma the child's mother must have faced in a time of aggression and ethnic cleansing."

The variety of genres written during the period is underscored in several essays as well. Milling and Copeland discuss Behn's farce *The Emperor of the Moon*. Myers and Crochunis explore Baillie's variations on gothic, tragicomic, and closet drama. A number of women playwrights—along with their male counterparts—adapted or translated earlier works, as Rizzo describes in her essay on Griffith's plays: *The Platonic Wife* was adapted from a tale by Marmontel that Griffith was translating at the time, and *The Double Mistake* was adapted from a work by George Digby, Earl of Bristol, who, in turn, had taken his plot from a play by Calderón. Betsy Bolton, in her essay on *A Bold Stroke for a Husband*, reminds us of Cowley's indebtedness to English works by Thomas D'Urfey and Thomas Otway.

In *A Literary History of Women's Writing in Britain, 1660–1789*, Staves concludes that "women writers must be judged by what they accomplished in their work, not merely sympathized with because they suffered from patriarchy or from misogynistic critics" (439). By bringing to light the considerable contributions of women playwrights of the Restoration and eighteenth century, this volume aims to demonstrate that their plays were essential to the development of drama during this period and crucial to our understanding of the London stage in the modern era. Furthermore, by providing resources that will enhance courses in British literature—as well as surveys of drama and theater history, introductions to women's literature, and courses in eighteenth-century British history—we hope to secure for these early women playwrights a place in college curriculums around the country and abroad.

Part I

Historical Contexts

Jane Milling

Working in the Theater: Women Playwrights, 1660–1750

The question of why women felt inclined to write drama for the public stage is a complex one. Elizabeth Howe, among others, argues that the presence of the actress on stage empowered women to write, and Angela J. Smallwood likewise suggests that the figure of the actress offered women a natural encouragement to the stage. Others consider the first women dramatists bold exceptions, reflecting that "the cultural pressures against trying to insert one's work into a previously all-male arena must have been enormous for the female dramatist" (Findlay and Hodgson-Wright 124). Whatever motivated women dramatists to write—and behind each decision there was some combination of commercial acumen, political passion, desire for fame or self-promotion, interest in the theater itself, or financial necessity—write they did.

But there is a danger that we might use the women dramatists of the long eighteenth century to fulfill our own intellectual agendas; that is, we should be wary of searching for a female solidarity underpinned by a latent feminism. Margarete Rubik plots a course through women's dramatic writing from 1550 to 1800 and argues:

> [Despite] the disparities between the various playwrights in plot, style and tone, a number of similarities emerge, which set women's plays off from the male canon and point to the existence of an—albeit muted—female tradition in English theatre. (*Early Women Dramatists* viii)

For her, the similarities include a greater interest in active female characters, a concentration on "female friendship and solidarity," and a reinterpretation of female stereotypes (199). Yet, even as she constructs this list of similarities, Rubik admits that such aspects are also found in male-authored work and that such elements provide only a very tenuous sense of tradition. Jacqueline Pearson, even when she was specifically looking for modes of feminism in the work of Mary Pix, Catharine Trotter, and Delarivier Manley, warned "they were not a school or even a close-knit group writing together with unanimity of purpose. It was only in 1695–6 that they lent each other consistent support" (*Prostituted Muse* 169). More recently, Jean I. Marsden has briefly looked at Pix, Trotter, and Manley and commented, "If we are searching for a distinctive *écriture féminine*, it is not here" (*Fatal Desire* 130). For Marsden the only distinctive, shared aspect of these three dramatists' work was their self-awareness as "women writing in a largely male profession" (130).

Undoubtedly some women playwrights did support one another in commendatory verses in published playtexts, and many reflect on the rarity of women's writing in dedications, prefaces, and prologues. This strategy also, of course, acted to increase the sense of their unique contribution and thus increase the value of their work in the theater. While many women dramatists of the period did identify themselves as women, not all of them were convinced they would benefit from identifying themselves as individuals in the developing literary sphere. Ariadne adopted a nom de plume, and Trotter initially figured herself as "one who conceals her name to shun that of Poetress. I wish I could separate them here, for then I should be proud to own myself to the World" (*Agnes*, Dedication n. pag.).[1] Paulina Kewes has argued that as the Restoration progressed, "playwriting could now be taken seriously by writers with literary pretensions" (31) and dramatists "were increasingly thought of as individuals who carried their own identity and authority, and from whom the printed artefact originated" (30). The resistance that some early female authors had to occupying an individuated position as female playwright was connected to literary concerns. The criticism that these writers expected was indeed on the grounds of their gender, but specifically because their gender had limited their access to education and other literary qualifications. Ariadne's preface protests her "unlearn'd, ignorant of any but her mother tongue . . . I am altogether unacquainted with the stage and those Drammatick rules which others have with so much art and success observed" (A2). Likewise, in the preface to *The Lost Lover*, Manley asserts, "I am now convinc'd that Writing for the stage is in no way proper for a woman, to whom all advantages but meer Nature are refus'd" (n. pag.). We should, however, be wary of reading these disavowals of learning as entirely inflected by gender. Male playwrights, particularly those new to the stage, were also attempting to negotiate this newly esteemed role of "dramatic poet"; as Thomas Dilke humbly acknowledges, "I am heartily willing to confess my want of Ability in writing" (A3). Nor do the apologies and confessions of inability keep the women writers from the stage. Trotter offers a second, "the next I bring upon the stage" (*Agnes*, Dedication n. pag.); Ariadne promises if *She Ventures and He Wins* meets with encouragement, "I will study in my next to deserve it" (A2v); and Manley's glorious preface to *The Lost Lover* promises her "Offended Judges" immediate satisfaction, since "there is a tragedy of mine Rehearsing" (n. pag.). So for the early women dramatists it was the negotiation between gender and literary qualification that they found the most perplexing. Gender inevitably inflected their experience of writing, but we should not overemphasize their presentation of gendered reticence.

Nor should we overstate the satiric vitriol expressed against women dramatists by their contemporaries. While there are some undoubtedly unpleasant satiric verses on female poets and playwrights, not least Robert Gould's highly sexualized "The Playhouse," the theatrical portraits of female dramatists are not so easily read as simple satiric denigration. The foremost theatrical satire of women dramatists was *The Female Wits*, an anonymous comedy produced by the Patent Company in 1696, in the wake of a spate of female-authored work staged by the Patent and Actors' companies during the previous two seasons. Marsilia (Manley), Wellfed (Pix), and Calista (Trotter) are pictured discussing their writing and in the playhouse at a rehearsal of Marsilia's tragedy. The satire is self-consciously in the mode of George Villiers, Duke of Buckingham's *Rehearsal* of 1671, but there is little in the portrayal of Marsilia, the central character of the satire, that Manley has not already commented on in *The Lost Lover*, through the figure of her "Affected Poetess," Orinda. In the preface to this play and her various writings, including *Letters Written by Mrs. Manley*, which also appeared 1696, as well as in her pseudo-autobiography *The Adventures of Rivella*, which appeared much later, Manley paints a picture of herself surrounded by sycophantic admirers and supporters, as well as men of sense. When satirized as Marsilia, she is courted by Lord Whiffle, Awdwell, the man of sense who sees the error of his ways, and Praiseall, who is a version of her own Sir Courtall. There is little negative in the portrayal of Marsilia that Manley has not already presaged herself.

Even the character of Phoebe Clinkett, in John Gay, Alexander Pope, and John Arbuthnot's *Three Hours after Marriage*, has redeeming features. Despite her hysterical collapse at the burning of her work, she is portrayed as understanding how to engineer access to the playhouse for her work: by passing it off as her male friend Plotwell's and by trying to draw in the support of the critic Sir Tremendous and the leading players. Played by the lively dancer Margaret Bicknell, Phoebe Clinkett would have had an undeniably active charm in performance. The desire to read her simply as a denigration of women's drama misses the broader commentary the triumvirate is making about pretentious spectacle and the political appropriateness of the kind of drama Clinkett writes. By the time Catherine "Kitty" Clive is writing *The Rehearsal; or, Bayes in Petticoats* (1750, Drury Lane), it should be clear that our understanding of the functions of theatrical satire needs reevaluating to encompass the possibilities of parody and pastiche as mechanisms of ironic self-promotion, celebration, and homage. Like *The Female Wits*, Clive's *Rehearsal* is a self-conscious reworking of Buckingham's *Rehearsal*, still a staple of the repertoire. Buckingham was writing from outside the industry he parodied, for political purposes in denigrating John Dryden's heroic versifying, but Clive was writing from a position of considerable power inside the theatrical industry. Her portrait of the playwright Mrs. Hazard matches the self-conceit and comic overreaching of Marsilia and Phoebe, always on the lookout for a hyperbolic simile and at the mercy of the actors; a portrait topped only by the representation of Clive herself, who is "so conceited and insolent" an actress that she will neither be tutored in her role nor deign to rehearse (15).

As images of women dramatists at work in the playhouse, both *The Female Wits* and Clive's *Rehearsal* present much that helps us understand the place of the female dramatist, above and beyond the satiric commentary on their hysterical self-conceit, the plague of playwrights male and female. Both plays find it possible to represent women directing rehearsals of their work, negotiating with managers, cajoling actors and actresses into roles, offering acting suggestions to performers, even taking to the stage to demonstrate the performance requirements of their plays, summoning audiences, and generating public attention for their work among the better sort. In this we can recognize a portrait not just of the female dramatist but also of the commercial dramatist at work—not as a literary figure disconnected from the mechanics of performance and the politics of the theatrical industry but as an active worker within the playhouse economy.

We can see a shift in the kind of woman who writes for the stage during the period 1660–1750, and this shift follows the development of the theater industry and echoes the experience of male playwrights.[2] In the early years of the Restoration, aristocratic men found access to the stage with a series of celebratory comedies or heroic tragedies reflecting on the court of Charles II. The first public performances of female-authored work came from Katherine Philips, a member of the gentry, whose translation of *Pompey* (1663, Dublin) and posthumously performed *Horace* (1668) caught the public mood. The gloriously eccentric Margaret Cavendish may also have aspired to see her work performed, although it only appeared in print. However, after the first few years of the Restoration, it was more common for aristocratic women to write for the closet: Anne Wharton's *Love's Martyr* (c. 1679); Anne Finch, Countess of Winchilsea's *The Triumphs of Love and Innocence* (c. 1682) and *Aristomenes* (1690); and Lady Mary Wortley Montagu's *Simplicity* (c. 1734) were not designed for the commercial stage (Rubik, *Early Women Dramatists* 25).

As with male playwrights, after the first decade of the Restoration there was an increase in the number of new professional women playwrights. These women dramatists were commercially minded. *The London Stage* records that Frances Boothby's tragicomedy *Marcelia* (1669, King's) and Elizabeth Polwhele's tragedy *The Faithful Virgins* (1671, Duke's)[3] were relatively successful one-offs (the only performed play from these authors), whereas the first tragicomedy by Aphra Behn, *The Forc'd Marriage* (1670, Duke's), only ran for six nights but set her on a writing career that was to span twenty years. In her spirited defense of her authorship in the preface of *Sir Patient Fancy* (1678), Behn confesses herself "forced to write for Bread, and not ashamed to owne it" (Av). Among several plays by unidentified writers—such as Ephelia's *A Pair-Royal of Coxcombs* (1679, Dancing School); "A Young Lady['s]" *The Unnatural Mother* (1697, Actors'); and Ariadne's *She Ventures and He Wins* (1695, Actors')—were the first plays from three enduring professional writers, Mary Pix's *Ibrahim* (1696, Patent) and *The Spanish Wives* (1696, Patent); Catharine Trotter's *Agnes de Castro* (1695, Patent); and Delarivier Manley's *The Lost Lover* (1696, Patent) and *The Royal Mischief* (1696, Actors') (see Van Lennep et al.).

By the time the theater industry had matured and had weathered the storms of William III's accession, the turbulent party fighting of Anne's reign, and the arrival of the Hanoverian kings, the kind of professional who was writing for the stage had changed; many more actors or those involved with management were trying their hand at playwriting. In the early eighteenth century, there was a healthy crop of women writing for the stage who had had some experience acting on it. Susanna Centlivre, one of the most prolific and successful women dramatists of the period, had, according to her romantic biographers, run away from home to join an acting troupe and met her husband while performing a breeches role at court in Windsor (Chetwood 140–41; Mottley 188). Whether credence can be lent to such picaresque stories, she herself describes "stroling with her Brat a Hundred Mile" in the prologue to her *Love at a Venture* (1706, Bath). Likewise, Eliza Haywood began her career as an actress in Dublin's Smock Alley Theatre in 1715, and she moved to Lincoln's Inn Fields in London in 1717. Her playwriting sprang from a long acquaintance with the stage as a performer and her connections with the theater managers. John Rich, her manager at Lincoln's Inn Fields, asked her to make Robert Hurst's *The Fair Captive* stage-worthy in 1721 (Haywood, "Advertisement"). Other important female dramatists of the period—Jane Egleton, Charlotte Charke, Susanna Cibber, and Kitty Clive—were all actresses first and foremost.

If we look at the pattern of women's dramatic writing over the period 1660–1750, it follows the structural shifts in the industry, that is, the number and composition of acting companies and playhouses. The sudden appearance of a welter of plays by four new women dramatists in the 1695 season seems to have been precipitated by the sudden demand in the market with the split of the Actors' Company from the United Company in 1694–95. Likewise, when the two-theater system went into crisis during the years 1707–10, there was little access for new playwrights to the stage—in the 1707–08 season, only seven new plays were staged by the struggling Queen's and Drury Lane companies (Burling, "New Plays" 22).[4] When the Little Theatre in the Haymarket opened in 1720, it offered an alternative venue for writers, as did Goodman's Fields in Ayliffe Street, opened in 1729. From the late 1720s to the late 1730s, most women's writing was showcased at the Little Theatre in the Haymarket. As Vincent J. Liesenfeld charts, when moves were made to limit the number of theaters (John Barnard's Playhouse Bill) and to restrict playing in the City of London, the number of opportunities for playwrights, male and female, correspondingly declined. Although Barnard's 1735 bill was thrown out, partly assisted by Robert Walpole's resistance, in 1737 the far more restrictive Licensing Act was passed as law, which answered the complaints of the patent houses and forbade all unlicensed playing in London and the provinces. This change of heart from Walpole and the ministry is usually attributed in part to Henry Fielding's political burlesques at the Little Theatre in the Haymarket. David D. Mann and Susan Garland Mann suggest that "many dramatists besides Fielding were displaced by this political manoeuvre, and for almost twenty years there was very little dramatic writing on the part of women; some, like Haywood, turned to prose fiction" (2). For all its bombast, the Licensing Act was not the end for unlicensed London theaters, as illustrated by the career of Charke, who had briefly established her own company in 1735 at the York Buildings and presented *Tit for Tat* at James Street in 1743, or Rachel Hoper, who wrote successfully for Goodman's Fields and the Haymarket in the 1740s (Burling, *Summer Theatre* 90; Mann and Mann 407).

Mann and Mann suggest that other structural mechanisms of the theater may have opened opportunities for women dramatists: "[I]t may have been the benefit nights of the mid-eighteenth century that motivated several female performers to write plays" (2). For an actress to differentiate her benefit night from the many others of the season by penning a brand new afterpiece, thereby maximizing audience interest and justifying a raised ticket price, was a canny commercial move. Of course, such possibilities existed only for those players from the established patent houses and only once the evening's program of multiple performance pieces (entr'actes, afterpiece, and music) had become current. Egleton, a stalwart performer at Lincoln's Inn Fields, wrote the unpublished two-act ballad opera *The Maggot* for her benefit night there on 18 April 1732. Clive wrote the afterpiece *The Rehearsal; or, Bayes in Petticoats* for her benefit night (15 Mar. 1750, Drury Lane). Her later three farces were also designed for one-off performances on her benefit nights, although some had a longer life in the company repertoire. Susanna Cibber translated and adapted the musical afterpiece *The Oracle* for a one-off performance at her benefit night on 17 March 1752 at Covent Gardens, although it was also revived for benefit performances thereafter (Mann and Mann 113, 3). These occasional productions represent a considerable investment of time, resources, and personnel from the companies involved and are a marker of the significance of the actresses to their companies.

Conversely, authors appear to have been tempted onto the stage to perform in their own plays for their author benefit nights on the third or, if they were lucky, sixth night of a run. Penelope Aubin delivered the epilogue to her play *The Merry Masqueraders* for her third-night benefit (11 Dec. 1730). Perhaps emboldened by her brief stint as an actress at Drury Lane, Elizabeth Cooper acted in her *The Rival Widows* at Covent Garden on the two benefit nights of her six-night run (Feb. 1735; Mann and Mann 45, 86). Such opportunities indicate a close relation between these writers and the companies that staged their works. To appear to perform one's own epilogue was a novel idea at this time. The traditional image of the dramatist presented by epilogues is as a figure quaking in the wings or the green room, too frightened to face the critical audience. The few authors who appeared in person to justify and commend their work to audiences tended to be the well-known fools or comics of the company. That the companies permitted these women to speak for themselves and, in Cooper's case, step into a lead part, indicates not only that these writers were respected for their theatrical acumen but also that they could be trusted in these delicate, financially significant roles.

All these considerations should encourage us to think of the women dramatists not as lone, literary figures but as active participants in the commercial networks and conversations of the theater industry. While structural changes caused the marketplace for plays to ebb and flow, access to that market remained open through traditional channels. Deborah C. Payne has drawn attention to the way that patronage endured as a powerful mechanism within the commercial theater ("Patronage"), just as it remained in the broader literary marketplace, as Dustin Griffin has argued. Access to the stage usually required recommendation through an intermediary, such as an influential patron, playwright, or actor or a direct approach to a theater-manager.

The networks of aristocratic connection and conversation described by George Farquhar in his *Discourse upon Comedy* were undoubtedly more difficult for women playwrights to access:

> 'Tis then whisper'd among his Friends at Will's and Hippolito's that Mr. Such-a-One has writ a very pretty Comedy; and some of 'em to encourage the young Author, equip him presently with Prologue and Epilogue; then the Play is sent to Mr. Rich or Mr. Betterton in a fair legible Hand, with the Recommendation of some Gentleman, that passes for a Man of Parts, and a Critick. In short, the Gentleman's interest has the play acted. (qtd. in Van Lennep et al. 1: cxlv)

Colley Cibber recalled that aristocratic patronage might influence the placement of plays in a competitive environment. After the success of

John Vanbrugh's *The Relapse* at Drury Lane (1696), Lord Halifax, whose interests lay with Betterton's company at Lincoln's Inn Fields, "having formerly, by way of Family-Amusement, heard *The Provok'd Wife* read to him in its looser Sheets, engaged Sir John Vanbrugh to revise it and gave it to the Theatre at Lincoln's Inn Fields" (Cibber [1889] 1: 217). Charting female access to such patronage can be difficult. One of the clearest cases is Katherine Philips who, as Maureen E. Mulvihill has outlined, was beneficiary of the patronage and support of Robert Boyle, Earl of Orrery. He masterminded and funded the appearance of her *Pompey* on John Ogilby's Smock Alley stage, as well as organized for musical arrangements and noble literary prologue and epilogue writers. Several women offer eloquent thanks in the dedication of their plays to aristocratic patrons, after the fact. For example, Trotter's encomium to Charles, Earl of Dorset, the lord chamberlain, describes her first work, *Agnes de Castro*, as

> first submitted to your Lordship's Judgment, Whether it shou'd be Stifled in the Birth, or preserv'd to try its Fortune in the world; and since 'tis from your sentence it has ventured thus far, it now claims a sort of title to your Lordship's protection. (n. pag.)

From such a conventional expression of gratitude, it is not possible to gauge the direct influence that Dorset might have exerted with the theater; he had actively intervened before to protect Thomas Shadwell during the Exclusion Crisis, but that Trotter was able to dedicate her play to the lord chamberlain of the day indicates her connection to a key theatrical network (Kewes 26).

Fellow playwrights' intervention was helpful in getting Cibber's *Love's Last Shift* (1696) onto the stage. In his dedication to Richard Norton, Cibber acknowledges: "That Mr. Southern's Good Nature (whose own Works best recommend his Judgment) engag'd his Reputation for the Success, which its Reception, and your Approbation, Sir, has since redeem'd" (n. pag.). In a similar manner, William Congreve was to prove invaluable to the developing careers of Trotter and Pix through a shared circle of Whiggish support at Lincoln's Inn Fields. Trotter cannily offered dedicatory verses for Congreve's extremely popular *Mourning Bride* (1697) and asked for his advice in revising her play *The Revolution of Sweden* in 1706. Congreve's support was to aid Pix in her battle over George Powell's plagiarism of her play *The Deceiver Deceived* in 1697. It might well have been the poet and sometime playwright Charles Beckingham who introduced Jane Robe's adaptation of Racine, *The Fatal Legacy*, to the stage in 1723. The dedication is unsigned, but the dedicator indicates the play was "written by a young Lady, and entrusted to my Management; I introduc'd it into the Playhouse for her Interest" (Robe [Web] v–vi); Beckingham provides the prologue. Perhaps the most successful mode of access was a direct approach to a theater manager, which appears to be how Manley brought in *The Lost Lover* (1696). Her preface waxes lyrical in "all due acknowledgement for Sir Thomas Skipwith's Civility, his Native Generosity and Gallantry of Temper, took care nothing on his part should be wanting to make it pleasing" (n. pag.). Her pseudo-autobiography written much later in her life, *The Adventures of Rivella*, suggests a close relation with Skipwith, with whom she engineered a meeting through a mutual gentleman friend.

The political patronage network is often neglected with regard to women dramatists. Political commitment seems to have driven some women's work, and the rise of influential political-party communities may have smoothed these authors' access to the stage. During the Exclusion Crisis from 1679 to 1682, the tussle between the nascent Whig and Tory parties was hard to miss in the dramatic outputs of both the King's and the Duke's companies, and Aphra Behn, the only woman dramatist writing during this period, was responding to and involved in generating those political discourses. Behn's Tory proclivities have been carefully explicated by recent scholarship (Kubek, "'Night Mares'"; Markley; Owen, *Restoration Theatre*) and are not just coded in the plots and characterizations she produced but outspokenly announced in her prefatory matter. Her dedication to *The City Heiress* (1682, United) asserted that the play is

> in every part true Tory! Loyal all-over! except one Knave. . . . It has the luck to be well received in the Town; which (not from my Vanity) pleases me, but that thereby I find Honesty begins to be come in fashion again, when Loyalty is approv'd and Whiggism becomes a Jest where'er 'tis met with. (n. pag.)

Behn could gloat at Tory triumph in the dying months of the Exclusion Crisis since it was clear by this stage that James would not be refused the throne. Later in the year, in August, however, Behn would fall foul of the lord chamberlain with a prologue and epilogue for the anonymous play *Romulus and Hersilia*. Her crime was excessive criticism of the Duke of Monmouth, who, despite his illegitimacy, had been trying to build a Protestant claim to the throne, with military backing, as an alternative to

James, Duke of York. Charles, for all his misgivings about Monmouth's resistance, was not prepared to see his son impugned. On the whole, the women dramatists of the period tended to have a settled political perspective and did not write pragmatically as suited the political climate. Behn's work was wholeheartedly Tory, and her run-in with the lord chamberlain indicates that even when one was on the winning side, political argument and events were finely balanced, and misjudged enthusiasm might still see a dramatist censored or worse.

On the other side of the political fence, Elizabeth Kubek's essay later in this volume looks in detail at Pix's expression of her Whiggish views in her playwriting. Susanna Centlivre was likewise a committed Whig and was supported and encouraged through prologue and epilogue provision, access to the stage, and dedicatee largesse by a Whiggish literary circle. She, too, encountered trouble from the Master of the Revels: her epilogue to *The Perplex'd Lovers* (1712) was refused a licence for being "notoriously whiggish" (Preface n. pag.), and her lively farce, *A Gotham Election* (1715), the first play to depict an election campaign and a model for Fielding's more muted *Pasquin* (1736), was completely refused production, a rare fate in the years before the Licensing Act. The play might have been handled so severely because it was fractionally too early in its championing of the Whigs in the delicate first year of George I's reign, because it placed the moral heart and political rationale of the play in the mouths of the lowest sort, or because it depicted but did not discipline an election riot (Milling).

Part of the success of the more enduring women dramatists was their sense of stagecraft. One important component was their inclusion of action and stage events appropriate to the genre of their work. An undoubted mistress of stage business was Behn, whose farce *The Emperor of the Moon* (1686, United) was an early example of harlequinade, a genre that became very popular in the eighteenth century. The physical demands her text placed on the performers were considerable and drew on the full clowning talents of Anthony Leigh (Scaramouch) and Thomas Jevon (Harlequin). In a "dark" scene, the two rivals for the serving maid Mopsophil creep into her chamber and then try to outwit each other in a series of acrobatic and madcap encounters, as "they go to fight ridiculously" (18). Behn's play draws not only on the physical resources of the actors but also on their abilities to manipulate complex stage props as well. After having been introduced in the first scene through the women of his household, the gullible virtuoso Doctor Baliardo, played by Cave Underhill, makes his entrance in the second scene "with all manner of Mathematical Instruments, hanging at his Girdle; Scaramouch [his man] bearing a Telescope twenty (or more) Foot long" (7). The possibilities of an entrance with such a prop (how much of the telescope emerges on stage before we finally find Scaramouch struggling under its weight? Who does it hit or miss as it is turned?) are topped by the magical games the young lover Charmante then plays with backlit glass paintings—an early magic lantern show—as much for the audience as for the duped doctor. This miniature magic is echoed by the final masque scene, which uses the full flying, scenic, and musical resources of the Queen's Theatre stage as the lovers enact a royal visit from the emperor of the moon.

Another aspect of the women dramatists' success was their ability to write plays that had a dynamic dramaturgy and that built mood and tension. Manley's *The Royal Mischief* (1696, Actors') plunges us straight into the heart of the matter by having the central character Homais confess her incestuous, adulterous love for her newly married nephew, Levan Dadian. The part was a gift for Elizabeth Barry, who must have played the punchy, breathless passion of Homais to the full. As Homais reveals her passion for Levan to the audience, "[s]he seems disorder'd during this Speech, and at length sinks down in a Chair" (3). By contrast, her mood on greeting her husband is so markedly cool, a row ensues. In act 3, Manley builds the tension before the passionate pair Homais and Levan meet for the first time. In a scene underscored by music, Homais appears first, and, unable to control "the Rage [her] Passion gives," she exits to wait for Levan (20). Levan enters on the opposite side: "I walk in Clouds, and breath the Air of Love," though he is troubled by black thoughts of incest (20). As Homais returns, the first meeting of eyes is cleanly framed on either side of the full width of the stage. The audience follows the erotic charge as the pair approach each other, and, when they make physical contact at center stage, it produces a melting that acts as metaphor for the sexual encounter:

> *Levan*. She faints, by Heav'n, I've caught the Poyson Too, and grow unable to support her. (*She sinks down in a Chair, he falls at her Feet.*) (22)

As the scene shuts on this image, Manley's work is done, and the audience cannot but imagine all that passion may unleash behind the scenes. The lovers' happiness is modeled by dancing Indians and a magical, musical garden.

As the acts roll on, however the scenes become shorter and the situation more urgent. In the final act, Manley uses multiple shutter scenes to indicate shifts in time and to compress the action as rival forces battle for control of the castle. The pace builds relentlessly toward the final moments of the play, when Homais and Levan's embrace is interrupted by her husband, who "enters with his Sword drawn, runs at her, and Kills her" (45). Within a few lines Levan throws himself on his sword and dies, leaving Homais's husband a brief lament, "O horrour, horrour, horrour!" before the play closes (47). Such exemplary building of tension, pacing of action, and creation of mood through stage placement and language demonstrate why plays from Manley continued to be welcomed on to the stage, at times despite her political affiliation.

Drawn from many different backgrounds and widely diverging in their choice of genre, political affiliation, style, and voice, the women playwrights of 1660–1750 do not form a unique female tradition of playwriting or even attempt to consciously construct themselves as a grouping. Their work for the theater was mostly commercially driven, alert to audience expectations and desire and attuned to the political and social moment of its staging. Because of the structure of the theater industry and the mechanisms by which plays reached the stage, each dramatist was to a lesser or greater extent aware of the foibles of theater managers, the talents of the various performers, and the staging possibilities of the playhouses. These parameters affected the dramaturgy of the women to varying degrees, and those who built the longest careers for themselves in the theater, like Behn, Pix, and Centlivre, had mastered these opportunities and limitations with a professional aplomb that ensured the survival of their work in the repertoire of future centuries.

Notes

1. All quotations from *Agnes de Castro* are taken from the 1696 printing found on *Early English Books Online.*

2. William Burling's electronic database "New Plays on the London Stage, 1700–1810" is an invaluable resource for tracking the productions of women dramatists. (The editors sadly report the passing of Bill Burling in spring 2009. His database can still be accessed through *Georgian Theatre Research Resources.*)

3. Like several works of lesser-known women dramatists, Polwhele's tragedy was never printed, but her unperformed comedy *The Frolicks* has been edited by Milhous and Hume.

4. A theatrical duopoly operated in London for most of the Restoration and early eighteenth century. The King's and Duke's companies were established in

1660, joining as the United Company in 1682. Christopher Rich's mismanagement prompted the leading actors to revolt in 1695, producing the Patent Company and the Actors' Company. When Vanbrugh opened the Queen's Theatre, Haymarket, he invited the Actors' Company into residency and imagined a theatrical union and monopoly. Rich resisted, and Drury Lane played on until 1706, when a proto-union split the companies on generic grounds—opera at Drury Lane, straight drama at Queen's. This division greatly reduced opportunities for playwrights, and the generic split (although housed in different playhouses) endured until 1714, when two acting companies ran at Lincoln's Inn Fields and Drury Lane and the King's Theatre, as the Queen's Theatre had been renamed, staged opera.

George E. Haggerty

Regendering the Restoration Stage: Women and Theater, 1660–1720

No one really knows the full effect of the revolution in acting that transpired in 1660 (or 1661) when women took the stage under the auspices of Charles II. Samuel Pepys famously mentions the first time he sees a woman on stage: "after that to *the Theatre*, where was acted '*Beggars' Bush*,' it being very well done; and here the first time that ever I saw women come upon the stage" (3 Jan. 1660/1661 2: 5). Other contemporaries make similar mention of the phenomenon. But few theater historians assess the effect of these new actors, and critics still have much to do to determine how plays changed as a result of the presence of women on the stage.

At first thought, the difference would seem obvious: women could "embody" female roles in ways that male actors never could. But that theory collapses when one considers the career of Edward Kynaston (see Haggerty, "Queen"). Kynaston in his female roles was as much an object of the theatrical male gaze as anyone on the Restoration stage. Pepys offers a useful comment on Kynaston's success in the role of Olympia in *The Loyal Subject*, by John Fletcher:

> Captain Ferres, my Lord's Cornet, comes to us, who after dinner took me and Creed to the Cockpitt play, the first that I have had time to see since my coming from the east, "The Loyall Subject," where one

> Kinaston, a boy, acted the Duke's sister, but made the loveliest lady that ever I saw in my life, only her voice was not very good. (18 Aug. 1660; 1: 224)

"The loveliest lady" moves the most "Compassion and Pity," it seems, because she is not a lady at all.

In the 1660–61 season, in addition to Olympia, Kynaston played Aglaura in *Aglaura*, by John Suckling (Rhodes Company at the Cockpit, Drury Lane); Arthiopa in *The Unfortunate Lovers*, by William Davenant; Princess Ismena in *The Maid in the Mill*, by John Fletcher and William Rowley (Rhodes Company at the Cockpit, Drury Lane); Princess in *The Mad Lover*, by John Fletcher (Rhodes Company at the Cockpit, Drury Lane); and in the 1661–62 season, he played Arthiopa one more time at least.

Kynaston could no longer play female roles because in the patents granted to Davenant and Thomas Killigrew,

> [a]ctresses are permitted. Because in the past "the women's parts have been Acted by men in the habits of women att which some have taken Offence," the King gives permission that "all the womens partes to bee Acted in either of the said two Companies for the time to come may be performed by women." (Milhous, *Thomas Betterton* 6)

This suggests that Kynaston had no choice but to turn to male roles. His career as an actor has special resonance for this reason. After his triumph in these women's roles, Kynaston did proceed to play male roles with success. His male roles, however, can be seen to be connected to his female roles both directly and indirectly. For instance, it is fascinating for anyone concerned with the assignment of gender roles at this crucial moment in stage history to recognize that Kynaston was assigned the title role in the revival of Ben Jonson's *Epicoene; or, The Silent Woman* (1609), which the King's Company produced at the Vere Street Theatre in January 1661. *Epicoene* was more popular during the early years of the Restoration than it had ever been for Jacobean audiences, and in addition to playing the title character in the 1660–61 season, Kynaston also played Dauphin, a foppish male character in the play, at court in 1666–67.

It is clear that Kynaston's career flourished even as women took over the roles that he had made his own. His transition is not the gender-reassignment project that it is made to seem in films like *Stage Beauty*, which equated learning male roles with learning heterosexuality. Kynaston was an actor, one of the last great actors of the Shakespearean tradition, and like the actors in those plays, he could take on and off gender roles, and in doing so he could triumph in any role. As Pepys said when he saw Kynaston in *Epicoene*:

> Tom and I and my wife to the Theatre and there saw *The Silent Woman*, the first time that ever I did see that excellent play. Among other things here, Kinaston the boy hath the good turn to appear in three shapes: 1, as a poor woman in ordinary clothes to please Morose; then in fine clothes as a gallant, and in them was clearly the prettiest woman in the whole house—and lastly, as a man; and then likewise did appear the handsomest man in the house. (7 Jan. 1661; 2: 7)

It helps to remember that if Kynaston could play such a complex role, then he could surely take on any of the roles that the Restoration playwrights presented him. What women were doing on the stage at this time would only complement and underline the rich acting tradition of which their presence was a part.

The real thrill of the Restoration was to see women on the stage. Women playing women's roles had special resonance for Restoration audiences, and many critics, like Elizabeth Howe, in her book *The First English Actresses: Women and Drama, 1660–1700*, discuss this remarkable transition. Howe considers whether the appearance of women on the stage had an effect on the portrayal of women in the plays of the period. Her answer is a profound yes, and I look at some of her examples below.

That women actors were joined by women playwrights complicated this shift in gender roles. By the end of the seventeenth century, several women had written plays, both comedies and tragedies, in which these "new" women actors could perform: Aprha Behn, Mary Pix, Susanna Centlivre, Delarivier Manley, and Catharine Trotter. These playwrights helped break one gender barrier in the theater, and they did so in a historical context in which gender—the interpretation of gender roles—was a primary motivating force of theatrical display. For Fidelis Morgan, "the advent of the actresses marked revolutionary change in the position women held in the theatre" (ix). Other questions also assert themselves: How are female roles depicted? How do women relate to one another? What versions of masculinity are held up to ridicule or praise?

Actresses Take to the Stage

The introduction of actresses after 1660 had a profound effect on theatrical production for the next forty years. J. L. Styan argues:

> [T]he presence of women on the English stage for the first time accounts for many of the new ingredients found in the comedy of the Restoration, and more than supplies an explanation for much of the streak of self-conscious exhibitionism running throughout the plays. (89; see also Bush-Bailey, esp. 27–50)

Howe expands on this observation:

> [T]he presence of women in the theatre did not only result in stage pornography and easy reinforcement of popular female stereotypes. In the outstanding plays of the period the sexual realism provided by the actress helped to promote a fresh, sensitive, and occasionally even a radical consideration of female roles and relations between the sexes. (37)

Throughout her study of actresses such as Nell Gwyn, Elizabeth Barry, and Anne Bracegirdle, Howe shows how certain roles were created for certain actresses and explains how these women, through their specific talents on stage, helped shape both comedy and tragedy in this rich dramatic period. She describes how Gwyn's "extraordinary dramatic talent" ("warm-hearted, witty and determined") worked particularly well with the comic actor Charles Hart, another member of the King's Company (70). Play after play was written and performed in which Gwyn and Hart played the central role of the witty, sparring, merry couple that makes Restoration comedy memorable. John Dryden's *The Secret Love* (1667) and Charles Sedley's *The Mulberry Garden* (1668) both contained scenes for Gwyn and Hart, and Gwyn in the former (as Florimel) was given special commendation by Pepys:

> The truth is, there is a comical part done by Nell, which is Florimell, that I never can hope to see the like done again by man or woman . . . so great performance of a comical part was never I believe, in the world before Nell does this. (8: 91; qtd. in Howe 70)

In the next decade, when Gwyn was no longer available as an actress, other actresses took up such roles and in the process shifted them slightly. In William Wycherley's *The Country Wife* (1675), the object of the libertine Horner's (Hart's) affection is the innocent-seeming Margery Pinchwife, played by Elizabeth Boutell, who was pretty, "with a Childish look" and a "weak, though mellow" voice (Betterton; qtd. in Howe 74–75). The different style of comic performance yields a very different kind of play and comic effect. Rather than a sparring couple, this play centers on an innocent girl who is likely to be seduced.

Often two women played off each other for considerable effect. The later actresses Barry and Bracegirdle acted together in fifty-six plays. Barry was the preeminent tragic actress, and her ability to move audiences, Howe claims, determined the "she-tragedy" genre that emerged in the 1670s. In Nicholas Rowe's classic she-tragedy *The Fair Penitent* (1703), Barry played the tragic heroine Calista, whom Lothario had seduced, while Bracegirdle took the role of Lavinia, the virtuous wife of Horatio (Howe 104–05). This contrast between pathetic fallen heroine and virtuous maid or dutiful wife is repeated in several plays. In the most famous tragedy of the 1680s, Thomas Otway's *Venice Preserv'd* (1682), Barry played the tragic heroine Belvidera, who also forms the center of values in the play. "Although threatened by rape like so many Restoration heroines," Howe notes, "Belvidera plays this to her advantage—the sexual jealousy that the rape engenders in Jaffeir sways him like nothing else" (52).

It is important to remember the role of theater in London life. As Peter Holland tells it, "Theatre-going was not an occasional rare practice for a lordly few. It was an habitual part of day-to-day living in London or visiting it" (5). Nor was theatergoing particularly gendered. Jacqueline Pearson talks about various roles that women performed in the theater: charwomen, candle women, dressers, dressmakers, orange sellers, and box keepers. She also offers an interesting perspective on the role of actresses:

> Actresses . . . were extremely popular in the theatre of the period, praised for their accomplishments as often as they were attacked for immorality. They were called on to perform prologues and epilogues, to play male parts, and occasionally to perform whole plays without male colleagues. They were usually paid less than their male colleagues. Despite this they exerted an important, sometimes a decisive, influence on plays and theatres of the period. (*Prostituted Muse* 31)

One of the most important ways in which women exerted influence, of course, was writing plays.

Female Playwrights

Aphra Behn, the best-known female playwright of the Restoration, used the theater for feminist purposes, as some critics have argued. Elin Diamond alerted theater scholars to the ideological dynamics of the Restoration stage. In her essay "Gestus and Signature in Aphra Behn's *The Rover*," Diamond argues that contemporary ideology is part of what is being performed in the Restoration playhouse. She shows how the theater apparatus objectifies the actress for a male audience and how it works to establish the erotic preoccupations of the entire culture. Following Bertolt Brecht, Diamond argues that certain "gestic" moments in performance can make "visible the contradictory interactions of text, theater apparatus, and contemporary social struggle" (519–20). Diamond centers her argument on the figure of Angellica, a high-class courtesan who has posted her portrait outside her house to attract a certain clientele.

If, as Diamond explains, the actress could be a figure of both admiration (for her craft) and calumny (for her sexual activity), then it is also worth considering how female playwrights could be similarly objectified and what that would mean for the theatrical apparatus itself. Restoration theater's spectacular elements—its elaborate sets and scenery, its costumes and lighting, the possibility of "discovered" scenes, everything that Diamond describes as a new scopic epistemology—could also be used to expose the cultural function of playwriting itself.

In *The Rover* (1677), Barry played the wily comic heroine Hellena, who is clearly a match for the abandoned libertine Willmore. Although the play's feminist concerns are for many muted in this portrayal of Angellica's tragic excess, they emerge more boldly in the ways in which Hellena matches wits with Willmore. As Howe explains:

> The Hart-Gwyn formula may have begun . . . as a series of bantering comic exchanges between lovers, but in plays like [George Etherege's] *She Would if She Could* [1668] and *The Rover* it became an important satiric means of conveying the female viewpoint in a relationship. (175)

Hellena is witty and wise, and she is as outspoken as most Restoration comic heroines are. In Barry's hands, she has clear power that she uses to manipulate the world around her (Howe 52). Early in the play, she confronts her brother Don Pedro who seems willing to make a match between their sister Florinda and the old and lecherous Don Vincentio. Hellena's defiance is breathtaking and memorable:

Hellena. (*Aside*.). . . Is't not enough you make a nun of me, but must you cast my sister away too . . .

Pedro. The girl's mad! It is a confinement to be carried into the country to an ancient villa belonging to the family of the Vincentios these five hundred years, and have no other prospect than that pleasing one of seeing all her own that meets her eyes: a fine air, large fields, and gardens where she may walk and gather flowers?

Hellena. When, by moonlight? For I am sure she dares not encounter with the heat of the sun; that were a task only for Don Vincentio and his Indian breeding, who loves it in the dog days. And if these be her daily divertissements, what are those of the night? To lie in a wide moth-eaten bedchamber with furniture in fashion in the reign of King Sancho the First; the bed, that which his forefathers lived and died in.

Pedro. Very well.

Hellena. This apartment, new furbrushed and fitted out for the young wife, he out of freedom makes his dressing room; and being a frugal and a jealous coxcomb, instead of a valet to uncase his feeble carcass, he desires you to do that office. Signs of favor, I'll assure you, and such as you must not hope for unless your woman be out of the way.

Pedro. Have you done yet?

Hellena. That honor being past, the giant stretches itself, yawns and sighs a belch or two as loud as a musket, throws himself into bed, and expects you in his foul sheets; and ere you can get yourself undressed, calls you with a snore or two. And are not these fine blessings to a young lady?

Pedro. Have you done yet?

Hellena. And this man you must kiss, nay you must kiss none but him too, and nuzzle through his beard to find his lips. And this you must submit to for threescore years, and all for a jointure.

(11–12; act 1, sc. 1, lines 95–127)[1]

I have quoted this scene at length because it shows the development of Hellena's character in a remarkable crescendo of speeches that leaves her brother almost speechless. This character is fashioned for triumph in the play, and in the course of it she masquerades as a gypsy and a boy. She turns out to be a match, although her emotion almost gets the best of her, for the libertine Willmore, and the play's happy ending also delivers Florinda from various emotional and physical assaults into the arms of her beloved Belvile.

The play may not be feminist in twenty-first-century terms, but Hellena speaks up for all the unhappy brides of her age; and if Angellica highlights the gender economy of the theater—the objectification of the actress and the ease with which members of the male audience could procure such women if they wanted to (Diamond, "Gestus" 524–27)—Hellena looks beyond the theater to the world of Restoration London at large.[2]

In Pix's *The Spanish Wives* (1696), a three-act "farce" according to the epilogue (183), two women and their ingenious female servants challenge assumptions about female fidelity, marital inequity, and cuckoldry.[3] The Governor, who seems a cuckold-in-waiting at the beginning of the play, gives freedom to his wife as a way of winning her faithfulness. And indeed the Governor's Lady loves him and hesitates to give in to the extravagant lovemaking of the English Colonel Peregrine:

Colonel. My Angel! by Heaven, I am raging mad; burnt up with violent love.—Thy shape—Thy every motion fires me,—but thy eyes—They set me in a blaze—Oh! I must die, unless the cordial of returning kindness save me!

Lady. Can you be so ungenerous to wrong this noble Governor, who is so fond of you, and even dotes on me?

Colonel. He has wronged thee more, when he condemned thy lovely youth to withered sapless arms.—Can little foolish tricks of fondness make amends for extasies, paintings, the joys innumerable of vigorous love?

Lady. I must not hear ye.

Colonel. You must, you must—I'll, kneeling, fix ten thousand burning kisses on thy beauteous hand; And the little wanton god swims and revels in thy sprightly eyes.

Lady. Why am I fastened here!—too rigorous Heaven! Take from this wondrous stranger his conquering charms, or give me more insensibility!

(145)

Without the outspoken freedom of Behn's Hellena, the Governor's Lady remains devoted to her husband, even as she contemplates deceiving him. And when she finally does decide to visit Colonel Peregrine clandestinely, even then she can say, "I swear I love this old Governor, and nothing but this charming Englishman could have tempted me to break my vows" (173). When the expression of love turns out to be a trick and her husband exposes her transgressive desire, she pleads that this is her only attempt at transgression, and she persuades him, by the use of their private loving language, to give her another chance. This odd moment of reconciliation defies many of the tenets of Restoration comedy, but it still has uncanny resonance. Pix paints a scene of female torture that seems to be the very aphrodisiac that the old Governor needs:

Lady. Do, lock me up; and next moment you are gone, I'll hang myself in my own garters, so I will.—Can you behold your Tittup hanged? her eyes goggling, her mouth you have bussed so often, gaping; and her legs dangling three yards above ground?—This is the sight you must expect.

Governor. Oh! I can't bear the thoughts on't—Stand farther off—farther yet—that I may rush upon thee with all the vigor of sixteen, and clasp thee from such danger—Thou resistless ruler of doting, fond old

> fool!—Here—I forgive thee—but if after this, I catch you staggering, expect no mercy. (174–75)

Tittup knows her husband well enough to understand how to turn him on and at the same time earn his forgiveness. Very few Restoration heroines manage their husbands so effectively.

The other heroine, Elenora, is married to a brutally controlling older man. But it seems she was actually betrothed to the Roman Count Marcellus, who is attempting to liberate her from the violent man who has stolen and sequestered her. The wife can resist her husband's demands, and even condemn his behavior, without seeming to violate the tenets of female respectability:

> *Marquess of Moncada.* You are a perpetual plague to me, I'm sure—You hate everybody that tells you your duty.
>
> *Elenora.* Inhuman Spaniard!—what wouldst thou have?—Am I not immured, buried alive? (148)

Elenora is finally liberated from the clutches of this wicked old man, and she enjoys the legitimate marriage with Marcellus to which she was already committed.

Both strands of the plot, then, give a female perspective on some of the most rigorous inequalities of marriage. The Governor's tendency to trust his wife is the position that comes off as most reasonable: neither the professing libertine nor the jealous husband offers anything of value. This simple play makes very vivid Pix's perspective.

In *A Bold Stroke for a Wife* (1718), Centlivre keeps her heroine, the wealthy unmarried heiress Mrs. (Anne) Lovely, offstage for most of the play and instead insists that Anne's suitor, Colonel Fainwell, win her hand by persuading four guardians that he is the right choice for her husband. The plot, which centers on his attempts to win over the guardians—a fashionable lord, a stockbroker, a virtuoso, and a Quaker—is finely drawn and the comedy rich and varied.[4]

In the scenes throughout which Anne Lovely appears, both when she is arguing with her guardians and helping Fainwell carry off his disguise and win her hand, she is a straightforward and engaging character in her own right. She argues with Mrs. Prim, Obadiah Prim's wife, in terms that are clear and direct:

> *Mrs. Prim.* Ah, Ann, Ann, that wicked Philip Modelove will undo thee. Satan so fills thy heart with pride during the three months of his guardianship that thou becomest a stumbling block to the upright.

Mrs. Lovely. Pray, who are they? Are the pinched cap and formal hood the emblems of sanctity? Does your virtue consist in your dress, Mrs. Prim?

Mrs. Prim. It doth not consist in cut hair, spotted face, and bare necks. O, the wickedness of this generation! The primitive women knew not the abomination of hooped petticoats.

Mrs. Lovely. No, nor the abomination of cant neither. Don't tell me, Mrs. Prim, don't. I know you have as much pride, vanity, self-conceit, and ambition among you, couched under that formal habit and sanctified countenance, as the proudest of us all; but the world begins to see your prudery. (207)[5]

This is bold speech, even for an early-eighteenth-century heroine, and a conversation like this between two women suggests that the heroine can hold her own in any context, and she does. She tells off her guardians and fights against those who would possess her, even at times against her lover, at least when she does not recognize him.

In the last scene of the play, Anne and Fainwell are finally working together to liberate her from the control of her guardians. She prevaricates and aids in subterfuge, she pretends to be converted to Quakerism, and she plights her troth to Fainwell in the very language she has been mocking:

Colonel. (*Aside.*) Admirably performed.—(*Aloud.*) And I will take thee in all spiritual love for an helpmeet, yea, for the wife of my bosom.—And now, methinks, I feel a longing—yea, a longing, I say, for the consummation of thy love, hum—yea, I do long exceedingly.

Mrs. Lovely. And very, verily, my spirit feeleth the same longing.

Mrs. Prim. The spirit hath greatly moved them both. Friend Prim, thou must consent; there is no resisting of the spirit. (250)

This open profession of sexual desire, which is celebrated even by the character it most mocks, is entertaining as a comic device, to be sure, but it also suggests the subtle point that a female playwright can make. Without forcing a feminist diatribe, which would be both unlikely and unsuitable to this story, Centlivre presents an intelligent and desiring female character who has a say in the disposition of her person and her wealth. If the energy of the play goes more richly into the variations on Fainwell's impersonations and deceptions, perhaps that suggests what a wonderful choice of husband she has made.

As these three comedies suggest, the plays by women do not vary greatly from the other comedies that were written and performed during the Restoration. But the subtle variations that they offer place greater emphasis on female choice, female self-determination, and female intelligence. Unreasonable brothers, husbands, guardians, and friends are dealt with severely in these plays, and even the heroes are put through their paces at least as energetically as they are in other comedies of the period.

Tragedy and heroic romance are another matter. In the she-tragedies of Otway and Rowe, women are victimized in a variety of ways. Often they end up invoking pity by a death both tragic and unfair. Even in heroic plays, women are usually abused and sometimes victimized. But in Manley's *Lucius, the First Christian King of Britain* (1717), Queen Rosalinda occupies a central and powerful role. Interpolated into her historical sources, this character is a Christian queen who converts the hero, Lucius, and marries him to become the first Christian monarchs of the formerly pagan kingdom (Rabb). As Melinda Rabb argues:

> [Rosalinda] represents a continuation of Manley's constant theme in all of her writing: the inseparability of sex and politics in the human struggle for power and love. The secret motives of love and religion, the play insists, may be reduced to the contending forces of men and women.

In this play female desire has all the significance of male desire, and a happy outcome is reached only when each character has sacrificed something for the other. Rosalinda gives up the grief she feels for her defeated and slain husband, Otharius, the king of Aquitaine; Lucius sacrifices the man he believes to be his father and in doing so signifies his conversion to Christianity. At a key point in their romance, they defend each other against Vortimer's lust (for Rosalinda) and fury (against his son):

Vortimer. (*Aside to Lucius.*) Yield up your bride to us, and thou shalt live.
Thy cursèd marriage may be disannulled,
And thou proclaimed our Kingdom's heir.
Lucius. Forsake my wife! It is not in my pow'r.
Mercy is cruelty when so disguised.
Vortimer. Then thou shalt die, rebellious hardened boy.
(*Aside to the Queen.*)
You know your charms, exert 'em now, be mine.
And Lucius, my curst rival, too shall live.
Queen. To save the Prince's life, I would do all
But break the sacred vow I plighted to him. (99)

This scene of mutual defiance sets them up for deliverance in the next scenes. The centrality of the female figure is as profound here as it is in Dryden's *All for Love* (1677) or Otway's *Venice Preserv'd* (1682). But in this case, neither the hero nor the heroine must die. They triumph in a joint marriage-conversion that places a woman at the origin of British Christianity.

In Trotter's tragedy *Agnes de Castro* (1696), several characters die, including the three central women—the Princess Constantia, Agnes de Castro, and Elvira, the jealous plotter who performs the murder that brings about the tragic denouement.[6] Agnes, the heroine of the play, has been brought to the Portuguese court from Spain. She is the favorite of the king and beloved by the prince and his friend and rival, Elvira's brother, Alvaro. But the key relationship recorded in the play is that between Agnes and the princess. Even when the latter is given (counterfeit) evidence that her friend is participating in a love affair with her husband, the princess can forgive her. Agnes's love for her is vividly requited. In the following conversation, the princess suggests that the prince loves her closest friend, and Agnes hopes that it is not she:

Princess. Ah! She who robs me of my Husband's Heart,
Is all a Charm, to plead for his Excuse;
Young, Beautiful, Discreet, and Chast, as Fair;
By Nature form'd to captive ev'ry Heart,
My Reason must approve the Prince's choice,
For I myself, prefer her to my self,
And love her too, as tenderly as he. . . .
Agnes. How very Miserable must I be
When I'm reduc'd to wish, you did not love me!
Those marks, of that peculiar, dear affection,
Which ev'ry day your partial kindness gave,
Are Witnesses which I would disbelieve;
Oh! Let me think your Friendship was divided,
Tell me you have another, nearer friend,
For I had rather lose your Love for ever,
Than be the wretched Cause of your misfortune;
Rather be hated by you, than deserve it;
Oh ease my cruel fears, and name some other.

(166; act 1, sc. 2, lines 213–19, 231–40)[7]

This language of female friendship is even more heartfelt when Elvira has stabbed the princess, thinking she is Agnes. Agnes cradles her dying friend in her arms: "Better all Womankind at once shou'd perish / Than you, the sole Perfection of the Sex, / The greatest Blessing, of the whole Creation" (185–86; 3.2.1122–25). And after the princess has died, she laments:

Oh! she's gone, she's gone, and left me here!
But I shall overtake my dear, dear Mistress.
This Ponyard, Purple with her precious Blood;
'Tis useless, Grief has kindly done its Work.
(*As she is going to kill her Self she falls in a Swoon.*)
(186–87; 3.2.1169–73)

There is no more beautiful account of female love in the Restoration, and all the other loves in the play pale in comparison. Even Elvira's murderous jealousy and madness seem pathetic next to the amorous devotion these women share.[8]

It would be misleading to end this discussion without mentioning the prolific playwright Margaret Cavendish, Duchess of Newcastle.[9] Cavendish wrote nineteen plays that were published in two large folio volumes (Shaver, Introduction 7). She chose not to produce the plays, but they could be imagined to hold their own on the Restoration stage. *The Convent of Pleasure* (1668) is a women-oriented play. As Anne Shaver describes it, the play "contains several recurring motifs: cross-dressing, pageantry, a powerful woman as the central character, strong arguments by women against marriage, and some male behavior that makes the reader see why women may object to marrying" (Introduction 12). Lady Happy articulates the case against marriage well:

> Put the case I should Marry the best of Men, if any best there be; yet would a Marry'd life have more crosses and sorrows then pleasure, freedom, or happiness: nay Marriage to those that are virtuous is a greater restraint then a Monastery. Or, should I take delight in Admirers? they might gaze on my Beauty, and praise my Wit, and I receive nothing from their eyes, nor lips; for Words vanish as soon as spoken, and Sights are not substantial. (218; act 1, sc. 2)

Cavendish's diatribe, like Hellena's in *The Rover*, tries to make a case for female independence, but even Lady Happy and Hellena accept proposals of marriage by the end of their plays. The protofeminism in these works is muted and circumscribed. But still, over the course of the late seventeenth century, the range of female behavior shifted, the pathos of female characters increased, and the value of actresses changed dramatically.

Female players, female playwrights, female perspectives: the Restoration discovered the value of shifting the emphasis in this way. Without these works, how would the great opportunities of female heroism that emerged in the eighteenth century have been possible? I am not thinking only of the great heroines of the theater, like Sarah Siddons, or great playwrights, like Hannah Cowley or Joanna Baillie; I am also thinking of the great heroines of fiction,. like Clarissa and Evelina, and the great female novelists, like Sarah Scott, Sarah Fielding, and Frances Burney. All these triumphs owe a great deal to the female achievements on the Restoration stage. Laura Brown has made a similar argument in *English Dramatic Form*. In talking about drama and the novel in the eighteenth century, she says, "The rise of the novel defines the decline of the drama. In this sense, the fates of the two genres are inextricably joined" (184). But rather than see a decline in one and a rise in the other, from the perspective of female artistic engagement we can see nothing but a rise.

Notes

1. All quotations from *The Rover* are from Frederick Link's edition of the play.

2. A useful feminist reading of the play is offered by Pilar Zozaya. She is particularly insightful about Angellica and builds on an argument that was originally made by Anne Russell: "[W]hen Angellica disrupts the exchange economy that defines her, she ceases to have a social identity" (119). Zozaya argues further that "in the social economy of the times, the three women involved exert 'whatever power they may have' so as to inscribe their right to enter and occupy areas so far restricted to men" (119). For a general assessment of Behn's place in Restoration theater, see Hughes, "Aphra Behn."

3. For a general discussion of Pix and a helpful reading of this play, see McLaren; see also Gómez. For a discussion of Pix's tragedies, see Collins.

4. For a general assessment of Centlivre, see O'Brien, "Busy Bodies"; see also D. Butler; Warren.

5. All quotations from *A Bold Stroke for a Wife* are from Katharine M. Rogers's edition of the play.

6. For a thoughtful consideration of Trotter as a playwright, see Backscheider, "Stretching"; see also Ready, "Damaris Cudworth Masham."

7. All quotations from *Agnes de Castro* are from Anne Kelley's edition *Catharine Trotter's* The Adventures of a Young Lady *and Other Works*.

8. It has been argued that *Agnes* is therefore a lesbian play, and Kendall maintains that the love between the princess and Agnes "is of a much more complex sensual identity then we are accustomed to finding in twentieth-century literature" ("Finding" 171). Elsewhere Kendall calls the play "the first lesbian play in English stage history" (*Love* 11). I agree with the spirit of this reading, but I resist the label "lesbian" because these two women love in a way that makes the label superfluous. Love, as it is used here, is of course erotic, and it declares itself as such. Anachronis-

tic labels distort the case for female affection. See also Kelley, for whom "a survey of letters of the period, between writers of the same sex, or different sexes, reveals a convention of extravagant compliment and affection which was rhetorical rather than sexual" (*Catharine Trotter* 124–25).

9. On Cavendish's drama, see A. Bennett, "Fantastic Realism"; see also Mendelson. Cavendish was also a highly respected poet; see Jankowski.

Jacqueline Pearson

Women Spectators, Playwrights, and Performers and the Restoration Stage

In 1988 I published *The Prostituted Muse: Images of Women and Women Dramatists, 1642–1737*, and writing this essay has given me the opportunity to review the changes in literary scholarship since then, as well as to rethink some of the assumptions I brought to the project. I suppose that when I wrote about the 1660s, I was thinking partly about the 1960s; after all, both had seen a sexual revolution resulting in radical innovation in the theater and new possibilities for women in the theatrical professions and in culture more broadly. I did not, perhaps, allow enough sense of the marked historical differences to emerge. In some respects, Restoration drama represented itself not as revolutionary but as a return to traditional values after the puritan revolution. As the prologue to the first play presented at court after the Restoration put it, "They that would have no *KING*, would have no Play," and Sir John Denham represents the new theater as continuing the glorious tradition of English drama as well as the English monarchy (Wiley 11). That this first play was Ben Jonson's *Epicoene; or, The Silent Woman* (1616) should also warn us that ideas about gender did not change abruptly with the Restoration but that, in some respects, an old "ideology of misogyny" remained accessible just beneath new ideas of politeness (Mendelson and Crawford 65).

In the 1980s I was looking for seventeenth-century women writers who shared my aspirations. I was interested in Margaret Cavendish, Duchess of Newcastle, for her heroines who gain power as military leaders and as cultural revisionists through their speech (and their silence). I was interested in her representation of relationships, even quasi-lesbian relationships, between women. Yet I could not ignore the fact that, like Shakespeare's, Cavendish's comic endings realigned desire with what in *The Convent of Pleasure* (1668) she calls "Nature." In consequence, the "Masculine" princess whom Lady Happy loves is, necessarily, really a prince; a capitulation to conventional gender ideologies is further marked by the fact that Cavendish's husband, the Duke of Newcastle, wrote considerable sections of the end of the play (234, 226, 238, 244). I was interested in Aphra Behn, for her bold heroines seeking freedom, but was less aware than we have since become of the fundamental contradictions in Behn's position:

> [C]ommitment to free love went hand in hand with an unflinching stress upon chastity; approval of patriarchal Royalism sat uncomfortably next to the effort to privilege individual female agency; and woman-centred aspirations, as delineated in Behn's prefaces and prologues, did not invariably square with the content of the plays. (Wray 11–12)

When I began my studies, Restoration drama had historically been constructed in the academy (and in the modern theater) by reference to the same half dozen dramatists: George Etherege, William Wycherley, William Congreve, John Dryden, John Vanbrugh, and George Farquhar. Consequently, when I began to work on Restoration drama in the 1980s, the number of women playwrights came as a revelation. About eighty plays by women were performed at commercial theatrical venues between 1664 and 1735 (the earliest London performances being Katherine Philips's tragedy *Pompey* early in 1664 and Frances Boothby's tragicomedy *Marcelia* in 1669). In addition, other female-authored plays were performed at private or semipublic venues, like Ephelia's *The Pair-Royal of Coxcombs*, performed at a dancing school in 1678; were published but not performed, like the massive oeuvre of Cavendish published in 1662 and 1668; or remain only in manuscript, like Anne Wharton's *Love's Martyr; or, Wit above Crowns*, written circa 1685. In particular, the decade from 1695 to 1705 (which produced at least twenty-eight plays by women) shows women playwrights vigorously shaping theatrical agendas. In this essay, I glance briefly at three new approaches that have begun to produce important insights into the drama of the Restoration and early eighteenth century: the gendered consumption of theatrical texts and performances, "intertheatrical" study applied to relations between women dramatists and women performers, and constructions of masculinity in plays of the Restoration and early eighteenth century.

Toward a Gendered History of Theatrical Consumption

Restoration and early-eighteenth-century women took a full part as consumers of theater and drama. Although conduct books and exemplary lives generally warned women against reading modern plays because they were "so Obscene" (Knight 32), ordinary women clearly bought and read plays. This is true not only of significant book collectors, such as Lady Ann Coventry and Frances Wolfreston (Perry; P. Morgan), but also of several obscure seventeenth- and early-eighteenth-century women known only from their book signatures. Sarah Ettricke owned a number of Dryden plays in 1733 (Folger Shakespeare Lib. 235-761); Ann Turneur owned and signed Mary Pix's *The False Friend* (Folger Shakespeare Lib. cs 1675); Mary Trenchard owned Etherege's works (Columbia U Lib. 1704). Books "have a special status within the early modern gift-exchange system" (Snook 135), perhaps especially for women, and, despite the disapproval of moralists, printed plays could cement a maternal lineage. Elizabeth and Francis Younge owned ten tragedies including some by Dryden, Nathaniel Lee, and Thomas Otway; these were originally a gift from Elizabeth's grandmother and were passed on to Francis, who was, perhaps, her daughter and who signed the title page in 1728 (Folger Shakespeare Lib. cs 174). This evidence is tantalizing but ultimately frustrating since it gives little information on the gendered experiences of reading plays or on the context in which such plays were read. Nonetheless, the evidence does demonstrate that, in defiance of strict ideas of propriety, printed plays were part of a female gift culture and were enjoyed by women readers throughout the period.

If the Jacobean public playhouse had symbolized the triple-decker universe—the earth in the center, heaven above, hell beneath—the post-Restoration playhouse functioned as a coded version of the English class and gender system made into bricks and mortar. Servants sat in the upper galleries, "Persons of Quality" in the front boxes, and the merchant class in the middle galleries (J. Pearson, *Prostituted Muse* 34). The Restoration "playhouse was filled with women," and these theatergoers were visible and influential (Lowenthal, *Performing Identities* 111). Samuel Pepys remarked on the "fine ladies" in the audience at two performances of 1667 and was amused and touched by their responsiveness to the plays, like the "very pretty lady" who "call'd out, to see Desdemona smother'd" in 1660 (qtd. in J. Pearson, *Prostituted Muse* 33).

Playwrights—especially but not exclusively women playwrights—appealed to women in the audience "as the arbiters of taste" (Lowenthal, *Performing Identities* 111), usually in tragedies, which it was believed women particularly enjoyed (J. Pearson, *Prostituted Muse* 37–39). Jane Robe in the prologue of her single play, *The Fatal Legacy* (1723), addresses the "Fair-Ones" in the audience on whom she "relies" for "Success," since "You're the best Judges, you are ever just" ([print] xii). Pix "[c]ourts the favour of the fair" to approve her lachrymose tragedy of 1698, *Queen Catharine* (73), and in the prologue of *The Double Distress* (1701) begs, "Be kind, ye Fair, since of the Fair she sings"; Delarivier Manley trusts that "the shining Fair" will give a kind reception to *Lucius, the First Christian King of Britain* (1717; prologue) and, ventriloquizing a male voice, solicits the approval of the "bright nymphs" in the audience of *Almyna* (1708; prologue).

Most elaborately, Catharine Trotter, in the prefatory material to *The Revolution of Sweden* (1706), emphatically equates femininity with moral virtue and creates a feminized space where women's political, cultural, and educational power is unassailable (as it is not in the main text of the play). Combining to create an alliance among women governors, writers, and consumers are the virtuous heroine, the virtuous dedicatee Lady Harriett Godolphin, women in the audience who care for the "Publick Good," the playwright who has taught moral lessons in the play, and the power and virtue of the queen actualizing this female power on the stage of national politics, "Great ANNA's Reign" (197–98, 200).

In the prologue to Susanna Centlivre's *The Wonder: A Woman Keeps a Secret* (1714), a comedy in which a heroic female character risks her own happiness to keep her word to a female friend, Thomas Burnet shows the playwright "[c]ommit[ing] her Cause" to "the bright Circle of the Fair." Women "first taught [men] to Love" and therefore have common cause and a common authority (120).[1] The epilogue, written by Ambrose Philips and spoken by the actress Hester Santlow, who played Donna Isabella—the romantic interest of John Mills, the actor who spoke the prologue—offers more combative conclusions based on the common cause among the female playwright, performer, and theatergoers. "Custom" and "Modern Laws" alone have given "Power despotick to Mankind," but the example of Violante, keeping a secret in defiance of stereotypes of talkative women and at the risk of losing her lover, proves women's strength and virtue in defiance of these negative constructions: "Women are not so weak, whate'er Men prate" (120). This is a highly effective theatrical epilogue, two-edged, ironic, and risqué (women's power, for instance, is embodied as the ability to foist secretly illegitimate children into lines of inheritance). But it also makes serious points about women's ability and nature and suggests that their potential can be partially fulfilled by a contract among the women who write, perform, and consume plays. Whether this contract ever worked effectively in reality is open to debate, but its rhetorical importance to women in the theater is clear.

Women's influence was also decisive—or was discursively constructed as decisive—in three important theatrical trends from the 1690s to the 1730s. First, women encouraged the introduction of increased amounts of Shakespeare into theatrical repertoires (Avery, "Shakespeare"), and consequently were praised for defending "Wit and Sense" against "Farce and Dulness" (J. Pearson, *Prostituted Muse* 41). Second, the popularity of tragedy and the rise of sentimental modes tended in contemporary writing to be attributed in large part to women theatergoers. Around 1703 a trend began for theaters to present stock repertoire plays allegedly specifically requested by "the Ladies." A clear picture emerges of a widely held belief that women preferred tragedy—*Hamlet* (1599) was requested thirty-three times and Otway's *The Orphan* (1680) thirty-two—and sentimental plays, like Colley Cibber's *The Careless Husband* (1705), the most popular of all, which was requested forty-three times (J. Pearson, *Prostituted Muse* 39–40).

At this distance in time, it is impossible to tell what was really at stake in this (alleged) public intervention by "the Ladies." Did these requests indicate real cultural power for women and even an authentic female taste, or did "the Ladies" only provide a conventional way of referring to "the moral element in the audience" (Scouten and Hume [1983] 61)? Can we learn about real women from these details or only about the economics of theater management and the mechanisms by which stereotypical constructions of gender difference were reconfirmed? The historical record suggests that gendered differences may not have been so clear-cut in reality. Women like Elizabeth Pepys and Lady Penelope Morley certainly attended comedies with every evidence of enjoyment (D. Roberts 49–64, 69–72), and Trenchard, Coventry, and Wolfreston owned comedies (Perry; P. Morgan). At the same time Morley was cautious to avoid obscenity, and perhaps Wolfreston was too, since all the comedies she owned were pre-Restoration, although she lived until 1677. Nonetheless, although some critics have claimed that women failed to give positive encouragement to plays geared to their tastes (Scouten and Hume [1983] 61), it is possible that the convention of requesting plays shows women supporting positive female role models and plays that avoid misogynistic obscenity.

Third, and perhaps most important, women theatergoers were identified with the movement for theatrical "reform." Spurred on by Jeremy Collier's *Short View of the Immorality and Profaneness of the English Stage* of 1698, several dramatists committed themselves to moral self-regulation to produce drama purged of obscenity and blasphemy. Choreographed gestures of protest against obscenity by women spectators go back as early as 1667 (J. Pearson, *Prostituted Muse* 35), and later playwrights protested that their plays failed because "ladies of stricter lives"—who were probably hypocrites anyway—boycotted them (Wycherley, *Plain Dealer* 3). The "reform" movement, though, split women writers as much as male. Trotter emphasized her dramatic function as a teacher of virtue, and Pix repeatedly drew attention in prologues, epilogues, and dedications to her commitment to "Reformation" or "reform" (*Innocent Mistress*; *False Friend*; *Double Distress*) in writing "innocent," "moral," "modest" plays (*Queen Catharine*; *False Friend*; *Ibrahim*; *Beau Defeated*). Conversely, Centlivre in the epilogue to her first play, *The Perjur'd Husband* (1700), insisted that the theater's function was to reflect life as it really was, and, unless society underwent a moral metamorphosis, it was unreasonable to expect "the Stage shall be reform'd."

Female Performers, Female Dramatists, and Intertheatrical Casting

Before the closure of the playhouses in 1642, the theater had been entirely male-dominated: as far as we know, all plays for public performance were written by men, and all performers, even of women's roles, were male. With the Restoration, there was a brief transition period when these protocols continued, but they were almost immediately challenged by two radical innovations: female playwrights and female performers, the earliest perhaps as Desdemona in late 1660 (Howe 19). The availability of female performers changed theatrical repertoires. Gender had become performable in new ways, and the body of the actress was, for the first time, a vital stage resource.

While in the early Restoration actresses were often regarded as little better than prostitutes (J. Pearson, *Prostituted Muse* 27), their status gradually rose, and famous performers, like Anne Bracegirdle, Elizabeth Barry, and Anne Oldfield, became the focus of an early celebrity culture, "objects of speculation and specularization" (Lowenthal, *Performing Identities* 112). As a result, "a communal, extratheatrical discourse" developed in which speculations about actresses' bodies offstage fed into the theatrical roles created for them and audience responses to those roles (112). Bracegirdle, for instance, had a reputation for chastity, and several roles were created to capitalize on that trait, though dramatists—like Thomas Southerne, who cast her as Trickitt in *The Maid's Last Prayer* (1693)—also sometimes cannily cast her against type, so gaining an effectively theatrical shock value.

It was not, however, simply "extratheatrical discourse" that helped dramatists shape roles for their performers. Audiences were also expected to develop an ability to watch plays in an "intertheatrical" way (Bratton, "Reading"), acquiring an awareness of the key roles performers had previously acted, and dramatists could exploit these earlier roles in "creating plays for an audience with preconceptions they could fulfil or frustrate" (Howe 7). Both extratheatrical and intertheatrical discourses, therefore, shape the way dramatists created roles and performers actualized them. This professional expertise was as available to female as to male playwrights and can perhaps be seen especially clearly in the two most prolific and professional women dramatists of the period, Behn and Centlivre. Centlivre, in particular, was criticized in her time and immediately afterward for a dull and plodding style, a lack of wit, and imperfectly developed characters; but all the evidence suggests that when the written role was filled out by the "artful Player" the result could be very effective (J. Pearson, Introduction xi–xii; Centlivre, *Wonder* 119).

When Behn began to write for the Duke's Company in 1670, she inherited a number of experienced and popular performers, including the leading man Thomas Betterton and his wife, Mary Saunderson Betterton. Their marriage was widely viewed as a stable and happy one, forming—unusually for theatrical people—a respectable family home. Behn capitalized on this by casting them as the romantic lead couple in several plays. At the same time, though, she achieved comic or tragic effects by casting them against type and so thwarting the audience's expectation that they would achieve a happy marital ending. In *Abdelazer* (1676), Thomas Betterton played the eponymous hero-villain and Mary Betterton his wife,

Florella, but this tragedy of blood becomes still more shocking when, far from enacting loving marital unity, Abdelazer manipulates his wife in his plots to gain the crown and betrays her with Isabella, who murders her.

In *Sir Patient Fancy* (1678), the exceptionally large cast and complicated cross-wooings are mediated by predictable casting, which then turns out to be less predictable than we had supposed. In two parallel plots, a mother competes with her daughter over a young man. Leander Fancy loves Lucretia Knowell but is being leaned on by his father to marry her mother; and Wittmore pretends to be a suitor to Isabella (actually in love with Lodwick Knowell) to cover his adulterous intrigue with her stepmother, Lady Fancy. Mary Betterton played Isabella, and Thomas Betterton played Wittmore. In act 5, scene 1, Wittmore, alone with Isabella, is still pretending he intends to marry her against her will and claims the "Authority . . . of a Husband," while she insists that "there will be danger" in forcing her to marry, for she will "Cuckold" him (61). At this point, Wittmore reveals his true intentions and hands her over to Lodwick.

This is a dark play, in which women's sexuality is seen as a site of danger or transgression. The youthful Lady Fancy, in love with Wittmore, has married the grotesque old hypochondriac Sir Patient for financial stability and intends to continue her relationship with Wittmore; but, thinking she is going to bed with him, she is deceived into having sex with the opportunistic Lodwick, her stepdaughter's lover. (There is, perhaps, some doubt whether this actually happens or whether they are interrupted.) Lady Fancy also appears to intend to steal her daughter's beloved (though, again, another narrative is available, that she merely tested their affection and helped them deceive Sir Patient). At the end of the play, Lady Fancy is revealed as an adulteress, her impoverishment and separation from her husband cutting across the usual protocols of the comic ending. In this world of coercion, deception, and oedipal conflicts, the audience's anxieties are, to some degree, assuaged because it would have known that the relationship between the Bettertons is safe, the "Authority . . . of a Husband" legitimate rather than coercive, the pretense of compulsion and cuckoldry manifestly only a pretense. Even if Lady Fancy's fate is separation from her husband, poverty, and the loss of reputation, the plot around Isabella remains within the canonical realm of comedy partly by the mechanisms of the casting.

Behn's casting strategies are especially interesting in *The Rover* (1677). Here she uses the Bettertons to create the chivalrous Belvile and Florinda—the meeker, less witty, and more vulnerable of the two sister heroines—and William Smith and Elizabeth Barry to play the contrasting couple, Willmore and Hellena. Casting the known married couple in the former roles gives a comforting predictability to their trajectory in the play, all the more necessary to maintain comic equilibrium in a play where Florinda is constantly in danger of rape. This casting creates a Florinda with a more stately, even matronly, appeal than modern readers might otherwise suppose. (Mary Betterton was twenty years older than her "sister" in the play.) The wittier heroine is played by the younger and more exuberant Barry, who had no known connection with Smith, and so the relationship between Hellena and Willmore must have seemed more edgy and uncertain. Barry would have been an unknown quantity who might act outrageously and unpredictably, qualities that would have been a positive advantage in her portrayal of the "gay," "wild," "mad" Hellena (480, 455, 477).[2] Barry was right at the start of her career: her first Behn role—perhaps only her second as a performer (Howe 178)—was Leonora in *Abdelazer*, but as her career developed she tended to specialize in passionate, dark, dangerous women. Had Behn written *The Rover* a few years later, she probably would have cast Barry rather than Anne Marshall Quin as the courtesan Angellica Bianca, but possibly these elements already add to the characterization of Hellena.

Smith, who was in the 1680s known for his Jacobite sympathies, might have offered a different kind of thickening of the character of the royalist Willmore. In her plays in and around the Exclusion Crisis of 1679–81, Behn regularly cast him as witty young gentlemen who figuratively or literally embody opposition to the bourgeois Whiggism that in Behn's mind fueled the crisis. In *The Feign'd Curtizans* (1679), for instance, she cast him as Sir Harry Fillamour, whose wooing of an Italian lady discredits the mindless antipopery of the puritan Tickletext and demonstrates that "hostility to Catholic countries is misconceived" (Owen, "Sexual Politics" 18). Smith also spoke the prologue to *The False Count* (1682), a play satirizing the Popish Plot, an alleged (but almost certainly in reality nonexistent) conspiracy by Jesuits to assassinate the king, whose publicity in 1678 generated Protestant paranoia and Catholic anxiety. This prologue pretends that Behn has made a surprising switch of political allegiance, "converted" to Whiggism, and written "a recantation play." The audience's knowledge of the actor's as well as the dramatist's political allegiance must have emphasized the transparent quality of the irony. In *The Rover*—and perhaps especially its second part (1681), dedicated to James, Duke of York, and responding to the Exclusion Crisis—Willmore, as played by Smith, may have produced an uneasy combination of a "feminist interrogation of the libertine ethos" and a fantasy of Stuart political potency (Owen, "Sexual Politics" 19), but it may be that in the original performances the casting made the latter more prominent than it can be for us.

The conclusion of *The Rover* is "problematic" (Szilagyi 438); it is significant that, when four years later Behn wrote a second part of the play, she could not imagine a place for Hellena in it and so had her disappear between parts, dying shortly after her marriage to Willmore. The second part of *The Rover* in some ways replays the first but significantly reverses the ending. Whereas in the first part Willmore must choose between a young, wealthy virgin and a courtesan and chooses the virgin, in the second part he instead chooses the courtesan. Any regret we might feel for the death of Hellena is minimized by the casting of the actress who originally played her, Barry, as the courtesan, La Nuche, who in the sequel is paired off with Willmore. If Behn is indeed the author of *The Revenge* (1680), this play again reverses the second part of *The Rover* by casting Barry as the prostitute Corina but having the Smith character, Wellman, reject her for a more conventional bride. Behn tracks her performers through her oeuvre, creating, repeating, and varying relationships within the rigid formulas of Restoration comedy to increase audience enjoyment; to capitalize on what they know (or think they know) about performers both within and outside the theater; and also, more seriously, to force the audience to examine self-consciously "the ways it 'reads' women" (Lowenthal, *Performing Identities* 119). That Barry could, with equal conviction, play the chaste Leonora in *Abdelazer*, the ruling-class virgin Hellena in the first part of *The Rover*, the courtesan La Nuche in the second, and the prostitute Corina in *The Revenge* may suggest not only the magic of the theater but also the subversive possibility that the apparently watertight categories into which the seventeenth century classified the idea of woman might very easily collapse.

Centlivre showed equal expertise in manipulating audience knowledge and thickening character and action through intertheatrical allusion, especially in the case of her most important leading man, Robert Wilks. Wilks's most famous role had been Sir Harry Wildair in Farquhar's *The Constant Couple; or, A Trip to the Jubilee* (1700), and Centlivre uses this role as the template for those she wrote for him, like Sir James Courtly (*The Basset Table* [1705]), Bellmie (*Love's Contrivance* [1703]), Sir George Airy (*The Busie Body* [1709]), and Felix (*The Wonder* [1714]). So overwhelming was the association of Wilks with Wildair that in *The Basset Table* Centlivre slips three times into referring to the character as Sir Harry rather than Sir James (J. Pearson, "Textual Variants" 44–47).

Centlivre capitalizes not only on Wilks's professional history but also on extratheatrical discourse, what she expected the audience to know about his private life. This has particularly striking results in *The Basset Table*. Here Wilks's character, Sir James Courtly, loves the "*Religious sober Lady*" Lucy (10), played by Jane Rogers. In act 5, however, as a stratagem to force the compulsive gambler Lady Reveller—the beloved of Courtly's friend Lord Worthy—to acknowledge her faults and reform, Courtly locks himself into a room with her and pretends to intend rape, on the grounds that a woman who "takes as much Pains to draw Men in to lose their Money, as a Town Miss to their Destruction" cannot "boast of Innate Virtue." If he offers her money for sex, is he therefore doing anything her behavior has not led him to expect? She learns the lesson, weeps, realizes that she has imperiled her "Honour" (45), and, when she is rescued by Lord Worthy, recognizes his worth and agrees to marry him.

Anne Oldfield, the leading actress of the day, whose double act with Wilks was hugely popular, played Lady Reveller. (While modern attention has tended to focus on Valeria, the female scientist, the casting reinforces the view that Centlivre imagines Lady Reveller as the central female character.) Centlivre responds to audience expectation that Wilks and Oldfield would be cast opposite each other by ostentatiously not doing so: the "rape" scene might gain an extra frisson from the audience's expectation that they would be cast as lovers, or its ability to disturb might be moderated.

Casting Rogers as Lady Lucy reprised the famous double act from *The Constant Couple*, where Rogers had played Angelica opposite Wilks's Wildair, but it also significantly downgraded Rogers's importance, since in *The Basset Table* this relationship is far from central. Rogers had a reputation for "Virtue and Modesty" (J. Pearson, "List" xxvii), which is no doubt drawn on to create the "*Religious sober Lady.*" But she was also famous as Wilks's ex-mistress and was probably the mother of his natural daughter. She had taken their parting badly and had allegedly bitten him onstage during a tragic love scene; she hated Oldfield, her successor as Wilks's leading lady, and orchestrated a riot against her in 1712. These crosscurrents must have generated in the audience a delightful uncertainty about how Rogers might behave, especially since the downgrading of her role must have seemed to mirror her downgrading in Wilks's personal life. This emotional turbulence likely added to the experience of the play's first performances, and Centlivre probably intended that it should, since it contributes so effectively to the play's uneasy comedy. The edgy and ambiguous rape scene, then, uses casting to generate an appealing theatrical intensity and suspense that is, nonetheless, not allowed to destroy the comic equilibrium; at the same time, the presence of Wilks's enraged ex-mistress, however contained within the role of a sober religious lady, allowed for the commercially appealing possibility that something outrageous and exciting might happen. Women playwrights could be very adept in manipulating extratheatrical and intertheatrical discourses. A more detailed and nuanced examination of these dynamics could cast real light on the gendering of dramaturgy and performance in the period.

Behn, Centlivre, Gender Stereotypes, and Masculinity

As I was already aware in 1988, women dramatists questioned the rhetoric and practice of heterosexual courtship and marriage, as well as the prevailing terms of gender discourse. In *The Rover*, Behn allows her "most problematic character" (Lowenthal 123), the courtesan Angellica Bianca, to claim she has given her "virgin heart" to Willmore (495), while the virgin Hellena gives a spirited and convincing performance as a roving gypsy. Behn implies that socially constructed roles and oppositions between respectable and unrespectable women have little to do with the complexity of real existence or with women's desires to "authenticate" themselves (Diamond, "Gestus" 533) and "move from subjection into subjectivity" (Pacheco 323).

But in 1988 I did not think enough about the possibility that the inauthenticity of socially constructed roles might apply to male as much as to female characters, and one of the most marked shifts in critical attention since the publication of *The Prostituted Muse* has been the opening up of masculinity as a field of scrutiny, no longer seen simply as the standard of normality from which the female is a deviation. Patriarchy, too, which seemed a relatively straightforward conspiracy of men against women in 1988, is now viewed in more complex ways, as a series of negotiations rather than a single force or structure, and within these negotiations women could in practice have "considerable flexibility" that might seem theoretically excluded (B. Harris 17). Early modern "patriarchal ideology" was not monolithic, and its social practices were "muddled, contradictory," so that "competing forms of manhood" were simultaneously available (Shepard 1).

The Rover thus stages competing models of masculinity and of patriarchy, and even considers the possibility that there might be a space outside patriarchy that men could inhabit. The banished English cavaliers stand quite explicitly apart from patriarchy, exiles deprived of land, with all structures of authority in their country in disarray. In Naples, too, as in England, "a legitimate patriarchal figure is absent" (Szilagyi 436), the effect being that patriarchy is shown to be theoretically powerful but comically impotent in practice. Behn is "reconfiguring patriarchy," imagining a "post-patriarchal" world where women can achieve their own agency (438).

Thus in *The Rover* Behn emphasizes the equality between the lovers. Belvile and Florinda repeatedly echo each other: in act 1, scene 2, Belvile does not recognize Florinda in disguise, while in act 4, scene 2, she does not recognize him in disguise; in act 4, scene 1, he is imprisoned, and in act 4, scene 3, she is imprisoned, and so on. The cavaliers, forced to occupy a nonpatriarchal space, are "implicitly 'feminized'" (Burke, "Cavalier Myth" 123), but at least for Belvile this effect is represented positively, allowing him to possess masculine courage but also to be chaste and, to use an adjective repeatedly used in the play, "modest." The play perhaps does not simply move from a patriarchal to a "fratriarchal" order (Szilagyi 443): it also, at least momentarily, tries to imagine what a world without patriarchy might look like.

It is one of the play's best jokes that the most literal of patriarchs, the father of Hellena and Florinda, never actually appears, and his orders constantly fail to be implemented. His son Don Pedro is in a state of "complicity"—to use R. W. Connell's terminology (76–81)—with patriarchy, hoping to become a ruling patriarch himself one day. Yet, although he appears powerful, "his authority is imaginary" (Szilagyi 438), and, as soon as this authority is opposed, it collapses. Although the symbolically phallic competition in act 5 shows him as having the longest sword, he lacks true patriarchal authority, and, at the end of the play, he hands Hellena over to Willmore: "I shall now be free from fears of her Honour, guard it you now, if you can, I have been a slave to't long enough" (518). While in the first act Florinda had accused Pedro of making a slave of his sister (456), it transpires that in Pedro's eyes he has been the slave all along, committed to the laborious effort of guarding his sisters' chastity. Now, freed from that obligation, Pedro is as much liberated as his sisters. Patriarchy again is revealed as an optical illusion, collapsing when it is acknowledged and opposed.

These contradictions become particularly tortured around the figure of Willmore, whose acquisitive royalist sexuality Behn both celebrates and undercuts. The most abiding critical disagreements about the play center on him: some critics see him as a glamorous outlaw figure embodying a "heroic" identification with royalist sexuality and politics (Szilagyi 441), while others see him as a fool, a "naive outsider," "a false knight," "a rapacious beast" (Burke, "Cavalier Myth" 123–24). The best reading will be one that acknowledges the contradictions of Willmore and the ideology of masculinity he embodies. His own self-image as a "Rampant Lion of the Forrest" satirizes a male lack of self-awareness if not masculinity itself (461). Willmore certainly cannot be said to embody patriarchy, and indeed, at the end of the play, his marriage to Hellena is built on a repudiation of patriarchal authority, at least in the sense that Don Pedro means it. Willmore is, he tells us, citizen of a "Nation, that are of opinion a womans Honour is not worth guarding when she has a mind to part with it" (518). For a moment, we are allowed to enjoy a utopian vision of an England where desire is free and uncoerced for both sexes and where the failure of patriarchal authority is not a political disaster but a personal triumph. That this vision is not quite in keeping with the rest of the play indicates the hard collision of brutal fact and fantasies of desire that often strikes us in Behn's writing.

I am aware that this essay, like *The Rover*, "leaves pressing questions . . . raised but unanswered" (Szilagyi 455). But my purpose has been to indicate some developments in approaches to the gendered Restoration stage since 1988 and to suggest some ways forward that might be worth pursuing. For me, these are a closer study of gender in the consumption of theatrical texts and performances (perhaps especially to gain more knowledge about play reading as a gendered practice); a more nuanced examination of the construction of masculinity and patriarchy in plays by women; and further investigation of how extratheatrical and intertheatrical discourses shape the way dramatic roles are created and performed.

Notes

1. All quotations from *The Wonder* are from Jacqueline Pearson's edition *Susanna Centlivre*.

2. All quotations from *The Rover* are from volume 5 of Janet Todd's edition *The Works of Aphra Behn*.

Catherine Burroughs

Women and Playwriting, 1750–1800

The history of British women writing drama between 1750 and 1800 has been told in several, somewhat contradictory, ways: one strand of this narrative emphasizes the impediments to commercial success; the other stresses how women playwrights, despite encountering obstacles, overtly and indirectly interrogated mainstream positions on nationalism, race, sexuality, gender, and class (see in this volume Milling; O'Quinn; Rizzo).

The facts featured obviously affect the tone of this history. On the one hand, according to Ellen Donkin, only approximately seven percent of London-produced plays between 1660 and 1800 were women's (1). The 1750s, in fact, mark the nadir of women writing for the British stage before 1900. Just a few plays from this time come to mind: Catherine Clive's *The Rehearsal; or, Bayes in Petticoats* (1750) and the attributed *The London 'Prentice* (1754; now lost), both at Drury Lane; Susanna Cibber's *The Oracle* at Covent Garden (1752); Elizabeth Tollet's unperformed musical drama, *Susanna*; and Frances Brooke's rejected play, *Virginia*, in 1753 or 1754 (see Donkin 41–56). Closet plays—dramas written to be read rather than performed—emerged as a mode for allowing both women and men to bypass the difficult process of getting a play produced, and the vogue was in full force in the 1790s. Yet the 1750s actually offered few closet dramas by women, among them plays by Sarah Fielding and Jane Collier, Elizabeth Harrison, and Charlotte Lennox.

According to David D. Mann and Susan Garland Mann, during the 1760s, however, a play by a woman was produced almost every year at one of the two patent theaters and the summer Haymarket; in 1763 Drury Lane brought out three plays by Kitty Clive and Frances Sheridan. The 1760s also ushered in the start of Elizabeth Griffith's successful career. Five comedies—*The Platonic Wife* (1765), *The Double Mistake* (1766), *The School for Rakes* (1769), *A Wife in the Right* (1772), and *The Times* (1779)—were performed at Drury Lane and Covent Garden between 1765 and 1779. In the 1770s—in addition to the better-known playwrights Hannah More and Hannah Cowley—Dorothea Celisia and Jael Henrietta Pye produced a tragedy and farce, respectively, at Drury Lane (in 1771), and Charlotte Lennox, Sarah Cheney Gardner, Elizabeth Craven, Ursula Booth, and Elizabeth Richardson each wrote plays that received commercial productions (407–08).

The 1780s was a decade of rich and varied play composition by women in both England and Ireland—from closet plays to staged dramas to private theatricals. These compositions ranged from Sophia Lee's extremely popular sentimental comedy *The Chapter of Accidents* (adapted from Diderot [1780]) and Frances Brooke's tragedy *The Siege of Sinope* (Covent Garden [1781]) to Harriet Horncastle Hook's burletta (or comic opera) *The Double Disguise* (Drury Lane [1784]) and Elizabeth Inchbald's first successes, *A Mogul Tale* (1784) and *I'll Tell You What* (1785), both at the Haymarket. Margaret Cornelys, Betsy Sheridan, Anna Maria Edwards, and Anna Ross each had professional performances of their plays in Dublin (Mann and Mann 409–10).

By the 1790s, the list of women writing plays for both the closet and the stage is long. In addition to Hannah Cowley, Elizabeth Inchbald, Elizabeth Craven, and Sophia Lee, new names join the scene, among them: Marianna Starke, Catherine Metcalfe, Maria Barrell, Anne Hughes, Margaret Turner, Amelia Opie, Elizabeth Pinchard, Jane West, Hannah Brand, Eliza Parsons, Sophia Burrell, Mary Deverell, Mary Robinson, Fanny Burney, Elizabeth Edmead, Lady Eglantine Wallace, Charlotte Turner Smith, Charlotte Sanders, Margaret Holford, Harriet Lee, Maria Thérèse DeCamp, and Joanna Baillie. In 1799, twenty play titles appeared, including translations, closet plays, and private and public stagings (Mann and Mann

412). Indeed, as Jeffrey N. Cox and Michael Gamer note, from 1770 until 1825, one "can trace an active presence of more than ninety women writers in the theater" (Introduction xii).

It is true that, after 1750, women still had to contend with the belief that the "professionalization of women in the theater [was], in fact, associated with the moral breakdown of the theatrical world in general" (Straub 100), and not until 1843 did "performers begin to be distinguished in law from vagrants" (Moody, *Illegitimate Theatre* 16). Nevertheless, "the increased prominence of women playwrights and the continued influence of actresses" underscore the degree to which women of the late eighteenth century "also chose to step on to the stage of the nation" (Bolton 3, 5). As George Taylor, Daniel O'Quinn (*Staging*), Gillian Russell (*Women*), Marjean Purinton (*Romantic Ideology*), Daniel Watkins, and others have shown, women playwrights frequently wrote plays that implicitly threatened the values of the state but managed to escape censorship. This fact counters traditional narratives about post-1750 playwriting as having been defanged by the Stage Licensing Act of 1737. Still, it is important to consider some of the long-lasting effects of this significant piece of legislation. As Margarete Rubik has noted, the Stage Licensing Act of 1737 was particularly hard on women, who, having "found a home in [Henry] Fielding's Haymarket Theatre," now "found themselves on the street" (*Early Women Dramatists* 119).

The Stage Licensing Act of 1737 confined the spoken canonical drama to Drury Lane and Covent Garden (and the Haymarket in the summer) and also solidified the position of the lord chamberlain, whose charge it was to censor politically sensitive fare (until 1968!). The results were significant. Because the number of stage plays was limited, the major theaters often presented the same work, turning theatrical productions and seasons into sportslike events in which actors competed to garner the best reviews. Even though we can see in acting styles "a gradual change from grand rhetoric toward everyday speech and from heroic to more homely emotions . . . between 1700 and 1790" (McConachie, "Theatres for Knowledge" 240), as the patent theaters grew to accommodate over three thousand spectators by century's end, actors struggled to convey emotional subtlety in the face of what Sarah Siddons called, in reference to Drury Lane, "a wilderness of a place" (qtd. in Baines and Burns xxxvi). In addition, the Stage Licensing Act resulted in a proliferation of productions of Shakespeare and consolidated power in the hands of theater managers whose tenure was often long and whose tastes controlled what did and did not get staged (Brewer 389–94).[1]

Moreover, until 1788, when the Enabling Act was passed—which allowed magistrates "to license theatrical performances for up to a year"—all theater in the provinces was technically illegal, though the Stage Licensing Act of 1737 did not "apply to purely musical performances, nor did it cover free, private dramatic performances" (Brewer 388, 385). Yet, as Bruce McConachie has pointed out, because the Stage Licensing Act "made no provisions for theatre outside of London," its "numerous loopholes also allowed fairground managers and other theatre entrepreneurs to produce plays for lower-class patrons that encouraged a range of antisocial behavior" ("Theatre and the State" 209). This development resulted in the passage of the Disorderly Houses Act in 1751, which ensured that "all places for entertainment of any kind within a twenty-mile radius of London had to display a license that certified that the managers took responsibility for the good conduct of their patrons" (209). Furthermore, this piece of legislation "moved theatrical regulation toward the Japanese model," since, "[l]ike the samurai, the English governing classes had come to recognize that lower-class 'immorality,' from their point of view, was inevitable" (209). But although legislation in 1752 required that popular entertainments in London be licensed as well, this "did not stop players [from] mounting a wide range of amusements . . . in theatres, taverns and music rooms, and at fairs and pleasure gardens" (Brewer 387; see also Bratton *New Readings*).

In Jane Moody's analysis, "the opposition between legitimate and illegitimate theatre constitutes the fundamental category of distinction" in plays written between 1770 and 1840 (*Illegitimate Theatre* 4). On the one hand, because the Stage Licensing Act of 1737 required late-eighteenth-century playwrights with commercial ambitions to obtain a license from the lord chamberlain, political, sexual, or religious debates had to be conducted in the context of historically distant periods and "exotic" geographic locations, such as Spain in the fifteenth century, classical Greece and Rome, or the Middle Ages. But certainly the creation of "illegitimate theatre" was a boon for an increasingly diverse demographic of playgoers. In the 1790s, for instance, the "Fall of the Bastille, and Britain's war against Napoleon, provided the minor theaters with a collection of topical, spectacular narratives perfectly suited to illegitimate representation," and "Astley's, the Royal Circus, and Sadler's Wells Theatre began to pioneer their own physical dramaturgy of war," featuring "military knowledge, technical innovation and topographical illusion" (Moody, *Illegitimate Theatre* 27). As Julie Carlson observes:

> [T]heatre in this period represents one of the most democratized and diversified cultural arenas at the same time that its various stage representations are active in shaping proper British subjects in the metropolis, provinces, and colonies. ("Theatre" 642)

This "illegitimate theatre" encouraged by the Stage Licensing Act also forced generic experimentation. Hybrid genres included burlettas; pantomime ("the most conventionalised illegitimate genre long established in the popular theatre" and a specialty of Sadler's Wells [Taylor 31]); equestrian drama at Astley's London Theatre, showcasing live horses; melodrama in 1802 (the term "came to designate . . . a highly sensational mode of drama which often pitted a victimized hero against a series of inequities" [Pascoe, "Romantic Drama" 412]); gothic drama; tragedy; sentimental comedy, or "comédie larmoyante"; harlequinade; extravaganza; farce; romance; nautical drama; and afterpieces such as Elizabeth Craven's *The Miniature Picture* (1780)—"first performed in the town hall at Newbury" (410). As Daniel J. Ennis and Judith Bailey Slagle's edited volume demonstrates, prologues, epilogues, curtain-raisers, and afterpieces were also an important feature of an evening of theater.

Betsy Bolton has noted that mixed genres "allowed women a voice in contemporary political debates as long as they disavowed political intentions" (5), and Moody has observed that "the confusion—and subliminal political anxiety surrounding mixed genres"—was a way to subvert, critique, and evade cultural and political censorship (*Illegitimate Theatre* 50; see also Taylor). Recent analyses bear out this observation. Several critics have focused on Mariana Starke's *The Widow of Malabar* (performed first as a private theatrical in 1790 and then at Covent Garden in 1791) to demonstrate the degree to which Starke was able to achieve commercial success in a play saturated with political and cultural relevance. The plot involves the Indian widow Indamora, whose husband's demise requires that she be burned on his funeral pyre, and various British characters, who attempt throughout the drama to stop the ritual. (For a summary of the several-layered plot, see Mann and Mann 354.) Anne Mellor reads Starke's dramaturgy as an example of "embodied cosmopolitanism"—"a commitment to universal human rights, to being a 'citizen of the world,' to 'cultural harmony through romance,'" even though Starke's "inter-racial love . . . must be Christian love" ("Embodied Cosmopolitanism" 297). Gioia Angeletti praises Starke for "exploiting the resources of stagecraft," successfully managing "to construct a double-edged Orientalist discourse, and produc[ing] a drama, fraught with historical-political innuendoes, which even-handedly interweaves conformity and disruption, conservative and radical overtones" (71). And Daniel O'Quinn interprets "the deliberate misreading of Starke's play in the press" as an indicator of the degree to which *The Widow of Malabar* "poses fundamental questions regarding the consolidation of masculinity that cannot be separated from the project of self-regulation that would become so important to British policy in India" (*Staging Governance* 267).

Especially for women, commercial success in the theater could produce ambivalent responses, underscoring the risk attendant on women who chose to engage in the most public of genres. Hannah More was especially fortunate as a writer of tragedy. Her *Percy* ran for twenty-one nights in 1777–78, was revived by Sarah Siddons in 1787, and was translated into German and French. Despite More's stage success, however, by 1801 she was "condemning the theater" while "endorsing the benefits of reading drama, in which context moral and spiritual issues could be made explicit" (Ready, "From the Stage" 204). More's discomfort with tragedy runs counter to an early-eighteenth-century trend, which resulted from Jeremy Collier and other critics' attacks on the bawdiness of the English stage: some women opted for tragedy precisely because it was "a genre generally believed to be more fitted for women dramatists on moral grounds" (Rubik, *Early Women Dramatists* 58). Yet Hannah More's embrace of closet drama—which many men also turned to during the last quarter of the eighteenth century, including William Wordsworth, Samuel Coleridge, John Keats, Lord Byron, and Percy Shelley—may reflect a belief that "there is something in the act of dramatization that tends to obscure doctrines impossible to embody adequately and whose embodiment encourages the viewer to focus on the corporeal rather than on the spiritual" (Ready, "From the Stage" 203). Regardless, the move to closet drama represented a bow to decorum by More.

Yet because a play could earn its author more money in the second half of the eighteenth century—Elizabeth Inchbald died a wealthy woman in 1821—writing for the stage was increasingly viewed as a profession that women could enter with a degree of respectability. The same is true for acting, which gradually became less disreputable in proportion to its increasing dissociation from prostitution (see Rosenthal in this volume).

By 1812, when Siddons retired from the London stage, she had long been idealized in paintings and reviews as "the female symbol of the entire nation, dressed as Britannia at the service in Saint Paul's to celebrate the recovery of George III from his madness" (Brewer 346). This image of undisputed respectability was reinforced by Joshua Reynolds's portrait of her as the tragic muse shown in 1784 at the Royal Academy, only two years after her second London debut. Siddons's ascendancy was certainly helped by David Garrick's efforts earlier in the century, as John Brewer writes,

> to establish himself as the model thespian—an actor-manager who was a public figure, a theatrical impresario who chose the repertory, a performer whose interpretation of great drama rivaled the literary critics', a gentleman of taste and discernment who led a respectable, domestic private life, and an Englishman with impeccable patriotic credentials. (406)

And while Kitty Fisher, Hannah Pritchard, and Susanna Cibber were celebrated at mid-century—with Frances Abington, Dorothy Jordan, Elizabeth Farren, Anna Maria Crouch, and Mary Robinson to follow—no actress sought to distance herself from scandal and to develop a respectable offstage persona more arduously than Siddons.[2]

As Robyn Asleson has noted in her extensive study of actresses' influence on studio artists between 1776 and 1812, actresses were

> essentially the only group of women in Georgian Britain with both the power and the license to orchestrate public perceptions of themselves—chiefly through carefully contrived stage performances, but also through myriad forms of personal propaganda and self-fashioning. (Introduction 1)

Siddons was especially determined to raise the status of the actress, and she did so through a conscious cultivation—in visual representation, in public appearances on and off the stage, and in the conduct of her private life—of "a larger-than-life, queenly image" that likened her to "the realm divine" (5). She achieved this persona even as she became the mother of five children, performing while eight months pregnant with her fifth child right before she made her second London debut. When she died in 1831, thousands of mourners attended her funeral.

Siddons was the queen of tragedy, but although women playwrights had over twenty tragedies produced between 1750 and 1800, the predominant dramatic forms were comedic, including farces, burlettas, burlesques, musical entertainments, and interludes. Yet, like many male dramatists of the period, a number of women who wrote for the stage also produced a range of other genres: poetry (see Joanna Baillie's extensive output); novels (see part 3 in this volume); periodicals (e.g., Frances Brooke published thirty-seven issues of *The Old Maid* in 1755 and 1756); and theater theory and criticism.[3]

Translations and adaptations—especially of the gothic plays of the French melodramatist René-Charles Guilbert de Pixérécourt and the German playwright August von Kotzebue—proliferated in the last quarter of the eighteenth century. Aside from Inchbald's translation of Kotzebue's *Lovers' Vows*, Anne Plumptre was "the foremost British translator" of his works, publishing seven translations between 1789 and 1798 (Moody, "Suicide" 267). Yet more so than German, Spanish, or Italian playwrights, French dramatists fueled the work of women dramatists—from Molière and Voltaire to Diderot and Beaumarchais. Sophia Lee's *The Chapter of Accidents* (1780),

> based on Diderot's *Le Père de famille* and Marmontel's moral tale 'Laurette,' stands out as one of the most popular adaptations of French materials in the period. Acted one hundred times through the end of the century [the play] was repeated almost every season until Lee's death in 1824. (Mann and Mann 4)

In addition to topics familiar to historians of British theater—how to negotiate marriages and maintain class hierarchies through economic gatekeeping—plays of the period interrogated nationalist and mercantile projects in an age of increasing travel and colonization, especially in India. The plots were notably inflected by a rise of liberal Enlightenment feminist writing in the 1780s and 1790s (by Catharine Macaulay, Mary Wollstonecraft, Mary Hays, Amelia Opie, and others), the American and French revolutions, the abolitionist movement led by dissenting churches, and the rise of the middle class in the wake of the Industrial Revolution.

The patent theaters were located in areas rife with prostitution, making them places that people flocked to but complicating women's presence there. While it is by now a commonplace that "the corruption of the theater, like the corruption of the actress, can be traced to the presence of feminine sexuality" (Straub 100), when one surveys plays written by women during the hundred years after Aphra Behn (in which female sexuality is so unequivocally center stage), female desire seems oddly less important in the late eighteenth century. That is, when moving away from the tradition established by Behn, Manley, Pix, and Trotter in the early eighteenth century through the plays of Centlivre, Griffith, Lee, Cowley, and More to Burney, Inchbald, and Baillie in the late eighteenth, one cannot help noticing that sexual pleasure as a female entitlement becomes less admired and the celebration of female virtue, honor, or chastity intensifies—to the point that "the fallen woman" is an obsession in Victorian melodrama. Deception as a strategy that the married woman must necessarily employ to have an erotic life—as in Behn's *Sir Patient Fancy* (1678), Pix's *The Spanish Wives* (1696), and Trotter's *Love at a Loss* (1700)—becomes less a value onstage, especially in comedy, and the woman who can reform her future husband for a domesticated sex life emerges as the heroine, as in Griffith's *The Times* (1779) and Cowley's *The Belle's Stratagem* (1780). While in Behn's plays and those by Trotter and Pix especially, eros may be found not so much between husbands and wives as between adulterous partners, by the latter part of the eighteenth century the erotic—like many male characters—is muted or channeled into the companionate marriage (see Burroughs, "Erotics").

Paradoxically, however, the move toward conceptualizing marriage as a more monogamous place for both women and men suggests that the home is potentially a more eroticized stage, one in which husbands and wives are encouraged to look to each other for all their sexual pleasure. As Misty G. Anderson has written, Cowley's and Inchbald's comedies are "not . . . about resisting marriage, but about negotiating the terms, literal and figurative, under which Restoration and eighteenth-century women existed within the institution" (2). These plays

> make marriages work by suggesting that although something may be wrong with the institution, it can be made right. As a group, these playwrights are more optimistic about the social and legal implications of contract thought for women than many of their male colleagues. (3)

According to Bolton, understanding the drama of the period undoubtedly "makes aesthetic sense as well as political sense only when seen in its larger cultural context" (238), what David Worrall calls "an anthropology of Georgian drama" (2) and Gillian Russell explores through the lens of "sociability." As more scholars and teachers turn to the second half of the eighteenth century, emphases will shift and narrative strands will be repositioned. For now, the most significant development in this area of study is the proliferation of knowledge destined to change the course of graduate and undergraduate classrooms everywhere.

Notes

1. Between 1747 and 1809, Drury Lane had only two managers: David Garrick (1747–76) and Richard Brinsley Sheridan (1776–1809); Covent Garden only three: John Rich (1732–61), John Beard (1761–74), and Thomas Harris (1774–1803).

2. For more information on actresses in the latter half of the eighteenth century, see Eger.

3. See Lennox's *Shakespear Illustrated* (1753); Griffith's *The Morality of Shakespeare's Drama Illustrated* (1775); Inchbald's critical prefaces to *The British Theatre* (1806–09 [see Nachumi in this volume]); and Baillie's numerous prefaces to her plays published between 1798 and 1836.

Part II

Individual Playwrights

Nancy Copeland

Aphra Behn in the Contemporary Theater

Aphra Behn and her work provide a unique opportunity to study the incorporation of a female Restoration playwright into the repertoire of the late twentieth and early twenty-first centuries. Plays by other women playwrights from the period have been revived, but Behn's prominence in the contemporary repertoire is exceptional. Mary Ann O'Donnell's list of recent productions, appended to the second edition of her annotated bibliography, documents nearly fifty productions of Behn's plays between 1979 and 2002, staged mostly in Great Britain and the United States by professional companies large and small, off-off Broadway and fringe groups, and conservatories and universities. Nevertheless, commentators on Behn's work have noted the challenge of transmitting its meanings into the contemporary theater, whether they concern gender relations, politics, or tone (Copeland, *Staging* 158–86; Goodman 176–78; Griffiths 26–27). On tone, Charles McNulty, reviewing productions of Behn's *The Luckey Chance* and Edward Ravenscroft's *The London Cuckolds*, observed that "[i]n the commute from one age to another, humour sometimes misses the connection."

Like the work of other early modern playwrights, Behn's plays are inevitably adapted in performance to suit the contexts of their production and reception, sometimes through extensive rewriting but more often through the less overt process that Alan C. Dessen terms "rescripting": "changes made by the director in the received text in response to a perceived problem or to achieve some agenda" (3). Such rescripting need not be textual: the elements of performance can have a similar impact. The process of staging any play from the past in a new context is a form of adaptation: not only have the material conditions of the production changed, but so have the circumstances in which it will be received. The production history of Behn's plays is a study of how they have been adapted in performance to convey meaning in new cultural contexts.

Behn's plays were thoroughly embedded in their original production context, the late-seventeenth-century London theater. Behn wrote in established genres: "Spanish" intrigue comedies, of which *The Rover* is the best known, with their complicated romance plots set in exotic Spanish or Italian locations; city comedies, like *The Luckey Chance*, that satirize the Whig opposition; farces, like the commedia dell'arte–inspired *The Emperor of the Moon*; tragicomedies; and even a tragedy, *Abdelazer.* Leading roles in these plays were crafted for the star actors of the Duke's Company and United Company, among them Thomas Betterton, Elizabeth Barry, and such comic performers as Anthony Leigh and James Nokes. The detailed stage directions in the published versions of Behn's plays indicate her skill as a theatrical craftswoman and the importance of complex staging to the meaning of her plays. Almost all of Behn's plays were performed at Dorset Garden, the Duke's Company's lavish purpose-built theater. Like the other late-seventeenth-century London theaters, Dorset Garden's stage was composed of a large forestage and a deep scenic area separated by a proscenium arch with one or two doors built into it on either side, each with a balcony above. Scenery took the form of perspective painting on wings and borders, which framed the stage, and on shutters, flat panels that slid on and off stage in grooves, meeting in the center to create a backdrop for a scene. The scenic area of the stage had several shutter positions, allowing for rapid transitions between settings and for "discoveries," in which the shutters were drawn apart to reveal a preset scene behind them. The theaters also had the capacity to accommodate "machines," that is, the apparatus necessary to fly scenery, properties, and performers (see Langhans).

Behn's plays provide excellent examples of how the resources of this stage were used in performance. The stage directions of act 2, scene 1, of *The Rover* (1677) illustrate the use of the stage's architecture. The setting is "The Long Street," which indicates that the entire depth of the stage was used (466).[1] Here it is the site for an active and colorful spectacle of rival groups of men, flowing on and off stage as they assemble in masquerade costume outside Angellica Bianca's house and then fight one another for the privilege of her attention. Angellica's house is represented by one of the stage doors and the balcony above it: her bravos hang "a great Picture" of her from the balcony and place two smaller ones on either side of the door (468; line 87). Angellica appears in the balcony above her pictures, inviting comparison between herself and her images and dominating the action below. When Willmore enters her house, he does so through the proscenium door, invading her carefully guarded domain literally as well as figuratively.

Act 3, scene 2, of Behn's satirical sex comedy *Sir Patient Fancy* (1678) is an outstanding example of how "changeable scenery" that is shifted in full view of the audience can create a cinematic effect (Southern). A complex sequence of scene changes moves the action rapidly through a succession of settings leading to the "discovery" of the adulterous Lady Fancy in her bedroom with a lover who has "just risen in disorder from the Bed," as the shutters draw apart to reveal the scandalous scene (37; 189). The act concludes with a different sort of spectacle: the scene "Changes to the long Street, a Pageant of an Elephant coming from the farther end" carrying the foolish Sir Credulous Easy, who arrives in this extraordinary fashion to serenade his mistress (41; 331).

Dorset Garden's capacity to accommodate stage spectacle was fully exploited in Behn's popular farce *The Emperor of the Moon* (1687), climaxing in an elaborate, masquelike entertainment in act 3 that supposedly represents the arrival of the Emperor of the Moon and the Prince of Thunderland. After the discovery of a vista showing "the Hill of Parnassus" and the descent of "Keplair and Gallialeus" in chariots, followed by "the machine of the Zodiac" (200; 455), "the Globe of the Moon appears, first like a New Moon; as it moves forward it increases, till it comes to the Full. When it is descended, it opens, and shews the Emperor and the Prince" (202; 549). After a song and dancing, "A Chariot appears, made like a Half Moon," carrying the "richly dress'd" Emperor and Prince, who then "descend and land" while the song continues (203; 576). Following a "very Antick Dance . . . the Front Scene draws off, and shows a Temple, with an Altar" (204; 588), where the play's heroines are married to their lovers, who have disguised themselves as the Emperor and Prince.

Behn's plays rarely receive such lavish staging today: they are most likely to be mounted by fringe companies on shoestring budgets. But even if the resources of the Royal Shakespeare Company or the Guthrie Theatre are available, as they were for John Barton's and JoAnne Akalaitis's productions of *The Rover*, the plays inevitably will be changed by being performed in new circumstances. As Linda Hutcheon notes, such "material considerations" are part of the process of adaptation (*Theory of Adaptation* 142). She cites Jonathan Miller's assertion, in *Subsequent Performances*, that a work of art "changes its character according to the physical format in which it is presented," so that changes in the physical arrangement of the theater will have as great an impact on a play as "reinterpretations of the spoken lines" (qtd. in Hutcheon 142). Since the mid-1980s, *The Rover* has been performed on the thrust stage of the Royal Shakespeare Company's Swan Theatre, on a sand-covered floor in a cavernous warehouse for the Women's Playhouse Trust production, and, for Akalaitis's version, on a set featuring "bubblegum–pink fabric penises" (Franklin) and a "crimson" scrim resembling "a hymen the size of a spinnaker" (Simons 11).

The modern production history of Behn's plays can be divided roughly into two stages. The first includes the high-profile productions that garnered widespread attention for Behn's work in the decade between 1984 and 1994: the Women's Playhouse Trust productions of *The Luckey Chance* (1984) and *The Rover* (1994), both directed by Jules Wright; the Royal Shakespeare Company's 1986 production of *The Rover*, adapted and directed by Barton; and Akalaitis's high-concept production of the same play for the Guthrie Theatre in 1994. The Royal Shakespeare Company's and the Women's Playhouse Trust's *Rovers* provide especially useful case studies for classroom use: they offer strong, contrasting interpretations of the play and are well documented, through the program-script of the Royal Shakespeare Company's production and the video of the Women's Playhouse Trust's staging, as well as in the scholarly literature.[2] The two productions also embody two different approaches to adapting the play for modern audiences: Barton extensively rewrote Behn's text for his production, making numerous and sometimes controversial changes, while Wright staged Behn's entire text but nevertheless conveyed a clear point of view on the play. Barton's adaptation, which is still frequently performed, moves the action from Spanish-ruled Naples to a Caribbean colony, where Belvile is a "black soldier of fortune" and Lucetta is a slave (Barton 5). Many of Barton's textual alterations, a substantial number borrowed from Behn's source—*Thomaso*, by Thomas Killigrew—accentuate the brutality of the play's environment, social relations, and language, but in performance his production became a crowd-pleasing, carnivalesque "romp" that evoked the swashbuckling conventions of pirate movies, particularly through Jeremy Irons's star turn as Willmore.

Wright's production, available on video, was explicitly conceived as a response to Barton's, which the production team felt neglected the "serious" side of the play—its "power politics" and violence, especially against women (Goodman 178). The setting in this case was postcolonial and the casting multiracial: the Englishmen were cast with white actors, the Spanish characters were represented by black actors, and Angellica was played by an Indian actress-dancer. The production's nontraditional casting and postcolonial interpretation, with its "carefully layered national and cultural identities" that reflect "gender and power relations in contemporary London" (178), effectively challenge expectations that late-seventeenth-century comedy will be remote from present-day concerns. The casting also makes visible the "outsider" status of both Angellica and Behn's Englishmen (178). The latter, with the exception of Belvile, frequently behave like boorish tourists, while Angellica's social isolation is embodied in her race, her Indian costume, and the dance movements with which she punctuates her monologues. Maya Krishna Rao's dignified and poignant performance conveys Angellica's vulnerability and the pain Willmore's betrayal causes her. Andy Serkis's impetuous, disreputable-looking, but basically decent Willmore helps the viewer understand the character's appeal, both for Hellena and for the actors and audiences that kept the play in the repertoire throughout the eighteenth century. Nevertheless, he inevitably participates in the male violence that pervades the production and culminates in the two attempted rapes of Florinda, which, in direct contrast to Barton's farcical staging of the same scenes, are starkly brutal. Wright's production vividly conveys the aggressive misogyny of the society in which Behn's female characters struggle to achieve autonomy and happiness.

Since 1994, *The Rover* has become a fixture of the repertoire: fifteen of the thirty-seven productions documented by O'Donnell were staged between 1995 and 2001, and Robyn Bolam lists six productions in 2005 alone (xxxi n33). While *The Rover* remains the most frequently produced of Behn's plays and *The Luckey Chance* is still sometimes performed, there has been some diversification in Behn programming to include *The Feign'd Curtizans*, *The Emperor of the Moon*, and, most recently, *Sir Patient Fancy* (see O'Donnell). Very often these comedies are "rescripted" through cutting designed not only to shorten the text but also to clarify the complicated plots and through the addition of music either composed for the occasion or selected from the turn-of-the-twenty-first-century repertoire.

Textual adaptations and appropriations of Behn's work have also proliferated during this most recent stage of her production history. *The Rover* predominates in this category as well: adaptations include the 1999 musical *Shake Your Groove Thing*, by William Massiolia (O'Donnell 656); a 1996 version by Gyllian Raby set during the Spanish Civil War; and Josh Costello's 2005 rendering, in which "four teenage girls act out the story during a slumber party," using Behn's play to negotiate their relationships and their "fears and dreams" about their futures (Costello). The highest-profile production of Behn's work in recent years was 'Biyi Bandele's adaptation, *Aphra Behn's* Oroonoko, staged by the Royal Shakespeare Company in 1999.

Behn's comedies have become staples of theater programs and fringe and off-off-Broadway companies since the mid-1990s. Reviews of many of these productions suggest that a consensus has developed on how to stage Behn's comedies: as "diverting" (Shore), often farcical comedies that emphasize the characters' youth and energy and the plays' opportunities for slapstick, exciting swordplay, and spectacle. The attempts to emphasize the serious undertones of Behn's comedies in the major productions of the late 1980s and early 1990s seem to have been replaced by an emphasis on their indisputable entertainment value and Behn's expertise as a *farceuse*. The sources of the plays' appeal for university and other noncommercial companies is suggested by Carol MacVey's explanation of why she chose *The Rover* for a production at Princeton in 1985: "I found it satisfied my needs for an undergraduate production—many young roles for college-aged actors, lots of comic shenanigans, sword fights, and women who prevailed" (393–94). The plays that get staged are those that can meet most, if not all, of these requirements. *The Feign'd Curtizans*, described by one reviewer as "a romantic comedy-farce" (Orel), resembles *The Rover* in having an Italian setting (in this case, Rome) and in featuring several intriguing young women, disguise, risqué situations, nighttime confusion, and swordplay. *Sir Patient Fancy*, while it is a royalist political satire of its titular alderman based on Molière's *Imaginary Invalid*, is also a sex farce that combines assertive female characters with skillfully constructed comic situations.

The inclusion of the spectacular *The Emperor of the Moon* in the not-for-profit repertoire epitomizes the association of Behn with light entertainment. Reviews of various recent productions suggest that this farce's renewed popularity lies in the virtuosic physical comedy and traditional masks of the three commedia dell'arte servant characters—Harlequin,

Scaramouch, and Mopsophil—who assist the young lovers in outwitting the moon-obsessed Doctor Balliardo, and in its fantastic plot, involving multiple disguises and transformations and possibilities for creative staging. The play's carefully constructed routines for the servants, with their continuing appeal for contemporary audiences, are further testimony to Behn's skill as a theatrical craftswoman and reveal the traditional antecedents of the farcical episodes that are prominent in many of her comedies, from Blunt's hapless encounter with Lucetta in act 3 of *The Rover* to the rake Wittmore's elaborate attempts to conceal himself in Lady Fancy's bedchamber in act 4 of *Sir Patient Fancy.*

The protofeminism that remains part of Behn's reputation finds expression in all-female productions. Particularly notable are those of the Brooklyn-based Queen's Company, a self-described "all-female ethnically diverse company" that staged one Behn comedy a year between 2001 and 2003 (Queen's Company). They have performed *The Rover* (2001), *The Feign'd Curtizans* (2002), and *The Luckey Chance* (2003) and workshopped *Sir Patient Fancy* in spring 2007. Their slogan is "all female! all the time! no apologies!" and Behn ranks second only to Shakespeare in their repertoire. They have explained their casting practice as a return "to Shakespeare's tradition of trans-gender casting," which allows them to "expand the performing opportunities for female actors, challenge gender assumptions and give new life and meaning to theatrical works" (Juggernaut). They describe their style as "populist" and characterize their productions as "an adrenaline shot kicking the classics back to life" (Queen's Company; Juggernaut). Rebecca Patterson, the director of these productions, explained in an interview about *The Luckey Chance* that the vigorous physicality of the performances is part of their challenge to the audience's "assumptions about gender": "these women 'really rough each other up,'" she commented (C. Byrne). The company's rambunctious style is an extreme example of the widespread practice of physicalizing Behn's comedy in performance.

Costello's adaptation of *The Rover*, first performed in 2005, also features an all-female cast. Costello's version is set in the bedroom shared by Hellena and Florinda, who are reimagined as contemporary teenagers aged about thirteen and fifteen. In a scene analogous to Behn's act 1, scene 1, Hellena goads Florinda and two of her friends to talk about love. She then engages them in a game that, according to Costello's synopsis, gradually turns into a reenactment of *The Rover*, "using props and costumes from a toychest, as if making it up as they go along." Willmore is played by the more "adventurous" of Florinda's friends, who believes that "men can be fun, but they're all jerks."[3] "Guys can't fall in love," she tells Hellena. "Not really. They don't know how." "[B]y playing this role," Costello explains in his synopsis, "the girl is trying to show the other girls that this is how men behave." The other friend plays Angellica. She believes that "women need to take control." "Don't fall in love," she advises Hellena; "get guys to fall in love with you." She "uses this role to show a powerful woman who uses her beauty and wit to control men," Costello comments. Other roles are filled by toys manipulated like puppets. The authority and credibility of Don Pedro and Don Antonio are undermined when they are ludicrously represented by a stuffed dog and duck, respectively, and Barbie and Ken are used "to dramatise Blunt's encounter with Lucetta" (Bolam xxxi), producing a farcical effect that can be glimpsed in the video montage posted on Costello's Web site.

Costello's version epitomizes recent trends in Behn productions, notably the focus on the female characters and the youth of the protagonists and the exploitation of the play's farcical potential; yet his adaptation seems to have been very successful in also conveying some of the serious issues raised by Behn's play. Costello comments in his synopsis that his adaptation works consistently on two levels: "Aphra Behn's story serves as a way for the girls to further their own agendas with each other, and the girls' agendas mirror and support the underlying themes of Aphra Behn's play." He emphasizes "the power of imagination" as the link between Behn's play and his adaptation; his young women all use imagination "to explore their questions about love and growing up."

Having the "jerk" Willmore played by a young woman foregrounds the play's exploration of gender roles and brings together the two levels of the action with particular force. Willmore's drunken assault on Florinda in act 3 becomes part of the girl's demonstration of "her point about men" (Costello), but their violent struggle, which Bolam reports "menacingly conveyed" this "potential threat of rape" (xxxi), is one of several actions that, Costello notes, "threaten to force the other girls to drop out of the game to stop her." The cross-gender casting lends homoerotic resonance to the relationship between Willmore and Angellica when Willmore's seductive lines near the end of act 2 lead the girl playing Angellica to kiss her friend passionately on the mouth, an impulse that surprises them both. Costello explains that this moment exposes the girl playing Angellica to "teasing from her friend, and also serves to mirror and support Angelica's reluctant infatuation with Willmore." The duality of the action is again brought into sharp focus in act 5, when, in place of the pistol with which Angellica threatens the perfidious Willmore, the girl playing the role substitutes the can of pepper spray she always carries "and seems to be about to use it on her friend." The young women then "use Aphra Behn's words to work through this crisis" in their relationship (Costello). Throughout, the two layers of the adaptation's action lend emotional immediacy and accessibility to the dilemmas of Behn's female characters while establishing present-day analogies for their situations.

Another high-profile production of Behn's work is Bandele's adaptation of Behn's novella *Oroonoko; or, The Royal Slave*, which was staged by the Royal Shakespeare Company in 1999. His *Oroonoko* is divided into two parts: the first, showing Oroonoko and Imoinda's life at court in Coramantien before they are enslaved, is inspired by Behn's text but is substantially original; the second, set like Behn's novella in Surinam, is adapted from John Hawkesworth's 1759 tragedy, which was in turn based on Thomas Southerne's tragicomedy of 1696 (Munns, "Reviving" 189).

Although Oroonoko's kingdom of Coramantien "existed in what is known today as Ghana," Bandele, a Nigerian playwright and novelist based in London, has set the first part of his "re-imagined *Oroonoko* in a Yoruba—which is to say Nigerian—setting" (Bandele 5). He explains that the characters' names are "recognisably Yoruba" (5), but the change of place also allows him to introduce "the performance of ceremonies from his own Yorubaland" that are the occasion for the drumming and dancing that were a highlight of the Royal Shakespeare Company's production (Cribb 173). Bandele's version of Behn's story mixes the archaic and mythic with the contemporary, notably an anachronistic late-twentieth-century feminism. Imoinda is articulate and self-possessed; when Oroonoko's misplaced loyalty to the Kabiyesi prevents him from intervening when she is sent the "Veil of Invitation," she temporarily defends herself from rape by castrating the old man, causing his death. Lady Inola, her surrogate mother and mentor, is an outspoken former concubine, whose "royal immunity" allows her to be a sarcastic critic of the impotent Kabiyesi and his corrupt court (Bandele 38).

The play as a whole has been criticized by Anne F. Widmayer for having "effectively silenced Behn's voice" by replacing "Behn's original with a more easily digestible version" (218). Elizabeth Kowaleski-Wallace voices a more positive view:

> Bandele's *Oroonoko* warrants our consideration not as an adaptation or a retelling of an old story but as a creative and important meditation on diasporic experience, on performance history, and on the history and future of transcultural contact. ("Transnationalism" 278)

Jessica Munns observes, "This story is one of the master narratives of colonial possession," and the repeated reworkings of it "suggest how important it was," and is, "to retell that story" ("Reviving" 192). As Hutcheon asserts, "[A]daptation is how stories evolve and mutate to fit new times and different places," thus helping keep their sources "alive" (*Theory of Adaptation* 176). This vital process includes not only appropriations like Bandele's *Oroonoko* and adaptations like Barton's or Costello's *Rover* but also the numerous productions both prominent and obscure that some of Behn's plays have received from the 1980s onward. The presence of her work in the contemporary repertoire is evidence of its continued ability to speak to audiences, adapting, in Hutcheon's biological metaphor, so that it may continue to flourish.

Notes

1. All quotations from Behn's plays are from Janet Todd's edition of Behn's complete works; stage directions are referred to by the line that they follow. For Behn's street scenes, see Lewcock, "Computer Analysis" 153.

2. See Aughterson 247–52; Copeland, *Staging* 167–82; Goodman; Munns, "Barton."

3. Dialogue is quoted from the video montage posted on Costello's Web site, from a live television remount of the original production that was broadcast in April 2005.

Elizabeth Kubek

Mary Pix, the London Middle Class, and Progressive Whig Ideology

Between 1697 and 1703, the Whig playwright Mary Pix wrote three comedies set in contemporary London: *The Innocent Mistress*; *The Beau Defeated; or, The Lucky Younger Brother*; and *The Different Widows; or, Intrigue All-a-Mode*. These plays serve as an index to the complex and changing network of relationships—political, personal, and professional—among women playwrights, theatergoers, and actors in late-Stuart London. Pix's London comedies are masterly examples of mixed comedy of feeling and intrigue, with strong roles for actresses. Taught using a combination of close reading and historical context, the plays also illustrate the topicality of late-Stuart drama and its importance as a site for women's participation in both political discourse and the construction of gender and class roles.

The Innocent Mistress and the Emergence of Mary Pix

Peter Motteux's epilogue to *The Innocent Mistress* (1697) teases its audience with the prospect of a new market for theatrical entertainment: the "grave" middle class, whose concerns and erotic practices are envisioned taking over both the space of the theater and the attention of the players. This demographic change in the London audience was a particular concern of the actresses and women playwrights of the late-Stuart era. Struggling for respect and success, these women were positioned awkwardly between the old system of aristocratic patronage (and often, for actresses, sexual exploitation) and a new competitive economy of professionalism and self-promotion. This transition reflects the larger social shift Michael McKeon describes as "the newly conceptualized antithesis between the 'landed interest' and the 'monied interest,'" a development he traces in part to "the new, quantifying forces of public credit created by the 'financial revolution' of the 1690s" (166). The shifting borders of class or status terminology (McKeon 131–75) inform competing analyses of late-Stuart comedy as "comprehending complex and incomplete processes of social differentiation" (Dawson 44). How were the urban middle classes distinct from the landed gentry, whose values and manners they often sought to emulate? Rather than seek assimilation, should London's merchant classes express their economic power in a distinct way? The wife of a merchant tailor, Mary Pix approaches these questions primarily through the figure of the economically powerful, middle-class woman. Although Pix's "Cits" (Londoners) and Ladies resemble traditional comic figures, they are updated to foster the emergence of "nice" and aspiring female consumers.

In her London comedies, Pix courted women's approval by employing careful exposition, comparisons between female characters, and topical and literary references. Although her origins were low relative to those of her friends Delarivier Manley and Catharine Trotter, Pix in her writing displays broad reading and social acumen. Moreover, through her relationships with Elizabeth Barry, Anne Bracegirdle, and Thomas Betterton, Pix was directly involved in the transformation of theatrical London. *Ibrahim*, her first play, was produced in 1696 at the Drury Lane Theatre by the remnants of the United Company. In 1695, this group had been split by a rebellion of its principal actors, led by Betterton and his two leading ladies, against serious mismanagement by its patentees (Bush-Bailey 95–100). Constance Clark argues that *Ibrahim* may have originally been written for Barry and Bracegirdle, before the company's split (220–21). Whatever her initial ties to Drury Lane, Pix found herself at the new theater in Lincoln's Inn Fields the following season, and she would write for Betterton's company for the rest of her career (Clark 183–287). Pix's work is thus strongly influenced by both the competition between the two companies and the composition of Betterton's troupe, especially the Barry-Bracegirdle partnership (Bush-Bailey 146–53, 180–84).

The Innocent Mistress opens with a pointed reference to this new atmosphere: "This season with what Arts both Houses strive, / By your kind presence, to be kept alive!" (Prologue). A blend of sentiment and intrigue, *The Innocent Mistress* contains lovers for every taste: Betterton and Barry starred as the sentimental hero and heroine, Sir Charles Beauclair and Bellinda, while John Verbruggen and Bracegirdle faced off as the rake Sir Francis Wildlove and the roguish Mrs. Beauclair, Sir Charles's niece. The Barry-Bracegirdle coupling, which inspired a generation of playwrights (Bush-Bailey; Howe 147–70), is here adapted to heighten the contrast between two virtuous heroines. Mrs. Prince and Mr. Hodgson represented a third, sensible couple: "Beaumont, an Honest Country Gentleman," and Arabella Venturewell, heiress to the fortune of her merchant father. A satiric counterpart to all this romance is offered by several mercenary and grotesque couplings,[1] through which the aspiring middle classes receive a series of lessons on manners and morals.

The play's opening scene establishes Pix's skillful use of exposition. Sir Francis defines for his friend Beaumont the various roles available in the London erotic market: "the Jilt," "the Mistress," and "the Coquette" are matched by "your Rake, your Cully, and your Beaux" (1–2). Sir Francis also confesses his attraction to Mrs. Beauclair, and he relates Sir Charles's "backstory": "a younger Brother," Sir Charles was coerced into marrying a rich widow before he acquired the family fortune and title. Beaumont supplies his own establishing narrative: he has come to London to help Arabella retrieve her fortune and to locate the missing heiress Mariamne Bellmour, a reader of romances in flight from a forced marriage. The witty dialogue of this expository scene helps disguise the reliance on convention that gives the play a popular appeal. By the time Sir Charles enters, the astute contemporary viewer would have been congratulating herself or himself on having guessed the main plot twists: the "Platonick Mistress" Sir Charles chastely adores is the missing Mariamne, and the first husband Lady Beauclair "hunted into the Indies" will turn up alive to release Sir Charles from his "Intolerable Plague of a Wife" (2–4).

Tellingly, Pix's most aristocratic characters, Mariamne and Sir Charles, are simultaneously idealized and gently satirized. Both are paradoxical victims of the aristocratic marriage system: she is the titular "innocent mistress," and he is a virgin husband, having refused to consummate his loveless marriage. All three of Pix's London comedies depict both men and women as objects of exchange in a mercenary and class-conscious marriage market. Pix's solution promotes progressive Whig ideology, in a form designed to flatter female Cits: wealthy women heroically counteract the injustices of aristocratic primogeniture by marrying or mothering good men.

Throughout *The Innocent Mistress*, Pix adapts comic conventions for her middle-class audience. Thus, when Mrs. Beauclair dons breeches to interrupt Sir Francis's assignation with Mrs. Flywife at Locket's tavern, she disguises herself as an apprentice: "I was put to an Attorney, but longing to turn Beau, have half-ruin'd my Master, wholly lost my Friends, and now am follow'd by the several Actions of my *Taylor*, *Sempstress*, *Perruke-Maker*, *Hosier*, and a long *Et cetera*." A disgusted Sir Francis remarks, "Tis monstrous to cheat honest Tradesmen in dressing up a Fop." Mrs. Flywife, however, allows herself to be decoyed away: "I think it is the prettiest Youth I ever saw, I have Wealth enough to supply his wants, what should then debar me?" (28). When Sir Francis challenges the supposed apprentice to a duel, Mrs. Beauclair unmasks and rebukes him as the dupe of a jilt. Pix uses her heroine's masquerade to denounce an urban black market of desire: the faithless mistress bestows her keeper's wealth on the apprentice who bankrupts his master. The episode thus provides a cautionary representation of the link between women's economic and erotic powers.

Yet the tavern scene also possesses a grim historical topicality. Sir Francis initially describes himself as one who would "sacrifice my life to serve my friend" (2), a rhetorical flourish that becomes disturbingly literal at Locket's, as the disguised Mrs. Beauclair has Sir Francis called away "on what concerns your Friend's Life." When Sir Francis reenters, to find Mrs. Flywife and the "apprentice" gone, he angrily demands, "[W]ho was that Impostor that told me my Friend Mr. *Beaumont* was taken up for a *Jacobite*, and the Mobb was pulling him to pieces?" (29). The reference is to the anti-Jacobite hysteria that followed the 1696 discovery of a plot to assassinate William III, in support of an invasion scheme on the part of James II and his patron Louis XIV (Garrett). Coming at a time of financial crisis, these events were closely covered by the popular press and led to a series of public attacks on real and suspected Jacobites (Ogg 428–29). The crisis intensified concern about the stability of the government, especially given the new system of succession established by the 1689 Bill of Rights; after the death of his wife Mary in 1694, William's claim to the throne depended entirely on an act of Parliament. Even within the emerging Whig party, William's taking precedence over his sister-in-law, Anne, was controversial, a point of instability that helped feed fears (or hopes) of a Jacobite restoration. Pix's reference to the angry "Mobb" thus interpolates contemporary paranoia into *The Innocent Mistress*'s relatively conventional network of deception and plots.

Beaumont's scheme to rescue Arabella and her fortune invokes further images of public brutality. Like Mariamne and Sir Charles, Arabella Venturewell is entangled in a forced-marriage plot, the result of a will forged by her former guardian, Lady Beauclair's father. When Arabella refuses to marry Lady Beauclair's brother Cheatall, she is imprisoned, but her maid Eugenia and Cheatall's servant Gentil conspire with Beaumont to terrorize Cheatall into freeing her. To this end, Beaumont masquerades as Arabella's bastard brother, a murderous pirate and self-proclaimed serial rapist, while Eugenia laments her mistress's apparent murder: "I went into the Room, where the Lady was lockt up: And there's at least a Pail full of blood—all the Water in the Sea will never wash the stains out" (34). Although Cheatall protests his innocence, later we hear a "Boy Without" marketing

> [a] full and true Relation of a horrid and bloody Murther, committed on the Body of Mrs. *Arabella Venturewell* . . . by one 'Squire *Barnaby Cheatall*, and his Man *Gentil*; shewing how they lock'd her up in the dark, then cut her to pieces, and carried the pieces away under their Cloaks. (42)

While a sequence of asides reminds the audience that the murder of Arabella is an elaborate gag, the viral spread of (mis)information recalls the everyday horrors unleashed by the discovery of the assassination plot, including the savage penalties for treason. Moreover, the image of "a pretty Lady" dismembered may allude to the vigilantism directed against urban women by such late-Stuart groups as the Society for the Reformation of Manners (see A. Hunt, ch. 1). *The Innocent Mistress* thus reflects the impact of violent events on a capitalist society in systematic political transition.

***The Beau Defeated* and the Cult of Princess Anne**

The next of Pix's London comedies, *The Beau Defeated; or, The Lucky Younger Brother* (1699 or 1700), was produced in a more stable social climate. The 1696 Act of Association, which amounted to a loyalty oath to William, had been employed to purge the government of Jacobites. Moreover, the 1697 Treaty of Ryswick bound Louis XIV not to support any challenge to William's reign, effectively isolating James II and his son (Ogg 426–39). However, Princess Anne, William's successor under the Bill of

Rights, was vulnerable both to suspicion of Jacobite sympathies and to accusations of unfeminine and unfilial conduct for supplanting her father. Yet Anne's difficulties also presented an opportunity for the creation of a political mythology that would legitimize women's claims to power. Carol Barash criticizes Tory poets' use of maternal imagery as making Anne "sound less like a monarch, more like middle-class kin" (225). But the image of bourgeois womanhood could be used by Whig writers to represent Anne as an alternative to traditional authority. The image of the powerful woman as an elevated version of the ideal middle-class wife and mother—practical, devoted, restrained, loyal—supports Pix's overall representations of women's role under progressive ideology. The progressive matron supports, and is defined by, a state system of reproductive, economic, and affective relations. Since the terms of Anne's succession derived from an act of Parliament and her fitness to rule was judged by her familial behavior and reproductive status, the future queen's legitimacy was confessedly defined by the same social forces that determined progressive class and gender relations. Pix's London comedies, then, represent powerful women as both commodities and consumers, on whose choices depends the moral well-being of society.

In *The Beau Defeated*, Pix again wrote lead roles for Barry and Bracegirdle, but this time she constructed a sentimental-satiric comedy around two female characters differentiated by the morality of consumption. Thus, while Bracegirdle played the virtuous Lady Landsworth, "A Rich Widow of the North," Barry enacted Mrs. Rich, "a Fantastick City Widow." The play begins with Mrs. Rich lamenting to her maid, Betty, that she has been publicly addressed as "Citizen" by "a beggarly Dutchess, at the end of an old Coach." Betty feigns astonishment:

> What! Madam, your Person shining all o're with Jewels, your new gilt Coach, your dappl'd Flanders with long Tails, your Coachman with cocking Whiskers like a Swiss Guard, your six Footman cover'd with Lace more than any on a Lord-Mayor's Day?

Mrs. Rich, whom Betty describes as "the Widow of an honest Banker, who got Two Hundred Thousand Pounds in the King's service" (1), is determined to become "a Woman of Quality" by marrying Sir John Roverhead, the titular beau: "there is Justice in what I design, Mr. *Rich* did not get his Estate too honestly; and 'tis some kind of Restitution, to raise up with what he has left me, one of the Ancients Families in the North" (3). This comment on the questionable honesty of bankers reflects an immediate concern of Londoners of all classes. William's administration had done much to regularize government finance, bringing lotteries under state regulation, attempting to control the "clipping" of coins,[2] and establishing—largely on the basis of a huge Stuart-era debt to the nation's goldsmiths and bankers—what would become the Bank of England (Ogg 418). Still, private bankers had many opportunities to raise money sub rosa. Mrs. Rich's desire to pass on her husband's money is thus by the play's standards not entirely without merit, but her attempts to gain "a Name" expose her to ridicule and worse; the "beau" and the "women of Quality" she cultivates are sharpers and frauds (3). Yet unlike Lady Beauclair, Mrs. Rich is balanced between folly and virtue. The end of the play sees her resigned to her new husband, a rustic but wealthy "Country Squire."

The play's main romance, however, involves the sentimental hero Clerimont, the squire's younger brother. Pix here takes on a favorite theme of progressive fictions, the plight of the younger brother under primogeniture (McKeon 218–20). The death of his father intestate has left Clerimont penniless. Nevertheless, when we first see him, he has just turned down a gift of gold from a "Mask in the Playhouse": "my Nature's quite otherwise, I cannot be oblig'd where I contemn, nor live so vile a way" (9). His landlady urges him to seek "private Chamber-practice," as so many of her "fine Gentlemen" have done: "if the young handsome Fellows were like you, there wou'd never have come so many of them to their Coach and Six." Clerimont's bitter retort—"if you think the Ladies will like me so well, take my Picture and hang it out at your Belcony" (10)—casts all mercenary love as prostitution while also feminizing the hero. The audience, however, knows that the "Baggage" to whom Clerimont is unwillingly attracted is, in fact, Lady Landsworth; Clerimont's virtue is never really at risk.

In *The Beau Defeated*, Pix conflates characteristics of both leads from *The Innocent Mistress*: like Mrs. Beauclair, Lady Landsworth uses masquerade for a virtuous end, while she resembles Mariamne in her idealism. In the earlier play, Beaumont attributes Mariamne's flight from an arranged marriage to her desire for "a Hero" possessed of "all *Scudries* accomplishments" (4).[3] This reference to romance is echoed in *The Beau Defeated* when Lady Landsworth describes to Betty her ideal second husband:

> *Lady Landsworth.* He should be Gentile, yet not a Beau; Witty, yet no Debauche; susceptible of Love, yet abhorring Lew'd Women; Learned, Poetical, Musical without one Dram of Vanity; in fine, very meritorious, yet very modest; generous to the last degree, and Master of no

Estate; mightily in Love with me, and not so much as know I am worth the Cloaths I wear.

Betty. Ha, ha, ha, to your Romances again Lady fair, 'tis only there you can converse with those Heros, this Town affords no such. (5)

But Lady Landsworth has already found her ideal in Clerimont, and her first marriage to an elderly and sickly "Debauchee" has "got" her enough wealth to test Clerimont's virtue by offering him both sex and gold. Far from being irrelevant to romance, the topic of money is crucial; when Clerimont refuses her advances, Lady Landsworth remarks, "He speaks, as my own Heart had Coin'd the Words" (20). This image plays on the idea of true coinage as a transparent medium of exchange, transcendentalizing the association of economic and moral value Pix laments in the play's dedication: "I wou'd have perswaded the World to prize Desert, before the Gifts of Fortune, but . . . few are so truly Noble to fix without Interest." Lady Landsworth demonstrates her moral value through the disinterested way she puts herself and her acquired wealth back into circulation.

The Beau Defeated ultimately demonstrates the triumph of middle-class values in the form of Mrs. Rich's "Citizen" brother-in-law, who angrily asks "if it would not be more decent for you to have a good grave Coach . . . than all this sumptuous Equipage, that makes People inquire who you are" (13) and attacks London's "*Beaux*" as "hav[ing] no more Credit, than they have Religion" (14). Mr. Rich, however, also speaks the play's closing lines, which envision a harmonious interrelationship of the classes:

The Glory of the World our British Nobles are,
The Ladies too Renown'd, and Chast and fair:
But to our Citizen's, *Augusta's* Sons,
The Conquering Wealth of both the India's runs;
Tho' less in Name, of greater Power by far,
Honours alone, but empty Scutcheons are;
Mixt with their Coin, the Title sweetly sounds,
No such Allay as Twenty Thousand Pounds. (47)

The play on financial terms reminds the audience of the dependence of William's new economy on credit and mixing—that is, banking, the constitutional monarchy, the mingling by marriage of Stuart and Orange and of merchant and gentry, and the fluid economic power wielded by women in a progressive society.

The Different Widows and the Last Stuart Succession Crisis

Although the title of Pix's last London comedy, *The Different Widows; or, Intrigue All-a-Mode* (1703), suggests another female pairing, the cast included neither Barry nor Bracegirdle. The leads are the romantic couple, consisting of the rake Sir James Bellmont and his virtuous betrothed Angelica. The play's elaborate plots, involving Angelica's masquerade as a kept mistress, are set in motion by Sir James's mother, Lady Bellmont, who endures much sentimental suffering to mortify and redeem her erring son.

The image of the heroic mother must have appealed to a generation of middle-class women raised on conduct books. Yet the play also alludes to a contemporary political crisis of particular concern to the Whig supporters of Anne, now reigning queen. The Jacobite threat had been reignited by two events: the death in 1700 of Anne's sole heir, the Duke of Gloucester, and renewed tensions between France and England, which had led to Louis XIV's recognition in 1701 of James II's son, the "Old Pretender." The 1701 Act of Settlement fixed the succession on the Protestant Hanoverians, through the electress Sophia, the granddaughter of James I (Ogg 459–85). Although Anne disliked Sophia's son George, who was suspected of having arranged the murder of his wife's lover (Hatton 50–61), she was under pressure to make some public gesture of support for the Hanoverian claim. Anne's conspicuous series of failures at motherhood, which included as many as thirteen miscarriages or stillbirths, brought to a head critical questions about constitutional monarchy: if the crown is no longer unalienable patrimony, what form of property is it? Moreover, on what grounds could a childless queen claim any role in the transfer of power? In 1703, the Duke and Duchess of Marlborough actively campaigned for a solution: Anne should "have the young Prince of Hannover & breed him as her own son" (Churchill 49; see Snyder, vol. 1). The idea of the queen's thus "breeding" an heir appealed to both Whigs and Tories, since Anne's half-brother, James Francis Edward, could also qualify by becoming a Protestant (Gregg 182–84; Hatton 73–78). The theme of heroic maternity allows Pix to address her progressive scenario to both constituencies, by creating a hero in whom the "Noble Seeds of Honour" bestowed by aristocratic patrilineage are developed by a reforming maternal agency (13). This image is tipped toward the Whig side of the scale, however, by Pix's representation of legitimate power as limited by legal document and precedent. With her will subject to the requirements of patriarchal law, the mother/queen must lead by example and self-sacrifice.

The Different Widows is dedicated to the Countess of Salisbury, whose "Heroick Vertue" "gives an *Idea* of those Noble *Roman Wives*, whose exalted Merit, in every Change of Life, was still the same"—a reference to Anne's having adopted as her motto Queen Elizabeth's "semper eadem" 'always the same.' The countess's virtue is especially manifest in her "unalterable Fidility to your Lord, and constant Suffering with him"; James Cecil, the fourth Earl of Salisbury, had been imprisoned (along with Marlborough) as a result of the forged "Flowerpot Letter" of 1692 ("Cecil"; F. Harris 66–67). Having reminded her readers of this Tory plot, Pix concludes by wishing that the countess "live to see Your Charming Son long possess his Honour, and increase That *Race* which always Adorn'd our Kingdom."

In *The Different Widows*, the mother is deemed virtuous precisely to the degree that she sacrifices her self for her "Race." We first meet Lady Bellmont visiting her sister Lady Gaylove, whom she reproaches with "conceal[ing] your Children as You do your Wrinkles, and for the same reason" (11). Having infantilized her children, Lady Gaylove is punished by their open rebellion. In contrast, Lady Bellmont forces maturity on her wastrel son, making Sir James "drink a deep Draught of Sorrow" so that he might be "weaned from these vain Pleasures" (46). The pain of watching him suffer leaves Lady Bellmont "almost Dead"; her one wish is that her son and Angelica "bring a smiling race to bless my Age." Yet Lady Bellmont's sacrifices are also practical: "I have been a Careful Mother, in hopes one day to see you reclaim'd, and have preserv'd enough to pay your Debts, and redeem your whole Estate" (57–58).

Although both sisters threaten their children with disinheritance, the "difference" between the widows is the degree to which they recognize the primacy of patriarchal law, especially the distinction between jointure and patrimony. While Lady Gaylove attempts to raid her children's inheritance, Lady Bellmont threatens only to withhold from her son "what you might expect from me" (51). Sir James for his part anticipates his mother's death: "Then there falls a swinging Joynture, which I intend to Mortgage before-hand" (3). Lady Bellmont's jointure is analogous to Queen Anne's assent as constitutional monarch to the Act of Settlement: it reflects her status, is within her gift, and can "redeem [his] whole Estate," but it is not patrimony.

Restored to fiscal health, a repentant Sir James kneels before his mother: "you have given me second Life, may it answer all your Hopes" (58). Yet her ability to give life is simply a restoration of inherited virtue: "the Noble Seeds of Honour . . . will in time Surmount," predicts Sir James's sentimental friend Valentine (13). Sir James's inevitable acceptance of his own nobility is signaled through this friendship: "our Affections agree, and how the Devil came our Constitutions to differ?" (2). Valentine, whose apparent murder is the final blow that inspires Sir James's repentance, represents the play's valorization of a sentimental masculine friendship with political implications. His name invokes both Shakespeare's *Two Gentlemen of Verona*, which similarly values friendship over the love of women, and the popular romance of Valentine and Orson,[4] in which civilized Valentine must reform his wild twin (Porter 34–36). Moreover, Sir James's reference to "constitution" plays on the Whig myth of the ancient British constitution, which, when supported by the true English prince, ensured the rights of subjects (Pocock). Later, Pix imbeds another Shakespearean reference that further grounds *The Different Widows* in this political mythology, as Sir James berates his footman: "Rascal, that are so fat with swilling Ale, and sleeping on Tavern Benches" (49). The reference to *Henry IV, Part I* casts the footman as Falstaff and Sir James as Prince Hal, the rakish heir who would become England's populist hero-king.

The Shakespearean references underline the play's ethical ambiguities: while *Two Gentlemen*'s conclusion praises both friendship and repentance, the allusion to *Henry IV, Part I*'s Hal reminds the audience that self-transformation can be politic. This point is brought home by the "*Machiavel*" Lady Loveman, who covers up her indiscretions by masquerading as her own male "Relation" and demanding that her Cit husband "learn to value Vertue" (39). Her motives are baldly economic: "For really a Woman parted from her Husband, especially if he's worth money, and will stand it out, is but a despicable thing" (40). Lord Loveman's closing declaration that he and "Cocky" are "new married" by their reconciliation casts an ironic reflection on Sir James's rebirth and establishes the extent to which progressive discourses of reform depend on the extension of credit.

Epilogue: Drama and the Commodification of the Role Model

At the close of *The Different Widows*, Angelica commands, "[B]ehold these Different Widows; my Lady *Bellmont*, the Wonder and Pattern of the

Age, the other the Shame" (61). Pix's London comedies illustrate the paradoxes of progressive individualism, which constructs virtue as an imitable "Pattern" of choices. An attentive student of Shakespeare's ambiguous histories, Pix simultaneously feeds her audience's desire for signs of sincerity and exploits the conventions of theater to expose these signs as performative (see Dawson 214).

As a commodity, the public identity of a person (whether an actress, a London wife, or a queen) derives its social value from the credit of others. The didactic and partisan discourses found in Pix's comedies exemplify women's struggles to legitimize their exercise of power in a public sphere that commodifies the performance of virtue and disinterestedness. With the same strategies of "authentic" self-representation now dominating the "me media" of reality television and social networking systems, contemporary students of late-Stuart drama may find the subtext of Pix's London comedies surprisingly familiar.

Notes

1. For different mappings of Pix's romantic schema, see Bush-Bailey 148–52; Finberg, Introduction xiii–xvi.

2. "Clipping" refers to the common early-modern practice of shaving off small amounts of gold or silver from coins before putting them back into circulation at face value.

3. Madeleine de Scudéry was the author of several highly popular multivolume seventeenth-century French romances, renowned for the exaggerated virtues and fantastic adventures of their heroes and heroines.

4. This French romance, originally translated into English by Henry Watson in the early sixteenth century, was frequently reprinted and widely available as a broadsheet at the turn of the eighteenth century.

Misty G. Anderson

Embodying Centlivre's Comic Vision: *A Bold Stroke* and *The Wonder* in the Classroom

Susanna Centlivre's later hit comedies, *The Wonder: A Woman Keeps a Secret* (1714) and *A Bold Stroke for a Wife* (1718), illustrate the intersection of Centlivre's very physical comic style with the weightier realities of the marriage contract. Centlivre possessed that Bergsonian comic gift for presenting "the mechanical encrusted on the living," in which the fate of the body expresses the social and cultural institutions that constrain it (Bergson 84). Centlivre's comic sensibility was enormously successful with audiences, and her three most popular comedies, *The Busie Body* (1709); *The Wonder: A Woman Keeps a Secret*, and *A Bold Stroke for a Wife*, were among the most popular of all plays in the century. Only Centlivre, William Congreve (who resented Centlivre's success), William Shakespeare, and John Vanbrugh could boast multiple plays among the most performed of the later eighteenth century. In London alone, *A Bold Stroke for a Wife* enjoyed 166 performances from 1718 to 1779; *The Wonder,* while it got off to a slower start, was one of the biggest theatrical successes between 1747 and 1779, with 130 performances in that period alone (Kavenik 119, 181).

The many great actors, including Robert Wilks, Anne Oldfield, Catherine Clive, Edward Shuter, Peg Woffington, John Philip Kemble, and David Garrick, who all gravitated to Centlivre's plays for revivals and benefits, helped maintain her plays' popularity over the century. Keeping the eighteenth-century star system in mind when teaching either of these plays, I first ask students to cast the plays with current actors and discuss their choices in small groups. Moving from that exercise, I acquaint students with *The London Stage* and the *Index to* The London Stage, valuable resources that can serve as the basis for short papers on casting, actors, or comparisons of the production histories of other plays. Seeing the long list of Centlivre's performance dates helps dispel the persistent myth that women writers were invisible in the eighteenth century. Establishing their popularity also situates the plays as part of a social imagination; just like contemporary popular romantic comedies on film such as *When Harry Met Sally* (1989), *Meet the Parents* (2002), or *The 40-Year-Old Virgin* (2005), Centlivre's comedies are the stories of her times, stories told about and to a particular social moment. The shameless comic rumination on dowries, estates, and portions in these two plays that is the food of, if not love, then marriage leads us to the Jamesonian question, "what happens when plot falls into history, so to speak, and enters the force fields of modern societies?" (Jameson 130).

The Broadview editions of *The Wonder* and *A Bold Stroke for a Wife*, edited by John O'Brien and Nancy Copeland, respectively, are wonderful teaching texts for the classroom, with useful introductions and appendixes.[1] The plays fit well into a variety of courses. I have taught them as parts of a drama survey, a Restoration and early-eighteenth-century course for English majors, a course on women writers, a graduate class on Restoration and eighteenth-century drama, and a seminar on faith and reason in the eighteenth century. In whatever context I teach these plays, I always present them as performance texts that held the stage for the entire eighteenth century, and I encourage my students to see for themselves what William Hazlitt deemed "the best of our acting plays" (143) and what Elizabeth Inchbald called "productions that depend on action" ("Remarks" 140). However hasty and on-book, in-class performance allows students to see, hear, and experience the ways that Centlivre materialized issues about marriage and gender relations on stage. There is a political edge to romance in these plays that displays a Whiggish belief in contract and extends it to women. *The Wonder* and *A Bold Stroke* were late volleys in Centlivre's extended conversation on contracts, and in them we witness a physical, even farcical comic energy up against the wall of the word of the father but determined to find a path around the obstruction. Centlivre's heroines negotiate the terms of their relationships in plotlines that find optimistic resolutions to the conflicts and contradictions in eighteenth-century marriage law. Her comedies allow me to walk students through this legal and cultural world and show them how the fate of bodies on stage is very serious (and very political) business.

Contracts and Centlivre

To teach Centlivre's accessible romantic comedies as useful artifacts in the history of gender relations as well as the history of genre, I need to educate my students a bit about eighteenth-century marriage law and how it intersects with the concept of contract after John Locke. The structure of both these plays gives us already united couples and heroines who are making arguments for their individuality. Unlike Millimant, who knows she will "dwindle into a wife," Violante asserts that she need not obey Felix yet (*Wonder* 79; act 3, sc. 1), and Anne connects her ability to negotiate with her future agency in marriage (*Bold Stroke* 60; 1.2). These women are not flirtatious, and they demand respect from their mates by proving themselves levelheaded, creative, and reliable. Centlivre's focus in these plots is less on the wooed but not wed couples than on the obstacles to marriage that must be negotiated from within (between the couple) and without (among fathers, guardians, and legal representatives). Through words as well as deeds, the couples come to agree on those "certain ingredients to be mingled with matrimony without which [they] may as well change for the worse as for the better" (*Bold Stroke* 60; 1.2). In so doing, they apply the logic of contract, which has a leveling force across genders as well as political relations. If the people at large can contract with a leader (through Parliament, to call or recall a king), then contract might also hold some equalizing force in a marriage.

Marriage, the main contract of Centlivre's comedies, is an institution that needs to be historicized. If students are slow to jump in on the issue, I might show a clip from the film *The Princess Bride* (1987) or *Four Weddings and a Funeral* (1994) to get them talking about what the authorizing moment or act for a marriage is, a live question in Centlivre's age, when the discrepancies between canon and civil law had destabilized the precise legal meaning of marriage. Centlivre sided with the civil principle that the agreement or contract, not the ceremony, was the fundamental feature of marriage and what validated it. Marriage law grew more confusing after the Commonwealth era with the Civil Marriage Act of 1653, which made marriage a civil institution but which was then invalidated in

1660. The post-Restoration problem involved conflicting legal precedents that referred to either civil or ecclesiastical authority. Clandestine or irregular marriages, which included any marriage outside church or outside canonical hours or seasons, were still legal before Hardwicke's Marriage Act of 1753, though they were not recognized by the church. Such marriages might involve a priest (or be solemnized at the chapel of the Tower of London or any chapel around Fleet Prison, which specialized in quick weddings), but they could simply be *contracts de presenti*, promises to marry made in the present tense between a man and a woman. Centlivre's comedies, like Aphra Behn's, present a disproportionate number of irregular marriages. Gellert Alleman's statistics reveal that a whopping sixty-nine percent of Centlivre's comedies, far more than any of her contemporaries, have clandestine marriages, which are usually revealed in act 5 (82). Notably, her three most popular plays all have clandestine marriages.

The relationship between Centlivre's plotting and her gender, the connection that Richard Steele and Hazlitt made in a condescending tone,[2] is one I encourage my students to reconsider (rather than dismiss) as good legal problem solving, in which Centlivre uses the elasticity of marriage definitions to preserve her heroine's agency. Both couples in *The Wonder* skate outside parental control with clandestine nuptials once they prove their intrinsic worth to their partner. If students have read other Restoration dramas for the course, I ask them what the implications of a clandestine marriage are as opposed to a tricked marriage, as in Behn's *The Lucky Chance* (1686), or even tricked sexual intercourse, as in William Wycherley's *The Plain Dealer* (1676). Centlivre's fascination with clandestine marriage maintains the validity of civil law, which sanctions the contractual agency of both men and women in their ability to enter into the marriage contract freely, instead of tricked marriages, which undermine that agency.

Another important legal concept that students can use to think about these comedies is coverture. Common law rendered a married woman a *feme covert*, which implied her loss of property and thus her loss of civil subjectivity, since she was "covered" by the legal identity of her husband. Two forms of marriage settlement—the strict settlement, which entailed a woman's estate on her future eldest son, and separate estate, which could take the form of property or an annuity, later called "pin money"—mitigated that concept by preserving property for women or their heirs, at least for the wealthiest people. But the lived reality of coverture, which governed marriage law before and after Hardwicke's Marriage Act of 1753, was even more varied than these arrangements suggest. Competing court jurisdictions (including manorial, ecclesiastical, chancery, and civil courts) interpreted the principle differently. Chancery (or equity) courts sometimes ruled in favor of widows suing for their husbands' estates on the basis of bonds or ancillary contracts, and ecclesiastical and manorial courts supported the property claims of wives by upholding conveyances (additional settlements of property or goods) that husbands made with their wives. Conveyancing manuals, including *Symbolaeography* (1594), *A Treatise of Feme Coverts; or, The Lady's Law* (1732), and *Precedents in Conveyancing* (1744), presented sample forms of settlements that preserved some of a wife's property through prenuptial contracts obligating the husband to pay sums to the wife or their children, either through his will or during his lifetime.[3]

I lecture briefly on these legal facts and prepare a handout of terms from Susan Staves's glossary to *Married Women's Separate Property in England, 1660–1833* to give my students a glimpse of the legal world of Violante (*The Wonder*), Miranda (*The Busie Body*), and Anne Lovely (*Bold Stroke*). These savvy women would have been aware of legal ways to have more independence and access to their fortunes than the dominant principle of coverture suggests. Other literary examples include the trust arrangement between Arabella and Mirabell in Congreve's *The Way of the World* (1700) and the bequest of Clarissa's grandfather that launches the plot of Samuel Richardson's *Clarissa* (1747–48). These arrangements imagine a *feme sole* who might persist into marriage, at least regarding her property. Such was the case when Lord Hardwicke ruled in Grigsby v. Cox (1750) that "where anything is settled to the wife's separate use, she is considered as a *feme sole*" (Staves, *Married Women's Separate Property* 152). Hardwicke's Marriage Act of 1753 made clandestine marriages such as those in *The Wonder* illegal, along with marriage between people under twenty-one without parental consent, thus vesting more control over marriage in the parents and guardians of wealthy families. For both pre- and post-1753 audiences, however, the contracts in Centlivre's play (and by extension the real financial arrangements) are between the lovers, who negotiate their way to a more egalitarian model of marriage in their private lives. The plays connect contract logic with romantic love, ameliorating what Staves called the "socially intolerable" aspects of contract ideas applied to marriage (4).

Promises, Promises, and *The Wonder*

The title of *The Wonder: A Woman Keeps a Secret* is the best point of departure I have found for teaching the play. I ask my students to parse it in class: what assumptions does it make, and what can you infer from the title about the author's perspective on those assumptions? How does it position the audience or reader? Does it make a difference that a woman rather than a man wrote it? The title speaks with mock surprise that a woman might be a reliable interlocutor, the kind of person whose word is good. The "wonder" of the play is an insider's joke about gender inequality that presumes men and women *can* negotiate and agree with each other for social as well as political purposes. The title also invites the viewer or reader to agree with Centlivre's position (of *course* women can keep secrets) to get the joke, a pattern of comic persuasion that runs throughout her plays. The play forwards some progressive notions: that the female character, Violante, deserves to control the plot; that marriage should be something that young men and women can equally contract; and that liberty, tempered by rationality, is a fundamental good. Taking time to talk about the title can help students begin to think through a truth widely acknowledged, that Centlivre's plays present Whiggish contractual models of marriage with something of a protofeminist slant.[4]

I then move to a discussion of motion, both the motion of bodies on stage and the motion of the plot. There is, as O'Brien has noted, less motion in *The Wonder* than advancing of a plot; it is a play in which characters are most often stalling to prevent another plot from unfolding (Introduction 14). This work slowdown is organized by Violante, and to a lesser extent Isabella, to keep them from falling into plots that fathers, families, and jealous lovers have devised. The play opens with Felix in hiding from a duel. Shortly thereafter, his sister, Isabella, throws herself from a balcony to escape her tyrannical father only to fall into the arms of Colonel Britton. One good scene for in-class performance is the end of act 2 (65–69), which gives students a chance to see the stage business of hiding or disguising the bodies that seem to be everywhere in this play. Felix has returned to visit Violante, but she is now hiding his sister in the next room. Blocking the scene with five student actors and taking a few moments to go over the ways that Centlivre uses the dash and the aside to give her actors room to move can yield delicious results. In small groups, I ask students to think about what they would do with each dash, either as directors or actors. The dashes indicate both motion and breaks in motion, the stalling of other plots until Violante and Isabella can find the time and means to bring their own versions of the story to fruition. Their performance decisions show students the ways the plays breathe and live on stage for generations of actors and directors. In this scene and others, the presence of the body does not mean what other characters think it means (Violante is not hiding a lover, Isabella is not having an affair). The scene sets up the theme of Violante's trustworthiness and what will be the struggle for the two lovers: whether Felix will trust her (and the validity of their "love contract") more than the circumstantial evidence he finds.

This scene is also a place for students to see how the play exemplifies what Shirley Strum Kenny called "humane comedy." For students who have read Wycherley's *The Country Wife* (1675) or George Etherege's *The Man of Mode* (1676), the contrast, particularly with Wycherley's famous "china scene," can help them develop a sense of literary history that weaves together social change and genre theory. The pleasures of Wycherley's play depend on a Brechtian alienation effect, in which comedy, as J. L. Styan observed, works because the audience is not emotionally involved with the drama. As in Wycherley's play, in Centlivre's *The Wonder* characters are concealed behind a door, a revelation occurs, and the knowing characters (Horner and Violante, respectively) must think fast to come up with a witty alibi. The differences, however, are everything, and I ask students to make a list of them. They tend to observe that Centlivre's scene is less mean-spirited, that the situation could be explained as reasonable and ethical, and that women are in control. Wycherley's cynical sex comedy plays with the bodies of the women (and men) in the scene in a libertine game aligned for the pleasure of the master gamer, Horner, who glibly controls the event. By contrast, the pauses, gaps, and revelations in *The Wonder* are all about the preservation of the integrity of all the bodies in the scene, male and female. Whereas the more materialist and libertine Wycherley presents a world of animal urges masked by a veneer of civility, Centlivre works out a plot to reconcile her embodied, conscious, feeling characters to the social world of laws, contracts, and promises.

But her Whiggish progressiveness does not mean that Centlivre downplays the body. If students do not bring it up themselves, I point out that Colonel Britton is fairly obsessive about women's "flesh" and that he sometimes refers to them as food (e.g., 51, 52; 1.1; 70, 71; 3.1; 82, 83; 3.2; and 104; 5.1). Britton's use of the term "flesh" underscores the way that embodiment deprives Isabella of agency. When she begs her father, Don Lopez, as his "Flesh and Blood" to put off the marriage to Don Guzman, he crudely replies that she "shalt have an Arm full of flesh and Blood to Morrow" (54; 1.1). Later in the play, Britton refers to Isabella as "Meat" (83; 3.2). This alienation of a rational, cognitive self from the body is something that Centlivre works to restore; her ideal is an embodied, Lockean self, an ideal with feminist implications. Britton is her pedagogical project and test case for the proposition that a sexist man can be reeducated. Though he prefers "the Conversation of Bodies" (83; 3.2) to that of minds and has a "tendency to the flesh" (104; 5.1), he develops an appreciation for Isabella's intelligence that grounds his excitement about her body and, as he eventually discovers, her wealth. All this "body talk" raises substantive questions about the nature of the self. The introduction of a little Locke earlier in the semester can make this connection even richer by placing it in the context of Lockean epistemology and the developing terms of sensory perception as a knitting together of body and mind that will become known as sensibility.

Centlivre's Whiggish nationalism holds out hope for a better world, with better marriages, and that world is called Great Britain. I ask my students to think about how an idealized American identity works in similar terms by collecting buzzwords from current political discourse and comparing them with similar buzzwords in *The Wonder.* If we have time, we also do keyword searches of other eighteenth-century texts, an easier task if they have access to *Eighteenth Century Collections Online*, or *ECCO*, the Gale database based on *The English Short Title Catalogue*. Shows like *The Colbert Report* and *The Daily Show* can help the more politically naive students with the contemporary side of the assignment. "Liberty" and "freedom" probably come up on both the eighteenth- and twenty-first-century lists, and comparing how they are used in direct political discourse as well as in indirect discourse (advertising most obviously) can help them politicize the marriage plot in *The Wonder.* "Freedom" or "liberty" in a White House press release has an overtly political purpose, but either term's ideological valence can also attach to descriptions of relationships between lovers, between parents and children, and between workers and bosses. Centlivre idealizes British liberty as the location of a just and free social order that includes women. Roman Catholic governments and tyrannical fathers stand in for bad, un-British governing principles, even though they are just an exaggeration of the realities of life in Protestant England. Against these Iberian constraints, England is the land where, Isabella imagines, "Duty wears no Fetter but inclination" (53; 1.1), and Frederick opines that "Women's Liberties are subservient to their Inclinations, and

Husbands seem of no Effect but to take Care of the Children which their Wives Provide" (52; 1.1). All these views are in some dialogue with the actual terms of early-eighteenth-century British gender scripts, illustrating for our students what Louis Althusser meant by ideology as "the imaginary relationship of individuals to their real conditions of existence" (109).

The Wonder's nationalism defines British identity beyond Englishness after the 1707 Act of Union, which joined England and Scotland to create a single kingdom, Great Britain. The attempt to rename Scotland and England as North Britain and South Britain ultimately failed, but Centlivre's choice of Britton as a name for her Scottish colonel reflects her enthusiasm for the idea. The play also boasts a comic Scot as Britton's footman; an English friend, Frederick (a nice German name that allies him with the house of Hanover); a Portuguese main cast; and a rich Dutch merchant as the unwanted groom, Don Guzman. Here, Britishness must speak for itself in a community of other identities and as a community unto itself. If you are lucky enough to have students who can read Britton with a Scottish accent against Frederick's English and Felix's Portuguese inflections, you can paint an aural portrait of cultural identity. Frederick, who exists to extol Britishness and set up Colonel Britton's lines, declares, "Liberty is the Idol of the English," and Don Lopez, the familiar (nearly stereotypical) stern father, agrees, with the caveat that liberty should not contradict "common Prudence," his euphemism for the forced marriage of Isabella to Don Guzman. As in Richard Steele's *The Conscious Lovers* (1722), Britishness here is intertwined with trade yet must be defined as more than (and other than) trade. The balance of bad foreign merchants against good English mercantile sensibilities involves cultural stereotyping that is familiar to students from the work of comedians like Carlos Mencia and Dave Chappelle. Such comparisons can help them think about how large colonial or multicultural nation-states talk about ethnicity in the national community, where some ethnicities appear to be more equal than others.

I always close the last class on *The Wonder* with act 5, scene 2, the reconciliation scene between Felix and Violante, to draw students' attention once again to the ways the play's stagecraft does ideological work. Felix's jealousy (and I remind them, he has *nearly* just killed a man in a duel) threatens to overwhelm the delicate stalling that Violante must do to bring both couples' plots to a happy conclusion. Felix must learn to moderate his passionate, Mediterranean responses in a more British fashion and channel this energy into a more rational affection, just as Colonel Britton, the earthy but tractable Scot, must come to realize that women are, to quote

Finding Nemo, "friends, not food." The scene is too long to run in its entirety for most classes, but beginning from the middle of page 107, just before Violante's outburst, gives a taste of this dream scene for the two actors playing Violante and Felix. The scene calls on Felix to reform believably, a reform that he has to signify with his body. Their dance of the chairs shows the characters moving back together, literally, as Felix decides to trust Violante's passion, both her love and her passionate stubbornness, traits that make them a wonderful match. Felix moves ever closer, an open hand on her leg as he pleads, "won't you—won't you—won't you?" and asks for her hand in return. Again, the dashes give the actor space to make some decisions, but the physicality of the scene, which recaptures the intimacy of the Restoration house for the much larger mid- and late-eighteenth-century theater spaces, is already in the text. His reformation is what we, along with Violante, have all been waiting for, and the couple's emotional truce bathes their mutual contract in soft focus. The reconciliation is like a cinematic kiss, a visual trope for their marriage of true minds materialized onstage as she chooses to give him, literally and symbolically, her hand.

Much as he loved the play, this scene may have proved too feminizing for David Garrick, who wrote himself a macho addendum some time in the early 1750s, in which a mock-drunk Felix pulls a pistol on Violante's father, Don Pedro. O'Brien has helpfully reprinted the scene, which was recorded in the Drury Lane Theater's prompt book and actually printed in John Bell's 1776 edition of the play. The added scene suggests that the plot reflects culturally female perspectives on marriage and gender roles and that at least one man wanted to write a more active role for himself in that plot. I ask students to read the added scene as they read the play, and then, in small groups, I have them discuss whether they like the play better with or without Garrick's added scene. If they have read *The Rover* earlier in the course, I ask at least one group to compare the added scene with Behn's act 5 scene in which Angellica threatens Willmore with a gun. Like Behn, Centlivre wrote witty and strong women, often giving them great power over their male counterparts: Violante trumps Felix in common sense and intelligence, and Miranda of *The Busie Body* takes the upper hand with her lover, George. Looking at Garrick's pistol scene in the light of these strong women can help students understand that we do not have to essentialize to see how women and men, for cultural reasons tied to their experience of gender scripts, might tell the marriage story differently.

Love for Sale: *A Bold Stroke for a Wife*

In *A Bold Stroke for a Wife*, Anne Lovely, the most restricted of all Centlivre's heroines, must find a way to rethink agency since her father's will has made it all but impossible for her to move through the romance plot. He "hated progeny" and has tried to thwart that basic impulse of comedy to renew and reproduce community by appointing Anne four irreconcilable guardians. To bring the lovers together, this comedy must unify the divisions in the father's will so that Anne can enjoy the privilege of her inheritance. She speaks pragmatically of the reciprocity that her money underwrites in this new relationship: "When the woman has fortune enough to make the man happy, if he has either honor or good manners, he'll make her easy. Love makes but a slovenly figure in that house where poverty keeps the door" (60; act 1, sc. 2). This is more truth than joke; the play between the hopes and the limits of contract expresses the Whiggish political philosophy Centlivre supports and supplies the primary source of the comic tension that fuels her plays. Anne sees her inheritance working like an implicit contract that balances power in her (future) marriage. She assumes that the authority of a husband is not absolute and that money can buy some privilege for women in marriage. Yet the contract represented by her father's will has only amplified patriarchal privilege, proving the resilience of patriarchal principles within contract logic. Anne is up against a bad contract that dampens the optimism of earlier works; she and Fainwell will have to turn outlaws (rather than work within the law) to find the "true" Whiggish spirit of contract as they negotiate their happy ending.

I ground this political view of the play in a discussion of the image of the fairy-tale castle stormed by the rescuing prince that comes out of this conversation, where the disappointment over the failure of contract logic is palpable. But heroine and playwright, neither of whom are prepared to surrender their hopes, reach cannily into fantasy narratives to plot their way out of the narrative dead end of the father's will. The fantastic appeal to "enchanted castles, ladies delivered from the chains of magic, giants killed, and monsters overcome" comes at a moment when reality proves unaccommodating (61; 1.2). Through this fairy-tale rhetorical frame, Anne's immobility can be scripted in positive terms as the plotting power shifts to the romantic hero (Fainwell) turned dragon slayer. This reference can also shed some light on Inchbald's claim that the overall effect of the play "is that of farce, and not genuine comedy" ("Criticism" 149), a claim that John Wilson Bowyer and Thalia Stathas both endorse. The play was adapted as a farce many times, including the 1741 *The Guardians Over-reached*, for which we have a text. But it is useful to press on about the concept of farce and to ask students what separates comedy from farce or, more generally, what are other moments when plays or films appeal to the unrealistic? Arden forest, *Death of a Salesman,* the ending of the film *Thelma and Louise*, and plenty of other examples that students generate mark those moments when narratives jump the tracks, so to speak, to show us alternatives to a constraining reality that are deliberately and purposefully unrealistic.

The class meeting before we are to start the play, I divide the class by guardian and ask each group (working independently outside class) to find props, costuming pieces, or suggest mannerisms that convey their character quickly. The exercise underscores the somewhat clownish commedia dell' arte approach to character that made the afterpiece and farcical adaptations of the play work so well, and it gives me a pool of "experts" on each guardian from which to draw in class discussion and performances. That the guardians are not more fully realized as characters is very much to the point; they represent ideas, faces of a patriarchal structure that fails to function organically and instead can be separated into component parts. Since the contract that they represent is also unfair, the scheme to cheat them out of their signatures is justified. Fainwell, as a soldier as well as the leading man, represents a hopeful, legitimate British identity that must overcome the illegitimate forms of power that still exist in the nation; his is a Whiggish mission to lead Great Britain forward into the political and social future, even if he has to trick ("fain") his way there. I also ask students to attend to the spaces in which this play unfolds for their guardian and for the others as they read through it. The scenes are, with the exception of those in the Prims' home, in very public spaces: taverns, coffeehouses, parks, and so forth. These settings are a notable contrast to the domestic spaces of most comedies of the day, something to draw out if one is teaching the plays in the context of a Restoration or eighteenth-century drama course. A Habermasian public sphere is on display, and it is largely a world of men.

With information about marriage and inheritance on the table and my experts ready to go, I explain the concept of "humours characters" and the contemporary notions of character in the *Tatler* and the *Spectator* (see Copeland, Introduction 23), and, in upper-division courses, I link these concepts to recent critical conversations about character and performance on the seventeenth- and eighteenth-century stage (Lowenthal, *Perform-*

ing Identities; Freeman, *Character's Theater*). I then proceed to teach through the guardians, calling heavily on the groups for discussion and for in-class readings. Depending on the size and nature of the class, I have all the students assigned to a particular guardian work as a performance troupe to present a scene in class. I want them to see how the guardians take part in the fantastic quality of the play; they are the cultural obstacle course Colonel Fainwell must navigate. To coach the groups along, I start with the question, How does this character represent an exaggerated aspect of patriarchy? I spend the least time with Sir Philip. The aging libertine-fop, with his pathetic francophilia, is obvious enough to students who have read through John Wilmot, Wycherley, and Etherege earlier in the semester and who can feel that the days of Wycherley's Horner are over. The overtly sexual face of patriarchy is the easiest to counter and the least threatening in this play; its substantive power resides elsewhere.

Tradelove's case is more complex. His greed and his involvement with the Dutch mark him as a foreign, ergo bad, model of merchant values, as opposed to the good, nationalistic commercial ventures of Freeman, who is aligned with British interests through Fainwell. I spend time with the stockjobber scene that opens act 4, which is unusual for comedies of the period in that it thrusts us into the public-sphere world of the eighteenth-century coffeehouse, a place to talk about how the Whiggish value of trade is at odds with the Whiggish value of liberty in this play. Copeland's introduction and appendix C provide good background material to start the discussion about coffee and the coffeehouse. If we have not already talked about "fuming liquor" and "fragrant steams" in the context of Alexander Pope's *The Rape of the Lock*, I point out that coffee was a tremendous force in eighteenth-century life, as it is in ours, both chemically and socially, and comes out of trade relations with much poorer countries. That companies like Equal Exchange have raised our consciousness about whether our cups of coffee are from fair trade beans is a reminder that our world has been shaped by patterns of eighteenth-century colonialism and its commodities. I then ask students to imagine bull pen traders from Merrill Lynch and TD Waterhouse walking through their local Starbucks hawking eBay, Apple, and even Starbucks stocks by calling out their prices; then we read through a bit of the scene with additional students chatting in the background to get a sense of the aural environment of the coffeehouse. It is the noise of the information economy, albeit an earlier version, as illustrated by Tradelove's relation to the news of the Spanish siege in act 4, scene 1. I also direct students to Daniel Defoe on stockjobbing, in the back of the Copeland edition; Ned Ward's *The Coffeehouse Mob*; *Tatler* issue 178 and other issues written "from Will's Coffee-House"; as well as William Hogarth's cartoon "The South Sea Scheme" (Paulson, *Hogarth: His Art* 74). The bubble had not burst yet, and Centlivre herself was hoping for some stock when she wrote the poem "A Woman's Case," in which she pled with Charles Joye to gift her some South Sea shares in the light of her service to the Whigs. Centlivre seems to be discovering personally that a free-market economy will not solve everything, and she materializes her concern about buying and selling Anne's and Fainwell's futures (as a female minor and a soldier, respectively) through the rapid and alienating exchange of stocks. Trade is a means to, not the end of, Centlivre's Whiggish values, which hold individual liberty and nationalism above the great stomach of early capitalism.

Periwinkle and the Prims provide the most fun material in a discussion of how Centlivre embodies her sexual politics on stage, but I have discovered students tend to have trouble placing Periwinkle, the virtuoso. A comparison with Jonathan Swift's "projectors," some information about the Royal Society, and the attitude toward collecting that gives birth to eighteenth-century museum culture (especially the British Museum and Sir John Soane's collection) are helpful, and links to those collections online work well to illustrate the basic point that collecting is an expression of global mastery as well as a potential form of mysticism as the collector fetishizes the object. Periwinkle's irrational belief in the properties of some of his objects goes hand in hand with his imperialistic impulse to assemble them. In an upper-division class, I sometimes discuss the mystical writings of Isaac Newton as a reminder that the great rational Enlightenment science project was not entirely rational. A portion of Periwinkle's scene with the girdle, act 3, scene 1 (82–90), rewards even a cold reading and illustrates the mysticism of the amateur scientist and collector. The scene's farcical premise builds on physical comedy for easy laughs, yet Centlivre manages to get broad comedy without cruelty. Periwinkle gets the humiliation he deserves as he "becomes invisible" because of his hostile and condescending attitude toward women. His infantile onstage game of peekaboo exposes his pseudoscientific obsession with artifacts as a dead end and a dead world. Like Anne's father, he seems to hate the next generation (he is glad his wife and child died), and the scene abounds with talk of death, embalming, and mummies. He is only reconciled to the idea of uniting the Colonel and Anne because their son "shall restore the art of embalming and the old Roman manner of burying their dead," and he is eventually tricked into signing the contract because he believes it is the last will and testament of his dead uncle, who has left him an inheritance to spend on more dead things (89). The humane vision that Kenny, Northrop Frye, and Brian Corman describe demands life and community, and so Centlivre turns the death-dealing Periwinkle into an animated puppet.

Periwinkle's interest in dead bodies dovetails with the Prims' hypocritical and entertaining attempts to deaden sexuality (though it is worth noting that Pentecostal students may find the satire offensive). The Prims come from a long line of hypocritical stage Quakers, including Charles Shadwell's *The Fair Quaker of Deal* (1710) and Charles Knipe's *A City Ramble* (1715), as well as treatises like John Gilpin's *The Quaker Shaken* (1653) and William Mucklow's *The Spirit of the Hat* (1673), works that suspected sexual desire lurked beneath the Quakers' practice of being "moved" by the spirit. John Gay's *Trivia,* with its couplet from book 3 on the nightwalker who poses as a Quaker, is relevant: "Nay, she will oft' the Quaker's Hood prophane, / And trudge demure the Rounds of Drury-Lane" (84; lines 279–80), as is Ronald Paulson's *Hogarth's Harlot.* Both provide more background on the connections between sexuality and religion in eighteenth-century popular culture. Later in the century, Bowyer and Inchbald charge Centlivre with immorality, probably for the rollicking scenes with the Prims. It is worth noting, however, that Anne expresses her greatest frustrations with them; she threatens to "tear her flesh," wishes that she were in her grave, and threatens to "turn papist and die in a convent." Her feisty replies are signs of extreme frustration with their governance and constant proselytizing, and she cries out that she will turn to the state and "try the power of an English senate" to see if they will set aside her father's will (122; 5.1). Her formulation of a separation of church and state is politically progressive, part of the unraveling of sacred and secular power that a Whig vision of the state involved. Even though she has little access to the public sphere, Anne Lovely still believes in it and prefers it to the stifling private space of the Prims' home and to their religious enthusiasm, which comes with its own laws about women's bodies.

Act 2, scene 2, is a good choice for in-class reading, especially if the student experts on the Prims have come up with costuming pieces that evoke Anne's fashionability and Mrs. Prim's stern dress. Mrs. Prim gets easy laughs for her biblical syntax and her sexually obsessed perspective that confirms Michel Foucault's insights about the discursive technology of desire. Depending on the class, I sometimes teach excerpts from the first volume of his *History of Sexuality* with the play. As Mrs. Prim inadvertently confesses, she intended for her ultramodesty to provoke desire (117; 5.1), at least in her younger days. The Prims' world is brimming with sex and desire: Tabitha and Tobias's affair; Obadiah's troubled "outward man"; and his clandestine meetings with Mary, in which he begs her to show him "a little, little, little bit of her delicious bubby" (74; 2.2). The Prims prove that sexuality will return with a vengeance when repressed, making a short path from religious enthusiasm to sexual desire. I always draw students' attention to the effect of costuming when Fainwell poses as Simon Pure in act 5; Anne and Fainwell both appear in Quaker dress, visual tropes of a false conversion and markers of a theatrical, performative model of identity that still does not overwhelm an inner, conscious agent whose freedom of choice (those Whiggish buzzwords that are still with us and still circulating around issues of sexuality) will find a way.

The physical, farcial humor of this act, particularly the dueling Simon Pures and the exchange in which Anne and Fainwell "hum" their way to greater intimacies, uses the Prims' technologies of control over the body as a way to complete the negotiation of their own legal and emotional union. Their mocking articulation of gender norms in their Quaker speech ("yea, I am become bone of thy bone and flesh of thy flesh" [113; 5.1]) and their ironic distance from the various identities they have performed over the course of the play alienates them from this social world and situates them as refugees seeking the imagined community of Britishness envisioned in the closing couplet: "'Tis liberty of choice that sweetens life, / Makes the glad husband, and the happy wife" (140; 5.1). This final optimistic gesture toward egalitarian marriage grows out of the farcical strategies of the play that exaggerated the guardians' blocking roles and set up the via media Britishness of Fainwell, who masters them all with the help of his trusty merchant sidekick, Freeman. Britishness delivers the fairy-tale ending, and, to some extent, it is the fairy-tale ending; both Fainwell and British identity turn out to mean what we want them to mean. We are left hoping that Anne does indeed get her wish for the happily ever after that makes her something more than another *feme covert* in marriage. I uphold the play as a true comedy with elements of farce in ways that anticipate the theatrical experiments of Henry Fielding at the Little Haymarket, but I also affirm for my students that farce, as Charlie Chaplin, Stanley Kubrick, and Terry Gilliam have all shown, can be thoughtful and richly political.

Notes

1. All quotations from *The Wonder* and *A Bold Stroke for a Wife* are from these editions of the play.

2. See also Jacob; Cumberland, "Life" and "Critique."

3. See Erickson 102–13 for a summary of the complex legal landscape established by these various instruments.

4. For critical work that identifies Centlivre's political affiliation as significant to her plays, see Lock; Frushell; J. Pearson, *Prostitued Muse*; Rosenthal, *Playwrights*; and M. Anderson.

Roxanne Kent-Drury

Performance and Philosophy in the Work of Catharine Trotter Cockburn

In a congratulatory poem attributed by Thomas Birch to John Hughes and appended in 1698 to the published version of her play *Fatal Friendship*, Catharine Trotter is described as assured immortality through her works, just as the warrior Camilla will be remembered for her role as defender of Aeneas:

Camilla shines
For ever bright in Virgil's Sacred lines
You in your own; —where to the World's last Date
You shall survive, and Triumph over Fate. (*Fatal Friendship* viii)

By 1754, however, in John Duncombe's poem "The Feminead; or, Female Genius," Trotter's reputation had dimmed considerably, with her name described as "undistinguished." Such ambivalence typifies critical attitudes toward Trotter, whom Duncombe remembered primarily as a defender of the philosophers John Locke and Samuel Clarke (lines 125–38).

Until recently, most literary historians have similarly dismissed Trotter's work. Anne Kelley's *Catharine Trotter: An Early Modern Writer in the Vanguard of Feminism* provides a detailed discussion of this reception over three hundred years. As Kelley argues, most assessments have suggested that Trotter's contemporaries were better playwrights, and critics have rejected her by often repeating the commonplace that she wrote failed plays on dull, moral subjects. Though recently considered sound, original, and cogently argued, Trotter's philosophical commentary on empirical philosophy, especially that of Locke, astonished her contemporaries primarily because it came from a woman's pen and not because her arguments were considered to be mounted in response to any serious challenge to Locke or his contemporaries. Her correspondent Thomas Burnet wondered, in a letter dated 18 February 1702, why she had responded to an attack so poorly argued that Locke himself had ignored it.

Why, then, given this critical assessment, is an essay about Trotter's work useful in a teaching volume such as this? Trotter's work should be reassessed for its integration of disparate cultural elements and their impact on women, as well as for her extension of Locke's empiricism, through which she establishes a cogent intellectual position for women within the male bastions of contemporary seventeenth-century thought. In rethinking the Restoration theater through British empirical philosophy, Trotter exhibits an almost protean ability to synthesize and embody complex cultural positions by transforming both genres and philosophical arguments to include women as thoughtful, rational individuals. Analogously, Trotter transformed herself from a marginalized female playwright with an ambiguous reputation to the respectably retired wife of clergyman Patrick Cockburn and a respected philosopher and correspondent of Locke and Gottfried Leibniz. In literary terms, she moved from teenage writer of a slightly prurient epistolary novel, *Olinda's Adventures; or, The Amours of a Young Lady*, to membership in the female triumvirate of playwrights to writer of moral plays to writer of philosophical treatises.

Through the positions her characters hold and the choices they make, Trotter constructs a place within traditionally male-dominated discourses from which to express concern about the limitations of women as subjects, but ultimately she articulates a place from which to speak, not as a woman ventriloquizing men, but as a woman. The conduct of her life and the content of her work represent a thoughtful though sometimes messy effort to syncretize opposing cultural currents, even as the woman remains shrouded in ambiguity that perplexed her contemporaries.

Catharine Trotter wrote five plays: *Agnes de Castro* (Drury Lane, 1695); *Fatal Friendship* (Lincoln's Inn Fields, 1698); *Love at a Loss; or, Most Votes Carry It* (Drury Lane, 1700); *The Unhappy Penitent* (Drury Lane, 1701); and *The Revolution of Sweden* (Queen's Theatre, the

Haymarket, 1706). Most of these plays have been dismissed as failures by later critics, beginning shortly after Trotter retired from the stage.

Yet measuring a playwright's success during this period in British theater history is difficult, since its theater records are notoriously incomplete. Although none of Trotter's plays entered the repertory, we have relatively complete records for her last play, *The Revolution of Sweden*, which ran for six nights (a success at this time, if the actor George Powell's epilogue to *Agnes de Castro* can be believed). For the others, we have only incomplete and unreliable records. During the 1700–01 season at Drury Lane Theatre, for example, when Trotter's *Love at a Loss* and *Unhappy Penitent* debuted, Judith Milhous and Robert D. Hume report that documentary evidence for the season exists for only 69 performances of 36 plays, primarily gleaned from the playlist of one theater patron. Yet Milhous and Hume estimate at least 50 titles were actually performed on 207 nights, adding that "[i]ncomplete performance records make more than an impressionistic estimate of their success impossible in most cases" (*London Stage* 5). In addition, despite the greater market for plays after Thomas Betterton and many of the other actors of the United Company left Drury Lane, why, if her writing was not considered viable, did theater managers stage five of her plays? If her plays had been unambiguous failures, it seems unlikely that a young woman barely out of her teens could have convinced profit-driven theater managers to stage her work over eight years, casting the best veteran actors at both major theaters. And, if she were considered a failed playwright, why was she thought prominent enough, with Mary Pix and Delarivier Manley, to be the target of *The Female Wits; or, The Triumvirate of Poets*, especially if, as Marta Straznicky suggests, the play was staged as revenge on Manley for her high-handed directorial practices (711)?

Aside from rethinking possibly overstated assessments that Trotter was not a viable playwright, examining the conditions of the stage during the last decade of the seventeenth century suggests other reasons to reconsider Trotter both as a woman writer and as a playwright negotiating a theatrical landscape alongside other playwrights of her time. Trotter first emerged as a playwright in 1695, after veteran actors of Drury Lane's United Company rebelled against Christopher Rich's management practices and took up residence at Lincoln's Inn Fields under Betterton's management. Conditions at Drury Lane had militated against the aspirations of new playwrights; the profit-driven management there had long preferred a conservative repertoire and exhibited skepticism toward unproved plays, preferring instead to stage work by earlier playwrights. Trotter and other emerging playwrights undoubtedly benefited when the company split, but this division alone does not explain why Trotter's work was staged. As Straznicky has also suggested:

> Like their male counterparts, these playwrights could succeed financially only if they cultivated working relations with other theater personnel . . . women fought and fought hard to keep their turf within the highly competitive theatrical world. . . . [T]hey were actively supported by some male colleagues in what was otherwise a homosocial network, and . . . they were equally caught up in the inter-professional rivalries of the theater business. (711)

In such a competitive atmosphere, plays must have been staged because they appeared promising, despite later judgments about their potential appeal to audiences.

While it is true that Trotter's plays did not enter the repertory, neither did anyone else's. John Harrington Smith, followed by Arthur Scouten and Hume, suggests that deciding what to stage was complicated because theater managers could not decipher the tastes of a fickle audience that demanded increasingly moralistic content dating from at least 1681, when "the ladies" lodged a protest against Edward Ravenscroft's *The London Cuckolds* (28). This trend toward morality on the stage accelerated with a pamphlet war that included Jeremy Collier's famous tract of 1698. With a Restoration-based repertory split unequally between two theater companies driving a demand for new material and with an audience (led by female theater patrons) newly incensed over immorality on the stage, theater managers must have been looking specifically for acceptable, morally appropriate material, perhaps written by literate women with at least nominally respectable reputations.

Trotter's perspective and work, then, may have been perceived by theater managers not as marginal but as desirable because of her gender, the moral content of her work, and her social position. Scouten and Hume observe that the trend toward a more moral stage was in full swing by the 1690s, well before Collier wrote. Extending Smith's argument, Scouten and Hume suggest that two factors led many plays to fail: reduced tolerance of bawdy language and, later, bawdy action, specifically in new plays (both tragedies and comedies) and not old ones, and responses of an inexplicably "cranky audience" ([1980] 54). As a result, few new plays were even performed by the United Company from 1682 to 1694, and from

1697 to 1703 nearly all new plays failed (59). In theater, failure is a relative term, and it is not surprising that Trotter's plays were staged repeatedly with outstanding casts even though they were not spectacular successes. Thus Trotter might have continued a promising career, even though she lacked a hit, had she chosen to remain in the theater rather than marry. Consequently, the cascade of unexamined comments that dismiss Trotter's work as unsuccessful may be historically uninformed.

With inadequate contemporary signposts by which to assess the impact of Trotter's work, then, how might a course in seventeenth-century theater place Trotter in a critical literary history that essentially has overlooked her work? One way to conceptualize Trotter's work is to reconsider the terms on which that history has been defined. Kelley writes that Trotter has been overlooked by feminist critics because she challenged patriarchal values less than other female writers did, such as Manley (*Catharine Trotter*). Kelley suggests that Trotter, viewed as more conservative in both her writing and her life choices, has been omitted by feminist critics as too mainstream.

Paradoxically, Marcie Frank suggests that Trotter has been written out of the history of literary criticism as not mainstream enough, a fate she has shared with other theatrical writers. Frank suggests that twentieth-century historians of literary criticism, favoring the novel, have traditionally begun with Joseph Addison and moved on through the essay-based criticism of Samuel Johnson. She believes that Trotter belongs firmly in a literary critical history that includes theatrical adaptations by Dryden, Behn, Trotter, and Manley of earlier works, which these later writers updated to reflect their own cultural idiom. Frank sees gender politics in these works as inseparable from theatrical performance.

Frank suggests that Trotter's theatrical adaptation of Aphra Behn's "Agnes de Castro," as well as the critical perspectives offered in Trotter's dedications and prologues, follows Dryden's critical stance toward literary history and that considering Trotter's work is crucial in elucidating the position of seventeenth-century women playwrights in the history of literary criticism (ch. 4). Trotter's adaptation of Behn's "Agnes" does not satirize but rather amplifies and dramatizes certain features for emphasis: the moral fortitude and relationships of several female characters, the weakness or even villainy of others, and the capriciousness and gullibility of authority figures. Although not parodic in the oppositional sense, Trotter's adaptation can be seen as parodic in the sense described in Linda Hutcheon's performance theory, which returns to the Greek concept of parody as a song (*odos*) that moves both with and against (*para*) (*Theory of Parody* 32). Analyzed as parody according to this definition, Trotter's *Agnes de Castro* can be reevaluated, rather than rejected as not sufficiently oppositional on the one hand and not sufficiently mainstream on the other. By reimagining a theatrical history inseparable from a history of gender criticism, Frank reestablishes Trotter, with Dryden, Behn, and Manley, as important partners in a discussion about gender in seventeenth-century society. At the same time, Frank reinforces Kelley's view, which sees Trotter as having been written out of feminist literary history because, unlike her colleague Manley, Trotter made choices in her plays and in her own life that appear conservative in reinforcing rather than challenging the masculine status quo.

Aside from her place in literary history and criticism, however, Trotter is important to the study of seventeenth-century literary history today because, beyond the level of plot and whether twenty-first-century scholars approve, her work displays the mind of a woman actively engaged in extending a system of moral philosophy that included women at the nexus of intertwined strands of contemporary political, philosophical, religious, and literary thought. Trotter's philosophical work, based on the writings of English empiricists such as Locke and Clarke, is recognized by philosophers today, not simply as elucidating or explaining these writings, but as actually extending them through original contributions (see Broad; Ready, "Damaris Cudworth Masham"; P. Sheridan, "Locke's Ethics" and "Reflection"; and Waithe). Kathryn Ready, in particular, believes that Locke's theories were attractive to women because

> Locke made it possible to conceptualize the self in terms other than the body and the soul—concepts that had long been implicated in arguments in favor of women's subordination. He shifted interest away from the body and soul toward the mind, which he believed was not gendered at birth. (563)

To read Trotter's plays against an interdisciplinary cultural backdrop, then, is to gain a greater understanding of her vision of the theater as a place where significant cultural conflicts might be resolved, as well as where literate women might induce change by prevailing on the public through the viewing audience.

Trotter's plays (four tragedies and one comedy) share several similarities. Although all of her sympathetic characters are members of the upper classes, all, perhaps like Trotter, are relatively powerless in civil society—they tend to be young women or subordinate men who are subject to the demands of parents, guardians, or superiors and who owe loyalty and duty to others through institutions such as marriage, position in the family, position at court, and citizenship in the state. All face dilemmas that essentially derive from a Lockean view of both human understanding gained through experience (*Essay)* and the nature of obligation in a civil society (*Second Treatise*). Trotter's characters generally have made an earlier choice—right or wrong—that places them in a vulnerable position in which they are tested when ordered to perform actions contrary to reason.

In Trotter's tragedies, the orders come from authority figures (e.g., parents, monarchs, generals) who, because they are human, are fallible. This concern about the fallibility of authority figures is consistent with Trotter's short treatise *Discourse concerning a Guide in Controversies*, in which she rejects the Roman Catholic doctrine of infallibility as inconsistent given the fallibility of the human beings invoking the power of this doctrine (Cockburn). The authority figures in Trotter's tragedies exert their influence on the basis of views clouded by false reports (including character assassination and forgeries in all the plays) or passion-driven, self-interested (frequently sexual) motivation (*Agnes de Castro*, *Unhappy Penitent*, *Revolution of Sweden*). Having committed earlier to a course of action, Trotter's sympathetic characters generally face a range of choices, all of which will result in negative personal consequences; the only positive outcome is intangible—in the mental well-being of the character who knows he or she has acted appropriately. Consequently, acting in the most moral and honorable fashion is its own reward. Acting in an immoral or dishonorable fashion equally results in unhappiness: the character's life unravels, as does the entire range of relationships built on trust within a civil society.

All five plays feature immoral actions that involve broken social contracts; in every case, a vow of friendship is violated, as is a vow of marriage or a stated intent to enter into a contract of marriage (the latter was also considered legally binding at this time, whether or not a ceremony had occurred). Violations of political loyalty to a leader or to the state, which also constitute immoral actions, occur in *Agnes de Castro, Fatal Friendship*, *Unhappy Penitent*, and the *Revolution of Sweden*. Regardless of the contract violated, tragedy ensues when characters indulge their passions rather than subdue personal inclination to reason.

In Trotter's plays, immoral actions result in tragic conclusions, such that a character of either gender or any class can assume the role of the tragic hero. This broad definition of what might constitute the tragic hero, familiar in George Lillo's later play *The London Merchant*, may be what led Trotter's critics to complain that her plays lacked decorum.

Trotter's drama also has a didactic purpose and so depicts moral exempla, in which men and women act morally, rationally, and in the best interest of the state by sublimating passion, love, and the inclinations of the heart. In all her plays, Trotter explores the need to act honorably and with loyalty in friendship, both same-sex and cross-gender, including the need to remain loyal to a friend even in the face of confusing evidence. She also challenges the received notions that men were ruled by reason, and women were ruled by passion, perhaps also an extension of Locke's view of the human being at birth as a tabula rasa on which sense impressions are recorded and organized through the exertion of reason. This gender-neutral formulation argues for the rational capabilities of women as well as the appropriateness of educating women, thereby permitting them to act from conscience and reflection as necessary precursors to formulating correct patterns of individual thought and action. Throughout Trotter's plays, even though several female villains appear, the characters most likely to behave with honor and restraint are women, and men are more likely to act impulsively to gratify the senses, dividing them permanently from happiness and the women they desire. Trotter's plays are also useful case studies of the fundamental conflict between pursuit of honor and pursuit of interest, as well as the complex of ancillary dilemmas that follow such decisions.

Although Trotter was more interested in the moral dilemmas investigated in her tragedies, her only comedy, *Love at a Loss; or, Most Votes Carry It* (1701), is the play most available in teaching volumes today. *Love at a Loss* explores the usual trajectory of social comedy—the negotiation of marriage—but does so, unlike the plays of many of Trotter's contemporaries, from the perspective of the female characters. In the process it suggests that satisfaction is rarely to be gained in marriage. This perspective is also expressed in Trotter's other work. Although her later marriage to Patrick Cockburn appears to have been happy, her earlier, semiautobiographical novel, *Olinda's Adventures* (1693), consists of a series of letters to a trusted male friend, to whom Olinda discloses her (mostly negative) encounters with men, her curiously unobservant mother's efforts to settle her in marriage, and her steadfast refusal to cooperate, vowing repeatedly to lovers that she will remain single. Trotter expresses similar views in her personal letters, such as her 7 July 1705 letter to her friend Burnet:

> [I] cannot imagine, what concern you suppose I might be in about settling my person. Certainly it is not my part to seek or take any pains

> for any Affair of that nature; and if I had been much inclined that way, there may have been some, who did not think a perfect agreement in opinion necessary to their happiness in it with me: But as I never had a thought towards it but for one, and that there are many obstacles against that, I believe I shall end my days as I am. Indeed, I have been always very fearful of putting my happiness entirely in the power of any one.

Love at a Loss relates the courtship negotiations among three couples. Lesbia and Beaumine have contracted a marriage, but, after having seduced Lesbia, the rakish Beaumine avoids following through by fabricating an objecting guardian. Miranda and Constant are engaged, but Miranda flirts shamelessly with Beaumine to avoid losing her liberty. Lucilia and Phillabell are a devoted couple, but Lucilia has compromised herself by sending bogus love letters to the "vain and affected" Cleon. The plot involves each couple's coming to terms with the loss of liberty inherent in marriage. Most intriguing is the Lesbia-Beaumine subplot, which is complicated by the presence of Lesbia's loyal former lover, Grandfoy, whom Lesbia still loves. Beaumine is willing to cede his interest, and Grandfoy is willing to overlook her indiscretion and marry her, but instead of choosing, Lesbia puts it to a vote. When the cast elects Beaumine, she eschews the happiness promised by Grandfoy and instead honors her contract with the ambivalent Beaumine.

Paula Backscheider has seen this plot as having the potential to be darkly satiric—with its possible antecedent the case of Mary Wharton, who sued for divorce in Parliament the same year and received it, "making her the only woman before 1801 whose marriage was 'dissolved.'" As Backscheider points out, "[S]he was also declared a virgin" ("Stretching" 443), which Restoration audiences must have seen as ludicrous.

Backscheider sees this and other contemporary comedies as turning on two underlying Hobbesian assumptions about human nature: that individuals crave novelty because it is pleasurable and that the capacity for human nature to change is limited (446). Described in these terms, the play becomes a series of debates about the unlikeliness of happiness in marriage because it involves loss of liberty and novelty, ideas Trotter expresses elsewhere. Backscheider reads the play's conclusion as laying bare the underlying cultural ideology that limited women's choices and tied them to unhappy marriages. As Backscheider points out, Lesbia simply goes along with the majority vote without declaring her feelings because she recognizes that Beaumine's right to her is indisputable (454).

Regardless of whether this conclusion is satisfying, however, given the trajectory of her tragedies, Trotter may also have seen Lesbia's fate as just and appropriate. For Trotter, morality lies in putting aside personal happiness, and, if *Love at a Loss* is read alongside *The Unhappy Penitent*, one sees the unsatisfying conclusion as unavoidable because Lesbia has made a choice, and, whether or not it is a good choice, it is her moral responsibility to honor that contract. In Trotter's other plays, tragic conclusions result when characters follow inclination rather than the dictates of reason, which are based firmly within the tenets underlying religious belief and civil law. In Trotter's tragedies, the moral choice is to sacrifice personal happiness to follow a rational course, and a promise to marry is a legal contract. Although Lesbia may regret her decision, she is now bound to Beaumine regardless of her chances for happiness.

Betty Rizzo

The Other Elizabeth Griffith

To glow with ardour and attempt with zeal
The reformation of the public weal
Is the high duty of the comic muse.

—Elizabeth Griffith, Prologue to *The Times*

Elizabeth Griffith had a difficult time establishing her literary persona, and to this day it remains confused and confusing. Not her first published work but the first identified with her, the *Series of Genuine Letters between Henry and Frances* (1757) established a protofeminist persona whose enthusiastic acceptance Griffith misunderstood. Balked thereafter of the right to express advocacy of woman's equality and requiring an accepting readership in order to support her family, for the rest of her long career she worked to forge a program through which she could permittedly, if covertly, express—the hidden agenda of the "other" Elizabeth Griffith.

At first in 1757 public approval must have been intoxicating to her, suggesting freedoms of expression not actually available to a woman at that time. The letters were indeed genuine, those written in Ireland between Griffith and her lover, Richard Griffith. From 1746 to 1751, their long and indeterminate love affair was fueled by his expectation of making a mistress of the clever but dowerless and socially inferior Elizabeth. Their sparkling correspondence was irresistible to both, as was her steely determination never to yield to him physically but in marriage. It was a struggle nearly to the death between ancient aristocratic prerogative and more modern standards of meritocracy. The correspondence continued after their marriage, in 1751, and they published further volumes of letters in 1760, 1761, and 1770.

In the early letters, Griffith espoused her protofeminist position, which after 1765 had to be masked for politic purposes and masked more carefully in her plays—which survived only by instant public approval—than in her other works. As Elizabeth and Richard wrote those early letters, Elizabeth could not accept the fact that Richard treasured the reputed difference between the intellects of men and women and, in fact, pardoned her for her effervescent wit only on those grounds. Richard and Elizabeth assumed the names of Henry and Frances in their published letters, and their statements therein are here attributed to these personas. In 1752 Henry summed Frances up thus:

> You have a very good natural understanding, a lively fancy, a quick apprehension, and an easy expression. Your judgment is rather delicate than strong, and may be better stiled a refined taste than a logical reason. (Griffith and Griffith, vol. 3, letter 364)

Frances, on the contrary, liked to quote Descartes's belief that reason has no sex (which she always rendered as "The soul has no sex," terms in which the issue was debated throughout the century), for, she notes, the creator would never have required "as great virtues from us, and subject us to as severe trials as men, without inspiring our minds with equal strength, or making our souls capable of as high moral perfection." Furthermore, women have shown "every manly virtue, even of personal courage, and contempt of death." She explains why examples of female heroism may be few:

> [A]re not the opportunities of exerting it as few also? I mean with regard to actions publick, and shining enough, for the notice of history; which, however, are neither more amiable, or more difficult than many virtues, you, vile men, give us the occasion of exercising in private life; to which you have arbitrarily confined the sphere of our activity.
> (vol. 1, letter 39)

Instead of Descartes, she may have been quoting more directly from François Poullain de La Barre—who in *De l'egalité des deux sexes* (1673) wrote, "The mind has no sex" (109)—when she presented herself to Henry not as a burden to be assumed but as a partner and equal contributor; he himself had written that their marriage was to be more an alliance than a conquest (vol. 1, letter 123). It is essential to recognize that she would always adhere to, though not further publish, these opinions.

And Richard would hold to his. In his *The Triumvirate* (1764), a novel published thirteen years after his marriage, one hero, Carewe, encounters at college Eloisa, a woman disguised as an undergraduate, and, unaware of her sex, assesses "him" as possessed "of no great logical faculties but a refined taste for poetry, painting, music, and the classics, with a remarkable facility for learning languages"; "and he applied himself with such diligence to this superficial part of literature" that he could read and speak with ease and correctness French, Italian, Latin, and Greek (2: 12). Carewe adds that, in the deeper studies and sciences, his friend was dull and slow, that he was fond of and curious about experimental philosophy, "but never troubled his head about the reasons of them," and he concludes, "Prithee, are not these the characteristics of a woman? And need she wear petticoats to declare her gender?" (2: 12). In the same novel, in his description of Miss Beville (a portrait of Elizabeth), he notes, "Her sense was of the right feminine kind, for it consisted rather in a quickness of apprehension, and a delicate taste, than a strong judgment" (1: 32). To this description, Frances objected:

> In the very Midst of your Panegyric, I find I could not escape without a Wipe. . . . "Her sense was of the true feminine Kind, it consisted rather in a Quickness of Apprehension, and a delicate Taste, than a strong Judgment." Pray . . . is this because I have never read Smiglesius? Or are you still so bad a Philosopher, as to distinguish Souls into Genders? (Griffith and Griffith, vol. 3, letter 364)[1]

Indeed Richard was "so bad a Philosopher," and so was almost everyone else. Moreover, it was the general belief that women's writing was the product of separate and inferior faculties. That belief made the writing of accomplished women perfectly tolerable and enjoyable to men like Richard.

A Series of Letters, when first printed in 1757, nevertheless won adulation for both authors. Elizabeth's independent considerations were fully accepted, but perhaps she did not understand that her consistent submission to Richard's authority and wisdom (he was, after all, five years older), not to mention her eventual subjection to him in marriage, won her pardon for her protests of equality. Richard clearly demonstrated that he was the mentor.

On his part, Richard let Elizabeth run on but never altered his conviction of the correctness of the age's ideology of masculine superiority with respect to reason, judgment, general knowledge, and the consequent unalterable difference between male and female intellectual capacities. But enchanted by her flow of words and her enthusiastic admiration of him and eager to keep the correspondence going, he allowed her an absolute self-expression: it was a lot more exciting to respond to; it made real work of his long and attempted seduction. And incidentally it enabled her, for the only period in her life, to express herself fully.

A rule for reading any eighteenth-century woman writer is to look for and to tease out from her published works the expression of her deeply held convictions that were deemed too unorthodox to state plainly, the chains of such expressions that sometimes seem like secret messages or like palimpsests, chains that have been called indirection.[2] Griffith, who on the face of things may look like a quisling, becomes on deeper inspection a successful spy in the conquering ranks—a spy never hanged but instead devoured by inward conflict.

There is first of all the absolute contradiction between her public persona as writer and her true self, a strong-minded person of steely determination who fought perpetually and almost always won. In 1749, when she was twenty-one, she understood that Richard—struggling heroically to support his parents and his sister by acting as a middleman (that is, as the lessee from the landholder of lands that he would then let to small farmers), going deeply into debt to establish a linen manufactory on his own precariously held farm in Kilkenny, and then mortgaging all to establish his sister in marriage—neither could nor would marry her. She found employment as Thomas Sheridan's ingenue tragedy heroine in his Dublin theater and, a merely competent actress, played there for two seasons (1749–51). Deeply in love with Richard, she nevertheless continued to fend him off, refusing his loving and selfish proffers of ruin for herself.

Elizabeth's latter-day public persona of the ideally subservient woman was constructed slowly through trial and error and is the picture that may linger in our minds, though her struggles to improve the lot of women illuminate the ideology of the period against which she had to perform.

To be published, Griffith became perforce the bellwether of the ewes, the upholder of the standards of obedience to the patriarchy. After her first unsuccessful and protofeminist works, she understood that these patriarchal standards must be followed if she wanted to earn by her pen.

When she began writing for money, she was in desperate need. In 1752 she was living at home with her family in Dublin, first secretly married and then pregnant. Her husband came to town from his Kilkenny farm only on occasion, visited her furtively, and could support her only surreptitiously and with difficulty. She needed lodgings of her own. Her first known work (apart from the letters) was a verse tragedy written in the sincere belief that she might as easily impose her standards on the world as she thought she had on Richard. When she set out as a playwright, she was determined to improve the treatment of women as she thought she already had done through the letters.

One device Griffith used to elevate the status of women was to make her tragedy's protagonist a courageous and noble-minded female. *Theodorick, King of Denmark* was adapted from the latter portion of Eustache Le Noble de Tennelière's novel *Histoire d'Ildegerte, reign de Danemark et de Norwege, ou L'amour magnanime* (1695), about an Amazon warrior, translated into English in 1721. Griffith concentrates, however, on the later life of Ildegerte the Amazon, during her reign as queen. The young queen is of inferior birth to her husband, King Theodorick, and she learns that she must free him to marry the Swedish princess if he is to save his throne. Griffith, full of thoughts about the inconvenience she posed her husband, was herself ruminating about suicide (Griffith and Griffith, vol. 5, letters 607–10), but in the play it is the high-minded Swedish princess who conveniently kills herself while Ildegerte redons her armor to fight for her husband. Griffith politicly named the play *Theodorick*, but she failed at the essential task of providing a starring role to be played by the theater producer, David Garrick in England or Sheridan in Ireland, and the play, never acted, was published—by "a young gentlewoman"—by a handsome subscription in Dublin in 1752 and then forgotten.

It was essential that Griffith earn money, but it took her a while to achieve this goal. In the course of her career, she wrote a great many unproduced plays, but her next published one, also never produced, was *Amana* (1764), adapted from a tale by John Hawkesworth that had been published in the *Adventurer* (nos. 72–73). Her heroine adamantly refuses to marry the sultan because she is engaged to a virtuous merchant. There might be actresses enough to play the part of the wise and magnanimous

Amana, but there was no theater manager interested in putting on the play. Griffith, however, who had contrived to move to London with Richard, famous with him for their published letters, had brought along a comedy, *The Platonic Wife*, which through the efforts of friends at Drury Lane was produced in January 1765. Its production became her most painful and instructive lesson.

Before *The Platonic Wife* was produced, Griffith had indeed become celebrated as the "Frances" of the *Series of Genuine Letters*. "Frances" had agreed with "Henry" that even after marriage she was to be treated as when she was being courted; she would remain equally polite to him. Griffith imagined she had struck an important blow for women, and she thought that as a playwright she could continue as woman's advocate.

The Platonic Wife was a she-comedy. The plot, like almost all of Griffith's plots (she always denigrated her talent for invention), was adapted from a model, "L'heureux divorce," a tale by Jean-François Marmontel that Griffith had lately been translating. Its female protagonist had been an attraction for her: the wife, married from the convent, never having had a chance to establish her character or her value as a person, demands time to realize herself, and the compliant husband moves out, leaving her free to entertain would-be lovers and incidentally, by her behavior, to win his respect. The theme could scarcely have been more feminist, and Lady Frankland, Griffith's heroine, even quietly insinuates a longing to know love and sexual passion.[3] What she learns through experience is what Marmontel already knew: there is no such thing as a romantic and disinterested passion; all men in love affairs have selfish ends. But in an age when female protagonists were, if virtuous, passive, this plot is driven by Lady Frankland and her desire. True, once she has gained her point and earned her husband's respect, she immediately subordinates herself to him, throwing herself at his feet: "In this, and every thing else, my pride and pleasure shall be, to obey my dearest lord."

> Too plainly have I prov'd that unconfin'd
> Our little skiff is toss'd by every wind,
> On rocks and quicksands often is it cast,
> And frequent sunk by cruel slander's blast;
> But when our pilot at the helm appears,
> With steady hand and compass when he steers,
> In full security we sail at ease,
> And fear nor driving winds, nor raging seas.
>
> (62; act 5, sc. 6)

Such a capitulation was no more than was necessary, but for the satisfaction of the male audience was far too little too late.

Indirection, in this case the uttering of indecorous truths by discountenanced persons, is a useful ploy: the raucous Lady Fanshawe attacks sacred marriage and says to Lady Frankland on her liberation, "next to the felicity of widowhood is that of being separated. However, there are, my dear, some material differences: While the tyrant lives to whom we have been bound, we never can forget we have been slaves" (15; 1.1).

It was difficult in any case for a woman playwright to write a successful comedy; she had to be decorous above all, and some parts of the first night's performance of *The Platonic Wife*—including a rape planned by a fortune hunter with the assistance of a French maid and some feeble sexual innuendos—had to be hastily written out for the second night's performance.

The complaisant husband and the liberated wife on a quest for self-realization outraged even the male players, who, in response to hoots and catcalls, stuck their heads out from behind the curtain and implored the audience to put an end to the play that very night (Davies 2). Instead, the play labored on through a sixth performance and then disappeared from the boards.

The Platonic Wife, a title that amused one critic as attributing to a woman a choice not hers to make, is Griffith's best and most original play. But money, none of which she had brought to her marriage, was her necessary object, and her further career demonstrates her adjustment to every obstacle to gain it. Thus she put her open advocacy for women aside.

The title of her second play, *The Double Mistake*, may well have implied an apology for *The Platonic Wife*. The play was produced at Covent Garden, where Griffith had at least one great friend, in January 1766. In every way, she showed she had learned her lesson. First, having been accused in her reviews of not understanding dramatic construction, she employed not a prose work but an earlier play as her model: *Elvira; or, The Worst Not Always True* (1667), adapted by George Digby, Earl of Bristol, from Pedro Calderón de la Barca's *No siempre lo peor es cierto* (1652). She had to slave mightily, however, over the adaptation from Spanish to English manners.

The plot of *Elvira* is overcomplex, and Bristol's play retains the Madrid setting and characters of the original. Betty Rizzo, in her introduction to *The Double Mistake*, summarizes Bristol's adaptation:

> Don Fernando, at the height of his happiness, imagines himself supplanted with his mistress, Elvira, when an intruder, Don Zancho, appears mysteriously in her chamber. Fernando runs Zancho through, but he recovers. Elvira, pure but dishonoured and threatened by her father, flies to Fernando for protection. Fernando secretes her in Valencia with his friend Don Julio, disguised as Silvia, the maid of Julio's sister Bianca. Elvira's father, Don Pedro, pursues her to Valencia and, assuming that Zancho has abducted her, appeals to Julio to help him get his revenge. Zancho, though temporarily attracted to Elvira, is in love with Bianca and Julio wants Fernando to help him trap Zancho during the latter's clandestine visits to Bianca. To protect Bianca, Elvira must take on herself the scandal of having admitted Zancho to the house, but she is finally exonerated when an interview between herself and Bianca is overheard. To their satisfaction, both couples are ordered to marry in order to preserve the honour of their houses. (66)

Transferring this action to England, Griffith had to alter the plot extensively. The male characters could no longer scheme to assassinate their enemies in the street and could no longer eavesdrop at doors. The passionate Bianca, wearing a stiletto, becomes the romantic but thoroughly misguided Louisa, who imagines she can devise her own love plot. Most important, while the calumniated but passive Emily does have the initiative to flee to her relation Lord Belmont for protection, she never demonstrates another iota of self-preservation. On the contrary, to protect the foolish Louisa, she seems to confirm her own misstep by falsely confessing to having secretly admitted Louisa's lover, Freeman, to the house. The adventurous and plotting Restoration heroines, of whom Lady Frankland was a worthy descendant, have been replaced by limp and self-sacrificing ladies. Plotting women like Louisa are wrong-thinking; she has been easily deceived by a tradesman intent on marrying her to improve his station. Even female pretensions to learning are thoroughly ridiculed in the person of Louisa's aunt, the pedantic Lady Bridget.

Perhaps in desperation for some female assistance, Griffith in this play both demonstrates and codifies a message she conveys for some time forward. It is even present in her last work, *Essays, Addressed to Young Married Women* (1782). The message: if a wife remains dependent and obedient, generous men may in turn enthrone them. Griffith also hoped to influence men: fine men, she attempts to establish, can be recognized by their generous behavior to women.

This was an unhopeful platform, but under the circumstances it was the best Griffith could do: "I never yet heard of a damsel in distress, that I did not wish to relieve her," says *The Double Mistake's* exemplary Sir Charles (86; act 2, sc. 1), who in fact will do his best to bring about the happy conclusion to the plot's complications. And the hapless Emily concurs: "by nature and by providence design'd, our helpless sex's strength lies in dependance; and where we are so blest to meet with generous natures, our servitude is empire" (116; 4.4). At last vindicated through no effort of her own, Emily is assured by her restored lover, "Transporting charmer! every way you have conquer'd, subdued me, by esteem, as well as love" (128; 5.4). These are instructions to gentlemen that they should reward rather than debase the women who willingly (abjectly) subject themselves. Before *A Wife in the Right* (1772), Griffith suggested that superior men would do so, and she must have hoped that many men would prefer to look superior in this way. Emily forgives her unjust accusers, including her lover, but she has done nothing to save herself; her female magnanimity has all but ruined her, and she is saved only by a stroke of providence—another hope Griffith held out when there was no other.

Louisa, that frail reed, is useful for providing one bit of indirection, surely a bitter reflection of Griffith's. The virtuous Lord Belmont expresses another of Griffith's prescriptions for marital happiness. The flame of marriage to fickle man must be carefully tended by his wife: "possession damps the ardor of desire; merit alone can keep the flame alive, and hinder every wanton gale from blowing it abroad; that, like the vestal fire, must be preserv'd by constant watching" (107; 3.4). Griffith, in her later work, insists on a wife's constant obligation to please. But here Louisa responds tartly, "By your account, my lord, a married woman has just as bad a life as a vestal, if her whole time is to be spent in keeping one spark alive."

A converted Louisa, in the epilogue, however, concludes significantly:

> When, after all our boast, we find, at length,
> To know our weakness is our surest strength,
> One path of science only, wise men say,
> Is left for female learning—to obey— (130)

One can follow Griffith's search for an answer to the problem: what *can* be done to ameliorate woman's miserable position? In this play Griffith first faintly delineates the faute de mieux prescription that she emphasizes in her next two plays. *The Platonic Wife*'s Lady Frankland is a self-reliant and autonomous heroine until her capitulation at the curtain. *The Double*

Mistake's Emily is entirely virtuous and limp. If a heroine renounces her self-reliance and autonomy, if she assumes a pleasing incapacity to become an echo to her husband, that husband, if a superior mortal, must honor her for it. Between this play and her next, Griffith consolidates the platform that was typically built to educate and alter the attitude of men. Lord Belmont, like all the admirable men of her dramas, notes that "all brave men shou'd engage on the weaker side" (94; 2.5).

After the disaster of *The Platonic Wife*, Griffith clearly and skillfully devised a platform that could win approval. Moreover, her authorship of *The Double Mistake* was carefully concealed. The play ran for twelve nights, and in February there was a royal command performance. The published play quickly ran into three editions and one Dublin edition. The play may have earned Griffith as much as £600, or approximately £60,000 in today's currency. Griffith had now codified her overt message, to be thereafter conveyed in drama, novel, short story, and essay, and she began in earnest to use indirection.

We can easily enough see the insincerity of her latter-day platform. But Griffith had come to believe that the path she advocated was not only the path acceptable to her male public but also the sole safe path for wives, the one by which they could earn the most privilege, and therefore the most security, in marriage. Other paths, she demonstrated in future works, often led to disaster. The arduous task of preserving even an unhappy marriage fell to women. Lord Belmont instructs:

> Men are naturally inconstant; and a husband may sometimes see a woman fairer than his wife; but 'tis her fault, if in the whole circle, he can find one that so well deserves his love; whose temper, manners, conduct, and behaviour, are so much suited to his sentiments; who knows no wish or will, but to please him—these charms, the homeliest woman may acquire; without them, the fairest form that ever struck our eyes, cannot retain one heart. (107; 3.4)

At this point, Griffith's platform depends not only on the entire submission of women to their husbands but also on the heightened sensibility of men that would lead them to reward and honor their wives for that submission. In her next play, Griffith incorporated into the rake husband's reformation his explicit awareness of the reverence due his wife.

Though Griffith labored in other genres—the third and fourth volumes of letters were published in 1766, and in 1769 she was completing her first novel, *The Delicate Distress*—the theater was always her first object, since it was potentially far more generous in its rewards. And in 1769 she achieved her greatest success. By playing the helpless mother, she had brought Garrick to heel at last (see my discussion of this manipulation in "'Depressa Resurgam'" 130–33), and he was collaborating with her on an adaptation of Pierre Beaumarchais's sentimental drama *Eugénie* (1767), based on the tale "The History of the Count de Belflor and Leonora de Cespedes" from the vastly successful *Le diable boiteux* (1707), by Alain-René Lesage. Belflor, a Spanish nobleman, falls in love with Leonora, the daughter of an ordinary gentleman, and, considering marriage to her impossible, subverts her governess and arranges a false private marriage. On discovering the situation, Leonora's father sends to the university for his son, Don Pedro, to avenge his family's dishonor. Pedro is, however, secretly in Madrid pursuing an unknown woman with whom he has fallen in love. Attacked in the street, Pedro is rescued by Belflor, who then asks Pedro to accompany him for a last visit to Leonora. When Pedro recognizes his own family, a general éclaircissement ensues, during which Belflor overcomes his pride, agrees to marry Leonora, and allows Pedro to marry his sister, who turns out to be Pedro's mysterious mistress.

Beaumarchais, a militant bourgeois, moved the action of *Eugénie* to England and made his protagonist, the aristocratic Lord Clarendon, a libertine who has been the ruin of many women. For the first half of the play, the tormented Eugénie alternates between joy and despair as Clarendon denies his approaching nuptials to an aristocratic lady. When at last she recognizes her position, she is further tormented by her brother's determination to fight Clarendon. Clarendon, however, is then subdued not by threats or vituperation but by the spectacle of Eugénie suffering; he obtains his father's permission to marry her and, presumably reformed, argues her into forgiving him. The play closes with the domestic circle, at odds with one another throughout the play, gathered harmoniously around the heroine. Beaumarchais, the son of a barber, thus justifies the new genre of domestic or sentimental comedy. And the heroine he devises for it is precisely the heroine Griffith has already constructed.

Griffith, however, had years of work to do before the play (which she called *The School for Rakes*) could be made truly English. She created for her hero, Lord Eustace, good and bad angels, Frampton and Willis. She introduced several servants and two comic characters and alternated sentimental and comic scenes. And she retained and enhanced the passivity of the heroine, Harriet, who blames only herself, never hates Eustace or considers resorting to the law or violence, remaining always what her lover refers to as "[m]y lovely softness" (160; act 2, sc. 1). Griffith had at last written a successful woman-centric play, for though Harriet is treated sadistically (probably the only way then to bring a heroine front and center), the final tableau is not the familiar young couple who has successfully wrested the power from their parents but the whole family grouped around the worthy and impeccable woman who has bested her rake lover. This scenario presents a different comic model entirely, one that establishes the primacy of the woman in the home and supports the standard of meritocracy rather than aristocracy.

Harriet has won by the complacency Griffith recommends, but she has been without the prerogative to plot her own survival, to act in her own behalf, throughout her distress. Her aunt has prevailed on her to make a secret marriage; her lover has duped them both. She remains gentle; she would entreat but not command, she says. Griffith thus reveals her belief at this time that the only means to feminine power is enacting powerlessness—and in her letters of the period she plays the same role, insofar as she, a strong director of the marital bark, can do so. The popular actor Thomas King, impersonating a woman as he delivered the prologue, instructed the audience, "Cowards spare none; but you, the truly brave, / Women, and children, will for ever save!" (144).

It remained Griffith's mission, given things as they were and had to be, to convince men that the best and bravest of them would always protect and nuture women—even in private, even in their marriages. But it followed that women could never threaten or challenge men. Though Griffith never said so, in her work from this time on she suggested that women must prevail through playacting and subtle manipulation. The advice is all but explicit, as is the best method for doing so, in her *Essays, Addressed to Young Married Women*. She might have certified her method by citing the sentence in a letter of 17 August 1766 that finally won over Garrick:

> [I]n attempting to wear the Sock, tho' I may fail to make it fit me, it was not vanity led me to the trial, but a young family & a small fortune, called for the assistance of a fond Mother, who would hazard much more than her fame, her life, for their service. (Letter 234–35)

The School for Rakes, then, underwritten by that best and bravest of men, Garrick, was vastly successful. There were eleven performances in February 1769, four more in the following months, and then the play entered the repertory to be acted in subsequent seasons. In April it had five performances, one the following year at the Theatre Royal in Dublin, and seven in Cork. There were three London and two Dublin editions and a further acting edition in 1795 that suggests the play was still performed in the provinces.

Wounding, perhaps, were the reviews that emphasized Garrick's part in the success. But the play must have grossed Griffith £700, a sum surely adequate to outfit her son Richard for his expedition to India (1770) as a writer for the East India Company, which was to result in independence for the family. She had in a way proved her prescription for women's triumph.

So many eager playwrights, so few slots for new plays—on average two for each theater a year—and Griffith's score of five plays produced at the two major London theaters represented a triumph of careful adaptation to the public taste. Garrick, Griffith now found, was determined never to produce a play of hers again. He had indeed labored mightily and considered that he had discharged his responsibility to this woman and her son.

So Griffith's next play, produced in 1772, went to George Colman at Covent Garden. The title, *A Wife in the Right* (provided by Colman—Griffith had named the comedy "Patience the Best Remedy"), seemed a somewhat unnecessary reference to *The Platonic Wife* (so clearly established to have been in the wrong). This wife was indeed as (apparently) unassertive as right wives should be. Lord Seaton, the rake who must reform, has married the woman of fortune rather than the woman he prefers, her friend Charlotte. Charlotte prudently leaves his house, but his wife believes she has done so only to receive her husband's visits more conveniently. The plot thus hinges on the wife's wise and restrained responses to the situation and, in fact, on the positive effect of her instrumentality. Seaton is also having an affair with the vicious Mrs. Frankly, with whom, unaware of her character, Charlotte has found refuge. Charlotte's lover Colonel Ramsey has returned from abroad and is seeking her; believing Seaton has misused her, he challenges him. Governor Anderson, Lady Seaton's uncle, a comically willful nabob, provides humor but no sensible government. Complete disorder reigns. At this point Lady Seaton appears, so composed and kind that her husband is converted and the duel averted. Lady Seaton is not only a most rational and right-thinking character but an active one: her two determined visits to Charlotte at Mrs. Frankly's precipitate the éclaircissement. She listens to and judges the evidence. She is not the passive heroine of *The School for Rakes* or *The Double Mistake* but takes necessary action to settle affairs. She is in great contrast both to her husband and to Governor Anderson. She has both reason and a heart that detects truth.

Thus a despised wife, through her delicacy, sensibility, right reason, and ability to take action, wins back her rake husband. By this time the only rebel against decency is Mrs. Frankly:

> [T]here is no such thing, on earth, as a friend, except money, child. Youth and beauty are bills of exchange. . . . [T]he utmost that is required of feeble nature, now-a-days, is barely to conceal the vices that we have, under the affectation of those virtues we are deficient in. (228–29; act 2, sc. 2)

And in this case once again Griffith uses indirection to provide an index to the powers that threaten. Mrs. Frankly's name suggests that the character speaks a kind of truth—the truth of perhaps the majority of society—and her standards, shared by Lord Seaton (who pursues beauty but who has married for money), make a dupe of the governor.

But Griffith is more peremptorily than ever emphasizing the fact that true men of honor appreciate and protect women. For instance, the exemplary Colonel Ramsey asks Lord Seaton of his wife, "How is it possible that you can allow her those merits which are to be the basis of your security and peace, and yet withhold from her the just reward of them, your tenderness and esteem?" (235; 3.1). Griffith has, however, adjusted her view that the exemplary heroine, to be admired, must be passive. Passivity alone, however, was not enough to preserve a marriage. Mrs. Seaton never reproaches her husband; she is, without complaining, as sadistically treated as any heroine of sentimental drama. Yet she brings about the dramatic climax only by the simple and acceptable feminine expedient of making two visits, both in search of a friend whom she has wronged. But it is an active expedient, suggesting a moral determination. And though the first visit leads to further complications, the second is amply rewarded—abetted, no doubt, by providence.

But the play failed. Its sentimental plot was vapid, and the half dedicated to a comic plot missed the mark. The meaty role of the nabob Governor Anderson, written, perhaps, for Garrick, was instead mishandled by the drunken Ned Shuter, who failed to learn his lines and lost the subtle thread questioning the worthiness of those men into whose hands government was entrusted. Colman withdrew the play after the first night. The reviews were terrible. In aggressive response the Griffiths mustered an impressive subscription list of over 530 people, including nobles and celebrities, and the reviews of the published play—identical to the performed one—were glowing and entirely regretful of its failure. But it was a vindication without financial reward.

For an author's great reward was a successful play, and it was only seven years later that Griffith saw her last play, *The Times*, produced. She had refused to produce another play with Colman, and Richard Sheridan, who had never liked her, was now manager in Garrick's place at Drury Lane; but in 1779 her old friend Thomas Sheridan was managing the theater in his son's absence, and he took her play.

The Times, an attack on contemporary gambling and profligacy, was an adaptation of Carlo Goldoni's *Le bourru bienfaisant*, about a crusty but benevolent bachelor who has repudiated his nephew and his wife because of their extravagance, which, unknown to his wife, has brought him to ruin. Unable to deprive her of any wish, he has allowed her to spend what he has not gambled away. Griffith adapted the play without most of the difficulties inherent in her earlier translations.

Lady Mary, guilty only of indulging in the extravagance of her peers because she has no idea she is overspending their income, on learning of her husband Woodley's ruin instantly proclaims her willingness to retire into the country with the husband whom she sincerely loves. She becomes a pattern of good sense. Simultaneously Woodley's uncle, Sir William, orders Woodley's sister Louisa to marry his forty-eight-year-old friend Belford; Sir William's plan is frustrated when Belford, apprised of Louise's understanding with Colonel Mountfort, generously refuses the match and takes the blame for the refusal.

Griffith has a new and braver point to make in this play. The complications of the twin plots are both caused by not keeping the women involved properly informed: Lady Mary has no notion of the financial situation of her husband until they are ruined; Sir William has not thought it necessary to consult Louisa about his marriage arrangements for her. To emphasize this point, the sometimes wrongheaded if warmhearted Sir William pronounces, "Women should ever be kept in ignorance to prevent mischief" (189; act 4, sc. 2). If Griffith cannot overtly demand that women be empowered, she can at least suggest the advantages of allowing them to share in the knowledge of family circumstances and to collaborate in the arrangement of their marriages—in short, to have a say in domestic matters.

Thus, as a woman playwright, Griffith fought her way through a difficult situation with indirection. Unable both to earn for her family and to demand autonomy for women with *The Platonic Wife*, she reestablished her popular credentials with the passive heroine of *The Double Mistake* and instituted a demand that superior males honor and revere the women that abnegate all autonomy, a demand made more explicit, yet not stridently, in *The School for Rakes* with its equally passive heroine. Griffith, however, must have recognized that servitude leads not to empire but invariably to further abuse. In *The Wife in the Right* a proper wife finds a proper way to eschew passivity and bring about happy resolution. Finally in *The Times* family disaster is averted only when a wife is informed about the true state of her family's fortunes and finds a means to respond and when the desires of a young marriageable woman are consulted. These points are so lightly inflected that it is doubtful that many of the theater audience noted them. Hence it was through the subtlety of indirection that Griffith had to make her points—as she had learned from her experience with *The Platonic Wife*, arguably her best play of all.

Notes

The volume editors would like to thank Beverly Schneller for her help reviewing this essay, whose author passed away before its publication.

1. Smiglesius (Martin Smiglecki [1560–1619]), author of *Logica Doctoris*, is noted by a fictitious persona, a student of logic, in Johnson's *Rambler*, who practices syllogisms and sleeps "every night with Smiglecius on my pillow" (144).

2. On indirection, the more subtle introduction of a point of view not to be directly expressed, see Poovey 40–47, 245, and 253n8, which cites several other important sources. Schofield 9–11 provides a bibliography of works on the secondary "woman's plot."

3. Quoting Pope's *Epistle of Eloise to Abelard*, "'Where thought meets thought, ere from the lips they part, / And each warm wish springs mutual from the heart, / This sure is bliss, if bliss on earth there be—'

Heigh ho! Why cannot I not repeat the rest?" (19; act 1, sc. 4). The rest is "And once the lot of Abelard and me," but Lady Frankland has never yet had that experience. As the roguish Clarinda notes at the start, "She dies for sentimental passion" (15; 1.1).

Cami D. Agan

Frances Sheridan: A Case Study for Mid-Eighteenth-Century Comedy

Despite contemporary inclination to view Frances Sheridan primarily as a novelist because of her successful *Memoirs of Miss Sidney Bidulph* (1761) and her association with Samuel Richardson, she was also closely connected to the theater through her husband, the actor-manager Thomas Sheridan. As one of the few authors of mainpiece comedy, female or male, of the mid-eighteenth century, Frances Sheridan makes for an intriguing case study in any classroom. Taken together, the success of her first comedy, *The Discovery* (1763), and the failure of her second, *The Dupe* (1763), reveal complex negotiations among an author's text, competing theatrical conventions, managerial whim, and an often unpredictable theatergoing public. Likewise, Sheridan's critical history reveals the power of later discourse to erase or devalue a theatrical era, in this case with sweeping readings based on the sentimental. Thus assigning a mid-century playwright like Sheridan allows students to examine the ways in which texts are affected initially by cultural conditions and subsequently by critical assumptions about an era.

Since her husband was constantly pursued by debts, Sheridan was a woman writer motivated by tangible economic as well as aesthetic factors that evoke the specific sociocultural conditions of 1760s Drury Lane. Jean Coates Cleary explains that the failure of Thomas Sheridan's Smock-Alley

Theatre in Dublin in 1758 resulted in "a massive £7,000 debt, a burden from which the Sheridans would not recover during Frances' lifetime" (x). Running for seventeen nights and guaranteeing the playwright three benefit evenings, *The Discovery* enjoyed a success on the stage that also led to more economic gain through its publication and later revivals, so that "for [Frances Sheridan], as for so many female writers, the needs of the family provided an excuse for venturing into publication" (Doody, "Frances Sheridan" 325). Sheridan's connection to literary and theatrical circles gave *The Discovery* entrée into the difficult world of Drury Lane, but such connections did not aid *The Dupe*, which failed after only three nights but had success in print. Undeterred by *The Dupe*'s stage failure, Sheridan wrote and submitted her third comedy, *A Journey to Bath* (1764), now extant in only three acts. When David Garrick rejected the comedy, also referred to as *A Trip to Bath*, Sheridan wrote a spirited letter in defense of her play. Robert Hogan and Jerry C. Beasley print both Sheridan's letter and Garrick's reply in full, reminding us "just what kind of arbitrary power aspiring and even established playwrights were up against at the hands of theatrical managers" (Introduction 26). Far from viewing herself solely as a novelist, Sheridan worked nearly concurrently on *Journey to Bath*, a sequel to *Memoirs*, and the "Oriental" *History of Nourjahad*. By now in exile in France—hiding from her husband's creditors—Sheridan continued writing until her early death in 1766.

Exploration of the theatrical production history of Sheridan's comedies offers a window into the complexities of theatrical production under the Stage Licensing Act of 1737, exposes the power of managerial control under Garrick, underlines socioeconomic concerns such as benefit evenings, and allows access to contemporary reviews and audience reactions. After reviewing primary source material found in *The London Stage*, Samuel Whyte's *Miscellanea Nova*, and Garrick's letters, students should more fully understand the difficulties mid-century authors faced in bringing new comedies to the stage.[1] Likewise, a focus on Sheridan's theatrical experience opens the classroom to questions about gender and the theater, about the economic pressures for women writers in the period, and about the necessity for theatrical or literary connections for first-time dramatists. By focusing on ways Sheridan wrote across literary forms, students can also discuss the treatment of genre: Is Sheridan a novelist? a playwright? a working writer? What are the results of such labeling? Recognizing Sheridan as a multigenre author allows students to reconsider the relations among genres and the potential erasure that results from privileging the novel.

Focusing student research on the critical treatment of Sheridan's comedies also exposes various ways in which the mid-century has been categorized, dismissed, and often erased from current theatrical scholarship and publication. Lisa Freeman begins her study of eighteenth-century theater by noting that, although

> dedicated scholars have amassed a vast historical record of eighteenth-century drama[,] . . . many of the scholars involved in these projects have turned a dubious eye toward the content of their subject matter and have expressed strong resistance to any efforts aimed at literary interpretation. (*Character's Theater* 1–2)

Lumped consistently in the sentimental category, defended or castigated according to their adherence to critical definitions of sentimentality, Sheridan's comedies, like those of her contemporaries, barely exist in the literary, scholarly, or pedagogical canons of eighteenth-century theater studies. As a female playwright who also wrote novels and who had a more successful playwright son, Frances Sheridan as dramatist now exists in critical shorthand only as "sentimental novelist and mother of R. B. Sheridan."

Through research into Sheridan's comedies and the mid-century theater, students may begin to realize how dangerous it can be to accept critical narratives, such as the sentimental construct that haunts mid-eighteenth-century comedy. Likewise, they may begin to consider the gaps in courses and texts not as natural spaces created necessarily by professors or editors shifting from one good work to another but rather as spaces that can expose vital tensions among historical, aesthetic, cultural, and critical discourses. By exploring those tensions, we can lead students to consider Sheridan's texts as feminist documents that attempt to negotiate a venue fraught with anxiety about representation of their audience's world and that seek to gain aesthetic or economic recognition for their author. In particular, *The Discovery* and *The Dupe* both employ the conventional courtship-marriage plot but also express anxiety concerning domestic spaces; both enact a concern with social performance, and both express a simultaneous awareness and mockery of audience taste.

The Discovery's use of the courtship plot stages the domestic space as containment for women, even as it suggests that they can still maneuver and gain their ends in that space. The comedy's primary plot concerns itself with Lord Medway scheming himself out of debt through the "selling" of his children to the highest marital bidder. Through Lady Medway's advice that Louisa obey her father and accept Sir Anthony, the text exposes a wife's despair and resignation at the limited options for women under eighteenth-century marriage constraints. Given what Ann Messenger calls the "patriarchal values" of Lord Medway (294), Lady Medway advises her daughter to capitulate: "you know your papa is absolute: I wish, therefore, you would endeavour to reconcile yourself to Sir Anthony." She prepares Louisa for Lord Medway's insistence on Sir Anthony: "I am commissioned to tell you, positively, you *must* accept of him for a husband" (48; act 1, sc. 3). Significantly, Lady Medway voices both traditional systems of feminine passivity—" 'tis certain you have no choice left"—and her clear dissatisfaction with her power within those systems: "I have already exerted my utmost influence over him, and that I am sorry to say is less, much less, than it ought to be" (49; 1.3).

In the scene that follows such advice, Lord Medway imposes his will on Louisa with biting mockery and a near violent attempt to silence her:

> Stay where you are madam.—When I condescend to talk with you, methinks you ought to know, 'tis your duty to attend to what I have to say. . . . But observe what I say; I forbid you to think, but even to think, of Branville. (50; 1.4)

Lord Medway's silencing of Louisa's voice parallels his thwarting of her will or choice in marriage. In fact, according to Patricia Meyer Spacks, "The scene . . . emphatically conveys male fears, as the man in possession of complete autocratic power imagines what his daughter *might* say, given the chance. Such imagining defines male vulnerability" (508). Despite his disordered state, it is Lord Medway's language that seems to rule the domestic space, and thus he both serves as the conventional parental figure in the courtship plot and succeeds in exposing anxieties about masculine control over women's lives.

Lord Medway's control is not complete, however, for Louisa and her mother have carved out a space of feminine comfort and potential power where they conduct their "evening meditations" (67; 2.1). Initially, Lady Flutter dismisses Louisa as "for ever poring over a book or a needle" (65) and makes reference to the women's "custom" of retiring to their "dressing-room," to which Lord Medway notes, "Oh, they read together every evening!" (67; 2.1). This reference to a "dressing-room" wherein the women work, read, and construct a kind of artistic and feminine space—although it may not undermine Lord Medway's ability to enter Louisa's room and silence her—does suggest a woman's locale apart from paternal domination. Lady Flutter's decision to reject that space puts her in the way of Lord Medway's schemes, from which, interestingly, only Lady Medway can rescue her. Thus while *The Discovery* employs typical characters and devices of the courtship plot, including the rake husband and tyrannical parent, the courtship model also stages anxiety about male power over space and language that is ultimately overturned by specifically female alternatives.

In addition to its depiction of courtship conventions, the comedy underlines social performances and the ways in which such masks inhibit the ability to distinguish between genuine behavior and show, particularly in gendered exchanges. In the secondary plot involving the Flutters, a married couple in constant battle, Lord Medway schools Sir Harry Flutter to act the imperious, hateful husband as he himself tempts Lady Flutter into a sexual liaison. Lord Medway suggests Sir Harry's mask:

> [T]here is a sort of sneering, ironical treatment, that I never knew fail of nettling a woman to the quick; and the best of it is, . . . let *them* deliver your very words, without the tone and air accompanying them, and there shall not appear the least harm in them. (46; 1.2)

Later, the play stages Sir Harry acting this part in a spectacle of masculine domination of language and space. Lady Flutter's fury at this display opens the door for Lord Medway's role as sympathetic listener-cum-seducer. Lord Medway's manipulation of the Flutters clearly exposes the power of theatricality to divide, to tempt, and to teach the role of male dominance, all to the detriment of Lady Flutter. However, one spectator Lord Medway does not envision for his social performance—his wife—observes his act of seduction and takes on her role of genuine adviser to Lady Flutter in the scenes that follow. As a result, Angela J. Smallwood notes, "The play discredits patriarchy by presenting Lord Medway's life as tyrannical, immoral, and doomed, and by contrasting it with Lady Medway's, which enshrines the antithetical principle of friendship and makes redemption possible" (244).

Once a passive observer of her daughter's plight, Lady Medway now finds that her "sympathy for another potential female victim compels her to discover ways of doing as well as being" (Spacks 509). With the knowledge of her husband's plan to seduce Lady Flutter, Lady Medway intervenes and cautions Lady Flutter about the spaces and facades she has been using:

> What do you think must be the consequence, if Sir Harry should discover that you have appointed a private place of meeting with my Lord? . . . If you will be ruled by me, Lady Flutter, for one week, nay but for three days, I'll engage that Sir Harry and you shall be as happy a couple as any in England. (75; 3.2)

Significantly, while Lady Flutter earlier "comments sarcastically on the fact that [Lady Medway] enjoys evenings spent reading in her dressing room with her daughter," the comedy eventually exposes Lady Flutter as "immature and counterproductive" and in need of a mature woman's advice (Smallwood 245). The comedy thus parallels male and female schooling of the Flutters: while Lord Medway maneuvers and stages their conflict to gain his own sexual ends, Lady Medway advises the use of conciliatory language and space to reunite them. As a result, Lady Flutter first only performs the part of agreeable wife, but then the act becomes genuine. Sir Harry subsequently realizes the absurdity of his masculine posturing, admitting, "Duce take me but I should think you prodigious agreeable, if you were always in good humour." Lady Flutter replies, "And, upon my life, I should think the same of you" (77; 3.2). On Lady Medway's advice, Lady Flutter achieves harmony through performance and exposes Lord Medway's scheme: "The tables are turned, my Lord; I'll whisper with nobody but Sir Harry" (78; 3.2).

The Discovery exposes no other social performance more ludicrous than that of Sir Anthony Branville, a buffoon committed to courtship's forms. His mask of delicate lover and worshiper of women makes him easy bait for Lord Medway's marital scheme. Louisa's early description of Sir Anthony's language—"the pomp and strange turn of his phrases, and the solemnity of his manner, is almost ridiculous" (48; 1.3)—is quickly confirmed in their first meeting. Sir Anthony cautions Louisa that "I by no means approve of those rash and impetuous lovers, who, without regard to the delicacy of the lady, would, (having obtained consent) as it were rush at once into her arms, you'll pardon me, madam, for so grossly expressing my idea" (81; 3.3). Louisa quickly sees that playing along with Sir Anthony's definition of courtship will enable her to escape the marriage, and she closes act 3 by underlining how well her mask may serve her: "Ha, ha, ha, I think I may now go, and very safely assure my papa, that I am ready to take my adorer whenever he pleases—this is fortunate beyond my hopes" (83). Both Sir Anthony's act and Louisa's role call into question the conventions of delicacy a mid-eighteenth-century audience expected of its comedy. His language is what any "conscious lover" would employ, but here the results are ludicrous and absurd. Louisa thus escapes one mode of masculine language (her father's) through the aping of another mode: the sentimental or chivalric.

That ultimately Sir Anthony is duped, schooled, and ruled by his former lover Mrs. Knightly only furthers his satiric use and the play's thematic concern with women's power. Mrs. Knightly's position as widow—free of the domestic and economic domination of a husband—aligns her with Lord Medway's economic power and offers an alternative to Lady Medway's "feminine" morality. Although initially imperious about keeping her sister Miss Richly from inheritance, Mrs. Knightly also finally thwarts Sir Anthony's designs on Louisa by claiming her former role as his adored object. She suffers his performance to open the possibility of happiness for Louisa. Messenger claims that one "innovation" of the comedy arises from the "gentle feminism, consisting in part of Mrs. Knightly's sudden change from jealous tormentor" to supporter of both Miss Richly and Louisa (293). The comedy's complex relation with the sentimental is embodied in Mrs. Knightly, for though she reverts to the good nature the sentimental ideal champions, she also exposes its language and its performance as subject to ridicule. Taken together, Lady Medway's more accepted feminine tactics and the widow Knightly's changeable, aggressive schemes represent two avenues of women's power in the comedy, one avenue that appears to adhere to accepted notions of femininity and another that employs a more powerful woman to expose Sir Anthony's fawning language as absurd.

Sheridan's second comedy, *The Dupe*, also explores problematic domestic space, which here is merely a facade. Sir John Woodall, the "dupe" of the title, does not recognize his wife, Mrs. Etherdown, publicly, and he is continually unconcerned with moral expectations about marriage and the domestic space. For example, he exults when he believes that his niece Emily has fled his house: "I warrant you'd have me be mighty anxious about her *virtue* now, and try to recover her, for fear she should be *ruin'd*, as you call it. Not I, by the mass! if the wench has a mind to take her fling, e'en let her, for me" (134; act 3, sc. 6). Sir John's refusal to value Emily's virtue undercuts typical conventions about a guardian's fixation on his ward's virginity. Giving her the right to "take her fling," Sir John dangerously equates masculine and feminine sexual desire and freedom by asserting Emily's right over her own movements and body. As such, the play seems to cast aside the social norms and fears about women's sexuality, for it thwarts conventions of the abduction trope and intriguingly complicates domestic space and conventional character. Given such a domestic scene fraught with disdain for cultural expectations, particularly about women, perhaps it is not surprising that the audience did not allow the play to succeed beyond its benefit evening.

With Mrs. Etherdown, Sheridan constructs a widow as Sir John's equal in deceit and the use of masks, a kind of monstrous woman who embodies aberrant social behavior. She unabashedly manipulates and exploits Sir John, seeking only to gain his fortune:

> I am so sick of [Sir John], and the continual disguise I am obliged to wear, that if I should once accomplish my point, I should rejoice to part from the beast. . . . How do you think I have made my money? Why by dipping him over head and ears in debt; appropriating every shilling he gave me for other purposes to my own use. (110; 1.2)

While she plays the role of pliable wife to him and appears willing to be shamed as his "whore" publicly, she reveals here what lies behind that disguise. As Messenger notes, *The Dupe*, particularly through Mrs. Etherdown, constructs a transgressive female character only "pretending to the kind of loving submissiveness that is genuine in Lady Medway" (296). Further, her use of a child she passes off as Sir John's heir taps into audience anxieties about legitimacy and inheritance. Here is no victim but instead a force worthy of opposing a rake, a figure who dons a multitude of masks or selves and casts aside those facades without moral consequence. Mrs. Etherdown never repents her actions, as is clear in her final speech:

> *Mrs. Etherdown*. . . . the farce is at an end between us; and you will find me quite a different creature from what you supposed. . . .
> *Sir John*. [*Stands and stares at her*.] . . . what the devil are you? a woman or a fiend?
> *Mrs. Etherdown*. . . . a woman, a woman of spirit, a woman of fashion, a woman of pleasure, expense, profusion, luxury! what do you think of me now? (143; 4.4)

Although Sir John attempts to demonize her as a "witch" or an "imp," Mrs. Etherdown remains brazen in her desire for power, wealth, and pleasure. Her use of theatrical metaphors, noting that the "farce" is over as she lays aside her "disguise," connects stage business to domestic relations. She triumphantly repeats "woman" in a verbal act of self-definition that must have shocked spectators, for she equates the desires of the whore unabashedly with "woman." Mr. Friendly does succeed in extricating Sir John from Mrs. Etherdown's control, but the audience never sees her defeated, and her powerful will is never completely overcome. The "monstrous" feminine characteristics that she embodies—sexual potency, economic desire, disguise and subterfuge—thus continue to register as powerful despite male attempts to contain or subvert her. Through this dangerous figure, *The Dupe* attempts to negotiate the line between the possibilities for a new active female character and audience expectations about what comedy and character should be.

Just as the conclusions of novels often fail to convince the reader that all is well, Sheridan's comedic resolutions lead us to consider more fully the dissonance created through the previous five acts. In both comedies the rakes reform as we expect, but only when forced to do so and not very convincingly even then. *The Dupe* also partially resists marital resolution, as Mr. Friendly agrees with Sir John that his maidservant, Rose, should not hold Sharply to his promise of marriage—"the woman's a fool who subjects herself for life to a man who must despise her"—and Sir John continues: "Rose, you see the banns are forbid on all sides. No more matrimony"(155; 5.6). Even the moral center of the play, Mr. Friendly, asserts that premarital sex and false promises are no reasons for marriage, at least for the serving classes. Clearly, the audience was unprepared for such dissonance. As the *Gazetteer and London Daily Advertiser* noted, the audience found "the persuading Rose and Sharply not to marry, highly immoral" (qtd. in Chew 198). Sheridan's decision to resist an easy closure for her comedy contributed to its failure, but it also suggests a writer interested in redrawing conventional boundaries in resolution and, through Mrs. Etherdown and Sir John, in characterization.[2]

Through critical reading, analysis, and discussion of *The Discovery* and *The Dupe*, students can observe clear tensions in the cultural, theatrical moment of the mid-eighteenth century. Not Restoration, not sentimental like Richard Steele, and not positioned as laughing or completely opposed to the sentimental, Sheridan's comedies are in between, a kind of "not, but" theatrical moment that marks anxieties about form, convention, content, and genre. This neither-nor position stands out starkly in the prologue and epilogue of both plays, which confront expectations about women writing, characterization, audience desire and power over the theatrical space, and the generic shift associated with delicacy. *The Discovery*'s prologue uses legal tropes to position Sheridan as a writer:

> A Female culprit at your bar appears,
>
> . . . .
>
> For, truant-like, she rambled out of bounds,
> And dar'd to venture on poetic grounds. (41)

Misty G. Anderson points out that such language exposes the belief that "women [writers] have encroached where they are not welcome and must beg a special day pass from the audience" (31). In *The Discovery*'s epilogue, Hannah Pritchard (the actress playing Lady Medway) addresses Sheridan: "Madam—excuse me—I don't like my part— / 'Tis out of nature—never drawn from life, / Who ever heard of such a passive wife?" (102). By questioning her perfection, the epilogue playfully undercuts Lady Medway, the virtuous paragon of the play, and complicates the play's relationship to her character's feminine ideals. In the epilogue to *The Dupe*, the notion of the form itself is undercut:

> Then you conclude, from custom long in vogue,
> That I come here to speak an Epilogue;
>
> . . . .
>
> All this you guess—and now you're out again:
> For to be brief, our author bid me say
> She tried, but couldn't get one to her play.
> (156–57)

Such intricate layers across text, actor, spectator, form, author, and gender achieved through the prologue-epilogue structure clearly open up further avenues of classroom discussion for students of mid-century comedy.

Because of Frances Sheridan's connection to R. B. Sheridan and the intriguing echoes of her comedies in his work, assigning her texts stands as a fruitful way to discuss a forgotten time before the supposed "laughing tradition" returned. In particular, reading Frances Sheridan's *A Journey to Bath* alongside her son's widely known plays, *The Rivals* (1775) and *The School for Scandal* (1777), suggests just how influential her texts were. Frances Sheridan created a Mrs. Surface in *Journey to Bath* who exhibits tendencies of counterfeiting similar to R. B. Sheridan's character of the same name. Even more intriguing, Mrs. Malaprop, perhaps R. B. Sheridan's most famous character, has direct roots in his mother's Mrs. Tryfort from *Journey to Bath*. Her lines—"To be sure he is one of *the* best bred, most polite, good humourd charming men living! . . . Oh in everything . . . he is a progeny!" (174–75)—foreshadow Mrs. Malaprop's hilarious description of Captain Absolute a generation later. Interestingly, *The Dupe*'s bold staging of "The Town's" immoral actions makes visual what *The School for Scandal* only refers to, and *Journey* reveals an interest in notions of public, classed, and theatrical space that R. B. Sheridan would exploit as well. Instead of assuming, along with critical tradition, that son improved on mother, we might instead encourage our students to look back through the lens of the son's texts into his source material, his mother's comedies.

In addition, courses that address connections between the dramas and novels of such authors as Frances Sheridan, Frances Burney, and Elizabeth Inchbald can raise intriguing questions about texts, authors, genre, and concerns of female authors in the eighteenth century. Is there a root difference between the private reading of a sentimental novel and the public viewing of a comedy's sentimental language, particularly in the 1750s and 1760s? In what ways does comedy as dramatic spectacle problematize notions of the domestic, of women, and of women authors by making the private public and shockingly visible? How do tropes in both genres—such as critiques of reading, the abduction trope, and the issue of parental authority—expose social anxieties about artistic production, representation, and women's position in public and private spheres? Examining Sheridan's comedies as case studies of mid-eighteenth-century theatrical negotiation reveals texts that concern women's power and that experiment with form, character, and language. Further, such exploration introduces a writer who saw the stage as the locus for both artistic and financial reward, reminding us that Sheridan was a woman writing for the stage and the page.

Notes

1. In the six-year time frame surrounding Sheridan's theatrical work, *The London Stage* (pt. 4, vol. 2) lists the new main-piece comedies as the following: Arthur Murphy's *The Desert Island* and *The Way to Keep Him* (1759–60); Samuel Foote's *The Minor* (three acts); George Colman's *The Jealous Wife* and Murphy's *All in the Wrong* (1760–61); William Whitehead's *The School for Lovers* (1761–62); Sheridan's *The Discovery* (1762–63) and *The Dupe* (1763–64); Elizabeth Griffith's *The Platonic Wife* (1764–65); and Colman and Garrick's *The Clandestine Marriage* (1765–66).

2. For a full discussion of the comedy's failure, see Samuel Chew's "*The Dupe*: A Study in the 'Low,'" which offers primary source evidence that the vulgarity of the play led to its failure, despite Samuel Whyte and Alicia Le Fanu's later claim that "some Theatrical cabals, fomented by a popular actress," assumed to be Kitty Clive, were the source (Whyte 117). *The London Stage*'s description of the play's reception (pt. 4, 2: 1025–26) supports Chew rather than later critics such as Bevis, who called the play "close to melodrama" (53).

Patricia Demers

Hannah More's Reformation of Romantic Theater

An evangelical Bluestocking and a "spiritually egalitarian" Tory who championed the abolition of the slave trade and the education of the poor, Hannah More (1745–1833), counterrevolutionary par excellence, was a figure of controversy and remains so today (M. Myers 239). One of the most influential and financially successful women writers in Georgian Britain, this poet, dramatist, essayist, tract writer, polemical reformer, and novelist cut her authorial teeth in writing for the stage, or, rather, for stages. While she was establishing a reputation as a poet, More published three different kinds of dramatic literature, performed on school, public, and private stages in either alternate rhyme or blank verse. They are a school play, *The Search after Happiness: A Pastoral Drama for Young Ladies* (1773); three tragedies, *The Inflexible Captive* (1774), *Percy* (1777–78), and *The Fatal Falsehood* (1779); and four plays and one monologue based on Old Testament stories, *Sacred Dramas* (1782). As early as 1774, the *Monthly Review* hailed her as one of the "British Nine" ("*Inflexible Captive*" 243), while the former pupil at the More sisters' Bristol school, the actor, poet, and novelist Mary Robinson, in her *Letter to the Women of England* (1799) conferred "the wreath of fame" for drama on "Miss Hannah More" (84). More certainly enjoyed a level of popularity for her plays. *The Search* went through thirteen editions before being included in her first *Works* in 1801. *Percy*, whose first edition sold out in less than two weeks, was "the most frequently performed tragedy by a woman" (Newey 83). *Sacred Dramas* ran to twenty-four editions; William Cowper maintained that these plays had "more verve and energy both in [their] thoughts and language than half the he rhymers in the kingdom" (227; 16 Feb. 1788).

In addition to her crisp, at times astringent views on social class, mainly articulated later in her career, More's strong evangelical convictions influence and complicate her attitude toward the stage, her first love. Drama's appeal to the emotions, deft speech, and ability to grapple with the responsibilities of existence infiltrate all her subsequent writing in multiple genres. Although critical comments customarily dismiss More's work for the theater as jejune apprenticeship or, worse, "a slum adventure" (Donkin 73), these first stages, "preoccupied with *the act* of emerging from private into public space," deserve careful study for several reasons (Burroughs, *Closet Stages* 79). As a participant in "women's ethical spectatorship of governance," More "engaged with the political life of the nation through media suited to forms of sociability deeply tied to the commercialization of culture" (O'Quinn, *Staging* 117)—in her case, through theater, tracts, and the novel. Drama not only launched her career but served as "a cross-classed site of cultural production, the public forum for the making and disseminating of cultural knowledge" (Purinton, "Gender" 117). In the three plays examined here, More was actually experimenting with innovations. *The Search*, the first pedagogical play specifically addressed to girls, vivified many of the principles More later enunciated in *Strictures on the Modern System of Female Education* (1799). Derived from Pierre-Laurent Buirette de Belloy's *Gabrielle de Vergy* (1770), *Percy*, whose twenty-one performances at Covent Garden constituted "an almost unprecedented achievement for a verse tragedy by an unknown author" (Stott 40), shows More's remarkable attentiveness to the nuanced language of tenderness, "filial piety," and "righteous retribution," while using a heroine's fate to illustrate trenchant criticism of patriarchal politics (More, *Percy* 175, 227). Forced into a loveless union, Elwina condemns her "barbarous father" who "dragg'd [her] trembling, dying, to the altar" (176). Rejecting malicious accusations of infidelity, she faces her accusers with the strength of Jacob and, "like the patriarch, wrestle[s] for a blessing" (184). A pacifist at heart, Elwina also exposes the Crusades' "sanctimonious garb of faith," labeling this "license[d] murder . . . tenfold guilt" (187). More's familiarity with the biblical plays of George Buchanan, Hugo Grotius, John Milton, and Pietro Metastasio in no way inhibited her bold experiments in *Sacred Dramas*, fashioned as "rescue dramas," where magic and "proto-scientific forces" interrogate the ethics of "nationalism and imperialism" (Purinton, "Gender" 119–20).

But perhaps the most intriguing and, in a way, vexing reason for considering More's plays is her ostensible renunciation of drama as a genre. By reading back from the "Preface to the Tragedies" (1801), which More nevertheless permitted to be included in the first and all subsequent editions of the *Collected Works*, I propose to examine what More was prepared to renounce and why. Her excitement about "the most intellectual . . . of all public amusements" (127), in which "the theatrical seed . . . is likely to shoot deep, spread wide, and bring forth fruit in abundance" (139), is palpable, as is her intuitive realization that doctrines are "embodied, made alive, furnished with organs, clothed, decorated, brought into sprightly discourse, into interesting action" (139). Kathryn Ready has examined the preface as More's "strategic" move to stimulate the growth of Romantic-era closet drama, "a medium through which women might compete for the same respect as men without violating gender roles" ("From the Stage" 186, 203). Aware of More's importance as a challenger of assumptions about women's intellectual inferiority and yet intrigued by the human messiness of the writer, who praised consistency so lavishly, I want to explore the combination of logic and ambivalence in More's progress through and across different stages.

Such an inventory reveals her countervailing influences of dramatic aesthetics and ethical ideas. Her retrospective commentary on the theater reads like an internal debate. The woman who placed such a high premium on intellectual pursuits admits that "a well-written tragedy is perhaps one of the noblest efforts of the human mind," underscoring that "of all public amusements, . . . it is almost the only one that has *mind* for its object" ("Preface" 127). Despite the qualifying "perhaps" and "almost," so uncharacteristic of Morean assertiveness and proclamation, this fundamental acknowledgment of mental enticement clears the way for a whole series of admissions about drama's appeal to the senses. Unlike pulpit delivery, "realised doctrines" on the stage are "enforced with all the energy of passion, adorned with all the graces of language, and exhibited with every aid of emphatical delivery, every attraction of appropriate gesture" (139). These are the constitutive elements of the "complicated temptation" of the theater, a label that reflects some conflictedness (139). While the aggregative levels of her admissions testify to the "complicated" nature of this attraction, the fact that More uses the morally charged term "temptation" evidences the powerful allure of the stage for More—even in her renunciatory state. As More sees it, the problem is the opposition between the Christian principles of humility, charity, and peace making and tragedy's preoccupation with anger, honor, and revenge. Gillian Russell understands this binarism as the threat posed to "the power of the word, . . . the biblical logos, . . . by the many voices, bodies, and images of the theatre" ("Theatre" 231). More also distinguishes seeing and reading a play, equating the latter activity with avoiding the "contagious and destructive" force of the uttered sentiments ("Preface" 152). Much as she endorses reading, More controls or restricts it to selected segments—in keeping with the expurgations recommended in *Strictures* and the practice illustrated by the Stanley children in her novel *Cœlebs in Search of a Wife* (1808).

My intent here is not to limit or circumscribe More's views but to offer a basis for understanding what appears to be her seriously considered ambivalence and to trace her logical path from the boarding school stage and the public theater to the private closet. Moreover, her awareness of the stage of discourse and the role of the affective in speech did not disappear but rather colored all her work. Instead of labeling closet drama as the "stable and static characterizations of neoclassical drama" (A. Richardson, *Mental Theater* 5), I suggest "disentangl[ing]" More from that category, seeing her instead as a promoter of "alternative theatre practice" (S. Bennett, "Outing" 173, 174), one in which strong impressions on the mind are designed to inculcate virtue and advocate reformation of conduct. More's envisioned reform of the theater, affecting both playwrights and audience, puts a particular and undeniably Christian emphasis on placing "imagination center-stage" (J. Carlson, *In the Theatre* 14).

More's imagination is always purposive. With all the changes and sharpening of focus in *The Search after Happiness: A Pastoral Drama*, which More composed as an eighteen-year-old junior teacher for the girls at her older sisters' school, she never dilutes the assertion that the pastoral aims to be instructive. In every version of the play, More retains her teenage reworking of *The Seasons* to stress both firmness of purpose and a largely female readership. Her epigraph adjusts the address in James Thomson's "Spring" (lines 1061–68) to the "delightful task" shared by "the Father's Lustre, and the Mother's Bloom" "to fix / The gen'rous purpose in the female breast" (249; Thomson had written, "to plant / The generous purpose in the glowing breast"). Indicating a striking maturity on the part of the young playwright, who may have polished the original manuscript before its first anonymous publication (when she was twenty-eight) as often as she continued to revise published versions, *Search* is a curious amalgam: a play in rhyming couplets devoted to the ideal of sequestered happiness that makes the pastoral setting of "a grove," "a cottage," and "a rural entertainment" the mere spots or pulpits from which the notion of happiness is addressed and interrogated (257, 264, 275); a didactic piece, using converts rather than genuine searchers, it nevertheless succeeds in conveying the process of learning. The all-female cast differentiates this school play from the Latin comedies performed as early as the fifteenth century by schoolboys at Winchester, Eton, and Westminster and from the native English comedies, *Ralph Roister Doister* and *Gammer Gurton's Needle*, entertainments for young gentlemen at Eton and Cambridge. The most popular "prize book for girls, second only to the Bible," *The Search after Happiness* also became "the most widely performed play" in schoolrooms in England "between 1780 and 1830" (Mellor, *Mothers* 47). Consisting of exchanges in which four "young ladies of distinction" (Euphelia, Cleora, Pastorella, and Laurinda) relate the reasons for the search, confess their past attempts and failings, and listen to the sage advice of the "antient shepherdess" Urania, along with interludes of song, *Search* is an oratorio-like play. Its imagery of cultivation and nurturance depicts learning as a deliberate blending of binary oppositions and organic growth, a combination of trial and error with amenability to instruction.

In remarkably colored, self-indicting language, the searchers explain their follies: "Bred in the regal splendours of a court," Euphelia shared her hours "betwixt the park and the play" as she "shunn'd Reflection, yet . . . sought Content" (More, *Search* 266); Cleora "sigh'd for fame, . . . languish'd for renown," and "long'd to burst female bonds" amid "abstruser studies" (267–68); Pastorella loved "pernicious novels" whose "pois'nous influence" made fiction her "guide" and romance her "law" (269); Laurinda's "slothful ease" left her "in size a woman, but in soul a child, . . . unfit to converse, and to books unus'd" (271–72). They seek Urania because "her virtues fire / [Their] ardent hearts to *be* what they admire" (260). This instructor is not retained by the girls' parents but sought after by the girls themselves. And Urania fills the bill. Her name is borrowed from Sidneian pastoral romance, blending the features of both the royal foundling reduced to poor shepherdess of the *Old Arcadia* and the "Heavenly Beauty inspiring Heavenly Love, the Muse of Christian Poetry" of the *New Arcadia* (Duncan-Jones 126). As the prologue had preferred "in a modish age . . . plain virtue to the boast of art," Urania offers "honest counsel, . . . / Though plain, well meant, imperfect, yet sincere" (More, *Search* 255, 277). She reformulates in a distinctive way John Locke's assertion that "'tis Vertue then, direct Vertue, which is the hard and valuable part to be aimed at in Education; and not a forward Pertness, or any little Arts of Shifting" (Locke, *Some Thoughts* 132). With precepts based on her own life ("What time has taught me, and experience shown" [More, *Search* 277]), Urania declares that "life's chief happiness and woe, / From good or evil education flow" (278). Urania's knowledge of real girls is likely based on More's firsthand experience of her sisters' Park Street school, which no doubt provided a rich source for characterization.

Urania's counsel, tailored to each aspirant and also universal, is memorable because of its troubling features. In what sounds like an anti-educational manifesto, she dissuades Cleora from her interest in science, as unsuited to female minds:

> You might be dazzling, but not truly bright;
> Might glare, but not emit a useful light;
> A meteor, not a star, you would appear;
> For Woman shines but in her proper sphere.
> Accomplishments by Heav'n were sure design'd,
> Less to adorn than to amend the mind:
> Each should contribute to this general end,
> And all to virtue, as their centre, tend. (283)

Urania's (and More's) position is ambivalent at best in this play, for in its third edition, in 1774, an epilogue appeared praising Elizabeth Carter, a translator of Epictetus, as "moral CARTER"; the poet Anna Laetitia Aikin as "faultless AIKIN"; one of the first critics of Shakespeare, Elizabeth Montagu, as "accomplish'd MONTAGU"; the female novelist Frances Brooke as "polish'd BROOKES"; and the female historian Catharine Macaulay as "fair MACAULAY" (225). This epilogue was deleted in the 1801 *Collected Works.* Although Urania's views are more tame than those expressed in More's *Essays on Various Subjects, Principally Designed for Young Ladies* (1777), especially in "Thoughts on the Cultivation of the Heart and Temper in the Education of Daughters" (a "juvenile" work More rarely permitted to be reprinted, considering it replaced by *Strictures*), Urania supplants learning with utility and self-reformation. Forceful personal conviction, advocating "not fame, but a life of dedicated benevolence, domestic good works, and conscious self-approbation" (Mellor, *Mothers*

48–49), characterizes her tribute to the figure we would recognize as the angel in the house:

> So Woman, born to dignify retreat,
> Unknown to flourish, and unseen be great,
> To give domestic life its sweetest charm,
> With softness polish, and with virtue warm,
> Fearful of fame, unwilling to be known,
> Should seek but Heav'n's applauses, and her own.
> (*Search* 285)

How can today's readers make sense of such utterances and of the junior playwright? More had finally said no to her dilatory suitor and received his annuity as a way of launching her writing career, yet she plies this discourse of domesticity as her way out of its restrictions and constraints. It is worth noting how the state of withdrawal is depicted in assertive, ambitious terms. It would be unjust to reject this seminal work or to dismiss it as inconsistent or reactionary. When it first appeared, attributed only to "a young lady," More's identity was soon disclosed. "On Seeing Miss H. More in the Title Page of the 2d Edition of *The Search after Happiness*: A Ballad," by William Buller, Bishop of Exeter, sewn into a late eighteenth-century commonplace book, warns "bachelors . . . briskly pursuing the sweet Hannah More" against plans for an easy conquest: "When to this Damsel, a wooing you go, / Pray be not dismay'd if she answer you no." Buller and More "were personally acquainted" (N. Smith, "Unpublished Poems" 598); in November 1773, he attended a performance of *Search* at the More sisters' Park Street school. Buller's ballad also alerts readers and spectators to a protean slipperiness about this witty damsel:

> And since this same prudence deals much in disguise,
> O trust not her words, but examine her eyes,
> Tis there you may learn what you wish to explore,
> And the sentiments learn of the sweet Hannah More.

In May 1774, *Gentleman's Magazine* praised *The Search*'s third edition, in which More first introduced her epilogue, as "a pleasing instructive little poem" ("*The Search*").

Because we are not accustomed to seeing the stage as teaching the theme of self-conquest, as More maintained in the prologue to *The Fatal Falsehood* (236)—her last work for the public stage—we need to make some effort to feel her internal debate over this powerful medium. Her perpetual struggle between "bright intellect" and "stern Puritanism" is one concise formulation illuminating the real promise and the tension of her playwriting (N. Pearson 856). In *Search* Florella's directive "to wean from earth" captures the play's complex thesis about learning and living, growth and nurturance (277). This scheme might also be read as a predictor of More's approach to or avoidance of theater: that is, withdrawing from earthboundedness and setting her sights elsewhere. Though rooted in the earth, learning and growth must ultimately be directed above. Figuring this disengagement as a way of accustoming oneself to doing without a mother's milk suggests that More had a grasp of both worlds of sense and spirit. She understood and genuinely sympathized with the young searchers' so-called follies; she also felt the keen attraction of virtue transcending mundane realities.

In the light of her continual tinkering with the text, More's comments to her sister on the occasion of the play's ninth edition in 1787, admitting shock "at the public taste, which has taken off ten thousand copies of a poem which I have not patience to read," seem a little disingenuous (W. Roberts 2: 52). Possibly, by the time of these remarks, More was already recasting her brief period of celebrity as a playwright for the London stage. She could not have been too embarrassed by her success since she allowed her three plays for the public theater—*The Inflexible Captive*, performed at Bath and Exeter in 1775; *Percy*, with its twenty-one-night run at the Theatre Royal in Covent Garden in 1777–78; and *The Fatal Falsehood*, with a foreshortened run of a few nights in 1779—to be reproduced in all her *Collected Works*. Her ease in "transfus[ing] the spirit of the Italian authors into her own language," having been acknowledged (N. Smith, "Unidentified Translation" 414), More adapted Italian and French sources: Metastasio's opera *Attilio Regolo* (1740) for *The Inflexible Captive* and Belloy's *Gabrielle de Vergy* for *Percy*. The unstinting patronage and mentorship of the retired actor-manager David Garrick, who arranged for the London performances of *Percy* and supplied its prologue and epilogue, were important—and, critics would add, the main—ingredients of her London acclaim. Dubbed "Garrick's Sappho" by the critic John Wolcot (3: 7), masquerading under the pseudonym Peter Pindar, More endured the snide remarks of Hester Thrale, who preferred Frances Burney as a playwright, and some social coolness from their mutual friend and supporter, Samuel Johnson, who "could not quite forgive More, perhaps, for attaching herself so firmly to Garrick" (Stott 42).

Garrick, "a leading proponent of the drama of sensibility" (Barker-Benfield 264), was as impressed by More's flattery as More was enabled by his theatrical network. What is remarkable about her three derivative and highly stylized tragedies is that, although "she was out of her depth in melodrama" (Stott 38) and likely found its "public spectacle of domestic plots" an intimate intrusion (Pascoe, *Romantic Theatricality* 59), she was experimenting, especially through her tragic heroines, with expressions of the boundedness and sorrow of their lives. *The Inflexible Captive*'s Attilia, faithful daughter of the captured Roman warrior; *Percy*'s Elwina, an obedient daughter who marries a man she does not love; and *The Fatal Falsehood*'s Emmelina, a daughter jilted by her fiancé, all make bold, high-sounding claims to courage and self-possession. But they live in worlds hostile to their virtue. Elwina is married to the pathologically jealous Douglas, and as a pale forecast of Gaetano Donizetti's mad, blood-spattered Lucia di Lammermoor, she accepts the poison that Douglas insists she consume as "[her] cup of bliss, [her] passport to the skies" (217). Attilia sinks down "the dread precipice of deep despair" (333), and Emmelina dies admitting "the afflicting angel has been with [her]" (303).

But in distinctive ways these heroines touch a moral pulse. More's adaptation of Metastasio's opera stresses the girlish rashness of Attilia, who nevertheless resigns herself to the hand of providence:

> Teach me to yield to your divine command,
> And meekly bow to your correcting hand;
> Contented to resign, or pleas'd receive,
> What wisdom may withhold, or mercy give.
> (*Inflexible Captive* 345)

Attilia also embodies the power of feeling, prompting a Roman consul to admit, "The softness of thy sorrow is contagious" (362). Arguments have already been advanced about the "liberating effect" of the sentimental novel "asserting the worth of feminine perceptions and values" (Rogers, *Feminism* 143). It is tempting to consider if More was experimenting with or gesturing toward the power of theater—comparable to rethinking on the role of the eighteenth-century epistolary novel—to generate a "new learning of empathy in operation" (L. Hunt, *Inventing* 42).

Percy's greater success—with speedy translations into French and German—is due to the protracted expressions of strong feelings, which, however, do not relieve a pervasive sense of doom. More was clearly impressed by the actors; she slipped into the Theatre Royal one evening just to "see Mrs. Barry in the mad scene in the last act of Percy, in which she is so very fine" (W. Roberts 1: 130). Although the tragedy has been written off by a late-twentieth-century reader as "priggish" (Rogers, *Feminism* 24) and More's retreat from theater dismissed as "no great loss" (Stott 47), I think we should pause to consider the complexity of dramatic tensions this tragedy animates. The opening scene introduces the marriage of Elwina and Douglas as a disastrous coupling:

> Ill are their spirits pair'd;
> His heart's the seat of frenzy, hers of softness;
> His love is transport, hers is trembling duty;
> Rage in his soul is as the whirlwind fierce,
> While hers ne'er felt the power of that rude passion.
> (167)

This is a play of vociferously displayed yet unchanging emotions; roles, attitudes, and dynamic tensions are announced and expanded. Equally ruinous as the forced union between Elwina and Douglas is Percy's and Douglas's inbred hatred of each other. The hero lashes out at his rival:

> Enough of words.—Thou know'st I hate thee, Douglas;
> 'Tis steadfast, fix'd hereditary hate,
> As thine for me; our fathers did bequeath it,
> As part of our unalienable birthright,
> Which nought but death can end. (212)

Though the meek "Resignation" of Elwina, "hopeless, yet uncomplaining" (168), distresses today's reader, accustomed to more vocal assertiveness, Elwina invokes a different ethic, banking on her response to the "cruel tyranny of tenderness" to explain to her lover Percy that she has married someone else to obey her father:

> Hast thou e'er seen a father's flowing tears,
> And known that thou couldst wipe those tears away?
> If thou hast felt, and hast resisted these,
> Then thou mayst curse my weakness; but if not,
> Thou canst not pity, for thou canst not judge. (198)

Accepting the domestic confines of Raby Castle as suited to her "humble, unambitious soul" (177), she begs forgiveness of "filial piety" for admitting that "that belov'd, that cruel father / Has doom'd me to a life of hopeless anguish" (175). Faithful yet maligned, Elwina proclaims, "I endur'd it all; and wearied heaven / To bless that father who destroyed my peace" (186). To compound the drama's sense of desolation it is this father, realizing he has murdered his child, who finally admits that such reversal of fortune is justified:

> A righteous God
> Has made my crime become my chastisement;
> And pull'd those mis'ries on my guilty head
> I would have drawn on others.—O, 'tis just!
> 'Tis righteous retribution!—I submit! (228)

There is a world of difference between More's tragedies—belabored, angst-driven adaptations for the public stage—and her *Sacred Dramas*, designed for private family, closet, or reading-theater enactment. Her source in *Sacred Drama*'s four blank-verse plays and one rhyming-couplet monologue is the Bible, a text she knew intimately and whose doctrines she revered. Such an affinity released a creative outpouring: assured versifying, nuanced and poignant characterization, hard-hitting opposition to the order of the state, an acute understanding of the gap separating public acclaim and private integrity, and a humbling, expressive recognition of fallibility. Although any criticism of More's dramatic work today only touches on her tragedies, her *Sacred Dramas* reveals the emerging power of More as a gifted, impassioned artist.

While in the "Advertisement" More reflects "with awe" on the "holy ground" she stands on (xxv) and defines her aim as being "at once useful and interesting" to a young audience, "in whom it will always be time enough to have the passions awakened" (xxvi), More, in her introduction to *Sacred Dramas*, does not shy away from the central concern of truth, however unfashionable its tenets:

> And shall no altars blaze, O TRUTH, to thee?
> Shall falsehood only please, and fable charm?
> And shall eternal Truth neglected lie,
> Because immortal, slighted or profan'd?
> Truth has our rev'rence only, not our love;
> Our praise, but not our heart: a deity,
> Confess'd, but shunn'd; acknowledg'd, not ador'd;
> Alarm'd we dread her penetrating beams;
> She comes too near us, and too brightly shines. (3)

The clear fervor of her address to "undebauch'd," "unsophisticate" youth (5) is one indication of More's self-assurance. The introduction's twinning of classical and biblical narrative is another indication of her confidence in the power of biblical story "to rouse a holy zeal, / . . . Correct th' irregular, reform the wrong, / Exalt the low, and brighten the obscure!" (6).

More brings a subtlety and deftness of character treatment to well-known stories in her plays *Moses in the Bulrushes*, *David and Goliath*, *Belshazzar*, and *Daniel*. Pharaoh's daughter represents a voice of solidarity for women; critical of her own father, she rescues the infant Moses and understands immediately the dilemma the child's mother must have faced in a time of aggression and ethnic cleansing:

> Who knows but some unhappy Hebrew woman
> Has thus expos'd her infant, to evade
> The stern decree of my too cruel sire.
> Unhappy mothers! Oft my heart has bled
> In secret anguish o'er your slaughter'd sons;
> Powerless to save, yet hating to destroy. (13)

This position results in a telling rebuke to her less compassionate attendant, Melita:

> How ill does it beseem
> Thy tender years and gentle womanhood,
> To steel thy breast to pity's sacred touch!
> So weak, so unprotected is our sex,
> So constantly expos'd, so very helpless,
> That did not Heav'n itself enjoin compassion,
> Yet human policy should make us kind;
> Lest in the rapid turn of Fortune's wheel,
> We live to need the pity we refuse. (19)

With her all-female cast in *Moses in the Bulrushes*, More makes a considerable effort both to individualize and to render some exchanges, such as these abrupt, tension-filled lines between Moses's mother, Jochebed, and his sister Miriam, flashpoints of anxiety and release:

Jochebed. Come and lament with me the brother's loss.
Miriam. Come and adore with me the God of Jacob!
Jochebed. Miriam!—the child is dead!
Miriam. He lives! He lives!
Jochebed. Impossible!—Oh, do not mock my grief;
See'st thou that empty vessel?
Miriam. From that vessel
Th' Egyptian Princess took him.

Jochebed. Pharaoh's daughter?
Then still he will be slain: a bloodier death
Will terminate his woes.
Miriam. His life is safe!
For know she means to rear him as her own. (23)

The predominantly male cast of *David and Goliath*—with the exception of the closing chorus of Hebrew women—also probes the consequences of war and aggression but mainly from the battlefront, the valley of Elah. Although David's opening song praises the shade and humility of his "lowly cot . . . remote from regal state" (37), with an attitude comparable to More's own delight in her retreat at Cowslip Green outside Bristol, most of the drama pits critical (Jesse) and vainglorious (Goliath and David's jealous brothers) views against each other. While the description of Goliath's "fearful stature," "helm of burnish'd brass" on his "tow'ring head," "capacious trunk," and "plaited cuirass . . . of massive iron" (53) recalls chapbook details of giants, Goliath's taunting speech to his opponent as "light boy," "stripling," "dainty-finger'd hero" (70), and "insect warrior" (72) emphasizes how little he understands David's power. In contrast to his brothers' "glozing speech" (50) and Saul's fearful reluctance to let David shine, the young shepherd's clear declaration of loyalty stands out: "Far higher views inspire my youthful heart / Than human praise: I seek to vindicate / Th'insulted honour of the God I serve" (62).

More's sense of oneness with her text in *Sacred Dramas* means that the doctrinal content is naturally high in a script that is both a palimpsest of biblical allusions and a series of comments on the challenges and upheavals of late-eighteenth-century British life. The rhetoric of her day, oscillating between revolutionary discontent and reform impulses, supplied a theater of public discourse that deeply engaged More. Not content to be part of a political audience watching "preferably in silence," she was unwilling "to sit back and partake vicariously in action from which [she] had been excluded" (Friedland 12). Through the warning of the prophet Daniel in *Belshazzar*, she voices concern about "the still-seeming safety of retreat" (117). Whether in ancient Babylon or Georgian Britain, political actors who purport to be working disinterestedly warrant careful scrutiny:

When selfish politicians, hackney'd long
In fraud and artifice, affect a glow
Of patriot fervour, or fond loyalty,
Which scorns all show of interest, that's the moment
To watch their crook'd projects. (143)

As an indication of where More's career was headed, it is significant that *Sacred Dramas*, with its strong connections between "the governance of the nation and the regulation of the passions" (Purinton, "Gender" 116), included the first appearance of her poem "Sensibility." Enshrining sensibility in the home as "thy true legitimate domain" (175), the poem concentrates on the quick, intuitive perception of "sweet SENSIBILITY!" as "unprompted moral! sudden sense of right!" "hasty conscience!" "prompt sense of equity!" "eager to serve," and "always apt to choose the suff'ring side" (173). Among the corrosive influences that destroy feeling, "Sensibility" catalogs a series testifying to the power of language and gesture: "the look oblique," "the sneer equivocal, the harsh reply," "all the cruel language of the eye," and "the guarded phrase" (176). These lessons More could have learned from the theater and from experience.

Although "Sensibility" has been dismissed for its "sentimental" prizing of "thin-skinned reactiveness" and "masochistic definition of woman" (Barker-Benfield 265, 384), I suggest that a closer attention to the poem's place at the conclusion of *Sacred Dramas* could provide another perspective on More's art and introduce some sense of the instability and incompleteness of our knowledge of this writer. It seems to me that in "Sensibility" More is translating in another largely secular medium her expansive and, yes, occasionally opaque views on the cultivation of the civil mind and feeling heart in everyday life. In subsequent hard-hitting essays, she pursues arguments about women's influence and the duties of the upper classes, in particular. Despite, or possibly because of, her apparent contesting of much of our feminist and postfeminist ideology, More, who inveighed against female indolence, passivity, and decorative accomplishments, does not deserve to be written off, mentioned and then hastily shunted aside as too pious or conservative or unsexy. Rather, I suggest that, by attending to the origins of her long career, her fascination and struggle with the corporeality of the stage, her steadfast determination to be a meliorist advocate for women's education, and her uplifting, new, though never fully realized, closet theater, we might extend the justice of critical and compassionate audience engagement to Hannah More.

Betsy Bolton

Hannah Cowley, Gender Identity, and *A Bold Stroke for a Husband*

An odd incident in the history of sentimental drama occurs as Hannah Cowley concludes the main plot of *A Bold Stroke for a Husband* (1783). In the fifth act, the cross-dressed heroine, Victoria, tricks her husband's mistress, Laura, into destroying her claim to Victoria's property—but then, having vanquished her rival, Victoria is startlingly conciliatory:

> *Victoria.*—To you, Madam, I fear, I seem reprehensible; yet when you consider my duties as wife and mother, you will forgive me.—Be not afraid of poverty—a woman has deceiv'd, but she will not desert you!
>
> *Laura.* Is this real? Can I be awake? (71)[1]

"Be not afraid of poverty": Victoria offers financial support to her husband's mistress, a woman who had intended to impoverish Victoria's entire family. This nod toward female bonding is so extreme that Cowley's audience must have wondered, along with Laura, how real the offer could be. Yet Victoria's apology and promise of support also underscore what might otherwise be overlooked as mere plot device: the sentimental heroine, the pure wife and mother, has acted in a way indistinguishable from the male rake. Seducing another woman under false pretences, Victoria has indeed behaved reprehensibly, and no degree of moralizing can erase that central problem. When, in her next breath, Victoria calls on Laura to reform, Laura quite rightly responds, "So, by a smooth speech about virtue, you think to cover the injuries I sustain. Vile, insinuating monster!" (72). Laura's insistence on her injuries, along with the extremity of the epithet "monster," suggests that Cowley and her characters take Victoria's male impersonation, her lesbian seduction of Laura, more seriously than one might expect.[2] This aspect of *Bold Stroke* makes the play a rich resource for graduate seminars on cross-dressing and gender identity in the eighteenth century, while the play's overall structure and stageworthiness suggest its inclusion in courses on eighteenth-century women playwrights.

Why does Cowley allow her villain to rebuke her heroine so strongly at this moment of plot resolution? Why does she allow the specter of this "vile, insinuating monster" to arise at all? Perhaps because the playwright was unwilling to abandon either one of two conflicting ideas structuring the comedy: an idealizing critique of gender relations and a performative critique of gender identity. Victoria's offer of financial support is consistent with Cowley's critique of gender: in Cowley's romance of female autonomy, women insist on alliances with other women, resisting men's attempts to divide and conquer. Yet Cowley's performative critique of gender identity disrupts the assumptions that would allow for this ideal unity of all women. Through cross-dressing, social masquerade, and conversation, Cowley highlights the performative, nonessential qualities of gender identity, dissolving some of the bonds between women. As Florio, Victoria is a better, more seductive man than the husband she seeks to regain, but how can two women become allies when one of them has been seduced and abandoned by the other? Sustaining two incompatible modes of critique as she interweaves her sentimental main plot and comic subplot, Cowley considers, from multiple perspectives, the question of what women want—only to enclose her outrageous answers within layers of conventionally gendered narratives.

Cowley's choices in *A Bold Stroke for a Husband* are somewhat more pointed than eighteenth-century historical trends. Randolph Trumbach, in his analysis of "London Sapphists," argues that, for most of the century, women "did not yet define their gender identities in terms of their relationship to other women. . . . Women were still given conventional female status because of the way they behaved with men" (130). Victoria exemplifies this double standard: as Florio, she seduces Laura but remains exaggeratedly devoted to her husband, Carlos, thus retaining her status as a virtuous wife. Yet Cowley's romance of female alliances pushes against this structure of identification: women's alliances in *Bold Stroke* are not sexual, but Cowley's emphasis on female relationships may still summon up the specter of the monstrous woman-loving woman. Kristina Straub's survey of "the guilty pleasures of theatrical crossdressing" at mid-century suggests that the cross-dressed actress served to criticize men for not living up to contemporary masculine ideals and to intensify the commodification of the actress's body even while evoking a "hateful idea" of feminine sexual desire exceeding the limits of "normal" heterosexual love (128, 134, 137). Cowley's cross-dressed heroine does, indeed, exploit the sexuality of the actress, though without ever acknowledging the fact: the virtuous wife Victoria was played by Mary Robinson, infamous for her affairs offstage. Yet Cowley displaces her criticism of men onto the figure of the femme fatale—the villain Laura—with the result that Victoria's cross-dressing also pointedly returns to the idea of a feminine desire that exceeds heterosexual norms.

Cowley's revision of gender relations and her critique of gender identity both come into sharper focus when one compares *A Bold Stroke for a Husband* with Cowley's source material: Thomas D'Urfey's *The Virtuous Wife* (1680) and Thomas Otway's *The Atheist; or, The Second Part of* The Souldiers Fortune (1684) (Genest 6: 271; Link, Introduction xxx). From D'Urfey, Cowley took the idea of a cross-dressed wife wooing her husband's lover and attempting to regain the riches squandered on that mistress. From Otway, Cowley took the figure of a husband fleeing an overly loving wife, whom he woos unwittingly, failing to recognize her beneath a veil. *Atheist* also includes two women, one cross-dressed, fighting for the affections of a single man. Most important for Cowley's idealized revision of gender relations, however, is *Atheist*'s odd masque episode, in which the widow Porcia has her lover kidnapped and brought to her house, which has been transformed into a palace of romance. Within this "very fair House, adorned with rich Furniture and Lights," Porcia's lover Beaugard is greeted by a dwarf:

> Welcome thou best-lov'd Man of the fair World. . . . My Orders are to lead you to repose in a Rich Bed prepared for Rest and Love. . . . Such are the Orders of the Power I serve. For you are come a long unmeasurable Journey. . . . Drawn by wing'd Horses through the untract Air. (31–32)

In this realm of romance, men are at women's disposal. Beaugard meekly undresses and is led off by two black women; his companion, Daredevil, asks the dwarf where they are and is answered, "A Chrystal Castle built by Enchantment in a Land unknown to any but the fair one that Commands it: The Spirits of the Air keep guard about it, and all obey her Charms" (40). Thus informed, Daredevil likewise submits to his "Enchantment." Yet this castle of female power is far from impregnable: Porcia's brother-in-law attacks the house, wounds Daredevil, and imprisons Porcia and her women in what should be their stronghold.

Cowley's *Bold Stroke* has no equivalent romance episode, but the play could be said to take place within a similar realm of romance. In the world of Cowley's play, women are granted the power of self-determination: Victoria succeeds in winning back her errant husband and the lands he squandered; Olivia successfully avoids unwanted husbands while bringing her chosen mate up to snuff in less than forty-eight hours; even the young Marcella is threatened with a repulsive marriage for only a few moments before being given a reprieve that lasts for the duration of the play. These women achieve control over their lives in part by exploiting the power of female alliances: Victoria is able to follow her husband to town because she can stay with her cousin Olivia; Olivia is aided in her performance as an unmarriageable "vixen" by the supporting performance of her maid Minette and the connivance of her neighbor Marcella (83). Indeed, when Olivia's father asks Marcella to keep the falsity of their engagement a secret from his daughter, Marcella rejects his overtures in favor of an alliance with Olivia:

> Enter into a league with a cross old father against a daughter! why how could he suspect me capable of so much treachery? I cou'd not answer it to my conscience. No, no I'll acquaint Donna Olivia with the plot; and, as in duty bound, we'll turn our arms against Don Caesar. (51)

Ironically, a failure to betray the father is reframed as treachery against the daughter: Marcella has no compunction—no conscience—about betraying Don Caesar's confidence, even though he could make her miserable by insisting on marriage. Women in *Bold Stroke* define their duty as a united front against male authority rather than as obedience to their fathers or husbands—and Cowley's plotting ensures that they do not suffer for it. This united front stands in strong contrast to the female characters of Restoration drama, each of whom seems primarily devoted to her own interests: Otway's Porcia and Sylvia may be cousins, but they lack the intimacy and mutual support that define Cowley's Olivia and Victoria. Cowley's insistence on female unity pushes beyond the familial unit, and even beyond a single social level, to include the servant Minette and reach out to the fallen woman Laura.

Only Laura resists the model of feminine unity promoted by Cowley's play—either because, despite Victoria's rhetoric, a fall from virtue is irrecoverable or because of Victoria's ambiguous position toward her own sex. The latter option is more telling: indeed, Victoria's possible sexual "monstrosity" highlights Cowley's performative critique of gender identity as it shows how differently cross-dressing signifies in Restoration and Georgian theater. D'Urfey's cross-dressing wife neatly exemplifies Straub's claim that "[d]esire between women was either constructed without a penis, in which case it was recuperable, or constructed with a 'penis' (or penis substitute) and brutally suppressed as a fraud" (144). D'Urfey's Olivia successfully woos her husband's mistress in his presence and, when challenged to a duel, successfully disarms her husband. Olivia's performance of masculinity is unabashed, her abuse of her husband's mistress unrepentant. In the unmasking scene, Olivia defines herself to her husband, Beverly, as

> [o]ne that to farther her revenge, has so long worn these fortunate breeches, that she can hardly consent to return to *quondam* Pettticoats again; one that has cur'd your jealousie by giving thee cause to be so, and, lastly, won your Mistriss in spight of your Sword, and Policy. (64)

In short, Olivia is more manly than her husband—and proud to be so. Yet in relation to his mistress, Jenny Wheadle, Olivia is necessarily less manly than her husband. She cannot fulfill her promise to marry Jenny:

> But for you Madam I vow to gad, 'tis an extream affliction to me, that I am utterly incapacitated of serving ye in that manner you, I know, expect, and passionately desire: 'tis alas a cheat Madam, that Nature has impos'd upon our Sex: you must needs think much against my own good liking. (64)

Olivia's contrition seems sarcastic: she highlights Jenny's sexual desires only to mock them; the promise of marriage was always a fraud, but here the fraud is licensed. In this Restoration comedy, female cross-dressing covers an absence: the punchline is the lack of a penis, and once the woman's sexual identity is revealed, the joke and the story end together. Though Olivia protests her wish to satisfy Jenny sexually, Jenny knows she is merely the butt of a joke and laments her own stupidity in falling for it (64).

Otway's cross-dressing Lucrece, by contrast, satirizes the paradoxes of male economic privilege; she spends more time describing her masquerade than performing it:

> If I go into the War, I shall have the privilege, when I return home, to talk of Marches, Battels and Sieges, which I never was at, nor understand any more than the Fools I tell my story to. If I stay at home, with the privilege of good Cloathes, Pertness and much Simplicity, will I set up for a Spark, grow familiar *at White-Hall,* and impudent with some great Man there or another; run in Debt with a high Hand, be terrible in eating Houses, and noisy all over the Town. (55)

Lucrece defines the performance of masculinity as a privileged (that is, unearned) relation to credit in the diverse forms of reputation and debt. Lucrece's demonstration of male speech underscores the connection:

> When I and another Spark meet; Dam me, *Iack*, says I. What times are there stirring? What ready to be had? What Caravans have you met with or what Loose lately managed? You Rogue, you look very high upon the Huckle. (55)

Money and sex—"ready" cash and "loose" women—are a man's major interests in this speech. When the maid demands, "[W]hat will all this Gibberish signifie?" Lucrece's translation underscores the economic bottom line:

> Signifie, you Fool! Why what it signifies already; Wit, Courage, Martial Discipline, Interest at Court, Pretence to Preferment, Free Quarter in my Lodgings, and Free Booty in every Cuckold's Shop, who shall trust me against his palpable knowledge, that I'm not worth a Groat; and never have the Impudence to hope to be Paid. (55)

The gratuitous insult of cuckold in the final item brings up the possibility of sexual transgression, but the conclusion shows this to be a red herring: the shopkeeper is cuckolded as the spark steals his goods rather than his wife's virtue. For Otway, Restoration masculinity is inseparable from aristocratic economic exploitation, and his cross-dressing woman is a man's man: a male playwright's satire of empty masculine privilege through a performance that conflates sex and money.

Cowley's use of the cross-dressing wife comes closer to Otway than to D'Urfey. Victoria, like Lucrece, spends as much time describing her performance of masculinity as she does enacting it, and her performance is largely excused by her husband's abuse of his economic privilege: his gift to Laura of Victoria's dowry. Whereas D'Urfey's Olivia takes pride in her masculine performance, Cowley's Victoria apologizes endlessly for her masquerade: "For myself, I wou'd not swerve from the nicest line of rectitude, nor wear the shadow of deceit—But for my children!—Is there a parental heart that will not pardon me?" (56). It is hard to imagine a Cowley heroine who would engage in a duel or resist a return to propriety—or be tempted to use her sword on her husband even after having disarmed him. Victoria as Florio does not duel or swagger; she merely dresses as a man and occasionally holds Laura's hand. Yet Cowley's cross-dressing woman represents far more than a joke about sexual absence: Victoria's performance may well be more muted than Olivia's and Lucrece's because it signfies more than its Restoration antecedents.

Indeed, if Otway's cross-dressing woman is a man's man, Cowley's cross-dressing woman is a woman's man or perhaps a woman's woman: she defines and discovers what women want, as shown in this exchange with her cousin Olivia:

Olivia. So suddenly to rob your husband of his charmer's heart! You must have us'd some witchery.

Victoria. Yes, powerful witchery—the knowledge of my sex. Oh! did the men but know us, as well as we do ourselves;—but thank fate they do not, 'twould be dangerous. . . . 'Tis in vain to attempt a description of what changed its nature with every moment. I was now attentive—now gay—then tender—then careless. I strove rather to convince her that *I was charming*, than that I myself was charm'd; and when I saw love's arrow quivering in her heart, instead of falling at her feet, sung a triumphant air, and remember'd a sudden engagement.

Olivia. [*Archly.*] Would you have done so, had you been a man?

Victoria. Assuredly—knowing what I now do as a woman. (20–21)

Victoria's performance as a man is strikingly feminine, not only in its individual elements, but also in its overall mutability. At the end of the eighteenth century, after all, femininity was equated with changeability. Cowley's *Belle's Stratagem* emphasized the plasticity of female character: stepping forth in propria persona to unite the characters of foreign charmer and English country bumpkin, Letitia Hardy insists to her lover Doricourt, "You see I *can* be any thing. . . . Shall I be an *English* Wife?—or, breaking from the bonds of Nature and Education, step forth to the world in all the captivating glare of Foreign Manners?" (81). William Hayley's mock-epic *The Triumphs of Temper* (1781) also tellingly underscored the shifting character of its heroine: "She's everything by starts and nothing long" (canto 1). Attentive, tender, gay, careless: Florio, like the heroines of the time, is everything by starts and nothing long.

But Victoria's performance in *Bold Stroke* exceeds a simple replacement of masculinity by femininity. The cross-dressed wife does not begin her deception knowing what women want: Olivia's closing question and Victoria's answer underscore a transformation in Victoria. What Victoria knows after her performance seems to encompass insights available neither to men nor to women who have not experienced the role of cross-dressed seducer. This passage asserts that it takes a woman to seduce a woman: femininity (attentiveness, gaiety, tenderness, carelessness—above all, mutability) in masculine garb is what women want. Or, at least, it is what a seductress like Laura wants. Even in this more limited formulation, such a suggestion is monstrous and too extraordinary to leave unchallenged.

Cowley's unmasking scene works to distract the audience from Victoria's performance and Laura's charge of monstrosity as soon as it is made. The villain promptly shifts from her injuries to her own malevolence: "Revenge is sweeter to my heart than love; and if there is a law in Spain to gratify that passion, your virtue shall have another field for exercise" (72). Gasper, the aged councillor, cancels that threat even as Laura exits ("No, no; you'll find no help in the law, charmer"). The mention of revenge serves primarily to blacken Laura's character and thus undercut her accusation against Victoria. Next, Carlos's sudden transformation back to loving husband distracts from the legal issue:

> Come, my Victoria—Oh, there is a painful pleasure in my bosom—To gaze on thee, to listen to, and love thee, seems like the bliss of angels cheering whispers to repentant sinners! (72)

This speech is clichéd and incoherent but well within the register of Beverly in D'Urfey's *Virtuous Wife*:

> Come to my bosom, thou art mine again—all—all my own, and shalt be so for ever—for from this moment, all base drossy thoughts, that soil'd the life and lustre of my Judgement, shall vanish. (64)

In both plays, hyperbolic male speech compensates for infidelity: words are asked to erase deeds and bring the cross-dressing woman back into the marital fold.

Ironically, the difference between the two plays lies in the sentimental drama's greater cynicism in its handling of this conversion. In D'Urfey's intrigue play, Olivia merely caps her husband's proclamation:

> This now is like a Husbands love; free as it should be;
> Which mine shall equal, and now I'll boldly say,
> Whensoe'er yours was, this is my Wedding day. (64)

The play then moves on to resolve its other romantic relationships. In Cowley's sentimental drama, by contrast, the scene of reconciliation ends by calling attention back to the original problem such hyperbolic nonsense works to dispel. Don Gasper's concluding remarks point out how unsatisfying this sentimental resolution is at heart:

> Lord help 'em! how easily the women are taken in! —Here's a wild rogue has plagu'd her heart these two years, and a whip syllabub about angels and whispers clears scores. (73)

As with Laura's rejection of Victoria's preaching, Gasper's summary of the scene is unexpectedly pointed. He goes so far as to begin a suggestion that women should be a little more stern with their men ("—'Tis pity but they were a little—") but brings himself up short with a claim that recapitulates the scandal inherent in cross-dressing: "tho', now I think on't, the number of these *gentle* fair ones is so very small, that if it was lessen'd, the two sexes might be confounded together, and the whole world be suppos'd of the masculine gender" (73). If Victoria were not a gentle dupe, then she'd be a man—or perhaps a monster—and there would be no way to distinguish women from men.

Monstrosity seems more likely than masculinity in this speculation, since Gasper's suggestion that a confounding of the two sexes would leave only "the masculine gender" runs counter to Cowley's handling of gender issues throughout the play. In their first appearance together, Laura informs her lover Carlos that "the vainest female, in the hour of her exultation and power, is still out-done by man in vanity.—'Tis more your ruling passion, than 'tis ours; and 'tis wounded *vanity* that makes you thus tremble with rage at being deserted" (18). "*Stamping*" and inarticulate, Carlos implicitly supports Laura's reading of his character. In addition, while Laura is not technically a cross-dressing figure, her description of romantic infidelity highlights the extent to which she acts a man's part in relation to Carlos:

> This rage would have been all cool insolence, had I waited for your change—the crime which now appears so black in me. Then, whilst, with all my sex's weakness, I had knelt at your feet, and reproached you only with my tears; how *composed* would have been your feelings.—Scarcely would you have deigned to form a phrase of pity for me; perhaps have bid me forget a man no longer worthy my attachment, and recommended me to hartshorn and my women. (18)

Laura offers Carlos only that "cool insolence" she knows to expect from a male lover who has moved on; her feelings are indeed composed, and the closest she comes to pity is her analysis of his wounded vanity. Part of what enrages Carlos, then, is the fact that Laura, by preempting the male role of unfaithful lover, leaves him only the feminine role of wounded vanity to perform. Straub suggests that the cross-dressed actress "is a divining rod for detecting the failure of men to live up to the demands of dominant masculinity" (137); Cowley intensifies this kind of critique by extending it to her unusually masculine femme fatale.

Here and elsewhere in *Bold Stroke*, masculinity as a distinctive quality becomes remarkably elusive, pointing back toward a confounding of the two sexes that replaces masculinity with the hybridity of cross-dressing or sexual counterperformance. Gasper, moments before his assertion that ungentle women would become men, identifies himself as a cross-dressing male, something at once more and less than masculine. Explaining to Carlos how she tricked Laura into destroying the deed to the family property, Victoria, dressed as Florio, notes Gasper's resemblance to her uncle Caesar, the basis for the liveried councillor's performance as that wealthy don. To this account Gasper adds a bit of bragging: "Yes, Sir, I was always apt at resemblances—In our plays at home, I am always Queen Cleopatra—You know she was but a gypsey Queen, and I hits her off to a nicety" (74). The danger in *Bold Stroke* lies in a confounding of sexes that might make the whole world not masculine but feminine—and this transformation threatens to remake femininity. What characters know as cross-dressing women (or feminized men) differs from what they might have known, as men or as women, in their previous, more conventional forms.

An oddity of *A Bold Stroke for a Husband*, then, is that the sentimental plot carries this radical critique of gender identity while the comic plot relies on a conservative model of fixed gender roles. The sentimental plot, normally a vehicle for conservative gender politics, ends with a double negation of gender: ungentle women may be indistinguishable from men, but men, vain and disempowered, are indistinguishable from women. More strikingly still, the marriage trouble in the sentimental plot of *A Bold Stroke for a Husband* has been resolved by a cross-dressed woman seducing her female rival with the aid of a man who would be queen. The heterosexual marriage is preserved only by figures who exceed or invert its sexual assumptions and constraints. For Cowley, even more than for her characters, this is a bold stroke indeed.

By contrast, the comic subplot of *Bold Stroke*, while it advances through an extended series of masquerades and performances, finally resolves by asserting an essential, conservatively gendered identity underlying the multiplicity of performance. Like D'Urfey's Olivia, Cowley's comic heroine Olivia talks a good game, but her many masquerades and performances dissolve in the closing scene. Throughout *Bold Stroke*, Olivia is something of a gypsy queen, dressed in fragments of other heroines. Claiming Xanthippe, the shrewish wife of Socrates, as an ancestor, Olivia professes herself unimpressed with the performance of Shakespeare's shrew:

> Catherine! Why she had not the spirit of a roasted chesnut—a few big words, an empty oath, and a scanty dinner, made her as submissive as a spaniel. My fire will not be so soon extinguished—it shall resist big words, oaths, and starving. (12–13)

Sure enough, when her father locks her up in her apartment, Olivia sees a possibility to escape (the garden door left open) but decides instead to outlast him, resisting his big words, oaths, and attempts to starve her: "I'll stay here two days, without once asking for my liberty, and you'll come the third, with tears in your eyes, to take me out" (77). Julio's presence in her apartment brings the comedy to an immediate resolution, however, so Olivia's resolution is never seriously tested. And Olivia's heroic antecedents include not only shrews but also a mythological figure of constant devotion: Penelope, with her "never-ending web" (33). As Penelope's weaving saves her from her suitors until her husband's return, so Olivia's false personae fend off her suitors until her chosen husband can be brought to propose.

But as Penelope reveals the trick of her (un)weaving once Odysseus returns, so Olivia's performances are unraveled by Julio to reveal her identity. As Minette and Caesar blacken Olivia's character to Julio, he protests:

> *Julio.* Oh, do not prophane her.—Where is that spirit which you tell me of? Is it that which speaks in modest, conscious blushes on her cheeks? Is it that which bends her lovely eyes to earth?
>
> *Caesar.* Ay, she's only bending 'em to earth, considering how to afflict me with some new obstinacy—she'll break out like a tygress in a moment.
>
> *Julio.* It cannot be—*are* you, charming woman! such a creature?
>
> *Olivia.* Yes, to all mankind—but one. [*Looking down.*] (82)

Olivia's traditional performance of sensibility—"modest, conscious blushes" and a modest downward gaze—is here taken to represent her true personality, even though her father sees it as merely a temporary intermission in the ongoing performance of the shrew. Julio, at once Olivia's chosen man and the man who can see through her vixen performance, becomes the perfect husband, Odysseus to her Penelope.

Yet this happy resolution necessarily ignores the duplicity of all performance, a problem first ironically established during Garcia's courtship of Olivia. Pretending not to have known Garcia's identity, Olivia shrewdly recants her performance as a shrew, speaking a truth she knows will not be believed:

> *Olivia.* Oh, Sir! All that is past was in sport; a contrivance between my maid and me: I have no spirit at all—I am as patient as poverty.
>
> *Garcia.* This mask fits too ill on your features, fair lady: I have seen you without disguise. (13)

At its most serious, Cowley's *Bold Stroke* wonders whether an existence "without disguise" is possible: the villain Laura proudly proclaims herself "above disguise" and avows her undisguised love for Florio—yet this admission only highlights the seductiveness of Florio's disguise (18). Furthermore, in the comedy's concluding scene, the ubiquity of disguise is utterly disavowed. Olivia's suitors now claim to recognize the constant character underlying her previous performance: " 'tis pretty clear now, *why* she was a vixen" (83). Bodies speak for hearts: Julio sees the real Olivia through her modest conscious blushes just as Olivia reads her cousin's fortunes on her face: "My friend, you are happy—'tis in your eyes, I need not ask the event" (84). Cowley is canny enough to present her heroines virtuously "above disguise" as she reaches her closing appeal to the audience. As Olivia remarks to Victoria, without the "approbation" of the audience "our labours have been vain; / Pointless my jests, and doubly keen your pain" (84). For Cowley's double-edged critique of gender to stand, it must pass muster with an audience unsympathetic to this kind of social vision.

Indeed, *A Bold Stroke for a Husband* is at once a more radical and less popular play than either Susanna Centlivre's *A Bold Stroke for a Wife* (from which Cowley adapted her title) or Cowley's *The Belle's Stratagem. The Belle's Stratagem* was performed 118 times in the 1780s and 1790s; *A Bold Stroke for a Husband* received a far more modest 27 performances between 1783 and 1800 (Hogan clxxi, 593–612). Setting the younger generation against the older, Centlivre's play produces laughter through a focus on whimsical extravagance, improbable plotting, and contemporary allusion instead of engaging any battle of the sexes or any possible transformation of sex and gender. Similarly, while Cowley's *Belle's Stratagem* and

Bold Stroke both use masks and performance to win or retrieve a beloved's affections, *Belle's Stratagem* contains its potentially transgressive energies strictly within conventional boundaries. Cowley's belle, Letitia Hardy, may flirt with (French) impropriety in her masquerade persona, but the monstrosity of cross-dressing remains unthought and effectively unthinkable. In Cowley's *Bold Stroke*, however, Victoria and Laura rebel against social convention implicitly but more thoroughly than Letitia Hardy needs or can imagine. In their willingness and ability to take on masculine personae and positions, Victoria and Laura are complicated women, perhaps too complicated for the comedy (or sentiment) of their time. Yet for teachers and students today, Cowley's *Bold Stroke* may sketch more suggestively how far the complexities of gender identity exceed the acceptable norms of comic structure, both then and now.

Notes

1. All quotations from *A Bold Stroke for a Husband* and *The Belle's Stratagem* are from Link's edition of Cowley's plays.

2. For histories of female cross-dressing and its relation to modern lesbian identity, see Straub; Trumbach, "London's Sapphists"; Dekker and Pol; Vicinus.

Nora Nachumi

To Write with Authority: Elizabeth Inchbald's Prefaces to *The British Theatre*

In his satirical poem *The Children of Thespis* (1786), Anthony Pasquin (a pseudonym for John Williams) takes aim at the players of the theaters royal at Covent Garden and Drury Lane. Of Elizabeth Inchbald he writes:

> To mangle poor Decency's breathless remains;
> To rob gentle Reason of all her domains;
> To give the last blow to expiring Propriety;
> To feed a base town with still baser variety—
> See delicate Inchbald assume the foul quill;
> And satirize Wisdom, by pleasing her will!
>
> (148)

Although Inchbald had not yet retired from the stage, Pasquin wastes no time on her skills as a performer; he reserves his ire for what he considers to be a far greater affront: her success as a dramatist. By 1788, when the fourth and last part of the poem was published, Inchbald had already seen several of her plays produced to acclaim at London's patent theaters. For Pasquin—who also takes issue with Hannah Cowley, Mary Robinson, Anna Seward, Charlotte Smith, and Ann Yearsley—Inchbald's temerity cannot be ignored. For him the pen is a masculine appendage. By assuming the "foul quill," Inchbald, he suggests, is performing something akin to transvestitism; a freak of nature, she is inadequate as a playwright and as a woman:

> Thus her mind like clear amber, condens'd by stagnation,
> Exhibits the dirt it imbib'd in formation:
> Like ungender'd abortions her plays have annoy'd;
> Which are born, see the light, and, when seen, are destroyed.
> (149)

Pasquin's language is brutal. By equating Inchbald's plays with "ungender'd abortions," he renders Inchbald an unnatural woman, someone who would rather give birth to bad plays than live babies.

Pasquin was not the only male writer threatened by Inchbald's incursion onto masculine territory. Twenty years later the playwright George Colman the Younger objected to several of Inchbald's prefatory remarks about his plays and his father's, published in a collection entitled *The British Theatre* (1808). "Madam," he begins,

> when I lately sold the copy right to *The Heir at Law* [1797] . . . I required permission to publish any prefatory matter, which might appear eligible to me. . . . I had reason to suppose that they would be put forth in a series of dramas, with *Critical Remarks by Mrs. Inchbald.* On this account I more particularly urged my *postulatum.*—I make no apology for writing Latin to you, madam; for, as a scholiast, you, doubtless, understand it, like the learned Madame Dacier, your predecessor.

Colman's use of irony is meant to be obvious. Unlike Anne Le Fevre Dacier—a French scholar and translator of classical texts by Homer and Terence—Inchbald, he implies, lacks the formal education, and presumably the intellect, requisite in a critic. As Colman well knew, his letter to Inchbald would be published in the collection alongside Inchbald's comments to his play. Thus he begins his defense by publicly challenging her authority as a critic.

Having thrown down his gauntlet, Colman proceeds to say:

> [A] little relative to those dramas of mine which have, already, had the honour to be somewhat singed, in passing the fiery ordeal of feminine fingers:—fingers which it grieves me to see destined to a rough task, from which your manly contemporaries in the drama would naturally shrink. Achilles, when he went into petticoats, must have made an awkward figure among the females;—but the delicate Deidamia never wielded a battle-axe to slay and maim the gentlemen.

Like Pasquin, Colman creates a reciprocal relation between Inchbald's literary deficiencies and her sex: she is inadequate as a critic because she is a woman and inadequate as a woman because she is a critic. Inchbald does not accept this equation. In fact, she uses her prefatory remarks in *The British Theatre* to defend women's participation in the theater as performers, playwrights, and—by example—critics. This defense is implicitly linked to other kinds of work accomplished by the prefaces. Throughout the collection, Inchbald's commentaries on performers and playwrights, her discussions of closet drama and the collaboration of live performance, and her opinions on political issues inform one another. They dramatize the extent of Inchbald's personal theatrical experience and so help validate her authority as a theater critic. For all these reasons, Inchbald's prefaces to the plays in *The British Theatre* are immensely important for both teaching and researching this period.

Inchbald's prefaces are not the first instance of theater criticism by a woman writer. Periodicals designed for women, like Eliza Haywood's *Female Spectator* (1744–46), included commentary on the theater, as did Frances Brooke's periodical, the *Old Maid* (1755–56). On occasion, periodicals for general audiences included theater criticism written by women. Like much theater criticism, most of these pieces are unsigned. Some, however—like Mary Robinson's remarks on the theater in her series of essays "The Present State of the Manners, Society, &c. &c. of the Metropolis of England" for the *Monthly Magazine* in 1800—include the name of the author. A few women wrote longer treatments of Shakespeare, including Margaret Cavendish, the Duchess of Newcastle, who published the "first sustained evaluation of Shakespeare as a playwright" in her *Sociable Letters* (1664) (Romack and Fitzmaurice, Introduction 2). Others include Charlotte Lennox, *Shakespear Illustrated* (1753–54); Elizabeth Montagu, *Essay upon the Writings and Genius of Shakespear* (1769); and Elizabeth Griffith, *The Morality of Shakespeare's Drama Illustrated* (1775). Not surprisingly, many of the women who wrote about the theater—including Cavendish, Griffith, and Lennox—were also playwrights. Like their male counterparts, female dramatists often incorporate expository remarks about the theater into the prefaces to the published editions of their plays. Frequently, they protest a double standard that allows more freedoms to male writers than to women. On occasion, they also inform their readers about the behavior of various performers and theater managers—especially when that behavior has affected the success of a production. If the play under discussion is an adaptation, the playwright may discuss what alterations she made and why she did so. At times, these prefaces criticize other plays or comment about the state of the British theater in general.

Nevertheless, Inchbald was still taking a risk when she accepted the invitation of Thomas Longman and his associates to write prefaces to the 125 plays that would make up the collection *The British Theatre.* As a theater critic, she would be entering a profession dominated by men. She would be passing judgment on the work of her fellow playwrights, most of them male, during a time when women's capacity to reason was still subject to debate. Moreover, as Colman surmises, Inchbald's education was typical of girls from the middle classes; while her two brothers were sent off to school, Inchbald and several of her sisters learned to read and write at home. This domestic education rendered her vulnerable to censure because it deprived her opinions of the authority formal schooling bestowed on male critics. Inchbald's earliest biographer, James Boaden, clearly was uncomfortable with Inchbald's status as a critic; in *Memoirs of Mrs. Inchbald* (1833), he declares that "there is something unfeminine . . . in a lady's placing herself in the seat of judgment." Although he admits that genius may be a characteristic of either sex, he notes that criticism is "more nearly allied to LEARNING than to GENIUS; and . . . as learning but seldom appears in female garb, it is commonly thought that criticism requires something beyond genius to arm itself fully for its awful task" (2: 84). Inchbald's feminine education, Boaden suggests, has rendered her unfit for such a masculine occupation.

Yet Inchbald was uniquely qualified to write the prefaces. Throughout her life, she set herself a rigorous schedule of reading to compensate for her lack of a formal education. Because she kept lists of her reading and annotated her copies, we know that she was a highly literate woman, well read in literature, biography, history, plays, and the classics. She also had years of experience as a professional actress. By 1789, when she retired from the repertory company of the Theatre Royal at Covent Garden, Inchbald had been a professional performer for seventeen years. In addition, she had already begun to make a name for herself as a dramatist. Between 1784 and 1805, Inchbald wrote eleven original plays and ten adaptations. Except for *The Massacre* (1792) and *A Case of Conscience* (1800), which were not published until 1833, all were produced during her lifetime. Sixteen were published; most were successful: "[f]ourteen . . . ran ten or more nights in their first season, and six ran twenty or more" (Backscheider, Introduction xi). By the late 1790s, Inchbald's career as a playwright was so well established that her "mainpieces generally brought her in the neighborhood of £500 to £600 through her three benefit nights," while "afterpieces usually earned her at least £100" (Donkin 123). Inchbald was also the author of two well-received novels, *A Simple Story* (1791) and *Nature and Art* (1796). Both were commercially successful, and her publisher was "prepared to pay £600 for their extended copyright before they were sold again in 1810 to Longman. In total, Inchbald earned over £1000 for the two novels" (C. Turner 115).

Thus, when Longman and his associates approached Inchbald to write the prefaces to the plays in *The British Theatre*, they were courting a well-known writer with extensive experience as a performer. Her name, as they knew, "would spark recognition from both the reading and the play-going public" (Waters 58). Inchbald herself seems to have found the task onerous; in 1806, shortly after beginning the project, she tried to get released from her contract, but Longman refused; he knew that her participation would help ensure the success of the collection. Consisting of 125 plays—none of which Inchbald selected—*The British Theatre* was initially published one play at a time beginning in 1806; in 1808, the entire collection was published as a set of twenty-five volumes. A short preface by Inchbald preceded each play, making the project the first "large collection of British drama in which literary criticism by a woman played a significant part"; in addition, because the plays initially were published in serial form, Inchbald's prefaces are the first instance of "ongoing, signed literary criticism by a woman writer" (Waters 59). Although Boaden insists that the prefaces "added but little to [Inchbald's] fortune and nothing whatsoever to her fame" (2: 87), the collection proved to be popular and financially successful. More to the point, it helped establish Inchbald's authority as a critic. By 1808 Inchbald had already contributed essays to the *Edinburgh Review* and to Prince Hoare's journal, the *Artist*. Subsequent to the publication of *The British Theatre*, she declined an invitation to become a regular contributor to the *Quarterly Review* and in 1809 rejected an offer to edit John Murray's journal, *La Belle Assemblée*. Inchbald did, however, agree to lend her name to two other collections: *The Modern Theatre* (1809) and *A Collection of Farces and Afterpieces* (1809). In both cases, she helped select pieces but did not contribute critical prefaces or any other observations. By this point, Inchbald and her publishers knew that the phrase "selected by Mrs. Inchbald" affixed to the title pages was enough to aid sales.

Despite their popularity, Inchbald's prefaces only recently have begun to receive the critical attention accorded her other literary productions. Scholars like Catherine Burroughs, Marvin Carlson, and Mary Waters have noted Inchbald's ability to comment on plays as both read and performed experiences. As Burroughs explains, the prefaces work to create a greater appreciation for apprehending both modes of drama (*Closet Stages* 84). Inchbald's attention to the contributions of actors, Waters contends, "stretches [her] drama theory beyond the closet/stage dichotomy into the issue of collaborative composition" (77). Scholars have also read the prefaces as political pieces. Cecilia Macheski finds them less political than Inchbald's novels while Anne K. Mellor and Waters regard them as extremely political. According to Mellor, Inchbald is one of several women writers who use their work to engage in discussions about social, moral, and national issues conducted in the public sphere (*Mothers*). Building on Mellor's contention, Waters reads Inchbald as one of several female literary critics who contributed to "establishing and revising the newly emerging literary canon, and to creating the literary values that made it possible to celebrate a native British literary heritage at one of the most divisive moments in British history" (16).

Finally, like the novels and plays, the prefaces have been scoured for evidence of protofeminist sympathies. As Katharine Rogers reads them, they depict Inchbald "as an individual and as a woman who achieved great success in a man's world and yet was intent on maintaining her femininity as her contemporaries defined it" ("Britain's First Woman Drama Critic" 278). Along similar lines, Burroughs examines the apparent conflict between Inchbald's portrayal of herself as a critic and her "preference for dramatic heroines of self-effacing rectitude" (*Closet Stages* 82). For Burroughs, however, Inchbald is a canny, self-aware performer who asserts "the value of women's criticism even while appearing to sacrifice her own achievements to make the point" (84). Anna Lott goes even further. Throughout the collection, she explains, Inchbald "celebrate[s] women who exist outside of familial constraint, refusing, despite strong pressure, to confess to misdeeds" ("Sexual Politics" 638). As a result, Lott concludes, the prefaces "present overtly sharp judgments about Inchbald's society and woman's essentially limited role in it" (638). Each of these topics is interesting in itself, but the three are also related. Throughout the prefaces, Inchbald's discussion of performers, playwrights, playwriting, and the plays themselves helps her render women's participation in the theater both respectable and important. Because these discussions help establish her authority as a critic, they also enable Inchbald to make observations about players, playwrights, and plays that are implicitly—and occasionally explicitly—political.

Throughout the collection, Inchbald repeatedly demonstrates that the emotional impact of the drama makes it a powerful means of moral instruction. Writing of *Macbeth*, she declares:

> [T]he scenery, costumes, music, and above all, the fear, the terror, the remorse—the agonized throbs and throes, which speak in *looks, whispers, sudden starts, and writhings* by Kemble and Mrs. Siddons . . . render this play one of the most impressive moral lessons the stage exhibits. (4: n. pag.)

She is equally vehement in her defense of *The Stranger* (1798), Benjamin Thompson's translation of August von Kotzebue's play *Menschenhass und Reue* (1789). We learn that Kotzebue has been criticized because the character of the adulteress, Mrs. Haller, is depicted with pity and she is ultimately restored to "her former rank in life, under the roof of her injured husband." According to Inchbald, some commentators alleged that this outcome "hold[s] out temptation . . . for women to be false to their husbands," but she disagrees. The play, she explains, eliminates this danger by depicting the "calamitous woes . . . as the consequence of illicit love." Not only the language but also the "plot and the incidents" of the play describe "with effect, those multiplied miseries which the dishonor of a wife spreads around." Her highest praise is reserved for the actors:

> Kemble's emaciated frame, sunken eye, drooping head, and death-like paleness; his heart-piercing lamentation that—"he trusted a friend who repaid his hospitality, by alluring from him all that his soul held dear,"—are potent warnings to the modern husband.
>
> Mrs. Siddons, in Mrs. Haller (the just martyr to her own crimes) speaks in her turn to every married woman; and, in pathetic bursts of grief—in looks of overwhelming shame—in words of deep reproach against herself and her seducer—"conjures each wife to revere the marriage bond." (24: n. pag.)

If the play's moral force resides in its ability to move the audience's emotions, then, Inchbald suggests, this effect is accomplished primarily through the spectators' response to the play in performance. Indeed, for Inchbald, the fact that plays like *The Stranger* are able to generate an immediate emotional response in theatergoers makes them powerful conduits for moral instruction.

Although Inchbald's defense of *The Stranger* may simply be read as a meditation of the moral effect of plays in performance, it is also an implicitly political statement. Kotzebue's plays enjoyed immense popularity in England, from about 1798 through 1810, a period characterized by discord over social and political issues raised by the French Revolution and its aftermath. Inchbald's contemporaries were divided about whether Kotzebue harbored Jacobin sympathies. They agreed, however, that his plays were characterized by a Rousseauesque strain of sensibility. According to Syndy McMillen Conger, Kotzebue "intensifies the ethic of sensibility to a pseudo-religion, absolutizes sentiment at the expense of older virtues, nature at the expense of culture, freedom at the expense of duty, passionate lover over prudent" (100). For conservative writers, Kotzebue's plays were, therefore, dangerous. They not only encouraged rebellion against established forms of authority but did so by making vice seem palatable. As Colin Pedley explains, writers who considered Kotzebue a threat repeatedly warned of the following scenario: "[T]he audience is seduced into acceptance by the grace of a performer; a position wins its place with us insidiously, bypassing moral filters in moments of emotional collusion" (307). Clearly, Inchbald is not of this opinion. Her remarks on the adaptations of Kotzebue's plays in *The British Theatre* indicate that she approved of the values espoused by his plays. Indeed, we see her approval of Kotzebue in her very successful adaptation of his play *Das Kind der Liebe* (1790), which she entitled *Lovers' Vows* (1798).

But Inchbald's negative remarks on Benjamin Moore's play *The Gamester* (1753) show that she recognized the danger of live performance. In the play's preface she warns readers against the emotional effect the play may elicit. Those who see it, she explains, are "deluded into pity by the inimitable acting of a Mrs. Siddons or a Mr. Kemble." Thus the audience "weeps with her; sighs with him; and conceives them to be a most amiable, though unfortunate pair." Yet a reader of the play, "blessed with the common reflection a reading should give, calls the husband a very silly man and the wife a very imprudent woman; and . . . the punishment of the author is rather expected with impatience than lamented as severe" (14: n. pag.). Reading a play, to Inchbald, is very different from watching it performed. A reader, she suggests, is able to evaluate the material from a detached perspective, whereas an audience spontaneously responds to a play in performance. Thus she shows her bias when she makes a distinction between plays like *The Gamester*, which, in performance, render vice appealing, and plays like *The Stranger*, which foster sympathetic responses that benefit the audience.

This force of example, Inchbald makes clear, often depends on the skill of the actors. Writing of Arthur Murphy's play *Know Your Own Mind* (1777), she notes:

> Millamour and Lady Bell are both admirable persons on the stage; although the reader, who never saw them there, may not conceive them to be so; for these whimsical lovers and all the occurrences in which they are concerned, are such that *depend upon action more than upon words.* The exposure of Millamour's verses by three different females at the same time—his pleasant unsteadiness of resolution upon every new desire that assails him, and his final rapturous submission to the melody of Lady Bell's vocal talents, are all incidents highly to be improved by *countenance and gesture*—in which the actor's colouring alone, brings forth the author's new design. (15: n. pag.; emphasis added)

To appreciate the play, Inchbald remarks, one must see it performed. The actors' gestures are as necessary to the meaning of this play as the words in the script. Often, she reserves her greatest admiration for the actor's ability to portray specific emotions. Writing of *The Wheel of Fortune* (1795)—Richard Cumberland's adaptation of *Menschenhass und Reue*—she commends the performance of her friend the actor John Philip Kemble. As Penruddock, Kemble "evince[s] himself . . . a complete master of his art," she declares. She then describes his performance:

> Old men, in love, have caused more laughter and derision on the stage, than, perhaps, any other common occurrence. . . . Here, astonishing reverse! Love, in the decline of life, constitutes a character deeply pathetic. . . . "You bear a strong resemblance to your mother" is a sentence, that seems to convey passion of no one kind that the heart recognizes yet, spoken by Kemble in this part, implies more tenderness, more rooted affection, than all the love that has filled plays and novels for the whole century past. (18: n. pag.)

These are strong words, written with conviction. With experience as a performer, a playwright, and a novelist, Inchbald is endowed with the authority to make such a claim.

Inchbald's efforts to render women's participation in the theater both important and respectable also are evident in her depiction of actresses and female playwrights. When Inchbald writes about actresses, she often cites Sarah Siddons, whose ability to move theatergoers was widely renowned, but Inchbald lauds the talents of actresses with less-than-sterling reputations as well. In her preface to George Farquhar's *The Beaux' Stratagem* (1707), she recounts how Mrs. Oldfield suggested that Farquhar "make some alteration . . . for that she was apprehensive [that] the free manner in which she had bestowed the hand of Mrs. Sullen upon Archer without first procuring a divorce from her husband, would offend a great part of the audience." Farquhar, who was then on his deathbed, gaily replied, "[T]ell her I wish she was married to me instead of Sullen; for then, without the trouble of divorce, I would give her my bond that she should be a widow within a few days" (8: n. pag.). Despite Oldfield's well-known liaison with the married Arthur Maynwaring, the actress appears more sensitive to what is morally right than does the author. Considered thus, Inchbald's decision not to mention Oldfield's relationship with Maynwaring seems less a reflection of her own delicacy than part of a deliberate strategy to recuperate the actress's reputation. Inchbald, in fact, has no problem mentioning illicit relationships when it suits her purpose to do so. She opens her discussion of David Garrick's play *The Country Girl* (1766) by speculating about the fact that William Wycherley—author of *The Country Wife* (1675)—was befriended by King Charles II, despite his alleged affair with the king's mistress, the Duchess of Cleveland. Yet in her considerable description of Dorothy Jordan as Peggy in *The Country Girl*, Inchbald makes no mention of the actress's ongoing relationship with the Duke of Clarence, focusing instead on Jordan's display of "such excellent sense, and such innocent simplicity, that her auditors were boundless in their plaudits." Moreover, Inchbald adds, "not a syllable that was spoken in Mrs. Jordan's commendation of this character was extravagant" (16: n. pag.). Thus Inchbald represents Jordan not as a mistress but as a talented and professional performer deserving of respect.

Inchbald does the same for the few women playwrights included in the collection. In writing of Joanna Baillie and Hannah Cowley, Inchbald emphasizes the relation between their artistry and the morality of late-eighteenth-century drama. Of Baillie's *De Monfort* (pub. 1798, perf. 1800) she writes:

> [F]rom hence is derived this most admirable moral—the proud man, yielding to every vice which pride engenders, descends, in the sequel of his arrogance, to be the sport of his enemy, the pity of his friends, to

> receive his life as a gift from the man he abhors, and to do a midnight murder! (24: n. pag.)

She finds Cowley's *The Belle's Stratagem* (perf. 1780, pub. 1782) superior to Farquhar's *The Beaux' Stratagem* because it is "humorous without ever descending to that source of humour, easy of access, and which is placed among characters in low life" (19: n. pag.). Although she admits that Cowley's *A Bold Stroke for a Husband* (perf. 1783, pub. 1783 or 1784) does not equal Centlivre's *A Bold Stroke for a Wife* (perf. 1718, pub. 1719) either in "originality of design, wit, or humor, it has other advantages more honourable to her sex and more conducive to the reputation of the stage" (19: n. pag.). As for Centlivre's play, Inchbald regrets that, "at the time the most ingenious and witty of the English dramatists lived, there was no restraint, as at this period, upon the immorality of the stage." Centlivre, she declares,

> falls more particularly under censure than her contemporary writers: though her temptations to please the degraded taste of the public were certainly more vehement than those of the authors who wrote at the time, for they were men whose fortunes were not wholly dependent upon their mental exertions; yet the virtue of fortitude is expected from a female, when delicacy is the object which tries it. (11: n. pag.)

At first glance, Inchbald seems to declare that Centlivre would have done better to starve than to write for money, but she is actually praising the playwright by comparing her favorably with her male peers. Centlivre may be guilty of indelicacy, but she alone wrote from necessity. Inchbald buttresses her point in the preface to Centlivre's *The Busie Body* (1709), recounting at length the hardships that drove Centlivre to take up the pen. Indeed, Inchbald remarks that

> when a man follows the occupation of woman, or a woman the employment of a man, they are both unpleasing characters, if they are guided in their pursuits by choice; but, if necessity has ruled their destinies, they are surely the objects of compassion and mercy should be granted to their want of skill in their irregular departments.

Centlivre, she contends, "encountered the masculine enterprise of an author" as an alternative to "female profligacy, or domestic drudgery" (11: n. pag.); Inchbald thus renders Centlivre's decision to work as a playwright virtuous and the playwright heroic. Inchbald also underscores the extent of Centlivre's talent in relation to the other playwrights—both male and female—included in the collection.

Throughout the prefaces, Inchbald's insistence on female virtue links her sex and her critical acumen; in differentiating between what is moral and what is not, Inchbald represents herself as someone capable of making such judgments. Thus she points out that Nicholas Rowe's *The Fair Penitent* (1703) is not aptly named since the heroine is

> no penitent, in a religious acceptation of the word; for, though she laments her fall from virtue with all the anguish of degraded pride, she is still enamoured of the cause from whence her guilt originated, and feels a deeper sorrow for her lover's abated passion (the natural consequence of her frailty) than from motives of contrition.

Overtly, at least, Inchbald's reflection on the fragility of female virtue echoes the observations of conduct-book writers like Thomas Gisborne and Dr. Gregory. Unlike these writers, however, Inchbald does not equate innocence with ignorance:

> Whatever reasons may be urged against the more elevated instruction of the sex at present, than in former days, one good consequence at least accrues from it—they are better qualified than heretofore to choose their lovers and husbands. It was in the age of female ignorance that the Lotharios and the yet viler Lovelaces flourished.—Now, enlightened by a degree of masculine study, women's taste and judgment being improved—this best consequence of all ensures—men must improve to win them. (10: n. pag.)

This observation is typical of Inchbald: her apparent agreement with conservative ideas about women's nature and roles actually furthers a different, more progressive agenda.

Nowhere is this strategy more evident than in her reply to George Colman the Younger. She apologizes for offending him but notes that she took the commission on the supposition that "no one dramatist could possibly be offended, by the cursory remarks of a female observer." Colman is thus trapped between a rock and a hard place. Either he is guilty of overreacting or Inchbald is a critic to be reckoned with. If the former, he is behaving like an overemotional woman; if the latter, Inchbald's sex does not invalidate her judgment. That Inchbald prefers the latter option is clear in the rest of the letter. She writes:

> Permit me, notwithstanding this acquiescence in your contempt for my literary acquirements, to apprize you—that in comparing me, as a critic, with Madame Dacier, you have inadvertently, placed yourself, as an author, in the rank with Homer. I might as well aspire to write remarks on *The Iliad*, as Dacier condescend to give comments on *The*

> *Mountaineers* [Colman's play, perf. 1793, pub. 1794]. Be that as it may, I willingly subscribe myself an unlettered woman.

Inchbald, of course, was not an unlettered woman, as demonstrated by her ability not merely to understand Colman's allusion but also to turn it to her advantage. While her apparent agreement with Colman's "contempt for [her] literary acquirements" renders her modest, it also indicates that Inchbald does not equate Colman with Homer. By following Colman's analogy to its logical conclusion, Inchbald reveals the extent of Colman's hubris and calls attention to his incompetence as a writer. In doing so, moreover, she dramatizes her intelligence as a reader and critic. Thus Inchbald provides the playwright with an example of irony that is far more sophisticated—and far more insulting—than his own heavy-handed comparison between her and Dacier.

Inchbald's prefaces to *The British Theatre* are a rich resource for scholars, teachers, and students interested in a variety of topics. In the classroom, they inform discussions of theater practices, particular playwrights and performers, and the reception of individual plays. They may be read as texts that contribute to the formation of a British dramatic canon (Waters 71) or examined for evidence of Inchbald's political sympathies or her position on the status of women in the theater. Finally, they demonstrate how a woman, working in a profession almost exclusively male, can exercise judgment and write with authority. To students who are honing their skills as critics and to scholars who regularly engage in critical discourse, Inchbald's prefaces may speak clearly indeed.

Victoria Myers

Joanna Baillie and the Theme of Trial

Joanna Baillie's 1798 collection *Plays on the Passions* provides an exciting culmination to several different kinds of courses in the undergraduate English curriculum. At many institutions, but especially the small liberal arts college, the number of English courses offered each term is limited. If we wish to teach British women playwrights with any frequency, we should be prepared to study them in different contexts. In this essay, I discuss how the theme of trial emerges in Baillie's drama theory and in the rhetoric and dramaturgy of *Count Basil*, *The Tryal*, and *De Monfort*, and I pinpoint the way this theme in her work exhibits the convergence of cultural developments in several areas of eighteenth-century thought and practice. I then sketch the prominent role Baillie can play in an eighteenth-century course on a mixture of genres and a Restoration and eighteenth-century drama course.

Baillie's "Introductory Discourse," in *Plays on the Passions*, explains her long-term project for a series of plays, each scrutinizing the operation of a master passion in the soul. For each passion, she couples a tragedy with a comedy, treating obsessive love in *Count Basil: A Tragedy* and its companion comedy, *The Tryal*, and obsessive hate in the tragedy *De Monfort* (its companion, *The Election*, appears in a later volume). Reflecting the spread of empiricism into all areas of thought in the eighteenth century, Baillie explains how this experimental investigation of the passions educates the public morally and improves the conduct of justice. While drawing drama toward the moral or scientific treatise, she nonetheless intends her plays to engage the audience's instinctual propensity to feel sympathy for other human beings and to treat them consequently as objects of curiosity. It is "sympathetick curiosity" that explains audience pleasure in the drama and must be understood for moral, psychological, and judicial progress (69).

To explain the spontaneous operation of sympathetic curiosity, Baillie describes a number of trial scenes from real life. A crowd watching a public execution will "eagerly mark . . . whether the motions of [the criminal's] body denote agitation or calmness" (70), subjecting the criminal to a trial of his moral stamina in the act of carrying out his sentence. Baillie argues for the primitiveness of sympathetic curiosity in a second example of trial: American Indians torturing a captive, a custom she believes is perpetuated less by "[r]evenge" motives than by the "universal desire in the human mind to behold man in every situation, putting forth his strength against the current of adversity" (70–71). This custom, "therefore, must be considered as a grand and terrible game" in which the contending tribes "try . . . the fortitude of the soul" (71). In a third example, Baillie brings the illustration of sympathetic curiosity closer to the everyday experience of her readers, scrutiny of a person under the sway of anger or other strong emotion. All of us, she urges, are fascinated even by a person who just begins to display "the smallest indications of an unquiet mind," and when we finally see the emotion full-blown, "how minutely will we endeavour to remember every circumstance of his past behavior! and . . . seize upon every recollected word or gesture, that is in the smallest degree indicative of the supposed state of his mind" (73). In these examples, "to try" attains diverse meanings: to inflict pain, to subject a person to scrutiny to discover his or her state of mind, to test to the limit of a person's endurance, to put to the test to find out a person's worth. Admitting that trying includes an element of cruelty, Baillie argues that, by scrutinizing a person, "we know what we ourselves might have been" in the same circumstances. She expects that this self-knowledge will work against the potential to be cruel; by exercising our natural propensity, we can "becom[e] more just, more merciful, more compassionate" and learn "to respect ourselves, and our kind" (74). The drama will lead spectators to "reflect and reason" and thus teach them to connect what would otherwise remain unsystematic observations (75).

Each of the plays in *Plays on the Passions* centers on the trial of a male character who is carried away by his passion to violate his duty, his integrity, or his nobility. In *Count Basil*, the title character undergoes a trial of the soul when he falls in love with Victoria, the daughter of the Duke of Mantua, who is using the unwitting princess to keep Basil out of an upcoming battle. Basil has hitherto centered his life on his military duty, earning fame and the devotion of his troops. His cousin and lifetime friend, Count Rosinberg, has willingly taken second place to promote Basil's career, delighting in Basil's growth into a man of sterling honor and skilled leadership. Rosinberg watches Basil anxiously as he postpones taking his troops into battle and extends his sojourn in Mantua day by day at the whimsical request of the vain princess. Rosinberg's repeated admonitions agitate Basil, who is stretched between maintaining his friend's approbation and attaining Victoria's love. Because Rosinberg reminds the hero of the incompatibility of his principles with obsessive love, Basil begins to perceive his friend as a trying person.

In teaching the trial theme, I involve students in an analysis of the dialogue and stage action, in which they find persuasion and resistance, passion and scrutiny of passion. In *Count Basil*, we analyze act 4, scene 3, the encounter between Basil and Rosinberg that forms the turning point of the play. At the opening, Basil is minimizing the danger of the mutiny he has just overcome. Rosinberg attempts to convince him that there remains a secret treachery—he suspects the duke's plot to keep Basil in Mantua—by recounting Albini's anxious efforts to warn him. Basil interrupts, eagerly interpreting Albini's manner as a sign of concern from Victoria herself and losing the point of Rosinberg's warning. In the midst of his rant, Basil notices Rosinberg "star[ing] upon" him (185; act 4, sc. 3, line 56). Rosinberg, distressed by this exhibition of Basil's continuing enslavement to love, asks, "So well, so lately try'd, what art thou now?" (line 61). Basil, in turn, is chagrined by Rosinberg's disapprobation and wants to avoid further scrutiny. Students analyze how Baillie has constructed the scene so that Basil experiences emotions rising in intensity as he attempts to parry Rosinberg's successively more penetrating discoveries of his infatuation. Basil feels manhandled as Rosinberg's words "push . . . with rough unsparing hand, / Where but the slightest touch is felt so dearly" (81–82), and later he feels that Rosinberg "contrive[s] but to torment! /

And hast a pleasure in the pain thou giv'st" (139–40). Suffering from increasing pain, Basil is prompted to attribute increasing degrees of cruelty to Rosinberg until, as the stage directions dictate, "Basil *walks up and down in great agitation, then stops, covers his face with his hands, and seems to be overcome,*" while "Rosinberg *looks at him earnestly,*" exclaiming, "O! blessed heav'n, he weeps!" (197). With Baillie's "Introductory Discourse" in mind, we can ask how Rosinberg's probing resembles or differs from the physical torture described in Baillie's second example: Does Rosinberg intend cruelty? Is his cruelty necessary? Is the cruelty only in Basil's perceptions? In pursuing this line of questioning, we uncover the complex moral valence of attempting to control others' actions through our withholding of approbation, as well as the integral part that approbation plays in maintaining social order.

To explore the thematic significance of this dramaturgy further, we compare *Count Basil* with its companion comedy on love. In *The Tryal*, the female tryer comes forward as the main character. An heiress of little beauty but much good humor, Agnes persuades her uncle Withrington to allow her and her pretty but poor cousin Marianne to exchange identities so that Agnes may escape fortune-hunting suitors and pursue "a reasonable woman's desire, . . . a respectable man, and a man who is attached to me" (220; act 1, sc. 1, lines 28–31). She has such a one in mind, a young idealistic lawyer named Harwood, who is attracted to her, persuaded she is the poor cousin, but pleased by her "good humoured way" with her uncle (227; 1.1.253). Harwood becomes more and more enamored of Agnes until he is as distracted as Basil. The trial theme emerges when Withrington provokes Agnes into proving Harwood thinks her more than "an amusing and good natured creature," and she engages to make him "think me a vixen and be pleased with me" (255; 3.1. 131–32, 134–35). Thus Victoria in *Count Basil* sets about making Basil love her "against his duty" and "against his reason's will" (147; 2.4.57, 59). Like Victoria, *The Tryal*'s Agnes succeeds only too well in pitting the hero's love against his reason and against the advice of his well-meaning friend. Withrington warns her that a man's "diseased" passion evidences no rational admiration for her (282; 5.1.47). She agrees that she must test him to determine whether "his love for me is stronger than his love of virtue" (283; 5.1.59–60), and (more cognizant than Victoria) she understands that she must undergo a simultaneous moral trial, to be willing to give him up if he does not come through successfully. She then devises a test of his moral fiber by conveying to him a contrived letter proving herself to be a vicious liar.

Although I usually teach *De Monfort* without the other two plays, it preeminently lends itself to a study of the trial theme because of the protagonist's crime. A tragedy about hate, it also targets love—homosexual or incestuous, detoured or repressed—and this doubling of obsessive emotion exhibits the theme in the complex agony of being scrutinized by an enemy who could be a friend, by friends who seem enemies. According to the backstory that De Monfort confesses to his sister Jane, he has hated Rezenvelt since their early youth, when, despite his lower status, the sociable Rezenvelt won the admiration of De Monfort's comrades. After inheriting a title, Rezenvelt seems even more obtrusive to De Monfort, who likely defends himself against a homosexual attraction to his rival (see Purinton, *Romantic Ideology* 156–57). Rezenvelt's parallel backstory, confessed to Count Freberg, reveals that Rezenvelt has deliberately baited and teased De Monfort, even at times targeted De Monfort's attraction to him, to make him lower his pride. De Monfort has let his resentment grow into an obsession. When the play opens, he is fleeing from the embarrassment of having challenged Rezenvelt to a duel and having lost, and he now borders on madness. His sister, with the help of Count Freberg, attempts to reconcile the two men and draw the savage De Monfort back within the pale of sociability. De Monfort goes through a series of trials. He is urged to explain his hatred to Jane, to whom he has a more than brotherly attachment and whose approbation he fears losing (see Burroughs, *Closet Stages* 121, 125). Then he is forced to have a reconciliation meeting with Rezenvelt, in which he must endure his rival's too eager moves toward friendship. Finally, from a townsman hoping to gain De Monfort's patronage by maligning Rezenvelt, De Monfort hears a rumor that Rezenvelt aspires to marry Jane.

In studying Baillie's dramaturgy of scrutiny and testing, students analyze these confrontational scenes as a trial of De Monfort's soul, much in the manner I described for *Basil* and *The Tryal.* Moreover, although I do not have my students read *The Election*, we locate within the grim plot of *De Monfort* some equivocally comic moments in Count Freberg's teasing his wife for her vulgar taste and Rezenvelt's baiting De Monfort for his arrogant detachment. The audience will laugh, but De Monfort, exhibiting a bitter misanthropy against what he calls "nature's man" (314; act 1, sc. 2, line 91), longs for social approbation, while Rezenvelt, playing the witty, sociable man, inflicts satire like an instrument of torture. In the minor plot, Lady Freberg longs for her husband's praise and is comically jealous of the more graceful Jane, but in taking petty revenge, she starts the rumor that Rezenvelt woos Jane—a rumor that destroys De Monfort's self-control. Both Lady Freberg's frustration and Rezenvelt's teasing help produce the murder to come. In this articulation of comedy with tragedy, students discover how the play focuses the tenuousness of sociability and civility.

The discussion of dramaturgy often raises questions from students about how the plays could have been performed in Baillie's day. This investigation entails a brief turn to the final pages of her "Introductory Discourse" and 1812 preface "To the Reader" to discuss the question of whether Baillie intended these plays to be closet dramas. While Baillie dispels that notion, she also rejoices in the fact that publication enables her readers to understand the plays as part of a systematic (moral) whole ("Introductory Discourse" 108–09). Moreover, she articulates her preference for a small, intimate theater, where the subtleties of facial expression and gesture would be more visible to the audience ("To the Reader" xviii–xxi). We look into brief descriptions of the patent theaters, acting styles of the major actors, criticisms of the stage, and the role of in-home theaters. Here I find Catherine Burroughs's *Closet Stages* most helpful to begin with, since it affords a bridge between theory and performance and makes students aware of how acting space, gesture, and intonation function in interpreting the plays. For reading more specific to *De Monfort*, I send students to chapter 6 of Paula R. Backscheider's *Spectacular Politics*, with its treatment of the actor's gaze and the style of Sarah Siddons, who played Jane in the London production of *De Monfort*, and to Paul Ranger's brief study of Baillie's stage directions, geared to the acting style of John Philip Kemble (98–103). While this approach allows a neat articulation of textual explication with historical research, I sometimes engage students directly in scrutinizing and being scrutinized by having them perform scenes. As an alternative to such a time-consuming project, I have enlisted students from the theater department to perform a scene from one of the plays and then let my students analyze how the performance has captured the theme of trial.

While these discussions take the students quite far in an appreciation of the rhetorical and dramaturgical aspects of the plays, I like to combine this approach with a historicist interpretation of the trial theme. Anticipating questions that usually arise in the course of interpreting Baillie's language, I explore several cultural changes. One change, the rewriting of moral philosophy in the sentiment movement, took form in David Hume's *Treatise of Human Nature*.[1] Agreeing with Francis Hutcheson, Hume premises that human beings receive pleasure from contemplating "generous and noble" behavior, pain from contemplating "cruelty and treachery" (296). Likewise, Hume describes a propensity to "sympathize with others, and to receive by communication their inclinations and sentiments" (316). Hume's version is mechanistic and epistemological, however. We receive the "ideas" or external signs of an emotion in others and, through our imaginations, spontaneously convert them into "impressions" with "such a degree of force and vivacity, as to become the very passion itself, and produce an equal emotion" in ourselves (317). Sympathy, in this mode, is a way of knowing the other. As Hume moves from epistemology to morals, however, his concept of knowing through sympathy becomes an equivocal concept of judging. Sympathy is the basis of social passions stimulating us to benevolent or noble actions; these produce pleasurable effects in others that we can contemplate in self-approbation (or approve in others when they perform such actions). In a further departure from Hutcheson, Hume maintains that sympathy also accounts for the antisocial passions: while we spontaneously feel pleasure in another's happiness, comparison with ourselves can spontaneously produce pain (envy) when we feel deficient in happiness. Remorse for such emotions, still more for actions resulting from them, begets "a kind of malice against ourselves" (376). Although Hume saw the social advantage of this self-castigation, for it blocked envy of the privileged from eventuating in violence, he also sensed that it afforded means for the propertied to use morality against the unpropertied; he placed greater emphasis, therefore, on the limitation of the passions through rational "general rules" (532).

Baillie's several accounts of trials in "Introductory Discourse" suggest that, like Hume, Baillie considered sympathy a spontaneous cognition coupled with judgment and designed to defend against its possible reversal into malice. I use brief excerpts from Hume's *Treatise* (294–98, 316–24, 372–80) to help students discover the implications of Baillie's concept of sympathetic curiosity. For Baillie, this propensity in human nature, which grounds the appeal of drama and its moral weight, packs two moments of human response into one movement: sympathy begets curiosity (67). Having students separate the cognitive from the emotional moment and then put them together again, under Hume's direction, brings forward Baillie's apprehensions about the social and antisocial passions available in the process of knowing the other. This complexity, in turn, proves important in understanding the ethical and social dimensions of Baillie's project and encourages a closer look at what Baillie means by moral theater. If "God Almighty has implanted" sympathetic curiosity within us (74), what is its purpose and how can drama further that purpose? If sympathetic curiosity has a potential for both cruelty and compassion, what kind of theater will produce a discriminating knowledge that will be usable in public (as well as private) life?

Although Baillie was preoccupied with the same moral concerns as Hume, she drew closer to Adam Smith, who followed Hume in initially deriving moral judgments from the operation of sympathy but denied that this operation occurs as spontaneously or produces as vivid an emotion in ourselves as in the person feeling it. For Smith, gaining sympathy becomes a task for the person ardently desiring the spectator's "fellow-feeling" (13). This premise grounds Smith's system of approbation, for people who desire sympathy must tone down their behavior and present their case in such a way as to gain that accord (36–37). Although he brings in general rules beyond sympathy, as Hume does, Smith describes how sympathy is elaborated into "the impartial spectator" (61). Not simply an empirical generalization of social behavior, this interior monitor represents the standard of morality in the community whose approbation each person desires (62, 157–61). Yet the possibility of devolution also exists, for Smith recognizes that the act of scrutiny often is felt not only as a testing of one's conformity to moral standards but also as an unendurable suspense of approbation. Like Hume, he sensed the power of approbation as social control: given the general tendency to defer to one's superiors, the "impartial spectator" could become a force for established power.

Reading excerpts from Smith's *Theory of Moral Sentiments* (9–19, 34–40, 61–66, 157–61) enables students to perceive the broad significance of Baillie's dramatization of control through approbation and to account for the hints of aggression in such scrutiny. In the specific scene from *Count Basil* analyzed earlier, I give an example of how students uncover the dynamic of approbation in Baillie's dialogue and dramaturgy. They can also discover the effect of (dis)approbation in the poignant dialogue of act 2, scene 2 of *De Monfort*, in which Jane pries from her brother a confession of his secret hatred of Rezenvelt. Although Jane desires to disburden De Monfort of this secret, claiming her right by nature and accustomed intimacy to know his troubles, he resists, because he fears in her the predominance of the impartial spectator over the partial sister. He says, in words that echo Smith's thesis, "thou wilt despise me. / For in my breast a raging passion burns, / To which thy soul no sympathy will own" (331; 2.2.78–80). Students see how stage action also echoes this thesis: De Monfort's confession and, worse, his refusal to relinquish hate physically propel Jane from him. She says, "I cannot speak to thee." He, in response, pleads, "Turn, turn thee not away! . . . Look on me yet again" (334; 2.2.181, 182–84). In relating the operation of Jane's sympathetic curiosity to the concept of the impartial spectator, students encounter Baillie's problematic of a moral theater—how to combine compassion with justice—which we later explore through her connection of psychology with law.

A second cultural change, linking Baillie's language of experiment to the new physiological psychologies, explains how it was possible for Baillie to believe that human beings, in a world of misunderstanding, could come to know one another.[2] Various scholars have traced Baillie's experiment to her knowledge of the work of her brother Matthew Baillie, a prominent London physician and anatomist (see, e.g., Burwick). His second and third Gulstonian lectures (1794) present several observations that translate into his sister's depictions of scrutiny, the most important of which was his view that the "emotions of the mind" stimulate the muscles, producing changes in countenance and gesture. The body thus "becomes a natural language," which one learns (imperceptibly) to use and interpret. Although emotion produces these readable appearances independently of volition, one can also repress and imitate such appearances, either voluntarily or involuntarily (146–48). Alan Richardson's interpretation of *Count Basil* in "A Neural Theatre" provides a vivid demonstration of how these premises underlie the references to body in Baillie's dialogue, as characters read the emotions of other characters, "artfully" construct the appearance of emotions, and screen themselves from being read (141).

With Richardson's essay and excerpts from Matthew Baillie, students can understand the physical trying of the soul that figures prominently in Joanna Baillie's plays. Asserting that "Basil's love" for Victoria "originates in her physical attraction," Richardson explicates Basil's rapt admiration as "one uniquely embodied sensibility" registering on him through "telling glances, gestures, and motions of the blood" (137). Much of this influence occurs below consciousness, hence the difficulty Basil experiences in resisting it. Since the body reveals the mind through its natural language, Basil believes he "read[s] [Victoria's] mind and character in her body" (139), but his social inexperience renders him inept at interpreting her "artful social style, alternately making and counterfeiting feelings" (141). Besides providing a guide to interpreting Baillie's dramaturgical clues to character psychology, Richardson recognizes that the embodied mind is also a social mind: although subjectivity is "thoroughly intertwined with . . .

the body," one's notion of oneself "can develop only through social experience . . . [and] remains dependent upon the acknowledgement of others . . . for its very continuation" (143). Richardson thus indicates an avenue by which Baillie fuses physiological psychology with Smith's system of approbation.

This excursion also turns up trial in a legal sense, marking a third change occurring in Baillie's day: the increasing admission of psychological expertise as testimony in criminal trials and the greater degree of psychological knowledge in the lay audience that might serve as jurors.[3] One of the most important features of eighteenth-century trial justice was the attempt to clarify the concept of intent, enshrined in a few landmark statements concerning the "constraints" (to use Thomas Green's term) that might render persons unable to exercise their reason (qtd. in Eigen 16–17). The legal definition of intent includes the will to do an act while being in possession of one's reason, indicated by the ability to distinguish right from wrong (see Blackstone 24–25). Insanity was among the constraints on intent, but the proof of insanity at the time of the act was difficult to evaluate in cases where the condition was interrupted by periods of lucidity. I send students to Joel Peter Eigen's *Witnessing Insanity* (chs. 3 and 4) to learn what sort of behavior was considered proof of insanity and how absence of intent was explained by various psychological theories. Baillie's preference for gradual development of a dominant passion, as well as her depiction of frantic behavior and distracted speech, suggests that she knew of the kinds of observations made in court by medical witnesses and family members of the accused. Baillie thus stands among the advocates for legal reform in a century dominated by the "bloody code," though she resists becoming an undiscriminating dispenser of compassion and takes up the challenge of making passionate characters interesting without palliating their crimes (104–05).

As indicated in her "Introductory Discourse," Baillie intends her theater experiment to educate the judge, magistrate, and civic leader (76). For my students to appreciate how Baillie produces this training, I have them use William Blackstone's distinctions among murder, justifiable homicide, and excusable homicide (180–91). By applying the definitions of each of these to De Monfort's killing of Rezenvelt, they discover that Baillie has carefully constructed the plot and the circumstances to make out a prima facie case of murder. We then try to determine, according to Blackstone's explanation, whether De Monfort could be exculpated by showing he is insane. Much in the other characters' descriptions of De Monfort, as well as in the stage directions, contributes to such an impression, but Baillie also provides elements in De Monfort's speech and actions that militate against this conclusion. In working out this case, we discuss legal definitions of intent and consider how physiological psychology, with its emphasis on reactions below the level of conscious will, might alter the application of this concept. What effect would such a psychology exert on the justice system, and how does Baillie handle this potential? In this light, we also evaluate Lady Jane's and Count Freberg's pleas at the end, one for preserving the character of the murderer, the other for sharing the blame.

Discussed in these ways, Baillie's work can play a role in a variety of eighteenth-century literature classes. Baillie holds a central place in my course Women in Restoration and Eighteenth-Century British Drama. This course begins with the emergence of women as important participants in theater and thereby as a social, political, and moral force in the reconstruction of the nation after the civil wars. We study their roles as actresses, playwrights, theater managers, and theorists of drama. During this era, theater was criticized as immoral and attempted to transform itself into a force for morality. I pose the question, Did women hinder or promote this project? In the first two-thirds of the term, we study this question by taking up plays by various dramatists in chronological order; in the last third we study Baillie intensively in the light of the issues developed earlier. The trial theme is dominant throughout the course.

We begin with a close study of Aphra Behn's *The Rover* (1677), which casts men and women in an adversarial relation: the brother attempts to control whom his sisters will marry, even whether they will marry, wanting to subdue them to a moral code that he freely violates. The sisters, using the opportunity of masquerade to seek out and test potential marriage partners, perform their desires through witty repartee and innuendo. Masquerade, however, also subjects them to a trial of their chastity and their self-concept. From Terry Castle's treatment, students learn how "[t]he classic features of masquerade—sartorial exchange, masking, collective verbal and physical license" (11)—lent themselves to "female emancipation" on the one hand and encouraged attacks on masked women on the other (33). Guided by brief excerpts from Peter Holland's *The Ornament of Action*, we analyze how stage scenery, both "as index of place" and "as commentary on the action," interprets the risks the women run as they move from the private chamber to the public street (19).

We discover similar adversarial relations within a context of masking in William Congreve's *The Way of the World* (1700). Where knowledge is power, characters engage in game playing, cruel teasing, and verbal torture to gain knowledge of others and deflect knowledge of themselves. The swift shifting of scenes underlines this elusiveness. This play, in which women betray women, also opens discussion of actresses, acting styles, and rivalries in the theater world (see Howe). The sexual openness of Behn's and Congreve's plays surprises many students and prepares them to take up the question, bruited about in this period, of whether the stage is immoral and carry it further, asking why the stage is obliged to be moral. Excerpts from Jeremy Collier, John Dennis, and Congreve stimulate a lively debate and review of the two plays already studied (see McMillin). Our next drama, Susanna Centlivre's *The Wonder* (1714), appears a direct reply to the trials described by Behn and Congreve—and to the accusations of stage immorality. Students immediately comment on the difference between Violante and the women in the earlier plays: to keep faith with a woman, she risks losing her fiancé, Felix. The nature of the trial subtly changes in this play since both Violante and Felix occupy the moral high ground, and at stake is not so much power as trust. Centlivre's running conceit of religious faith still is shaded, however, by the stage business of hiding and spying.

When we move to the latter part of the century, students find some decided changes in stage morality reflected in the trials women undergo—and impose. In Elizabeth Inchbald's *Every One Has His Fault* (1793), the questions change: Can authority give way to mercy? Can we forgive offenses against our dignity and our love? There are continuities with the early plays—lying, concealment, and cruelty abound, to protect the weakness of persisting love and to exercise male authority—but there are differences as well. In staging, the explicit mask is gone, as well as the action of hiding and spying. Hiding is predominantly verbal, and in Inchbald's dramaturgy characters expose their feelings, sometimes deliberately, to have them soothed, as when Mr. Solus seeks Mr. Placid's pity because he is lonely without a wife or when Mr. Irwin bitterly reveals to Mr. Harmony that fashionable friends have turned him away or when Sir Ramble expresses anxious uncertainty over whether his wife will receive him. Inchbald strips away the protective pretenses at the end, revealing an equal emotional need between men and women. Also a theater theorist, Inchbald exposes a change in stage morality in her prefaces in *The British Theatre*. Those for Centlivre's *The Busie Body* and *A Bold Stroke for a Wife* exhibit Inchbald's expectations of "taste and morality" in the choice of plot, action, and language and her recognition that personal circumstances make writing for the theater a trial of one's own "delicacy" (*Remarks* 3, 4).

Baillie accepts without argument the expectation of the time, voiced by Inchbald, that writers for the stage should avoid licentious language and action. Baillie's concept of trial, nonetheless, launches some severe challenges to the eighteenth century's concept of morality: sympathetic curiosity produces cruelty as well as compassion, and the system of approbation harbors repression as well as compassion. We also investigate the changes in the physical space of the theater and acting styles since the early eighteenth century and discuss how Baillie's moral project demands a theatrical reform. Her preference for smaller theater spaces constitutes her training ground for compassionate leaders; at the same time, smaller performance spaces implicate the audience in the characters' mental pressure on each other. In this respect, we then consider in what ways Baillie works within a theatrical tradition, focusing on her retention of issues and motifs from earlier plays. Her treatment of the masquerade in *Count Basil*, for example, retains the erotic impetus of *The Rover*, and the dialogue in the infatuation scenes recaptures, to a certain extent, the game playing from *The Way of the World*. Yet Baillie, like Inchbald, aims at compassionate reading of the verbal and behavioral clues given by persons in pain.

In the second course where I teach Baillie, Restoration and Eighteenth-Century Literature, the "Introductory Discourse" and *De Monfort* serve as the culminating assignments, pulling together our semester-long exploration of civility and cruelty in the making of British concepts of civilization. John Dryden's *An Essay of Dramatic Poesy* sets us on our course with its dialogic form, its gentlemanly code of "candour and civility" (34), and its inclusive interpretation of aesthetic rules—all against a battle setting, the defeat of the Dutch, and the outward movement of British power after the revolutionary upsets of the seventeenth century. This foreground of civility and background of violence form the initial structural pattern, which is varied and interrogated in other works in the course: Dryden's ethos of moderation, Alexander Pope's celebration of the British commercial empire and ambiguous philosophy of the middle way for the lords of creation, Jonathan Swift's rational utopia.

In the second part of the term, we study the sentiment movement, first in general as a reformation of manners and critique of British commerce and justice, then more closely with Samuel Richardson's *Clarissa* to bring out the paradoxes of sensibility, the body as language of the soul and focus of an exploitative gaze, the bankruptcy of the aristocratic ideology, the drive to test virtue to destruction, the treachery of the heart. The trial theme begins to emerge with this focus, and here we study Hume's experimental treatment of sympathy and Smith's absorption of sympathy into a system of approbation, along the lines discussed above.

Baillie's "Introductory Discourse" and *De Monfort* take up motifs developed throughout the course—the ethos of moderation, the history of savagery, self-knowledge, the master passion, the language of the body, the destructive gaze, the ambiguity of sympathy. Students who have been observing how civility and cruelty interweave will notice that Baillie does not resolve the ambiguities of the earlier works, though she treats them with explicit critical and analytic consciousness. Sharing the Enlightenment's cultural self-consciousness, she nonetheless makes it a point to salvage that savagery not far below the surface of sociability and to show that civilization depends on a propensity to sympathy that has both benevolent and aggressive potentials. In her theatrical project, more than a mirror of the British condition, she joins the reforming impulse of an age of revolution to a drive for knowledge and order.

Notes

1. The treatment of Hume and Smith described in the following paragraphs and their connection to Baillie's "Introductory Discourse" are more fully developed in V. Myers, "Joanna Baillie's Theatre." The application to Baillie's *De Monfort* is made in V. Myers, "Joanna Baillie: Speculations."

2. See A. Richardson, ch. 1 of *British Romanticism*, and Weiner for useful background on the emergence of new psychologies.

3. See V. Myers, "Joanna Baillie and the Emergence," for more extensive development of the ideas in this paragraph and the next.

Part III

The Playwright-Novelist

Michelle Ruggaber Dougherty

Frances Brooke's *The Excursion* and Eighteenth-Century Women's Theater

A particular challenge facing teachers of eighteenth-century women's literature is students' lack of exposure to the period. Sadly, eighteenth-century studies often receive inadequate attention in general curricula, and it is not rare to have a class of undergraduate English majors who have little or no knowledge of any eighteenth-century works, much less eighteenth-century women's writing. A productive teaching technique in such situations is to link the knowledge that students do have with new information. Therefore, a useful way to introduce students to eighteenth-century women's drama is to start with a study of Frances Brooke's *The Excursion* (1777). This work fits into literary traditions to which students may already have been exposed—the courtship novel and the female bildungsroman, for example—but it also dramatizes some of the barriers limiting women's access to the dramatic literary marketplace. A central scene in *The Excursion*, featuring the heroine Maria's ill-fated interactions with the famous actor and manager of Drury Lane, David Garrick, mirrors some of Brooke's own difficulties with Garrick, and the resolution of Maria's story can be read as Brooke's solution to women's problems with theatrical life in London. By linking a discussion of women's drama with *The Excursion*, instructors can build on students' familiarity with the novel as a genre, raise elements of social history that affected the success of women in the literary marketplace, introduce prominent theoretical debates regarding women's positions as authors, and develop sufficient background knowledge for further study of women's drama.

Brooke's involvement with the London theatrical world began with her attempts to have her tragedy *Virginia* produced by Garrick's Drury Lane sometime in the early 1750s. Historically, Garrick has a justifiably strong reputation as a supporter of women in drama. During his twenty-nine-year career, he produced fifteen plays by women (Donkin 30–31). Brooke's early interactions with Garrick, however, proved unsuccessful. When she approached Garrick with *Virginia*—based on Livy's tale of the rape and kidnapping of the Roman girl Verginia by Appius Claudius—she learned that Garrick had already received two other scripts adapted from the same story, one of which was produced in February 1754, and he declined to read hers (Donkin 41). Brooke then appealed to Covent Garden, the only other licensed theater in London, and was rejected from there as well. Ultimately, she gave up on seeing *Virginia* performed, and she published it in 1756, turning her literary efforts toward starting a periodical. For thirty-seven weeks in 1755 and 1756, Brooke wrote *The Old Maid*, under the pseudonym Mary Singleton, Spinster, through which she provided commentary on social conventions, politics, and the arts, often including theater reviews. In the 13 March 1756 issue, for instance, she criticized the choice of both licensed theaters to produce Nahum Tate's severely edited version of *King Lear* and unfavorably compared Garrick's performance of the lead with that of the rival actor Spranger Barry's. Brooke wrote:

> I think [Mr. Barry] was perfectly right to take the *Lear* which is commonly play'd, that the competition between him and *Mr. Garrick* in this trying part, may be exhibited to the public upon a fair footing; I have not yet been so fortunate as to see the latter in it, whose performance, I doubt not, is no less justly, than generally, celebrated and admired; but the advantage *Mr. Barry* has from his person: the variety of his voice, and its particular aptitude to express the differing tones which sorrow, pity, or rage, naturally produce, are of such service to him in this character, that he could not fail of pleasing. (103–04)

As Ellen Donkin has noted, although Brooke's criticism seems even-handed and fair, Garrick appears to have taken great offense, going so far as to advise her fellow author Marie-Jeanne Riccoboni, whose work Brooke had previously translated, to have nothing more to do with her professionally (47). Nearly twenty years later, in 1772, Brooke again tried to have a work of hers produced, this time the opera *Rosina*, and, again, she was rejected from the major theaters, including Garrick's Drury Lane. In a letter to a friend, Brooke suggested that her rejection may be some sort of plot—"theatrical tyranny"—and considered applying to the lord chamberlain for permission to produce the opera on her own (Donkin 50–51). Perhaps inspired by her difficulties as a playwright, Brooke joined with her friend Mary Ann Yates to manage King's Opera House in 1773. She and Yates successfully managed King's for four years, but they were never granted a license to produce plays, which limited their productions to operas.

Nearly thirty years after her first attempts to have a play produced, Brooke at last saw her works on stage at Covent Garden. First, her tragedy *The Siege of Sinope* was produced in 1781. Moderately successful, it was performed ten times, reviews suggested that it was received warmly by the audience, and it earned Brooke a few hundred pounds (McMullen 189–94). Then in 1782, ten years after Brooke initially tried to bring *Rosina* to the stage, it was produced (Shield). This time, Brooke's writing elicited great popularity and an enthusiastic critical response. *European Magazine* noted that on opening night "many of the songs were encored," and it was ultimately performed 201 times by 1800, making it one of the most popular comic operas of the time (qtd. in McMullen 201). By Brooke's death in 1789, twelve editions of *Rosina* had been published (201–03). Another opera, *Marian*, first performed in 1788, was Brooke's last production, and it, too, enjoyed critical and popular appreciation, although not to the extent of *Rosina*.

Between her management of King's Opera House and her success with these plays, Brooke published *The Excursion*, her third novel, in 1777. The heroine of *The Excursion*, Maria Villiers, leaves her country home for London with two goals in mind: to return home "with a ducal coronet on her coach" (10) and to achieve literary fame by selling an epic, a novel, and a tragedy, which she also assumes will provide comfort and wealth. As her living expenses increase and her money decreases, Maria decides it is time to approach theater managers with her tragedy, and, after hearing that another tragedy, *Braganza*, is playing at Drury Lane with great success, she "anticipated her own success . . . and congratulated herself on the happiness of having written for the theatre at a time when it was so evidently the interest of the managers to take new pieces" (53).

Despite her naïveté regarding other aspects of the literary marketplace, Maria does recognize one impediment to her success: propriety. After seeing the tragedy at Drury Lane and deciding that Garrick is the manager to whom she wishes to show her play, she notes, "One only difficulty remained, that of finding some respectable man of learning; for a man of learning she determined it should be, who could with propriety introduce her to the acting manager" (57). When Maria's landlady reveals her friendship with Mr. Hammond—"[o]ne of the sublimest poets, and most judicious critics, this enlightened age has produced" (59)—Maria considers her problem solved. Yet when Mr. Hammond returns several days later, he reports that when he asked Garrick if he had even read the play, Garrick stammers, "Why—a—um—no—not absolutely read it—Such a multiplicity of affairs—Just skimmed the surface—I—a—Will you take any chocolate, my dear friend?" (81). Garrick then proceeds to criticize its lack of comic vision (until reminded that it is a tragedy), and he dismisses Hammond with a vague promise to produce it in 1782—seven years later (81–82). A heartbroken Maria publicly reacts to this news with a "tear of blended resentment and distress" but privately fantasizes how, when she achieves her (ultimately unsuccessful) goal to be married to her current suitor, Lord Melvile, she will

> make a present of her piece to the other house; letting the manager who had treated her so contemptuously know, *whose* play it was he had not condescended to read. . . . Lady Melvile's play would be *received*, though Miss Villiers's had not even been *read*. (83, 86)

In short, Maria daydreams of getting her revenge on Garrick.

Brooke's commentary on Garrick continues in a footnote she added to this scene after he had announced his retirement. In it, she calls him a "great theatrical luminary" and assures her reader that "the various excellencies of his performance will be remembered with delight." Yet she also indulges in the wish that "new Shakespeares, new Sophocleses, new Garricks, [may] arise, under the auspices of a manager who has sufficient genius to be above envy, and sufficient liberality of mind to be incapable of avarice" (85), suggesting that Garrick is not a manager in that vein.

Brooke's characterization of Garrick in *The Excursion* is sharp and witty, but it may also have been ill-timed. Given the proximity of Garrick's retirement to the publishing of the book, many contemporary reviews of the novel strongly criticize Brooke for being mean-spirited in her portrayal of him. A commentary in the *Monthly Review*, which Lorraine McMullen argues was likely written by Garrick himself, protests, "The public owe [Garrick] too many obligations, and we owe too much to the public, not to endeavour to remove the obloquy with which this lady has loaded him, in his late capacity of manager" (qtd. in McMullen 175–76). In 1785, Brooke published a second edition of *The Excursion*, and the most heavily revised section is the Garrick scene. In the revision, Garrick's voice is completely removed, and Mr. Hammond relates the details of his meeting with Garrick entirely in third person and in far less detail. Brooke replaces Garrick's stammering speech with Mr. Hammond's reasoned explanation:

> [T]here is, it seems, an etiquette in respect to the reception of theatrical pieces, of which I was not aware. . . . This etiquette precludes even the perusal of an offered play, till a certain limited time before the season in which, if approved, it may, in rotation, be accepted. (qtd. in McMullen 173)

The replacement of Garrick's comic stuttering with Mr. Hammond's calm explanation significantly softens the reader's perspective of Garrick and places the blame on Mr. Hammond's ignorance of conventions rather than on Garrick's rudeness. In both versions, however, Brooke makes clear the challenges proper women faced in trying to enter the theater marketplace. Once Maria realizes that her dreams of theatrical success will not likely come true in London and having been rejected by Lord Melvile, she decides to return to her uncle's country estate where the novel began.

After students have read *The Excursion* and have discussed Brooke's historical relationship to Garrick and to theatrical history, an instructor may wish to introduce them to some of today's critical appraisals of the novel, many of which express concern about the conclusion of the book. Brooke gives her novel a happy ending: in the last few pages, Maria is saved from her economic troubles by an anonymous benefactor; she returns to the estate on which she grew up; and she meets and falls in love with Colonel Herbert, the brother of a family friend. She even declares to her sister, "If I should marry him, . . . it would be the most extraordinary commencement of a matrimonial engagement that ever happened" (150). These are her last words in the novel. The question of whether she will continue to write is only answered obliquely, when Mr. Hammond suggests they build a theater on the estate, where "Miss Villiers and I will, in defiance of managers, write tragedies, and play them ourselves" (152). Many feminist critics view this conclusion with concern and generally read it as Brooke's abdication of the notion that a woman can be commercially successful as a dramatist. After all, Maria so strongly connects her self-image with others' perception of her writing that Mr. Hammond's plan, no matter how conveniently it removes obstacles, also seems to remove the social aspect of writing that Maria finds attractive. She writes her tragedy with the intention of seeing it produced on the London stage. She is "[c]ertain of [it] being received with rapture by the managers [of both theaters]" (16); she writes the part of the hero for Garrick and the heroine for Mary Ann Yates (16, 61); and she rejoices when she hears that the tragedy *Braganza* is sold out "till the thirtieth night . . . anticipat[ing] her own success in that of the estimable author [of *Braganza*, Robert Jephson]" (53).

I suggest that an instructor read a few of these critics who criticize the novel's conclusion and select provocative statements for use in class discussion, perhaps placing several excerpts on a handout prepared for students to read at the beginning of a class session. Katharine Rogers complains that at the conclusion of *The Excursion* "Maria's passionate vocation for authorship . . . unfortunately drop[s] out of sight; the last we hear about it is her maidenly fear that it will be revealed to her family" ("Sensibility" 169). Jodi Wyett describes Maria's future dramatic activities as done "merely for the benefit and amusement of her friends and family, not as part of an economic exchange necessary to survival" (150). Emily Bowles considers Maria's return to the country "a reinstatement of the status quo"; Bowles also suggests that Mr. Hammond's desire to have Maria perform for him is tantamount to

> draw[ing] [her] into a circuit of secluded, privatized sexual exchange: she will write for him, for her guardian, for her . . . husband, and for her sister, but she will not participate in literary culture broadly or publicly. . . . Maria silently acquiesces to what is literally a patriarchal system of enclosure. (140, 140, 150)

After reading such arguments, students can discuss the fairness of these conclusions. Is Brooke selling out by removing Maria from the theater marketplace?

This discussion is also a good opportunity for an instructor to provide additional context about the social elements of eighteenth-century London that made public success difficult for young female dramatists. (Alternatively, an instructor could introduce the following information earlier in the class, but explaining it after or during the above discussion may serve to temper strong opinions and highlight the complexities inherent in Brooke's conclusion.) In eighteenth-century London, a proper young woman's freedom was limited at best, which is a point that Brooke emphasizes. Paula Backscheider and Hope Cotton note Maria's confinement to domestic life even in the public world of London:

> Tied to the few people she believes respectable, Maria must wait for introductions and invitations. . . . As her money dwindles and her acquaintances drop her, she is imprisoned in Mrs. Merrick's house, and Brooke depicts her pacing and discomfited. (xxii)

London offered women like Maria the possibility of becoming involved in the theater industry firsthand, but the limits of propriety that prevented Maria from making her own acquaintances and from going out into society unchaperoned would also have prevented her from actively entering the theater world. Although women playwrights were not uncommon in the late eighteenth century, any woman wishing to enter the public literary arena would be, in Mary Poovey's words, "jeopardiz[ing] modesty," since public writing "cultivates and calls attention to the woman as subject, as initiator of direct action, as a person deserving notice for her own sake" (36). Further, playwriting was a particularly risky activity for women to participate in because of the combination of elements it required: "composition, publication, reading, and performance widespread," in addition to the discussion of ideas that occurs when writing is presented in a public setting (Davis 18). Donkin adds:

> Playwriting, as a profession, violated all the rules of conduct. It conferred on women a public voice. It gave them some control over how women were represented on stage. It required that they mingle freely with people of both sexes in a place of work that was not the home. It made ambition a prerequisite, and, perhaps most importantly, it offered the possibility of acquiring capital. (18)

In the light of these difficulties, students may wish to reevaluate the criticisms of Maria's decision and to analyze the realistic options available for many women struggling to be economically and artistically successful in London's literary marketplace. Brooke's removal of Maria from the economic world of playwriting also removes her from the potential of scandal and into the acceptable worlds of marriage and family, but is her new position necessarily a relegation to a situation in which her writing will only be heard by family and friends, without having an influence on the larger society? Some dramatists, like Yates and Brooke, were able to find theatrical success; others, however, undoubtedly shrunk away from the stresses of a theatrical life. How can we reconcile the historical success of some women with the story of Maria and other women like her?

A helpful pedagogical approach here is to introduce students to the public-private debate prevalent in discussions of eighteenth-century literature. The crux of the critical debate on *The Excursion* is whether private theatricals are inferior to public writing. Many of Brooke's modern-day critics seem to think so, but Brooke was writing in a social context that did not necessarily lead to this conclusion. The second edition of *The Excursion* was published in 1785, just before the dramas of Joanna Baillie and other Romantic women were gaining in popularity, and Maria's resolve to retire to the country belongs in this tradition of plays that were meant to be read or performed privately—but are still important.

As with the critical debate on *The Excursion*, I suggest here, too, that an instructor provide students with brief summaries or excerpts of social theorists to give students an overview of the critical debate. I begin with Jürgen Habermas and his claim that the public sphere in the eighteenth century consisted of "private people who related to each other in it as a public" and that the literary public sphere "provided the training ground for a critical public reflection still preoccupied with itself—a process of self-clarification of private people focusing on the genuine experiences of their novel privateness" (28–29). Habermas's writing can be dense for undergraduates, but this idea that the public world consists of private individuals engaged in public reflection is crucial. If we believe that "private" equals "hidden" or "unknown," then private theatricals have little significance outside their immediate audience. If we think of the public world as composed of private individuals coming together, however, then the experiences of private citizens can reach further. Next, I include critics like Tracy Davis who discuss sociability, the notion that since one's society is made up of a small and intimate audience of close friends that cannot be separated from the larger public world, the private flows into the public. The individuals in any private setting are part of the public institutions that constitute society, and, because of blurred distinctions between public and private spheres, writing for the family or domestic audiences can have more widespread influence. Debates and conversations can take place in the home among several people who engage in various public activities; although the location is private, the ideas are public. "Thus," as Davis argues, "the authoring of a play is an act of the associative public sphere, necessarily implicating publicity (publicness), whether it was bound for publication, home theatricals, professional production—or utter obscurity." Playwriting, then, "in common with other kinds of public acts," is an act of vocalizing ideas (22).

Next, Lawrence E. Klein's "Gender and the Public/Private Distinction in the Eighteenth Century" questions the usefulness of binary distinctions. Klein believes that terms like "masculine/feminine" and "public/private" are hastily dichotomized; while distinctions between these terms did exist in the eighteenth century, they were understood not only in opposition to each other but also in opposition to several other words and meanings (99). "Man," for example, could be opposed to "woman," but it could also be opposed to "boy," "child," "baby," "animal," and so forth. Klein similarly points to differences in the meaning of the word "public," concluding that in the eighteenth century a "civic public sphere" existed that encompassed all behavior involving society as a whole (104). Klein concludes by emphasizing that people in the eighteenth century most often functioned in an associative public sphere and that "public" actions were simply actions that were not performed alone; those public actions could take place in a drawing room, a coffeehouse, a public square, a private home—or, if we apply Klein's theory to theater history, a private theater in a private home. As long as the actions performed were open and transparent, Klein argues, they were public in eighteenth-century terms (104–05). Considering Klein's terminology concerning "public" and "private," we can see that a writer's private dramatic activity, while centered in the home, would not necessarily restrict her from communicating her ideas publicly.

Finally, I include a theorist like Catherine Burroughs, whose discussion of the public-private debate specifically addresses the theater (*Closet Stages*). Writing is an undeniably active pursuit, and the private theatrical allows women the chance to explore more identities and communicate more ideas about the world than they might be allowed to in a traditional public setting. Burroughs explains:

> Those who made theater in their homes between 1770 and 1810 confronted the performative aspects of their actual experience through the process of self-consciously adopting roles for the private stage. For women, especially, whose performance of femininity was tested perhaps most stringently in the semipublic spaces of the domestic sphere, the private theatrical provided often unlooked-for opportunities to analyze how social identities are constructed and represented. (151)

For women like Maria, private theatricals are the answer to the problem of how to write without subjecting oneself to the social difficulties present in the literary marketplace. Writing, even private writing, allows a woman to construct a variety of situations and identities that she would not otherwise be able to experience.

Once students have read and discussed the above excerpts, an instructor can again ask questions about the conclusion of *The Excursion.* Does Maria's relegation of writing to a private stage mean that no one will hear her ideas? What are the advantages of private theatricals over plays performed in public theaters like Drury Lane and Covent Garden? While Maria is not participating in the literary world of London when she writes and performs her private theatricals, she is still participating in a public life of letters. She will have an audience, she will write about ideas that are important to her, and she will likely inspire conversation and discussion of those ideas outside the confines of her private theater.

By exploring the above aspects of *The Excursion*, an instructor will be able to set the stage for a discussion of other late-eighteenth- and early-nineteenth-century women playwrights, such as Frances Burney, Frances Sheridan, Hannah More, Hannah Cowley, Elizabeth Inchbald, and Joanna Baillie. What led some of these women to be public successes and others to write closet plays? What difficulties did Cowley have with Garrick or Inchbald with the theatrical manager Thomas Harris? Why did Baillie write plays that could be read as closet plays even as she expressed a wish to see these plays performed publicly, as in her "Introductory Discourse"? Why would Brooke work to be recognized publicly but be satisfied with the private writing of her character Maria?

My purpose here has been to offer instructors a new way of introducing students to the social and theatrical history surrounding eighteenth-century women's drama in general, rather than to give advice on teaching any specific plays. I hope that my suggestions will lead to animated classroom discussions about the decisions that female authors made or felt forced to make as they strove to enter the theater marketplace and that instructors will challenge their students to expand their understanding of eighteenth-century literature and women's place in it.

Catherine Ingrassia

"The Stage Not Answering My Expectations": The Case of Eliza Haywood

Eliza Haywood published more than fifty novels and at least five plays during her nearly forty-year career.[1] The relevance of her publication in multiple genres (she also wrote poems, conduct manuals, and periodical essays, among other things) remains largely undiscussed, partly because of modern literary history's tendency to flatten the fluid relationship among genres during this period. Too often we study genres discretely, rather than integrating them into a dynamic relationship that might more accurately capture the experience of reading and writing in the early eighteenth century. Readers and authors moved rather seamlessly among the then contiguous available genres in a commercial world not yet preoccupied with niche marketing. Haywood, like her predecessor Aphra Behn or her contemporary Henry Fielding, undertook a wide range of activities as an author. Possessing a clear recognition of what Paula Backscheider describes as "the cultural capital and exchange value of each genre" ("Literary Culture" 505), Haywood wrote theatrical texts simultaneously with prose fiction, deploying each in a way that best served her professional, commercial, and aesthetic goals.

Haywood had a material and discursive presence in the commercial marketplace of the London literary world. A writer of prose fiction,

Haywood was also intimately involved with the mechanisms of the print trade throughout her career. She exemplified the bookseller-author with a "common overlap of authorship, publishing, and printing" (McDowell 53). That involvement culminated in 1741, when, at her own bookselling shop located at the Sign of Fame in Covent Garden, Haywood sold texts she had written and assembled herself.

Her involvement in the theater, though less discussed, is similar. As an actress, Haywood consistently appeared on the stage from her debut in Dublin in 1714 through her arrival in London in 1717 (playing the title role in her *A Wife to Be Lett* in 1723) until the Stage Licensing Act of 1737. She was a competent and recognized actress with considerable experience. Kathryn Shevelow describes her as "well-known and genuinely talented," bringing skills "Fielding must have welcomed" (240). She worked at Fielding's Little Haymarket as both actress and author, and her collaborative ballad opera *Opera of Operas* (1733), an adaptation of Fielding's *Tragedy of Tragedies* (1730), had a successful run.[2] A benefit performance of Fielding's *Eurydice Hiss'd* and *Historical Register* was held for "Mrs. Haywood the Muse, Author of Love in Excess, and many other entertaining Pieces" on 23 May 1737, the night before the Licensing Act went into effect (Scouten 674). Patrick Spedding also asserts it "seems likely" that Haywood was a strolling actress or a manager of a company of strolling players during the 1720s and 1730s (345). She strategically "used her notoriety as an author . . . as a commodity on the stage," suggests Susan Staves, and "theatrical appearances functioned as advertisements for her books" (*Literary History* 189). Her 1735 text *The Dramatic Historiographer* (reissued in 1747 as *A Companion to the Theatre*) fully demonstrates both her commanding knowledge of the English dramatic canon and her insight into the politics of the London theatrical world. Yet Haywood is consistently misrepresented as someone who was, at best, marginally successful in the theater.

Perhaps Richard Savage's depiction of her in *Authors of the Town* (1725) as a less-than-successful theatrical maven—"A Printer's Drudge! / Flush'd with Success, for Stage-Renown she pants" (10)—contributed to that misapprehension. The idea also might stem, in part, from a 1721 letter Haywood wrote to a potential patron in which she represented her move from the theatrical to the literary marketplace as one of economic necessity: "The stage not answering my Expectations has made me turn my Genius another way."[3] That language is specifically designed to extract a financial contribution. In fact, the theater was an institution that could provide an author with great profit more quickly than any other art form. The theater provided Haywood with a consistent income, and many of the benefit performances for her netted financial amounts that compare favorably with those cleared by "the performance of well-established plays" (Spedding 311). Further, the theater as an institution, drama as a literary text, and the performative aspects of a dramatic career informed Haywood's works throughout her professional life, during which she moved seamlessly, if at times imperceptibly, between the two genres. Elizabeth Eger suggests that an actress-author like Haywood demonstrates "a remarkable capacity for self-invention across a range of literary genres" (36).

Just as Haywood's dramatic texts share qualities with her fiction, her novels owe a great deal to the theater, specifically in terms of the representation of gender and social interaction. A rich intertextuality infuses her work. Vivien Jones reminds us:

> [I]f we are to do justice to the full variety of women's experiences of eighteenth-century print culture, "literature" must be used flexibly to cover not simply the productions of a cultural elite (which would include the majority of novels), but also those popular and more ephemeral genres. (Introduction 3–4)

To help our students understand an author like Haywood, we need to situate her fiction within the cultural field of her dramatic writings and the commercial and material presence of the London theatrical tradition. This context profoundly enriches the discrete texts studied in the classroom and, more important, reveals the degree to which drama and the performative mode of the period influenced the texts people read, shaped authorial discourse, and informed social interactions.

We could readily identify numerous moments of intertextuality throughout Haywood's oeuvre that would potentially yield revelations in terms of her appropriation of previous and contemporaneous texts. What I would like to do here, however, is explore the mutually informing relationship between her drama and her fiction. Haywood establishes a consistent pattern of fictional female characters who are self-consciously actresses, powerfully suggesting the performative nature of social interaction and also revealing Haywood's familiarity with contemporary acting theory. Similarly, her best-known novel, *The History of Miss Betsy Thoughtless* (1751), strategically uses theatrical allusions to provide the reader with additional layers of signification, drawn from contemporary theatrical models. Finally, a representative dramatic text, *A Wife to Be Lett* (1723;

pub. 1724), simultaneously anticipates and echoes Haywood's previous and subsequent dramatic and fictional work in its representations of marriage and male-female relationships. It suggests how, for eighteenth-century readers and authors, dramatic and fictional texts constituted a dynamic continuum.

Fantomina; or, Love in a Maze (1725) begins in a theater, where "A Young Lady of distinguished Birth, Beauty, Wit, and Spirit, happened to be in a Box one Night" (227).[4] The unnamed woman, who will come to be known as "Fantomina," is fascinated by the social performance of several gentlemen in the pit who were "entertaining a Woman who . . . might easily be known to be one of those who come there for no other Purpose, than to create Acquaintance with as many as seem desirous of it." Desiring the "Gratification of an innocent Curiosity," Fantomina dresses herself "as near as she cou'd in the Fashion of those Women who make sale of their Favours" (227). Her success is unparalleled, and, using "Aids from Nature, join'd to the Wiles of Art" (238), she is able to seduce the desirable Beauplaisar four times, each as a different character. Fantomina, like Haywood, is simultaneously actress and playwright, creating "plots" that require her to assume disguises and act appropriately. Fantomina alters her physical appearance through clothing and a clear displacement of her class. As Celia, a serving maid, she dons "a round-ear'd Cap, a short Red Petticoat, and a little Jacket of Grey Stuff" and adjusts her physical and vocal features:

> [A] broad Country Dialect, a rude unpolish'd Air, which she, having been bred in these Parts, knew very well how to imitate, with her Hair and Eye-brows black'd, made it impossible for her to be known, or taken for any other than what she seem'd. (234)

No one recognizes Fantomina because of her successful acting and because of the "vast Disparity . . . between their Characters" (228).

Her skills transcend mere dissembling and disguise, however; Fantomina "knew so exactly how to form her Behaviour to the Character she represented, that all the Comedians at both Playhouses are infinitely short of her Performances" (238). The language that describes Fantomina's performance echoes that of contemporaneous acting manuals by Aaron Hill and Thomas Betterton; Hill urges the actor to "act a passion" by using the face, body, voice, and gesture to represent emotion (*Essay* 9). While, ideally, the actor will "attempt [an] imitation" of a passion "till his fancy has conceived so strong an image, or idea, of it, as to move the same impressive springs within his mind," Hill concedes that some actors may need to take a "*shorter road*" (15). In that case, the actor needs only to "annex" the "*look* to the *idea*," which will also create "the image, the look, and the muscles" necessary to represent the emotion. In discussing "the Art of Action or Gesture," Betterton advises actors to express "the Nature of the Things you speak of" with eyes, eyebrows, mouth, and hands; "make the Gestures supply Words, . . . joining these significant Actions to the Words and Passions justly drawn by the Poet" (97, 104).

Here, Fantomina is her own poet, and she "disclos'd by the Gestures with which her Words were accompanied, and the Accent of her Voice so true a Feeling of what she said" (Haywood, *Fantomina* 237). She possessed "the Power of putting on almost what Face she pleased": "she could vary her very Glances, tune her Voice to Accents the most different imaginable from those in which she spoke when she appeared herself" (238). Fantomina represents women from every point of the social spectrum—wealthy widow, prostitute, serving girl. Each time her performance elicits a different reaction from the same man in a way that clearly illustrates the very class-specific nature of male-female relationships and the power of Fantomina's acting.

Anti-Pamela; or, Feign'd Innocence Detected (1741) similarly focuses on a heroine gifted in dissimulation and acting. Certainly Haywood traded on the name recognition of Samuel Richardson's phenomenally popular novel *Pamela* (1741); her fictional response is, in part, an incisive critique of Richardson's didactic novel. Yet it also dissects the highly performative quality of women's virtue and other desirable feminine characteristics for women in eighteenth-century culture. Syrena Tricksy, raised to make her fortune with her beauty, functions as an actress from the very beginning of the novel. By age thirteen, "she excell'd the most experienc'd Actresses on the Stage, in a lively assuming all the different Passions that find Entrance in a Female Mind" (54). Like an actor following the techniques urged by Betterton and Hill, Syrena internalizes a powerful emotion that manifests itself physically:

> Her young Heart affected with imaginary Accidents . . . gave her whole Frame Agitations adapted to the Occasion, her Colour would come and go, her Eyes sparkle, grow Languid, or overflow with Tears, her Bosom heave, her Limbs tremble; she would fall into Faintings, or appear transported, and as it were out of herself; and all this so natural, that had the whole College of Physicians been present, they could not have imagin'd it otherwise than real. (54)

Haywood underscores the performative nature of Syrena's feigned social interaction with theatrical language: Syrena embarks on the "Stage of Life" (58); she sets the "Scene of Mischief" (114); her Mother "highly applauded" her performance and "gave her fresh Instructions for perfecting their most detestable Plot" (115).

Haywood—as she does elsewhere—here uses familiar dramatic texts as cultural points of reference for both her characters and her readers. Syrena, for example, working as a housekeeper for the virtuous, elderly merchant Mr. M—, is discovered reading Richard Steele's *The Conscious Lovers* (1722), a popular sentimental comedy in which the apparently orphaned (and thus sexually vulnerable) Indiana is in love with the honorable Bevil, who is engaged to the wealthy Lucinda. Bevil simultaneously remains faithful to Lucinda and treats Indiana with nothing but virtuous generosity. Haywood describes *The Conscious Lovers* in *The Dramatic Historiographer* in lengthy detail, finally offering unequivocal praise: "All the Persons of the *Drama* conclude their Parts with the utmost Satisfaction, but can counterfeit no more than what a virtuous and polite Audience must feel in Reality at so agreeable and moral an Entertainment" (54). In a gesture that heightens the performance of social interaction, Haywood likens the reaction of the spectators within the play—the persons of the drama—to the spectators of the play—the "polite Audience." Both "feel" satisfaction with the sentimental conclusion of the drama.

In *Anti-Pamela*, the play functions as a marker of an idealized and nostalgic representation of male-female relationships. While Syrena feigns interest in the play—"it pleased me" (176)—Mr. M—, who likens Syrena's merits to Indiana's ("You have as much, and perhaps more" [177]), questions Bevil's behavior. While "most People" find the drama pleasing, Mr. M—thinks "there is somewhat in Characters of *Bevil* and *Indiana* not quite agreeable to Nature" (176); Bevil is

> less self-interested than we Men are capable of being to the Object we love . . . it does inspire what is commonly called Generosity, . . . but then that Passion that makes us so liberal, makes us also desire something in return—we cannot content ourselves with rendering happy the Object of our Affections, but languish for something more than Gratitude. (176–77)

This observation simultaneously serves as commentary on Steele's *Conscious Lovers*, sexual relationships in *Anti-Pamela* (and eighteenth-century culture generally), and Haywood's previous discussion of the text in *The Dramatic Historiographer*. Mr. M—'s comment more accurately represents an attitude toward male-female relationships consistent with Haywood's fiction. It also suggests an eighteenth-century reader who is familiar with texts from multiple venues, one perhaps who has read Steele, Haywood's theatrical commentary, and, now, Haywood's fiction. The intertextuality extends from drama to reference work to fiction.

Similar moments of intertextuality also enrich *The History of Miss Betsy Thoughtless* (1751), a novel that chronicles the social actions of Betsy Thoughtless, a wealthy, beautiful, but unreflective young woman whose coquettish behavior costs her social capital and threatens her personal success. Throughout the novel, Haywood directly and liberally quotes from the English dramatic canon, both revealing her striking command of the texts and suggesting the average reader's shared frame of reference. She draws on some of the most popular plays of the period, those performed consistently throughout the eighteenth century. A reader of Haywood's fiction lacking a "literary" or reading knowledge of these dramatic texts might have seen them performed or have read about them in Haywood's *Dramatic Historiographer*.[5]

While Haywood directly quotes more than a dozen plays, a resonant moment of her strategic use of theatrical example occurs at the center of the book, when Betsy's most appropriate suitor, Charles Trueworth, sends a letter ending the relationship, deeming her unsuitable and urging "very small retrospect on some remarkable passage in your own conduct" (246). The letter arrives while Betsy is at the theater seeing "that excellent comedy, called *The Careless Husband*" (247). Haywood praised Colley Cibber's dramatic text previously, claiming:

> Never was poetical Justice more strictly observ'd than in this Play: Every Error finds its Punishment in Proportion; and singular Virtue is singularly rewarded. The excellent Moral, together with the happy Choice of Characters, natural and gentile Diction, and that Spirit of Gaiety which runs through the whole, will undoubtedly maintain the Reputation this Piece has so justly acquired, as long as Theatrical Representations shall exist. (*Dramatic Historiographer* 46)

The power of the theatrical experience provokes an atypical moment of reflection for Betsy. Imagining "she saw herself in the character of Lady Betty Modish," she "came home full of the most serious reflections, on the folly of indulging an idle vanity, at the expence of a man of honour and sincerity" (247–48).

In this frame of mind, she is confronted by Trueworth's letter. The dramatic text offers a clear model for behavior: Lady Betty, feigning indifference for the beloved Lord Morelove, recants her treatment of him and begs his forgiveness. She is recuperated into the social order when her behavior changes from coquettish to normative. Yet Betsy, when urged in the letter to reflect on (and thus change) her own behavior, instead criticizes the ill treatment she has received at Trueworth's hands. As a result, she will endure a horrific and abusive marriage before she is united with Trueworth. In a sense, Haywood implicitly provides her readers with two paths for behavior: Lady Betty's and Betsy's.

Haywood's *A Wife to Be Lett* (1724), her second play, explores gender relations, courtship, and the institution of marriage in ways that anticipate or echo her prose fiction. The text takes as its central metaphor an issue explored in most of Haywood's fiction: "the hard uncoveted condition of [a] Wife" (14). The plot uses the figure of the miserly older husband who is willing to prostitute his wife for financial gain (a pattern Haywood repeats in *Betsy Thoughtless*). Mr. Graspall seeks to profit from his lovely young wife, Mrs. Graspall, and thus "rents" her to the charming Sir Harry Beaumont with whom she is really in love. Beaumont is secretly married to Amadea, who disguises herself as a young man to gain access to him. The play incorporates many stock characters from Restoration comedy—the lascivious widow, the affected fop, the virtuous if imperiled wife—and its familiarity may have contributed to its popularity: "[T]he fact the play continued to find new readers and new audiences long after it was first acted says something of its popularity" (Spedding 128). The initial popularity may also have been enhanced by Haywood's appearance as the title character. Although advertised as a result of "the Indisposition of an Actress" (Avery, *London Stage* 731), her appearance more likely was planned. The prologue reminds critics that "A dangerous *Woman-Poet* wrote the Play":

> Measure her Force, by her *known Novels*, writ
> With Manly Vigour, and with Woman's Wit.
> Then tremble, and depend, if ye beset her,
> She, who can talk so well, may act yet better.
>
> (4)

Haywood's powers translate into multiple venues: she writes, she talks, she acts.

The stock types common to drama of the period are joined in Haywood's play by devices such as disguise that are simultaneously dramatic and novelistic. Amadea circulates as a man (allusive of Hellena in Behn's *The Rover* [1677] or any number of other breeches parts), and the servant Shamble impersonates a gentleman (echoing Waitwell's disguise as Sir Rowland in William Congreve's *The Way of the World* [1700]). Jenny, a former prostitute of sorts, "found Trading in publick grew somewhat slippery" (11), and, like Fantomina or Syrena, she transforms herself into the "housekeeper" Dogood: she is "metamorphos'd, fine Lace Pinners transmogrify'd into a round-ear'd Coif and a high-crown'd Hat—a Gold Watch into a Pincushion, and a Tweezer into a Scissar-Case" (11). She trades the accoutrement of vanity and sexual circulation for those of domestic virtue. That "Change of Habit" shares much with Fantomina and Syrena (13), further underscoring the performative and ultimately artificial markers of virtue and domesticity.

In addition, Haywood points directly to the challenges of the written, fictional rather than performed, dramatic text. "How small a Relief can Books afford us when the Mind's perplex'd?" asks Mrs. Graspall, played, of course, by Haywood.

> The Subject that our Thoughts are bent upon, form Characters more capital and swelling, than any these useless Pages can produce—and 'tis no matter on what Theme the Author treats; we read it our own way, and see but with our Passions Eyes. . . . These Opticks too are Traytors, and conspire with Fancy to undo me. (27)

As in *Betsy Thoughtless*, where a dramatic text provides a powerful prompt for reflection and behavior, so too here Haywood seemingly highlights the limitation of reading—the imagination and the passions make the pages "useless" and "conspire" to undo her. Haywood as author, actress, and dramatic character appears to privilege the immediacy of the dramatic over the discursive text—lines that gain a greater resonance when literally uttered by Haywood. The appearance of Haywood on the stage, in this play or any other, foregrounds the simultaneous dissonance and continuity between the stage and the (novelistic) page. Writing consistently in both genres, while also offering sustained commentary on dramatic texts in *The Dramatic Historiographer*, Haywood had a keen sense of the power and limitations of each. The immediate gratification a performance potentially provides the viewer, the playwright, and the actor differs significantly from the necessarily deferred gratification of the reader and writer of fiction.

Perhaps Haywood's incorporation of the two modes was an attempt to diminish the distance between them.

Notes

1. For a full bibliography of Haywood's work, see Spedding.

2. See R. Hume's discussion of their connection in *Henry Fielding and the London Theatre, 1728–1737.*

3. The original document for this oft-quoted line is in the Public Record Office, London, State Papers Domestic 35 22/54.

4. All quotations from *Fantomina* are from Paula R. Backscheider and John J. Richetti's edition.

5. The plays Haywood quotes directly or alludes to include the following (plays with asterisks are those discussed in *The Dramatic Historiographer*): Susanna Centlivre's *The Busie Body** and *Mar-plot; or, The Second Part of* The Busie Body; Colley Cibber's *The Careless Husband**; William Congreve's *The Mourning Bride**; John Dryden's *All for Love**, *Amphitryon**, *Aureng-Zebe, Conquest of Granada, The Indian Emperor, The Spanish Friar** and *Tyrannic Love*; Richard Estcourt's *The Fair Example*; George Farquhar's *The Beaux' Stratagem**; Thomas Otway's *The Orphan**; Nicholas Rowe's *The Fair Penitent** and *The Tragedy of Jane Shore**.

Francesca Saggini

Teaching *Evelina* as a Dramatic Text

After about two centuries of oblivion, Frances Burney's four comedies (*The Witlings* [1779–80], *Love and Fashion* [1798], and *The Woman-Hater* and *A Busy Day* [c. 1800]), three complete historical tragedies (*Edwy and Elgiva* [1788–90] and *Hubert de Vere* and *The Siege of Pevensey* [1790–91]), and dramatic fragment (*Elberta* [1791]) have finally been made available in Peter Sabor's thoroughly annotated collected edition, *The Complete Plays of Frances Burney*. Burney's dramatic works elicit growing scholarly attention (Sabor's *Cambridge Companion to Frances Burney* has a full chapter on Burney as dramatist); her comedies are at last making it onto the stage; and the *Burney Newsletter*, published by the flourishing Burney Society, regularly records professional and amateur productions performed on both sides of the Atlantic.

This enlargement of and challenge to the ideologies of the literary canon make a compelling case for a timely—and radically new—look at Burney's complete oeuvre but particularly *Evelina; or, The History of a Young Lady's Entrance into the World* (1778), the author's debut novel, the most successful of her works in her lifetime, and the one that has remained the most widely known and taught. This essay draws attention to the presence of elements of theater and drama in *Evelina* from a twofold point of view. On the formal level, it analyzes the plot as a structure of five narrative units reminiscent of dramatic acts, all of which bear similarities to eighteenth-century stage genres. On the thematic level, it engages with Burney's "hybrid" or "double-voiced" style, a discourse that is characterized by the presence of a dramatic subtext. I demonstrate that Burney's narrative technique adapted clearly recognizable dramatic situations, stock resolutions, and typified characters to the printed page. These interacted in accordance with well-defined acting rules and conventions to create meaning. I also consider such components of writing for the stage as movement, gesture, and the use of space, as well as analyze the embedding of eighteenth-century theater in *Evelina* by addressing the following textual ingredients: the London representational spaces frequented by the characters of *Evelina*; the relation of the novel to contemporary plays (dramatic transtextuality); stage business and characterization (the application of contemporary acting techniques to the epistolary narrative manner of *Evelina*); and, finally, the implicit (mental) mise-en-scène.

London Performance Spaces

After a brief introductory dramatization in letters of Evelina's family problems (exposition in action), the first volume of the novel quickly moves on to the girl's London apprenticeship. After leaving Berry Hill and the protection of her guardian, Mr. Villars, Evelina encounters the sophisticated world of the city under the wing of her surrogate mother, Mrs. Mirvan. During this early period in London, she meets Lord Orville and Madame Duval, her grandfather's widow, a loud and eccentric frenchified beldam who threatens to frog-march her to Paris.

The adventures of volume 1 are followed in volume 2 by a later sojourn in London during which Evelina, accompanied this time by Madame Duval, comes in contact with the more vulgar representatives of her mother's family (the grotesque Branghtons) and learns to maneuver her way through the treacheries that mark a girl's entrance into society. The social gatherings in which Evelina takes part provide further opportunities for her to become better acquainted with Lord Orville. The nobleman is visibly attracted by the young woman's ingenuous nature and closely observes Evelina as she moves about a hostile and insidious world whose rules she does not know.

The third and last volume of the novel provides the epilogue to the story. While staying at the Bristol Hotwells with Mrs. Selwyn, Evelina receives a marriage proposal from Orville. This happy ending is followed—and thus socially sanctioned—by Sir Belmont's public recognition of his daughter once a serious misunderstanding is providentially cleared up.

The division of the story into three volumes emphasizes Evelina's personal development—achieved by way of her attendance of the London entertainments. Burney takes up and revises the conventional city-country dualism, a staple of Restoration comedy since, at least, George Etherege's *The Man of Mode* (1676). The moral topography of *Evelina* charts a clear-cut distinction between the ideal world of the countryside—the idyllic setting of Evelina's childhood—and the chaotic yet dangerously seductive world of London. By frequenting the capital's fashionable and not-so-fashionable amusements, Evelina not only completes her social *Bildung* but also learns how to behave in the beau monde and to evaluate the people she meets. The varied representational spaces of the city—both theatrical and performative, institutional and social—are summed up in the subtitle of the novel by "world," a term with clear thespian connotations, commencing from *The Way of the World*, by William Congreve (1700); Burney uses Congreve at more than one level in her novel.

Evelina's catalog of London's places of public entertainment follows a hierarchical spectacular decorum, which applies neoclassical dramatic rules to the capital's spaces of leisure. Burney's urban drama clearly separates the higher-class social gatherings attended by the aristocratic Mrs. Mirvan (vol. 1) from the lower-class shows appealing to Madame Duval and the Branghtons, as the embodiments of the parvenu cits (vol. 2).

As illustrated in the table, the theatrical performances and elegant gathering places Evelina visits in Mrs. Mirvan's company are the inverse of those she attends with Madame Duval. Evelina visits the opera house in the Haymarket twice—first in aristocratic company and later with the Branghtons. The juxtapositions of these episodes offer more than comic parentheses at the expense of the Branghtons' vulgar *noblesse de robe*. From a historiographic point of view, we may notice that the composition of the late Georgian theatrical audience was, in fact, volatile and hardly homogeneous in tastes and membership (see Emeljanow). It included members of various social groups who intermixed without restriction in the space of a single dramatic evening. This social mingling reflected deep-seated economic transformations, born of a culture irretrievably altered by the early Georgian cult of social mobility and aggressive business ethics.

Evelina's double vision reminds us that the power of money commanded by the Branghtons and by the rich widow Duval had irreparably

***Evelina*'s Performance Spaces**

	Mrs. Mirvan	Madame Duval
Enclosed Performance Spaces	Drury Lane Theatre • David Garrick in *The Suspicious Husband* (1747) • William Congreve's *Love for Love* (1700) • David Garrick in *King Lear* Haymarket's Opera House (unnamed performance)	Little Theatre in the Haymarket • Samuel Foote's *The Minor* (1760) • Samuel Foote's *The Commissary* (1765) Haymarket's Opera House (unnamed performance)
Extensible Performance Spaces	Pleasure Gardens • Ranelagh • Kensington Social Gatherings • Pantheon • The Mall of St. James's Park • Ridotto Attractions • Cox's Museum • *Fantocini* (puppet show)	Pleasure Gardens • Vauxhall • Marylebone • Kensington Social Gatherings • White-Conduit House • Long Room at the Hampstead Spa Attractions (does not visit)

changed the commissioning of theatrical works and the cultural demand for them. In *Evelina* there appear two distinct yet coexisting groups of spectators: the polite audience able to appreciate David Garrick's impassioned renditions of the Shakespearean repertory and the less-refined spectators who enjoyed the farcical comedy of the self-styled English Aristophanes, Samuel Foote. The diversified composition of the Georgian audience implied that different horizons of expectations, frames of reference, and cultural and dramatic competences coexisted at any given show. *Evelina*'s ideal audience of readers—knowingly moving along with Evelina herself between the two adjoining cultural worlds of the Mirvans and the Branghtons—might reflect the Georgian playgoing audience, who might have enjoyed afterpiece farce and tragedy, dramatic opera and harlequinades, satire and bourgeois drama in the space of a single evening's entertainment.

The opposition between Garrick's legitimate theater and the unpatented theater of Foote is equally of interest. Foote, popular for his farcical shows featuring impersonations of fellow actors (including Garrick), was connected to a popular comic theater and to environments such as the Little Theatre in the Haymarket, in which the actors performed on the fringes of the patented monopoly at hours when the Theatres Royal were closed (e.g., during the day). The dramatic and social pairing of Garrick and Foote is thus rich in multiple connotations. The sparring between these two figures takes up the infighting between patented and unpatented theater, a crucial point in the history of the Georgian theater. Foote's rough lampoons and coarse parodies—lacking the subtlety and finesse for which Garrick's acting was celebrated—worked as a form of long-range social mirror according to which newly acquired bourgeois wealth and ostentation seemed to provide the illegitimate mimicry of the social habits and tastes of the more refined upper classes.

The Dramatic Structure of *Evelina*

The topological and chronological subdivision of the novel into five distinct sections (a circular route encompassing Berry Hill–London [Mirvan]; London–Berry Hill; Berry Hill–London [Duval]; London–Bristol Hotwells [Selwyn]; Bristol Hotwells–Berry Hill) parallels the structuring of the plot into three principal moments and two secondary ones, which I respectively label acts and entr'actes. During the acts, set in the city, the action proceeds according to a threefold forward movement (chronological, spatial, and narratological) that is undercut by the entr'actes—two brief interludes set in the countryside that release the tension.

During the first act (protasis, or exposition), set in London, Evelina makes her debut in society. Her inexperience is cause for a series of embarrassing social situations, while her participation in diverse forms of social entertainment allows her to mingle with such members of high society as the conceited Mr. Lovel, the rakish Sir Clement Willoughby, and the incomparable Lord Orville. Moreover, the solicitous concern of Lady Howard, Mrs. Mirvan's mother, sets in motion the other major plot of the novel, Belmont's eventual recognition of Evelina's legitimacy. The unexpected meeting with the frenchified Madame Duval leads to ongoing skirmishes between her and the patriotic Captain Mirvan, which are marked by a high degree of physicality.

The squabbling between Madame Duval and the captain continues throughout the first *entr'acte*, set in Howard Grove, working in a crescendo of comical situations and burlesque scenes (*lazzi*) to the terrible punishment inflicted by Mirvan and Willoughby on the woman. Disguised as bandits they assault her, leaving her bound and battered in a muddy ditch:

> Her head-dress had fallen off; her linen was torn; her negligee had not a pin left in it; her petticoats she was obliged to hold on; her shoes were perpetually slipping off. She was covered with dirt, weeds, and filth, and her face was really horrible, for the pomatum and powder from her head, and the dust from the road, were quite *pasted* on the skin by her tears, which, with her rouge, made so frightful a mixture, that she hardly looked human. (165–66)

The coarseness of the practical joke—a favorite episode of the novel, often privately theatricalized by Burney's family friends and also used as a frontispiece to the second volume of the first edition of *Evelina*—enhances the corporal aspect of Burney's characters, whose flaunting physicality recalls the energy of the actors of farce. Furthermore, in devising Madame Duval's cosmetic catastrophe, the author seems to allude light-heartedly to a rich network of theatrical references ranging from the tradition of the older dames in Restoration comedy to several eighteenth-century popular roles in drag. These include Garrick's impersonation of Lady Brute, from his adaptation of John Vanbrugh's 1697 comedy *The Provok'd Wife*, illustrated by the artist Johann Zoffany in a famous painting widely reproduced—also as an engraving ("Sir John Brute in The Lady in Disguise scene")—at the time. Similarly, both of the Foote farces mentioned by Evelina included roles in drag, which the comedian usually played himself, incorporating into them his typical uproarious histrionics. The most notorious of them was, without doubt, Mrs. Cole, the procuress in *The Minor* (1760). Thus Madame Duval appears as a deeply theatrically typified character, constructed as a kind of well-recognizable tribute to eighteenth-century high comedy and farce.

In the second act (epitasis, or crisis), Evelina returns to London accompanied by Madame Duval. The new social embarrassments to which she is subjected by her grandmother and the Branghtons find a counterpoint in her evermore problematic legitimization. These highly emotional episodes function to provide several sentimental incidents in which Evelina's sensibility may shine, thus increasing the narrative's tension.

During the second entr'acte, set at Berry Hill, Evelina indirectly reveals her love for Orville to her friend Maria Mirvan, Mrs. Mirvan's daughter. The development of this love interest is completed in the third act (peripeteia, or turning point, and denouement of the story), set in Bristol, during which the two basic situations of the action—love and family—are resolved. Evelina and Orville are joined in marriage (unknotting), but not before Belmont has recognized Evelina (anagnorisis) and is reunited with her in dramatic encounter, which thrilled the reading public of the time (climactic tableau).

The plot of *Evelina*, accordingly, interrelates four distinct levels of the dramatic action. These have been measured in such a way that each prevails on the others. We may define these four dramatic levels as follows:

comedy of manners: Evelina's entrance into society
sentimental comedy: her relationship with Orville
domestic drama: her legitimacy and the origins of Belmont's mysterious refusal
farce: the violent physical skirmishes involving Mirvan, Willoughby, and Madame Duval.

The novel is thus structured on a dramatic continuum balanced through the harmonious alternating of tragic, comic, and farcical tones. The careful mixing of these stage genres is echoed in the storyline by the multiple theatrical references that provide groundwork for the narrative discourse.

Dramatic Transtextuality

Evelina's transtextuality (or textual transcendence; Genette 3–5) is threefold: formal, intertextual, and metatextual.

The Formal Relationship

In the formal relationship, the time of telling coincides with the time of the action so that the episodes of the novel are, in fact, frequently constructed as scenes. Dialogue predominates, and the time axis shifts to the present. Narration (in particular of emotional and mental states) is replaced by ostension (showing). The novelistic scene, therefore, transforms into a microsystem of interacting codes, while the characters are no longer filtered through the pen of Evelina, the first-person narrator. They autonomously emerge as actors on a mental stage (mise-en-scène) and are defined by a dramatic typifying language (idiolect) and precise bodily interactions.

The Intertextual Relationship

The intertextual relationship refers to a case of overt reference in which the narrative episode contains a direct quotation from or an allusion to other plays. For instance, the crucial reunion between Evelina and Belmont intentionally reevokes such analogous scenes as the one between Indiana and Mr. Sealand in *The Conscious Lovers* (1722),[1] a popular moral comedy by Richard Steele, as well as that of Lucy and Mr. Wealthy in Foote's *The Minor*. Also, the figure of Captain Mirvan belongs to the swarm of sailors who invaded the English stage at this time. Charles Dibdin's *The Friendly Tars* (1777) is a well-known example, published just one year before *Evelina*. The frenchified English spoken by Madame Duval—a factor of dramatic characterization common in the eighteenth century—draws from and revises the dramatic idiom of Monsieur Canton, a character in *The Clandestine Marriage* (1766), by George Colman and Garrick.

Eighteenth-century conventions of identification also characterize the gallant Mr. Lovel, a mollified lover of luxury and refinement who has much in common with the fops of the previous century. The fop's bland sexuality was typically contrasted with the rake's aggressive dissolution and brutal virility. Burney—very much aware of a dramatic tradition that she knew firsthand[2]—highlights this gender contrast through the twofold juxtaposition Lovel-Willoughby/Lovel-Mirvan. Interestingly, Mirvan draws heavily from Garrick's rendition of the crude and bullish Sir John Brute, as the mid Georgian revision of the figure of a boorish and dissolute husband.

As pointed out by Susan Staves, however, during the eighteenth century the fop ceased to be a favorite of the public and became the butt of often aggressive ridicule ("Few Kind Words" 426–27). *Evelina* duly reproposes this change in taste with the terrible joke played on Lovel by the cruel Mirvan, who presents him with a snappily dressed monkey, introduced by a coarse innuendo, "Why now, Ladies and Gentlemen, I'll be judged by you all! — Did you ever see any thing more like? Odds my life, if it was n't for the tail, you would n't know one from t'other" (444).

The Metatextual Relationship

An effective example of the metatextual relationship is the episode concerning the performance of Congreve's *Love for Love* (86–92). Evelina goes to the Drury Lane Theatre accompanied by her chaperone, Mrs. Mirvan; the inseparable Maria; and the bothersome Captain Mirvan. Once at the theater, Sir Clement Willoughby, Mr. Lovel, and Lord Orville join their party. A series of pointed comments on the play they have just seen highlights the comedy-novel metatextual relationship. The first opinion we hear is Evelina's:

> The play was *Love for Love*, and though it is fraught with wit and entertainment, I hope I shall never see it represented again; for it is so extremely indelicate . . . that Miss Mirvan and I were perpetually out of countenance. (87)

Similarly, Mrs. Mirvan, as the spokesperson of the moralistic Georgian audiences, politely condemns the licentiousness of the play: "Want of entertainment . . . is its least fault, but I own there are objections to it, which I should be glad to see removed" (89).

Unlike his wife, Captain Mirvan openly praises the play, which amused him very much: "I'll maintain it's one of the best comedies in the language, and has more wit in one scene, than there is in all the new plays put together" (89). Yet, with a well-timed reference to the contemporary diatribe between sentimental and laughing comedy, of which Oliver Goldsmith's "An Essay on the Theatre; or, A Comparison between Laughing and Sentimental Comedy" (1773) was the best-known example, Mirvan reluctantly admits that perhaps the ladies did not enjoy the play because, "it is not sentimental enough" (89).

The negative judgment expressed by Evelina predictably conforms to the ideas (and ideals) of Lord Orville, who, when invited by Willoughby to express his views, states, "I could have ventured to answer for the Ladies . . . since I am sure this is not a play that can be honoured with their approbation" (89). Here Orville revives the harangue begun at the turn of the previous century by the Reverend Jeremy Collier, whose *A Short View on the Immorality and Profaneness of the English Stage* (1698) is commonly considered the most vocal assault against the lewd excesses and the amorality of Restoration comedy, in particular that promoted by Vanbrugh and Congreve.

The characters of *Evelina* are thus divided into three distinct groups according to the aesthetic and ethical stance they take toward Congreve's play, which serves as an overt comment on the narrated action. The close link between the dramatic subtext (hypotext) and narrative situation (hypertext) is further indicated by Evelina's concluding words, "The curtain drew up, and our conversation ceased" (91). The dialogue exchange in the box at Drury Lane is interrupted by the beginning of the stage afterpiece. This narrative artifice would seem to suggest that the curtain has, in fact, opened on the characters of the novel itself, interrupting what was only a rehearsal of the play underlying *Evelina*.

The Embedded Stage

The description of the second encounter between Evelina and her father is the highlight and most theatrical part of the novel (422–29). Burney connects it in an interesting way to *King Lear*. In her journal letter to Villars of 5 April, Evelina makes a brief annotation:

> Thursday night.
>
> We are just returned from the play, which was King Lear, and has made me very sad. We did not see any body we knew.
> Well, adieu, it is too late to write more. (42)

Evelina's laconic remarks are arguably prompted by her reaction to the story of King Lear, the tragic tale of an erring father who disowns his virtuous daughter. The production of *King Lear* Evelina attended at Drury Lane was based on Nahum Tate's adaptation (1681), later significantly altered with great success by Garrick (1756). According to neoclassical theories of poetic justice, the adapted *Lear* had a notorious happy ending, which rewarded Cordelia's daughterly virtue and Lear's reformed fatherhood. The altered *Lear* had, in fact, taken on several features that would be very recognizable—and indeed palatable—to the eighteenth-century conception of family drama. Jean Marsden remarks that Garrick's *Lear*, centered as it was on the relationship of a reformed father and a virtuous daughter, "reverses the emphasis on female pathos and replaces it with an appeal to sympathy, particularly through the figure of the distraught father and his devoted daughter" (*Re-imagined Text* 93).

Burney writes two journal entries on Garrick's *Lear*, one of which particularly agrees with Evelina's feelings. On 9 February 1773, Burney writes:

> We had yesterday—I know not whether to say the *pain* or *pleasure*,—of seeing Mr. Garrick in the part of Lear. He was exquisitely Great—every idea I had of his talents, although I have ever idolized him, was exceeded. (*Early Journals* 1: 242)

The admiration Burney felt for Garrick's performance echoes the audience's fascination for the new acting style developed by the actor. This highly physical technique exteriorized emotions and states of mind through a body grammar of animated passion, scientifically declined through a gallery of gestures, expressions, and tones of voice that operated as the onstage transubstantiation of the characters' internal world.[3]

From the point of view of theatrical communication, it is important to underline that the passions were represented through a rational process of impersonation that solicited the visceral and deeply moving interaction between actors and members of the audience. Garrick's sensibility was, in fact, to remain untouched so that the audience's sensibility might be moved. Characteristically, one auditor described this rewakening spectatorial *sympateia* in physical terms: "Methinks I share in his [Lear's] calamities, I *feel* the dark drifting rain, and the sharp tempest" (Downer 1015). Evelina's response to Garrick's performance provides new evidence of the correctness of her taste:

> Such ease! Such vivacity in his manner! Such grace in his motions! Such fire and meaning in his eyes!—I could hardly believe he had studied a written part, for every word seemed to be uttered from the impulse of the moment. (28)

Arguably, the fascination and cathartic identification created by Garrick in his audience are the implicit emotive models for the reunion scene between Belmont and Evelina, the long delayed confrontation on which the girl's destiny has hung suspended throughout the novel. On the formal and thematic level, Burney was probably inspired by ancient models, particularly by two fundamental moments in the structure of classical tragedy, of which she offers a creative parallel: the recognition of the tragic guilt of the hero and the agnition scene. Aristotle states that peripety and discovery are the turning points of a drama:

> A Peripety is the change from one state within the play to its opposite of the thing described. . . . A Discovery is, as the very word implies, a change from ignorance to knowledge. . . . The finest form of Discovery is the one attended by Peripeties. (11)

In accordance with classical poetics, the interview between Belmont and Evelina is a rite of acknowledgment, which sanctions both the reformation of the unwittingly erring father (a Georgian reworking of the classical *hamartón*) and the social rehabilitation of the virtuous daughter.

The crucial encounter suggests a strong visualization. "The time-of-utterance *now*, and location of utterance *here*," which Keir Elam considers as the markers of dramatic discourse, are present (125). The meeting takes place in a drawing room, while the epistolary writing to the moment and the dialogue form orient the tense toward the present. Evelina's and Belmont's physical and psychological states are consistently displayed through body movement. Burney's use of such exemplary speech acts as "kneeling," "embracing," "starting," "rising," "walking hastily," "casting oneself" recalls implied stage directions that assist the readers' visualization.

Evelina enters, holding a letter—written by her mother, Caroline Evelyn, on her deathbed—which she presses to her lips. The physical presence of this letter and the way it is continually referred to may be considered a further theatrical expedient. Not merely a stage prop, the letter is, in fact, transformed into a third virtual stage presence that gives the reader the ultimate proof of both Belmont's guilt and the legality of his secret marriage with Caroline Evelyn. This latter question offers another topical dramatic reference. Lord Hardwicke's Marriage Act of 1753 had offered much needed legal systematization to the validity of marriage and the legitimacy of children. Secret marriages were a favored dramatic topos of the age, as exemplified by Colman and Garrick's *The Clandestine Marriage*, a comedy Burney mentions at least four times in 1778, the year she composed *Evelina* (*Early Journals* 3: 13, 49, 116; *Diary* 1: 96).[4] Once again, *Evelina* opens up to a multilayered critical approach that positions the novel at the center of a complex web of intertextual and intertheatrical echoes.

Burney uses classical references to aggrandize Evelina and Belmont's meeting and to enhance the solemnity of the scene. If Caroline Evelyn's letter is a sign that succeeds in persuading Belmont, Evelina may be definitively identified by her face, on which her mother's features are indelibly impressed: "[n]ever was likeness more striking!—the eye—the face—the form" (428). The voice of reminiscence cuts deeper than the mechanical testimony provided by the letter, however highly symbolic this token may be. According to Aristotle, the third kind of discovery operates through memory. It moves from "a man's consciousness being awakened by something seen or heard. Thus in *The Cyprioe* of Dicaeogenes, the sight of the picture makes the man burst into tears" (16).

The fateful encounter also comes to a pause and then concludes in a display of emotion. Belmont weeps, overcome with emotion and remorse, and so does Evelina, overcome with sheer joy at finally being recognized. We may expect that the readers too would participate in this deeply moving fictional scene by weeping their applause and shedding real tears of catharsis.[5] The tears of Lear, the fragile old king who weeps with sorrow and rage while cursing his aberrant issue, ideally mix with the tears of Belmont, the baronet blinded by error now reunited with his adoring daughter—a double act of recognition, remembrance, and interpretation, on both the readers' and the characters' part, which seals the intertheatrical and the interactive dimensions of *Evelina*.

Notes

I have adapted portions of this essay, including the table, from chapter 2 of my book *La messinscena dell'identità. Teatro e teatralità nel romanzo inglese del Settecento.*

1. Pedicord records 96 performances of *The Conscious Lovers* at Drury Lane and 29 at Covent Garden from 1747 to 1776 (198–99, 220–21).

2. In July 1771, Burney took part in a private theatrical production of *The Careless Husband* (1704), by Colley Cibber, the comedy that launched the character of Lord Foppington (Burney, *Early Journals* 1: 159–63). The parodies of the fop played by Garrick must have been equally familiar to Burney, who in 1770 played the role of Tag in a private production of *Miss in Her Teens*, Garrick's 1747 farce (1: 116).

3. The lexicography of expressions compiled in 1698 by Charles Le Brun (*Méthode pour apprendre à dessiner les passions*, pub. c. 1702) furnished visual artists as well as actors with precise visual norms toward representation of twenty-four passions. The treatise, which was strongly indebted to Descartes's *Les passions de l'âme* (1649), appeared in English translation in 1734 as *A Method to Learn to Design the Passions.* It remained the most influential reference book for actors and painters alike throughout the eighteenth century, along with Foote's *A Treatise on the Passions, So Far As They Regard the Stage* (1747), John Hill's *The Actor; or, A Treatise on the Art of Playing* (1750, rev. and enl. 1755), and Aaron Hill's essays in *The Prompter* (1734–36) and his essay "The Art of Acting" (1746).

4. Pedicord records 86 performances of the comedy from the year of its opening to 1776 (198–99).

5. Branaman quotes a comment by Arthur Murphy, who reported, "[*King Lear*], as it is altered, will always be most agreeable to an Audience, as the Circumstances of Lear's Restoration . . . must always call forth those gushing Tears, which are swelled and ennobled by virtuous Joy" (55).

Gillian Skinner

Class, Gender, and Inheritance in Burney's *A Busy Day* and *The Woman-Hater*

"Whoever knew that Fanny Burney wrote a play?" So wrote Richard Hornby as recently as 2001 in a review of a production of Frances Burney's *A Busy Day* for the *Hudson Review* (629). Many students would probably echo the sentiment today, for while Burney's fiction is well established in university courses, her drama remains almost wholly unknown. Yet Peter Sabor's edition *Complete Plays* (1995), an excellent full-length study of Burney as dramatist by Barbara Darby (1997), and commentary by both Margaret Anne Doody and Janice Farrar Thaddeus in their biographies (1988 and 2000, respectively) testify to scholarly interest in Burney's plays. Two were performed for the first time in the 1990s—*A Busy Day* in Bristol, England, in September 1993 and *The Witlings* at the College of Staten Island in November 1994. *The Woman-Hater* had its world premiere at the Orange Tree Theatre, Richmond, London, in December 2007.

Burney's comedies significantly broaden our understanding of her treatment of class, developing concerns well explored in her novels, such as the status of trade (and those who engage in it) and anxieties about lack of breeding. Comparison especially with her novel *Evelina* suggests that the "radical ambivalence" detected by Darryl Jones in Burney's fiction is equally evident in the comedies and possibly most apparent in their conclusions.

None of Burney's four comedies was performed in her lifetime, although the second, *Love and Fashion* (1798), reached rehearsal stage at Covent Garden. A combination of paternal disapproval and unlucky circumstances ensured that Burney's comedies remained unperformed, facts that in themselves offer fruitful material for teaching. Questions about the status and reputation of women dramatists—and women's writing more broadly—can be raised, as well as the contingency of what makes up our university syllabi. Sabor and Geoffrey Sill, in the introduction to their edition of *The Witlings* and *The Woman-Hater*, remind us that Oliver Goldsmith was advised to suppress *She Stoops to Conquer. The Rivals* was roundly criticized on its first performance and withdrawn as a result, but, eleven days of revision later, Richard Sheridan restaged it, to general acclaim. We can never know how Burney's comedies would have been received by a contemporary audience or—crucially—how that reception might have molded their final incarnations. Darby speculates, "Had Burney's comedies been produced, she might have redirected her career entirely toward the stage, as she perfected her craft and enjoyed the monetary rewards that accrued to dramatists" (3).

An important vehicle for the exploration of class in Burney's comedies is the issue of inheritance, a concern that also runs through all her novels. In *Evelina* (1778), the heroine is reunited with her father and restored to her inheritance in scenes of high emotion; *Cecilia* (1782) sees the orphan-heiress struggle with the terms of her inheritance and the pride of the Delviles; Sir Hugh Tyrold, in *Camilla* (1796), tries unsuccessfully to manipulate the consequences of his choice of heir by arranging strategic marriages; Juliet, in *The Wanderer* (1814), eventually and after many "difficulties" attains respectability and social position as the heiress of her uncle the Admiral. Burney's novels return repeatedly to inheritance as the elusive—or possibly illusory—key to identity and security as well the source of profound misery and frustration. It is thus both something to be desired and something to wish to escape from, an ambiguous good whose relation to happiness and freedom is never uncomplicated.

The plotlines of all Burney's comedies are also underpinned by questions of inheritance, and the required happy endings are tied to their resolutions. In using inheritance as a lynchpin of both plot and character, Burney was not only following a path taken by many of her contemporaries but also employing a standard comic motif. Comedies end in marriage: if they end in marriage with a rightfully restored fortune thrown in, so much the better. Yet her plays investigate not just the financial or dynastic implications of inheritance but also its social and behavioral aspects. Nature and nurture come under scrutiny, with results that are not always consistent.

It may be useful here to say a brief word about Burney's class position and her politics. Her association with many literary luminaries of the day and her service at court as keeper of the robes to Queen Charlotte make it easy to forget or discount her family's relatively lowly status. Judith Lowder Newton, in a telling phrase, calls Burney's family "uneasily genteel" (24). Her father, as Thaddeus points out, "gave music lessons and for fifteen years appears to have been 'proprietor of Gregg's Coffee House.'" She goes on: "Burney was acutely aware of [the social] scale, in all its permutations and its more cruel distinctions" (33).

At the age of twenty-three, Burney received a proposal of marriage from a Mr. Barlow, "an unremarkable young man," Newton explains, "whom she had met at tea four days before and whom—it is hardly surprising—she was eager to refuse" (25). But her status as a dowry-less young woman precariously dependent on her father was forcibly brought home to her when her female relatives; her other "daddy," Samuel Crisp; and even her beloved father urged her to consider the proposition seriously as a way of establishing herself financially. In response to a letter from Crisp, Burney wrote of her shock at the views he expressed, commenting, "God knows how I shall have Courage to answer it" (*Early Journals* 2: 120). In his letter, Crisp exclaimed, "Oh Fany this is not a marrying Age, without a handsome Fortune! . . . —Suppose You to lose yr Father—take in all Chances. Consider the situation of an unprotected, unprovided Woman" (123). Although Burney successfully resisted the pressure—and persuaded her father to support her decision—the episode could not have ended, Newton suggests, "without leaving its trace, without putting Fanny in some doubt about the inviolability of her status and freedom" (26). The impact of class and inheritance (or its absence) on people's lives, particularly those of women, was thus something of which Burney had poignant personal experience.

Traditionally, Burney has been seen as largely sharing the conservative politics of her father. Feminist critics have challenged this reading and pointed to the problems in simply taking the views of the conservative and royalist Dr. Burney to be those of his daughter. Doody, for example, quotes Burney's November 1791 letter to her sister Susanna: "I feel always *democrate* where I think Power abused" (*Frances Burney* 300). Darby notes that feminist interpretations tend to share a view of Burney's identity and works as "characterized by ruptures and divisions, the simultaneous pull of conservative and radical ideologies, the contradictory strategies of rebellion and apparent submission" (5). Certainly the plays do not, any more than the novels, lend themselves to easy labeling.

The question of inheritance becomes particularly important in a storyline Burney returned to with renewed interest after a twenty-year gap. Like *Evelina*, *A Busy Day* and *The Woman-Hater* (both c. 1801) use the trope of the daughter removed from her origins in her infancy as a key element, but the ramifications of the situation are explored differently. In *A Busy Day,* the heroine Eliza is the heiress to an £80,000 fortune and is engaged to the aristocratically connected Cleveland. Her adoption as a small child and her upbringing have distanced her from her original class position: plucked from a lowly mercantile background, she was taken to India by the wealthy Mr. Alderson. Eliza's return to London and reunion with her birth family, the Wattses, exposes the contrast between her roots and her present position. Cleveland, on seeing Eliza with her family, asks in amazement, "[F]rom weeds so coarse can a flower so fragrant bloom?" (351; act 3, lines 599–600). The Wattses, embarrassingly nouveau riche, recall the vulgar Branghtons of *Evelina*. Where in *Evelina* the heroine's reunion with her aristocratic father confirms the essential parity between her demeanor and her origins, Eliza's shows the disjunctions between hers. As the play progresses, Eliza is always ill at ease, the anomalies of her class position painfully expressed in her almost permanent discomfort.

Discomfort is about the only thing Eliza shares with her father. Explaining the trials of affluence to his cousin Joel Tibbs, Mr. Watts confesses that ever since he gave up his business, he's "never known what to do"; his wife and daughter have

> made me give up all my old acquaintance, because of their being so mean; and as to our new ones, it's plain as ever you see they only despise me: for they never take off their hats if I meet them in the streets; and they never get up off their chairs, if I ask them how they do in their own houses; and they never give me a word of answer I can make out, if I put a question to them. (341; 3.276–81)

Watts is by no means an admirable character, but neither is he completely unsympathetic. His puzzlement at the unintended and unforeseen results of his success (boredom and social ostracism, not to mention lack of control over the once submissive women of his family) questions the realities of social mobility and puts a different slant on the period's perennial concerns about class.

Darby points out that both *A Busy Day* and *The Woman-Hater* "foreground . . . anxieties about class distinctions, which were becoming increasingly fluid at the end of the eighteenth century" (147). The anxiety that commercial success would enable the lower classes to dress as their betters and confuse the natural order of things had long been commented on. In an essay on the late Restoration playhouse, Cynthia Lowenthal observes that the actress Elizabeth Barry "became a target of satiric abuse precisely because she cultivated a carriage so noble that her mean birth was in danger of being obscured" ("Sticks" 231). A hundred years later, the actress and writer Mary Robinson was provoking a similar reaction, as Paula Byrne suggests: "A Mrs Robinson who was better dressed than a duchess raised troubling questions about class and status. . . . When fashion was open to all, it became hard to identify people's social standing from their appearance" (207).

Yet *A Busy Day* appears to suggest that this anxiety is overplayed: imitating your social superiors is not so easy as it looks. Barry may have had a convincingly noble "carriage," and Robinson may have successfully imitated (or, indeed, triumphantly outdone) a duchess, but such achievements were not commonplace. The Watts family fails dismally in their attempt to ape gentility, as Cleveland's reaction testifies. While illustrating the practical difficulties involved in upward mobility, the play somewhat undermines the category of gentility altogether, as the bad manners of all classes and particularly the antics of Joel Tibbs reveal.

Tibbs, a man of business, still holds a clear place in the world and suffers none of the confusions experienced by his cousin. His response to Watts's complaints is both bullish and pragmatic: "Why then don't take off your hat to them; and don't get off your chair to them; and don't answer them when they speak to you" (341; 3.282–83). His finest moment comes in act 5, a brilliant end to the play, in which Burney engineers a confrontation between classes under the guise of a social occasion. The resulting scene sees the upper-class characters determinedly ignoring their social inferiors in the ways already described by Watts, while the Wattses awkwardly attempt polite behavior and then become increasingly confounded by the rudeness they encounter. Tibbs, however, cheerfully eats all the party food and then bets Miss Watts sixpence he can imitate upper-class manners. Lady Wilhemina, Cleveland's aunt, becomes his unwitting stooge:

Mr Tibbs. . . . How do do?
Lady Wilhemina. (*Starting*.) What?
Mr Tibbs. I hope you are confounded well?
Lady Wilhemina. Heavens!
Mr Tibbs. (*Ludicrously imitating* LORD JOHN.) O the doose, and the devil, and the plague and consumed!
Lady Wilhemina. What inscrutable effrontery! I'll look him into a statue. (*Fixes her eyes upon him, and frowns*.)
Mr Tibbs. How do, I say? (*Nodding familiarly*.)
Lady Wilhemina. Dignity is lost upon such ignorance. 'Twill be better to awe him by authority — (*imperiously*) Draw me that sofa this way, sir!
Mr Tibbs. Sofa? (*singing*) Tol de rol.
Lady Wilhemina. Astonishing! Did you not hear me, sir!
Mr Tibbs. O the Doose!
Lady Wilhemina. This is a class of person beyond any I have met with yet!
(391; 5.678–93)

As Doody suggests, the comic sympathy in *A Busy Day* is unstable, moving "towards any character who is being thrust into a subordinate and inferior position" (*Frances Burney* 299). The limits of this shifting sympathy are clear, however. When Miss Watts, for all her unattractive faults, laughs at the end of this episode, the audience very definitely laughs with her—something that never occurs with Lady Wilhemina, who, with her husband, Sir Marmaduke, stands wholly outside the circle of comic sympathy.

In *A Busy Day*, Burney depicts an entrenched upper class that is self-serving and unfeeling. The rising middle class is hardly more attractive, except when its members are shown as victims or exposers of upper-class intolerance. Eliza, originating in one class but brought up in another, is left dangling awkwardly between the two, alienated from her roots but unable to escape them or to be wholly accepted in her new position.

In *The Woman-Hater*, Burney turns again to the plot of inheritance and the daughter removed from her origins in infancy, but with different results. Sir Roderick, jilted seventeen years ago by Miss Wilmot (now Lady Smatter, a widow) and incensed by his sister Eleonora's marriage soon after to Miss Wilmot's brother, has become a confirmed woman hater and plans to leave his estate to Young Waverley, a distant relation, on condition that he never marry. The opening scene reveals that Wilmot is coming home from the West Indies with his daughter, Sir Roderick's niece. Meanwhile Young Waverley has fallen for the beautiful daughter of a mysterious widow recently arrived in the district. The "widow," we discover later, is Eleonora. In contrast to the passive figure of the abandoned Caroline Belmont in *Evelina*, Eleonora fled from Wilmot's violent jealousy and wrongful accusation of infidelity, taking her daughter, Sophia, with her. The daughter Wilmot brings back to England is, in fact, the child of the Wilmots' nurse, substituted for their daughter just as Polly Green was substituted for Evelina. Polly Green, however, becomes the meek Miss Belmont, a shadowy figure conveniently married off to Evelina's half-brother Mr. McCartney, whereas Miss Wilmot, once revealed as Joyce, becomes a key figure in the play's commentary on class, gender, and inheritance.

The opening scene of act 2 takes place in a room at an inn, with a "table covered with Books. WILMOT is discovered reading, and MISS WILMOT with a Book in her hand" (211). Wilmot throws his book down and paces around, expressing his regret at his treatment of Eleonora, whom he now believes innocent; intermittently he speaks to Miss Wilmot, who is virtually monosyllabic throughout. Her father comments, "Poor fearful Girl! thy timidity subdues thy faculties!" (212; 2.1.28). When a message brought by a rural simpleton, Bob Sapling, causes Wilmot to leave the room, however, she transforms. Having checked with the nurse that he is out of earshot, she jumps up, singing:

> Then hoity, toity, whiskey, friskey,
> These are the joys of our dancing days—
>
> Come, now let's get rid of all this stupifying learning! so march off, Mr. Thompson! decamp, Mrs. Chapone! away, Watts' improvement of the mind, and off! off! off! with a hop, skip, and a jump, ye Ramblers, Spectators, and Adventurers! (*throwing about the Books, and dancing round them*) (214; 2.4.33–38)

Freed from her father's oppressive presence, Miss Wilmot gladly abandons the role of proper young lady. Boisterous and loud, she affectionately teases the nurse and flirts with Bob Sapling. In a later scene with her aunt, the literary-minded (but comically forgetful and imprecise) Lady Smatter, Miss Wilmot tells her she hates books and study. Lady Smatter asks, "Perhaps you hate every thing?" to which Miss Wilmot retorts, "O no, I don't. I like a great many things; but my first best favourite of all is dancing. It makes one so light, and so blyth . . . !" (239; 3.10.62–65). She then lists singing, swinging, walking, running, and jumping as among her favorite things and scandalizes her aunt with her vulgar fondness for food and drink: "And then, when one's famished, and empty,—how delightful are minced veal, and Pancakes! . . . And O! when one's parched, and faint—how delightful is a Glass of lemonade!—or Punch! Punch, Aunt!" (240; 3.10.99–100, 103–04).

In her playfulness and frank enjoyment of physical pleasures, the character of Miss Wilmot recalls the youthful Camilla, with a mind "which to dance, sing, and play could enliven to rapture" (*Camilla* 16), or indeed Jane Austen's ten-year-old Catherine Moreland, who "was . . . noisy and wild, hated confinement and cleanliness, and loved nothing so well in the world as rolling down the green slope at the back of the house" (*Northanger Abbey* 2). Both Camilla and Catherine, no less than Miss Wilmot, have to learn to suppress these aspects of their characters as they grow into young women, but where the two former succeed (if that is the right word) in internalizing enough of propriety to enable them to act it convincingly and to gain the approval of the men in their lives, Miss Wilmot only ever learns to feign proper femininity temporarily and abandons it whenever she gets the chance. Darby astutely identifies problems with Burney's critique of class here:

> While Burney's characterization of Joyce suggests that gentility can be successfully imitated, it also reveals a sense that there is a "natural" class identity that specifies Joyce's social place as closer to that of the nurse than to Sophia, Wilmot, or Lady Smatter. . . . The qualities of lower-class people are repeatedly characterized here as predominantly physical and almost belligerently anti-intellectual. . . . All the talk in the play of the books that represent "culture" implies that class positions are constructed rather than inherent, yet we are reminded that Joyce is able to take on the physical trappings of gentility, but few of the intellectual ones. (159–60)

Darby's reservations are understandable, but elements in *The Woman-Hater* and comparison with *A Busy Day* indicate that there may yet be more to be said.

After the initial shock, Miss Wilmot experiences her change of status not as a disaster but as a liberation. The nurse, once she knows that Eleonora and Sophia are in the neighborhood, realizes that her deception will be discovered and decides to tell her daughter the truth about her origins. Bursting into tears, Miss Wilmot sobs:

> What must I do?—what will become of me?—I can't scrub rooms . . . And I can't turn ballad singer, and—(*suddenly brightening*) yes, I can, though! that I can, Nurse! and if I must be something—I had rather be a ballad singer than anything else. (251; 4.8.81–85)

After this scene, Miss Wilmot becomes Joyce in the stage directions. Joyce sees nothing but advantage in the new state of affairs, rejoicing in her release from the restrictions of living the life of a proper lady and relieved to find that the nurse she has always loved is her mother, while the father she has always feared and who has required such alien behavior from her is not related to her at all.

It is true, as Darby says, that Joyce roundly rejects the intellectual trappings of gentility. The nurse urges her to get Sir Roderick to settle some money on her, while he still believes that she is his niece. Joyce tells Sir Roderick that such an old man can't have much use for money, whereas she will "whisk it about! I'll go to plays, . . . —I'll go to puppet-shews,—I'll see all the wild beasts, I'll eat all the tarts at the Pastry Cooks" (267–68; 5.4.88–91). Sir Roderick is outraged until she promises to make a "gigantic bonfire of all Aunt Smatter's Books and Authors," to which he cries, "Will you, faith?" and leaves Joyce triumphant (268). But if Joyce has no time for books, she has taken more from her upbringing than simply the ability to "take on the physical trappings of gentility." In the first half of the play, in the presence of all but her supposed father, she clearly has a confidence and a habit of command resulting from her social position, and this attitude does not desert her when she learns of her real birth. She tells the nurse she plans to marry Bob Sapling:

> *Nurse.* Fie, Miss, fie! if I a'n't ashamed to hear you!
>
> *Joyce.* Why he's as good as I am! so I won't be cooped up any longer. I want my liberty, Nurse!
>
> *Nurse.* O, my dear,—
>
> *Joyce.* Don't contradict me, I say, for I'll marry Bob!—I shall like that a great deal better than always studying Books; and sitting with my hands before me; and making courtsies; and never eating half as much as I like,—except in the Pantry!—And I'll make Bob do everything I bid him; and you shall be my house-keeper! (275; 5.12.23–31)

The desire to marry as part of a desire for liberty is one generally treated with healthy skepticism—if not downright contempt—in Burney's work. The narrator in *Camilla* is plainly irritated by the foolish Miss Dennel, who languishes "for the complete power which she imagined a house and servants of her own would afford" (391). Yet for Bob and Joyce in *The Woman-Hater*, the notion does not seem so far-fetched, since marriage would offer Joyce an escape from values she had been forced to accept.

Although Eliza and Joyce have both been transplanted from one social class to another as infants, their situations are very different, as the plays' endings indicate particularly graphically. Eliza and Cleveland's love story is at the crux of *A Busy Day*. Accordingly, at the end of the play, Eliza and her marriage are central to the play's resolution, even if that resolution is somewhat strained by the clash between the vulgarity of Eliza's original family and the snobbery of Cleveland's, especially of his aunt, Lady Wilhemina.

In *The Woman-Hater*, by contrast, no one couple is central to the resolution. At the end of the play, Joyce stands outside the resolution; despite her avowed intention to marry Bob, he is not on stage in the final scene. There is no shortage of couples for the closing tableau: Sir Roderick and Lady Smatter, Wilmot and Eleonora, and Young Waverley and Sophia are all paired up. Joyce is alone, however—Bob was last seen being chased off stage by Sir Roderick, and the nurse ran away from Wilmot when her deception was revealed. Wilmot dutifully assures Joyce "of [his] inalterable interest in [her] welfare" (282; 5.22.4–5), so we know that she will be provided for even if Sir Roderick's money goes elsewhere (as Joyce thinks likely—seeing him again she remarks humorously, "La! it's old Sir Roderick that was going to give me so many thousand pounds!" [282; 5.23.22–23]).

The end of *The Woman-Hater* suggests the difficulty of assimilating Joyce into the comic resolution. Neither of the people she loves would fit into the group who are onstage in the final scene; certainly neither of them could accept Lady Smatter's invitation to "adjourn to [her] house" (285; 5.23.111). Just what Joyce's social position will be remains unclear; the kind of provision Wilmot intends is unspoken. Eliza internalizes the mores of her adopted class; Joyce's resistance and her choice of Bob could suggest "innate" class characteristics, but given the contrary example of Eliza in a work composed during the same period, Joyce can also be read as the expression of a playful yet earnest rejection of the restrictions of gentility.

Anna Lott

Elizabeth Inchbald's Revolutionary Writings

During the last third of her life, Elizabeth Inchbald became increasingly concerned with public conflicts and events. Her final diaries chronicle events in France throughout the Napoleonic era. In 1792, she wrote *The Massacre*, a never-performed play about the French Revolution and the resulting violence to the family unit that occurs. *The Massacre* portrays the helplessness of individual family members (and their ideals) when faced with the Paris mob. The play was suppressed from publication or performance because of its pointed social criticism: the tragedy was considered too controversial for performance, and George Woodfall and John Robinson "resolved to suppress it altogether" from publication (Boaden 2: 305). Although *The Massacre* was read by some as reactionary, Inchbald's stance seems clearly progressive in a later unpublished play, *A Case of Conscience* (1800), set in Spain during the Inquisition. Inchbald had intended *A Case of Conscience* to be performed by her friends Sarah Siddons and John Kemble at Drury Lane Theatre, but Kemble had quarreled with the proprietors there, as well as those of Covent Garden, and James Boaden explains that the play "fell to the ground in the change of scene and contention, and was never acted" (2: 295). *A Case of Conscience* depicts

Inchbald's fear of despotism, encapsulated in a tyrannical father so moved by jealousy that he nearly causes the tragic dissolution of his family. The family's private struggle to resolve its "case of conscience" echoes larger themes in contemporary politics and suggests the great damage caused by public despots such as Louis XVI and Napoléon.

Perhaps in response to the fate of plays such as *A Case of Conscience* and *The Massacre*, Inchbald later argued in her 1807 letter to the journal the *Artist* that it is easier to write novels than plays because the novelist is not subject to uncertainties such as official censorship, actors' performances, and audience response. Thus, "whilst the poor dramatist is . . . confined to a few particular provinces . . . the novel-writer has the whole world to range" (348). Like many other dramatists, Inchbald often negotiated these constraints by disguising her plays' subject matter in adaptations of already established works or works with exotic settings that would not be associated easily with her liberal stance. (An exception to this method was her successful play *Such Things Are* [1787], which, as George Taylor has noted, "combined radical content with an identifiable portrait . . . John Howard, the penal reformer imprisoned himself in France during the seven-years war" [38]). In *A Case of Conscience*, Inchbald uses the historical and remote setting of the Spanish Inquisition to blur—but not entirely to hide—her disgust with arbitrary tyranny, both private and public. In *The Massacre*, as Wendy C. Nielsen has observed, Inchbald "[t]hrough footnotes . . . veils these specific events [the September Massacres] and sets *The Massacre* in a town outside sixteenth-century Paris during the massacre of the Protestants, a curious choice for a Catholic writer" (280).

Inchbald's liberal stance is apparent in much of her writing (her plays, novels, letters, and diaries), yet also clearly evident is her dislike of any sort of public or private violence. Boaden writes that "however the new doctrines might attract her, she has expressed with suitable horror her utter detestation of the murderers of the King and Queen of France" (1: 314). This detestation is particularly evident in a letter that Inchbald wrote to Frances Phillips on 26 August 1813, lamenting the death of Germaine de Staël's son, who was killed in a duel while acting as an aide de camp to Napoléon's marshal, Jean-Baptiste Bernadotte. In the letter, Inchbald remarks that a few days before this calamity, she had visited Staël and had envied her blissful relationship with her children—a relationship that Inchbald, who had no children, would never experience: "she [Staël] then so forcibly depicted a mother's joys, that she sent me home more melancholy at the comparison of our situations in life than could have arisen from the consequences of riches or poverty." When Inchbald visited Staël again, two days later, she was told that her friend was ill and would not see her. She read of Staël's son's death in the next morning's newspaper. In the letter, Inchbald extols the son's virtues and his position in Staël's extended family, including her father, Jacques Necker, finance minister to Louis XVI. Staël's son was, Inchbald bewails, "the most beautiful young man that ever was seen, only nineteen,—a duel with sabres, and the first stroke literally cut off his *head* / Necker's grandson."

Evidently, Inchbald did not view violence as an appropriate solution to tyranny: she described its far-reaching, destructive effects in plays such as *The Massacre* and in her letters, novels, and pocket diaries. And though Inchbald struggled to find an effective, nonviolent response to despotism, she seems to locate in the individual family unit a model for appropriate, nondespotic governance that could extend to the public sphere. She hoped that changes in the immediate family would affect the extended family and that those family members would influence a larger, even global, community. In her play *Every One Has His Fault* (1793), for example, the despotic father, Lord Norland, is influenced by his son-in-law Irwin's apparent suicide to forgive his daughter for her socially unequal marriage and to accept Irwin into the family. According to Matthew J. Kinservik, Norland learns that "while vice is bad, it must be understood and sympathetically corrected, not punished" (207). This lesson begins in the family and then extends to larger issues of justice and punishment. As Annibel Jenkins explains, the situation of the impoverished Irwin (who has returned home after fighting for the British in the American Revolution) "is a comment on the army as well as his father-in-law" (336). Norland's inhumane treatment of his family is analogous to the actions of the inhumane public militia that for Inchbald functioned as kind of negligent, cruel father.

In Inchbald's novel *Nature and Art* (1796), we see a similar insistence on understanding and forgiving individual transgressions; here the form of the novel enables Inchbald to make unambiguous her social statement. *Nature and Art* spans three generations, and the list of characters includes a son named William, who has received from his father both affluence and an unquestioning assumption of his own privilege. William abandons his pregnant lover, Hannah, who ultimately becomes a prostitute and a thief so that she can support herself and her son. At the end of the novel, William, who has become a powerful judge, sentences Hannah to death for an inept attempt at counterfeiting money. When Hannah is brought before William for sentencing, he does not recognize her, so drastically altered is her appearance by poverty, aging, and hard labor. Like Irwin in *Every One Has His Fault*, the forsaken Hannah is driven by poverty to steal; unlike Irwin, she does not receive forgiveness or even recognition from her accuser. As Shawn Lisa Maurer notes in her introduction to *Nature and Art*, the depiction of Hannah's fate "anticipates recent feminist criticism by demonstrating the crucial intersection of gender and class" (19): men do not become pregnant, and they do not generally become prostitutes. Because of William's moral blindness, he misses an essential opportunity not just to rescue Hannah but also to practice a form of individual philanthropy that could redeem Hannah and future generations. (Hannah's son dies from grief shortly after her execution.)

In the same novel, Inchbald offers a depiction of William's cousin Henry and Henry's wife Rebecca that serves as a powerful alternative to William's self-serving ideology. At the end of the novel, Henry and Rebecca discuss the idyllic state of their own poverty when compared with the stresses caused by wealth and social prominence—stresses encountered by William and also by Norland in *Every One Has His Fault*. Henry pronounces at the end of *Nature and Art* that social injustices are reinforced by unconsidered adoration of wealth and all of its trappings—an adoration perpetuated by both rich and poor: "Let the poor," he argues, "no more be their own persecutors—no longer pay homage to wealth—instantaneously the whole idolatrous worship will cease—the idol will be broken" (154). The novel leaves open the possibility that the children of Henry and Rebecca might lead the way to a more egalitarian future, one based on merit not wealth, in which individuals take responsibility for one another.

The daily accounts in Inchbald's private pocket diaries seem to reinforce this model of using personal actions to instigate broad social change, particularly her association of her private world with the public and political unconscious. In the diaries (available in the Folger Library and in a recent edition by Ben P. Robertson published by Pickering and Chatto), Inchbald records private events such as tea with a friend concomitantly with public milestones such as the birthdays and deaths of royalty (in England and abroad). If we consider her diaries as an intentionally crafted series of narratives, rather than as a haphazard collection of temporal observations, then the order in which she records public and private events (as well as the specifics she chooses to include in each entry) becomes a significant detail that helps shape our understanding of her political and private attitudes. Personal events (news of a family member) frequently appear on the same page as entries about public figures or events. Inchbald often includes herself as spectator when she describes historical events about which she is not individually concerned. On 25 January 1808, for example, she notes that the "funeral of Lord Trafalgar passed going to St. Pauls" (*Diaries* 83). In other entries, her observations seem more immediate and private, as when she notes on 14 August 1807 that "a child fell down . . . opposite me in Somerset House and was killed" (47). (Later in the same entry, she repeats the information, this time identifying the child as female, stating simply that "a little girl [was] killed opposite my window.") Inchbald's other diary entries for the same week contextualize the child's death in both the public sphere (Napoléon's "return to Paris," which was "in the paper" on 11 August) and Inchbald's private sphere (copying her will on 12 August and, on the same day, having dinner with her sister Dolly and quarreling "about Bonaparte").

The inclusion of the details of her private life ("beef tea for dinner wine and water for supper" [48]) in the context of public events ("the Prince of Wales's birthday" [47]) suggests that Inchbald did not view her private life as necessarily separate from the public events that she read about in the newspaper and addressed in her published writings. The diaries function, certainly, as a memoir of Inchbald's personal history, but they also blur the distinction between personal and political. Inchbald purposefully saved her diaries, and, though her intended audience is unclear, Katherine S. Green has suggested in an intriguing footnote that Inchbald, always concerned with her public persona, actually edited her diaries, with the apparent expectation that they would be scrutinized later:

> A close comparison of Inchbald's and Godwin's diaries for 1793 raises the suspicion that at some later date Inchbald copied her diary over, possibly editing out some material. The date tabs at the edge of her "Pocket Memorandum Book" have been razored off, and there are discrepancies in the number of Godwin's visits and the dates she records for them, as compared with those he records.
> ("Mr. Harmony" 50n14)

Green's suggestion that Inchbald significantly edited her diaries challenges some of our earlier assumptions about Inchbald's personal life and her political stances. Inchbald's often quoted 1779 journal entry written in the year of her husband's death—"began this year a happy wife . . . finished it a wretched widow" (Boaden 1: 104)—may indeed be a type of performance meant to leave Inchbald's audience with the impression that she was an inconsolable private widow instead of a public, pragmatic figure who resumed acting on the stage just weeks after her husband's demise.

Women who kept any sort of journal in the eighteenth century were, as Felicity A. Nussbaum has suggested, using the form of the diary to express themselves in a way that a public forum would not allow. "In writing to themselves, eighteenth-century women . . . could create a private place in which to speak the unthought, unsaid, and undervalued" (154). According to Nussbaum's logic, Inchbald's diaries might have been intentionally obscure, intentionally deviant from an established form that Inchbald had clearly mastered. Hélène Cixous has explored the possibility of a female form of writing that is inexplicable to an audience accustomed to an ordered syntax:

> Such is the strength of women that, sweeping away syntax, breaking from the famous thread (just a tiny little thread, they say) which acts for men as a surrogate umbilical cord . . . women will go right up to the impossible. (886)

In Inchbald's novel *A Simple Story*, Miss Milner also deviates from established forms of expression, relying on gesture and facial expression instead of the more linear, verbal forms of expression used by the men of the novel—Dorriforth and his mentor, Sandford. As Eleanor Ty has argued:

> The pre-verbal, semiotic language of gestures, exclamations, looks, and manners, which would have been particularly familiar to Inchbald, who had dramatic training, constitutes a large part of Miss Milner's means of communication and is an element of her attractiveness and her enigma. (90)

Miss Milner's reliance on theatrical conventions is reminiscent of the author's career on the stage, during which Inchbald worked to overcome a serious speech impediment. As she explains in the preface to *A Simple Story*:

> [I]t has been the destiny of the writer of this Story, to be occupied throughout her life, in what has the least suited either her inclination or capacity—with an invincible impediment in her speech, it was her lot for thirteen years to gain subsistence by public speaking. (55)

As Dwight Codr has noticed, Inchbald's description of "vocal stuttering" is particularly striking in a preface to a "literary work" (368). Codr's essay considers *Nature and Art* and *A Simple Story* through the prism of disability studies. Offering another perspective, Emily Hodgson Anderson has challenged us to view Inchbald's stammer in the first performance of her play *The Mogul Tale* (1784) as "a performance within a performance, a feigned recreation of a defect for which she was well known that serves, perhaps, as a purposeful yet subtle puff for her play" ("Revising" 18). Inchbald, according to Anderson, may have intentionally called attention to herself as author of the play first by her stammer and then by her subsequent nervous laughter. Anderson's essay suggests an understanding not only of Inchbald's performative career but also of the theatricality in *A Simple Story* and other works, including her novel *Nature and Art*, her diaries, her plays, and her essays.

A Case of Conscience, though never performed, functioned as another kind of forum enabling Inchbald's developed and nuanced reactions to the incidents she recorded in her diaries. Set in Spain during the Inquisition, *A Case of Conscience* is about a husband's complicated ploy to gain revenge for his wife's supposed adultery. The play is reminiscent of Shakespeare's *Othello*, a tragedy that Inchbald admired in *The British Theatre*; she writes in her preface to the play that she appreciates Shakespeare's skill in "delineating the rise and progress in the human breast that a young and elegant female is here represented, by his magic pen, as deeply in love with a Moor,—a man different in complexion and features from her and her whole race" (5: n. pag.). In *A Case of Conscience*, Adriana and Romono are divided not by race but by the fact that Adriana's father has already betrothed her to another man, Cordunna. Adriana explains to the priest who secretly married her and Romono that "Romono, the Marquis of Romono, came from the field of glory, and with superior claims of person as of fame, seized on my heart by force, and perforce made me feel I had never loved till then" (308; act 2, sc. 1). At the play's beginning, Adriana and Romono have been happily married for seventeen years, but Romono, like Othello, is made vulnerable by his inability to trust his wife's fidelity, a vulnerability that Bonnie Nelson has identified as typical of what she terms "Othello plays" (132–67), a group of plays written between 1729 and 1739 that echoed Shakespeare's play in both plot and message. The Othello plays documented by Nelson clearly prefigure *A Case of Conscience*. Inchbald's Cordunna, like Shakespeare's Iago, plans and executes a revengeful plot against the married couple, presenting to the jealous Romono seemingly incontrovertible evidence of Adriana's betrayal. Instead of a handkerchief, the smoking gun is a miniature portrait of Adriana that Cordunna claims Adriana has recently given to him. Romono, like Othello, is easily duped by the ploy and plans revenge against his wife. Romono's intended victim, however, is not the supposedly unfaithful wife but the couple's son, Oviedo, mistakenly believed to be the child of Cordunna and Adriana. Romono sends a message to the Grand Inquisitor ordering that Oviedo be imprisoned and sentenced to death because of his mother's supposed adultery.

In the play's first scene, we see that a culture of violence surrounds not only Romono and Adriana but also Oviedo, who is returning from fighting in Portugal, presumably participating in the ongoing struggle for Spanish occupation. According to Oviedo's servant, Girone, "in our very last engagement we stormed and took a city" (297; 1.1). After Oviedo's return from the war, we see that his aggressive martial feats have been inspired by his intense need to please his father. Oviedo explains that his military decorations are significant only if his father approves of them: without this approval, "they would in my estimation hang like the gaudy trappings of a may-day puppet, and I should blush at the decoration" (315; 2.1). Oviedo's triumphant homecoming is tainted by his father's mistaken belief that his mother is an adulteress. When Romono announces that "this son *shall* be the sacrifice for her guilty love" (343; 4.2), Oviedo becomes the potential victim of the sort of atrocity he had perpetuated in battle in his attempts to gain Romono's favor.

Oviedo's courtship of Eudora, to whom he has been betrothed since childhood, seems almost inevitably as violent as his parents' apparently was. When Girone rescues Eudora from the convent where Romono has sent her, the liberation is so sudden, violent, and uninvited that it resembles abduction rather than the welcome release Oviedo had intended. Girone brags, "Don't you hear the sound of distress in that bell, and see it in the black flag displayed on the roof? We have terrified the nuns, half-killed the abbess, and taken the fair Eudora prisoner" (330; 4.1). Girone defensively attributes his aggressive methods to the example Oviedo set on the battlefield: "It was following you to the camp which taught me these arts" (332; 4.1). Oviedo's perception of himself is more peaceful than that held by Girone, and he insists that his "designs were to do nothing by force; but all by gentle means" (331; 4.1). Oviedo's public battlefield persona, however, has led Girone to assume otherwise and to kidnap rather than liberate Eudora.

When I teach *A Case of Conscience*, the violence surrounding Oviedo's and Romono's private courtships and public battles causes my students to lack sympathy for either of the men, although they do acknowledge that

Oviedo may be trapped somehow by the oppressive masculine ethos created and maintained by Romono. Students also lack sympathy for Lord Elmwood in *A Simple Story* during a horrific scene of violence against Lady Elmwood's former lover, Lord Lawnley, that leaves Lawnley "so maimed, and defaced with scars, as never again to endanger the honour of a husband" (225). In describing Elmwood's vindictive, frenzied behavior, Inchbald shows her deep concern for the perpetrator of violence as much as her concern for the recipient of the violence. Students' disgust with Romono is similarly increased after the following graphic and cruel speech by the Marquis:

> Heaven is my witness, Manuel, I bear the young man no resentment. (*pathetic*) His parents are the persons I mean to slay in his execution; his mother and his father—Cordunna and Adriana! (*raging*) The groans of the youth shall sound in their ears, and reach their guilty hearts—and while the ministers of justice shall bind him to the instruments of torture, shall lacerate his tender flesh, or dislocate his well-formed joints—then—then—(*Case* 337; 4.2)

When my students encounter this impassioned and conflicted speech, they immediately rely on anachronisms to describe Romono's paranoia and suspicion: "verbal abuse," "relationship violence," even "child abuse." When they finish the play, many are horrified, not delighted, to discover Romono reunited with his family, telling his wife, Adriana, to turn "from that sight of horror!" where Oviedo was to have been tortured. Romono's eventual remorse does little to redeem him. This "honeymoon phase," my students predict, will be short-lived and will return to the erratic rage and confusion Romono displayed at the play's beginning.

Without denying the truth of these familiar patterns, I try to guide students to a more sympathetic understanding of Romono's internal battle, a battle caused by false information given to him by Cordunna. Romono's jealous fury is consistently mitigated by his obvious struggle to disguise or suppress his love for his family. His responses vacillate rapidly between "trembling" for his son's safety and "looking sternly" at Adriana, but he consistently longs to "trust the power [Oviedo] has over [his] heart" (339; 3.3). Inchbald emphasizes the frightening power of the despot while simultaneously revealing that his masculine masquerade disguises paternal feelings that in the end drive his choices. As he explains to Oviedo, "It is my reason that has erred. My heart always acknowledged thee" (350; 5.2).

Romono's struggle and the play's eventual happy ending are reminiscent of Inchbald's drama *Wives as They Were, and Maids as They Are* (1797), in which we see a struggle similar to that undergone by Romono; when the patriarch Sir William stands by as the authorities take his daughter to jail because of her gambling debts, we watch him struggle to maintain a self-protective, uncompromising facade that hides his paternal love (see Lott, Introduction 40). As Miss Dorrillon leaves for prison, she says, "I forgive you," though she does not yet know the disguised Sir William is her father. When she is gone, Sir William says, "And perhaps I can forgive you. But I must not. No, this is justice—This is my Duty—this is strength of mind. This is fortitude—fortitude—fortitude" (68; act 4, sc. 3). Like Romono in *A Case of Conscience*, Sir William realizes near the play's end that he has mistakenly trusted a linear logic (a reason "that has erred") instead of his instinctive love for his daughter. Inchbald explores similar masculine struggles between reason and emotion in her novel *A Simple Story*, where Elmwood protects himself from any sort of paternal emotion when he allows his daughter, Matilda, to stay in his house but only on the condition that she never come within his sight. Our recognition of Elmwood's genuine concern for his daughter must be based on almost unrecognizable hints, such as the care that Elmwood takes in choosing books for her female servant, Miss Woodley. The narrator tells us that Miss Woodley "reasonably supposed Matilda's reading, and not hers, was the object of his solicitude" (288; see Lott, Introduction 38). Elmwood's genuine love for his family is most evident when Matilda faints in Elmwood's arms. Elmwood is so distraught that he can barely speak (reminiscent, again, of Inchbald's speech impediment), and "his long-restrained tears burst forth" before he can manage to command his servant to remove Matilda's grasp from his coat (289).

Though in many of her novels and plays, Inchbald depicts despotic patriarchal control as dangerous and initially inflexible, in *A Case of Conscience* she specifically alludes to issues central to revolutionary rhetoric in 1790s France, such as the legal tyranny of parents and especially the tyranny inherent in the lettre de cachet, a sealed letter authorizing imprisonment or death of a named person, often a family member of the letter's author. For Inchbald and others, the lettre de cachet functioned as a metonym for despotism in England. As Lynn Hunt explains:

> Images of state and familial power were perhaps most closely intertwined in the controversy over lettres de cachet that developed during the eighteenth century. The king could use lettres de cachet to

> imprison or exile anyone who threatened public order, and lettres de cachet could be solicited by parents to incarcerate their children, without a hearing, for the sake of familial order and reputation. (*Family Romance* 19)

Lettres de cachet had been abolished after the French Revolution but were reinstituted by Napoléon. In a famous lettre de cachet, Honoré Mirabeau's father wrote a letter ordering his imprisonment in the dungeon at Vicennes. Mirabeau's writings on lettres de cachet (*Des lettres de cachet et des prison d'état* [1782]), published after his release from prison, were translated into English and widely circulated in England under the title *Enquiries concerning Lettres de Cachet: The Consequences of Arbitrary Imprisonment, and a History of the Inconveniences, Distresses, and Sufferings of State Prisoners: Written in the Dungeon of the Castle of Vincennes* (1787). Excerpts from this translation help students of *A Case of Conscience* contextualize Oviedo's predicament and Romono's anguish. Mirabeau argues that "wherever despotism prevails," people will be vulnerable to "spies, informers, and an effectual inquisition, decorated with a milder name; and it will always be on the reports of such men, branded with infamy as they are, that Lettres de Cachet will in general be issued" (21).

The Inquisition in *A Case of Conscience* echoes Mirabeau's description of an "effectual inquisition." In *A Case of Conscience*, Romono sends a message to the grand inquisitor ordering that Oviedo be imprisoned and sentenced to death: "Take this ring as a proof you come from me; and to my message add, that the rightful posterity of a noble house depends upon this my request" (343; 4.2). Later Romono explains to a priest who has been a longtime family friend and adviser:

> I yield him up to the full rage of the inquisition; Let the holy council know I do; and add in secrecy, that though, as his nominal father, I cannot sit as one of the judges in his cause, yet, would custom allow me to give a vote in his punishment, it would be death. (336; 4.2)

When Oviedo learns scattered pieces of his father's letter and his actions, he assumes naively that any message from his parent must be for his benefit. After Oviedo has been taken prisoner by the guards of the Inquisition, a servant explains to Romono that "they hold him in such close custody, they will permit no one to speak to him: but he requests most anxiously to have an audience with you" (337; 4.2).

When Oviedo understands what Romono has done, he confronts his father and invokes the family, particularly Adriana, in his plea for mercy:

> And will my father, without one effort, yield me up to the rigid trials of an Inquisition. . . . And must I expiate my faults not only by death, but by ignominy? Oh! If not for the honour of your noble family—your former love to me—my reverence toward you—for my mother's sake!— (338; 4.2)

Oviedo's unwitting reference to his supposedly adulterous mother only increases Romono's anger, which so confuses Oviedo that he cannot finish his sentences when he discusses his estrangement from his father. He explains to Adriana that he received "a cold reception" from his father (324). To Romono, he stutters, "My Lord, I—I—, please your Lordship" (325; 3.3). Oviedo's halting speech delays Romono's quest to have his son tortured and murdered, and it creates in the audience a sympathy for Oviedo that spectators would not necessarily have if they based their judgment solely on his triumphs in battle.

Romono's letter brings to mind an incident from Inchbald's novel *A Simple Story*, in which Miss Milner (now Lady Elmwood) leaves a deathbed letter asking her husband to accept their daughter, Matilda, into his household despite Miss Milner's former adultery. The letter is as successful as Miss Milner might have hoped; Lord Elmwood agrees to grant the letter's request that Matilda be allowed to live in his house, as long as he never has to see her. For Matilda, who has no knowledge that the letter effectively sentences her to a kind of prison, the letter functions as a lettre de cachet similar to the one Romono writes in *A Case of Conscience*. When Matilda is asked if she knows what her mother's request was, she replies, "Not entirely. But she told me her letter concerned none but me" (241). Yet the letter requires that Matilda must (by her mother's decree) live in the house of a despotic man she has only briefly met and who will not acknowledge her presence or even her existence. Matilda's figurative imprisonment resembles Oviedo's literal imprisonment in *A Case of Conscience*. In both works, the familial struggle is resolved finally by a renewed appreciation of responsibility to the second generation but only after a good deal of anguish and suffering.

A few of my students notice the grace displayed by the wrongly accused Adriana, a part that was to have been played by Inchbald's friend Siddons, renowned for a stage presence so powerful that her audience either left the theater in tears or fainted and had to be carried away. Inchbald, in her preface to Nicholas Rowe's *Tamerlane*, explains that Siddons's performance evoked such strong psychological or even physical responses because her portrayal was so convincingly realistic:

> Mrs. Siddons has, indeed, the power of inspiring a degree of horrible wonder in the dying scene; when, dropping down dead at the Sultan's feet, she gives, by the manner and disposition of her fall, such assurance of her having suddenly expired, that an auditor of a lively imagination casts up his eyes to heaven, as if to catch a view of her departed spirit. (10: n. pag.)

As Julie Carlson has noted, Siddons was able to sustain such forceful illusions by maintaining a public persona as the epitome of beauty and intelligence: "the most famous actress of her period, Sarah Siddons, is celebrated for her strength of intellect, dignity, force, and the nature of her beauty is characterized as both feminine and sublime" ("Remaking" 291). Siddons's performances swayed not only her individual audience but also, according to Shearer West, a larger political climate:

> [I]n a culture undergoing an epidemic of private and public crises, with the madness of George III, the profligacy of the Prince of Wales, the "delicate investigation" into the Princess of Wales' infidelity and an anxiety about radical thinking in the wake of events in France, Siddons provided order amidst the chaos. (208)

An Adriana played by Siddons would have offered a powerful model of forgiveness and hope that emphasized Inchbald's optimistic vision.

Inchbald particularly admired the didacticism of Siddons and her brother Kemble (who was to play Romono in *A Case of Conscience*). In her preface to Shakespeare's *Macbeth*, Inchbald writes admiringly of the pair's performance in the play:

> [T]he agonizing throbs and throes, which speak in looks and whispers, sudden starts, and writhings, by Kemble and Mrs. Siddons, all tending to one great precept—Thou shalt not murder,—render this play one of the most impressive moral lessons which the stage exhibits. (4: n. pag.)

Since Inchbald intended to cast *A Case of Conscience* with the same actors she admired in *Macbeth*, it seems likely that she had a similar "moral lesson" in mind for her play, although her choice to end it with redemption rather than tragedy emphasizes her hopeful confidence for her nation.

At the moment when Romono has been informed of his son's imprisonment by the Inquisition, Adriana confronts him with the widely divergent consequences of his potential actions. Her speech expresses exactly what is at stake not only for Romono and his family but also for a nation facing the beginnings of the Napoleonic Wars:

> I am come to kneel or rave! To be most humble, or most haughty! All gratitude, or all indignation! To love, or to hate you, Romono, while thought retains its station. Which of all these will your conduct exact? You know the subject—answer me. Am I to live a mother, bless'd beyond heaven's common bounty in my offspring? Or am I in a few days, or hours perhaps, to become childless? (*Case* 341; 4.2)

Because Adriana rises above Romono's accusations, forgiving him even as he threatens her and her family, she saves her family from dissolution, and her power echoes the political and social sphere of influence that Inchbald and others granted to any stage performance. When Adriana is told that her son (whom Cordunna describes to her as "*your* pride, and the nation's glory") is dead by her husband's decree, Adriana insists on being taken immediately to Romono: "to console him for his loss—to join my tears with his—he will require my comfort" (347; 5.2). Even in the moment of her greatest anguish (before she learns Oviedo is alive), Adriana does not insist on revenge for Romono's crime. Instead, she offers a powerful model of forgiveness and hope that would have influenced her audience as much as it does Romono in the play.

A similar moment of understanding and mercy occurs in *A Simple Story* when father and daughter are reconciled despite their relationship marked by turbulence and despotism. Inchbald's narrator speculates that "these were the happiest moments she had ever known—perhaps the happiest *he* had ever known" (334). At the end of the novel, when Elmwood's nephew asks for Matilda's hand in marriage, Elmwood demonstrates his moral growth when he allows his daughter to choose her own life partner: "on your will his fate shall depend" (340). By enabling Matilda to direct her future and that of his nephew, Elmwood establishes a pattern of trust and goodwill that will extend well beyond this particular generation. Like *A Case of Conscience, A Simple Story* conveys an optimistic message, as Siddons did on the stage. Likewise, Inchbald's stage presence as well as her diaries, novels, essays, and plays function collectively as a kind of personal memoir of her aspirations and hopes.

Part IV

Comparative Approaches

Pilar Cuder-Domínguez

Gender, Race, and Party Politics in the Tragedies of Behn, Pix, and Manley

Many early modern women dramatists tried their hand at writing tragedy. Jane Lumley translated Euripides's *Iphigenia at Aulis* around 1550. Mary Sidney closely adapted Robert Garnier in her *Tragedie of Antonie* in 1592, making it the first play by an Englishwoman to be published, while Katherine Philips's adaptation of Pierre Corneille's *Pompey* became the first play by a woman to be staged in the commercial theater. The first original play written by an Englishwoman was also a tragedy: Elizabeth Cary's *The Tragedie of Mariam* (1613). Some writers wrote mostly tragedies rather than comedies, like Catharine Trotter and Delarivier Manley (see Findlay and Hodgson-Wright).

As the seventeenth century wore on, the theory and practice of tragedy—and, indeed, of all drama—in England underwent considerable transformation. French theorists and practitioners such as Corneille contributed to rethinking the themes and conventions of tragedy, and John Dryden aimed to reformulate the field in England. Although Dryden's 1677 tragedy *All for Love* would bear a long-lasting influence on the English stage, with its account of a hero torn between public duty and private desire, during the previous decade Dryden had staged several heroic plays, from *The Indian Queen* (1664) to *Aureng-Zebe* (1674). It was in this period that women playwrights entered the public stage and became professionalized. In the season of 1670–71, three women boldly premiered their plays: Frances Boothby, Elizabeth Polwhele, and Aphra Behn. Of them only the last would go on to fulfill her promise and make her living by the pen.

Behn was aware that she was writing for a theater world that had been revitalized by the introduction of women players and renovated by the use of mechanical contraptions, such as shutters (with powerful scene-changing effects), that came to join the more traditional but always entertaining use of music and dance. She was also quick to pick on themes and trends, introducing, for example, exotic settings, particularly in combination with heroic plots. The exoticism of Mediterranean cultures had made a strong impression on Restoration London theatergoers since William Davenant's *The Siege of Rhodes* (1663), and it was rekindled in the 1670s by plays like Dryden's *The Conquest of Granada* (1671) and Elkanah Settle's *The Empress of Morocco* (1673). Yet this development can hardly be considered new, since Restoration writers were tapping into a spatter of Elizabethan and Jacobean plays on the Mediterranean Muslim kingdoms. Trade with the Mediterranean region had prospered in the late sixteenth century so that the English had increasingly more contact with Muslim trade partners, particularly the Kingdom of Morocco and the Ottoman Empire. These locations, though dangerous, offered beguiling prospects to enterprising subjects (Vitkus 29–31). Not surprisingly, Moors and Turks were soon featured in the plays of the time with similarly ambivalent connotations, awakening fear and admiration.

In the season of 1670, Behn decided to use these materials by adapting the anonymous 1661 play *Lust's Dominion; or, The Lascivious Queen*, set in medieval Spain and featuring Christians and Moors involved in a heroic plot, like Dryden's *The Conquest of Granada* (see Cuder-Domínguez, "Of Spain"). *Abdelazer; or, The Moor's Revenge* (1677) follows the conventions of revenge tragedy: the Moorish prince of the title has been deprived of his inheritance by the Spanish royal family and now seeks revenge on them by exploiting Queen Isabella's passion for him. Playing the several parties at court against each other, Abdelazer manages to wreck the kingdom before dying a villain's death. At the death of the old king, two opposing concepts of monarchy emerged at court, each of them represented by one of the young princes. Ferdinand, the older son, privileges private joys over the public good and would rather devote all his energies to lovemaking. The younger brother, Philip, appropriately bears the old king's name, for he boasts the same kind of soldierly feats of conquest that brought his father his laurels. Philip is just arrived from the wars to find that his father has died, and, much like Hamlet, his words highlight his mother's wantonness and his father's warrior virtue:

> My Father whilst he liv'd, tir'd his strong Arm
> With numerous Battles 'gainst the Enemy,
> . . . .
> Whilst you, . . .
> . . . .
> Suffer'd his Bed to be defil'd with Lust,
> Give up your Self, your honour, and your vows,
> To wanton in yon Sooty Lecher's arms.
> (255; act 1, sc. 2, lines 83–91)

Above all, Philip embodies the virtues of leadership and courage that must adorn a true king. The idea of "discernible superiority" has been identified by Susan J. Owen as "a commonplace of the heroic plays of the 1660s and 1670s" (*Restoration Theatre* 127), and it allows Philip to finally gain the upper hand over the malcontent Abdelazer, whose characterization as ungrateful also features prominently in the dramatic language of Tory politics around the time of the Exclusion Crisis,[1] since "the patriarchal model suggests that subjects should be as grateful for the benefits of kingly government as children are to parents" (131). Therefore Behn's play establishes a clear antagonism not only between villain and hero, Abdelazer and Philip, but also between a monarch blinded by a pursuit of private pleasures to the conspiracies raging at court and a monarch better equipped to restore the kingdom to its pristine situation of justice at home and conquest abroad. Behn's Toryism would lead her to support the Duke of York's much debated claim to the throne by conjuring up the figure of a deserving younger brother engaged in the fight against the forces of evil.

Yet Behn's party politics create dissonances in the play, particularly in how they clash with her feminist politics (as evidenced in her comedies) and her antiracism (as underscored by her novel *Oroonoko*). That Behn's play demonizes a dark-skinned character has been problematized by critics who, like Susie Thomas, feel that the author of *Oroonoko* could not possibly have written "an overtly racist play" (25). To save Behn from such an accusation, critics usually compare it with its source, *Lust's Dominion*, and thus can conclude that the older play's racial script is much more reactionary. Thomas argues that Behn made important ideological alterations, downplaying the blackness of Abdelazer and emphasizing the queen's agency (21). Virginia Mason Vaughan concurs on both counts and contends that Behn's Abdelazer dies "a proud prince of Africa, not a devil from Hell" (140).

Though Behn may have slightly altered the racist script in *Lust's Dominion*, she did not materially resist the characterization of women as either passive virgins or forward adulteresses. As Derek Hughes has remarked, "Women die in the bedroom, sexually threatened or sexually expectant" (*Theatre* 57). Thomas may find that the queen's having more to say and do in Behn's adaptation is a positive trait, but the queen's agency and loquacity can also indicate female monstrosity as long as passivity remains the paradigm of female normality. Like the source, Behn's play sees in Isabella the threat of unleashed lust, as Philip points out, and even a female succubus, as Abdelazer suggests in the first scene (lines 53–59). Even though other female characters in the play display submissive conformity, they can hardly be said to fare any better. The Infanta Leonora hardly speaks, and Abdelazer's wife Florella's speeches are few and perfectly conventional. Only once, when commanded to kill the king, is Florella shown to harbor individual thoughts and to resist Abdelazer's will (275; 3.1.222–31). Like elsewhere in the play, here, too, royalist sentiments take precedence over all other duties and ties. Behn did not introduce major modifications in the representation of women. The basic types—virgin or whore—remain in place. In fact, women characters are of consequence only insofar as they oppose the royalist cause (Isabella) or advance it (Leonora and Florella). If the former, they are villains who must perish; if the latter, they may survive (Leonora) or die as martyrs to the cause (Florella). Women's villainy, and their final silencing, is the price Behn has to pay here to strike the royalist moral home. That *Abdelazer* turned out to be her only tragedy is significant. From then on, Behn would turn away from the straitjacketing of dramatic tragedy to explore the tragic mode in another genre, fiction (see Carnell), while she continued to provide us with challenging portrayals of Restoration womanhood in the more flexible genre of comedy.

For several years after Behn's death, London theaters were missing the regular input of a female playwright. The 1680s and early 1690s were difficult for the theater in general, since the political atmosphere immediately before and after the Glorious Revolution of 1688 was not conducive to seeking or providing entertainment. By the mid-1690s, an increasing stability coincided with changes in theater management to facilitate the staging of women's plays. Judith Milhous has noted how the competition between the King's Company and the Duke's Company during Charles II's reign influenced the amount and the kind of drama then produced (*Thomas Betterton*). When the two companies merged in 1682, such competition ceased. There followed a conservative period when few new plays were produced. When Thomas Betterton broke away from the United Company in 1695, establishing a rival company in a new playhouse, Lincoln's Inn Fields, the immediate result, as Milhous records, was "a flood of new plays (again more than twenty each year)" (ix). In the 1695–96 season, four female playwrights had their plays produced by one or the other company: Catharine Trotter (*Agnes de Castro*), Mary Pix (*Ibrahim, the Thirteenth Emperor of the Turks*), Ariadne (*She Ventures and He Wins*), and Delarivier Manley (*The Lost Lover* and *The Royal Mischief*). Unlike those women first entering the stage in 1670–71, this later generation was already well aware of belonging to a tradition of women's writing, within which two authors, Philips (known as "Orinda") and Behn ("Astraea") stood out. They also outspokenly supported each other in what was a man's world.

It is remarkable that, with the exception of Ariadne, these women writers would turn toward tragedy in their premiering works.[2] Manley started out with a comedy (*The Lost Lover*), but in the same season she also had her tragedy *The Royal Mischief* performed. Jean Marsden has attributed the resurgence of serious drama in these years to two causes. First, the popularity of she-tragedies by Thomas Otway and John Banks in the 1680s had "shifted [drama's] emphasis from the hero to the heroine, usually a virtuous woman beleaguered and overwhelmed by sorrows" ("Tragedy" 236). Second, interest in tragedies would have been spurred by the box-office success in the previous season of Thomas Southerne's *The Fatal Marriage; or, The Innocent Adultery*, based on Behn's novel *The History of the Nun; or, The Fair Vow-Breaker* (238). The shift from male-centered heroic plays to women-centered pathos was easily accommodated by theater companies, whose casting strategies included pairing off actresses with diverse strengths. Elizabeth Barry and Anne Bracegirdle at Lincoln's Inn Fields and Frances Knight and Jane Rogers at Drury Lane were two such celebrated pairs; one actress skillfully acted out passion while the other embodied virtuous demureness (Howe 152–61). More and more often, passion was to be condemned in a cultural climate that, unlike the libertinism of the early Restoration period, emphasized morality and virtue. During the reigns of the later Stuarts, societies for the reformation of manners proliferated, and the theater came under attack by moralists who regarded it as nursing libertinism and irreligion (Staves, *Literary History* 107).

Despite all these changes, some overall continuity can be established in the topics and concerns of this later generation of women writers. In devising their first tragedies, both Pix and Manley made renewed use of the Eastern script of earlier Restoration playwrights. Although the writers' politics differed, Pix's *Ibrahim* and Manley's *Royal Mischief* feature strong women whose desires interpellate the social order of a kingdom and, though supposedly far away from England, betray anxieties much closer to home.

Pix's *Ibrahim, the Thirteenth Emperor of the Turks*, despite its title, is less about Ibrahim than about his mistress, Sheker Para, who involves him in her revenge against virtuous Amurat for daring to reject her advances. Unlike the queen in Behn's revenge tragedy, Sheker Para is the agent of the action and not a mere collaborator. She is a strong woman who uses whatever means necessary to obtain her desires and boasts of her power and influence over the emperor. Using her skills, Sheker Para has managed to defeat a gender economy that turns women's bodies into disposable objects for the emperor's consumption, but, to do so, she must join that very economy and cater to Ibrahim's appetites. Bridget Orr finds Sheker Para fascinating because "her role reflects the eclipse of the traditional source of female authority, maternity (as embodied in the Queen Mother), and reveals the fissures in masculine identity through her manipulation of Ibrahim" (89). Yet Sheker Para may also repel, particularly because she is ready to victimize other women to advance her own agenda. She punishes Amurat's rejection by bringing the existence of his beautiful fiancée, Morena, to the attention of Ibrahim, knowing full well that the emperor's lust accepts no boundaries. Morena's violated female body acquires emblematic value and comes to stand for everything that is wrong in the political order. A rebellion puts an end to Ibrahim's tyranny but is ultimately unable to rescue Morena from dejection and self-loathing. Pix's play betrays her Whig sympathies because, like other post-1688 works, it justifies active resistance against tyranny (Orr 86). Pix's gender politics, however, reveal ambivalence and contradiction. Cynthia Lowenthal has underlined Morena's courage against the tyrant, for, in the scene immediately preceding her rape, Morena marshals rhetoric, violence, and even the threat of rebellion in her defense. Consequently, Lowenthal contends, Morena represents a new kind of female hero who fights against the tyrant for her self-preservation, even if she finally and conventionally swoons, overwhelmed by her plight (*Performing Identities* 169–72). Yet one must concur with Marsden that Morena's status as a new kind of hero is somewhat compromised by the fact that her violence is ultimately directed against herself, not the tyrant (*Fatal Desire* 109).

Pix seems to be caught in the same double bind that Behn was. Patriarchally defined virtue leaves women exposed to male violence, while their agency can only be figured as deviancy. *Ibrahim* resounds with unresolved gender anxieties, most of them linked to the character of Sheker Para, whose ambition is conveyed in terms of excessive masculinity. When she propositions Amurat, she describes herself as wishing she were "a Man, your Companion / in the War" (12), and in act 5, as the rebellion rages, she wishes once more to be a man to fight for her lord. Sheker Para has no trouble adopting the heroic language of war just as she has proved apt in the power politics of the kingdom. In contrast, dignitaries like the Mufti and Mustapha complain in act 1 of the feminization of the realm, ruled by a "degenerate" man because "softness and ease, / Flatterers and Women, fill alone our Monarch's Heart" (1). Morena's violated body is paraded as a sign of the kingdom's corruption in the last two acts of the play. It is exposed again and again, first to her father and her fiancé's father, then to her fiancé and his friend. The continued male gaze onstage also stands figuratively for the spectators'. The effectiveness of this display as a theatrical device is beyond doubt, but by objectifying women's bodies and exposing them to lustful looks, Pix comes close to acting out Sheker Para's role when, at the beginning of the play, she gives orders for twenty young virgins to parade before the emperor. Eroticism and pathos are closely imbricated in this play, and it could be argued that they result in the victimization of women (see Marsden, "Rape").

Manley's *The Royal Mischief* echoes similar anxieties but resolves them differently. Here, too, a *femme forte* engineers the plot, this time set in contemporary Persia (Orr 118–30; R. Herman 188). Homais, married to the old Prince of Libardian, nurses a passion for the younger Prince Levan Dadian after hearing of his heroic feats in the war against the Abcans and viewing his portrait. Unlike Sheker Para, Homais is under strict surveillance by her husband, who so distrusts her that when he goes to war he leaves her under heavy guard in their castle. Both Sheker Para and Homais are women who dare be the subject of desire rather than its object, and therefore their main motivation is sexual, but for Homais it is mingled with resentment over her confinement instead of with ambition.

These overall similarities in plot and characterization indicate that Manley is working here with the contrasting pair of forward versus demure women that we have encountered in the other two tragedies. Like Behn and Pix, Manley seems caught in the bind of condemning women's sexual agency and endorsing women's passivity. Nevertheless, Manley paints all shades of gray in this play. All her characters (women and men) are flawed somehow, and all fail to embody extremes of virtue or of evil. Thus Levan Dadian, unlike Amurat in Pix's play, falls into temptation and commits adultery with Homais as well as incest, for she is his aunt by marriage. But perhaps the best example of the many fractures in the ideological script of Manley's tragedy is the Prince of Libardian, the jealous husband who keeps his wife strictly confined and forbids all visits. This feature works toward undermining his status as a figure of virtue and righteousness in the spectators' minds, as he conforms to the stereotype of oriental jealousy and tyranny. But the author's Tory politics influence the play's ending, in which Manley manages to bring about a final restoration of order, rather than leaving the kingdom in utter disarray as Pix does in *Ibrahim*. Ruth Herman has contended that Manley's plays became the arena where she debated her political positions and worked out her doubts and that, in *The Royal Mischief*, the Prince of Libardian came to stand for the exiled James II (189–90). Although the play's prince may not be perfect, he performs a sacred mission in restoring harmony and dispensing punishment to the forces of evil, including the execution of his adulterous wife, Homais. As a result, although Manley may have seen some truth in popular claims about James II's irregularities and overbearing behavior, her play was implicitly counterarguing that this was not enough cause to remove the kingdom's ruler.

A decade later Manley once more turned to an Eastern location to sound out her gender and party politics preoccupations. *Almyna; or, The Arabian Vow* (1707) is loosely based on the framing story in the *Arabian Nights*, which had recently reached England in French translation (R. Herman 193). The Spanish-sounding sultan Almanzor, enraged by his wife's adultery, has taken a vow to marry a woman each night and to have her executed the following morning. The vizier's eldest daughter, Almyna, a woman who has received a privileged education, decides to marry Almanzor and convince him to go back on his vow, thus saving many women's lives. Rather than acting impulsively out of sexual desire or personal ambition like Homais in *The Royal Mischief*, Almyna is motivated by selflessness. Consequently, some critics consider the play of little interest, accuse it of being "more lecture than drama," and even argue that Almyna is a Christ-like figure (Marsden, *Fatal Desire* 128–29). It is certainly true that Manley's later tragedy is less sensually titillating than her first, and passion only features as a vice to be avoided by women, for "passions . . . but seldom mend a wrong" (*Almyna* 26). Such a radical shift from passion to reason is remarkable for Manley and makes the play more interesting than current critical neglect might lead one to suppose.

Most striking, Manley lets go of the contrasting pair of women and settles for two equally virtuous sisters. Although the cast is still built on the acting strengths of Barry and Bracegirdle, Almyna and her younger sister, Zoradia, do not convey the habitual contrast between forwardness and demureness. The already familiar pattern of female rivalry over a man is here canceled out by the sisters' strong alliance. Act 2 focuses on their tender friendship, in an intimate garden scene in which Zoradia reveals to her caring older sister that she is in love with Abdalla, Almanzor's younger brother and heir, and that they have been secretly engaged. She further informs her that, though he has now shifted his attentions to Almyna, she cannot possibly hate her beloved sister as she should hate a rival. Thus Zoradia masochistically turns her hatred toward herself like other virtuous heroines, and her body becomes a living emblem of her suffering.

Although Zoradia corresponds to the stereotype of the passive victim and thus will suffer the general fate of death, in Almyna, Manley has managed to create a female character that has agency and is outspoken without becoming monstrous. At the beginning of act 4, she exhibits courage and determination, daring to upbraid both the sultan and his brother for their behavior and to demand justice and changes. Her main objective consists of dispelling the sultan's strong conviction that women do not have a soul, and so her case is carefully constructed on former examples of female heroism. Powerless to cancel the sultan's vow, she must walk the narrow path toward martyrdom, meekly accepting death for the sake of all her peers. But Manley contrives to bring about a happy ending; we find the sultan is only testing her virtue to the breaking point when he declares himself "[q]uite vanquished, by thy heroic Deeds" (65). Here as in no other play, Manley has managed to reconcile her gender and party politics. Almyna, a woman who speaks up for a just cause, a champion of women's sisterhood, is rewarded with the highest position in the kingdom, while the more passive woman who accepts maltreatment dies an accidental death. Almanzor is able to rectify his mistakes and to restore order and satisfaction in the kingdom, but his less deserving heir dies, allowing Manley to keep the Tory script in place. This tragedy, composed so close to the death of the last Stuart and to the Hanover settlement, powerfully resonates with Jacobite echoes, particularly in the scene in which Almanzor appoints Abdalla as his successor. Perhaps the Tory overtones explain the lack of popularity of a play that must have made many people at court uncomfortable, although, in her preface to the publication, Manley attributed the play's discontinuation to Bracegirdle's retirement.

In the season previous to Manley's *Almyna*, and approximately thirty years after Behn's *Abdelazer*, Pix used similar materials for a completely different end in *The Conquest of Spain* (1706), a tragedy featuring once again a country torn between the Islamic and the Christian parties. It is not unreasonable to suppose that the earlier play had some impact on Pix, since she must have seen the revival of *Abdelazer* at Drury Lane in 1695, the same year she launched her career as a playwright. Pix's play is vaguely set in the early eighth century, when the Christian Goths ruled the Iberian Peninsula and had to resist the invasion of successive bands of Moors from across the Strait of Gibraltar. Pix's choice of topic and plot may not be incidental, for England was at this point in the middle of the War of the Spanish Succession. Indeed, as Orr points out, "the play was produced after the capture of Gibraltar and the victory at Blenheim" (179). Although probably inspired by such current affairs and influenced by Behn, Pix used as her direct source William Rowley's *All's Lost by Lust*, which in turn romanticizes details of a story told in Spanish medieval romances, such as the *Romance de la Cava* (see Cuder-Domínguez, "Islamization").

The Conquest of Spain tells how the virtuous Jacincta is raped by the lustful King Rhoderique while the kingdom is being invaded by Moorish forces led by Mullymumen. Like Morena's in Pix's earlier tragedy *Ibrahim*, Jacincta's violated body powerfully brings into sharp relief what is wrong in the kingdom. But while in *Ibrahim* the action takes place within the seraglio, that is, the private section of the palace, here Pix plays with the contrast between Rhoderique's castle and the battlefield outside, the private and the public. Jacincta approaches her father disguised as a Moorish woman, which hints at the defilement and alienation she has undergone and also projects a symbolic image of the future of Christian Spain. Under cover of her Moorish veil, she movingly denounces the wrong she has suffered while offering a titillating picture of sexualized femininity (34). Yet her father refuses to act against the villain once he learns it is the king.

Although Pix skillfully exploits the tensions between both parties in the play's action, the ideological import of Christians and Moors is fairly interchangeable. One can hardly tell the difference between the hero Theomantius and the invader Mullymumen, for instance. Both adhere, in words and deeds, to a chivalric code of behavior. Both want to possess Jacincta and are willing to wreak havoc in the process. What is at stake in the main plot is, after all, a mere trafficking of women. Male rivalry over women and the country thus seals the trope of woman as nation, which Pix successfully uses in *The Conquest of Spain*, whereas in *Ibrahim* the political implications of the plot were perhaps less obvious. In both plays the king has failed to protect the kingdom; immersed in hedonistic pleasures like Emperor Ibrahim in the earlier play, Rhoderique has been careless in his duties and has left the kingdom open to a foreign invasion. The familiar symbols of kingship and warrior heroism, so deeply entwined with the dramatic genre of tragedy, are here deflated. Ultimately, Spain ceases to exist from now on as a Christian nation, just as Jacincta's defiled body is not recuperable, and in act 5 she dies an accidental death (rather than a self-inflicted one like Morena's) in the confusion of the battle.

Although Jacincta is a passive character, the emblem of victimized femininity and thus very far from the active assertion of Sheker Para in *Ibrahim*, the parallelism between the ravished female body and the invaded nation allows Pix to question both monarchy and patriarchy by showing them as equally abusive and oppressive. It is remarkable that in *The Conquest of Spain*, as in Manley's *Almyna*, there is no instance of female deviancy. The only other major female character, Margaretta, functions as a perfect mirror of Jacincta's virtue, producing a doubling effect in the play rather than the slight contrast achieved by Manley. Margaretta must also resist the unwanted advances of a man who uses deceit to get into her bed, and she too remains perfectly loyal to the man she loves. She is luckier than Jacincta, however, and is saved from "pollution" in the nick of time. Such lack of female deviance in Pix's world suggests that women's agency is not at fault for the collapse of the social structure. Instead, women's virtue is subjected to arbitrary fate and mere chance in a corrupt political system that would require substantial reform.

Pix's use of pathos in *Conquest* disrupts the surface message that the violated woman transmitted in her earlier play. Although the male gaze is present here as well and the ravished woman on stage may become a visual source of erotic pleasure, Pix endows her with several new meanings. Rape in this play is the means of exposing the inconsistencies of a patriarchal structure that fails to protect those who live within its fold. As Dympna Callaghan has remarked regarding Renaissance tragedy:

> [Female tragic characters] are frequently constructed as catalysts of tragic action, throwing moral order into confusion rather than merely ratifying its boundaries; they serve not just to define limits but also to uncover the limiting structures of society. (63)

Therefore, through these five plays one can trace meaningful changes in the way that Behn, Pix, and Manley handled their materials, at the level of both aesthetics and politics. A thread of continuity is their choice to turn toward exotic settings and characters. As Jacqueline Pearson has observed, ethnic otherness held particular interest for women dramatists of the Restoration because "racial and ethnic difference provided useful tropes for gender difference" ("Blacker Than Hell" 15–16). Nevertheless, the racial script often hid more immediate concerns and imbrications with the political agenda of these dramatists' day and time, as well as a permanent engagement with the performance of women's lives. As the situation of women changed over that period, so did these writers' handling of the dramatic conventions of tragedy and their use of the ethnic other. In Behn's generation and in Pix's and Manley's early work, the tragic pattern seems to have functioned as a kind of straitjacket against which the authors chafed, since they were compelled to write within the limits of a virgin-versus-whore characterization. In their later plays, both Manley and Pix manage to infuse more complexity into the tragic mold. Whether their party politics were Whig or Tory and whether they emphasized pathos or preferred a more outspoken feminist viewpoint, one can tease out from their work how party, gender, and racial scripts were coming together in new ways at the beginning of the eighteenth century.

Notes

The author wishes to acknowledge the support provided by the Spanish Ministry of Education in funding the writing of this essay (Research Project HUM2006-09252/FILO).

1. The term "Exclusion Crisis" refers to Parliament's attempts to have King Charles II's heir, the Duke of York (later King James II), excluded from the succession after he made public his conversion to Catholicism.

2. Nothing is known of the person writing under the pen name Ariadne, and no further plays under this rubric seem to have been written or produced for the stage.

Tassie Gwilliam

Disguise, Fantasy, and Misrecognition in *The Belle's Stratagem* and *Fantomina*

To gain a lover, hid behind a mask!
What's new in that? Or where's the mighty task?
—Hannah Cowley, *The Belle's Stratagem*

Fantomina; or, Love in a Maze (1724), Eliza Haywood's newly canonical distillation of the masquerade of femininity,[1] works well as a companion and introduction to Hannah Cowley's *The Belle's Stratagem* (1780).[2] In a multigenre course on women writers of the Restoration and eighteenth century, the interplay of this novella and this comedy encourages students to map out and explain some contradictory uses of disguise and masking that are crucial (and ubiquitous) in the literature of the long eighteenth century. In this essay, I sketch ways that *Fantomina* can open up a reading of disguise, fantasy, and misrecognition in *The Belle's Stratagem*.[3]

For me, *Fantomina* is a particularly useful text because it explicitly confronts the problems that certain forms of disguise attempt to solve: female resentment against men in general; women's conflicted sense of their superiority; the supposed incompatibility of female and male desire; and women's exasperated, half-willing subjection to the demands of masculine desire. Despite the brevity of Haywood's novella, it is marked by an insistent repetition that not only embodies but also comments on these issues, beginning with the conflict between men's desire for variety and women's desire for sameness. Haywood constructs her story around the idea that, because male and female desires are incompatible, the young Lady must compulsively refashion herself first to create and then to re-create a man's desire.[4] Cowley's heroine engages in an equivalent protean display to renegotiate her relationship with the man she is destined to marry. Both *Fantomina* and *The Belle's Stratagem* focus on this need to accommodate female desire to masculine nature—a trope that endures in such self-help books as John Gray's *Men Are from Mars, Women Are from Venus*—and both offer similar investigations of the pain and pleasure for women inherent in such accommodation.

To show how this mixture of feeling is articulated in the two texts, I take a passage from each. In *The Belle's Stratagem*, Letitia rants about her first meeting with the adult Doricourt:

> Men are all dissemblers! Flatterers! Deceivers! Have I not heard a thousand times of my air, my eyes, my shape—all made for victory! And today, when I bent my whole heart on one poor conquest, I have proved that all those imputed charms amount to nothing; for Doricourt saw them unmoved. A husband of fifteen months could not have examined me with more cutting indifference. . . . I will touch his heart, or never be his wife. . . . [I]f there is spirit or invention in woman, he shall [fall in love with me].
> (224, 225, 227; act 1, sc. 4, lines 117–23, 145–46, 210–11)

And *Fantomina*'s young Lady rages about the evidence of Beauplaisir's treachery:

> Traytor! (*cry'd she.*) as soon as she had read them [the two letters to her two different personas], 'tis thus our silly, fond, believing Sex are serv'd when they put Faith in Man: So had I been deceiv'd and cheated, had I like the rest believ'd. . . . But I have outwitted even the most Subtle of the deceiving Kind, and while he thinks to fool me, is himself the only beguiled Person. (par. 20)

Both speeches demonstrate a volatile amalgam of vengefulness, injury, desire, and triumph. But why does disguise seem to be the solution to the heroines' problems? In these passages, the young women suggest that their disguises respond to and imitate earlier wrongs against which they must defend themselves and their sex. When Letitia labels all men "dissemblers" and the young Lady refers to "the deceiving Kind," students will also catch an echo of another discussion of disguise from an earlier author. The narrator's introductory remarks in Aphra Behn's novella *The History of the Nun* (1688) give a similar story of the origins of disguise:

> Nay, what woman, almost, has not a pleasure in deceiving, taught, perhaps, at first by some dear false one, who had fatally instructed her youth in an art she ever after practiced in revenge on all those she could be too hard for and conquer at their own weapons? (139)

Behn presents deceit for women as imitation, self-protection, and revenge, thus defending them from the accusation of being naturally or originally inclined to dissimulate.

Fantomina's heroine openly celebrates outwitting Beauplaisir through her disguises, presenting them as revenge on behalf of those members of her sex who are unable to fight back; this context can also allow us to bring to light the hostility that Cowley leaves only partially buried in the portrayal of Letitia. Disguise seems to express anger as well as playfulness in this context, even in Cowley's lighthearted romantic comedy. Letitia presents the roots of her recourse to disguise as a kind of arming for battle with an adversary of the opposing force—an opposing force that has used dissembling and deceit against her. Cowley, like Haywood, however, suggests that this righteous indignation may lead to darker consequences.

Both writers create plots that associate the disguising women with figures of debased desire. Once the heroines begin to meddle with their identities, danger to female sexual reputation emerges, and the female authors appear to begin a process of disavowal. For both heroines, significantly, disguise is associated with prostitution; although neither character is a prostitute, Fantomina skates very close to the line. And while the old identification of the mask and the prostitute is no longer primary by the time *The Belle's Stratagem* was published, the association of actress and prostitute still apparently requires repudiation and negotiation. Cowley, on the one hand, disavows the insinuation that disguises put on to express female desire equal illicit sexuality, but, on the other hand, she leaves traces of prostitution throughout the play. For the young Lady, her equivocally inaccurate identification as a prostitute is openly treated as prophetic: Beauplaisir, echoing a long line of antitheatrical writers, "did not doubt, . . . but that in the End she would be in Reallity, the Thing she so artfully had counterfeited" (par. 6). Haywood makes the link between theatrical performance and illicit sex at the very opening of the novella. The protagonist's desire is initially mimetic; she attempts to reproduce the spectacle of desire and desirability that she watches being performed by the playhouse prostitutes. While Letitia, in contrast, is unequivocally pure, her mistaken identification as a kept woman serves not only to delay the consummation of the marriage plot but also to keep the negative associations of female performance alive.

Aside from the explicitly refuted mischaracterization of Letitia as a kept mistress, disguise as prostitution circulates most explicitly in *The Belle's Stratagem* through Kitty Willis, the scapegoated double for the virtuous Lady Frances of the secondary plot. When the scheming Courtall thinks he has trapped the aristocratic new bride in his rooms, he actually has only Lady Frances's tawdry simulacrum—the whore as counterfeit lady. Courtall, the ostensible target of the substitution trick, is laughed out of the play because of his failure to distinguish between whore and lady, but his misrecognition links him to Doricourt, who also cannot tell lady from whore. In an impressive display of homosocially induced blindness, Doricourt credits the most lamebrained character in the play, Flutter, when he claims that the masked Letitia is a kept mistress. Flutter's status as the exemplary figure of the masculine failure to penetrate disguise is underlined by his speech at the beginning of the masquerade: "A mask is nothing at all to me," Flutter says, before going on to misidentify virtually everyone (254; 4.1.81).

Fantomina allows us to see the interrelations of male misrecognition and female performance through its plot and then to map that perception onto *The Belle's Stratagem*. Among the most striking and crucial aspects of *Fantomina* is Beauplaisir's failure to recognize that the different women he has had sex with are not only the same woman but also the young aristocrat he has seen at court and at the theater. While this kind of challenge to realism would (and regularly does) go unremarked in a play (again suggesting the theatrical affinities of the tale), Haywood calls attention to the artificiality by simultaneously underlining the transparency of the lady's disguise and defending its impenetrability. Haywood, in her trademark lavish style, describes Beauplaisir watching the spectacle of the young Lady immediately after leaving the "languishing Fantomina":

> Lac'd, and adorn'd with all the Blaze of Jewels, has he, in less than an Hour after, beheld at the Royal Chapel, the Place Gardens, Drawing-Room, Opera, or Play, the Haughty Awe-inspiring Lady—A thousand Times has he stood amaz'd at the prodigious Likeness between his little Mistress, and this Court Beauty; but was still as far from imagining

> they were the same, as he was the first Hour he had accosted her at the Playhouse, though it is not impossible, but that her Resemblance to this celebrated Lady, might keep his Inclination alive something longer than otherwise they would have been; and that it was to the Thoughts of this (as he supposed) unenjoy'd Charmer, she ow'd in great measure the Vigour of his latter Carresses. (par. 8)

This (literally spectacular) passage switches dizzyingly back and forth between recognition and misrecognition and between resemblance and difference. Beauplaisir's celebrity fantasy at the end suggests the extent to which the young Lady has succeeded in becoming a prop for his autoeroticism, but Haywood does not rest there. She comes up to the edge of exposing the machinery of disguise but then underlines the investment that both characters have in the performance; Beauplaisir's refusal to see what is hiding in plain sight suggests his unconscious complicity in his own duping—and signals the duplicity of the identifications Haywood offers her readers. While that desire for the same thing over and over again but in different packages demonstrably overrides his ability to perceive correctly, we succumb to the young Lady's dazzling performances. The reader of *Fantomina* thus gets to have "female" and "male" pleasure, enjoying the spectacle of a series of animated sexual encounters powered by (her) constant love and (his) excitement at new conquests and by her skillful disguise and his blindness. *The Belle's Stratagem* also allows the spectator to identify with Letitia Hardy's quest to reveal her true self to Doricourt through disguise while enjoying the spectacle of her (and the actress's) successive disguises.

Both Haywood and Cowley lament and confront the masculine blindness and obliviousness that allow these mixed pleasures, although for somewhat different purposes. Doricourt is prevented from seeing what is in front of him by the false (and foreign) image of femininity he has constructed; the fantasy figure he desires blocks his perception. He declaims about the woman he could love: "She should have spirit! Fire! *L'air enjoué* [sprightliness]! That something, that nothing, which everybody feels, and which nobody can describe, in the resistless charmers of Italy and France" (220; 1.3.61–64). Letitia, on first viewing, is, in contrast, "a fine girl, as far as mere flesh and blood goes. But—. . . She's *only* a fine girl; complexion, shape, and features, nothing more" (220; 1.3.58–59). His more patriotic friend, Saville, stands up for "true unaffected English beauty" and laments that "Miss Hardy, with only beauty, modesty, and merit, is doomed to the arms of a husband who will despise her" (221; 1.3.84–85). Biases against the women of his own country and a disabling fantasy (rather than Beauplaisir's innately masculine drive for variety) create Doricourt's blindness, but these responses work just the same to galvanize Letitia's disguises. Doricourt's blindness looks as if it can be cured; Beauplaisir's presumably is hardwired and cannot be corrected.

The heroines of both works produce stories of origin for their particular disguises. Masquerade is a choice the women make, however much that choice appears to be forced on them by necessity. The young Lady in *Fantomina* attempts to reproduce the tumultuous initial moment of being desired by her compulsive self-transformation. She is precipitated into the eighteenth-century equivalent of multiple personalities by nostalgia, pushed forward by looking back:

> [R]emembring the Height of Transport she enjoyed when the agreeable *Beauplaisir* kneel'd at her Feet, imploring her first Favours, she long'd to prove the same again. . . . Her Design was once more to engage him, to hear him sigh, to see him languish, to feel the strenuous Pressure of his eager Arms, to be compelled, to be sweetly forc'd to what she wished with equal Ardour, was what she wanted, and what she had form'd a Stratagem to obtain. (par. 9)

The young Lady achieves a remarkable painful-pleasurable blending of domination and submission; trying to reclaim what she has lost, and knows she will lose again, she generates multiple identities. Dipping further into the underlying feminine sadomasochism, she also conflates the positions of betrayer and betrayed when Beauplaisir cheats on her (as Fantomina) with herself (as the Widow Bloomer).

Although Letitia does not have the specifically sexual memory that animates *Fantomina*'s heroine, she does evince remarkably similar nostalgia. She recalls her childhood impression of Doricourt—"the blooming boy, who left his image in my young heart"—and then laments a present lack in terms that echo the young Lady's (225; 1.4.126–27). When Mrs. Caroline Racket, the experienced widow, mocks her disappointment at the reunion with her intended husband, she replies, "He should have looked as if a sudden ray had pierced him! He should have been breathless! Speechless! For, oh, Caroline, all this was I!" (225; 1.4.136–38). It is that missing desire of his that her "stratagem" of disguise aims to produce.

These writers show that eliciting male desire requires a lot of work; the usual gender binary of feminine passivity and masculine activity is clearly being remixed in both texts. Beauplaisir imagines he is in pursuit, but he is, in fact, only participating in an artfully constructed scenario that calls on him to produce newly animated desire on the young Lady's schedule. Doricourt, the faux-continental dandy, at first makes a virtue of his passive acceptance of his bride, but, once Letitia starts her initial disguise as a sexually aggressive country hoyden, he pretends to threaten suicide ("I shall certainly set off for Bath, or the other world tonight" [224; 3.1.155–56]) and later incompetently feigns madness in a weak, unconvincing attempt to escape the marriage.

Haywood articulates the collision between passive male obliviousness and female activity by explicitly confronting a male reader who doubts Beauplaisir's continuing blindness. She produces a paean to the young Lady's acting skills:

> It may, perhaps, seem strange that *Beauplaisir* should in such near Intimacies continue still deceiv'd: I know there are Men who will swear it is an Impossibility, and that no Disguise could hinder them from knowing a Woman they had once enjoy'd. In answer to these Scruples, I can only say, that besides the Alteration which the Change of Dress made in her, she was so admirably skill'd in the Art of feigning, that she had the Power of putting on almost what Face she pleas'd, and . . . that all the Comedians at both Playhouses are infinitely short of her Performances. (par. 16)

Interestingly, despite the ostensible purpose of this passage—to defend Beauplaisir from the accusation of blindness—the invocation of the "Comedians at both Playhouses" does not exactly call up the image of a chameleonlike submergence in a part; instead, it points to protean, metamorphic acting for an audience appreciative of a flamboyant display, very much like the performance that Letitia gives for Doricourt at the masquerade and the one the actress playing Letitia gives for the theater audience at *The Belle's Stratagem*.

But what is the difference between a woman putting on disguises portrayed by an actress in a play and a woman putting on disguises described as an actress in a narrative? How many layers are there, and how do the layers relate to one another? We can try to pinpoint when the performance breaks down or reveals itself as a performance as one step in this investigation: When does the dupe know that he is watching a performance? When does misrecognition turn to recognition for the two men, and what happens then to desire? Here the novella and play diverge. As critics such as Emily Hodgson Anderson have pointed out, when the young Lady of

Fantomina puts on a mask and flaunts the fact of her performance in her final role of "Incognita," Beauplaisir refuses to continue his (unknowingly repetitious) pursuit ("Performing"). This is the only disguise in the novella that fully embodies the explicit awareness of theatricality that is intrinsic to the stage and that permeates *The Belle's Stratagem*, and, significantly, it ultimately fails.

At this point in our investigation, students can begin to see some ways that genre differences shape the stories; in particular, the endings dictated by the genres produce quite distinct effects. Like Beauplaisir, Doricourt is presented with a succession of women who are all the same woman, and, again like Beauplaisir, he fails to identify them as the same, for reasons intrinsic to the mechanics of the plot and for the larger reasons of multiple identifications sketched above. Perhaps because Doricourt needs to be humbled, have his eyes opened, and reform to become a proper husband, Cowley stages the conclusion as a moving scene in which mutual recognition ends the need for disguise; Cowley insists that Letitia and Doricourt now can see each other as they really are. In contrast, at the end of *Fantomina,* Beauplaisir is the baffled spectator at a scene of forced unveiling supervised not by the heroine but by her angry mother. Beauplaisir is briskly dispatched, bemused by the strange episode, presumably to resume his rakish ways. He is not required to understand what has been happening to him. Strangely enough, although Beauplaisir is both the object of desire and the cause of action, he is ultimately shown to be less an agent than an adjunct to the young Lady's exploration of sexual desire and desirability. In keeping with the social inclusiveness and forward projection of comedy, Doricourt, in contrast, must be present to our imaginations beyond the ending.

Cowley suggests that Doricourt needs to see that Letitia is willing to be a series of different women to win him. At the masquerade, Letitia says:

> Why then I'd be anything—and all! Grave, gay, capricious—the soul of whim, the spirit of variety—live with him [the man worthy of her love] in the eye of fashion, or in the shade of retirement—change my country, my sex. (250; 4.1.278–80)

But Cowley plays a double game. At the end, she first has Letitia spell out that her masking has been an unmasking:

> This little stratagem arose from my disappointment in not having made the impression on you I wished. The timidity of the English character threw a veil over me you could not penetrate. You have forced me to

> emerge in some measure from my natural reserve and to throw off the veil that hid me. (277; 5.5.229–34)

Letitia then offers, somewhat alarmingly, to continue to be a fantasy—a phantom like Fantomina:

> You see, I *can* be anything. Choose then my character; your taste shall fix it. Shall I be an *English* wife? Or, breaking from the bonds of nature and education, step forth to the world in all the captivating glare of foreign manners? (277; 5.5.237–40)

Doricourt, of course, refuses this offer, claiming that he wants her only to be herself. The play presents this ending as a recognition scene: "Your person, your face, your mind, I would not exchange for those of any other woman breathing" (278; 5.5.244–45). The young Lady of *Fantomina* gets no such recognition: Beauplaisir, brought to her childbed and accused of being her seducer, stammers that she "was a Person whom he had never, more than at a Distance, admir'd" (par. 29). But does Doricourt have a deeper understanding of who Letitia is than Beauplaisir does of the young Lady? His curtain speech suggests that he does not and that, further, Cowley feels the need to overcompensate for challenging feminine modesty through the masquerade. Doricourt announces:

> It was a strange perversion of taste that led me to consider the delicate timidity of your deportment the mark of an uninformed mind or inelegant manners. I feel now it is to that innate modesty English husbands owe a felicity the married men of other nations are strangers to. It is a sacred veil to your own charms; it is the surest bulwark to your husband's honour, and cursed be the hour—should it ever arrive—in which British ladies shall sacrifice to foreign graces the grace of modesty! (278; 5.5.266–73)

By finishing with an effusion of gendered nationalism, and replacing the veil Letitia had lifted, Cowley appears to repudiate the behavior of her own heroine, which has not in fact been characterized by "delicate timidity." It seems more honest or at least consistent to send one's female protagonist off in disgrace to a "Monastery in *France*," as Haywood does (par. 29). At this point, we might remember other disturbing moments in *The Belle's Stratagem*: the insistent association of the heroine with prostitution and the almost frantic succession of disguises, for example. The pleasure of Letitia's exuberant manipulation of identity may turn sour at this ending, and a sober discussion of the self-constraints women writers still labored under in the later eighteenth century may become the morning-after task of a class on *The Belle's Stratagem.*

Notes

1. In addition to Broadview's Fantomina *and Other Works* and Oxford's *Popular Fiction by Women, 1660–1730: An Anthology*, *Fantomina* appears in the following more general collections: *The Norton Anthology of Literature by Women: The Traditions in English* (Gilbert and Gubar), *The Broadview Anthology of British Literature* (Black), Blackwell's *British Literature: 1640–1789* (DeMaria), *The Norton Anthology of English Literature* (Greenblatt), and *The Longman Anthology of British Literature* (Damrosch and Dettmar). Online versions of the texts are also available at University of Pennsylvania's *Celebration of Women Writers* (http://digital.library.upenn.edu/women/haywood/fantomina/fantomina.html) and at the Rutgers University, Newark, site (http://andromeda.rutgers.edu/~jlynch/Texts/fantomina.html). In my classes and in this essay, I use the Rutgers text, edited by Jack Lynch. Lynch uses paragraph numbers rather than page numbers in his online edition; I follow his system here.

2. Juliette Merritt and Wendy Arons discuss femininity as masquerade in *Fantomina* and *The Belle's Stratagem*, respectively. The concept is ultimately derived from Joan Riviere's 1929 article "Womanliness as a Masquerade."

3. The two texts of *The Belle's Stratagem* that I have used in teaching are in the collections edited by Katharine M. Rogers and by Melinda C. Finberg. I quote from the Finberg edition here.

4. We never learn the real name of the heroine of *Fantomina*; when she appears in her own person, she is called only "the young Lady."

Kathleen Leicht

Comparing Early and Late Plays

Comparing and contrasting the work of late-eighteenth-century women playwrights with that of earlier, Restoration-era women playwrights enhances the instruction of both periods. Aphra Behn's *The Luckey Chance* (1686) and Hannah Cowley's *The Belle's Stratagem* (1780) provide engaging material for such a comparison. Both plays appear in *The Other Eighteenth Century*, edited by Robert Uphaus and Gretchen Foster, as well as in *The Broadview Anthology of Restoration and Early Eighteenth-Century Drama*, edited by J. Douglas Canfield. Asking students to explore the relations of love and marriage, gendered identity, and English identity in these two plays will lead them to historical insights about the cultural work performed in both periods by women writing plays.

While both *The Luckey Chance* and *The Belle's Stratagem* follow the comic convention of addressing love and marriage, their treatment of these subjects illustrates different social and political climates associated with the Restoration and the late eighteenth century. In *The Luckey Chance*, Behn portrays marriage as a risky enterprise for men and a necessary evil for women.[1] Marriage is largely a social performance for members of both genders, who pursue their individual interests by any means available.

The old men in Behn's play represent the corrupting influence of such self-interest. Sir Feeble Fainwou'd, having tricked Leticia into marrying him by lying to her about her lover's death, plans literally to lock her up upon marriage (257; act 3, sc. 1, lines 505–06).[2] He hopes that his friend, Sir Cautious, will restrain his wife, Julia, by means of a chain (243; 2.2.202). Sir Feeble contemplates consummating his marriage like a bird of prey: "Adod, I'm as yare as a Hawk at the young Wanton" (245; 3.1.27–28). The lascivious yet childish language Sir Feeble uses to address Leticia, reminiscent of Antonio's "Nicky Nacky" language in Thomas Otway's *Venice Preserv'd* (1682), rounds out Behn's portrait of Sir Feeble as an unattractive and predatory husband. Sir Cautious Fulbanks is similarly exploitative, treating Julia as a commodity and gambling her away for three hundred pounds in a scene that will remind students of movies such as *Indecent Proposal* and *Honeymoon in Las Vegas.*

With the possible exception of Courtall, *The Belle's Stratagem* does not include any characters as lascivious and predatory as those in Behn's play. Marriage in Cowley's play reflects the increasingly polite society of the later eighteenth century and insists more directly on love and sincerity as components of marriage. Cowley makes clear that some performative aspects of marriage are still relevant, but more influential is the idea that everyday social interactions with women may exert a refining, civilizing influence on men (Carter 66–70). While characters still follow their individual interests, other English citizens and the rules of polite society play a greater role in regulating their effectiveness at doing so. The only husband in the play, Sir George Touchwood, is guilty of releasing his wife's favorite bullfinch from its cage, but he does so because he is jealous of his wife's affection for it. Other characters respond by calling him cruel and barbarous (29; act 2, sc. 1).[3] Although he means to keep Lady Frances in the country, as Pinchwife does with his wife, Margery, in William Wycherley's Restoration-era *The Country Wife* (1675), Sir George's friends once again respond negatively and prevent him from carrying out his plan.

In *The Belle's Stratagem*, Cowley portrays feeling and emotion as integral parts of marriage, even though some of her modern editors characterize the play as part of a "laughing comedy" revival designed to "eschew sentimental comedy and melodrama" (Canfield, *Broadview Anthology* 1825–26). This characterization, however, presents a false dichotomy (R. Hume, *Rakish Stage* 312–55); individual plays display varying degrees of humor and sentiment throughout the eighteenth century. Rather than being a foil for sentimental comedy, *The Belle's Stratagem* illustrates differences between the tastes of Cowley's audiences and Behn's. After examining the expressions of feeling in both plays, few students will mistake Cowley for a Restoration playwright. In contrast to the blocked marriages of Behn's play, for example, nothing impedes the marriage of Letitia to Doricourt except her own reluctance to have his hand without his heart: "I will touch his heart, or never be his wife," she vows (15; 1.4). She appears to take this feeling seriously: "never to be his wife will afflict me less, than to be his wife and not be belov'd," she tells Mrs. Racket (35; 3.1).

Though their portrayals of marriage differ from each other, both plays depend on a fluid conception of identity that characters manipulate through disguise. In *The Luckey Chance*, manipulating one's identity through disguise is essentially a survival skill, while, in *The Belle's Stratagem*, it is a luxury closely regulated by English polite society. Both Behn's and Cowley's heroines seem to find disguise empowering, though in neither case is it an unalloyed empowerment. Male characters in both plays also disguise themselves, and their disguises have the potential to disrupt women's lives and plans.

Like most of Behn's plays, *The Luckey Chance* is full of disguises: Bredwel disguises himself as the devil; Gayman disguises himself as Wastall; and Bredwel, Gayman, and Belmour all disguise themselves as ghosts. Julia's disguise provides the most intriguing commentary on gendered identity, however. Julia disguises herself as an unknown to assist Gayman with money and to test his fidelity; these activities allow her to exercise her compassion and test her understanding of Gayman's character as she circumvents the oppressive restrictions of her husband. Gayman's impersonation of Sir Cautious, however, ultimately causes Julia to sacrifice her honor. Disguise empowers Julia, but her lover attempts to use it against her. In a well-known article, Catherine Gallagher argues that Julia, like Behn, uses the apparent loss of honor for her own ends. By disguising her reaction to Gayman's trick—appearing to be angry rather than pleased—Julia creates "a second order of reality," in which she remains free to refuse or accept the sexual demands of both her husband and her lover (34). Julia's position at the end of the comedy is unconventional: neither fully married nor fully unmarried, Julia faces a future that seems to exist outside the usual parameters of comedy. Disguise is available to all in Restoration comedies, but it carries no guarantee of success in the changing and dangerous world portrayed. Behn leaves the audience wondering whether Julia's prospects for happiness are any better than those of Leticia and Diana, whose plots end more conventionally with marriage.

The Belle's Stratagem contains a formal masquerade to draw attention to identity issues. Cowley's Letitia masquerades as a foreign beauty to captivate Doricourt in a move that some students may see as ultimately reinscribing a traditional feminine role and others may see as exhilarating: Cowley's portrait of a woman's ability to control her identity and play with the materials of culture. Masquerades were enormously popular entertainments, and they could be dangerous, precisely because guests altered their identities in "an intoxicating reversal of ordinary sexual, social, and metaphysical hierarchies" (Castle 6). Courtall illustrates the danger when he attempts to ruin Lady Frances by disguising himself as her husband.

While Sir George expresses his fear that London society has become "a meer chaos" and "one universal masquerade" (27; 2.1), the masquerade in *The Belle's Stratagem* proves the opposite: English society regulates itself very well. Courtall's disguise does not ruin Lady Frances because Saville unselfishly rescues her. Sir George's fears about allowing his wife into society, while not entirely unfounded, prove outdated, as Mrs. Racket does not hesitate to point out. She opposes Sir George's definition of a fine lady with an updated one of her own, dismissing his with the comment, "Twenty years hence, one might have forgiven such a libel!" (25; 2.1). Villers, too, comments on Sir George's fears, saying that "Sir George is metamorphosed into a sour Censor; and talks of Fashionable Life with as much bitterness, as the old crabbed Fellow in Rome" (46; 3.4). Despite these remonstrances from friends, only his wife will be able to update Sir George.

Lady Frances is not a character from a Restoration comedy; she should not be locked away. Beginning to suspect that her husband "painted Fashionable Life in colours so disgusting, that I thought I hated it," she finds that, "on a nearer view, it seems charming." When Mrs. Racket tells Lady Frances, "I am impatient to introduce you to that Society, which you were born to ornament and charm," she tries to convince the young wife that her desires coincide with her duty (26; 2.1). Saville envisions a similar role for her when he states that "Lady Frances was born to be the Ornament of Courts" (77; 5.5). After her rescue by Saville, Lady Frances decides that she will assume her place in polite society, but by her husband's side, not in the independent style of Mrs. Racket. By assuming the ornamental role that seems to be waiting for her, Lady Frances provides a different, more fixed model of feminine identity from that which Letitia Hardy explores through disguise. Cowley encourages readers and audiences to see the newly educated Lady Frances as both a potential regulator of polite society and a decorative part of it. Her charms reform Sir George, who updates his views by the end of the play and sees himself as having "recovered one Angel" (82; 5.5). English femininity thus exerts an almost spiritual significance in the ideology of Cowley's play.

The representations of men and masculinity in the two plays are tied to English politics. Behn's political agenda can be confusing to students, largely because she often presents her Tory agenda with some ambivalence (Hughes, *Theatre* 161). In *The Luckey Chance*, Sir Feeble and Sir Cautious—two aldermen—are Whiggish London citizens and the objects of Behn's satire. The logic of Behn's play demands that, in addition to his relative youth, Belmour must possess Tory sympathies and a dashing Cavalier style. Belmour's previous participation in a duel, his subsequent flight from England, and his daring return all testify to his Cavalier sensibility.

England as portrayed in *The Luckey Chance* is the politically rancorous and corrupt place we would expect it to be in 1686. Few can be trusted, and individuals must fend for themselves in all arenas: romantic, financial, and political. Instability and political difference are dominant features of the many references to governmental and political structures in Behn's play. Gayman, for example, professes his faithfulness to both Belmour and Julia during Belmour's absence, but he does so by casting aspersions on the City: "'Twas high time the City should lose their Charter, when their Wives turn honest" (222; 1.1.74–75). His use of the pronoun "their" instead of "its" works to cast some distance between him and the City alderman he seeks to cuckold. Belmour capitalizes on the fears of cits like Sir Feeble when he makes up the story that "the City's up in Arms Sir, and all the Aldermen are met at *Guild-hall*; some damnable Plot Sir" (247; 3.1.128–29). Leticia, seeking to avoid her wedding-night obligation to Sir Feeble, furthers Belmour's stratagem with an appeal to the king's safety: "And shall his Majesty's Service and his Safety lie unregarded for a slight Woman Sir?" (248; 3.1.145–46). Leticia's appeal to Sir Feeble's loyalty and his indecisive, reluctant demonstration of it show that she would be better matched with the Tory Belmour than with this City alderman. In a later scene, Sir Cautious also demonstrates weak loyalty to the king; he pretends to harbor "some prohibited Goods that [Sir Nicholas Smuggle] has stoln the Custom of, and cheated his Majesty" (275; 5.2.147–48). Thus the old men lack royal fervor in addition to youth and virility, and their capitulation to the younger generation represents a political as well as formal logic.

The Belle's Stratagem illustrates the more securely hegemonic nationalism of nearly a century later and makes Englishness "the ultimate aphrodisiac" (M. Anderson 6). In the late eighteenth century, England's opposition to its external enemies largely replaced the internal divisions of Restoration politics. The play enacts elements of the historian Linda Colley's thesis that Francophobia worked to unite Britons during the second half of the eighteenth century. Cowley's characters are nothing if not united by the end of the play, and the English femininity represented by Letitia Hardy and Lady Frances Touchwood is largely responsible for uniting them.

As Doricourt learns the proper value of English women's charms, the other characters preserve and disseminate English wisdom and sensibility, frequently opposing it to dangerous French influences. Though Doricourt is infatuated with French fashions, his tastes are salvageable, as Cowley takes pains to point out. When Saville criticizes Doricourt's French servants as "that flock of foreigners . . . with their parchment faces and snuffy whiskers" (7; 1.3), Doricourt disparages English servants in terms that are actually quite flattering: "An Englishman reasons, forms opinions, cogitates, and disputes" and is "conscious of equal importance in the universal scale with yourself" (8; 1.3). Furthermore, while admitting that he is captivated by French women and servants, Doricourt confesses, "I have never yet found any man whom I could cordially take to my heart, and call Friend, who was not born beneath a British sky, and whose heart and manners were not truly English" (10; 1.3). Though Doricourt arrives back in England infatuated with all things French, he is still an Englishman at heart, and the right Englishwoman may be able to reclaim him. Showing that England is no place for those who do not live up to its ideals, Courtall flees to Paris when Saville humiliates him and exposes him as a villain (63; 4.1). The implication is clearly that good Englishmen belong in England and that France is adequate for villains and rogues.

The ideology of a polite society in which the common good is paramount permeates *The Belle's Stratagem.* Perhaps no character provides a better example of this ideology than Saville. Admiring Lady Frances from afar, he does not try to cuckold Sir George, as a Restoration character might do. Instead, Saville protects Lady Frances from Courtall. His stratagems are, in a sense, for the good of England rather than for his own good. Letitia's stratagem for captivating Doricourt also becomes a common project. Although Letitia initially conceives the idea for sparking Doricourt's passion, Mrs. Racket, Mr. Hardy, and Saville also contribute to it. Restoration characters frequently provide incentives, positive or negative, to their coconspirators, whereas Cowley's point is precisely that Mrs. Racket and Saville cooperate without such incentives.

The play also corrects the selfish ideology of Sir George Touchwood, who learns that "the most tenderly-anxious Husband could not wish to banish his Wife" from the British court, where Queen Charlotte provides a "bright Example . . . the splendour of whose rank yields to the superior lustre of her Virtue" (77; 5.5). This tribute to the queen underscores the correction of Doricourt's French tastes to English ones and Sir George's outdated tastes to current ones.

While the differences between the two plays may be their most instructive features, the common ground between Behn and Cowley is also worth exploring. In *The Luckey Chance*, Pert warns Gayman about asking too many questions of the disguised Julia before him: "You know, too much Curiosity lost Paradice" (249; 3.1.183). Letitia in disguise says nearly the same thing to Doricourt in *The Belle's Stratagem*: "Beware of imprudent curiosity; it lost Paradise" (55; 4.1). The plays thus present disguise as a potentially dangerous tool, powerful when used by skilled women. Both playwrights also feature major characters who confront others—and implicitly the audience—with disarming questions about identity. Belmour asks Sir Feeble, at the end of *The Luckey Chance*, "Belmour—or Francis—chuse you which you like, and I am either" (281; 5.2.341–42). Cowley's Letitia presents Doricourt with a strikingly similar choice when she reveals her stratagem:

> You see I can be anything; chuse then my character—your Taste shall fix it. Shall I be an English Wife?—or, breaking from the bonds of Nature and Education, step forth to the world in all the captivating glare of Foreign Manners? (81; 5.5)

Belmour and Letitia, like their creators, draw the audience's attention to the ways society constructs identity in the two historical periods.

In both periods, such construction is always gendered. The choice Belmour presents to Sir Feeble is not really a choice at all; by asserting, "I am either," Belmour claims his place in England and his victory over the older characters. Letitia's question, however, presents her victory more conditionally. Though she sounds confident that she can please Doricourt, she acknowledges his ability to "fix" her character. Letitia—and the audience—must wait while he decides that "You shall be nothing but yourself" (81; 5.5). Taught together, these two plays encourage students to consider the construction of identity in the Restoration, in the late eighteenth century, and in their own time.

Notes

1. See Gill for a brief overview of Restoration representations of marriage in comedy, especially 193–94, where she focuses on Behn.

2. Page numbers for *The Luckey Chance* refer to the edition of the play in Janet Todd's *Works of Aphra Behn*.

3. Frederick Link's edition of Cowley's plays, cited throughout this essay, does not provide line numbers, and plays are paginated individually.

Emily Hodgson Anderson

She Stoops to Stratagem: A Comparative Approach to Eighteenth-Century Comedy

I want to begin with a discussion of titles. The first is the one appended to this essay, since it is a title about titles, a kind of portmanteau phrase taken from Oliver Goldsmith's comedy *She Stoops to Conquer* (1773) and Hannah Cowley's comedy *The Belle's Stratagem* (1780). "She Stoops to Stratagem" is meant to be a nod to the comparative approach I use in the classroom: I teach these two plays in tandem, focusing on female stratagems. But my title also reflects on my role as a teacher of these plays, as ultimately I use the gendered plotting that motivates both comedies to theorize my strategic classroom methods. I will state the first part of my stratagem right up front: I choose to teach these plays because they are funny. Eighteenth-century drama can be a hard sell to undergraduates, but these plays make students laugh. And when we laugh, we learn.

What do we learn? To answer that question, I turn to the title of Gail Finney's edited collection of essays on gender and comedy, *Look Who's Laughing*. The phrase focuses our attention on the audience response, but aside from the reference to one-upmanship, Finney's title asks us to think about how laughter, or its absence, can teach us something about audience demographics and, specifically, gender divisions: one goal of Finney's volume is to document that "not only men but also women can laugh" ("Unity" 1). But the audience response also reflects on who is telling the joke, and Finney's other goal is to query whether "the gender of the creator of the comedy can make a difference in the kind of comedy produced" (1). Who's laughing, and who isn't, can tell us as much about the jokester as about the audience.

When I teach these plays, I look at pedagogical moments in the texts that are conducted through humor. My focus has two goals. First, following Finney's lead, it lets me use comedy as a way into discussions about gender difference. Second, thinking about comedy as a form of pedagogy allows me to relate pedagogical moments in the text to pedagogical moments in the classroom. By the end of this essay, I hope to show that these two goals are related. Teaching the teaching, as it were, allows my classes to have more refined discussions about how gender is figured in these plays; it also allows them to move beyond standard readings that present the heroines of these plays as either empowered or subjected to patriarchal norms, feminist or antifeminist (see, e.g., Brooks; Arons; Isikoff). Teaching the teaching also exposes tensions in how we talk about and teach gender: it exposes the assumptions about gender that underline our decision to teach plays by women in comparison with plays by men.

Nowadays, we teach or anthologize texts in a comparative context to challenge assumptions about gender difference, and, if I teach these plays because they are funny, I also teach them because students find them similar (and thus similarly accessible). It is interesting to note that students have a much easier time understanding *The Belle's Stratagem* when they read it after *She Stoops to Conquer*. The language and action of Cowley's play are more complex than Goldsmith's, and when I teach *The Belle's Stratagem* on its own, my explication often kills the humor (imagine trying to laugh at a joke you did not understand the first time around). When I teach it after Goldsmith, though, students quickly recognize the similar plot trajectory and can grasp Letitia's stratagem on their own; they take pleasure in the comedy of the play and the fact that they understand the joke. Thus the Goldsmith and Cowley plays provide fertile ground in which to test Finney's argument that "as many features link comedy by male and female writers as distinguish it" ("Unity" 10–11). Both plays take their titles from the actions of the female lead, and Goldsmith—famously undecided about what to call his play—considered using the title that Cowley chose (Ferguson 26). At one point, then, both plays were conceived of as *The Belle's Stratagem*, an allusive nod to George Farquhar's 1707 play *The*

Beaux' Stratagem and a connection that suggests the plays and their heroines have at least a source text in common.

There is more: both plays feature heroines who use their stratagems to educate the male protagonist. Betrothed to the painfully shy Marlow, a man "doomed to converse with the only part of the sex that he despise[s]," Goldsmith's Kate Hardcastle pretends to be a barmaid to "teach [her lover] a little confidence" (357; act 2, sc. 1).[1] As a barmaid, she can engage Marlow in conversation, and, throughout the play, she gradually modifies her behavior and her status from servant girl to poor relation. By the end, then, she has taught him more than confidence; he has learned to respect the woman and the manners that so terrified him. As Kate hypothesized correctly at the beginning of the play, "Can't he be cured of his timidity, by being taught to be proud of his wife?" (337; 1.1).

Cowley's Letitia Hardy also masquerades to teach her fiancé to respect the decorum and manners of a British lady. In the Cowley play, Doricourt has returned from the grand tour enamored of "foreign graces," and he finds Letitia's restraint and modesty stultifying by contrast (278; act 5, sc. 5, line 272).[2] Letitia designs a stratagem to disabuse Doricourt of this notion and to inspire him with passion for her; she achieves her goal by interacting with him through various disguises. By the end of the play, when all stratagems have been revealed, Doricourt concludes, "I feel now it is to that innate modesty English husbands owe a felicity the married men of other nations are strangers to" (278; 5.5.268–70).

Ideally, this pedagogical process in the plays expands outward to include the audience. In both plays the intricate charades that make us laugh also have an important didactic function: as comedies, the plays reach their climactic revelations through elaborately constructed jokes. This statement may sound like a commonplace definition of the comic genre, until we remember that Goldsmith frames his play as unique in its ability to elicit laughter. This uniqueness is certainly suspect, and Robert Hume has rightfully qualified Goldsmith's assertions, made in the 1772 "An Essay on the Theatre; or, A Comparison between Laughing and Sentimental Comedy," that his comedy represents a definitive shift in dramatic trends ("Goldsmith" 238). Yet Goldsmith's essay, which I teach in our first class on *She Stoops to Conquer*, does position his brand of humor in contrast to distinctly unfunny comedies that the playwright sees as lacking a certain, unspecified "efficacy" (762). Even when read as purposefully polemical, Goldsmith's fears that we will be "deprived of the art of laughing"—coupled with the pedagogical function of laughter in his play—suggest that, if these fears were fulfilled, we as audience members would be deprived of more than just entertainment (Goldsmith, "Essay" 763).

To support this reading, we spend some time discussing when, if ever, comedy can be "efficacious" and what exactly this term might mean. Students have lots to say on this topic; after all, they are well schooled in programs such as *The Daily Show*, *The Colbert Report*, and *South Park,* which use comedy to convey searing social critique. I encourage students to use these touchpoints to think generally about how we, as audiences, respond when commentary is presented as comedy. To return to our primary texts, we then look at the different jokesters in Goldsmith's play and ask what purpose, if any, the jokes serve. Here, students love to discuss Tony Lumpkin, the blockhead who forswears learning in favor of liquor yet emerges as one of the most savvy characters in the play (339; 1.2). Tony's first prank—in which he convinces Hastings and Marlow that Mr. Hardcastle's house is an inn—seems motivated by pure mischief, but his later jokes are more utilitarian. Thus the pranks he designs to assist the elopement of Miss Neville and Hastings come to resemble Letitia's plans in Cowley's play; they function not just as jokes but as stratagems. Those who laugh at these jokes—Tony himself, Miss Neville, Hastings—are in the know, and their laughter signals not only their amusement but also their stratagem's success.

But who isn't laughing? Being the butt of a joke (as opposed to being the audience of one) is never much fun, and Tony's mother, a constant dupe, rarely cracks a smile. Yet Marlow and Doricourt, Goldsmith's and Cowley's respective male protagonists and laughingstocks, respond differently. In the Goldsmith play, everyone but Marlow is soon aware of Kate's plan, and Kate has to plead with her father not to "laugh [Marlow] out of his resolution" to pursue her (379; 4.1). Laughing at someone can backfire, and, at end of the play, when Kate does mock her lover, she almost scares him away. Kate's last lines are "ha ha ha," to which Marlow responds, "Oh, curse on my noisy head. I never attempted to be impudent yet, that I was not taken down. I must be gone." Only Mr. Hardcastle's command keeps him in place: "You shall not stir, I tell you . . . take courage, man" (395; 5.3). Cowley's Doricourt, on the other hand, is thrilled to discover that he has been made a dupe, though in the process he has been jeered by Mrs. Racket, Flutter, and even his friend Saville. As Letitia details how and why she has tricked him for five acts, Doricourt can only respond, "I am yet in a state of intoxication . . . speak on, sweet angel!" (277; 5.5.235–36).

As Finney suggests, who is or isn't laughing can tell us as much about the joker as about the audience, and students ascribe these varied responses to the slightly different stratagems that each heroine adopts. These differences begin to emerge in our classroom discussions of titles. Despite the temporary titular overlap, Goldsmith ultimately chose another descriptor for his play, and the contrast in titles hints at deeper contrasts in plot. *She Stoops to Conquer* reveals the outcome of the play—Kate conquers—whereas Cowley's title is more ambiguous. We know there will be a stratagem, but we do not know how it will turn out. Cowley's title is a phrase, whereas Goldsmith's title is a sentence with an active verb: "she" is the subject, and the subject is doing something. But the verb is problematic; despite the redeeming "conquer" at the end, she is "stooping." This verb had several meanings in the eighteenth century, and while Goldsmith certainly invokes its sense of subordination, I sometimes mention that "stoop" also refers to the motion of a bird of prey descending on its victim (see "Stoop"). This sense may make the title less paradoxical. Goldsmith's Kate also recalls a much earlier Kate, Shakespeare's heroine in *The Taming of the Shrew*, whom Petruchio specifically compares to just such a bird: "My falcon now is sharp and passing empty, / And till she stoop she must not be full-gorged" (act 4, sc. 1, lines 180–81). In this usage, Petruchio describes the process whereby birds were trained to stoop—not to prey but to lures (and thereby tamed). When I teach Goldsmith in a drama survey, I often begin with *The Taming of the Shrew*; Petruchio's soliloquy and the play's ambiguous power dynamics provide extra context for our discussions of these issues in *She Stoops.* "She" acts only to subordinate herself, a contradiction missing from the Cowley title.

These differences expound with analysis. Goldsmith makes Kate's stratagem relatively simple: she will dissemble as a low-class character and gradually modify her behavior so that the too-modest Marlow is lulled into conversing with an upper-class woman before he is even aware of it. In this play, Kate "conquers" without aid from mask or makeup. She meets Marlow first in her simple "housewife's dress," without any of the "superfluous silk" or "trimmings" that her father finds so indulgent (335; 1.1). (The epilogue, composed by Goldsmith and spoken by Kate, reinforces that she has "gain'd a husband without aid from dress" [398].) Her "unveiling" is thus gradual, metaphorical, and accompanied by no onset of nerves; her final stage direction specifies that she deliver her lines "in her own natural manner" (395; 5.3).[3] In the Cowley play, by contrast, the stratagem has two parts. Letitia Hardy also poses for some of the play as an ill-bred rustic, but, unlike Goldsmith's Kate, Letitia uses this role to repulse her lover so that she can attract him later as a masked incognita. Letitia, as the incognita, relies heavily on a masquerade costume complete with actual vizard. Her unmasking is therefore literal—she enters the final scene still in masquerade garb—and represents "the most awful moment of [her] life" (277; 5.5.221). Yet even as she unmasks, Letitia states, "You see I *can* be anything" (277; 5.5.237). From these comparisons, Kate Hardcastle emerges as a simplified, unmasked, "natural" woman, while Letitia remains a complicated, dressed-up chameleon (she can, she asserts, if Doricourt wishes, even change her sex [258; 4.1.280]). Goldsmith thus exposes an idea of femininity that is stable despite its social trappings; Cowley presents us with the trappings but leaves the woman inaccessible.

The progression from observations about the dramatic characters to claims about the playwrights reveals that there are strategists who lie behind these heroines. They are, of course, the authors, and classroom discussions that focus on the different performance techniques adopted by these heroines highlight the different ways in which Goldsmith and Cowley treat gender. We end up talking about authors—just as we began the course. When I introduce the plays, I assign biographical presentations on the playwrights, and in them students often refer to the (perhaps apocryphal) account of Goldsmith's own Marlow-like confusion of a squire's house for an inn, as well as Cowley's early relationship with David Garrick and her subsequent experiences as a female playwright without this male mentor.[4] The presentations highlight connections between text and author and provide important cultural context—indeed, Melinda C. Finberg contrasts Ellen Donkin's biographically influenced chapter on Cowley to other more theoretical work, calling it "the most intriguing Cowley scholarship in print" (Select bibliography lix). Finberg's biographical work is also very useful, especially her observation that the negative reception of Cowley's subsequent play, *A School for Greybeards* (1786), forced the playwright to "retreat behind a veil of decorum" (Introduction xlvii). Cowley the woman seems to disappear behind the guise of English modesty, and yet Letitia's response to this same threat makes Cowley's retreat less oppressive. Given this context and my emphasis on titles, students are led to speculate that the "belle" of *The Belle's Stratagem* is Cowley herself and, if she shares Letitia's chameleonlike abilities, that her ultimate adoption of social conventions—a conclusion that resonates with Letitia's status at the end of Cowley's play—registers as simply another performance.

That our discussions of gender in these plays connect back to the playwrights introduces a potential payoff: if a comparison of male and female playwrights can lead to new conclusions about eighteenth-century drama or to broader theoretical conclusions about gender and its relation to social contexts, then perhaps more of our colleagues will want to teach these plays by women, either in tandem with plays by men or alone. But this comparative rubric also asks that our pedagogical and scholarly discussions start with the gender of the author and use this lens to examine the plays. To what extent should authorial gender guide or preface our interpretation of text? Finney asks in the introduction to her edited volume, "Is women's comedy anything more than comedy by women?" ("Unity" 11). If we conclude that it is not anything more (Finney suggests that "as many features link comedy by male and female writers as distinguish it" [10–11]), then have we done these plays a disservice? Or, in our eagerness to show a kind of feminist unity in these female-authored plays, do we risk effacing other compelling reasons to teach them? If we approach the plays with a sense of feminist unity already in place, then does our syllabus design become governed by a desire for equal representation of male and female playwrights but not necessarily by any more substantial analytic goals?

Our students are not privy to the queries and assumptions that go into crafting a syllabus; they do not know if we have added a play simply to keep the ratio of male to female playwrights intact. Indeed, in my experience, a syllabus that consciously favors a comparative approach to male and female playwrights predisposes students to acknowledge some kind of gender difference—or to assume that any differences we discuss in connection to these plays are linked to authorial gender. In a recent class on *The Belle's Stratagem*, for example, one of my first-year students noted that, unlike Goldsmith's Marlow, Cowley's Doricourt takes pleasure in the fact that he has been deceived; the student then speculated, as I do above, that the different attitudes of the male protagonists might have something to do with the gender of the playwright who created them. The student explained that, after finishing her reading, she asked all her friends how they would respond to the types of deception advocated by both plays: her female friends said they would not be bothered by it; her male friends would. While I started this paper with the assumption that these plays are funny, this student's poll indicates that not everyone finds them amusing. Humor again hints at complexities in gender: my student's sampling suggested to her that Doricourt could *only* be the production of a woman author. Does an author's gender matter? For this student, at least, it does.

These comparative textual pairings encourage this type of observation, but they can also complicate it. For if only a woman could create a Doricourt, this same woman has devoted her play to destabilizing the concept of femininity, or the concept that a stable feminine essence can be located beneath or apart from the fluid markers of costume and behavior. In class we explore this destabilizing as consistent with eighteenth-century theories of theatricality and staged femininity, which complicate the sense that the author's sex is crucial to or determinant of anything. When I teach these plays to advanced undergraduates or graduate students, I pair them with excerpts from Dror Wahrman's book on eighteenth-century concepts of identity, which I juxtapose to Judith Butler and to Joan Riviere's essay "Womanliness as a Masquerade." Wahrman argues that theater practices in the better part of the eighteenth century reflect the eighteenth-century concept of identity as something protean and superficial—something constructed from without. Butler and Riviere both apply this idea specifically to gender, in that social acts of masquerade and performance produce the gendered identity that they seem to express. I use these readings first to demonstrate how we can link a historical analysis of theatrical practices to current theoretical meanings of performance and performativity and then to enrich our discussions of Letitia as a protean character: Does her malleability make her a purely superficial character? Does Cowley seem invested in any sense of the individual or individual agency? How would this belief, if present, work with the sense that Letitia's character is constructed by her performances? So while students' assumptions about gender difference guide the discussion of other differences between these texts, our textual analysis simultaneously encourages them to challenge these initial assumptions.

I want to emphasize, though, that my classes do not just coax students toward some notion of performativity. Instead, we tend to reframe the relation of gender to performance as something reciprocal: we recognize how gender influences eighteenth-century conceptions of theatrical performance but also how these varied conceptions of performance (Kate's ability to act in her natural manner versus Letitia's strange inability to unmask) affect contemporary depictions of gender as theatrically performed. This reciprocal understanding of gender's relation to performance allows us to move beyond the strict feminist/antifeminist dichotomy that governs most scholarship on these plays.

This progression, ideally, is the payoff of my stratagem in the classroom and in this essay. But I would like to make one more conceptual reflection on what it means to have a stratagem in the classroom: Have I "stooped" in doing so? Does the fact that I guide my students toward conclusions undermine the idea of the individual and thus the potential for individual agency? Of course not. A good class encompasses a dynamic play between our pedagogical plan and our students' ability to affect this plan, and this observation gives me a way to understand the paradox of Goldsmith's title, if not my own. While "conquering" is a rather militaristic term for teaching, we certainly "stoop" (in that we subject ourselves to the viewpoints of others) and direct (in that we exert control as we would in any rehearsal space) in the classroom. To a certain extent, we are both students and teachers, and to be good teachers we must occupy both roles: we must be open-minded if we are to teach effectively. And as part of this open-mindedness, we need to acknowledge that the choices we make in designing a class reflect just as much about us as teachers as they do about what it is we want to teach. The self-reflexiveness of teaching mirrors that of pedagogical comedy; both reveal as much about their creator as they do about their audience. Studying these particular comedies thus illustrates that, by teaching the teaching, we can learn something more about our subject matter—as well as something more about the state of our profession and ourselves as scholars in it.

Notes

1. All quotations from *She Stoops to Conquer* are taken from David Lindsay's edition.

2. All quotations from *The Belle's Stratagem* are taken from Melinda C. Finberg's edition.

3. Interestingly, this stage direction is not in the Larpent manuscript, which was licensed under yet another title: *The Novel; or, Mistakes of a Night*. It does appear in the first edition of the play, which was published as *She Stoops to Conquer; or, Mistakes of a Night*.

4. I refer students to Ellen Donkin's chapter on the apparent competition that existed between Hannah Cowley and Hannah More for Garrick's attentions and urge them to contrast Cowley's perceived abandonment by Garrick to her subsequent success with *The Belle's Stratagem* (57–76).

Part V

Classroom Strategies

Marie E. McAllister

Using Production to Teach Women Playwrights

Almost all plays are written in hopes that actors will someday perform them for audiences—preferably paying, and ideally cheering, audiences. In literature courses, however, it can be easy to forget that playscripts are blueprints for production, not stand-alone texts. Plays by Restoration and eighteenth-century women playwrights offer such rich ground for analysis that a class could spend an entire semester discussing texts without ever getting to drama as a performative art. Because much scholarship on these playwrights still focuses on gender at the expense of genre, courses involving secondary reading might end up even less attentive to performance. Such an approach, though, would be unjust both to students and to the writers of the plays. Without sacrificing what they already do well, instructors can easily bring production into the classroom. I offer here suggestions for helping students think about performance, production history, and performance theory in ways that are especially rewarding for the study of women playwrights.

A simple yet very successful starting exercise asks students to watch the beginning of the wonderful 1965 BBC live television production of *The School for Scandal*, by Richard Brinsley Sheridan (1777). The video opens with act 2, scene 1, in the play (which students should have read first) and depicts the Teazles' daily quarreling as a form of flirtation. After briefly discussing what the class has noticed or found interesting in the scene, I have students list other ways in which it might have been interpreted: a struggle for power, the showing up of a foolish old husband, a critique of spoiled wives, one more symptom of a dying marriage. We then discuss which interpretations would work best on stage and why. Students who have been thinking solely about character consistency or how this scene fits with the rest of the play suddenly find themselves considering performance and audience reaction.

A more advanced exercise asks students to work with an excerpt from Judith Milhous and Robert D. Hume's *Producible Interpretation*, one of the earliest texts to focus on the interrelation of production choices and interpretation. The chapter on William Wycherley's *The Country Wife* (1675) is a lovely self-contained example of their method. Reading it, students immediately grasp how our interpretation of the entire play can be altered simply by casting Horner as a "dashing scamp of 25," a "glamourous Truewit of 35," or a "debauchee of 40+" or by playing Pinchwife as a tyrannical bully rather than a blustering idiot (103). A less advanced class might simply examine Milhous and Hume's table of three ways to interpret *The Country Wife*: as farce, libertine comedy, or satire (see table). Once students have argued for the column they prefer or for a mixture of all three, I explain how Milhous and Hume use their knowledge of the original cast to make an educated guess that the play was originally staged as a libertine comedy. Students are usually fascinated to hear of the archival research that leads scholars of Restoration drama to such conclusions; few have ever thought of financial records and playbills as tools for interpreting literature.

At this point, students are ready to start creating a case study of their own. Aphra Behn's *The Rover* (1677) makes an excellent choice, both because it comes relatively early chronologically and because it offers so much to discuss. Even first-time readers pick up on the troubling aspects of the play and are eager to talk about Don Pedro's treatment of his sisters, the two scenes in which Florinda is nearly attacked, and Angellica's role in the play. Having students talk explicitly about production complicates their initial reactions, although those reactions may already be varied across a class. In act 3, should Florinda be struggling in true alarm, or should she merely be furious with a Willmore so comically drunk that he poses no threat to anything but her planned elopement? At the end of act 4, should the audience believe that Blunt and Frederick are fully prepared to commit rape (in their parlance, "ruffle a Harlot" [506]),[1] or should Florinda

Various Character Treatments for *The Country-Wife*

Character	Farce	Libertine Comedy	Satire
Horner	dashing scamp of 25	glamorous Truewit of 35	debauchee of 40+
Harcourt	moonstruck lover	romance convention lover	serious lover
Dorilant	(parallel to Horner)	(parallel to Horner)	(parallel to Horner)
Sparkish	stupid clothes horse	arrogant courtier	obnoxious ass
Pinchwife	roaring booby	threatening bully	wife-beater
Sir Jaspar	doddering butt	complaisant butt	smug dupe
Quack	cheery accomplice	smooth accomplice	society leech
Margery	silly newly-wed	budding Hoyden	victimized innocent
Alithea	comically blind	romance convention lover	serious lover
Lady Fidget	bored young wife	sexy lady on the prowl	amorous older woman
Dainty	receptive ingenue	easy pickings	amorous spinster
Squeamish	giddy adolescent	younger easy pickings	hypocritical young cow
Lucy	wide-eyed auxiliary	practiced schemer	experienced go-between

Note: Reprinted with permission from *Producible Interpretation: Eight English Plays, 1675–1707*, by Judith Milhous and Robert D. Hume, table 3.1 (103). ©1985 by the Board of Trustees, Southern Illinois University.

be so obviously Blunt's superior that the audience laughs all through his threats? What should the audience feel during these scenes: alarm and relief, outrage, smug confirmation of male stupidity? Should Angellica, in turn, be a tragic figure or a self-dramatizer? How does the play change if she is played as an empowered businesswoman, a self-loathing victim, a wounded lover, or a rejected outsider—and which interpretations are best justified by the play's text and context? Once students have found textual evidence supporting their decisions, we talk about how seemingly small production choices can change the entire tone of a play and the reactions of its audience. Students soon see that there are many valid ways to interpret any play, although some choices are more historically accurate or lead to a more interesting and successful performance than others.

Because *Producible Interpretation*'s eight studies include only male authors, a good follow-up assignment asks students to prepare their own table for a female-authored play, either *The Rover* or a play to be read later in the term. In Elizabeth Griffith's *The Times* (1779), for example, should Sir William be a kindly old crank or a misogynistic petty tyrant? Is Woodley best played as an ineffective milksop who cannot even speak honestly to his wife or as a gullible but good-hearted counter to the corruption around him? Is Lady Mary's conversion—probably the weakest moment in the play—more believable if she has been portrayed as blindly self-centered or as merely silly? Not every play, of course, lends itself to radically different possibilities; while different interpretations by the lead actors might make for very different versions of Joanna Baillie's *De Monfort* (1800), it is hard to imagine Mary Pix's *The Innocent Mistress* (1697) as, say, serious social satire. If students get interested in this project, they can move on to researching a play's production history and test the plausibility of their alternative interpretations.

By this point, I have usually paused to give students some insight into the historical contexts in which women's plays were written and performed. An overview lecture might include the reopening of the theaters, the appearance of actresses on stage, the issue of reputation for both actresses and women playwrights, the physical conditions in which plays were performed, the audiences, and so forth, through the Licensing Act of 1737 and on to late-eighteenth-century drama. With so many excellent resources available—Susan Owen (*Companion*) and J. L. Styan are particularly accessible—students could introduce background material in short solo or group presentations. Instructors could also shape future discussions by assigning topics related to production or specific to women playwrights.

All along, too, I try to include activities designed to help students develop their visual imaginations and picture possible production choices when reading, rather than merely think about the words on the page. Some literature students are longtime theatergoers, and a few may have acted in high school or taken a college drama class. At many institutions, though, most students have seen little or no live theater. Kinesthetic learning, learning that involves the body as well as the mind (in contrast to the traditional classroom of immobile students), especially benefits those new to theater. Getting students actively involved helps them associate appropriate movements with the events on the page. Certainly nothing breaks the ice faster than having an entire classroom of students stand up and try out a few simple stage moves: curtseying, drawing an imaginary sword, taking a pinch of snuff from an invisible snuffbox, peeping from behind a fan. Part of the pleasure for students, of course, lies in watching their teacher demonstrate such antics. After they have mastered a simple bow, we do it again while keeping track of an imaginary wig and turning a sexy calf toward the audience. A basic curtsey turns more formal in an imagined unbending corset. The class quickly becomes more attuned to the language of gesture and pose, especially if we follow up by having a few volunteers act out a scene using the gestures we have just learned. There is a funny moment in act 2 of Behn's *The Feigned Courtesans* (1679) where the trickster Petro teaches Tickletext and Sir Signal Buffoon to take snuff before he picks their pockets. Swordfight scenes are easy to locate, especially in Behn (whose duels tend to turn into all-out battles), while nearly any scene involving an entrance or exit offers opportunities to practice a bow or curtsey. Some cross-gender casting increases the level of hilarity during gesture training and also plants the first seeds for thinking about gender as performative.

Likewise, students think more carefully about performance after just a few minutes spent discussing and demonstrating how close two characters should stand when flirting or arguing or how a stage coterie might use physical space to show that they are allied against an outsider. As the students analyze specific scenes, I stop them occasionally to ask what stage directions are stated or implied, how the characters should be grouped, and what else the actors might do while saying certain lines. It also works to have students draw a fast sketch of what the audience might be seeing at a given moment: Who is standing or sitting? Who is attentive to whom? How does the audience know who is the center of attention? Who holds power over whom?

Dramatic reading can be used in many ways to deepen literature students' understanding of plays. A very little cajoling usually results in a handful of volunteers willing to stand and read a scene aloud, book in hand, not trying to act but simply carrying out whatever stage directions are implied. Even more effective is to break the class into groups and assign each a single page or column from a key scene, giving them fifteen minutes to choose roles, decide on some simple stage actions, and try a run-through before reading their scene for the rest of the class. Using the term "dramatic reading" helps allay communication anxiety by distinguishing this exercise from full-fledged acting. It is important to stress that talent is not required and to remind students that their goal is merely to help everyone visualize the play as theater. I start with a comic scene to get everyone laughing and take a small part myself—an obsequious or stupid servant role offers plenty of room for being silly. Follow-up questions focus on the play rather than on the performers (e.g., What is one thing you saw that was more interesting than when you just read the words on the page?). Because women students are often a majority in humanities courses, plays by Restoration and eighteenth-century women are ideal for dramatic reading: they raise issues about self-definition, independence, and sexuality to which women students can often relate. They also tend to include excellent female roles.

Dramatic reading can take many forms. A course that emphasizes oral presentation might include prepared and graded readings, with a rubric focused on interpretation, collaboration, and ideas rather than theatrical skill. A course in which production is largely a means of helping students visualize and enjoy drama might keep readings ungraded. Starting class with a short dramatic reading can lead to discussion of a particular scene or idea; ending with one gives students the chance to see that day's critical remarks brought to life. Repetition can be productive: just as one might have two different students read a poem aloud before discussing it, one can have two different groups do a dramatic reading of the same scene then ask the class to discuss similarities and differences. Likewise, if two groups happen to pick the same passage for a performance assignment, the class can talk about how the productions reflect each group's interpretation. Another approach is to ask the class to make connections between different production scenes. Did the first group envision the lead actress in the same way as the second? Did both groups choose to emphasize similar themes, or have the important ideas of the play shifted from one act to the next? Some plays work better when read aloud than others; scenes with complex language or intricate puns are probably best saved for textual study. But almost any variation on dramatic reading produces thoughtful reflections on how production and interpretation intertwine, as well as plenty of classroom entertainment.

Combining dramatic reading assignments with writing assignments strengthens students' skills and critical understanding. Large lecture courses might need to allow a few groups of volunteers to do a performance in place of a more traditional assignment, and courses with twenty-five to forty students might need to shorten the presentation times suggested below. In courses with fewer than twenty-five students, the following assignment can easily be used twice during a typical semester—perhaps once for a comedy and once for a serious play. I start by dividing the class into groups of five to seven students and either assign a play to each group or have each choose a favorite. With the help of a handout, each group then moves through four stages in preparing their play:

Reviewing what genre of drama the play falls into, how it fulfills the goals of that genre, and what students see as the major themes, ideas, or conflicts it presents.

Discussing particular scenes: Which most effectively bring out the themes of the play? Which are funniest or most moving or most provocative? Which are particularly memorable in other ways?

Choosing a few pages from one scene and planning the production: How should the audience feel when this scene ends? What actions and speeches in it are most important? What actions are implied by the stage directions and the lines themselves? What else might the players be doing during the scene? How should the different players deliver their lines? What goals does each character have during this scene? What alliances or conflicts exist among the various characters?

Selecting a group member to play each role and one or two people to talk afterward about the choices the group made.

Assuming that a class has already talked about the plays, this discussion need take no more than thirty minutes: steps 1 and 2 will be largely review and—unless a battle breaks out over who gets the best role—step 4 takes only seconds if the class has become comfortable enough that students willingly volunteer for parts. For residential institutions, where students can get together later, instructors can put this exercise at the end of class and then send students off to rehearse and locate a few minimal props. (I set a budget limit of one dollar per group member to ensure that no one will feel pressured; I also loan out the toy swords and funny hats I have accumulated over the years.) If most students commute or have full-time jobs and families, it makes more sense to start with discussion and then allow students the rest of the period to practice. One or two students might act as directors at this stage, making suggestions to the rest of the group. When the class comes back together, each group has eight to ten minutes to give their dramatic reading, after which students who did not read parts have five minutes to explain why the group made the performance choices it did. Each participant then writes his or her own short paper about what the group was trying to bring out and how; what they found most difficult and most successful; and perhaps what they might do if given time, a budget, and professional actors to work with.

Another topic that merits discussion in any course is the almost complete absence of stage directions in older plays. Students sometimes appear to believe that, unless an action was spelled out, actors just stood there declaiming their lines until the next "exeunt," so it helps to remind them that actors on stage are always doing something, even if that something is just listening to another character. Is the listener in motion or frozen, tense or relaxed, attentive or careless, sneering or turned away, fiddling with some prop? Such decisions need to grow organically out of a play and not be arbitrary; they signal the interpretation of character, theme, and tone. If the campus theater has a friendly director, she or he might be willing to come talk about the process of deciding on stage business for each scene. It also works well to show several different versions of a famous speech from a much-filmed playwright like Shakespeare. What exactly is Hamlet doing, for instance, as he asks his famous question, "To be, or not to be?" Students quickly see how the tone of the scene shifts if Hamlet is touring a crypt, as in Franco Zeffirelli's 1990 *Hamlet*, or experimenting with possible angles for a bullet through the head, as in Michael Almereyda's 2000 version.

Another aspect of performance that deserves attention is the intersection between theater and performance theory, particularly as the latter relates to gender and sexuality. Women playwrights from the Restoration and eighteenth century push us to consider gender as performative by explicitly raising the issue of whether gender is innate or assumed and, if assumed, whether our gendered behaviors are assigned by society, chosen by us, or both. Breeches parts make the question most obvious—do clothes make the man?—but every time a female character must disguise herself or act a part, we are asked to think about how female identity is determined, assumed, or assigned. In Hannah Cowley's *The Belle's Stratagem* (1780), for example, Letitia Hardy presents herself in turn as a modest English girl, a sexually eager country hoyden, and a masked mystery women of exotic tastes. The play asks us directly which is the real woman and whether Letitia's identity is revealed by such acting or imposed by society and the man she woos. Scholarship on women playwrights thus discusses gender as socially constructed and performative.

Many women playwrights call attention to the performance of class as well: through servants successfully disguised as members of the aristocracy, like Sir John Roverhead and Lady La Bassett in Pix's *The Beau Defeated* (1700); through citizens trying to ape the manners of the upper class, like Mrs. Rich in the same play; or through well-born ladies disguising themselves as gypsies (*The Rover*), prostitutes (*The Feigned Courtesans*), kept mistresses (*The Beau Defeated*), or male pages (*The Rover* again). Self-referential moments—such as the prologues and epilogues in which the audience is jokingly reminded that they are spectators at a play—also offer good sites for drawing attention to the performative.

Writing assignments also offer many ways to help students think about production. Using no more than *The London Stage* and *A Biographical Dictionary* (Highfill, Burnim, and Langhans), students can often learn a fair amount about the original production history of a play and the kinds of roles usually played by its stars. Scholarship on individual plays often includes some discussion of original productions as well. Instructors can ask students to summarize their research findings in a short exercise or have them incorporate their research as part of a longer interpretive essay. In either case, it is important to warn students that good information is not always available and to provide an acceptable alternative for students who get stuck. Classes can also use *The London Stage* and even the incomplete *The London Stage, 1800–1900* (Nelson et al.) to study the later performance history of a play: how many nights it ran, how often it returned to the stage, whether it was ever chosen for a benefit performance, which actors played the leads in subsequent productions, and, occasionally, what viewers had to say. Today's renewed interest in early women's plays has conveniently coincided with the explosion in electronic resources, so it is often possible to find newspaper reviews of recent productions. Plays by Baillie, Behn, Frances Burney, Susanna Centlivre, Cowley, Elizabeth Inchbald, Pix, and Catharine Trotter have been produced since 1995, both at college theaters and at professional companies of various sizes. Some reviews of these productions offer only a short biography and a plot summary, but a few discuss production choices. Enterprising students might even try to contact directors or actors with their questions.

If an instructor has devoted class time to considering what its drama says about an age, one interesting possibility is to ask students to consider the differences between what a Restoration or eighteenth-century audience might have wanted to see in a play and what would need to be done to adapt one of these plays for a modern audience. We cannot know whether the original audience for Behn's *The Rover* felt any qualms when watching first Willmore and then Blunt and Frederick threaten Florinda with rape, but because twenty-first-century students often find those scenes deeply troubling, a group of students might want to consider how a modern production could preserve a comic tone in those scenes—or whether it should emphasize those scenes' potential grimness. Similarly, audiences in the age of sensibility probably felt less skeptical than we do about Lady Mary Woodley's quick conversion in Griffith's *The Times*, which has this fashionable spendthrift suddenly agreeing to a modest country retirement with her formerly submissive husband. Students can be asked to find ways to play this and preceding scenes so as to make Lady Mary Woodley's change believable to a modern audience. Many Restoration plots feel rather cruel today, so students might consider how to prevent a certain nastiness from creeping into Miranda's extended flirtation with her old guardian in Centlivre's *The Busybody* (1709), another Miranda's teasing of Constant in Trotter's *Love at a Loss* (1701), Lady Landsworth's testing of Younger Clerimont in Pix's *The Beau Defeated*, or Charlotte's outlandish testing of her new husband's loyalty in Ariadne's *She Ventures and He Wins* (1695).[2]

One stimulating variation on the traditional research paper takes students back to Milhous and Hume's *Producible Interpretation* by asking them to appraise a scholarly theory about a text based on its producibility. For this assignment, students examine the existing scholarship on a play and use questions about production to test the persuasiveness of different interpretations. Is it possible to produce the play in such a way as to bring out these ideas? Would such a production please an audience, or does it somehow go against the grain of the play's appeal? As mentioned earlier, even though women playwrights from the Restoration and eighteenth century were highly successful in the theater, much scholarship on their work still focuses chiefly on theme or on the intersection of theme and biography. Attending to performance is thus one good way to evaluate scholarly interpretations: which interpretations work in the theater and which work only on paper? Of course, an interpretation that works only on paper can be fascinating and even revelatory, but one that also works in performance is probably closer to the playwright's ideal.

Once instructors begin introducing production into the classroom, they will quickly find exercises, assignments, and discussion questions that work for them. Students will add wonderful ideas of their own as they discover that talking about text and talking about performance can be complementary. A production-based approach to teaching drama makes a perfect lead-in to thinking about gender as performative, drama as a performative art, and women's role in theater history.

Notes

1. This quotation is from Janet Todd's edition of *The Rover* in *The Works of Aphra Behn*.

2. Charlotte first makes Lovewell think he has been tricked into marrying a prostitute, then gets him arrested for her supposed debts, and finally pretends she wants to be released from her vows to marry his best friend.

Laura J. Rosenthal

Cultural Studies in the Classroom: Behn's *The Rover*

In the 1990s, cultural studies emerged as a popular approach to reading the long eighteenth century. Scholarly work on the period's theater history has benefited from this expansion, giving us studies of not just the plays themselves but also phenomena such as riots on the Dublin stage, the ubiquitous figure of Harlequin, circum-Atlantic performances, constructions of national identity on stage, the mobilization of spectacle, the disturbing presence of the female body, the celebrity of and sexual suspicions around performers, theater's engagement with colonial expansion, and the multiple meanings of dramatic authorship.[1] The opportunities opened up by cultural studies have been particularly useful to feminist critics, whose work has long considered the way texts shape (and have been shaped by) gendered experience. But while much work has suggested ways of thinking about women in this period's drama in an expansive cultural context, less has been written about how this kind of approach might transform the classroom. Culturally oriented scholarship does not necessarily take the text as the focus of study; most literature department curricula, however, remain organized around periods and genres. Access to nonliterary materials for the classroom is a problem as well, although some publishers have recognized the opportunity to bridge this gap. Bedford has published excellent cultural editions, but none so far on a play by an eighteenth-century woman. The unavailability in print of plays by women once formed a serious barrier to teaching, but this situation has improved. Individual editions of women's plays as well as important anthologies offer new opportunities to teach plays by women. *The Broadview Anthology of Restoration and Early Eighteenth-Century Drama*, expertly edited by J. Douglas Canfield, offers, for example, a far more balanced representation of the period than earlier anthologies.

But while the availability of women's plays has become less of a problem, the incorporation of contextual material remains a challenge. An instructor still has the option of contextualizing through lectures, although this strategy does not provide students with the opportunity to analyze primary documents. Scott McMillin's *Restoration and Eighteenth-Century Comedy*, which includes only one play by a woman (Aphra Behn's *The Rover* [1677]), nevertheless provides an excellent example of the kinds of documents an anthology can include, such as the *Spectator*'s disapproving comments on *The Man of Mode* (1711), Jeremy Collier's critique of the stage (1698), and William Congreve's defense of it (1698). In trying to give students a sense of the cultural context of these plays, I have found such documents much more useful than either lectures or the critical essays sometimes included in editions. Critical essays can become dated, are now easily found on electronic databases, and may not speak to the particular issues that I hope to raise in a given semester. (I include critical essays as part of the work in upper-level undergraduate courses, but I change them for each section.) In future anthologies, then, it would be wonderful to see more space devoted to primary documents or even—dare one dream?—a companion paperback volume to the Broadview filled with such resources pointing to the range of cultural and gendered experience around Restoration and eighteenth-century drama. Lacking such a volume, I have created an ad hoc document collection using copy services and course Web pages.

Assuming the intervention of culture and gender into a traditional genre-focused course would not be the only option for teaching. One could offer a course on women, theater, and theatricality in the long eighteenth century, in which students would read actresses' biographies; Charles II's decree demanding that women play women's parts; Colley Cibber's *Apology* (1740), which comments extensively on actresses; *The Female Wits* (1704); *The Juvenile Adventures of Miss Kitty Fisher* (1759), an anonymous prostitute biography threaded with theatrical adventures; journalistic articles from the period on female performance; plays by women that focus on theatricality, such as Hannah Cowley's *The Belle's Stratagem* (1780); plays by women that focus on gender, such as Susanna Centlivre's *The Wonder* (1714); and even novels with crucial theatrical scenes, such as Jane Austen's *Mansfield Park* (1814), Eliza Haywood's *Fantomina* (1725), and Daniel Defoe's *Roxana* (1724). Such a course could explore the way actresses transformed the English stage in the Restoration, the changing meaning for women of a career in the theater, the theatricality of everyday female life, the theater's place in the cultural construction of sexuality, authorial issues particular to writing for the stage, and the specific ways in which the theater defies the emergent division between gendered spheres. While a few public spaces permitted the participation of women, after Charles II's decree about actresses the theater actually required the presence of women. As a public space, the theater may have been unique in this respect. Such a course would be more consistent with recent scholarship published under the rubric of cultural studies, since it would seek to reconstruct and interpret a broad range of cultural phenomena. Plays written by women could hold a prominent place, but the end point of the course would not necessarily be a reconstruction of female literary history in drama or a close reading of a series of plays.

I have not taught such a course, which probably appears only rarely, because most undergraduate programs continue to be organized around genre and period, despite the new directions that research has been taking. Further, while some institutions would allow the course just described as a special topics section, the heavy demands of preparation might limit the instructor's incentive. Traditional genre courses, however, can provide the opportunity to think about women, gender, and cultural issues as well, and I devote the rest of this essay to this more readily available option.

Fortunately, it is nearly impossible to avoid questions of gender and sexuality in teaching any plays from this period, especially the Restoration comedies that begin most courses. If, for example, a course opens with John Dryden's *Marriage à la Mode* (1673), in which two couples consider sleeping with each other's spouses or intended spouses; then moves to William Wycherley's *The Country Wife* (1675), in which the main character feigns impotence to seduce a higher class of mistress; and then turns to George Etherege's *The Man of Mode* (1676), in which the main character displays his supreme pleasure in the anger of cast-off lovers, discussions of gender and sexuality will never seem like irrelevant feminist impositions on timeless art that contemplates transcendence. In my experience, students raise the cultural issues themselves. After teaching a few commonly anthologized plays by male authors, I turn to Aphra Behn for comparison. I have found that Behn's plays teach extremely well, and I have had success with *The Feign'd Curtizans* (1679) and *The Luckey Chance* (1687). Here I focus on ways to contextualize *The Rover*, perhaps Behn's most popular and most widely anthologized play and an excellent choice to follow Dryden's, Wycherley's, and Etherege's plays. By the time we get to our third play, *The Man of Mode*, students usually have noticed that Restoration comedies often begin with some kind of scheme made clear to the audience but not to all the characters. In *The Rover*, however, unlike in the other plays, they notice that the schemers are the women. Thus whether or not students read the play as a feminist intervention, they notice at least a structural difference. We can then move on to exploring other differences. *The Rover* clearly takes advantage of some of the same dramatic types found in the other plays, but it also interrogates them. (Students often insist that Restoration comedies are all alike, so I try to focus on the ways in which the plays creatively vary some central themes.) I make comparisons throughout the course between the traditionally more familiar male playwrights and women writers such as Susanna Centlivre, Elizabeth Inchbald, and Hannah Cowley. With each playwright, I also try to have students think about any differences in the specific context of the historical moment. I contextualize *The Rover*, then, with two salient issues that have particular significance to the Restoration: libertinism and prostitution.

Libertinism

Much criticism of *The Rover* has struggled to define Behn's intervention into libertine philosophy. In my course, I set up the context for thinking about Restoration libertinism with primary documents, recent criticism, and even the representation of libertinism in current popular culture. The touchstone for many undergraduates for this subject has become the popular film *The Libertine* (2004), although fewer are familiar with the play on which it is based. I have shown trailers in class downloaded from *YouTube*, but possibly a full screening could enhance classroom discussion. *The Libertine* provides an intriguing combination of mythologizing and demythologizing the Restoration, which could be balanced with recent scholarly accounts of libertine court culture. James Turner and Jeremy Webster could be productively paired, since they offer opposing views of libertinism's gendered significance. Basing his arguments on extensive consultation of primary documents (some of which students could explore through *Early English Books Online*, if available, or documents posted on a course Web page), Turner explores the misogyny embedded in much libertine writing and shows how distinctions between artistic eroticism and abject pornography constantly threaten to collapse during this period. Webster takes another perspective, suggesting that libertinism held, within some undeniable limits, liberating potential for both men and women.

To show students more explicit forays into libertinism than we find in the plays, I have used "A Satyr against Reason and Mankind" (1674), by John Wilmot, the earl of Rochester (94–101). I like to show them objecting texts as well, such as Edward Ward's 1709 poem *The Libertines Choice; or, The Mistaken Happiness of the Fool in Fashion* and the anonymous 1673 *Remarques on the Humours and Conversations of the Town*. I have also used Thomas Shadwell's brilliantly outrageous play *The Libertine* (1676), available in Deborah Payne Fisk's excellent *Four Restoration Libertine Plays*, which attacks libertinism by following it through to its presumably logical conclusion. Students often love this play for its absurdity, sometimes finding it more immediately accessible than the subtle complexities of Wycherley and Etherege.

While the representation of libertinism in many plays of the period aligns with party divisions, with Whigs attacking rakes as abusers of power and Tories offering a more sympathetic (although far from uncritical) exploration,[2] Behn's depiction of Willmore—modeled, according to rumor, though now much disputed, on the ur-libertine Rochester—offers a complex and ambivalent portrait. Questions of sexual freedom take on new dimensions in this play. I like to ask students, sometimes on a quiz, whether they would have known this play was written by a woman if they hadn't seen the author's name, which prompts them to think about similarities and differences with the other plays we have read. Reading the way Hellena responds to Willmore's attempts at seduction—she refuses to have sex with him outside marriage because of the unwelcome possibility of single motherhood—opens up discussions about why the potential physical consequences of sex draw so little attention in the other plays, something that usually goes unnoticed until we read Behn's confrontation of it. To be sure, this is not an issue that only women think about—reproduction comes up in Congreve's *The Way of the World* (1700) and Thomas Otway's *Friendship in Fashion* (1678) in parallel plots about marrying off potentially pregnant mistresses. Yet Hellena's direct statement about her physical predicament, in a response that defies the expected balking at virtue or reputation, differs dramatically from the male track-covering plots in the other plays. Why doesn't the possibility of pregnancy occur to Bellinda or Mrs. Loveit in *The Man of Mode*? Canfield has argued that the threat of the confusion of lineage haunts many Restoration cuckolding plots (Introduction). Nevertheless, when in *Marriage à la Mode* the four lovers discuss and reject the possibility of a secret agreement to allow access to each other's spouses, pregnancy plays no role in their deliberations.

The figure of the rake, of course, also serves as an excellent point of comparison between Behn and her male contemporaries. Here a pairing of opposing critical perspectives can help students refine their own views. I have paired Robert D. Hume's essay "The Myth of the Rake in 'Restoration' Comedy" with Michael Neill's "Heroic Heads and Humble Tails: Sex, Politics, and the Restoration Comic Rake." Hume argues that, despite the reputation of this period's drama, few of the plays actually promote libertinism, since many of the rake figures either reform or end up looking absurd or vicious. Neill, by contrast, argues that libertinism challenges the patriarchal status quo. After reading these essays, we think back to the rakes we have encountered, asking whether they ultimately support or undermine the given hierarchy. What kind of rake, I ask the students, does Behn give us, compared with the rakes imagined by her male contemporaries? At first glance, Willmore appears to differ little from other rake heroes, and Behn's political loyalty to her banished Cavaliers could not be clearer. Behn, however, splits the figure of the romantic hero and rake into two different characters (Belvile and Willmore), offering masculine possibilities absent in most other plays of the time.

We also discuss some of the parallels between Willmore and the foolish Blunt, both of whom have a difficult time navigating the foreign culture in which they find themselves. In particular and unlike Belvile, neither has much talent for discerning the difference between marriageable ladies and prostitutes. The crucial scene between Angellica Bianca and Willmore, in which he declares that he would never sell himself, provides the opportunity to ask students to weigh Angellica's answer (men approve a system of commodification in marriage) against Willmore's claim. I eventually ask students if there is any sense in which Willmore does sell himself. The astute readers notice that Angellica not only refuses to charge him but also pays him for sex shortly after he claims he would never sell himself. Are there differences, I ask them, between his acceptance of Angellica Bianca's gold and her self-commodification in the marketplace? I also discuss with students Willmore's final choice of Hellena over Angellica Bianca. Often students at first take Willmore at his word: he has fallen in love with Hellena, and his agreement to marry her has nothing to do with her wealth. A closer look, however, suggests that Willmore is not fully disclosing his knowledge in this scene and that Angellica, of all people, has inadvertently revealed to him Hellena's true identity, assuming that he had already figured it out (he had not).

While Willmore's humor, charm, and job as marine escort to Charles II garner him considerable audience sympathy, he has a darker side that makes for interesting class discussion and gets at some of Behn's mixed feelings toward libertinism. When Willmore drunkenly stumbles upon Florinda, he tries to rape her, and, when she resists, he offers to pay her. One of the most antilibertine moments in the play comes when Belvile utterly rejects the excuse that Willmore thought Florinda was a whore. While Rochester's satire suggests that human beings should revel in their similarities to animals, Belvile turns this figure around, accusing Willmore of acting like a beast. Students, however, sometimes pay less attention to Belvile's condemnation and tell me that "back then" a woman standing outside by herself would simply have been vulnerable to this kind of treatment.[3] Yet Belvile's condemnation makes clear at least the possibility of different perspectives.

By the time we get to discussing the second rape scene, students often see more nuances. On the one hand, they grasp and enjoy the fast-paced comedy of Florinda's attempts to escape from Blunt's aggression. On the other hand, the possibility that Florinda will be raped by her brother particularly complicates this scene for them. Why, I ask them, does Behn threaten her comic heroine with the possibility of incestuous rape? Ideally this question leads them to consider some of the familial and political structures that Behn explores. Does rape mean the same thing in Behn's play as it does in our own time? Much information about rape in the seventeenth century remains inaccessible, but I ask them to consider that rape would have been seen as a crime not just against the woman but also against the victim's father or husband (Bowers). Thus Don Pedro would also suffer from the violation of the woman he has spent so much time trying to protect by way of an honorable marriage to his friend. Echoing the earlier scene, Florinda's vulnerability stems from her temporary lack of protection: by stepping into a no-man's-land, so to speak, between the protection of her father (in this play taken on by a brother who undermines the father's authority in arranging what he sees as a more suitable marriage) and the protection of a husband, Florinda lacks an identity that would protect her from assault. Is it significant that Behn sets this predicament in a Catholic country, which she has in other ways represented as more traditional than Prostestant England? What is the importance of Hellena's experience in this no-man's-land compared with Florinda's? What about Angellica Bianca, also poised throughout the play between male protectors? Do other plays explore the possibility of women in such a position? Even the plotline with Lucetta, though she is overseen by a lover and a pimp, traces female movements in the no-man's-land briefly outside masculine protection. Blunt's violent response, transferred to Florinda, suggests the precariousness of Lucetta's position.

In a good semester, this line of questioning leads to general considerations of specific forms of cultural knowledge and the various ways a text can represent them. While I try not to reduce a comparative reading of *The Rover* to the woman's perspective on libertinism, the question of sexual freedom clearly raises different issues from different perspectives. This usefully complicates the students' sense of culture—that is, there was no more one culture than there was one attitude toward rape, female independence, or sexual freedom.

Prostitution

The Rover also explores the cultural meaning of prostitution. Prostitutes and prostitution certainly appear in plays written by Behn's contemporaries, but less commonly as important characters. The dialogue of Wycherley's *The Country Wife* leads us to understand that Horner consorted with prostitutes before he came up with his scheme to seduce elite ladies; in Etherege's *The Man of Mode*, Dorimant receives a barely literate note from a whore asking for money. It is impossible not to notice, however, that Behn gives the two prostitutes in *The Rover* (Angellica Bianca and Lucetta) not only more attention but also a more complex perspective. To contextualize prostitution as well as libertinism, I have found it useful to remind students that, despite the sexual freedom apparently advocated in some of the plays from the period, serious opposition appeared at the time as well. To compile a rich cultural description, I sometimes have them read something like Josiah Woodward's 1699 *Account of the Societies for Reformation of Manners*, which describes, in admiring detail, the violent Christian vigilante societies that sprang up at the end of the century to police suspected prostitutes and other sinners. Richard Ames's *The Female Fire-Ships; or, A Satyr against Whoring* (1691) and Richard

Head's *Miss Display'd for All Her Wheedling Arts* (1675) offer bawdy and blatantly misogynistic attacks on prostitution. Other somewhat more complex representations include John Garfield's *The Wandring Whore* (1660); the anonymous *Crafty Whore; or, The Misery and Iniquity of Bawd-Houses, Laid Open in a Dialogue between Two Subtle Bawds* (1658); and, my personal favorite, *The Whore's Rhetorick* (1683). These can be accessed through *Early English Books Online* and then copied, placed on reserve, or posted on a limited-access course Web page. They are also available on microfilm. While materials from the Societies for the Reformation of Manners and the misogynist attacks suggest how some contemporaries identified prostitution as the greatest enemy to emergent forms of capitalism for how it supposedly disrupted family life and thus both bourgeois and laboring-class discipline, *The Whore's Rhetorick* and a few other texts from the period suggest, with various levels of irony, that prostitution is identical to—and even a model for—other forms of commercial enterprise.[4]

In some of the plays written by Behn's contemporaries, prostitution functions as an extension of libertinism: Dorimant's whore in *The Man of Mode*, for example, is simply the lowest woman on a ladder that rises from her to Mrs. Loveit to Bellinda to Harriet. The play suggests the whore's humble position through her illiteracy and Dorimant's casual payment to her, in contrast to Harriet's mastery of language and independent fortune. Students often pick up the analogies Behn makes between marriage and prostitution. Indeed, *The Rover* confronts this similarity directly when Angellica challenges Willmore on his insistence that, unlike her, he would never sell himself. Nevertheless, students often assume that the money flows in one direction and the sexual service in another in both marriage and prostitution in predictably gendered ways. Then I ask them, Why does Willmore rattle his gold as he walks out of Angellica Bianca's house? What does Willmore know about Hellena when he asks her to marry him? Does money play any role in his decision?

Returning again to the confrontation between Angellica Bianca and Willmore, I ask students to think back and explore whether any couples in the plays we have read actually meet Angellica Bianca's ideal of entirely noncommercial desire. Why does Behn put this argument in the mouth of a prostitute? Further, what do we make of this declaration in contrast to Angellica's public advertisement of her services? The text identifies her as a courtesan, but placing her picture and her price in the street for all to see is certainly very uncourtesanlike behavior. Comparison with some of the primary accounts of prostitution suggests that it might even be odd behavior for a prostitute. Angellica's public advertisement links elite courtesanship with an almost parodic version of public prostitution, thus collapsing differences in the ladder of women that *The Man of Mode* proposes.

A central point that emerges by historicizing both libertinism and prostitution, then, is that the works of women playwrights in this period can best be understood comparatively. If some women novelists in the nineteenth and twentieth centuries have been able to see their writing as part of a distinct tradition of women authors, no such possibility existed for Behn. While some eighteenth-century women playwrights certainly looked back to her for inspiration, they too did not seem to think of women's plays as forming a separate literary tradition. Behn's version of feminism and the extraordinary complexity of her best plays become most clear in the broader context of the other great comedies written for the stage at the time and the culture that she and her male contemporaries shared, shaped, and contested.

Notes

1. See Burke, *Riotous Performances*; O'Brien, *Harlequin Britain*; Roach; O'Quinn, *Staging*; Marsden, *Fatal Desire*; Straub; and Rosenthal, *Playwrights*.

2. On this point, see Owen, *Restoration Theatre* 176.

3. In matters of gender, perhaps more than anything else, I find that students often assume a static, misogynist past in implicit comparison with their own enlightened present. I try to remember to ban the phrases "back then" and "in those days" from classroom discussion. Somehow, it becomes harder for them to generalize when they have to begin with a phrase like, "in late-seventeenth-century England. . . ."

4. See Rosenthal, *Infamous Commerce*, esp. chs. 1 and 2.

Ellen MacKay

Performance Theory: Attending to the Monkey Wrench in Centlivre's *The Busie Body*

> Th[is] authoress needed no indulgence as a playwright on the score of her sex, for not one among the dramatists contemporary with her better understood the construction of light comic actions, or the use of those conventional figures of comedy which irresistibly appeal to the mirthful instincts of a popular audience. (A. W. Ward 489)

The question that dogs women's writing has long been some version of this one: Having recovered a sizable canon, what do we do with it? Wedging "authoress[es]" alongside famous authors in our anthologies and syllabi raises the specter of asymmetrical treatment that A. W. Ward's defense of Susanna Centlivre is unequal to dispel. Yet courses and collections that treat women's literature as a separate (but equal) subject are no less haunted by unhappy insinuations. So for the critics working this once lonely but increasingly traversed field, perhaps a more searching way of posing the same question is, What does this literature do for us? Self-scrutiny in the discipline has mainly proved a lesson in what women's literature ought not to do: namely, reify an essential, transhistorical idea of woman; reflect back to us our own desires for female agency, resistance, and critique; cordon off women's work from discussion under other rubrics; or flatten out the influence of other categories and contingencies. As a result, the womanliness (whatever that is) of women's literature has become a dubious, and therefore an inefficacious, quality; by now, it is impossible to make an unqualified claim about what women's writing in its capacity as women's writing is doing.

Drama, though, is another matter. As a blueprint for performance (e.g., "*Embraces her in Extasie*," "*[she] struggles and flings from him*" [Centlivre, *Busie Body* 789; act 2, sc. 1, line 275]),[1] it possesses an obvious instrumentality that the more readerly forms of poetry and prose lack. The extent to which its program of action is tied to issues of gender is, of course, open to debate, but since Elin Diamond's influential account of the sign of the Angel in Aphra Behn's *The Rover*, the gestures, deeds, tableaux, and postures that women playwrights demand from their productions help raise the prospect of what Diamond calls "gestic" playwriting, "the purpose of which always is to denaturalize and defamiliarize what ideology—and performativity—makes seem normal, acceptable, inescapable" (*Unmaking* 47). Repurposing the theories of Bertold Brecht for feminist critique, Diamond labels "gestic" any moment in which a playwright makes self-conscious use of the artifice of theatrical performance. She mines rich significance from those occasions: by reminding us of the way theatricality estranges what it shows, rendering identities or conditions an act rather than a natural fact, Diamond proposes that women's dramatic work tends to prove how cultural truths, and especially cultural truths about women, amount to performed fictions.

In the spirit of Diamond's project, this essay scrutinizes a gestic moment in the canon of eighteenth-century women's drama. My aim, though, is not just to lay out the politics of the resulting alienation effect (or *Verfremdungseffekt*, to use Brecht's term) but also to show how received accounts of this dramatic corpus have tended to normalize what is odd, unsettling, and especially gestic about it. The playwright I have chosen to discuss is Susanna Centlivre, an "authoress" who has suffered unjust acclaim for her dramaturgical conformity: as Ward puts it, no one rivals her mastery of comedy's "conventional figures." To dispel this fallacy, I take up the example of Miranda, a heroine of Centlivre's 1709 comedy, *The Busie Body*, and, in particular, her peculiar manner of speaking to the title character, one Marplot by name and avocation, who is rendered in the dramatis personae as "a sort of silly Fellow, Cowardly, but very inquisitive to know every Body's business, generally spoils all he undertakes, yet without Design" (780). Like Miranda, Marplot is an orphan and a ward of Sir

Francis Gripe, but unlike Miranda, who suffers Gripe's jealous keeping of her person and her fortune, Marplot is begrudgingly paid an allowance. Thus absolved of the Restoration hero's quest for financial security, Marplot can indulge his singular trait—a relentless desire to be part of the intrigues that take place around him, coupled with an utter inability to play along.

Recall that Miranda is very nearly undone by Marplot's plot marring when, having completely misunderstood the assignation, he leads Gripe back into the house where the dashing Sir George, at Miranda's behest, has just arrived to declare his affections and procure the lady's rescue (805; 4.3.84). At the sound of the approaching steps of Marplot and Gripe, Miranda hides Sir George behind the chimney board of her fireplace, where the gentleman hastily "condescends" to "lie close" (lines 88, 92). But alas, the troublesome Gripe enters eating an orange and offers to dispose of the peel "behind [the] Lady's Chimney-board" so as to not "litter her chamber" (113, 114). Despite the valiant effort of Miranda's maid, who pleads to eat the trash to save the gentleman from discovery ("Oh pray Sir, give it me; I love it above all things in nature," she says [116]), Gripe is unyielding in his progress toward Sir George's hiding place, and Miranda is left with no choice but to summon up her wits and contrive some excuse that will prevent imminent disaster:

> Hold, hold, hold, dear Gardee. I have a, a, a, a, a Monkey shut up there; and if you open it before the Man comes that is to tame it, 'tis so wild 'twill break all my China, or get away, and that wou'd break my Heart; for I am fond on't to Distraction, next to thee, dear Gardee. (120–25)

In the grand tradition of lascivious guardians, Gripe makes an ass of himself by believing this story. But Marplot, at the prospect of a monkey, cannot contain himself. "A Monkey, dear Madam, let me see it," he cries, "Oh how I love the little Miniatures of Man" (129, 131). Apparently he is quite prepared to help himself to the sight, for the stage directions read that Miranda "strive[s] with him" when she replies, "Be quiet, Mischief, and stand farther from the chimney—You shall not see my Monkey" (132–33). The upshot of this struggle leaves Marplot nearly throttled for his obstinacy; after being told to "let [his] Chargee's Monkey alone" or suffer a clout from Gripe's cane (141), he petulantly waits until both Miranda and Gripe have left the room before he makes for the chimney, raises the board, and is frightened witless by the cramped and crabbed personage of Sir George. When he screams like a fishwife at the surprise

("Oh Lord!" "Thieves," and "Murder" [158–59]), he summons Gripe back to the scene of the old man's deception. But just when all seems lost, Marplot prevents disaster by covering Sir George's exit with an uncharacteristically deft lie:

> I beg of you to forgive me: Longing to see the Monkey, I did but just raise up the Board, and it flew over my Shoulders, scratched all my Face, broke yon' China, and whisk'd out of the Window. (168–72)

As the author prophesizes in her prologue, critical opinion accounts *The Busie Body* an "inspired" comedy ("If with such scenes an audience had been fir'd / The poet must have really been inspired" [780; lines 3–4]), albeit a slight one, and therefore, over the long but lean history of judgments pronounced on the play, it has been something of an obligatory exercise to offer an account of whence the inspiration for it may have come. From Laura Rosenthal's work on the subject, we know that women playwrights of the long eighteenth century are peculiarly "vulnerable to the charge of plagiarism" (*Playwrights* 12), and Centlivre suffers this suspicion more acutely than most for the combination of her susceptibilities: she is not just a woman but also an actress of humble birth and (it has been alleged) of multiple marriages,[2] too protean of surname and too subject to the marketplace to be taken for the proprietor of her own fictions; she is, in sum, too little self-possessed to be possessing. Thus, writes David Womersley, who includes *The Busie Body* as the final play in his anthology *Restoration Drama*:

> [S]cholars have hunted for sources for the play, but aside from one or two touches lifted from Jonson's *The Devil is an Ass*, and some very general parallels with Molière's *L'Étourdit* and Dryden's *Sir Martin Mar-all*, they have returned empty-handed. (Introduction)

While Womersley retraces here the network of indebtedness that he dismisses as the pursuit of a wrong-headed line of scholarship, he has a different interpretation of Centlivre's impressionism to influence: to Womersley, *The Busie Body* derives from "lengthy experience of what works in the theatre, rather than . . . hard reading in the study." In other words, Centlivre cannot be said to have cribbed the work of fellow authors, because she is never part of that intellectual fellowship; she is a creature of the stage rather than the study, and she has learned her business in a milieu in which petty thievery is not a hazard but something of a professional obligation. By her functionalist commitment to "what works," we can assume Womersley means that Centlivre borrows for her own use the conventions of late Stuart comedy—among these, saucy double entendre, multiple disguisings, and a denouement that features the punishment of elderly lechery and the reward of young love. And while this practice is hardly extraordinary, her accomplishment is the fluency of the resulting pastiche. For corroboration of this assessment, Womersley enlists the faint praise of William Hazlitt, who pronounces *The Busie Body* lacking in profundity but "admirable" for its "ingenuity of contrivance"; as Hazlitt analogizes, "the situations succeed one another like the changes of machine in a pantomime" (qtd. in Womersley, Introduction). The rationale for the play's inclusion in the canon of *Restoration Drama* is thus its extraordinary ordinariness; as Womersley concludes, "it is a consummately professional piece of work, and as such sheds clearer light than do other perhaps more profound or subtle plays on the taste and expectations of theatre-goers during the reign of Queen Anne."

While Womersley's claim is in many respects unexceptionable, I want to rethink Centlivre's longstanding reputation as a professional of the stage, a designation that cannot help but seem a derogation when we keep in mind that excluded from its reference are male poet-scholars like John Dryden, George Farquhar, and William Congreve, the last of whom happens to peer out from his burnished study, book in hand, in the Richard Van Bleeck portraït that graces Womersley's anthology's cover. More particularly, I want to reconsider the allegation that Centlivre's (meager) achievement is her knack for picking over for her own reuse the best "contrivance[s]" that her comic forbearers had to offer. To do so means returning to the scene in which Miranda, Sir George, Gripe, and Marplot face off over the imaginary monkey.

Given Hazlitt's view that Centlivre's best characteristic is the smooth operation of her stolen plots ("the situations succeed one another like the changes of machine in a pantomime"), what interests me about the monkey interlude is the awkwardness of its start. In her effort to halt her guardian in his trip to the hearth, Miranda thrice tells him to "hold" and five times repeats the indefinite article "a" before she conjures up the monkey that will keep him at bay. From these circumstances, we can safely conclude that this stutter is therefore not of the type that warrants therapeutic treatment, for Miranda's faltering does not sound like the inopportune emergence of a speech impediment. It isn't that Miranda can't speak but rather that she is scrambling, rather witlessly, for something plausible to say. Therefore, the "a" that keeps repeating here works something like a pianist's vamp for a nervous singer—it is a cue for a performance that is repeatedly deferred and thus becomes the score, or the metronomic index, of Miranda's stalled invention. The effect is comedy by excruciation: with each failure to yoke her "a" to an object, Miranda renders the possibility of her problem's smooth resolution increasingly remote and the prospect of an impropitious lie increasingly likely. In these five maladroit syllables, then, the play's happy ending teeters on the brink.

For all its compact force, though, "Hold, hold, hold, dear Gardee. I have a, a, a, a, a Monkey shut up there" has failed to attract the plaudits earned by the theater's more distinguished repetitive phrases—from Shakespeare's *Macbeth*, "Tomorrow, and tomorrow, and tomorrow" (2613; act 5, sc. 5, line 19), for instance; from David Mamet's *Glengarry Glen Ross*, "get the *chalk*. Get the *chalk*. Get the *chalk*" (63); from Suzan-Lori Parks's *Top Dog/Underdog*, "who-see-thuh-red-card-who-see-thuh-red-card? I see thuh red card" (18); or from Samuel Beckett's *Happy Days*, lovingly satirized in Christopher Durang's *The Actor's Nightmare*, "pause, pause, pause" (165). Whereas Mamet, Parks, Beckett, and Shakespeare render repetition a mark of the poet, in Centlivre's case, repetition is the mark of the poet's embarrassing absence. Miranda's stutter is the written transcription of words' failure; it is the sound a tongue makes when it has lost traction with the world of ideas, which happens also to be the sound that an actor makes when she has lost track of her lines. As the work of a playwright characterized as machinelike in her efficient succession of contrivances, the exhibition of the stammering Miranda therefore presents us with a provocative contradiction between dramatic reputation and dramatic action. And thus it demands we give Centlivre's dramaturgy a second look.

Miranda's line is important on two counts: first, for its novelty—in my anecdotal experience, it is the first instance I have encountered of this kind of scripted incoherence—and, second, for the shock it must therefore occasion, since with the same deliberation that she rhymes a couplet, Centlivre ruptures the comic routine. When Gripe dismisses Mrs. Scentwell's request for his orange peel, Miranda's awkward attempt to resolve her misfortune signals, by its very awkwardness, the intrusion of contingency in a closed world of carefully rehearsed social performance. That stammer, in other words, is the sound of artful contrivance hitting the skids; in it we hear a spanner dropped in the production's works. There is, moreover, an audible willfulness to this rupture, for the line guards against the possibility that it be misperceived as merely an accident of performance. Since surely no one playing the ingenue's role could manage to forget the word "Monkey" in this sentence or to trip in so ungainly a fashion over its untricky pronunciation, Centlivre scripts Miranda's fumbling to sound like scripted fumbling, so that her "a, a, a, a, a" marks a decision to break with the customary glibness of laughing comedy. And thus, for the briefest moment, she raises the possibility that *The Busie Body*'s smooth course to its foregone conclusion is not a done deal.

This effect, however fleeting, conveys the fundamental difference I want to delineate between the dramaturgy of *The Busie Body* and that of the genre Centlivre is said to mechanically epitomize. By sending Miranda to her wit's end and by leaving her there to hem and haw in a manner unbecoming of a leading lady, Centlivre shows her audience that wit has an end, or at least a clearly demarcated edge off of which she leaves her heroine to dangle. The effect is to force her audience to notice that the blistering bon mots and the brilliant sallies that characterize eighteenth-century comedy's ritual courtships continue only so far as Centlivre labors to invent them. We could call this the tyranny of an author over her dependent creations, but what I suggest instead is that, by inserting a burst of static in her play's patter, Centlivre confronts us with the mechanics of her dramatic construction, rather as Toto exposes the tootling machinery of the Great and Powerful Oz. She draws the curtain on the elaborate artifice of the genre she practices, exposing a world as artfully contrived and as utterly inauthentic as the scenery of a pantomime.

How then can we account for the play's critical reception? I suggest that when Hazlitt recollects for us a *Busie Body* that is a feat of theatrical engineering and Womersley collects for us a *Busie Body* that is an exemplar of professional proficiency, they prove how effectively Centlivre evokes the elaborate mechanicity of the tradition in which she works. Its briefest malfunction, rendered here like five skips of a broken record, is enough to expose eighteenth-century comedy, when professionally (and not poetically) composed, as a clockwork genre. For these critics, such a revelation can only mark the limits of Centlivre's artistry; when Womersley writes in his introduction that *The Busie Body* "sheds a clearer light than do other perhaps more profound or subtle plays on the taste and expectations of theatre-goers during the reign of Queen Anne," he makes the playwright's selling point—that is, Centlivre's "ingenuity of contrivance"—an important talent only insofar as it reveals to us the shallowness of her audience and her epoch. But another way of understanding Womersley's observation is that if *The Busie Body* illuminates theatergoers' "taste and expectations" in the contrivances it is famous for exhibiting, the harsh glare of the play's mechanicity exposes those same tastes and expectations in Diamond's denaturalizing light. Unlike those study-bound playwrights (again, Dryden, Farquhar, and Congreve come to mind) whose plays prescribe what is "normal, acceptable, inescapable" (Diamond), Centlivre, in her association with "construction," "convention" (Ward), and "contrivance" (Hazlitt), highlights the man-madeness of what those playwrights pass off, and their audiences perceive, as natural and true. Even more intriguing, the popularity of Centlivre's plays suggests the possibility that, as in Brecht's prewar Germany, the alienation of that which has heretofore seemed normal, acceptable, and inescapable was precisely what appealed to audiences' tastes and expectations.

Admittedly, this seems a lot to claim for the halting delivery of five "a"s, regardless of their originality. But instead of dismissing Miranda's stutter as too small a break with convention to merit our critical interest, we need to remember how prominently the trippingly spoken speech—as opposed to one that is tripped over and mangled—shapes our idea of the theater. Thanks to Hamlet's advice to the players ("Speak the speech, I pray you, as I pronounced it to you—trippingly on the tongue" [1708; act 2, sc. 2, lines 1–2]), which is by now something of a theatrical prime directive, there is a pervasive belief that an actor's job is to get out of the way of the script, checking any idiosyncrasies at the playhouse door. Somewhat further along the same line of thought is the assumption that a great script can rise above the contingencies of performance, muscling aside an actor's incompetence to charm the audience. To see how entrenched this notion has become, we need only consult that high-water mark of theater mythology, *Shakespeare in Love*, wherein the world is presented as a succession of cruel accidents for which the stage is the cure.

Those who know the film well will recall that one of its running jokes is the appalling amateurism of Henslowe's bit players, for the theater manager settles his debts by offering stagestruck creditors roles in his original production of *Romeo and Juliet*. Much to young Shakespeare's dismay, Henslowe casts his tailor to recite the sonnet prologue, despite the man's misfortune of an outrageous stutter. In rehearsal, the afflicted actor never gets past the *t* of "Two households," but when he makes his debut, words pour effortlessly from him; suddenly he turns into the masterful thespian of Hamlet's description. The implication is that a miracle happens when an actor is in the grip of dramatic greatness: as if possessed by the fineness of the poetry he speaks, he transcends the flaws of his earthly body to render his lines appropriately immortal. The boldness of Centlivre's dramaturgy is cast in high relief by comparison, for in *The Busie Body*, the pleasing fiction of drama's glitchless, hitchless world is turned on its head. The play shows instead that the glib life some male authors have scripted to take place behind the apron or inside the proscenium is an unsustainable performance.

It is worth emphasizing that the claim I am making for Centlivre is not epistemological—the world the comic theater depicts in 1709 is hardly at risk of being mistaken for real life. What I mean is that the *The Busie Body* exposes the labor, not to say the laboriousness, behind the period's most reflexive teleology. For the hitch in Miranda's assured progress from wealthy orphan to lover to wife is a hiccup in a tale that may be unmistakably fictional but is also creepily mandatory: by the fiat of an unyielding comic imperative—we might call this the law of "what works"—it serves as the stuff that the culture's dreams are made on, since, judging by its dramatic offerings, post-Restoration England's happiest fantasy is a parentless heiress. So while her march to the altar is but momentarily disrupted, the sudden flummoxing of Miranda—her wit and grace heavily vanished, like the nymphs at Prospero's banquet—is a momentary but memorable disenchantment of a cherished fiction. Or to put a finer point on it, the scene turns a cherished fiction into a marred plot.

Eventually, which is to say in a matter of mere seconds, Miranda recovers from her stammer. Five "a"s are sufficient for her to dream up the monkey whose imagined effects—china smashing, defenestration—are reason enough for Gripe to discard his orange peel elsewhere. The breach in *The Busie Body*'s dramaturgy is thereby repaired, and the play resumes its progress toward its compulsory comic closure. But once having brought to mind the play's comic artifice, the ensuing scene has the strange effect of raising it all over the place. For as Womersley notes in his gloss, Miranda's excuse, when she finally spits it out, is inspired by William Wycherley's *The Country Wife* (also included in Womersley's anthology), in which "china" is the watchword for several adulterous trysts and monkeys are the insult of the libertine Horner masquerading as a woman-hater: "Oh women, more impertinent, more cunning, and more mischievous than their Monkeys, and to me almost as ugly" (205; act 4, sc. 3, lines 154–56). To

Womersley, Centlivre's use of these charged terms is simply her recycling of Wycherley's randy coinage; in his gloss, the monkey who will "break [Miranda's] china" means the man who will "ravish [her]," the idea being that Miranda is taunting her dull-witted guardian with the imminent theft of her virginity (805). And yet, as Beth Kowaleski-Wallace writes, "china tropes the male body" in *The Country Wife*: "Like expensive china, Horner's body is sought after by the ladies. The 'hardness' of the china makes it an appropriate phallic image" ("Women" 156). This meaning makes Miranda's lie a little perplexing, as well as the monkey's shift from figuring women to figuring a man. If having china means having her way with the gentleman she desires, how is it that Miranda can have her china, in Wycherley's sense, and have her monkey break it too? The allusion to *The Country Wife*, while certainly audible, fails to set in a second motion the double entendres that are Wycherley's claim to fame and leaves us feeling that we have missed the dirty joke, or, more unsettling, that the dirty joke that Centlivre refers to has disappeared under the renewed scrutiny of her play's allusion to it.

To my mind, this unsatisfaction is precisely the pleasure of *The Busie Body*. In the vein of Miranda's stutter, the interdramatic episode plays out as a dramatic failure, for it depletes Wycherley's celebrated china scene of all its titillating éclat. Always the literalist, Marplot even goes so far as to turn the winking innuendo of "china" back into teacups and dinner plates when he breaks some to punctuate George's escape. But the effect of letting Restoration drama's cheeky conceits sputter and stall out is to champion a new form of comedy, one that challenges the preordained plots of Wycherley and his ilk by turning the play over to its titular busybody—that bumbling hero of unknown parentage and unfixed ideas who is so fittingly named. Under the influence of Marplot, Centlivre's play proposes that the faltering of comic conventions—indeed, the wholesale marring of them—makes for happier endings.

Of course, there are more conspicuous strategies that women playwrights use to challenge the expectations and tastes whetted by their male rivals. It is hard to miss the way Elizabeth Griffith's *The School for Rakes* (1769) and Hannah Cowley's *The Belle's Stratagem* (1780) turn the tables on gender roles that are already fixtures of the social and dramatic repertoire (thanks to Molière's *School for Wives* and Farquhar's *The Beaux' Stratagem*, respectively). A more trenchant but less overt example of this same tactic occurs in *The Rover*, when Behn invents a trick bed as the centerpiece of a scene that dispenses a neat corrective to romantic comedy's infamous bed trick.[3] But I find Centlivre's stutter to be especially ingenious for the way it invites us to reassess established dramatic conventions: rather than invert or revise comedy's devices, *The Busie Body* momentarily brings them to an unsteady and uncomfortable halt. In her capacity as the consummate professional of the eighteenth-century stage, Centlivre takes a hard look at the theater's ingenuity of contrivance, then does us the favor of tossing a monkey wrench into the works.

Notes

1. All quotations from *The Busie Body* are from David Womersley's *Restoration Drama: An Anthology*.

2. Centlivre's marital history is a matter of gossip and conjecture, since there is insufficient documentation of her early life to ascertain whether she married any of the men with whom she has been associated before Joseph Centlivre (Finberg, Introduction).

3. I am referring to scene 2, act 3, of *The Rover* (in Womersley's anthology), in which Lucetta's bed "descends" from her darkened chamber, while Blunt, groping blindly to consummate the assignation he has contracted, stumbles down a trap and falls into the "Common-Shoar," getting "his Face &c. all dirty" in the process (359–60; lines 65, 121). The conventional bed trick is the substitution of one woman for another in a prearranged sexual assignation. Best known for its centrality to Shakespeare's *All's Well That Ends Well* and *Measure for Measure*, the bed trick is a sufficiently common device that Marliss Desens dedicates an entire book to its study.

Thomas C. Crochunis

Pre- and Postrealist Dramaturgy: Women Writers, Silence, Speech, and Trauma

Throughout the history of women's dramatic writing, traumatic experiences serve as central incidents. While traumatic events might also be said to be a staple of the long legacy of male writers' tragic dramaturgy, women writers pay particular attention to the traumas suffered by women that are related to their gendered societal roles. Even in comic forms, women's plays often build on disturbing situations related to pressures to marry, crises of reputation, and problems resulting from desires for autonomy prohibited in particular social systems. This essay, however, is concerned with how we can teach the long history of the way women playwrights have employed innovative dramatic forms to present on the public stage the kinds of profoundly disturbing traumatic experiences for which realistic representation proves inadequate. To what extent can connecting pre- and postrealist dramaturgy help students understand the problems of dramatic representation for women writers? In particular, I want to suggest ways that Joanna Baillie's *Orra* (1812) and Elizabeth Inchbald's *The Massacre* (writ. 1792, pub. 1833) might be taught alongside a series of dramatic texts by women writers that stage women's traumatic experiences—plays such as Florence Bell and Elizabeth Robins's *Alan's Wife* (1893), Susan Glaspell's *The Outside* (1917), Paula Vogel's *How I Learned to Drive* (1997), and Adrienne Kennedy's *The Ohio State Murders* (1992), as well as graphic fictions such as Marjane Satrapi's *Persepolis* (2003). By inviting students to examine how each of these dramatic pieces relates to psychological realism, we can help them explore ways to relate Baillie's or Inchbald's dramatic strategies to women's postrealist dramaturgy.

An interesting place to begin is with scenes from contemporary graphic fiction. Examining Marjane Satrapi's dramatic strategies in *Persepolis* provides an effective way of seeing the different rhetorical approaches possible in representing stories through images of characters, their words, their bodies, and their settings. Satrapi establishes several different dramatic-rhetorical figures: the representational realism of (drawn) photographs, stylized images of social movements, caricatured pastiches that show key moments in social change, and moments of direct character address to the reader-viewer-audience. The book begins with a drawing of Satrapi as a girl in Iran and the caption, "This is me when I was 10 years old. This was in 1980." The playful fiction of objective representation is soon exchanged, however, for a different rhetoric. In the third frame of the first page, Satrapi presents a stylized drawing of a group of Islamic revolutionaries with arms raised at visually synchronized angles. While the captions continue to narrate—as if in voice-over—her personal history within the history of cultural change, Satrapi introduces yet another rhetorical strategy in the fifth and final panel of her first page. A group of children are shown dispersed and playing in the schoolyard, each engaged in some form of refusal to wear the newly instituted veil with appropriate solemnity. After several panels that further chronicle the social changes under fundamentalist Islam while reworking these three strategies of rhetorical representation, Satrapi ends her book's opening with a direct address to the reader: an image of herself as a girl looking as if she is speaking directly to us with the caption, "And that was that." By opening her book with this rhetorical overture, she establishes the dramaturgical possibilities of her medium, making clear that *Persepolis*'s way of engaging us as readers will use dramatic forms not limited to realist representations of characters and their circumstances.

Beginning with graphic fiction allows students to get a sense immediately that dramatic forms are rhetorical, that events represented in serious dramas need not be related as tales of painful experiences that unfold as if inevitable. Two questions emerge from consideration of Satrapi's dramatic narrative approach: How could we enact scenes from Satrapi's fiction, using her images as clues to bodily performances that could suggest the shifting tones of her story? How does pushing the boundaries of representational memoir enable Satrapi to engage her readers more effectively? Regardless of how the class comes to answer these questions, considering them carefully helps prepare us to discuss similar questions when exploring why women writers such as Baillie and Inchbald chose to write in dramatic forms in a novel-reading era that presented a woman writer with all manner of social and practical challenges to getting her plays staged in the theatrical venues to which she aspired.

After students read *Persepolis* and consider its shocking cartoonlike drawings of the torture and mutilation of political prisoners, they can do a simple assignment that prepares them to consider how powerful the act of writing down dramatic enactments can be. To underscore this point, I ask students to make lists of traumatic incidents that strike them as real-world horrors. For this assignment, it is important to outline clearly the steps that are to follow, including which parts of the assignment will be shared with someone else and which parts will not be. When students each have a list of four or five possibilities, I ask them to choose the one on their list that is most troubling. I then have students write a sentence-length summary of the traumatic incident envisioned; I encourage them to write as objective a characterization as possible on an index card. Next, I invite everyone to place the index cards into a stack and ask each student to draw one card. Before students look at the cards, I remind them that the card draws will lead to one of two kinds of writing: its recipient will either write a simple script that represents the traumatic incident in stage or shot directions and dialogue or write reflectively about the feelings, beliefs, or experiences that lead him or her to choose not to represent the incident. Discussion following the exercise can focus on student observations about the general point that dramatic writing can be dangerous even if never enacted. Students will then understand better what some of the women playwrights we study already knew: how high the stakes can be in dramatic writing.

In sequencing a syllabus, I begin with realist plays that foreground the difficulties of representing characters that have experienced trauma. Florence Bell and Elizabeth Robins's *Alan's Wife* provides a valuable starting point. The play's center is Jean Creyke's increasingly painful predicament. Having willingly given up her aspirations to a middle-class life by marrying Alan, a worker in the town's factory, Jean is devastated by his death in an industrial accident at the end of scene 1. Confronted with caring for her crippled and congenitally ill child, she decides to put young Alan out of his misery in the harrowing end to scene 2. Finally, in scene 3, facing the law's inquiry into the child's death, she becomes silent, only gesturing the meanings the script conveys through a combination of stage directions and otherwise conventional-looking lines of dialogue that readers are told is "a stage direction of what she is silently to convey" (367):

> *Mrs. Holroyd.* [T]hink, Jean, think, honey! It may be you could tell them something that would save you.
> *Jean.* (*silent—stares vacantly into space*) I can tell him nothing.
> *Colonel Stuart.* Nothing you can say, of course, will clear you now; but, for the sake of the memory you will leave behind you, can you give no sort of reason, no explanation of the impulse that led to your terrible crime? (*Jean shakes her head*) (368)

With Robins creating the role of Jean in the original production, the play sought to find in gesture a language through which suffering could speak. Only at the end of the play does Jean speak aloud again, in her final lines, telling her mother that she accepts her death sentence:

> You do not think I could live after this, do you? I had to do what I did, and they have to take my life for it. I showed him the only true mercy, and that is what the law shows me! Maybe I shall find him up yonder made straight and fair and happy—find him in Alan's arms. (370)

On first reading, the play may seem merely melodramatic, but when we begin to reconsider Jean's gestural speech in scene 3, the play seems almost an object lesson in realism's difficulty both with telling a story centered on traumatic events and with finding a dramaturgy and language that do not neutralize the trauma in the telling. For Jean's voice to be presented, however, the dramaturgy had to be driven by legal inquiry—a representative of the court had to pose questions that Jean's gestures could answer, though of course her bodily answers convey a range of feeling that exceeds the factual information requested. In this play, students begin to see how realist dramatic forms can be at odds with representations of traumatic experiences and how playwrights such as Bell and Robins convey a character's suffering by going beyond the protocols of realistic theatrical speech.

Building on *Alan's Wife*, the course then turns to Susan Glaspell's *The Outside*, a short play that both provides a realistic setting for its traumatized characters and serves as a symbol for the characters' state of mind created through the evocation of its borderland Provincetown seascape. *The Outside* centers on two women who, as they struggle with the pain of past losses, are living in what was once an active lifesaving station on the margins of land and sea. While the women are poetic, even cryptic in their silences (Allie) and contorted speech (Mrs. Patrick), Glaspell juxtaposes them with the realistic behaviors of the lifesavers, men who drag back bodies from the sea to revive them. In fact, by putting characterizing descriptions of the women in the men's mouths, Glaspell shows us just how different a pragmatic, realist view of trauma and its evocative staging can be. For instance, Bradford, a lifesaver, tells of how Allie Mayo came to work for Mrs. Patrick:

> And then she wanted somebody to work for her. "Somebody," says she, "that doesn't say an unnecessary word!" Well, then Bill come to the back of the store, I said, "Looks to me as if Allie Mayo was the party she's lookin' for." Allie Mayo has got a prejudice against words. Or maybe she likes 'em so well she's savin' of 'em. She's not spoke an unnecessary word for twenty years. She's got her reasons. Women whose men go to sea ain't always talkative. (51)

It is helpful to contrast Bradford's narrative explanation of the background of the two women's relationship with how Allie Mayo characterizes the world they occupy together, when Mrs. Patrick indicates that she has sought the margins:

> *Mrs. Patrick.* This is the outside—these dunes where only beach grass grows, this outer shore where men can't live. The Outside. You who were born here and who die here have named it that.
>
> *Allie Mayo.* Yes, we named it that, and we had a reason. He died here (*reaches her hand toward the closed door*) and many a one before him. But many another reached the harbor! (*slowly raises her arm, bends it to make the form of the Cape. Touches the outside of her bent arm*) The Outside. But an arm that bends to make a harbor—where men are safe. (53)

When Allie Mayo's arm significantly makes the shape of Provincetown's cape shore, once again gesture provides a way for realistic dramaturgy to get beyond the limitations of character speech about past trauma. Through their verbal confrontation at the end of the play, Allie Mayo and Mrs. Patrick move beyond silence and toward an epiphany about what the "savers of life" might be able to show them about "meeting the outside" (53)—that facing the outside, nature, and death may simply be the other side of harboring or nurturing life on the inside, in human society, and in relationships with others. The pain of loss can turn and become the basis for human connection.

Students can consider the ways that these plays move between representing realistic silences surrounding traumatic memories and enacting growth and healing that audiences can feel as well as rationally understand. By examining how Bell and Robins and Glaspell push the limits of realist dramaturgy, we can help students look more carefully at the logical assumptions underlying realism, such as the following:

> The past traumas of characters can be adequately expressed through realistic behavior and speech about those characters in realistic social settings.
>
> Audiences can integrate characters' past and present experiences through making rational connections and inferences about characters' emotions.
>
> Performers can best engage audiences with characters through representing their behavior (including speech) in realistic social environments.

Assumptions like these, in the light of reading *Alan's Wife* and *The Outside*, can be the subject of critical examination. I remind students of the varied dramatic rhetorics employed in the opening of Satrapi's *Persepolis* and ask them to consider how rhetorical alternatives to realistic character representation could change the kinds of feelings, political stances, and identifications audiences experience in response to characters' suffering.

Having complicated students' understanding of realistic dramaturgy a bit, I turn to two prerealist plays: Inchbald's *The Massacre* and Baillie's *Orra*. For me, these plays are the centerpiece of the historical reevaluation of the lineage of women's formal struggles with the social issues surrounding dramaturgy and trauma. Before there was poststructuralist, Marxist, and feminist dramatic theory to question whether the assumptions underlying realist dramaturgy could allow for compelling representations of women's responses to violence, cruelty, and violation, there were dramatists working on these theoretical issues in practical, dramaturgical terms. Inchbald and Baillie are central figures in the history of this feminist praxis.

In introducing plays such as Inchbald's *The Massacre* and Baillie's *Orra* to students, instructors may find it helps to weigh carefully the dramatic predicament the two authors bring on themselves. Inchbald wrote her thinly veiled dramatic report on the violent public massacres in France during the height of British anxiety about how the events in France would affect homeland security. Although it is hard to know for sure, I suspect that Inchbald knew when she wrote the play that it could not be staged. But even given the cultural context in which Inchbald was writing plays in the early 1790s, *The Massacre* is a startling play; its compression into a "time of representation" of "one day" and division into three short acts with two breaks in time and only one change of scene gives it the urgency of a one-act play. Though set in the time of France's 1572 Saint Bartholomew's massacre, the play clearly parallels political events in 1790s France. Beginning in medias res as the family of Eusèbe Tricastin nervously awaits his return from Paris, the play's action is soon accelerated when it is reported that there has been a massacre of citizens believed to have the wrong factional sympathies. Eusèbe arrives safely, easing concern, but paints a picture of the slaughter he has witnessed. Though act 1 ends with young Tricastin, his father, his wife, and their children resolved to flee the country, at the opening of act 2 word comes that they are too late, for the crowds of revolutionists are roving the countryside and are reported to be in search of young Tricastin. Old Tricastin pleads with his son to make one last attempt to conceal himself for his wife's and children's sakes, but efforts at concealment fail, and only Eusèbe's improvised lie deceives the vigilantes into believing that his wife is merely a servant and better left behind.

After a brief street scene in act 3, scene 1, the act's second scene opens in a law court with Glandève sitting in judgment and taking a critical view of the brutal proceedings initiated by the crowds. His goal in taking the position of judge, he asserts, has been to institute justice, not factional interest. After a series of threats and counterthreats, the violent revolutionary Dugas calls on his soldiers to claim their victims, and all seems lost; but the troops assert through a spokesman that they "are all . . . ready to enter the field of battle against an insulting foe, and boldly kill him; but . . . we have not one hangman." Just when it seems the massacre is scotched, the soldiers reveal that they have discovered Madame Tricastin and her children already stabbed and dying; they carry in their bodies. Glandève's assurances that those responsible for these heinous crimes will be brought to justice notwithstanding, the play ends with the mourning Tricastin men following the bodies as they are carried off while a dirge is sung. Thus Madame Tricastin, who opened the play anxious that her husband might have been the victim of violence, ends the play as a silent, lifeless representative of the revolution's disregard of the domestic and familial relations made central to the Tricastin family's crisis.

This summary of Inchbald's plot gives some sense, I hope, of the headlong pace of her play. *The Massacre*'s characterization and language suggest intensely emotional performances, particularly in the more developed characters of Madame Tricastin, Eusèbe Tricastin, Old Tricastin, Dugas, and Glandève. As the director and performers of a staged reading of the play at the North American Society for the Study of Romanticism at the University of Colorado, Boulder, in September 2004 discovered, the play requires a combination of theatrical points to highlight the key passions of the major characters and supporting performances that move the practical business of the play forward through timely entries and announcements.[1] While the play's brutal events help explain the emotional intensity of the action, for a play written without any immediate likelihood of performance to depend on moments of heightened histrionics raises many questions to explore with students.

When Inchbald submitted *The Massacre* to both of London's major patent theaters, she knew that neither Thomas Harris nor George Colman would produce it. Why would a writer so well aware of the political and social constraints placed on dramatic writing have even written such a play? Inchbald surely understood that *The Massacre*—largely because it was a play—would disturb her radical friends Thomas Holcroft and William Godwin by casting in a negative light situations strikingly similar to those in France. For Inchbald, writing the play was a political act. The play is an unusual hybrid falling somewhere between an incomplete work of art (a romantic fragment) and a politically controversial memo. It exerted all the more pressure on readers such as Godwin because the unlikelihood of its being staged or published in its era raised questions about what kinds of political discourses surrounding gender and revolution were possible.

And yet, having considered the play's historical situation as a politically (though not theatrically) unperformable text, instructors can further explore the play with students by asking them to identify key moments in the play's action and, working in groups, stage them as tableau images meant to communicate key passions, relationships, and themes through embodied frozen moments. By finding ways to create selected three-dimensional pictures, students not only interpret the political ideas behind the theatricality but also encounter the emotional energy created by the movement from page to stage. In working out the physicalization of key moments, students can begin to hypothesize about what Inchbald is trying to reveal to her readers through dramatizing the trauma of revolutionary violence and yet purposefully closeting the play's passions.

They might ask, What were Inchbald's reasons for making women's and men's bodily experience of revolutionary violence seem both imaginatively present and yet transgressive? How might Inchbald's threatening to publish *The Massacre* have provoked radical readers such as Godwin and Holcroft to reconsider constraints on British women's opportunities to speak about the politics of revolution?

Baillie's *Orra* is a less histrionic authorial performance, but it nonetheless troubles the waters of public enactment of (gendered) passions that the playwright had established as her particular concern when she published the first volume of *Plays on the Passions* in 1798. By the time *Orra* appeared in the third volume in 1812, Baillie had established herself as a published dramatist, though she had also taken pains to assert her desire for theatrical production through offering detailed discussions in her prefaces of the stagecraft she thought might benefit her plays. For Baillie, the continued reference in the introductions of her plays to the theater maintained for her readers a sense of the virtual or simulated theatricality of her dramatic works. Both Inchbald and Baillie, then, developed their plays not simply as carefully wrought stage dramaturgy but also as rhetorical exploitations—of the stage as a symbolic public venue, of actors as virtual figures, and of dramas as potentially unrepresentable enactments of trauma.

Baillie's *Orra* is a striking prerealist drama about the effects of psychological trauma on its central character. Introducing her two tragedies on the passion of fear, *Orra* and *The Dream*, Baillie justifies her view that this passion can, in fact, make the subject of an interesting play:

> It has been thought that, in Tragedy at least, the principal character could not possibly be actuated by this passion, without becoming so far degraded as to be incapable of engaging the sympathy and interest of the spectator or reader. I am, however, inclined to think, that even Fear, as it is under certain circumstances and to a certain degree a universal passion (for our very admiration of Courage rests upon the idea), is capable of being made in the tragic drama, as it often is in real life, very interesting, and consequently not abject.
> ("To the Reader" [1851] 228)

Because Baillie wants her tragedies on fear to provoke audience interest in the character's passion rather than dismissive judgment of her or his weakness, she portrays Orra as a lively, intelligent, and independent woman whose verbal quickness and confidence in her views make her a compelling figure. Her one weakness is her superstitious belief in gothic stories about murders and hauntings. When Hughobert—her guardian and the father of Glottenbal, the man to whom Orra is betrothed—loses patience with her refusals and begins to fear that she is becoming too close to Theobald, another suitor, he conspires with Rudigere (a bastard relative of Hughobert who has his own designs on the heroine) to send Orra away to a castle in the forest, aiming to frighten her and weaken her resistance to marrying his son. Though Orra effectively resists their efforts to weaken her resolve, fear causes her to lose her grip on reality, and the play ends with her seeing dead people rise up:

> They close upon us.—Oh! the void
> Of hollow unball'd sockets staring grimly,
> And lipless jaws that move and clatter round us
> In mockery of speech!—Back, back, I say!
> Back, back!
> (*Catching hold of Hughobert and Theobald, and dragging them back with her in all the wild strength of frantic horror, whilst the curtain drops*)
> (164; act 5, sc. 2, lines 218–22)

Orra, then, raises important questions for discussion in class: How might using the language and thinking of the sane inhibit a playwright's presentation of the meaning of a character's trauma? What possibilities does madness open up for a playwright seeking a more impassioned form of discourse to engage audiences emotionally and intellectually with a character's traumatic experiences? One provocative way to invite students to consider the dramaturgical possibilities of madness is to ask them to think back to the traumas they identified as possible subjects for dramatic scripts early in the course. What form would the madness of the victims of those traumas take—what language would they speak, what movements would they make? By asking students to draw images, write lines, or—for the boldest—improvise short solo scenes, I lead them to consider how staging madness like Orra's provides Baillie with an alternative form of dramatic discourse that translates the protocols of representation of realistic character into an impassioned performance of suffering.

Once plays such as Inchbald's and Baillie's have been examined in relation to later realist dramas and students have had a chance to explore how dramaturgy before realism employed heightened theatricality to communicate the complex situation of characters, they are prepared to analyze how contemporary dramatists rework realist dramaturgical conventions to layer character stories with our responses to varied sequences of events, distance from narrated events, and performer identifications. I introduce them to modern plays such as Sarah Daniels's *Masterpieces* and Rebecca Gilman's *Boy Gets Girl*—both realistic treatments of women's traumatic experiences—and then Paula Vogel's *How I Learned to Drive* and Adrienne Kennedy's *The Ohio State Murders*, two plays that explore alternatives to performing traumatic stories realistically. Vogel's and Kennedy's plays, while not radically avant-garde, both introduce a narrative frame that allows the posttraumatic representation of their central characters—Li'l Bit and Suzanne Alexander, respectively—to remain distinct from the versions of themselves that experienced the trauma. *How I Learned to Drive* has the actress who plays the adult Li'l Bit in her thirties or forties also play the part of the teenage Li'l Bit, who was drawn into a sexualized relationship with her Uncle Peck. The play's dual movement is handled in such a way that the ambiguity of the relationship between the two becomes more and more uncomfortable as the action moves both forward in time—toward college-age Li'l Bit's breaking away from Peck and leaving him to suffer on his own—and back in time to reveal earlier and earlier incidents of Uncle Peck's sexual assaults on Li'l Bit. Because Li'l Bit is played by an adult woman, the complexity of trauma's effect on the character and on the audience's empathy drives the play more than do less ambiguous judgments of Peck as a vile abuser. Vogel's dramatic structure is critical to the play's emotional effect.

Likewise, Kennedy's Suzanne Alexander, in *The Ohio State Murders*, is both the teller of her story and the main character in it. Invited to speak at her alma mater about the violent imagery in her work, Alexander tells, and the play enacts, the story of her college years, the racist attitudes she confronted, and the traumatic murder of first one and then the other of the twins she bore as a result of her relationship with their killer, a university lecturer. Kennedy uses the hallucinatory reassurance of Suzanne's voice in the present to lure her audience into the play's story in a way that illuminates the psychological state in which the young Suzanne drifts toward her trauma.

Kennedy's and Vogel's plays represent innovative postrealist techniques of staging traumatic stories. In the context of the entire sequence of readings and activities outlined here, these plays can make a new kind of historical sense, revealing the ongoing challenges of representation and audience engagement that women writers have faced when dramatizing women's traumatic experiences. Baillie and Inchbald are essential parts of that history, and their significance can be best understood through connecting their work to a longer piece of women's dramatic history.

Note

1. The director of this staged reading, Andy Garrett Grapko, wrote in an e-mail message after the production: "The very nature of the piece demanded physicalization. When I got the actors on their feet and they tried reading in a more contemporary and familiar acting style the script just seemed ridiculous. . . . There were certain points of discovery that were crucial, for example, realizing that the intense moments of passion had to be expressed with complete physical expressions of the heightened emotion. For these moments I asked them to play with a technique I know as 'checking' which comes from Asian theatre tradition (you see it at the Beijing Opera). To 'check' means that the performer, in those particular moments of most heightened emotion, . . . hits a dramatic pose as all actions/bodies point to the actor expressing that moment. [T]he actor in focus 'checks' in with the audience metaphorically, as if to say 'see this, are you looking, do you get it?' Those moments just seemed to come naturally and also felt very authentic for the period."

Vimala C. Pasupathi

Contexts for Teaching Margaret Cavendish's *Bell in Campo*

In the 2000 MLA volume *Teaching Tudor and Stuart Women Writers*, Anne Shaver described the numerous classroom contexts in which she taught Margaret Cavendish's *The Blazing World*. Not content to defy the phenomenon described by Elaine Hobby and Bill Overton in their 1994 study "'There Is Not Space for Margaret Cavendish and Dryden,'" Shaver boldly declared that Cavendish's works "deserve an entire course to themselves" ("Margaret Cavendish" 195). Covering information on available editions and approaches to teaching specific texts, Shaver provided the tools to make such a course a reality.

Resources for the study and teaching of Cavendish have grown considerably since the publication of that volume. Such growth owes much to Shaver and the International Margaret Cavendish Society, whose members have produced numerous books and articles on Cavendish and her works in recent years.[1] But if resources abound, opportunities to teach single-author courses remain limited; and though we may no longer be compelled to choose between Dryden and Cavendish in our reading lists, we may still lack opportunities to share the Cavendish canon with students in a way that does justice to its size and scope. While I think any work by Cavendish has something to offer teachers and students of premodern drama, I argue here for the particular rewards of teaching *Bell in Campo*, a two-part drama that appeared in the duchess's first published collection of plays.

The play's primary plot follows the exploits of a general's wife and other women who defy early modern social expectations by accompanying their husbands as they go off to war. More than merely the "beauty in the camp" implied by the play's title, these women respond to their marginalization there by forming their own army, a military unit whose discipline and potency prove superior to the male army of their own kingdom as well as that of the enemy. Rescuing their male counterparts from certain defeat, the female army earns the respect of the male soldiers as well as praise from the king, who, after its disbandment, gives its commander, Lady Victoria, an opportunity to grant its members rights and privileges unprecedented for women in Cavendish's time.

Populated by a variety of allegorically named characters (Lady Victoria, Madames Passionate and Jantil, and Doll Careless) and rival kingdoms (Reformation and Faction), *Bell in Campo* provides a highly literary but also accessible account of both gender and political conflicts in an extremely complicated period of English history. Given the prominence of military affairs in today's political world (and the corresponding prevalence of such affairs in art, media, and other forms of culture), it is not difficult to imagine that *Bell in Campo*'s plot and themes will resonate with students. Yet *Bell in Campo* has more to offer a class than topicality; in fact, one of its greatest strengths lies in stimulating students' interest in the past, particularly in the extent to which the playwright's creation—and ultimate dissolution—of a military unit of women is politically progressive. Indeed, *Bell in Campo* prompts students to consider the complexity of early forms of feminism and the historical conditions that enabled and limited those forms.

I can provide no better evidence for this claim than to share student responses to my general prompt for their thoughts on the conclusion of *Bell in Campo*. One student expressed frustration at the fact that Cavendish does not allow her all-female army to remain intact after it achieves a major victory: "Why give women an army if you only plan to relinquish it later anyway?" Another student responded by arguing that the army is, for Cavendish, simply a means to an end, since the king rewards its demobilization with several social gains. A new legislative act solidifies these gains, declaring in one clause that its members will now sit at the head of their households and, in another, providing "a blank for the female Army to write their desires and demands" (163; pt. 2, act 4, sc. 18). Countering a classmate who was critical of the ending, she wrote, "[W]eren't these some pretty big gains as far as women's rights are concerned?" Praising the playwright's decision to have her characters read the new legislation aloud from a stone tablet, she argued, "[L]isting out those rights is a clever way for Cavendish to list out the way it should be for women (or, I assume, how she thinks it should be)."

Another student quickly objected to this defense of the playwright, insisting that parts of the act were troubling; in fact, one clause demotes the social status of women who were not members of the army, and another implies that they deserve harsh punishment. Another student expressed disapproval that many of the rewards indicated in the legislation benefit only the army's commander. Citing the act's clause that grants Lady Victoria "as much as can be given either from Kings, States, or Poets" (163; pt. 2, 4.18), she reminded her classmates that "Lady Victoria is still being 'given' her honor and privileges by masculine figures. And her treatment is merely an exception rather than the rule." "Is Cavendish consciously making these anti-revolutionary statements," this student wondered, "or is she merely censoring herself?"

Recognizing several points of contradiction in an ostensibly protofeminist play, my students were able to raise, with little prompting, the same questions that literary scholars have wrestled with for decades: Why does Cavendish demobilize Lady Victoria's army? What does it mean that Cavendish privileges some women's choices and actions over others? And how can her Amazonian protagonists simultaneously insist that women deserve equality with men while still glorifying male authority? Students also expressed quite a bit of uncertainty; the student disappointed in Cavendish's ending wondered whether the playwright was fully conscious of its implications, and even Cavendish's most confident advocate had to admit that she was making some assumptions about the playwright's intentions and beliefs.

Certainly, by itself, *Bell in Campo* offers little sense of whether the female army's rewards would have represented "pretty big gains" for women in the early 1660s. Nor does it provide a clear reference point for what constitutes a "revolutionary statement" or the reverse. But the greatest challenge that comes with teaching *Bell in Campo* can also be the source of its greatest pleasure. Indeed, what is most gratifying about sharing it with students is not providing firm answers to their excellent questions but rather giving them an opportunity to explore and develop their own answers. We can enrich students' experiences with the play by helping them situate *Bell in Campo*'s two parts in a variety of overlapping contexts—textual, biographical, historical, cultural, and literary—that may underpin Cavendish's artistic decisions and the contemporary reception of her work.

Because the play's printing coincides roughly with the reemergence of the public theater, *Bell in Campo* provides an excellent starting point for a study of Restoration and eighteenth-century playwrights. Appearing in print in 1662 in the first collection of dramatic works by a woman (*Playes*), the play reflects, in many ways, a unique moment in the history of England and English drama. Although *Bell in Campo*'s publication year places the play firmly within the Restoration, Cavendish's most recent biographer follows her predecessors' contentions that Cavendish composed it while in exile on the Continent during the civil wars and interregnum (Whitaker 209). The play stages a fictionalized account of the events of the previous decades; depicting war between the kingdoms of Reformation and Faction for an England that had survived real-life battles between king and Parliament, it offered a historical account of Stuart civil conflict for those who lived to see a Stuart Restoration. Although the theaters reopened when Charles II returned to the throne, Cavendish's dramatic works were probably never performed.

By accessing the full text on either *Early English Books Online* (*EEBO*) or on microfilm as part of the *English Short Title Catalog* (*ESTC*), teachers and students can read both parts of *Bell in Campo* in the form that Restoration readers would have encountered them. The 1662 volume is also available on the *Women Writers Online* database (*WWO*) as part of the Brown Women Writers Project. Examining the play as part of a larger collection of plays not only allows students to see *Bell in Campo* as part of a substantial dramatic canon but also gives them access to the prefatory matter that introduces the plays within, primarily in the form of letters to readers and to her husband William, Earl, Marquis, and, ultimately, Duke of Newcastle.

These epistles feature Cavendish's theories on a variety of subjects, from conditions of performance and strategies for reading plays aloud to generic conventions and gendered assumptions about appropriate subject matter for female writers. Alternately self-deprecating and self-promotional, this prefatory material provides a useful beginning to explore historical shifts in the institution of the theater in England. While the material helps emphasize the strangeness of writing plays in a time without a national stage, it offers an even more compelling frame for *Bell in Campo*, a so-called closet (or at least unperformed) play that posits public action as the only real way to serve the public good.

The dialogue between the play and the paratexts is also reproduced, albeit in a necessarily limited way, in two excellent modern editions of *Bell in Campo* by Anne Shaver (The Convent of Pleasure *and Other Plays* [1999]) and Alexandra Bennett (Bell in Campo *and* The Sociable Companions [2002]). Both editions provide excerpts from Cavendish's epistles in appendixes, allowing instructors to juxtapose Cavendish's anxieties about issues of performance and dramatic authority with the forcefully confident victories of *Bell in Campo*'s female army. Both editions also contain student-friendly introductions, as well as timelines that place the play in its historical framework.

Along with the dedicatory epistles, the appendixes in Bennett's edition include excerpts from Cavendish's autobiography, *A True Relation of My Birth and Breeding*, a text that expresses anxieties similar to those articulated in the letters preceding *Playes* regarding writing and her public persona. In this text (also available in full on *WWO*, *EEBO*, and *ESTC*), Cavendish writes proudly of her brother, a prominent commander in the royalist army, but deploringly of civil conflict. She gives vivid reports of its detrimental impact on domestic life and therein provides an important, if implicit, reminder that the play's two warring kingdoms, Faction and Reformation, are not just plot constructs for political allegory. For Cavendish, the conflict was not one of merely abstract ideas; it was a war that took the life of her brother and devastated the Lucas family estate. Read alongside *Bell in Campo*, *A True Relation* brings the martial realities behind the play's war plot into sharp relief, fleshing out the former's sometimes glib or comedic statements about war with lived experience.

That her brother and the man she would eventually marry held officer positions in the forces of Charles I is also significant, since it helps foreground both Cavendish's adherence to—and sometimes rejection of—royalist doctrine in the play. Instructors wanting to further explore royalist politics and military aspects of the civil wars will find Bennett's edition of *Bell in Campo* particularly useful for its pairing of the play with *The Sociable Companions*, a work published in Cavendish's second volume of drama, *Plays, Never Before Printed* (1668). Following the fate of cashiered soldiers after the civil conflict has been resolved, this later play provides a chapter of English history that complements the events staged in *Bell in Campo.*

In addition, Bennett's edition contains documents in appendixes that help instructors contextualize the time period, including excerpts from contemporary letters about real-life women who took up arms in civil conflict. These letters offer students a glimpse of the kinds of evidence scholars have used to identify the women who may have inspired Cavendish's fictional viragos (see Scott-Douglass; Tomlinson; K. Jones; Whitaker).

Of course, excerpts from either edition cannot provide students with extensive knowledge of the civil wars in England, and though students can deal substantively with the play without such knowledge, I find that helping them acquire a better sense of these conflicts greatly enhances their understanding and appreciation of the play's political complexity. In courses in which subject matter dictates extra attention to military issues—a course on war literature, for instance—instructors can assign individual or collaborative research projects that culminate in short in-class presentations that help contextualize *Bell in Campo*'s engagement with martial affairs. Giving students an opportunity to explore a particular topic in greater depth—such as the careers of significant civil war commanders, the rules of martial discipline, and debates over standing armies—can provide great insight into the play's representation of camp life, warfare, and demobilization. In courses that focus on themes other than warfare, such topics can be expanded to include larger political issues that the play explores, among them the role of the monarch in state governance, the institution of marriage, the status of widows, and women's property rights.

The last two topics in this list are particularly ripe for student investigation, since *Bell in Campo*'s subplot depicts the fates of three wives who stay at home and lose their loved ones to combat. These women either die of grief or remarry only to witness the depletion of their households by prodigal husbands. Students' research can help shed light on the extent to which Cavendish's harsh treatment of war widows—women who, not coincidentally, decline to go to war themselves—reflects the dictates or constraints of English law or the playwright's rather unfair punishment of women whose choices do not conform to her values.

As Lisa Hopkins reminds us, however, we need not commit solely to "fostering readings that do nothing but historicize" (398). *Bell in Campo* has several thematic, literary, and rhetorical aspects that provide excellent fodder for discussion and writing assignments on the text itself or on the text in comparison with other literary works. In her use of allegorical names, for instance, Cavendish deploys a technique celebrated in playwrights such as Jonson and Shakespeare, inviting students in drama or general literature surveys to consider the persistence of the technique as a method of characterization and a mode of literary invention.

In Shaver's edition, *Bell in Campo* appears alongside additional plays by Cavendish that allow for other compelling comparisons and contrasts. *Loves Adventures* features a young woman who takes up a disguise and arms to fight alongside the man whom she loves; in addition to contrasting with *Bell in Campo*'s armed female collective, Cavendish's use of the dramatic convention of female cross-dressing invokes parallels with Shakespearean heroines such as Rosalind and Portia. *The Bridals* and *The Convent of Pleasure* demonstrate, like *Bell in Campo*, Cavendish's interest in all-female communities, "dramatic utopias," as Erin Lang Bonin deems them, that pointedly explore feminine behavior and female political potential in the absence of male influence.

Instructors may also find it productive to have students examine the rhetorical aspects of the long speeches in *Bell in Campo*; alternately conventional and unique examples of martial oratory, Lady Victoria's speeches to her female troops are worthy of analysis in close-reading exercises in class or in formal essays. Students may examine these speeches on their own merits or in comparison with speeches by soldiers and women in Cavendish's *Orations of Divers Sorts* (1662) or with those in other plays with soldier-statesmen, from *Antony and Cleopatra* to *Henry V*. Lady Victoria likens women's lack of action to "aborted" potential, deems Fortune a "midwife" for facilitating the women's entrance into warfare, and exhorts her charges to give birth to their own heroism and become "Mothers of Glorious Action" (143; pt. 2, 1.3).

In contrast to Shakespearean orators, Cavendish's Lady Victoria exhorts her soldiers into the breach, where they are not the "shrill-shriking daughters" that may fall victim to war in *Henry V* (act 3, sc. 3, line 35) but full and active participants in military action and social reform. In those speeches—and in *Bell in Campo*—students can see that Cavendish wields her pen as deftly as her Amazonian soldiers wield the sword. Her play does not simply bring women into the camp; it brings students there to explore the full range of possibilities for a country and its subjects in a female-authored political world.

Note

1. The International Margaret Cavendish Society's annual convention facilitates scholarly exchange and provides a venue for performances of dramatic works.

The society's Web site maintains a bibliography of critical studies and modern editions of Cavendish's works. Recent entries include monographs; biographies, such as Katie Whitaker's *Mad Madge: Margaret Cavendish, Duchess of Newcastle, Royalist, Writer, and Romantic* (2002) and Emma Rees's *Margaret Cavendish: Gender, Genre, Exile* (2003); collections of essays, such as Stephen Clucas's *A Princely Brave Woman: Essays on Margaret Cavendish, Duchess of Newcastle* (2003), Line Cottegnies and Nancy Weitz's *Authorial Conquests: Essays on Genre in the Writings of Margaret Cavendish* (2003), Ben van Benden and Nora de Poorter's *Royalist Refugees: William and Margaret Cavendish in the Rubens House, 1648–1660*, and Katherine Romack and James Fitzmaurice's *Cavendish and Shakespeare, Interconnections* (2006; see esp. Pasupathi); and Susan James's edition of Cavendish's political writings (2003) and Fitzmaurice's edition of *Sociable Letters* (2004).

Cynthia Richards

To Whom Does the New World Belong? Teaching Behn's *The Widow Ranter*

Teaching Restoration drama is not for the faint of heart. The genre's reliance on witty wordplay, bad boy theatrics, and insider knowledge of the Restoration stage (and the court politics that gave it its urgency) makes it a hard sell for any undergraduate classroom. But in a liberal arts college of approximately two thousand students located in southwest Ohio—where teaching the Restoration and the eighteenth century can only happen once every other year—this endeavor can seem downright foolhardy. Why then compound the problem by teaching one of the lesser-known works of the Restoration's premier female playwright, Aphra Behn—*The Widow Ranter; or, The History of Bacon in Virginia*, written in 1688 and published posthumously in 1690?[1] Why select a play that even one of her strongest proponents has rather bluntly framed as "not particularly good" (Hughes, *Theatre* 189) and that has generated some of her most divisive criticism, when it is not more generally ignored?

The answer may be apparent in the play's subtitle. *The Widow Ranter*'s colonial setting makes it one of the few Restoration dramas likely to hit home—literally. In addition to being the first play set in the colonies, it is the first, as Peter Herman argues, to treat the colonies as "a separate cultural space, different from and possibly superior to England," the first to grapple with the idea of being "American" (254). That Behn is widely believed to have at least stopped in Virginia on her way to the British colony of Surinam lends weight to these speculations, even for the most literal-minded students, and forces an unexpected confrontation with American cultural identities at their nascent stage and filtered through a foreign perspective. Although some critics continue to read the play as representing a standard diatribe against the crass individualism and resulting incivility of the western colonies or as merely reflecting Behn's late-life disenchantment with the old-world hierarchies central both to her career and her professional identity, such positions are increasingly in the minority. Rather, in recent criticism, *The Widow Ranter* has assumed a more prominent position in colonial and transatlantic literature, offering a rare substantial portrait of the New World.

Margarete Rubik argues that Europeans were not used to seeing themselves as "somebody else's 'other'" at the time of *The Widow Ranter*'s performance and that the play's chief virtue lies in its willingness to force on British audiences this unfamiliar perspective ("Estranging" 35). The same can certainly be said of most students enrolled in my Restoration and eighteenth-century classroom. They are not used to seeing themselves as somebody else's other or in the drama of this period. Yet *The Widow Ranter* clearly reflects the homegrown cultural politics of the students' communities while presenting them from an unfamiliar perspective. From school board elections to presidential politics, my students have long learned to overlook the vagaries of the democratic process to herald its overriding virtues. To see that process treated suspiciously in this text awakens them to its initial difference. At the same time, the play's ability to evoke for my students a possession of the text through its American setting while repeatedly reminding them of an originating dispossession—that America was not really theirs to begin with—provides fertile ground for exploration. It is why, I think, the following question has never failed to elicit an engaged and complex discussion in the classroom: According to this play, to whom does the New World belong?

Critics have long acknowledged the conflicting loyalties of this play.[2] Does Behn champion the rebel Nathaniel Bacon, who is a compromised hero at best in the history of colonial Virginia, but who, in Behn's play, emerges more as a classic hero displaced in a new world driven by mercantile values? Or does she most admire the Native Americans, whom she directly equates with fallen monarchs? Yet it is the colonial council, composed of former convicts and lower-class citizens, that arguably wins in the end, and, despite their satiric names, one can detect a grudging respect on Behn's part for the colonists' scheming ways, especially as associated with the women in the play, women like the Widow Ranter, who are clearly empowered by the loss of traditional notions of male honor and power in the New World.

I begin the lesson simply enough by writing these various groups on the board: the English gentlemen, who include Bacon, the newly arrived younger son Hazard, his adviser and fellow second-born, Friendly, and Bacon's two lieutenant generals, Daring and Fearless; the lower-born and generally unsavory "Americans"—none too subtly named Dullman, Timorous, Whimsey, Whiff, Boozer, Brag, Grubb, and Dunce; and the Native Americans, the Indian queen Semernia and the Indian king Cavarnio. The women in the play fit all three of the above types yet function as a discrete entity in the text. The Widow Ranter leads Madame Surelove and Chrisante in their quest for proper mates, but their quest is never far from that of the high-born Semernia, who similarly transgresses because of her love for Bacon, and the lower-born tavern keeper Mrs. Flirt, who is just as determined to maintain "the best house" in Virginia as her more marriageable female compatriots are (*Widow Ranter* 253). Students soon discover that all four of these constituencies have a proper claim to the New World and that the question of to whom the New World belongs has no one correct answer.

Still, the value of the question lies equally in its insistence that students determine for themselves the proper possessor. In fact, I begin the class by asking students to vote on which answer they believe to be the right one. The play is sufficiently detailed regarding the rights of each of these constituencies that each category never fails to elicit its staunch supporters. Moreover, the vote produces a personal investment in the answer and heightens both the students' search for proper evidence and what they believe to be at stake in the discussion. Indeed, if all goes well, the conversation can even get a bit heated. It is precisely this democratic process that Behn critiques in her depiction of the colonial American council: voting is just as likely to produce entrenched self-interest as it is to further the common good. That Behn mocks this democratic process in the play makes it all the more important that it be performed—and, of course, reflected on later.

The case for the English gentlemen is fairly transparent and hinges on Behn's unusual depiction of the English general Nathaniel Bacon. In the official version of Bacon's rebellion (generally believed to be Behn's source material)—*A True Narrative of the Late Rebellion in Virginia, by the Royal Commissioners, 1677*—Bacon acts opportunistically. Seeking to secure his plantations and taking advantage of the absence of the appointed governor, Sir William Berkeley, Bacon and his supporters raid neighboring Indian camps, even those of the Pamunkey Indians, longtime allies of the English, flagrantly disregarding Berkeley's authority and using aggressive tactics against the Native Americans. Bacon succeeds in taking Jamestown but soon dies of dysentery, in effect abandoning his men to their swift executions by hanging. By contrast, in Behn's play, Bacon's cause is unquestionably just: "finding here my inheritance," he tells none other than the Indian king Cavarnio, "I am resolved still to maintain it so," language clearly intended to evoke the prerogative of James II at a time in which the queen's pregnancy had intensified challenges to his throne (*Widow Ranter* 269).

Yet what my students notice are not these old-world echoes of monarchal privilege but rather how favorably Bacon contrasts with the Americans. Whereas he is willing to take a stand, the Americans' loyalties are easily swayed (hence the names Whiff and Whimsey); whereas Bacon acts out of principles of self-actualization, the Americans merely manifest self-indulgent interests (hence the names Boozer and Grub). In short, Bacon acts a lot like my students' image of an American Revolutionary hero. That the Indian queen Semernia finds him "pleas[ing]" affirms his right to this new land (269): as in Disney's *Pocahontas* (1996), only the right foreigner will attract the attention of the native woman and become the true American. Yet in Behn's play, Bacon is not an American hero but an English one. Thus students arguing for his rightful possession of American land may be driven by their sympathy with his rebellious nature. But if they are paying attention to Behn's characterization of her hero, they necessarily make the case for an old-world sense of honor and duty. In fact, if they are reading closely, they will note that all the dispossessed second sons—like Hazard and Friendly and even Bacon's lieutenant general Daring—are possessed of estates by the end of the play through advantageous marriages and that their argument has put them in unwitting agreement with Friendly's imperial assessment that this new land "wants nothing but to be peopled by a well-born race to make it one of the best colonies in the world" (256).

The case for the English gentlemen may be the most transparent, but it is not typically the most popular. The category of Native Americans tends to get the most votes. In part, its popularity registers my students' happy surprise that a late-seventeenth-century text written by a white subject of a colonial power would even allow for such a position. How refreshing to be able to vote on this question and be on what students now know is the right side! And although the scenes describing the Indians are few, Behn's play gives them much to work with. These scenes are largely adulatory, the language of Cavarnio and Semernia elevated and beautiful. It is Cavarnio who speaks most directly to my question, providing this history of his people to a sympathetic Bacon:

> [T]hat we were monarchs once of all this spacious world; till you an unknown people landing here, distressed and ruined by destructive storms, abusing all our charitable hospitality, usurped our right, and made your friends your slaves. (269)

Cavarnio's speech may not resolve the question of to whom the New World belongs, but it goes a long way toward answering to whom it should belong. As students are quick to note, the pageantry afforded the Indians in the play would reinforce their power on the stage. We first find "the Indian King and Queen sitting in state, with guards of Indians, men and women attending to them" (269). By contrast, the English gentlemen are more likely to be seen in disarray, their swords removed or even appropriated by the women on the stage.

But as the conversation progresses, enthusiasm for this category tends to wane, especially once the focus turns to the play's representation of women. The students frankly lose patience with Semernia. By the end of the play, she seems a thin product of Behn's fantasy of the New World, dying mistakenly by Bacon's hands while thanking him for killing her. The historical record will amply support student suspicion. As Heidi Hutner details in *Colonial Women*, Bacon aggressively pursued the Pamunkey queen and English ally Cockacoeske. Yet even without that historical record, students begin to suspect that Behn's representation of the king and queen speaks more to a desire to find in this natural kingdom a substitute for England's declining monarchal honor than to a sincere statement of native rights. If I am lucky, some students even begin to question how their own fantasies of Native Americans are similarly compromised.

Not surprisingly, given the names of the play's characters, the least popular category tends to be the Americans. But I have found that, by calling this group Americans rather than colonists or even Virginians, they never fail to garner a few votes. (Interestingly, when I taught this text in conjunction with a class at the University of Exeter, none of the British students saw these characters' hidden virtues, while my American students seemed all the more determined to do so.) Once encouraged to take this argumentative leap, the American students find much to support this position. For one, the American side seems to win. Bacon dies not in battle but by his own hand, and, although this death is intended to give his life the arc of a classical hero's, it represents defeat nonetheless. By contrast, the Americans seem remarkably down-to-earth, their humor frequently puncturing the stale heroics of the less grandiose but recently arrived English gentleman, Hazard. Much of the humor of the play circulates around Hazard's having drawn his sword on the perception of a verbal slight in the first act of the play. Taken to court, he protests, "I wear a sword to right myself" (289). But, as Timorous points out, a sword has yet to make him stand upright, and throughout the play Behn takes similar comic stabs at an old-world faith in individual heroics to save the day. However laughable, community allegiances, though shifting and self-serving, prove the stronger of the two. Indeed, once Bacon—"he that could have conquered all America"—dies, Daring simply quits (322). Janet Todd calls Bacon an "anachronistic" hero, but, for my American students, he is simply out of place ("Spectacular Death" 82). In early America, there is little room for "great men" (*Widow Ranter* 256), and even today my American students find the old-world heroics of the English gentlemen comic by contrast to the real-world practicalities of individual self-interest and opportunistic alliances.

Regardless of how the debate begins, it typically ends with students feeling that the women have the upper hand. Behn's America may not support great men, but it does allow for free-spirited women. In fact, Behn appears to have stacked the cards in their favor, for no matter which group wins the vote, the women win, since they occupy positions in each category: the women include English daughters like Chrisante, daughter of Captain Downright; Native American queens like Semernia; and unapologetic American businesswomen like Mrs. Flirt. But most notably, this group includes the Widow Ranter, whose amorphous behavior suggests that the group is intended to function as a separate category. Ranter borrows from all three categories: she fights nobly like the Indian queen; she profits from the American trade of tobacco and participates in its homegrown pleasures of punch, smoke, and spirited council; and she retains enough old-world honor to make her capture—along with those of the other women—a source of outrage for the fighting men. My students adore her, for, unlike Hellena in *The Rover*, whose freewheeling ways seem restricted to the time of Carnival, the Widow Ranter seems poised to sustain her freedom, her behavior even turning my question about the rightful possession of the New World on its head. For if no one can answer this question with certainty, then it is at least possible to imagine that it belongs to the traditionally dispossessed, the women. It is Daring, students point out enthusiastically, who encourages Ranter to wear breeches, and the other English gentlemen, such as Hazard and Friendly, seem just as eager to support the women's protean ways by joining their ranks through marriage at the end of the play. Indeed, through marrying these wives and daughters of earlier colonial American settlers, the English gentlemen reverse the standard marriage plot: through marriage, their identities are changed, as they cease to be second-born English gentlemen and become, instead, landed Americans.

Once again, Behn's view bears only a modest relation to the truth. The Virginia colony did have its share of strong and independent women, but its policies toward women could be just as and sometimes more repressive than England's. As Kathleen Brown points out, although many women rallied around Bacon's revolt against English authoritarian rule, the rebellion is more properly viewed as an attempt to restore patriarchal authority, to allow male plantation owners such as Bacon to protect their properties against excessive English taxation and raids by Native Americans. Furthermore, from 1660 to the time of the rebellion, Governor Berkeley was particularly interested in curtailing female speech, especially in the form of religious dissent. By giving the widow the name Ranter, a term that can mean both "rake" and "one who rants, declaims noisily or bombastically, esp. in preaching" ("Ranter"), Behn makes this character the target of those repressive policies while suggesting Ranter's desire for greater sexual and intellectual or spiritual liberty.[3] Yet what my students appreciate most about the question of to whom the New World belongs and the surprising answer that the New World may belong to the women is just how accommodating the New World proved to Behn's fantasy of female mobility and uncompromised agency. And no wonder, as many of my Ohio students will openly admit, for they share the same dream.

By the end of the class, the blackboard is quite full and sympathies continue to be divided. No one leaves the class assured of having the right answer. But students do not leave empty-handed: they have an understanding of the complexities of the New World and how those complexities continue to affect their national identities. When asked to reflect on this question, my students unfailingly discover that claims to the New

World are many and competing and that their more conventional notion of an American history in which the struggling commoner successfully and rightfully challenged aristocratic privilege does not evolve from a clean narrative line. Moreover, they find that the wild card in all this mix is the female voice and perspective, both Behn's and those of her vocal female heroines. Thus prompted, students emerge eager to know about the ways in which women shaped not just Restoration drama but also the politics of the New World. Amid this drama's distant history and geography, they even find a place that they can call home.

Notes

1. I have adopted the standard American spelling, *The Widow Ranter*. European articles typically cite the original spelling of the play, *The Widdow Ranter*.

2. For help laying out these conflicts, see Bridges; Hendricks; Hughes, *Theatre*; Ross; Todd, "Spectacular Death"; and Visconsi.

3. Brown's chapter "Vile Rogues and Honorable Men: Nathaniel Bacon and the Dilemma of Colonial Masculinity," in *Good Wives, Nasty Wenches, and Anxious Patriarchs*, can be particularly useful in laying out these gender tensions for the class.

Anita Pacheco

Teaching Behn's *The Rover*

When teaching Aphra Behn's *The Rover; or, The Banished Cavaliers* (1677), one of my main aims is to help students grasp Behn's consummate talent as a dramatist. Ideally, I would like them to take from their study of the play a well-developed sense of what Derek Hughes refers to as her "supreme skill—unrivalled in her lifetime—in using all the resources of meaning offered by the theatre" (*Theatre* 11). This objective necessitates acquainting students with the main properties of the theater for which Behn wrote, which can be done through a brief guide to the Restoration theater, made available to students as a handout and, if possible, on the course Web site. Here students should be able to find a description, supplemented with images, of the principal features of the Restoration stage: the apron stage, with one or two doors on either side, divided by the proscenium arch from the scenic area behind, whose painted wings and shutters allowed for scenery that was at once spectacular and changeable. A valuable online resource for compiling such a guide is the University of Saint Andrews Web site *Restoration Theatre*. The guide might also include information on the Globe and the Rose, so that students can get a sense of the way the theater in England developed from the late sixteenth to the late seventeenth century—from open-air theaters with little if any scenery to smaller indoor spaces with a forestage that generated intimacy between actors and spectators and with scenery and scenic changes as integral parts of the performance. Many students will already be aware of another significant change from pre-1642 theaters: the appearance of actresses in the female roles.

The guide can also usefully inform students about Behn's position in the Duke's Company, for which she wrote all her plays until the two Restoration theater companies merged in 1682. I include brief accounts of the original cast of *The Rover*; students should know that the role of Willmore was taken not by Thomas Betterton, who first played Dorimant in George Etherege's *The Man of Mode*, but by the Duke's Company's other leading actor, William Smith, who specialized in playing "dashing heroes" who were often "sex-mad scamps" (Milhous, "Smith"). This fact opens up a crucial aspect of the characterization of Willmore: he is at once the play's libertine hero and a bit of a fool. Betterton took the role of Belvile, and Cave Underhill that of Blunt. Underhill is another interesting casting choice, described by Colley Cibber as excelling at playing "the Stiff, the Heavy, and the Stupid" but also as more than capable of conveying brutishness, "ill-nature," and "perversity of spirit" (*Apology* [1740] 128, 129). Did Underhill bring this combination of stupidity and threat to the role of the would-be rapist Blunt? The principal women's roles are also touched on, in particular the fact that Hellena was played by Elizabeth Barry, widely considered the greatest actress of her age, who created many witty comic heroines, playing them with a "graceful, easy, genteel style" (Backscheider, "Barry"). Angellica Bianca, meanwhile, was played by Anne Marshall Quin, whose "forte was in tragic and passionate roles" (Hughes, *Theatre* 91). Such details about the play's original actors and company not only shed light on how its main characters may have been represented when the play was first performed but also place Behn in a theatrical context that complicates the still prevalent picture of her as a woman writer inevitably excluded from and vilified by the mainstream.[1]

It is a good idea for students to read the theater guide before the play, to help them approach the text as a blueprint for performance created with a particular kind of theatrical space in mind. The aspects of *The Rover* about which students regularly complain—its myriad characters, the proliferation of disguises, the often hectic stage action—tend to become less objectionable when students are more aware of the play as a text produced to be acted on a stage; indeed, it is not unheard of for students to come to appreciate the play's most crowded and least readable scenes as evidence of Behn's skill as a dramatist. The task of reading the play with the Restoration theater very much in mind is made easier if students use an edition that foregrounds performance issues, such as the Oxford World's Classics The Rover *and Other Plays*, edited by Jane Spencer, to which I refer in this essay. Spencer's edition gives a great deal of help with the staging of the play, both in its introduction and in the notes, and is reasonably inexpensive.

Students might find it helpful to have a list of questions to ask while they read the play: Is *The Rover* set mainly indoors or outdoors? What is the impact of its scene settings? What kind of stage directions does the play contain? Are there many asides? How about other kinds of stage action, such as fights or songs and dances? What do you think is the impact of these? The point is to encourage them to focus on the ways in which Behn uses the stage to create a compelling theatrical experience. This exercise serves not only to increase students' appreciation of Behn's stagecraft in *The Rover* but also to change their way of reading drama. In my experience, many students approach plays as if they are novels, in which all the meaning derives from the words on the page. By encouraging them to attend to setting and stage directions, we enable them to recognize that in drama meaning derives from staging as well as from the words the actors speak.

In seminars, it is useful to divide students into groups and get each group to act out a particular scene, in whole or in part, depending on the length of the class session. Any scene will bring its own revelations, but I have often assigned act 2, scene 2, Willmore's conquest of Angellica Bianca; act 3, scene 1, when she witnesses his betrayal; act 3, scene 5, the first of the play's attempted rape scenes; and act 4, scene 5, when Florinda happens on the now vengeful Blunt. With longer, more complicated scenes like act 3, scene 1, it is advisable for the group to talk the class through some of the most significant aspects of the staging while restricting their performance to a particular episode. If space permits, students can mark out (roughly) the forestage and the scenic area on the classroom floor with chalk or masking tape. As students work on their respective scenes, the instructor can move from group to group, to give assistance and guidance with performance decisions. Each presentation is followed by class discussion of the main issues that the performance has raised.

Act 2, scene 2, is the audience's first close encounter with Angellica Bianca and with Willmore in full seductive flow. So how does Behn stage the scene? Students generally make an effort to convey that this scene is indoors, set in "[a] fine chamber," and so the painted wings and shutters, along with Angellica's costume, need to offer visual confirmation of the wealth that this expensive courtesan enjoys (27). Yet students might also grasp that the significance of a setting partly derives from its relation to what preceded it. In this case, Angellica's "fine chamber" follows a scene set in "the long street" (19), when both sets of shutters would have been opened to reveal the full depth of the stage. Perhaps, then, Angellica's "fine chamber" feels claustrophobic by contrast and so suggests precisely what the action of the play will soon force her to recognize: the prostitute's lack of genuine power and freedom. Staging the scene allows students to think as well about where the action should take place, and the numerous asides spoken by Angellica and Willmore locate the scene mainly on the forestage, where the actors could directly address the audience and where the verbal sparring in which Willmore engages with both Angellica Bianca and Moretta could be most clearly and forcefully conveyed to the audience. The scene highlights the play's critique of mercenary marriage as a form of commodification of women akin to prostitution, and students often point out the link with the opening scene and its attack on contemporary marriage practices. Students also tend to notice that the asides are divided fairly evenly between Willmore and Angellica in this scene, prompting consideration of the function of asides: Do they necessarily work to establish intimacy between character and spectator? Do Willmore's asides in this scene arouse audience support for the duplicities of the rake hero or encourage us to side with Angellica?

Performing the scene leads students to attend carefully to Behn's stage directions, which make clear the physical forcefulness with which Willmore approaches this seduction: on two occasions the stage directions tell us that he "holds her" (29, 30; lines 71, 127), and this physical roughness is visually reinforced by the bloody shirt he is wearing after his brawl with the Spaniards in the previous scene. Students are often struck by the aggressiveness of Willmore's language here, the way in which he attacks the Petrarchan mistress for the suffering her beauty inflicts on her male admirers. His assertiveness, verbal and physical, clashes with his apparent romantic abasement when, late in the scene, he "kneels and kisses [Angellica's] hand" (31; line 151). Is Behn using the stage action to imply the hollowness of courtly love conventions or the animosity that underlies them? Students, of course, have to make decisions about how aggressive they want Willmore to be in this scene, which drives home the fact that a dramatic performance is a kind of negotiation between playwright and director.

The following scene, act 3, scene 1, is one of the play's many "busy" scenes, and it illustrates well Behn's skill in manipulating the resources of the Restoration stage. It returns the action to "the long street" and its expanded acting space. Although the stage is crowded, the action focuses on several discrete groups of characters, each of which takes center stage and then relinquishes it to another group. This is also an eavesdropping scene, as Hellena watches Willmore emerge from his tryst with Angellica Bianca and as Angellica watches Willmore pay court to Hellena. All this activity necessitates that students think carefully about the position and movement of characters on the stage, the way Behn uses the entire stage area for this street scene, and how to handle the many entrances and exits.

Most of the characters are in masquerade, which opens up discussion of the play's carnival setting, with its numerous outdoor scenes and plentiful disguises (see Franceschina 29–36). Students are likely to notice the props in the scene as well: the gold that Angellica has given Willmore and that he proudly displays to his comrades; the jewel that Florinda gives to Belvile, which turns out to be her portrait. These items can stimulate discussion of the function of the play's numerous visual signifiers: the jingling gold is clearly a sign of Willmore's sexual triumph, and students often feel that Florinda's jewel represents her exalted value as an upper-class virgin. That the jewel is also her picture provokes comparisons with Angellica and so reinforces Behn's interest in establishing parallels between her gentlewomen and her prostitute. This example illustrates how classroom performance can illuminate the way in which dramatic themes emerge in part through carefully crafted scenic links and echoes (Ikegami 309). Willmore kneels at the end of this scene too, on this occasion to kiss Hellena's hand. The class can consider the way this kneeling repeats the action in act 2, scene 2, but also deviates from it: this time Willmore is ordered to kneel by Hellena, who, in an aside, makes it abundantly clear to the audience that she is not fooled by Willmore's seductive idiom for a moment. There is obviously a lot of scope for examining Behn's representation of the libertine hero here. This comparison can also spark discussion of the contrast the scene establishes between Hellena's good-humored worldly wisdom and Angellica's tragic despair, as Behn constructs the female character capable of turning her rakish hero into a husband and exposes the painful fragility of Angellica's self-construction as powerful Petrarchan mistress.

Act 3, scene 5, is an important one for students to explore through performance, for it raises various difficult questions about Behn's use of attempted rape scenes in this comic play. The students will need to decide how the Restoration stage would have been likely to represent "the garden in the night" through its painted wings and shutters and with its actors pretending to be in darkness (43). The scene is interesting as well in terms of the play's use of indoor and outdoor space; the garden is a liminal area, outside the house but protected by a wall and a door that Florinda unlocks at the start of the scene, only to find that it is not Belvile who enters but the drunken and rapacious Willmore. Behn uses her indoor and outdoor settings to comment on women's social position: as the play's opening scene and Pedro's role throughout the play make clear, a gentlewoman's male relations seek to control her by locking her up in the home (see Hughes, *Theatre* 13, 93–95). But if domestic space is oppressive in the world of the play, the streets in carnival time are also dangerous—but how dangerous? Students working on this scene soon discover that they have to make some tricky decisions about precisely how funny and how threatening they want Willmore to be here. It might be worthwhile to encourage them to approach this problem by thinking about what Willmore says in this scene and what the dialogue suggests he is doing. His speeches insist that this advance is not a rape because Florinda is asking for it: why else would she be out alone at night? Yet Florinda's "wicked man, unhand me" (44; line 41) and the stage direction "[s]he struggles with him" (45; line 67) indicate that, as in act 2, scene 2, Willmore is applying a certain degree of physical force. By considering the tension between Willmore's words and actions—if Florinda is so willing, why does he need to manhandle her?—students begin to grasp that this troubling scene, although it can clearly be played for laughs, has a serious underlying meaning; its words and stage action work together to reveal a dramatic world in which rape rarely happens to women of quality. Deprived of the signifiers of high social status, a woman will be read as a whore who can be sexually assaulted with impunity (Pacheco 332–35). Students often remark on the significance of Florinda's jewel box here: having placed it in a "jessamine" (jasmine) bush for safekeeping (43; line 9), Florinda has no visible sign of her high rank.

Belvile enters in the nick of time, and this two-hander (scene with only two characters) suddenly becomes crowded as male characters pour onto the stage. Students will need to consider how to stage the fight that breaks out between Spaniards and English. They will know from their guided reading that this skirmish is the play's fourth fight and that there will be four more before it is over, two of them between Belvile and Willmore. The prominence of outbreaks of violence in the play speaks volumes about

Behn's interest in masculine rivalry, even between ostensible comrades and especially over women.

Act 4, scene 4, is one of Behn's much-loved discovery scenes, in which the first set of painted shutters is drawn back to "discover" actors in front of the second set (Spencer, Introduction xii; Lewcock, "More for Seeing" 70–71). It seems important for students to have an opportunity to work out, with guidance, the mechanics of such scenes. This indoor scene also promotes further discussion of the gendered meaning Behn gives to space in the play: Florinda, out on the streets again, looking for Belvile and being pursued by Pedro, enters an open door to escape his "tyranny" (65; line 2) only to happen on the gulled and vengeful Blunt, who threatens to rape her; by the end of the scene she has been confined in a room by Blunt and Frederick. Once again, Behn uses scene settings to indicate the kindred dangers awaiting women both in and out of doors (Hughes, *Theatre* 93–95). As with Willmore in act 3, scene 5, students will need to decide how ridiculous and how sinister they feel Blunt should be in this scene. The stage directions will help here, for they tell us that Blunt is discovered "sitting on a couch in his shirt and drawers, reading" (65; line 1) and, a few lines later, that he "[p]uts on an old rusty sword, and buff belt" (line 6). Clearly, he is being made into a figure of fun, though the casting of Underhill in the role might well suggest that an element of genuine menace would not be out of place. Students will have to think about the movements of the characters on stage, in particular those of Blunt, who starts off in the scenic area, at some distance from the audience, and ends the scene on the forestage, locking one of the proscenium arch doors and exiting by the other door. Students will certainly pick up on Behn's use of props in this scene: the old rusty sword as a signifier of Blunt's failed masculinity and the ring that Florinda gives Blunt, which in the short term saves her from rape by identifying her as a "maid of quality" (68; line 122). Students will also notice the way the scene echoes act 3, scene 5: the combination of physical force (Blunt twice "pulls Florinda rudely" [66, 68; lines 45, 105]) with assertions that Florinda must be a whore, the meaning of which is neatly summed up in Frederick's "'twould anger us vilely to be trussed up for a rape upon a maid of quality, when we only believe we ruffle a harlot" (68; lines 121–23).

There are, of course, other effective ways of organizing students' performances of sections of the play. Assigning two or more groups the same scene yields differing interpretations that will generate lively and constructive discussions. Using their background knowledge of the original actors, students can work in groups and cast the play themselves, providing justifications of their choices. I also attempt to ensure that students spend some time thinking specifically about the language of the play. Students are often reluctant to analyze dramatic language, especially in a non-Shakespearean play written mainly in prose. They need to be encouraged to recognize that in a play, as in a poem, it is not just what a character says that matters but also how he or she says it. What follows are a few ideas for getting students to attend closely to aspects of the language of *The Rover*. They probably work best for first-year undergraduates, who particularly need a nonintimidating introduction to the analysis of dramatic language.

I choose a few extracts from the play, of about fifty to sixty-five lines, photocopy them, and cut them up into the individual characters' speeches. Then I divide students into groups and give each group an extract to work on, asking them to put the speeches back together in the order they were written, without consulting the text of the play, of course. This is a good way of getting students not only to read carefully but also to enjoy doing so. It can work well with scenes like act 1, scene 2, lines 126–97, and act 3, scene 1, lines 126–81, both episodes of flirtatious dialogue between Hellena and Willmore in which the two characters use numerous discourses and speak in sometimes elaborate metaphors. Once students complete the exercise, they will have become very familiar with the dialogue and its playful humor. I then ask them, still working in groups, either to paraphrase the extract or to write an early-twenty-first-century version of it. Rewriting the dialogue requires students to engage, for example, with Willmore's sexual innuendo in act 1, scene 2, and with his wont to adopt a Christian persona and talk like a preacher, even though he is trying to get into Hellena's bed. This episode leads to a discussion of the way Behn makes comedy out of having her thoroughly disreputable rake hero press Christianity into the service of his sexual appetite. It is only after the students have examined the language of the extract in depth that I introduce *discourse* as an effective analytic term to use in describing Willmore's language in this extract. The same kind of procedure will help the students recognize the extended use of metaphors of food and eating in act 3, scene 1, and also perceive how the language of this episode follows up the exchange in act 1, scene 2. Another passage that might be similarly approached is act 2, scene 2, in which Willmore seduces Angellica Bianca, since it is full of commercial metaphors (such as Willmore's "Thou hast sold plenty of thy stale ware at a cheap rate" [28; line 33]) and various courtly love idioms, close analysis of which will enable students to think carefully about Willmore's seductive strategy with Angellica Bianca and why it proves so spectacularly successful.

One last exercise involves Angellica Bianca's and Willmore's verse speeches in act 5, scene 1, lines 282–308. Copies of these speeches can be given to students, again working in small groups, with some crucial words removed and blank spaces left in their place. The students' task is to fill in the missing words, choosing from a list of possibilities (which can contain more items than the number of blank spaces to be filled). The point is to invite students to think carefully about what each character is saying and also about the kind of poetic devices Behn is using to construct two of her principal characters. Students will also have to be alert to the question of meter in making their choices. Once they have supplied the missing words, they explain their choices: how did they know, for example, that the word "spoil" belonged in line 290 or the word "idol" in line 292? For those unsure of their ability to engage with poetry, the discovery that they have been responding to the passage's figurative language can provide a valuable boost in confidence.

It has generally been my experience in teaching *The Rover* that what students find most interesting about the play is the complexity of Behn's representation of the relationship between the upper-class virgin and the prostitute, those two types of women who are in some ways similar and in others poles apart. Becoming familiar with Behn's theater and attempting to stage some of the play's central episodes allow students to appreciate the artistry with which Behn gives that theme and others dramatic form. This appreciation can only be enhanced by study of *The Rover, Part Two*, centrally concerned with the same issues. Even if the teaching schedule is too tight to accommodate the sequel, students will certainly find it gratifying to know that Behn once again presents Willmore (now a widower) with the choice between a gentlewoman and a prostitute—only this time she lets the prostitute win.

Note

1. Students might also learn about this theatrical context by researching the play's first actors themselves. This project could be tackled in small groups, each group being assigned a principal role. Students would thereby gain valuable experience of doing research in the library and in presenting their findings in a concise, well-focused oral presentation.

Melinda C. Finberg

Centlivre and the Stage Sodomite

All our students of English literature and theater studies ought to know Susanna Centlivre. Her comedies were loved by audiences for their wit and scintillating dialogue and by actors for the fabulous characters she gave them to portray. What I want to explore here is how we, as teachers, can make Centlivre's comedies come alive so students will see them not just as words on a page but as works of living theater. As a dramaturg, I work with theaters on bringing historical plays to life on the professional stage. Many of the approaches that I use in the theater have applications for the classroom. A dramaturg educates the director, cast, designers, and audience about the language and historical background of the play. A dramaturg must help the production stay true to the integrity of the work while keeping in mind the artistic, physical, and economic realities of the present-day theater. But a dramaturg has one other crucial job, especially when the play is from another century: to make sure the story of the play is being communicated to the audience. A dramaturg always must be asking, What is the play's relationship with the audience?

By focusing on this question, we can lead our students into an active dialogue with the play. Here I use *The Busybody* (1709),[1] one of Centlivre's best and most popular comedies, to illustrate some ways this approach can work. I examine aspects of both the specific social and political history of her time and the physical history of the English stage to demonstrate how *The Busybody* connected to its contemporary audiences and how productions of it can connect to audiences today.

The early English eighteenth-century stage differed from the standard proscenium stage we think of today and was more similar to the thrust stage, with the audience on three sides. The London stage of Centlivre's day was what the theater historian Allardyce Nicoll refers to as a "tripartite" theater (25–34). The theater was divided into three spaces: the house, the scene, and the platform. The house was the domain of the audience; the scene was the back area of the elevated stage, where most of the backdrops and scenery were placed; and bridging the two was the platform, the area of the stage on which most of the acting was performed. The boundaries of the house and the platform were not strictly rectangular or even clearly fixed. The house would encroach on the platform because there was very desirable seating along its sides and in raised boxes above it. From the platform, the actor, surrounded on three sides by audience members, could speak in a natural voice and easily be heard by them. This intimate relationship lent itself to asides and allowed the actor to aim pointed jokes at the spectators, or even to address them directly.

Centlivre wrote *The Busybody* with the physical dynamics of this theater in mind. Teachers can introduce students to the ways in which the physical setup of a theater influences the comedy by having them get up and read a scene, such as act 2, scene 1 (Miranda's silent interview with Sir George, observed by Sir Francis), first by having the readers-actors at a distance from the rest of the class and again by having them read surrounded by the class on three sides and directing their asides to these intimate observers. Everyone will immediately experience how Centlivre writes to include the audience in the action and how distancing the audience makes it difficult to convey the humor. Even when played in a large theater, a production will benefit from creating, at least, the illusion of intimacy.

Understanding the actor-spectator dynamic inherent in the comedy will help students find the subtext of the comedy from the inferred and physical humor of the script. But students also need to learn about the script-specific social history of the time so they will get the jokes. Centlivre was not a playwright who shied away from controversial issues, and teachers can begin to explore this aspect of her work by examining the thinly veiled controversy in the subtext of *The Busybody.*

The title character of the play, Marplot, the busybody, was so beloved by audiences that Centlivre wrote a sequel just for him, *Marplot; or, The Second Part of* The Busybody (1710). Marplot has been called "one of the most attractive of literature's simpletons" (Bateson 70). Throughout the century it was a choice role for actors, including David Garrick. Marplot is good-natured, well-intentioned, eager to be of any service to his friends, but insatiably curious. He has no overt romantic interests of his own and is essentially a voyeur. Although some critics have described Marplot as "desexed" (Kinney 95), as a "curiously unmale figure" (J. Pearson, *Prostituted Muse* 210), a "gender misfit" (Haggerty, *Men* 45), a "desexualized, innocent, a kind of wild child" (Bratton, "Reading" 20), or as "a kind of antitype of the hyper-sexualized rake hero of Restoration comedy" (O'Brien, "Busy Bodies" 181), he can also be seen as an early-eighteenth-century homosexual stereotype. More specifically, Marplot follows in the tradition of such overtly gay comedic characters as Sir Jolly Jumble, the "old Goat" in Thomas Otway's *The Souldiers Fortune* (1680), and the Abbé, in Thomas Southerne's *Sir Anthony Love* (1691), who are also go-betweens and establish a pattern of voyeurism among "stage sodomites" (Senelick 43–44).

Marplot is a successor to the character of Maiden in Thomas Baker's *Tunbridge-Walks; or, The Yeoman of Kent* (1703), whom Susan Staves cites as a new type: an obviously homosexual character portrayed as an ultraeffeminate fop ("Few Kind Words" 415). Marplot is not as overtly effeminate as Maiden, but he has traits that would signal his orientation to the audience of his day, such as being cowardly, gossipy, overly concerned with his appearance, and having an exaggerated fondness for small animals. Centlivre called attention to Marplot's connection to Baker's Maiden by asking Baker to write the prologue to *The Busybody* and by advertising this prologue as "by the author of *Tunbridge-Walks*" (*Busybody* 78). She seems to be pointing out to spectators and readers that, if they liked Baker's play, they will also like hers. Marplot's sexual otherness is part of his function in the plot; to miss this aspect of his character is to miss much of Centlivre's humor.

Centlivre never directly addresses the question of Marplot's sexuality—even her use of Baker is oblique—partly because of the social history and politics of her time. In the early eighteenth century, the concepts of gender consciousness and sexual subdivisions were undergoing radical change (McCormick 117). The overtly bawdy Restoration period celebrated "polymorphous lechery" (Senelick 47), of which the quintessential example was John Wilmot, Lord Rochester (1647–80), the debauched and pornographic poet, who was never limited in his sexual conquests by the mere matter of gender. As Randolph Trumbach explains, Rochester's affairs with young men were never viewed as effeminate or specifically homosexual—rather, they were the signs of his insatiable sexual appetites: "Before 1700, in London and at court, wild rakes such as Lord Rochester had had wives, mistresses, and boys. Such characters could in the 1670s even be presented occasionally on the public stage" ("Sex" 189).

Likewise, the character of the stage fop was not necessarily connected with effeminacy. A fop was a man overly vain about his appearance, dress, and manners, but he could still be heterosexual and active on the marriage market. All this changed over the course of the 1690s.[2] By the end of the decade and continuing into the early part of the eighteenth century, a new view of male sexuality came to dominate popular culture: masculine men were viewed as desiring only women; fops and any other effeminate males were viewed and depicted as sodomites or homosexuals (or, as Staves claims, "asexual" ["Few Kind Words" 414–15]). Homosexuals or "mollies" were considered aberrant personalities, living depraved lifestyles (McCormick 117), and homophobia began to be expressed among certain social groups (in ways that might seem particularly current to early-twenty-first-century students). As early as 1694, societies for the reformation of public manners began calling for the suppression of the London playhouses because of their connection to and their staging of sodomites. Both 1699 and 1707 saw "homosexual pogroms," as Laurence Senelick calls them, which included raids on suspected homosexual gathering places, arrests, prosecutions, and even executions of accused "sodomites" (50).

Theatrical audiences, subjects of the attacks of the societies for the reformation of public manners, were hardly likely to be sympathetic to the political agendas of such groups. Nor was a playwright such as Centlivre, who used the preface of her first play, *The Perjur'd Husband* (1700), to attack Jeremy Collier's *A Short View of the Immorality and Profaneness of the English Stage* (1698). Centlivre saw the stage as a reflection of society, not a model for it, and considered the purpose of plays to be entertainment, not moral education.

With this background, we can now return to *The Busybody* and examine what Centlivre is doing with her eponymous character, Marplot. At first glance, the comedy is not about him at all. It is a double-plot comedy in which two couples navigate difficult obstacles to their marriages. In many ways, Marplot is not necessary to the plots—all he does is try to help his friends, and, in doing so, he endangers the chances of the marriage plots concluding successfully. Marplot is completely other, and Centlivre never comes out and directly tells the audience what the nature of Marplot's otherness is. We must look for the subtext to discover it. I examine here two of Marplot's scenes to demonstrate how Centlivre creates this subtextual dialogue with the audience.

In the first scene in which Marplot appears, Centlivre fills his dialogue and the discussion Sir George and Charles have about him with coded language:

Sir George. Pugh, yonder's a fool coming this way, let's avoid him.

Charles. What Marplot? No, no, he's my instrument. There's a thousand conveniences in him. He'll lend me his money when he has any, run of my errands and be proud on't; in short, he'll pimp for me, lie for me, drink for me, do anything but fight for me, and that I trust to my own arm for.

Sir George. Nay then he's to be endured; I never knew his qualifications before.

Enter Marplot with a patch across his face

Marplot. Dear Charles, yours. (*Aside*)—Ha! Sir George Airy, the man in the world I have an ambition to be known to. (*To Charles*) Give me thy hand, dear boy—

Charles. A good assurance! But hark ye, how came your beautiful countenance clouded in the wrong place?

Marplot. I must confess 'tis a little mal a-propos, but no matter for that; a word with you, Charles. (*Takes Charles aside*) Prithee, introduce me to Sir George. He is a man of wit, and I'd give ten guineas to . . .

Charles. Well, on condition you'll give us a true account how you came by that mourning nose, I will.

Marplot. I'll do it.

Charles. Sir George, here's a gentleman has a passionate desire to kiss your hand.

Sir George. Oh, I honour men of the sword; and I presume this gentleman is lately come from Spain or Portugal by his scars.

Marplot. No, really, Sir George, mine sprung from civil fury. Happening last night into the groom-porters, I had a strong inclination to go ten guineas with a sort of a, sort of a—kind of a milk sop, as I thought. A pox of the dice he flung out, and my pockets being empty as Charles knows they sometimes are, he proved a surly North Briton, and broke my face for my deficiency.

Sir George. Ha, ha! And did not you draw? . . .

Marplot. . . . I avoid fighting, purely to be serviceable to my friends, you know—

Sir George. Your friends are much obliged to you, sir, I hope you'll rank me in that number.

Marplot. Sir George, a bow from the side box, or to be seen in your chariot, binds me ever yours.

Sir George. Trifles, you may command 'em when you please.

Charles. Provided he may command you—

Marplot. Me! Why I live for no other purpose. Sir George, I have the honour to be caressed by most of the reigning toasts of the town, I'll tell 'em you are the finest gentleman—

Sir George. No, no, prithee let me alone to tell the ladies—my parts.

(82–83)

Before Marplot even appears on the stage, the audience hears that he is a fool, a go-between, and a coward. These descriptions, in combination, tip off the knowing audience members that they are about to meet a man very different from the two virile young men on stage. When he appears, with his face bandaged, his language is overflowery, full of "dear Charles" and "dear boy," as compared with the more sexually joking style of Charles's first greeting to Sir George: "Ha! Sir George Airy! A-birding thus early? What forbidden game roused you so soon? For no lawful occasion could invite a person of your figure abroad at such unfashionable hours" (80). Charles teases Sir George that he must be hunting a young woman for an assignation if he is in Saint James's Park so early in the morning. Moreover, Charles mocks Marplot's flowery style, his vanity, and his bandages when he asks, "[H]ow came your beautiful countenance clouded in the wrong place?" and when he introduces him to Sir George with "here's a gentleman has a passionate desire to kiss your hand." To refer to a man's face as "beautiful" is effeminizing, as is the description of Marplot's "passion" to kiss Sir George's hand. Charles and Sir George are laughing at Marplot's effeminacy behind his back and egging him on. Sir George knows full well that Marplot's wounds are not those of a soldier, but he is trying to goad Marplot into explaining his injuries. When Marplot tells him about the scuffle with the Scotsman and that he avoids fighting solely to be able to come to the aid of his friends, the joke about Marplot's cowardice is shared among Sir George, Charles, and the audience.

Does Marplot acknowledge to the audience that he knows everyone thinks he is a coward, or is he unaware? It is helpful for students to experience some of the different choices possible by getting up and reading the exchange in several ways. While Marplot is not as overtly effeminate as Baker's Maiden, he clearly does not embody the manliness of the two men with whom he is trying to ingratiate himself. In case his effeminacy has not been suggested strongly enough, when Marplot brags about being in with the most fashionable women (preferring the society of women is also a sign of effeminacy in the stage sodomite) and offers to put a good word in for Sir George, Sir George rebuffs him, as if afraid of what being associated with Marplot might do to his own reputation.

Although similar hints and coded language occur whenever Marplot appears, the signals get raised to a higher pitch in the monkey scene, in which Sir George is concealed behind the chimney board to hide from Miranda's guardian, Sir Francis, and Miranda tries to keep Sir Francis and Marplot away from the fireplace by claiming she has a monkey trapped behind it:

> *Miranda.* Hold, hold, hold, dear Gardee! I have a . . . a . . . a . . . a . . . a monkey shut up there, and if you open it before the man comes that is to tame it, 'tis so wild 'twill break all my china, or get away, and that would break my heart, for I am fond on't to distraction, (*in a flattering tone*) next thee, dear Gardee.
>
> *Sir Francis.* Well, well, Chargee, I won't open it. She shall have her monkey, poor rogue . . .
>
> *Marplot.* A monkey, dear madam? Let me see it. I can tame a monkey as well as the best of them all. Oh, how I love the little miniatures of man!
>
> *Miranda.* Be quiet, mischief, and stand farther from the chimney. You shall not see my monkey—(*striving with him*)—why sure—
>
> *Marplot.* For heaven's sake, dear madam, let me but peep, to see if it be as pretty as my Lady Fiddle-Faddle's. Has it got a chain?
>
> *Miranda.* Not yet, but I design it one shall last its lifetime. (126)

The humor of this exchange is all in the subtext, which an early-eighteenth-century audience would grasp immediately. Monkeys are traditionally used in art to represent lasciviousness, and a chained monkey historically has been used as an emblem of subjection to lust. Miranda's and Marplot's references to the monkey thus contain a number of double entendres that operate on several levels. While the eighteenth-century audience would recognize that Miranda's reference to designing a chain for her monkey refers to her bringing Sir George under her subjugation through marriage, there are also numerous seventeenth-century literary references to monkeys both as homoerotic images and as male substitutes for single or otherwise unsatisfied women (Gordon Williams 900–02).

Marplot's "miniatures of man" is an echo of Rochester's "A Letter from Artemisia in the Town to Chloe in the Country," in which Artemisia recounts the story of a "fine lady" who exclaims passionately to her pet monkey, "Kiss me, thou curious miniature of man! / How odd thou art! How japan! / Oh, I could live and die with thee!' (Wilmot 108, lines 143–45). ("Die," of course, carries the double entendre of having an orgasm.) Thus the original audience of Centlivre's play would see Miranda and Marplot working at cross-purposes—in their physical fight over the chimney piece but also, intentionally and unintentionally, in the suggestive qualities of their imagistic language about taming monkeys. While Miranda's language substitutes "monkey" for "Sir George," Marplot's creates images of sex toys and maybe even an unacknowledged desire for Sir George himself. Miranda's innuendos are heterosexual, Marplot's homoerotic.

Centlivre uses another sexual reference when Miranda expresses her fear that the monkey will break all her china—a common metaphor for the loss of virginity as well as an overt allusion to the famous china closet scene in William Wycherley's popular *The Country Wife* (1675), in which the word "china" becomes a code word between the supposed eunuch Horner and Lady Fidget for Horner's actual sexual potency. Just as Lady Fidget and Horner engage in ribald banter with each other and Sir Jasper Fidget about how Lady Fidget is determined to get a piece of Horner's china, so the mention of breaking Miranda's china calls the audience's attention to how the different levels of banter regarding Miranda's monkey take on increasingly phallic connotations. The exchange culminates after Sir Francis is sent on his way and Marplot is brought to understand how he has undermined his friends' assignation. Marplot tries to exculpate himself by saying, "And when you talked of a monkey, who the devil thought of Sir George?" and Miranda scathingly dismisses him with "A sign you converse but little with our sex" (127)—"converse" being yet another double entendre for sexual intercourse.

Awareness of the physical stage, the social context, and the jokes of the time brings Centlivre's comedy to life. Though we cannot expect today's audiences to pick up on all the popular culture allusions that the original audience got without help, if the actors understand what they are saying or doing, the humor will be communicated.

Of course, students need to realize that no one interpretation of *The Busybody* is necessarily the definitive one; every production involves dramaturgical choices. Does Marplot believe he is keeping his sexual orientation from the other characters in the play? from the audience? Does he have a sexual interest in any character on the stage? Or is he asexual and completely unaware of how he is the butt of others' humor? It is questions like these that we and our students must ask about each reading and production of a play that makes for living theater. And it is because Centlivre's plays open themselves up to so many different kinds of questions, all with fascinating possible answers, that they are so worthy of our attention.

Notes

1. While the 1709 first edition of Centlivre's play is titled *The Busie Body*, the edition I cite is from *Eighteenth-Century Women Dramatists*, edited by Melinda C. Finberg and part of the Oxford's World's Classics Drama Series, whose policy is to modernize spellings.

2. For discussions of how and why this transition happened, see Staves, "Few Kind Words"; Trumbach, "Sex"; McCormick; and Senelick.

Jones DeRitter

On Using *Thelma and Louise* to Teach Centlivre's *The Wonder*

I teach in a midsize department at a regional comprehensive university in the Northeast. Our English major is organized around a traditional model of English and American literary history, but the gateway course for our first-year students is designed to emphasize close reading, forensic argument, and classroom discussion. Those of us who teach this course are not required to use a common reading list or to include any particular writer or era. Rather, we are expected only to cover some drama, some poetry, and some prose and to expose our students to a variety of genres and historical periods. Because of these requirements, we all expect to spend most of our class time discussing works that are outside our specialty areas, but each of us also includes some material that reflects his or her particular tastes and interests. In other words, anyone who teaches the course will approach most of the reading list from the perspective of the enthusiastic amateur but will also examine one or two texts from the perspective of the professional scholar. The first situation brings us a bit closer to our students in the classroom—like them, we may sometimes struggle with the sense that we do not know everything we need to know to fully grasp what we are being asked to do as readers—and forces us to rely on our most basic analytic skills. On the other hand, when we have the chance to demonstrate how our scholarly pursuits can be useful in the undergraduate classroom, we have to find ways to explain our research without seeming too pedantic or (as our students sometimes say on their course evaluations) too dry.

This is not to say, however, that everyone who teaches our gateway course is starting out from the same place. When our Shakespearean teaches the course, he can safely assume that his students have read *Macbeth*, *Julius Caesar*, and probably *Romeo and Juliet*. Likewise, our medievalist can assume that her students have probably encountered the General Prologue to *The Canterbury Tales* and some version of *Beowulf*; our nineteenth-century specialists can assume that their students have read one Dickens novel, and our Americanists can anticipate that each year's crop of new majors has read a little Poe, a little Hawthorne, and the same handful of poems by Whitman and Dickinson. In my case, however, because very few recent graduates of American high schools have either read or seen a performance of any English play written between 1660 and 1800, I have to assume that we are starting from scratch.

Faced with this circumstance, I was tempted at first to lecture for an hour or so about the closing and reopening of the London theaters, the Restoration, the first English actresses, the rake and his female counterpart, the fop, the booby squire, Calvin and Hobbes (and Locke and Shaftesbury), the Glorious Revolution, Jeremy Collier, the city and the country, the Whigs and the Tories, satire and sensibility, the marriage plot, homosociality, the heroic couplet, and what exactly it was that made John Gay rich and John Rich gay. There are at least two good reasons to resist this temptation. First, in a first-year course, almost any display of scholarly erudition, even if it succeeds in being informative and entertaining rather than self-indulgent and obscure, will lead many students to conclude that the professor would rather listen to his or her own voice than to theirs. Second, since there are always many other works on the reading list that (at least from a student's perspective) need little or no introduction, the attempt to provide a respectable scholarly background for an eighteenth-century English play may lead students to conclude that the work in question cannot be understood, much less enjoyed, unless the reader has mastered what appears to be an atypically complicated set of political, economic, and literary contexts. If I am going to include an eighteenth-century stage comedy on the reading list for an introductory-level course, I need to provide a way in to the text, the genre, and the period that does not involve a sudden shift away from everything I have worked to create in the classroom up to that point.

For the past three years, I have taught Susanna Centlivre's *The Wonder: A Woman Keeps a Secret* (1714) in our gateway course. Centlivre's comedy replaced Oliver Goldsmith's *She Stoops to Conquer*, which I had often paired with Shakespeare's *The Taming of the Shrew* to form a unit that one of my students once referred to as "those theater-as-therapy plays." I made the switch partly because the theater-as-therapy discussions were beginning to feel a little stale, partly because I had had good success with *The Wonder* in my Restoration and eighteenth-century theater elective, and partly because Broadview had just published John O'Brien's excellent stand-alone edition of the play. The final impetus for the change, however, came from Adelphia Cable, which, in late spring 2005, was including two stations in their basic package that seemed to be running Ridley Scott's 1991 outlaw-buddy-road film *Thelma and Louise* on heavy rotation. I watched the film twice on television and then bought the DVD, and, the more I looked at it, the more it seemed to me that there were similarities between Centlivre's script and Callie Khouri's screenplay that might be worth exploring in the classroom. (I also thought that if I was having trouble escaping it on the small screen, the same was probably true for many of my students. If the film was familiar to them, perhaps I could use it to make the play seem familiar as well.)

Most undergraduates think of Hollywood films as instances of straightforward representational storytelling, and, when they are asked to describe and interpret what they have seen, they usually begin by focusing more or less exclusively on issues related to plot and character. In the case of *Thelma and Louise*, my students have applauded the evolving relationship between the two leads (played by Susan Sarandon and Geena Davis) and approved of Harvey Keitel's detective. They have laughed at the temptation represented by a nineteen-year-old Brad Pitt and at the increasing bewilderment displayed by Christopher McDonald's Darryl. The more sophisticated students debate the claim of Sarandon's Louise, made shortly after shooting the drunk who tries to rape Davis's Thelma, that they would not be able to get a fair shake from the authorities. Some argue that the final overreaction by the police suggests that the statement should be taken at face value, and others that Louise's backstory—though it is never spelled out for us in detail, she was apparently the victim of a similar assault when she lived in Texas some years earlier—explains why she would jump to a conclusion that does not always make sense to the audience members in relation to what they see and hear from Keitel's Hal Slocumb. They understand that, once Thelma begins to rob grocery stores and gas stations, the deaths of the two protagonists are a foregone conclusion, though students are not always sure where they get that sense of inevitability.

When my students begin reading *The Wonder*, they recognize immediately that the female friendship at the center of the plot is structured like the one in the film, with Isabella playing the impulsive, childish Thelma to Violante's more mature and sensible Louise. This characterization is especially obvious in the opening moments of act 4, where Isabella cheerfully announces her plan to marry Colonel Britton while Violante frets about her own situation. In the jargon of Hollywood screenwriters, Isabella and Colonel Britton "meet cute"—she leaps out of an upstairs window as he just happens to wander by, so he catches her—and on the basis of this first encounter and one later conversation, Isabella concludes that he is "a Man of Sense, Generosity, and good Humour, in short . . . every Thing that I cou'd like in a Husband" (87–88). Though Pitt's J.D. is clearly not marriage material, Isabella's behavior with respect to Colonel Britton resembles Thelma's behavior with respect to the young hitchhiker, just as Violante's comment to Isabella—"I can't for my Life admire your Conduct, to encourage a Person altogether unknown to you" (88)—sounds very much like an eighteenth-century version of the warnings Louise delivers to Thelma, both when they meet J.D. and when they are drinking at the Silver Bullet earlier in the film.

Students also understand that in Centlivre's Lisbon the social system is controlled by the tyrannical fathers of the two heroines and that the analogue in the movie is what one student described as the "weirdly all-male" police task force headed by Stephen Tobolowsky's Max. Students have consistently been very interested in Frederick, a secondary character who serves as a *raissonneur* in the play, as a version of Keitel's sympathetic detective. In the opening scene of the play, Frederick tries unsuccessfully to persuade Isabella's father, Don Lopez, not to force his daughter to marry a rich and ugly fool (48–49), and, because Frederick argued on her behalf in that earlier scene, he is later accused by Don Lopez of having helped Isabella to make her escape. In the film, Slocumb tries more than once to persuade Thelma and Louise to surrender peacefully, expresses sympathy for both women based on his knowledge of what happened to Louise in Texas, and vents his frustration on J.D., who has placed the two women in dire circumstances by stealing their getaway money. In the final scene of the film, Slocumb tries desperately to persuade Max to control all the cops who have their weapons trained on Thelma and Louise. "How many times, Max?" he asks, "how many times them women gonna be [abused]?"

Students also recognize that Frederick and Slocumb are outnumbered and outranked by men whose attitude toward women is condescending and proprietary. In the play, both aspects of this attitude are expressed most explicitly by Don Lopez (48, 55), and the proprietary side of it is later reiterated by his son Felix. At the outset of the play, Felix is in hiding because of his involvement in a duel he fought over his refusal to marry a woman his father had chosen for him, but when his opponent is safely out of danger and Felix is able to move about freely once again, he thinks nothing of joining the pursuit of his sister and lamenting the perceived injury she has inflicted on the family's honor (78). In the film, the most explicit expression of this attitude occurs in a conversation at Darryl's place when Max and Slocumb are trying to tell Darryl how to talk to Thelma when she calls to check in. When Slocumb asks Darryl whether he has a "good relationship" with his wife, Darryl explains that he is "about as close as I can be to a nutcase like that." In response, Max suggests that when Thelma calls, Darryl should "just be gentle, you know, like you're really happy to hear from her, like you really miss her," and then adds that "women love that [stuff]." After a brief pause, all three men dissolve into nervous laughter, perhaps because Max's slip has exposed casual insincerity as a form of aggression.

Of course, character-based analogies will get us only so far, and on all three occasions when I have pursued this line of discussion in the classroom, there have been students who argued essentially that the similarities between the characters in the play and the characters in the film do not seem to mean very much in the long run, because, after all, the film ends with the deaths of both title characters while the play ends with the marriages of Violante to Felix and Isabella to Colonel Britton—marriages that, in the patriarchal world of the play, would seem to require that the women value their husbands more than any of their friends. This claim is worth exploring in some detail, and, if we have even a few good readers or film enthusiasts in the room, we might work our way to and through the following three points.

First—and remember, these students are just out of high school—not all fictional marriages should be taken as surrenders to an oppressive and hidebound social system, and not all fictional deaths should be taken as confirmations of failure. On both the stage and the screen, style and circumstance should count for something. In her commentary on the DVD of the film, the screenwriter Khouri says that she wanted the ending to be like the ending of *Butch Cassidy and the Sundance Kid* (1971), where the two outlaw heroes are frozen in time just before the volley from dozens of Bolivian soldiers tears them to bits. In other words, the end of *Thelma and Louise* is intended to elevate the two heroines to mythic status; they go up into a burst of light, and they never come down.[1] With respect to the play, we have to evaluate the marriages in relation to the events and emotions that preceded them. Has Felix or Colonel Britton changed in any noticeable way over the course of the play? Does Violante ever repent of her decision to hide Isabella from her brother and her father? Will Violante and Isabella maintain their friendship even after they get married? The first of these questions is relatively easy to answer. Though there is no proviso scene in *The Wonder*, there is an important scene in the middle of act 5 wherein Felix and Violante clasp hands to acknowledge that, after all their disputes and misperceptions, their love finally leaves each of them with no choice other than to trust the other (108). In his next to last speech, Felix also disavows his earlier comments about Isabella on the grounds that "Love has taught me to know, that every Man's Happiness consists in chusing for himself" (116). The answers to the questions about Violante and Isabella are perhaps a little more complicated, but here again the comparisons to the film can help.

My second point about the different endings of the play and the film is that genre conventions extend well beyond questions of plot and character. Both *The Wonder* and *Thelma and Louise* use physical space as a means of shaping our responses to plot and to character. The various settings of Centlivre's comedy suggest that indoor spaces can be controlled by women but that independence can only be gained outdoors. For most of the play, Violante struggles to manage the comings and goings of Isabella, Felix, Colonel Britton, and the two fathers so that no one but she fully grasps everything that is going on. The misperceptions that threaten at regular intervals to separate Felix and Violante forever are always presented as incursions from the street into the house; even when the intruder is her father, he is presented as having left the house and returned unexpectedly because of a mechanical problem with his carriage (108). Yet the weddings that finally remove both heroines from the oppressive custody of their unreasonable fathers take place outdoors in the Terreiro de passo (the Royal Palace Square). In *Thelma and Louise*, of course, the iconic landscape of the American West is used to signal the two heroines' growing sense of independence and self-sufficiency. We understand that the film's ending is meant to be uplifting partly because Thelma and

Louise choose to die in the open, as opposed to living in jail. In the play, both Isabella and Violante ultimately take control of their marital destinies by meeting Colonel Britton and Felix in a public space before their fathers can arrive to break things up.

Finally, both film and theater are industrial art forms. With respect to mainstream Hollywood films and to professional theater companies, the contributions of many individuals are required to produce a single work of art, and those individuals rely on the commercial success of their collective effort for their livelihoods. Screenwriters and playwrights who want to see their works produced are asking to gamble with other people's money and other people's careers; it stands to reason that some of those other people might wish to hedge their bets by catering to popular tastes. In her commentary on the DVD, Khouri expresses some unhappiness with the presentation of the tank truck driver whose rig is blown up by Louise shortly before the final chase begins; Khouri apparently wanted the driver to be more threatening and less clownish. Centlivre had been dead for a long time when David Garrick revived her play in the 1750s, so she was spared the pain of seeing him shift the focus of the play away from her heroine and toward Felix's manly efforts to control his passions. Even during her lifetime, she had battled with the actor Robert Wilks because he felt that one of her earlier male characters (Sir George Airy in *The Busie Body*) had not been dignified enough (M. Anderson 115–16). In fact, the fiery personality of the original Felix may represent an attempt to give this actor more opportunities to enact what he thought of as more masculine behaviors. Khouri does not seem to be more than mildly exasperated about the truck driver, and Centlivre continued to work with Wilks, and neither writer ever complained in public about the genre conventions that dictated the endings of these works. (Janet Maslin reported in the *New York Times* that when Khouri accepted the Academy Award for Best Screenplay of 1991, she told "everyone who wanted a happy ending to *Thelma and Louise*" that "for me, this is it.")

To return to the original student comment: though the genre conventions of the twentieth-century American road movie and the eighteenth-century British stage comedy dictate different endings for these stories, *Thelma and Louise* and *The Wonder* share a great deal more than a few character types. In both works, the more levelheaded of the two leading women continues to help and protect her more vulnerable friend despite repeated indications that she would be better off betraying that trust. Thelma and Louise's kiss and clasped hands just before driving off the cliff are one way of showing this, as is Isabella's statement to Violante—uttered just before the two of them run off to the Terreiro de passa to be married—that "I know not how to express my Thanks for what you suffer'd for my Sake, my grateful Acknowledgments shall ever wait you; and to the World proclaim [your] Faith, Truth, and Honour" (97). In each case, the destination is a foregone conclusion, but both works manage to suggest that some friendships enable some few of us to confront those inevitabilities on our own terms.

Note

1. In another extra on the DVD, the director Scott explains that the crew had actually filmed a much longer take of the '66 Thunderbird falling toward the earth, only to cut away to an earlier shot of Thelma and Louise driving across the desert floor. According to Scott, the long fall was perceived as too depressing, so they went with the quicker cut.

Marjean D. Purinton

Teaching Burney's *The Witlings*

What should we make of *The Witlings*? This funny play, which Frances Burney wrote in 1779 at age twenty-seven, was suppressed by her father, the distinguished musicologist Charles Burney, and her father's friend, the critic Samuel Crisp; produced for the first time in 1994; and published for the first time in 1995. Claire Harman points out that Burney did not admit to composing *The Witlings* until the beginning of 1779, although she was probably secretly writing it well before then (132). Why would she feel compelled to be so secretive about the play? What does it mean for Burney to have taken the enigmatic pseudonym "A Sister of the Order" as the author? Margaret Anne Doody maintains that the subject of *The Witlings* is the intellectual self-consciousness of would-be wits, the "Order" suggesting Bluestocking clubs, often characterized as salons of hypocritical, shallow, stupid women professing knowledge (*Frances Burney* 70).

Is Burney, a Bluestocking member, engaged in self-satire, self-reflection, or self-criticism, and what possible use might *The Witlings* have in our undergraduate and graduate classes? Kate Chisholm records that *The Witlings* was read aloud in 1779 at Chesington Hall by an ensemble that included Burney's sisters Susan and Charlotte, and so the play was circulated in what might be called a limited pedagogical setting (87–88). In the world of the play's "witlings," however, real information is repeatedly lost in discussions that do not come to any satisfactory resolutions. As Barbara Darby points out, "Burney presents in the literary witlings a set of people who seek to imitate the responses of an educated class of readers" (35). What then might our students discover in a play about nonsense and pseudolearning? We can explore these and other puzzles of Burney's satire with the Broadview Press 2002 edition of Burney's *The Witlings* and *The Woman-Hater*, edited by Peter Sabor and Geoffrey Sill, an excellent teaching text of the plays.

One approach to teaching *The Witlings* is to present it as a comedy about education and learning, both in its historical moment of late-eighteenth-century London (satire on literary clubs, especially the Bluestockings, and Georgian anxieties about women's reading, for example) and in the context of today's societal discussions (liberal arts education versus job training, the accountability of learning outcomes and assessments to legislative and tax-paying publics, and the value of service learning).[1] Here I want to explore how students might get to conceptual and thematic issues in the play by examining the ways that spaces, structures, and geographies operate textually; how notions of industry, intellect, and time function as dominant tropes; and, finally, how the Esprit Party featured in *The Witlings* can be read as an analogue to today's educational enterprises in humanistic studies.

Time and space operate as key components in *The Witlings*. The play has an unusual setting, occurring in different interiorized geographies, and I want to examine how the location of all five of its acts might be defined as female or domestic spaces. Act 1 takes place in Mrs. Wheedle's milliner shop, and act 2 occurs in Lady Smatter's drawing room. Act 3, the heart of the play, is set in the most intimate of female spaces, Lady Smatter's dressing room. Act 4 brings us to Lady Smatter's library for the meeting of the Esprit Party literary club, and act 5 occurs in Mrs. Voluble's parlor. The spaces of the play's setting begin in the domestic, public venue of a woman's shop, then draw us into the privacy of the dressing room—a space signifying female sexuality—and back out again to the familial arena of the parlor. This movement among dramatic spaces charged with psychological and social meanings is important; as Cynthia Wall has demonstrated, the stage's fourth wall invites spectators into these interiors and domestic scenes with increased intensity (115). Darby's discussion of the "censored women" in *The Witlings* asserts that Cecilia is a character who is literally "out of *place*" (33), a woman with no control over her position in society (34–35).

The geocritical pattern of spatial and temporal relations is also important to the larger context of the play's setting in fashionable London at the end of the eighteenth century. For the geography of the City, like the geographies of the setting in *The Witlings*, is connected to class mobility, gender identity, and national intellect. According to Karen Harvey, forms of geographical or spatial knowledge facilitated gendered relations and gendered codes of movement in Georgian England (132). Michèle Cohen adds that eighteenth-century practices of sociability generated "social spaces," tea tables and assemblies, for example, that were ambiguous and unstable for the publicity of women and the fashioning of gentlemen (66). Moreover, Alan Robinson emphasizes how the democratization of consumer pleasures, "with its accompanying leisure and market-mediated consumption," fostered Georgian anxieties about class and gender leveling (103). Indeed, the emergent metropolitan London is omnipresent in the backdrop of the comedy. At the very beginning of act 1, Mrs. Wheedle tells those in her shop that she will send a cap and "other things to Mrs. Apeall in the Minories" (47; act 1, lines 15–16) and then remarks to Miss Sally, "it will do well enough for the City" (16–17). The Minories signifies the part of London that was seen as the center of trade and finance. Mrs. Voluble explains to Miss Jenny how the orphan Cecilia Stanley, having recently achieved age and fortune, "came to spend the Winter in Town with Lady Smatter" and fell in love with Mr. Beaufort, Smatter's nephew (50; 1.87–88). The fashionable set, like Cecilia, would want to be in London during the winter season, November through May. Jack, the foolish young man too busy going places to get anything done, has just been at the Royal Exchange in the City, the center of British business, where he learns that the banker Stipend, Cecilia's guardian and banker, has gone bankrupt. Now seemingly penniless, Cecilia has no reason to be in London, and Lady Smatter recommends that she return to her friends in the country, for "London is a dangerous place for Girls who have no Fortune" (90; 3.108–09). Because Cecilia's financial state makes her no longer desirable for London residency, she hopes to move "far away from this hated City" (147; 5.236), and she describes herself as a devalued commodity for the city market: "I must hide myself from the World" (148; 5.275).

Thus the play's structure draws our attention to particularized, feminized, and intimate spaces at the same time that its textual clues make us mindful of the larger geographic scenes in which the comedy's seemingly silly activities occur, making expansion and isolation keys to its structural and thematic issues. When students are attentive to the play's geographic patterns, its interior spaces as well as its references to commercial London outside the play's settings, then they can see how Burney constructs intersections of interior and exterior spaces in which attitudes about education and leisure are put into question. *The Witlings* interrogates the values of education, particularly for women, and whether time spent on reading, writing, and discussing literature can be valuable when industry and consumerism are inflected with greater cultural significance. With this particular attention to the play's spatial structuring and its geographic and temporal references, an instructor can help students learn to make close textual readings, furthering their critical skills and their appreciation of how eighteenth-century geography informs the play's thematic concerns.

A feminist reading of *The Witlings* also exposes the closet, an intimate female space. *The Witlings* is a "closet drama" in the sense that Catherine Burroughs recognizes in Joanna Baillie's theater: a limited space where societal identities can be constructed, represented, interrogated, and rehearsed (*Closet Stages* 150–51). Act 5 of Burney's comedy draws on the closet trope when Mrs. Voluble presses Mrs. Sapient into the parlor closet where she is "Crampt to Death!" in the "strange place" amidst the hurriedly cleared dinner and cutlery (156; 5.537). While Bobby and Jack mistake her for a cat entrapped in the cabinet, Mrs. Voluble discloses who is in the closet to everyone, enabling those assembled in the parlor to speculate how Mrs. Sapient has used her time there in the darkness. Censor suggests that she has applied herself to "the Study of the Occult Sciences" (172; 5.1036), implying that this space is somehow not natural, as the space where something sexual is bound to take place. In fact, this deeply interior, mysterious space represents the climax of what a feminist reading would call the male penetration of female spaces occurring throughout the play. The scene provides additional titillation in its rendering of the possibility of two women being closeted in the cabinet, implying a sexual encounter involving same-sex desire.

Another way to read this male penetration of female spaces is to see *The Witlings* in the tradition of "rescue dramas." Cecilia looks for Beaufort to rescue her from her wicked mother-in-law-to-be and from the prospect of working for a living as a traveling companion to Mrs. Hollis. For Cecilia, marriage is the panacea, and she is demoralized by what she believes is Beaufort's impotence—his refusal to rescue her—and so she renounces him, saying, "[N]othing can extenuate the coldness, the neglect, the insensibility of his conduct" (110; 3.781–82). Lady Smatter dehumanizes Cecilia in her shallow promise to protect "the poor Thing" (90; 3.124), that "poor Girl of Fashion" (83; 2.607–08), that "most insipid thing" (84; 2.650) whom she never really liked. Janice Thaddeus has suggested that Cecilia's need to wait for her man is linked to prevailing ideas about women's powerlessness and loneliness (55). But all the relationships in the comedy rely on the need to be financially rescued: Cecilia depends on marriage to Beaufort, Beaufort depends on his Aunt Smatter's financial support, both Cecilia and Beaufort depend on the intervention of Censor, the milliner shop women depend on the fashionable ladies to pay their bills, Dabler depends on the Esprit Society for his writing, and its members depend on him for their criticism. Everyone in this comedy relies on an unhealthy dependence from which she or he seeks rescue, and these dependences are played out in the small spaces of closeted interactions.

Within the metropolitan London spatial background, we find that, by the end of the eighteenth century, modes of production shifted from task-oriented labor to timed labor. The result was a time discipline that Burney sees absent in the Esprit Party even as this discipline became a status symbol as the emerging work ethic. Sandra Sherman asserts that this reconceptualized time puts the value of leisure into question and that Burney's comedy explores the status of leisure and time devoted to industry (401–04). During the Industrial Revolution, time was transformed into currency, an equation that will undoubtedly prompt students to see postmodern analogues to the commodified time of the age of information and technology.

Furthermore, Britain's emergent colonialism exploited the industry of others so that its middle classes might acquire the commodities that signaled privilege. Uncomfortable as they are in the milliner's shop, Censor asks Beaufort, "[I]s not a man's person his own property?" (50; 1.101), and Censor blesses the stars that he is "a *Free Man*" (51; 1.135). Censor is, of course, a man free of the burden of making a living. In the comedy's final act, Mrs. Wheedle complains about fine ladies who "keep ordering and ordering, and think no more of paying than if one could Live upon a Needle and Thread" (140; 5.5–7). We learn that Cecilia is not the only one in financial debt, for Mrs. Voluble laments, "Ah, this is a sad World!

a very sad World indeed! nothing but ruination going forward from one end of the Town to the other" (lines 18–20). All the play's characters are anxious about money, production, and consumerism.

In a compelling study entitled *The High Price of Materialism*, Tim Kasser demonstrates how our twenty-first-century culture is driven by the desire to consume goods and services. He argues that, despite the belief that commodification leads to personal pleasure—an idea inherited and reworked from the Georgian past—strongly materialistic people often feel controlled and alienated in several aspects of their lives. Consumer culture, he details, makes us possessive, narcissistic, and destructive (1–95), the same qualities we see Burney's characters dramatize.

In the midst of the economic crises marking the end of the eighteenth century, it is ironic that Burney's comedy features nothing of the industry and middle-class work ethic of the period; instead, *The Witlings* promotes wasted time with the frivolous antics of the Esprit Party. Codger grumbles, "I have no Time for reading; and I hold that these sort of things only turn one's Head from matters of more importance" (75; 2.362–64). If one has money, then time is surplus. Mrs. Sapient sallies, "[I]t is a pity to waste Time" (76; 2.400–01), and adds, "[T]he thought of losing one's money is extremely serious, for as far as *I* have seen of the World [i.e., London], there's no living without it" (80; 2.520–22). Stressed about Cecilia's material deficiencies, Beaufort finds that the activities of the Esprit Party are "useless, idle, ludicrous disquisitions" (135; 4.680) and take time from "affairs of real interest and importance" (line 681); he frets, "[I]s this a Time to talk of Books and Authors?" (87; 3.25–26). Lady Smatter demonstrates her class status with the comment, "[W]hen I am preparing a Criticism, I sometimes give a whole Day to poring over only one Line" (89; 3.96–98), even though she concedes that "there may be other things of greater utility in common Life" (73; 2.292–93). Similarly, Jack accuses the Esprit Party of wasting time: "You good folks who sit here talking by the Hour together, must lead strange dull Lives; I wonder you don't lose the use of your Limbs" (125; 4.334–36). While Tara Wallace suggests that *The Witlings* expresses Burney's suspicions about the new economic system, its resulting new class distinctions, and its reconceptualization of leisure and utility (67–69), the themes students will see in *The Witlings* are the values of humanist knowledge and knowledge making in the age of technology.

It seems to me that the economic question at the center of *The Witlings* is a postmodern epistemological one as well: What value does society wish to bestow on intellectual industry? While Burney's comedy stages the issue satirically, the serious matter of value for intellectual property and the process of knowledge construction arise in our day. Lady Smatter impresses on Cecilia how much time and effort she gives to her research, concluding, "[I]f my pursuits were not made public, I should not have any at all, for where can be the pleasure of reading Books, and studying authors, if one is not to have the credit of talking of them?" (65; 2.24–27). She tells Beaufort that the world can little appreciate the "secret labours," "private hardships," and arduous "figuring" necessary for a Belle Esprit's "brilliancy of Conversation" (67; 2.67–69). When Beaufort damns Smatter's eternal books, she asks, "How? do you mean to depreciate Books? to doubt their general utility, and universal influence?" (135; 4.669–70). Smatter stands on the platform formulated from her studies that "a noble mind, as I was reading the other Day, is always superior to misfortune" (84; 2.654–55).

The satire here reminds me of our difficulties today in making academic work transparent to the general public and therefore worthy of time and funding. According to Eric Rauchway's editorial in the *New Republic*, American research universities, particularly land-grant universities, face the same problem they did at the end of the nineteenth century: funding. The true exemplum of *The Witlings* suggests that knowledge is an investment, a valuable process, resulting in practical skills (jobs) and time well spent, something necessary for fostering self-dependence, the "most useful of all practical precepts" (172; 5.1053–54). In this context, the stasis and confined spaces of the comedy suggest that the Industrial Revolution, like our technological revolution, will exact a price, economic and human, for its increased production and faster-paced lifestyles. The play examines what kind of value will be placed on intellectual activity in a society that rewards the production of commodities and that, like today's culture, conceives of education in the language of customers and assesses intellectual outcomes in terms of customer satisfaction, a trend some educators are resisting. The recent reaffirmation of general education in the undergraduate curriculum at Harvard University, for example, emphasizes liberal arts as the locus of study in which students acquire curiosity and inquiry that readies them for lifetime learning. In an article for the *Boston Globe*, Anthony Kronman admonishes teachers of humanities to reconsider the nature and value of their work, to confront the ways in which the modern research models devoted to graduate education and grant acquisition have deformed or weakened our efforts to teach the art of living. John Gravois's *Chronicle of Higher Education* report includes a statement made by a professor of English at Emory University lamenting that professors have few incentives to focus on undergraduate teaching and that the university is less committed to cultivating engaged, critical citizens than to providing job training. Burney's *The Witlings*—as well as her later comedy *The Woman-Hater* (1802), which also features the Esprit Party—can be read in the context of today's debates about the teaching mission and curricular directions of higher education and the value we place on reading, learning, and thinking as processes rather than products.

The Witlings is also engaged profoundly with ethical matters, such as slander, libel, plagiarism, and censorship in their specific historicity and location as well as in their conceptual connections with the modern academy as the site of intellectual production and learning, where time and space are valued in terms of learning assessments and external financial support. Burney's indictment of education and her critique of class consciousness under construction at the end of the eighteenth century resonate in the early twenty-first century, when notions of liberal arts education might be seen as becoming as meaningless as the intellectual pursuits of the witlings' Esprit Party. Burney's fictitious salon, modeled on her participation in the Bluestocking circles of late-eighteenth-century London—heterogeneous groups of "visiting foreigners, popular writers of the day, a sprinkling of the nobility, scholars and prelates, a few actors and musicians" (Clifford 334)—is strikingly similar to the faculty we may find in our divisions of humanities and colleges of liberal arts. Like Burney toiling secretively on her comedy about pedants in the mid-1770s, today's faculty members often work behind closed classroom doors at an educational enterprise that the general public finds mysterious and esoteric. Similarly, the critique of learning and the value of knowledge that are staged in the interior spaces of *The Witlings* can be interrogated in our intimate closets known as classrooms, where postmodern consumption culture comes head-to-head with the price and the purpose of liberal arts education.

Note

1. According to Jacqueline Pearson, Lady Smatter represents Burney's anxieties about being thought ostentatiously bookish, since Burney was surrounded by books in her father's library (as many as twenty thousand volumes in 1798 [*Women's Reading* 128–31]). As Karen Harvey remarks, for women of the eighteenth century reading was considered a potential threat to both body and mind (142).

Daniel O'Quinn

Scarcity and Surplus: Teaching Inchbald's *Every One Has His Fault*

In a theatrical world where state censorship and commercial considerations trumped all else, Elizabeth Inchbald managed to forge a playwriting career that was as remarkable for its aesthetic achievement as for its complex representation of social upheaval. Teaching Inchbald's *Every One Has His Fault* provides the opportunity to test much of the received wisdom about political theater and about women's role in the commercial public sphere. But helping students recognize and assess Inchbald's politics is a difficult task, even though the circumstances of the play's initial production were thoroughly politicized. The play was in rehearsal when the Edict of Fraternity was passed, and Thomas Harris, the manager of Covent Garden, postponed the debut of Inchbald's *Every One Has His Fault* (1793) for fear of coinciding with the French regicide.[1] The play opened three days before Britain's declaration of war with France, but much of the play's intervention in the debate surrounding the morality of Britain's war with France hinges on the utterance of four words—"Provisions are so scarce" (44; act 1, sc. 2, line 37). While I have written elsewhere about how Inchbald's play interrupts the political discourse surrounding the commencement of the war (O'Quinn, "Bread"), here I suggest ways to help students appreciate how Inchbald uses the sexual economy of five-act comedy to allegorize and explore political issues that would be explosive in the hands of any playwright, let alone a woman.

With the recent publication of Jeffrey N. Cox and Michael Gamer's superb edition of *Every One Has His Fault*, teachers can now set up exercises for students to combine primary-document research regarding the composition and reception of the first productions with close readings of the play. This essay offers practical instructions for such exercises in the hope that the experience with the newspapers, the lord chamberlain's papers, and the play will give students a sense of the possibilities nascent in a performance-based theater history. This type of theater history uses key elements of performance studies, cultural studies, and social history to develop large-scale theses about political representation that are, nevertheless, responsive to the minute details of the script and its enactment. Because scarcity is a theme of the play, we can begin by addressing the methodological problem of scarcity that besets any form of theater criticism—from the scarcity of dramaturgical information to the transient moments of audience sociability in which the play is received. In the process, I argue for a more nuanced approach to understanding women's role in the public life of the nation at this historical moment.

Theater historians are continually beset by two related problems: a nagging sense that the incompleteness of any theatrical archive undercuts the certainty of arguments that reconstruct a particular moment of production and reception and a terrifying recognition that the intense sociability of the theater renders it a site of multifarious and proliferating signification. In short, working on theater means continually grasping for missing information and attempting to decide which elements of the surrounding cultural and social noise should enter into the discussion. The methodological implications of careering between archival scarcity and the surplus of information afforded by microhistory are deeply challenging, especially for students whose primary training takes place in literature departments. Although I teach in a department that has a distinct and innovative theater program, my experience teaching eighteenth-century and Romantic theater, and Inchbald in particular, has been confined to period-based courses in a largely text-based English program. Thus most of my students have little or no training in how to think not only about such obviously crucial issues as performance, space, bodies, and archives but also about issues that should be crucial to literary study in general, including the production, circulation, and reception of cultural commodities. My students are also unfamiliar with the social and the political history of the late eighteenth century. This situation is a problem for teaching the theater of this period, because, as Gillian Russell has demonstrated with extraordinary rigor, understanding the pleasures afforded by these plays requires both topical knowledge of the world they represent and a hawklike attention to the intense integration of theatrical sociability—the social experience of going to the theater—and theatrical representation (*Women*).

Inchbald's plays were performed for an audience that was continually evaluating its relation to itself by seeing the dynamics of social exchange represented on a nightly basis in two state-controlled theaters. As David Worrall has reminded us, from 1737 onward the state regulated not only what kind of experiences could be represented on the stage but also what kind of social interactions could be prompted, sustained, or critiqued in the playhouse (33–68). But this kind of direct censorship by the lord chamberlain was arguably less important than the internalization of state scrutiny by theatrical managers, playwrights, and performers. And this internal calibration of what was presentable was further complicated by the fact that the theater in the eighteenth century was the preeminent cultural commodity, subject to intense economic speculation and critical evaluation. Plays cost money to stage, and their success or lack of it was a crucial issue for the theater. My students are not used to thinking about cultural artifacts as commodities, nor are they inclined to translate the economic and material imperatives of theatrical production into how they visualize performance. Nor are they used to thinking about how commodity circulation impinges on reception. The aesthetic experience from my students' lives that comes closest to eighteenth-century theatrical reception is the cinema. I often make this comparison to get them to realize how deeply the theater of this period permeated everyday life; after all, when conversation flags, one can always revert to movies and celebrity gossip. But this comparison captures none of the restrictions imposed by theatrical licensing. On any given night, London theatergoers in the 1790s had to choose primarily between Covent Garden and Drury Lane or perhaps the Kings Theatre for opera. As Jane Moody has argued, illegitimate houses were proliferating at this moment, but the entertainments on offer had to circumvent the prohibition against certain spoken dialogue written into the Stage Licensing Act of 1737, so these became venues for nascent forms of musical theater, melodrama, and spectacular displays of physical and technological mastery (*Illegitimate Theatre*).

I have just realized that I am repeating one of the cardinal errors of teaching. I have started to tell you about the theatrical enterprise, rather than introduce you to it. In courses where I have needed to deal with an Inchbald play quickly—say, in a class or two—this method is inevitable. But let us assume for a moment that we have a couple of weeks to examine a representative play in an upper-level seminar. My institution is fortunate enough to have access to the *Early English Newspapers* microfilm collection for the period in question, so the first thing I do is send my poor students off in search of reviews of *Every One Has His Fault* and of its competitor on opening night. I ask them to read the review and then examine the paper from which it is taken. This exercise is not simply a matter of sadism—although I think it is valuable to give students a sense of the labor involved in dealing with the archive—but rather a crash course in both the methodological problems of social history and the perplexing problems of reception. The sadistic thrill comes when you tell them, after the fact, that Cox and Gamer have reprinted the reviews in a very helpful appendix. But I would argue that seeing the advertisements and adjacent reports of events in France and India very quickly locates the students in the historical moment. Doing a full workup of reviews is beyond the scope of most students' schedules, so I tend to assign two or three papers per student and then have them talk as a group about what they found.

As it turns out, there is a great deal of juicy controversy associated with Inchbald's play. The ultraloyalist *True Briton* accused Inchbald of "democratic" tendencies, and a vigorous debate ensued regarding the play's relation to events in France. The controversy was sparked by the repetition of four words: "Provisions are so scarce." The reviewer for the newly operative *True Briton* immediately objected to allusions "to the dearness of provisions in this Metropolis" and declared that "in several sentences the *Democrat* displays a cloven foot" (30 Jan. 1793). The *Morning Chronicle*'s retort to the "lynx-eyed sedition-hunter" was quick and withering:

> Certainly any compassionate allusion to the distresses of the poor, at a time when an impending war threatens to aggravate them all, may be very good *treason by construction*; and we trust Mr. REEVES and his associates will look to it, or at least send an *anonymous letter* against the Author to the Secretary of State. (31 Jan. 1793)[2]

The students also discover that the audience on opening night was actually dressed in mourning for the recently executed French king, so the papers are remarkably useful for giving the students a sense of how social performance and theatrical performance are in dialogue. This research prompts the students to find out more about the context until they realize that the conventional, and rather lazy, distinction between text and context, which tends to prevail in our teaching practice, simply does not hold. Any full understanding of *Every One Has His Fault* requires that one engage with the papers, and any real examination of the papers forces one to confront the complex intersection of public representations, private desires, and the social forces that both drive and limit their expression.

So an afternoon chained to a microfilm reader has rendered your better students wary of any of the tactics for productively limiting cultural analysis to a discrete set of resolvable problems. Authorship is under immense pressure because it is clear that the players, the manager, and the state are integrally involved in the play's realization. The text is under considerable scrutiny because the published document is not only distinct from the examiner's text, which Cox and Gamer give us a clear sense of, but also from what may or may not have been spoken on that night. The context proves extraordinarily messy because the daily papers do not agree on the events that are unfolding around them. And finally, the audience is composed of whom exactly? And what are its members doing? Are they even present for the entire play? Or did they come with other interests and objectives in mind? This point is helpful in sketching out the multifarious structure of an evening at the theater, and the very mixed house. And it is a superb place to complicate students' notions of the public sphere, because one can discuss the related yet distinct publics generated by print and performance. In the past, I have often kept a running discussion on Jürgen Habermas and his critics throughout the entire syllabus, and this moment is useful for discussing not only the gendering of print culture but also the gender dynamics of public space. At this point, students are equipped to start asking some pithy questions about the place of women in these different public realms.

After exploring some of these large-scale arguments about public life and commercial culture, most of the students become acutely aware that the messy sense of reception derived from their time with the papers continues to haunt their ability to articulate how the play operates. At this time I draw their attention to the specific merits of the script. *Every One Has His Fault* is arguably Inchbald's finest play: the dialogue is extremely cunning, and her manipulation of the formal elements of five-act comedy is innovative and elegant. Incorporating Richard Brinsley Sheridan's *The School for Scandal* (1777) or Oliver Goldsmith's *She Stoops to Conquer*

(1773) into the syllabus will give students valuable comparators from which to analyze Inchbald's formal preoccupations as well as her complex intervention in the sexual economy of eighteenth-century theater. For my literature students, this comparison allows them to build on one of their strengths—close reading—while forcing them to imagine the play in performance. In fact, I have frequently asked students to find what they believe to be roughly comparable scenes in *Every One Has His Fault* and *School for Scandal*—scenes where key characters are introduced, such as act 1, scene 1 of both plays, or scenes where the sexual plots are complicated or resolved. Then, after breaking them into groups, I have students work up staged readings of small segments of those scenes. Such quick performances allow for a series of searching questions about formal innovation and the difference that gender makes in the scripting of these scenes.

After this exercise, I ask students to look at how the newspapers read the play. I get them to use their skills as discourse analysts to sort out how the papers represent theatrical experience. The controversy initiated by the *True Briton* generates explicit and self-aware analyses of specific speeches in papers such as the *Morning Chronicle*:

> I cannot but express my astonishment, to find in a newspaper, now on the table before me, a most unjust accusation of Mrs. Inchbald, imputing to her an ill-founded charge. I will state the very words of the play as they were spoken on Tuesday night.
>
> > There is not a fraud, a theft, or hardly any vice committed, that you do not take the criminal's part, shake your head and cry, "Provisions are so scarce!" And no longer ago than last Lord-mayor's day when you were told that Mr. Alderman Ravenous was ill with an indigestion, you endeavoured to soften the matter by exclaiming, "Provisions are so scarce!"
>
> Could anybody imagine that those words, would be so misunderstood, or so warped as to induce any man of sense or candour to find in that passage a *democratic* sentiment? The whole context imports the very reverse; it is a nice stroke of satire on those who see many men guilty of actions of an evil tendency, and yet have some *cant phrase*, by which they hope to varnish over the conduct of the wrong doer.
> (1 Feb. 1793)

This call for contextual reading is curious not only because it implies verbatim knowledge of an as yet unpublished play but also because it elides both the immediate context for the utterance and the broader implications of Inchbald's intervention. These lines are spoken by Miss Spinster, who can hardly be considered a neutral conveyor of information about Mr. Harmony. In her eyes, "all this pretended philanthropy renders [Mr. Harmony] ridiculous," and she ultimately "condemn[s] that false humanity, which induces [him] to say many things in conversation which deserve to stigmatize [him] with the character of deceit" (43–44; 1.2.33–45). Although the cruel Mr. Norland is critiqued throughout the play, his traditional limitation of legitimate feminine roles in act 3, scene 1 to "widow, maid and wife" reflects a broadly held opinion regarding the nonnormativity of "spinsters" (57; lines 364–65). Inchbald's position regarding unmarried older women may be more complex, but throughout the scene Miss Spinster is ridiculed for her vanity, her unsociability, and her severity toward her servants. Her critique of Mr. Harmony's philanthropy is explicitly tied to class relations:

> *Miss Spinster*. I will not forgive you for thus continually speaking in the behalf of every servant whom you find me offended with. Your philanthropy becomes insupportable; and, instead of being a virtue, degenerates into a vice.
>
> *Mr. Harmony*. Dear Madam, do not upbraid me for a constitutional fault.
>
> (43; 1.2.1–6)

The pun on "constitutional" clearly marks Mr. Harmony's politics, so why is the *Morning Chronicle*, the voice of Foxite opinion, "varnish[ing] over the conduct" of both Mr. Harmony and Inchbald? Is it simply a matter of ensuring that the play stays on the stage and skewering the *True Briton* in the process? Or does Inchbald's intervention engage more troubling political concerns that both sides of the press would like to see disappear—albeit in different ways?

Such readings of small segments of the play and of the reviews give students a clear sense of the complexity of comedy as a vehicle for social critique, as well as the interlacing worlds of the theater and the newspapers. Most of my students tend not to think of the press as partisan, so one benefit of this exercise is that they have to recognize and identify the political distinction between the *Morning Chronicle*'s Whig opposition and the ultraconservative *True Briton*. This intensive work on the press also underlines the value of close reading to any broader project of cultural analysis. From here it is instructive to send the students to the excellent criticism of this play—especially the work by Misty G. Anderson (171–200), Ellen Donkin (110–31), Lisa Freeman ("Social Life"), Amy Garnai, and Katherine S. Green ("Mr. Harmony")—not simply to sort out the progress of largely feminist writing on Romantic theater but also to recognize which elements of the theatrical-social scene the critics avoid or downplay to make their arguments. This kind of exercise helps students learn how to deal with the aforementioned combination of surplus and scarcity of cultural information. How one deals with the archive requires a self-conscious combination of repression and speculation that opens onto the most valuable pedagogical moments imaginable.

We recognize that close reading—here understood as a careful attention to the details afforded by the archive—instantiates both an opening onto history and an articulation of theory. Inchbald offers a particularly apt occasion for this lesson. Her plays are deeply involved not only with the representation and evaluation of British society but also with the complex task of theorizing the dynamics that give shape to social and cultural exchange. As her role as the editor of the *The British Theatre* (1806–09)—the most comprehensive anthology of English plays hitherto compiled—might suggest, Inchbald's intimate knowledge of theatrical and social practice led her into a career whose manifest achievements are theoretical. An adept political and social theorist, she wrote plays that are consistently pitched at resolving or exploring manners through their representation. Like many other Enlightenment thinkers, Inchbald saw an integral relation between the practice of everyday life and the conceptual structures of governance and social exchange. To be a bit polemical, I would argue that the Inchbald canon amounts to an enactment of social criticism akin to Adam Smith's *The Theory of Moral Sentiments* (1759). She and Smith are not similar thinkers, but they share a similar project in relation to the social and moral world. Inchbald's explorations of the generic possibilities of five-act comedy amount to a form of social theory.

It is not difficult to fold *Every One Has His Fault* into an ongoing discussion about the implications of the French Revolution, and the play teaches particularly well next to William Godwin's novel *Caleb Williams* (1794). But my favorite move with *Every One Has His Fault* is to set up a more complex historical intervention. After reading the reviews, students cannot help considering how the play relates to events in France. But the play's plot does not seem to lend itself to such a straightforward analysis. Rather, Inchbald's analysis of Britain's relation to revolutionary France travels by way of a historical analysis of the social upheaval generated by the American war. As noted above, the *Morning Chronicle* emphasized that finding sedition here requires the eyes of a lynx. Because lynx are particularly good at seeing fast movements in the dark, I encourage my students to read the dark bits of the play with a similar paranoid intensity.

The Irwin plot is extremely disturbing, and much of it takes place at night and in the dark, enclosed spaces of either a tavern or the Irwins' rented rooms. Irwin is a military man on half pay, returned from service in the American war and alienated from British society. In a state of utter depression, he contemplates suicide, but instead, wearing a disguise, he eventually assaults his father-in-law in the street and robs him. The Irwins' difficulties are tied to an unresolved crisis in national subjectivity following the American war and specifically to Irwin's inability to sustain his family. Captain Irwin does his duty in America, but, when the war is lost, he is forced to return to London an indigent and friendless man. It is important to remember that friendship is a fundamental component of British theories of political association and civil polity. As a refugee from previous bad military and foreign policy, Irwin figures for the damaged empire, and thus his violence is tied to past and present political errors. Inchbald's simultaneous critique of nonnormative familial relations and the emasculation of military men gives this play political purchase. This reading is most evident in the play's treatment of Mr. Placid, the other character with an American past. He is utterly ruled by his wife, and his attempts to reassert his masculinity are the focus of another key subplot. His strategies for dealing with Mrs. Placid, and the accommodation that resolves their marital tension, are fascinating because they work through a series of suspect sexual roles. I ask my students, What do the Placids' American careers have to do with Inchbald's representation of their marriage and ultimately with the larger political problems posed by the play? With remarkable rapidity, students begin to realize that matters of sexuality cannot be separated from the representation of politics.

One salutary aspect of this kind of reading is that it asks the students to think about how the play's sexual economy allegorizes political problems besetting Britain at this time. This attention to allegory is crucial not only because it captures a key aspect of theatrical reception in the period but also because it is through this indirect path that Inchbald's theorization of social relations takes place. Allegory enables Inchbald to stage struggles between men and women in the marriage state as interventions in the politics of the day without incurring the wrath either of the censor or the public at large. By capitalizing on the interpenetration of public and private, Inchbald puts the lord chamberlain and the loyalist papers in the position of having to read into the script and thus recognize the implicit similarities between the example of failed policy in America and the potential for similar failure in the ministry's bellicose reaction to French affairs. In short, the play calls the state to account, both in the small world of theatrical affairs and in the greater world of national and imperial fantasy.

From here one can stage one further lesson. After establishing this complex reading of how the play explores the psychic damage incurred during the American war as a way of addressing the political and social crisis prompted by events in France, I simply ask my students to support the reading with evidence from the reviews they have already read. What they discover is that the press does not recognize the Irwins or the Placids as figures for ongoing or unresolved national crisis. Nor is there much reference to America. The students are left with a compelling reading of the play's allegorical gestures that is based on a careful analysis of the script and the social dynamics of late-eighteenth-century life but that does not seem to match the reception history gleaned from the press. They have a surplus of argument and a scarcity of reception evidence. This contradiction raises fundamental theoretical issues pertaining to evidence and the notion of theater history and makes students aware of how arguments, no matter how persuasive, need to be constantly tested.

As someone who has argued in print for this reading of the play's engagement with the American war, I have implicitly suggested that the argument can be sustained in the face of scarce evidence. My conviction arises from my sense of the argument's internal coherence, my knowledge of the surrounding cultural dynamics, the importance of allegory to theater at this time, and ultimately the fact that the press does not represent reception in a direct way. The papers, no less than the plays, require one to look carefully at what is not presented, at what lies in darkness, for these occluded elements are themselves revealing. If pressed, I tend to argue that Inchbald is tapping into a reservoir of cultural memories that remain traumatic enough to resist direct articulation but that have the capacity to drive thought. Or, alternatively, I argue that accepting Inchbald's equation of the two revolutions required the press to tacitly accept a critique not only of the ministry but also of the fantasies of national cohesion and imperial dominance and that such an acceptance may have been felt but not represented in print. In short, I attempt to enact the risk and the responsibility that attends any act of cultural criticism.

Notes

1. On 19 November 1792, the National Convention issued the Edict of Fraternity, which offered French military assistance to all "subject peoples" attempting to overthrow their government. The edict abetted war with surrounding Continental powers and contributed to Britain's entry into war with France.

2. The reviews of Inchbald's play in *True Briton* and the *Morning Chronicle* are listed under the title "Rev. of *Every One Has His Fault*" in this volume's list of works cited.

Jean I. Marsden

Imagining a Course: Teaching Women Dramatists

Each of us has a dream course; mine is teaching women and drama in the Restoration and eighteenth century. In this essay I map out a plan for such a course, articulate my goals, and sketch out a syllabus with primary and secondary readings as well as tentative assignments. Although the course is planned for upper-level undergraduates, I also show how it could easily be adapted for graduate students.

Goals

My main goal is to create a course that covers a variety of women playwrights during the changing theatrical eras of the Restoration and eighteenth century. The course focuses on the drama, providing students with the opportunity to explore a range of writers and genres. I have designed it around careful reading of the texts, which will enable students to understand the language and conventions of what, for most of them, is an unfamiliar age. Including opportunities for students to read aloud or to act out scenes is vital since these moments bring the plays to life and demonstrate that, even three hundred years after they were written, the works of these women continue to have the ability to affect an audience.

A second goal is to place these writers and their works in the changing theatrical, literary, and social contexts of the Restoration and eighteenth century. It was in this age that playwriting was the most lucrative way to earn a living by one's pen and that women first became professional writers (and most of the women on my syllabus saw themselves as professional writers). Thus it would be important for students to learn about the era's theaters, actors and actresses, and audiences. It would be equally important to provide students with an understanding of literary and political events. It is difficult to understand the action of *The Rover* without some knowledge of the English civil wars and how Aphra Behn's status as a staunch Royalist affected her writing. Likewise, Frances Burney's *The Witlings* would lose some of its effect if students lacked information regarding the Bluestockings or Burney's connections with Elizabeth Montagu.

Such a course depends on connecting the readings with the lived experience of women in the Restoration and eighteenth century, an experience very familiar to playwrights whose works are the subject of the course. My ultimate goal is not to provide my students with a set canon of works but rather to challenge the concept of a canon of this period's drama, which, until the turn of the twenty-first century, excluded the women playwrights discussed here.

Structure and Content

In constructing this course, I originally contemplated a thematic approach to the material, creating units, for example, on modes of tragedy, on social comedy, or on the "female wits"; in the end, I adopted a more traditional, chronological approach. Thus the course begins shortly after the reopening of the theaters with Aphra Behn, moving through the era of the Stage Licensing Act of 1737 and into the later eighteenth century. Such an approach helps students see each play in its theatrical, historical, and social moment and enables them to understand the ways in which a woman writer interacted with this environment. To ignore such topics is to relegate women to an apolitical and ultimately limited realm, even though I deviate from strict chronology occasionally, as needed to shape the course. In any course there are practical issues—as well as philosophical and pedagogical concerns—at play that affect the shaping of a syllabus. One important concern is workload: how much I can reasonably expect students to read, digest, and enjoy. I decided that a reading load of roughly one play a week, supplemented by numerous short historical and occasionally theoretical readings, would be optimal. A second concern arises from the mundane but critical issue of texts. To some extent, all teachers are constrained by the availability of specific works, and this limitation is especially true of women's drama, whose works have been out of print for many years. While anthologies of women's drama do exist, notably *Eighteenth-Century Women Dramatists* (Finberg), *The Meridian Anthology of Restoration and Eighteenth-Century Plays by Women* (Rogers), and *Major Voices: Eighteenth-Century Women Playwrights* (Caines), the number and range of plays they offer are limited. Almost inevitably, the teacher of a course on women's drama will have to arrange for copies to be made of a play that is not readily available; in my proposed course, for example, neither Catharine Trotter's *Agnes de Castro* nor Delarivier Manley's *The Royal Mischief* has been recently anthologized, although the latter has been republished in Pickering and Chatto's multivolume collection *Eighteenth-Century Women Playwrights* (Hughes), and the former appears in Anne Kelley's facsimile edition of some of Trotter's works.

The plays on the syllabus were selected on the basis of their popularity, influence, or, looking backward, importance. The plays in Joanna Baillie's *Plays on the Passions*, for example, were not widely influential in their day, yet today Baillie's works, if not canonical, are recognized as important meldings of poetry, drama, and contemporary theories of sympathy. Personal prejudice will always play a role in the design of any course, and my proposal is no exception. My syllabus includes Behn's dark comedy *The Luckey Chance* not because it was popular or influential but because I find it a rich source for discussion regarding the status of women in the later seventeenth century. Likewise, my decision to include Susanna Centlivre's *The Wonder* rather than *A Bold Stroke for a Wife* stems, in part, from the fact that I find the women in *The Wonder* more interesting.

The other component of the syllabus is supplementary readings. For an undergraduate class, most of these readings consist of secondary materials providing historical or literary background along with additional primary materials that illustrate the world in which—and for which—the plays were staged. These readings might be as diverse as outlines of women's legal status, responses to specific plays or authors, and even fiction or poetry. When appropriate, the syllabus also includes theoretical readings, such as Catherine Gallagher's essay on the figure of the woman playwright as prostitute, or responses to specific topics, such as discussions of female friendships in the later seventeenth century (see weeks 4–5).

Syllabus

This class is designed as a small (fifteen to twenty students), upper-level undergraduate course aimed at English majors and dramatic arts or women's studies students. Because of its small class size, the course focuses heavily on discussion interspersed with lectures when appropriate. The syllabus includes the central dramatic work for the week along with a collection of suggested supplemental readings, both primary and secondary.

Week	Topics and Readings
1	Introduction to the Restoration stage; background materials on the stage and acting during the Restoration Selections from Howe, *First English Actresses*; Fisk, "The Restoration Actress"
2	Behn, *The Rover* (1677); Woolf, excerpt from *A Room of One's Own* (1929); Diamond, "Gestus and Signature in Aphra Behn's *The Rover*"
3	Behn, *The Luckey Chance* (including preface) (1686); excerpt from *The Laws Respecting Women* (1777); Gallagher, "Who Was That Masked Woman?"; Rosenthal, excerpt from *Playwrights and Plagiarists*
4–5	Trotter, *Agnes de Castro* (1695); all the prologues by female wits, plus Congreve's prologue to *Agnes de Castro*; Spencer, *Behn's Afterlife*, chapter 4 ("Women Writing after Behn"); Faderman, excerpt from *Surpassing the Love of Man*; Kendall, "Finding the Good Parts: Sexuality in Women's Tragedies in the Time of Queen Anne"
6	Manley, *The Royal Mischief* (1696); excerpt from *The Female Wits* (1704); Merrens, "'Unmanned with Thy Words': Regendering Tragedy in Manley and Trotter"
7	Pix, *The Beau Defeated* (1700); modern responses to Pix: short selections from Hughes, *English Drama, 1660–1700*, and Findlay and Hodgson-Wright, *Women and Dramatic Production*
8	Centlivre, *The Wonder: A Woman Keeps a Secret* (1714); Dibdin, excerpt from *A Complete History of the Stage* (1800); Inchbald, remarks on *The Wonder* (1808); "A Life of Mrs. Centlivre," from *The Works of the Celebrated Mrs. Centlivre* (1760); Scouten, excerpt from introduction to part 3 of *The London Stage* (on the Stage Licensing Act)
9	Burney, *The Witlings* (c. 1779); selections from the letters and journals
10	Griffith, *The Times* (1779); Brooke, selections from *The Excursion* (1777); Donkin, *Getting into the Act*, chapter 1

11	Cowley, *The Belle's Stratagem* (1780); Kowaleski-Wallace, "Theatricality and Cosmopolitanism in Hannah Cowley's *Belle's Stratagem*"
12	Inchbald, *Such Things Are* (1788); Green, "'You Should Be My Master': Imperial Recognition Politics in Elizabeth Inchbald's *Such Things Are*"
13	Baillie, *De Monfort*, from *Plays on the Passions* (1798); excerpts from Baillie, "Introductory Discourse"
14	Presentation of final projects

As designed, the course divides roughly into two parts: the plays of the Restoration (weeks 1–7) and the plays of the eighteenth century (weeks 8–14). It opens with Behn's *The Rover*, the most canonical play by a Restoration or eighteenth-century woman playwright, introducing the topic of the woman writer as a successful professional, an issue expressed both in the preface to *The Luckey Chance* and in Woolf's homage to Behn in *A Room of One's Own*, in which she famously states, "[A]ll women together ought to let flowers fall upon the tomb of Aphra Behn, for it was she who earned them the right to speak their minds" (113–14). Behn's status as a major literary figure (playwright, poet, and novelist) prompted me to include a second work by Behn, *The Luckey Chance*, a play that more explicitly than *The Rover* depicts the problems faced by women in a world that sees them as sexual and financial commodities. The supplementary legal readings for this week help students understand the restrictions on women.

The fourth week turns to the topic of how society perceived the woman playwright. Gallagher's controversial essay, which argues that the woman playwright saw herself, and was seen, as sexually tainted, and Laura Rosenthal's rejection of this argument are prompts for discussion. The syllabus builds on this issue by including the prologues and prefatory material by the so-called female wits—Catharine Trotter, Delarivier Manley, and Mary Pix—in which they address the topic of the woman as playwright, pointing to their vision of themselves as the successors to Behn. William Congreve's prologue to *Agnes de Castro* is included for contrast. From there the course focuses on the diverse works of the female wits, including an excerpt from the satire in which they were first given that sobriquet.

The second half of the course begins with Susanna Centlivre's *The Wonder*. Although written not long after the comedies of Pix, *The Wonder* presents an opportunity to introduce students to the changing mores of eighteenth-century audiences, especially as seen through commentaries by later critics on the indecency of Centlivre's comedies. With its Mediterranean setting and plot, the play also provides a useful counter to the bawdy *The Rover* as well as to the more "decent" plays of later playwrights. Arthur H. Scouten's *The London Stage, 1729–1747: A Critical Introduction* provides a concise explanation of the 1737 Stage Licensing Act; students could also be referred to Vincent Liesenfeld's book-length study on the subject. Burney's *The Witlings*, the next work on the syllabus and the only play unstaged in its time included in the course, builds on these concerns of decency and the implications that playwriting held for respectable women.

The next three weeks showcase a group of comedies by Elizabeth Griffith, Hannah Cowley, and Elizabeth Inchbald. This module begins with a selection from Frances Brooke's novel *The Excursion* (see the essay by Michelle Ruggaber Dougherty in this volume), depicting a young woman's unsuccessful attempt to get her play performed. Brooke illustrates the business of theater during the second half of the eighteenth century—an age when powerful managers such as David Garrick controlled the theater—and the difficulties faced by an aspiring playwright without theatrical connections. In contrast to the social comedies of Griffith and Cowley, the final two plays, Inchbald's *Such Things Are* and Baillie's verse tragedy *De Monfort*, add a more serious and intensely emotional note that effectively brings the century to a close. Where Inchbald's use of emotion to promote social reform represents a break from the social satire of earlier comedy, Baillie's focus on feeling and the workings of sympathy provides a contrast with the earlier tragedies of Trotter and Manley and links the playwright to the emergence of Romanticism, as can be clearly seen in her comments on the interplay of sympathy and dramatic composition in "Introductory Discourse."

The final week is dedicated to the in-class presentation of students' research projects. The (ideally) diverse presentations would provide a fitting conclusion to the course.

Assignments

I envision this course to be what my university designates a writing-intensive course, with a mixture of short, informal assignments and larger, more creative, research assignments designed to make students explore the world beyond the text of the play.

Response Papers

This assignment entails a series of frequent ungraded papers on a specific topic or topics directly related to the day's readings. I have found that such an assignment encourages active responses to the material and stimulates discussion in addition to providing an opportunity for assessing students' writing. (I first began assigning these short responses in desperation when faced with a silent, unresponsive class.) One obvious assignment would be to ask students to react to the arguments posed by Gallagher and Rosenthal concerning the role of the female playwright as public object. Other potential topics could include asking students to discuss the relationship between Constantia and Agnes in *Agnes de Castro*, to respond to Derek Hughes's claim that Pix "distinguished herself as a slavish upholder of male authority" (*English Drama* 419), or to follow Baillie's plan of paired plays and speculate on what a comic parallel to *De Monfort* would look like.

Brief Oral Reports

Possible topics for five-minute oral reports would be Charles II and the Cavaliers for *The Rover*, inheritance law for *The Beau Defeated*, or the Bluestockings for *The Witlings.* A performance history of the week's play would also be an option, as would a specific aspect of Restoration or eighteenth-century theater, such as the actor or actress who made a particular role famous (or infamous). Students would provide their classmates with a handout containing illustrations, a brief bibliography including both primary and secondary works, and an outline of the presentation. I would expect my students to have consulted *Eighteenth Century Collections Online* (*ECCO*) for these presentations.

Research Papers

The final assignment would be an eight-to-ten-page paper focusing on a specific critical issue related to a playwright, performance, or performer. The paper would build on research skills students had developed in their oral reports (and might be an offshoot of the same topic). Each student would be required to turn in a bibliography containing both primary and secondary works, along with an outline of the project, two weeks before the final paper is due. I would expect the student to incorporate both eighteenth-century responses to the material (possibly including other writings by the playwright) and recent critical studies. The final phase of the project would occur during the last week of class when students present their research to the rest of the class.

Graduate Seminar

Any graduate seminar dedicated to Restoration and eighteenth-century women dramatists would obviously have a greatly expanded scope, in terms of both primary and secondary readings and research expectations. In such a course, it would be important to include not only more drama by women but also more reading on the culture of the theater in the Restoration and eighteenth century, as well as on the position of women as writers, as performers, and as audience members. Thus the syllabus would include roughly twice as many primary materials, such as an additional play by Behn, possibly *The Rover II* (1681), *The Feigned Courtesans* (1679), or *Emperor of the Moon* (1687); Pix's popular tragedy *Ibrahim* (1696); Hannah More's *Percy* (1778); Inchbald's *Wives as They Were, and Maids as They Are* (1797) or her adaptation of August von Kotzebue's *Lovers' Vows* (1798); and all three of the plays in Baillie's *Plays on the Passions.* A seminar would also include more extensive historical readings on the theater (the Blackwell *Companion to Restoration Drama*, edited by Susan J. Owen, is especially useful because of its broad range of supplementary texts), as well as more detailed readings on women's lives during the Restoration and eighteenth century (beginning perhaps with a source book such as Vivien Jones's *Women in the Eighteenth Century: Constructions of Femininity*). A final addition to the syllabus and to class discussions would be theoretical texts related to gender, sexuality, and performance. I have found the feminist film theory of Laura Mulvey and Teresa de Lauretis effective in opening up texts and Deborah C. Payne's concept of the "fragmented gaze" a useful corrective to the blanket application of such theory ("Reified Object"). The canonization of women's drama, both inside feminist studies and out, is a challenging issue explored in essays such as Susan Bennett's "Theatre History, Historiography and Women's Dramatic Writing" and Jacky Bratton's "Reading the Intertheatrical; or, The Mysterious Disappearance of Susanna Centlivre." Other readings could include Misty G. Anderson's *Female Playwrights and Eighteenth-Century Comedy: Negotiating Marriage on the London Stage* and Elin Diamond's *Unmaking Mimesis: Essays on Feminism and Theater* or collections of essays such as *Women and Dramatic Production, 1550–1700* (Findley and

Hodgson-Wright) and *Women, Theatre and Performance: New Histories, New Historiographies* (Gale and Gardner).

Assignments would include the fairly traditional weekly response papers, oral reports, a shorter midterm paper, and a longer term paper. For one of the reports, I would ask students to research a play that is not on the syllabus and then present that play to the class along with a handout providing a bibliography and other information relevant to the play, the author, and major issues. These reports serve to expand the syllabus and can be the basis of the shorter, more historical, midterm paper. I would want students to ferret out as much information as they could about the experience of women theatergoers and the response to specific plays and playwrights (the eighteenth- and nineteenth-century descriptions of Behn as a "wanton hussy" are notorious examples) and, whenever possible, to apply this information to drama, remembering that theater is a living entity, an experience as well as a text.

One thrill of teaching is discovering which works and which authors excite twenty-first-century students and which texts pose the greatest problems. While the plays on my syllabus are diverse in style and content, they are united in their ability to depict richly drawn female characters, characters whose struggles, wit, and triumphs resonate with a modern audience. Though few of us have had the opportunity to teach an entire course devoted to Restoration and eighteenth-century women playwrights, it is my hope that this essay will prove useful in presenting an example that will become a reality for a whole new generation of teachers and students.

Notes on Contributors

Cami D. Agan is professor of English and chair of the Department of Language and Literature at Oklahoma Christian University. She has published on the eighteenth-century actress Catherine "Kitty" Clive and is continuing work from her dissertation on Frances Sheridan. Her work on the medieval York and Wakefield cycles has appeared in *Studies in Philology*, and her work on Tolkien has appeared in *Mythlore*.

Emily Hodgson Anderson is associate professor of English at the University of Southern California. Her publications include articles in *Eighteenth-Century Fiction*, *Eighteenth Century: Theory and Interpretation*, *Journal for Early Modern Cultural Studies*, *Studies in the Novel*, and *English Literary History*. She is the author of the book *Eighteenth-Century Authorship and the Play of Fiction: Novels and the Theater, Haywood to Austen*.

Misty G. Anderson is associate professor of English at the University of Tennessee, Knoxville. She has published essays on John Cleland, Margaret Cavendish, and Jane Austen. She is the author of *Female Playwrights and Eighteenth-Century Comedy: Negotiating Marriage on the London Stage*. She is currently at work on a book about Methodism and eighteenth-century British identity, and she coedits the journal *Restoration: Studies in English Literary Culture, 1660–1700*.

Betsy Bolton is professor of English literature at Swarthmore College. She is the author of *Women, Nationalism and the Romantic Stage: Theatre and Politics in Britain, 1780–1800*, and her articles have appeared in *English Literary History*, *Studies in Romanticism*, *Eighteenth Century: Theory and Interpretation*, and *European Romantic Review*.

Catherine Burroughs is Ruth and Albert Koch Professor of Humanities at Wells College and visiting lecturer in English at Cornell University. In addition to articles on British Romantic theater and drama, her publications include *Reading the Social Body*; *Closet Stages: Joanna Baillie and the Theater Theory of British Romantic Women Writers*; and *Women in British Romantic Theatre: Drama, Performance, and Society, 1790–1840*.

Nancy Copeland is associate professor of drama at the University of Toronto. Her publications include *Staging Gender in Behn and Centlivre: Women's Comedy and the Theatre* and an edition of Susanna Centlivre's *A Bold Stroke for a Wife*, as well as articles on Behn's comedies and twentieth-century productions of late-seventeenth-century drama.

Thomas C. Crochunis is assistant professor of English at Shippensburg University. He has had articles published in *Romanticism on the Net*, *Gothic*

Studies, *European Romantic Review*, and *Victorian Studies*. He is coeditor (with Michael Eberle-Sinatra) of the Web project *British Women Playwrights around 1800* and the forthcoming *Broadview Anthology of British Women Playwrights, 1777–1843* and editor of the collection *Joanna Baillie, Romantic Dramatist: Critical Essays*. He has helped organize preconference workshops on Romantic-era drama and theater history held in conjunction with the North American Society for the Study of Romanticism annual conference.

Pilar Cuder-Domínguez is associate professor at the University of Huelva. She is the author of *Margaret Atwood: A Beginner's Guide*, the editor of the collection *Exilios femeninos*, and the coeditor of *La mujer del texto al contexto*, *Sederi XI*, *Espacios de Género*, and *The Female Wits*. Her study of Stuart women playwrights between 1613 and 1713 is forthcoming.

Patricia Demers is University Professor at the University of Alberta. Recent publications include *Women's Writing in English: Early Modern England*; an edition of Hannah More's *Cœlebs in Search of a Wife: Comprehending Observations on Domestic Habits and Manners*; and the edition *From Instruction to Delight: Children's Literature to 1850*. She was the first female president of the Royal Society of Canada (RSC: The Academies).

Jones DeRitter is chair of the Department of English and Theatre at the University of Scranton. He is the author of articles on Aphra Behn, George Lillo, Nicholas Rowe, Henry Fielding, and Charlotte Charke and the book *The Embodiment of Characters: The Representation of Physical Experience on Stage and in Print, 1728–1749*.

Michelle Ruggaber Dougherty has taught at Marquette University and Ohio Dominican University. Her publications include a contribution to the book *Auto-poetica* and an article in *Notes and Queries*. Her research interests include eighteenth-century women's novels and eighteenth- and nineteenth-century domestic fiction.

Melinda C. Finberg is a professional dramaturg. She was awarded the 2006 Elliott Hayes Award for the 2005 production of Hannah Cowley's *The Belle's Stratagem* at the Oregon Shakespeare Festival and has been instrumental in reviving the plays of historical women playwrights for productions and readings in Washington and New York. She is the editor of *Eighteenth-Century Women Dramatists* and visiting assistant professor of English at Swarthmore College.

Tassie Gwilliam is associate professor of English at the University of Miami. She is the author of *Samuel Richardson's Fictions of Gender* and articles in the book *Body and Text in the Eighteenth Century* and the journals *Novel*, *Representations*, *Journal of the History of Sexuality*, and *ELH*.

George E. Haggerty is professor of English at the University of California, Riverside. His books include *Gothic Fiction / Gothic Form*; *Unnatural Af-*

fections: Women and Fiction in the Later Eighteenth Century; *Men in Love: Masculinity and Sexuality in the Eighteenth Century*; and *Queer Gothic*. He has edited (with Bonnie Zimmerman) *Professions of Desire: Lesbian and Gay Studies in Literature*; *Gay Histories and Cultures: An Encyclopedia*; *Music and Sexuality in Britten: Selected Essays of Philip Brett*; and (with Molly McGarry) *A Companion to Lesbian, Gay, Bisexual, Transgender, and Queer Studies*.

Catherine Ingrassia is professor of English and executive associate dean for Research and Graduate Affairs in the College of Humanities and Sciences at Virginia Commonwealth University. In addition to articles on early-eighteenth-century literature and culture, her publications include *Authorship, Commerce, and Gender in Early Eighteenth-Century England: A Culture of Paper Credit*; *"More Solid Learning": New Perspectives on Alexander Pope's* Dunciad; an edition of Haywood's *Anti-Pamela*; and *A Companion to the Eighteenth-Century Novel and Culture*. She is also coeditor (with Paula R. Backscheider) of the anthology *British Women Poets of the Long Eighteenth Century*.

Roxanne Kent-Drury is director of the English graduate program and associate professor of English at Northern Kentucky University. Her areas of research and publication include eighteenth-century performance as cultural practice, women's writing, and the literature of exploration and travel.

Elizabeth Kubek is associate professor of literature and chair of the Department of Languages and Literature at Benedictine University. Recent publications include an article on Mary Pix's novel *The Inhumane Cardinal* and articles on John Cleland and Eliza Haywood. She edited Pix's *The Beau Defeat'd* for the *Broadview Anthology of Restoration and Eighteenth-Century Drama* and is currently working on a contribution to a collection on book illustration and the visual image.

Kathleen Leicht is associate professor of English at the University of Central Missouri. She is working on a study of Restoration and eighteenth-century representations of duelling in British fiction and drama; a section of this work appeared in *Studies in Philology*. She has served as the secretary-treasurer of Midwestern American Society for Eighteenth-Century Studies since 2002.

Anna Lott is professor of English and coordinator of women's studies at the University of North Alabama. Recent publications include an edition of Elizabeth Inchbald's *A Simple Story* and an article on Jane Austen's *Mansfield Park* in *Studies in the Novel*.

Ellen MacKay is assistant professor of English at Indiana University, Bloomington. She has published on the Canadian theater, the performance of self-translation that the Immigration and Naturalization Service require, the theater's propensity for burning, and the disciplinary legacy of *Dionysus in '69*. Her book, *Persecution, Plague, and Fire: Fugitive Histories of the Stage in Early Modern England*, is forthcoming.

Jean I. Marsden is professor of English at the University of Connecticut, Storrs. In addition to articles on women and drama, she is the author of *Fatal Desire: Women, Sexuality, and the English Stage* and *The Re-imagined Text: Shakespeare, Adaptation, and Eighteenth-Century Literary Theory* and the editor of *The Appropriation of Shakespeare: Post-Renaissance Reconstructions of the Works and the Myth*.

Marie E. McAllister is professor of English at the University of Mary Washington. She works on women's drama, the novel, travel writing, and venereal disease in literature. Her publications include articles in *Eighteenth-Century Fiction*, *Eighteenth-Century Life*, *Age of Johnson*, and *Eighteenth-Century Novel*. She is editing Ann Flaxman's travel journal for Romantic Circles Electronic Editions.

Jane Milling is senior lecturer in drama at the University of Exeter. She has written on women dramatists, actors, and performance in the Restoration and early eighteenth century. She coedited volume 1 of *The Cambridge History of British Theatre* with Peter Thomson and *Extraordinary Actors* with Martin Banham. She also works in the modern period and has published on theories of performance and devised theater.

Victoria Myers is Blanche E. Seaver Professor in the Humanities at Pepperdine University. She has written numerous articles on eighteenth- and nineteenth-century literature and culture. Her most recent publications include a series of articles treating Romantic dramatists' reproduction of the language and issues of real-life trials. She has coedited (with Robert Maniquis) the collection *Godwinian Moments: From the Enlightenment to Romanticism* and is currently coediting the diaries of William Godwin.

Nora Nachumi is associate professor of English at Stern College for Women. In addition to articles on eighteenth- and nineteenth-century British women writers, she has written about film adaptations of Jane Austen's novels and about teaching women's studies and women's literature courses at a religious institution. She is the author of *Acting Like a Lady: British Women Writers and the Eighteenth-Century Theater*.

Bonnie Nelson is associate professor of English at Kansas State University. She is the winner of two Excellence in Teaching Awards from the College of Arts and Sciences, as well as the department's SAGE award for graduate teaching. She serves on the women's studies faculty and has published articles on gender and drama in such periodicals as *Theatre Survey*, *Keats-Shelley Journal*, and *Women's Writing*.

Daniel O'Quinn is professor in the School of English and Theatre Studies at the University of Guelph. He is the author of *Staging Governance: Theatrical Imperialism in London, 1770–1800*. He coedited the *Cambridge Companion to British Theatre, 1737–1840* with Jane Moody and edited *Travels of Mirza Abu Taleb Khan*. His articles have appeared in *ELH*, *Studies in Romanticism*, *Texas Studies in Literature and Language*, *Theatre Journal*, *European Romantic Review*, and *Romantic Praxis*.

Anita Pacheco is a senior lecturer in the English department at the Open University. She has published on Aphra Behn and is the editor of *A Companion to Early Modern Women's Writing*.

Vimala C. Pasupathi is assistant professor of English at Hofstra University. Her work has appeared or is forthcoming in *Modern Philology*; *English Literary History*; *Cavendish and Shakespeare, Interconnections* and *Research Opportunities in Medieval and Renaissance Drama*. She is currently working on a monograph on military obligation in sixteenth- and seventeenth-century English drama.

Jacqueline Pearson is professor of English literature at the University of Manchester. She is the author of *The Prostituted Muse: Images of Women and Women Dramatists, 1643–1737* and *Women's Reading in Britain, 1750–1834: A Dangerous Recreation* and has published on Aphra Behn, Susanna Centlivre, Margaret Cavendish, Aemilia Lanyer, Mary Pix, and Jane Barker. She is currently completing a book on seventeenth-century conversion narratives.

Marjean D. Purinton is professor of English and associate dean of the University Honors College at Texas Tech University. She is the author of *Romantic Ideology Unmasked: The Mentally Constructed Tyrannies in Dramas of William Wordsworth, Lord Byron, Percy Shelley, and Joanna Baillie*, as well as articles on British Romantic drama and nineteenth-century British women writers. She is working on the book project "Staging Grotesque and Ghosts: Techno-Gothic British Romantic Drama."

Cynthia Richards is professor of English at Wittenberg University. She is editing, with Mary Ann O'Donnell, the MLA's "Approaches to Teaching Behn's *Oroonoko*." Recipient of the 2002–03 ASECS Innovative Course Design Award, she publishes on issues of pedagogy as well as on Aphra Behn and Mary Wollstonecraft.

Betty Rizzo was emerita professor of the City College of New York and the CUNY Graduate Center at the time of her death in 2008. Her books and essays include work on Christopher Smart, Sarah Scott, and Frances Burney. She edited the plays of Elizabeth Griffith and completed biographies of Elizabeth Griffith and Frances Greville. She leaves a legacy of fine scholarship and generosity.

Laura J. Rosenthal is professor of English and associate chair at the University of Maryland, College Park. She is the author of *Infamous Commerce: Prostitution in Eighteenth-Century British Literature and Culture* and *Playwrights and Plagiarists in Early Modern England: Gender, Authorship, Literary Property*. She is working on a study of eighteenth-century cosmopolitanism, with particular attention to gender, travel, and theater in the British empire.

Francesca Saggini is associate professor of English literature at the Università della Tuscia and honorary research fellow at the University of Glasgow. She is the author of numerous contributions on eighteenth- and nineteenth-century theater and of *La messinscena dell'identità. Teatro e teatralità nel romanzo inglese del Settecento*, which was awarded the 2005 prize for best scholarly work by the Accademia dei Lincei and the 2005 Walker Cowen Memorial Prize by the University of Virginia Press.

Gillian Skinner is a lecturer in English at Durham University. She is the author of *Sensibility and Economics in the Novel, 1740–1800: The Price of a Tear*, as well as articles on eighteenth-century fiction.

Works Cited

Alleman, Gellert Spencer. *Matrimonial Law and the Materials of Restoration Comedy*. Philadelphia: U of Pennsylvania, 1942. Print.

Althusser, Louis. Lenin and Philosophy *and Other Essays*. Trans. Ben Brewster. New York: Monthly Review, 2001. Print.

Ames, Richard. *The Female Fire-Ships: A Satyr against Whoring: In a Letter to a Friend, Just Come to London*. London: E. Richardson, 1691. Print.

Anderson, Emily Hodgson. "Performing the Passions in Eliza Haywood's *Fantomina* and *Miss Betsy Thoughtless*." *Eighteenth Century: Theory and Interpretation* 46.1 (2005): 1–15. Print.

———. "Revising Theatrical Conventions in *A Simple Story*: Elizabeth Inchbald's Ambiguous Performance." *Journal for Early Modern Cultural Studies* 6.1 (2006): 5–30. Print.

Anderson, Misty G. *Female Playwrights and Eighteenth-Century Comedy: Negotiating Marriage on the London Stage*. New York: Palgrave, 2002. Print.

Angeletti, Gioia. "Mariana Starke's *The Widow of Malabar*: Orientalist Discourse in Romantic Women's Drama." *La questione Romantica: Il dramma storico delle donne tra Rivoluzione e Restaurazione* 14 (2003): 55–72. Print.

Ariadne. *She Ventures and He Wins*. London: Hen. Rhodes, J. Harris, and Sam Briscoe, 1695. Print.

Aristotle. *On the Art of Poetry*. Trans. Ingram Bywater. 1920. Oxford: Clarendon, 1951. Print.

Arons, Wendy. "Performance, Mobility, and the Domestication of Female Desire in *The Belle's Stratagem*." *1650–1850: Ideas, Aesthetics, and Inquiries in the Early Modern Era* 11 (2005): 251–64. Print.

Asleson, Robyn. Introduction. Asleson, *Notorious Muse* 1–21.

———, ed. *Notorious Muse: The Actress in British Art and Culture, 1776–1812*. New Haven: Yale UP, 2003. Print.

Aughterson, Kate. *Aphra Behn: The Comedies*. Houndmills: Palgrave, 2003. Print.

Austen, Jane. *Mansfield Park*. Ed. James Kinsley. Oxford: Oxford UP, 2003. Print.

———. *Northanger Abbey*. 1818. Oxford: Oxford UP, 1985. Print.

Avery, Emmett L. *The London Stage, 1660–1800: Part 2, 1700–1729*. 2 vols. Carbondale: Southern Illinois UP, 1960. Print.

———. "The Shakespeare Ladies Club." *Shakespeare Quarterly* 7.2 (1956): 153–58. Print.

Backscheider, Paula R. "Barry, Elizabeth (1656x8–1713)." *Oxford Dictionary of National Biography*. Ed. H. C. G. Matthew and Brian Harrison. Oxford: Oxford UP, 2004. *Oxford Dictionary of National Biography*. Web. 23 Nov. 2007.

———. Introduction. Backscheider, *Plays* 1: ix–xlv.

———. "Literary Culture as Immediate Reality." *A Companion to the Eighteenth-Century English Novel and Culture*. Ed. Backscheider and Catherine Ingrassia. Oxford: Blackwell, 2005. 504–34. Print.

———, ed. and introd. *The Plays of Elizabeth Inchbald*. 2 vols. New York: Garland, 1980. Print.

———. *Spectacular Politics: Theatrical Power and Mass Culture in Early Modern England*. Baltimore: Johns Hopkins UP, 1993. Print.

———. "Stretching the Form: Catharine Trotter Cockburn and Other Failures." *Theatre Journal* 47.4 (1995): 443–58. Print.

Backscheider, Paula R., and Hope D. Cotton. Introduction. Brooke, *Excursion* ix–xlvi.

Baillie, Joanna. *Count Basil: A Tragedy*. Baillie, *Plays* 115–213.

———. *De Monfort*. Baillie, *Plays* 299–387.

———. "Introductory Discourse." Baillie, *Plays* 67–113.

———. *Orra*. Cox and Gamer 133–64.

———. *Plays on the Passions*. 1798. Ed. Peter Duthie. Peterborough: Broadview, 2001. Print.

———. *A Series of Plays: In Which It Is Attempted to Delineate the Stronger Passions of the Mind—Each Passion Being the Subject of a Tragedy and a Comedy*. 3 vols. London: Longman, 1812. Print.

———. "To the Reader." *The Dramatic and Poetical Works of Joanna Baillie*. London: Longman, 1851. 228–35. Print.

———. "To the Reader." 1812. Baillie, *Series* 3: iii–xxxi.

———. *The Tryal: A Comedy*. Baillie, *Plays* 215–98.

Baillie, Matthew. *Lectures and Observations on Medicine*. London: Richard Taylor, 1825. Print.

Baines, Paul, and Edwards Burns. "The Playhouses of London, 1768–1821." *Five Romantic Plays, 1768–1821*. Ed. Baines and Burns. Oxford: Oxford UP, 2000. xxxiv–xxxviii. Print.

Baker, Thomas. *Tunbridge-Walks; or, The Yeoman of Kent*. London: Bernard Lintott, 1703. Print.

Bandele, 'Biyi, adapt. *Aphra Behn's* Oroonoko. Charlbury: Amber Lane, 1999. Print.

Barash, Carol. *English Women's Poetry, 1649–1714: Politics, Community, and Linguistic Authority*. Oxford: Oxford UP, 1996. Print.

Barker-Benfield, G. J. *The Culture of Sensibility: Sex and Society in Eighteenth-Century Britain*. Chicago: U of Chicago P, 1992. Print.

Barton, John, adapt. *An Adaptation of* The Rover (The Banished Cavaliers). By Aphra Behn. London: Methuen, 1986. Print.

Bateson, F. W. *English Comic Drama, 1700–1750*. Oxford: Clarendon, 1929. Print.

Beaumarchais, Pierre. *Eugénie. Drame . . . avec un essai sur le drame serieux*. Paris: F. Grasset, 1768. Print.

Behn, Aphra. *Abdelazer; or, The Moor's Revenge*. Todd, *Works* 5: 239–315.

———. "Agnes de Castro." *"The Fair Jilt" and Other Stories*. Todd, *Works* 3: 120–61.

———. *The City Heiress*. London, 1682. *Early English Books Online*. U of Exeter Lib. Web. 1 Oct. 2007.

———. *The Emperor of the Moon*. London, 1687. *Early English Books Online*. U of Exeter Lib. Web. 1 Oct. 2007.

———. *The Emperor of the Moon*. Todd, *Works* 7: 153–207.

———. *The False Count*. Todd, *Works* 6: 299–356.

———. *The Feign'd Curtizans*. Todd, *Works* 6: 83–159.

———. *The Feigned Courtesans.* 1679. Lyons and Morgan 2–101.

———. *The History of the Nun; or, The Fair Vow-Breaker.* Oroonoko *and Other Writings.* Ed. Paul Salzman. Oxford: Oxford UP, 1994. 138–90. Print.

———. *The Luckey Chance; or, An Alderman's Bargain.* Todd, *Works* 7: 209–84.

———. *The Rover.* Todd, *Works* 5: 445–521.

———. *The Rover.* Womersley, *Restoration Drama* 338–84.

———. *The Rover, or, The Banished Cavaliers.* 1677. Ed. Frederick Link. Lincoln: U of Nebraska P, 1967. Print.

———. *The Rover; or, The Banished Cavaliers.* Spencer, The Rover *and Other Plays* 1–88.

———. *Rover II.* Vol. 1 of *The Works of Aphra Behn.* Ed. Montague Summers. London: Heinemann, 1915. Print.

———. *Sir Patient Fancy.* London, 1678. *Early English Books Online.* U of Exeter Lib. Web. 1 Oct. 2007.

———. *Sir Patient Fancy.* Todd, *Works* 6: 1–81.

———. *The Widow Ranter.* Oroonoko, The Rover, *and Other Works.* Ed. Janet Todd. London: Penguin, 2003. 249–325. Print.

Bell, Florence, and Elizabeth Robins. *Alan's Wife. Female Playwrights of the Nineteenth Century.* Ed. Adrienne Scullion. London: Dent, 1996. 347–71. Print.

Belloy, Pierre-Laurent Buirette de. *Gabrielle de Vergy.* Paris: Dychesne, 1770. Print.

Benden, Ben van, and Nora de Poorter, eds. *Royalist Refugees: William and Margaret Cavendish in the Rubens House, 1648–1660.* Antwerp: Rubenshuis, 2006. Print.

Bennett, Alexandra G., ed. Bell in Campo *and* The Sociable Companions. By Margaret Cavendish. Peterborough: Broadview, 2002. Print.

———. "Fantastic Realism: Margaret Cavendish and the Possibilities of Drama." Cottegnies and Weitz 179–94.

Bennett, Susan. "Outing Joanna Baillie." Burroughs, *Women* 161–77.

———. "Theatre History, Historiography and Women's Dramatic Writing." Gale and Gardner 46–59.

Bergson, Henri. *Laughter: An Essay on the Meaning of the Comic.* Trans. Cloudesley Brereton and Fred Rothwell. New York: Macmillan, 1917. Rpt. in *Comedy.* Ed. Wylie Sypher. Garden City: Doubleday, 1956. 61–190. Print.

Betterton, Thomas. *The History of the English Stage from the Restoration to the Present Time, including the Lives, Characters and Amours of the Most Eminent Actors and Actresses.* Comp. Edmund Curll and William Oldys. London, 1741. Print.

Bevis, Richard. *The Laughing Tradition: Stage Comedy in Garrick's Day.* Athens: U of Georgia P, 1980. Print.

Birch, Thomas, ed. *The Works of Mrs. Catharine Cockburn.* 1751. 2 vols. London: Routledge, 1992. Print.

Black, Joseph, gen. ed. *The Broadview Anthology of British Literature.* 2nd ed. Peterborough: Broadview, 2009. Print.

Blackstone, William. *Commentaries on the Laws of England.* Facsim. of 1st ed. Introd. Thomas A. Green. Vol. 4. Chicago: U of Chicago P, 1979. Print. 4 vols.

Boaden, James. *Memoirs of Mrs. Inchbald: Including Her Familiar Correspondence with the Most Distinguished Persons of Her Time, to Which Are Added* The Massacre *and* A Case of Conscience. 2 vols. London: Richard Bentley, 1833. Print.

Bolam, Robyn. Introduction. *The Rover*. By Aphra Behn. Ed. Bolam. London: Black, 2005. xi–xxxiv. Print.

Bolton, Betsy. *Women, Nationalism, and the Romantic Stage: Theatre and Politics in Britain, 1780–1800*. Cambridge: Cambridge UP, 2001. Print.

Bonin, Erin Lang. "Margaret Cavendish's Dramatic Utopias and the Politics of Gender." *Studies in English Literature, 1500–1900* 40.2 (2000): 339–54. Print.

Bowers, Toni. "Suing for Rape: Complicity and the Meaning of Seduction in Old Bailey Rape Trials, 1700–1742." MLA Annual Convention. Marriott, Philadelphia. 29 Dec. 2004. Address.

Bowles, Emily. "Frances Brooke's Erotic-Didactic Garden: Desire, Shame, and Sensibility in *The Excursion*." *Eighteenth-Century Novel* 4 (2005): 139–62. Print.

Bowyer, John Wilson. *The Celebrated Mrs. Centlivre*. Durham: Duke UP, 1952. Print.

Branaman, George. *Eighteenth-Century Adaptations of Shakespearian Tragedy*. Berkeley: U of California P, 1956. Print.

Bratton, Jacky. *New Readings in Theatre History*. Cambridge: Cambridge UP, 2003. Print.

———. "Reading the Intertheatrical; or, The Mysterious Disappearance of Susanna Centlivre." Gale and Gardner 7–24.

Brewer, John. *The Pleasures of the Imagination: English Culture in the Eighteenth Century*. New York: Farrar, 1997. Print.

Bridges, Liz. "'We Were Somebody in England': Identity, Gender, and Status in *The Widdow Ranter*." O'Donnell, Dhuicq, and Leduc 75–80.

The British Theatre; or, A Collection of Plays, Which Are Acted at the Theatres Royal, Drury Lane, Covent Garden, and the Haymarket, with Biographical and Critical Remarks, by Mrs. Inchbald. 25 vols. London: Longman, Hurst, Rees, and Orme, 1808. Print.

Broad, Jacqueline. *Women Philosophers of the Seventeenth Century*. Cambridge: Cambridge UP, 2002. Print.

Brooke, Frances. *The Excursion*. 1777. Ed. Paula R. Backscheider and Hope D. Cotton. Lexington: UP of Kentucky, 1997. Print.

———. *Old Maid* (1755–56). Print.

———. *The Old Maid, by Mary Singleton, Spinster*. 13 Mar. 1756. Rev. ed. London: A. Millar, 1764. Microfilm. *Women Advising Women, Part I: Early Women Journals, c.1700–1832*. Bodleian Lib., Oxford: reel 8.

———. *The Siege of Sinope: A Tragedy: As It Is Acted at the Theatre-Royal in Covent-Garden*. London: T. Cadell, 1781. Print.

———. *Virginia, a Tragedy, with Odes, Pastorals, and Translations*. London: A. Millar, 1756. Print.

Brooks, Christopher K. "Goldsmith's Feminist Drama: *She Stoops to Conquer*, Silence and Language." *Papers on Language and Literature* 28.1 (1992): 38–51. Print.

Brown, Kathleen. *Good Wives, Nasty Wenches, and Anxious Patriarchs: Gender, Race, and Power in Colonial Virginia*. Chapel Hill: U of North Carolina P, 1996. Print.

Brown, Laura. *English Dramatic Form, 1660–1760: An Essay in Generic History.* New Haven: Yale UP, 1981. Print.

Buller, William. "On Seeing Miss H. More in the Title Page of the 2d Edition of *The Search after Happiness*: A Ballad." *Commonplace Book.* 1795–1805. M.a. 179. Folger Shakespeare Lib., Washington.

Burke, Helen M. "The Cavalier Myth in *The Rover*." Hughes and Todd 118–34.

———. *Riotous Performances: The Struggle for Hegemony in the Irish Theater, 1712–1784.* South Bend: U of Notre Dame P, 2003. Print.

Burling, William. "New Plays on the London Stage, 1700–1810." *Georgian Theatre Research Resources.* Missouri State U, 2006. Web. 7 Oct. 2009.

———. *Summer Theatre in London, 1661–1820, and the Rise of the Haymarket Theatre.* London: Assoc. UP, 2000. Print.

Burnet, Thomas. Letter to Catharine Trotter. 18 Feb. 1702. Birch, *Works* 2: 160.

Burney, Frances. *A Busy Day.* Sabor, *Complete Plays* 1: 287–397.

———. *Camilla.* 1796. Oxford: Oxford UP, 1989. Print.

———. *Cecilia; or, Memoirs of an Heiress.* Ed. Peter Sabor and Margaret Anne Doody. Oxford: Oxford UP, 2008. Print.

———. *The Diary and Letters of Madame D'Arblay.* Ed. Charlotte Barrett. 6 vols. Basingstoke: Macmillan, 1904–05. Print.

———. *The Early Journals and Letters of Fanny Burney.* Ed. Lars Troide et al. 3 vols. Oxford: Clarendon, 1988. Print.

———. *Evelina; or, The History of a Young Lady's Entrance into the World.* Ed. Margaret Anne Doody. Harmondsworth: Penguin, 1994. Print.

———. *Love and Fashion.* Sabor, *Complete Plays* 1: 103–89.

———. *The Wanderer; or, Female Difficulties.* Ed. Margaret Anne Doody, Robert L. Mack, and Peter Sabor. Oxford: Oxford UP, 1991. Print.

———. *The Witlings: A Comedy by the Sister of the Order.* 1779. Sabor and Sill 43–172.

———. *The Woman-Hater.* Sabor, *Complete Plays* 1: 191–285.

Burroughs, Catherine. *Closet Stages: Joanna Baillie and the Theater Theory of British Romantic Women Writers.* Philadelphia: U of Pennsylvania P, 1997. Print.

———. "The Erotics of Home: Staging Sexual Fantasy in British Women's Drama." *Women's Romantic Theatre and Drama: History, Agency, and Performativity.* Ed. Lilla Maria Crisafulli and Keir Elam. Farnham: Ashgate, 2010. 103–21. Print.

———, ed. *Women in British Romantic Theatre: Drama, Performance, and Society, 1790–1840.* Cambridge: Cambridge UP, 2000. Print.

Burwick, Frederick. "Joanna Baillie, Matthew Baillie, and the Pathology of the Passions." Crochunis 48–68.

Bush-Bailey, Gilli. *Treading the Bawds: Actresses and Playwrights on the Late-Stuart Stage.* Manchester: Manchester UP, 2006. Print.

Butler, Douglas R. "Plot and Politics in Susanna Centlivre's *A Bold Stroke for a Wife*." Schofield and Macheski 357–70.

Butler, Judith. "Performative Acts and Gender Constitution: An Essay in Phenomenology and Feminist Theory." *Performing Feminisms: Feminist Critical Theory and Theater.* Ed. Sue-Ellen Case. Baltimore: Johns Hopkins UP, 1990. 270–82. Print.

Byrne, Christopher. "Transformative Theater." *Gay City News* 25 Apr.–1 May 2003: n. pag. Web. 20 July 2006.

Byrne, Paula. *Perdita: The Life of Mary Robinson*. London: Harper, 2005. Print.

Caines, Michael, ed. *Major Voices: Eighteenth-Century Women Playwrights*. New Milford: Toby, 2004. Print.

Calderón de la Barca, Pedro. *No siempre lo peor es cierto*. Madrid, 1652. Print.

Callaghan, Dympna. *Woman and Gender in Renaissance Tragedy*. New York: Harvester Wheatsheaf, 1989. Print.

Canfield, J. Douglas. Introduction. *Tricksters and Estates: On the Ideology of Restoration Comedy*. Lexington: UP of Kentucky, 1997. 1–30. Print.

Canfield, J. Douglas, gen. ed., with Maja-Lisa Von Sneidern. *The Broadview Anthology of Restoration and Early Eighteenth-Century Drama*. Peterborough: Broadview, 2001. Print.

Canfield, J. Douglas, and Deborah C. Payne, eds. *Cultural Readings of Restoration and Eighteenth-Century English Theater*. Athens: U of Georgia P, 1995. Print.

———. Introduction. Canfield and Payne, *Cultural Readings* 1–12.

Carlson, Julie. *In the Theatre of Romanticism: Coleridge, Nationalism, Women*. Cambridge: Cambridge UP, 1994. Print.

———. "Remaking Love: Remorse in the Theatre of Baillie and Inchbald." Burroughs, *Women* 285–310.

———. "The Theatre." *Romanticism: An Oxford Guide*. Ed. Nicholas Roe. Oxford: Oxford UP, 2005. 642–53. Print.

Carlson, Marvin. "Elizabeth Inchbald: A Woman Critic in Her Theatrical Culture." Burroughs, *Women* 207–22.

Carlson, Susan. *Women and Comedy: Rewriting the British Theatrical Tradition*. Ann Arbor: U of Michigan P, 1991. Print.

Carnell, Rachel K. "Subverting Tragic Conventions: Aphra Behn's Turn to the Novel." *Studies in the Novel* 31.2 (1999): 133–51. Print.

Carter, Philip. *Men and the Emergence of Polite Society, Britain 1660–1800*. Harlow: Pearson, 2001. Print.

Cary, Elizabeth. *The Tragedy of Mariam, 1613*. Oxford: Oxford UP, 1992. Print.

Castle, Terry. *Masquerade and Civilization: The Carnivalesque in Eighteenth-Century English Culture and Fiction*. Stanford: Stanford UP, 1986. Print.

Cavendish, Margaret. *Bell in Campo*. Shaver, Convent 107–70.

———. *The Convent of Pleasure*. 1668. Shaver, Convent 217–47.

———. *Orations of Divers Sorts Accommodated to Divers Places*. London, 1662. Print.

———. *Playes Written by the Thrice Noble, Illustrious and Excellent Princess, the Lady Marchioness of Newcastle*. London, 1662. Print.

———. *Plays, Never before Printed Written by the Thrice Noble, Illustrious, and Excellent Princesse, the Duchess of Newcastle*. London, 1668. Print.

———. *The Sociable Letters*. 1664. Ed. James Fitzmaurice. New York: Garland, 1997. Print.

———. *A True Relation of My Birth and Breeding*. Excerpts. A. Bennett, Bell 205–09.

"Cecil, James, fourth earl of Salisbury." *Oxford Dictionary of National Biography*. 1912–21. Print.

Centlivre, Susanna. *The Basset Table.* J. Pearson, *Susanna Centlivre* 1–52.

———. *A Bold Stroke for a Wife.* 1718. Ed. Nancy Copeland. Peterborough: Broadview, 1995. Print.

———. *A Bold Stroke for a Wife.* 1718. Rogers, *Meridian Anthology* 187–259.

———. *The Busie Body.* 1709. Womersley, *Restoration Drama* 779–813.

———. *The Busybody.* 1709. Finberg, *Eighteenth-Century Women Dramatists* 75–143.

———. *Love at a Venture.* London, 1706. *Eighteenth Century Collections Online.* U of Exeter Lib. Web. 1 Oct. 2007.

———. *Love's Contrivance.* London, 1703. *Eighteenth Century Collections Online.* U of Exeter Lib. Web. 1 Oct. 2007.

———. *Marplot; or, The Second Part of the* Busybody. 1710. Print.

———. *The Perjur'd Husband.* London: Bennett Banbury, 1700. Print.

———. *The Perplex'd Lovers.* London, 1712. *Eighteenth Century Collections Online.* U of Exeter Lib. Web. 1 Oct. 2007.

———. "A Woman's Case." Centlivre, *The Wonder* [O'Brien] 132–39.

———. *The Wonder: A Woman Keeps a Secret.* Ed. John O'Brien. Peterborough: Broadview, 2004. Print.

———. *The Wonder: A Woman Keeps a Secret.* J. Pearson, *Susanna Centlivre* 113–73.

———. *The Works of the Celebrated Mrs. Centlivre, with a New Account of Her Life.* 3 vols. London, 1760. *Eighteenth Century Collections Online.* U of Exeter Lib. Web. 3 Sept. 2009.

Chetwood, William Rufus. *The British Theatre.* London, 1750. Print.

Chew, Samuel. "*The Dupe*: A Study in the 'Low.'" *Philological Quarterly* 18.2 (1939): 196–203. Print.

Chisholm, Kate. *Fanny Burney: Her Life, 1752–1840.* London: Chatto, 1998. Print.

Churchill, Sarah. *An Account of the Conduct of the Dowager Duchess of Marlborough, from Her First Coming to Court, to the Year 1710.* London: J. Bettenham for G. Hawkins, 1742. Print.

Cibber, Colley. *An Apology for the Life of Mr. Colley Cibber.* 2nd ed. Vol 1. London, 1740. Print.

———. *An Apology for the Life of Mr. Colley Cibber.* Ed. R. W. Lowe. 2 vols. London: J. Nimmo, 1889. Print.

———. *The Careless Husband: A Comedy.* London: W. Davis, 1705. Print.

———. *Love's Last Shift.* London, 1696. *Early English Books Online.* U of Exeter Lib. Web. 1 Oct. 2007.

Cibber, Susanna. *The Oracle: A Comedy in One Act: As It Is Acted at the Theatre-Royal in Covent Garden.* London: R. and J. Dodsley, 1763. Print.

Cixous, Hélène. "The Laugh of the Medusa." Trans. Keith Cohen and Paula Cohen. *Signs: Journal of Women in Culture and Society* 1.4 (1976): 875–93. Print.

Clark, Constance. *Three Augustan Women Playwrights.* New York: Lang, 1986. Print.

Cleary, Jean Coates. Introduction. *The Memoirs of Miss Sidney Bidulph.* By Frances Sheridan. Ed. Patricia Koster and Cleary. Oxford: Oxford UP, 1995. vii–xxxiii. Print.

Clifford, James L. *Hester Lynch Piozzi (Mrs. Thrale)*. 2nd ed. New York: Columbia UP, 1987. Print.

Clive, Catherine. *The Rehearsal; or, Bayes in Petticoats*. Dublin, 1753. *Eighteenth Century Collections Online*. U of Exeter Lib. Web. 1 Oct. 2007.

Clucas, Stephen, ed. *A Princely Brave Woman: Essays on Margaret Cavendish, Duchess of Newcastle*. Aldershot: Ashgate, 2003. Print.

Cockburn, Catharine Trotter (*see also* Trotter, Catharine). *A Discourse Concerning a Guide in Controversies*. 1707. Birch, *Works* 1: 1–42.

Codr, Dwight. "'Her Failing Voice Endeavoured, in Vain, to Articulate': Sense and Disability in the Novels of Elizabeth Inchbald." *Philological Quarterly* 87.3-4 (2008): 359–88. Print.

Cohen, Michèle. *Fashioning Masculinity: National Identity and Language in the Eighteenth Century*. London: Routledge, 1996. Print.

A Collection of Farces and Other Afterpieces, Which Are Acted at the Theatres Royal, Drury-Lane, Covent-Garden, and Hay-Market: Printed under the Authority of the Managers from the Prompt-Book: Selected by Mrs. Inchbald. 7 vols. London: Longman, Hurst, Rees, Orme, and Brown, 1815. Print.

Colley, Linda. *Britons: Forging the Nation, 1707–1837*. New Haven: Yale UP, 1992. Print.

Collier, Jeremy. *A Short View of the Immorality and Profaneness of the English Stage*. London: S. Keble, R. Sare, and S. Hindmarch, 1698. Print.

Collins, Margo. "Feminine Conduct and Violence in Mary Pix's She-Tragedies." *Restoration and Eighteenth-Century Theatre Research* 18.1 (2003): 1–16. Print.

Colman, George. "To Mrs. Inchbald." *The Heir at Law*. *British Theatre* 21: n. pag.

Colman, George, and David Garrick. *The Clandestine Marriage: A Comedy*. 2nd ed. London: T. Becket and P. A. De Hondt, 1766. Print.

Conger, Syndy McMillen. "Reading *Lovers' Vows*: Jane Austen's Reflections on English Sense and German Sensibility." *Studies in Philology* 85.1 (1988): 92–113. Print.

Congreve, William. *Love for Love: A Comedy*. London: Jacob Tonson, 1695. Print.

———. *The Way of the World*. McMillin 251–319.

Connell, R. W. *Masculinities*. Cambridge: Polity, 1995. Print.

Cooper, Elizabeth. *The Rival Widows*. London, 1735. *Eighteenth Century Collections Online*. U of Exeter Lib. Web. 1 Oct. 2007.

Copeland, Nancy. Introduction. Centlivre, *Bold Stroke* [Copeland] 7–39.

———. *Staging Gender in Behn and Centlivre: Women's Comedy and the Theatre*. Aldershot: Ashgate, 2004. Print.

Corman, Brian. *Genre and Generic Change in English Comedy, 1660–1710*. Toronto: U of Toronto P, 1993. Print.

Costello, Josh. *The Rover*. *Josh Costello*. Costello, n.d. Web. 8 June 2007.

Cottegnies, Line, and Nancy Weitz, eds. *Authorial Conquests: Essays on Genre in the Writings of Margaret Cavendish*. Madison: Fairleigh Dickinson UP, 2003. Print.

Cotton, Nancy. *Women Playwrights in England, c. 1363–1750*. Lewisburg: Bucknell UP, 1980. Print.

Cowley, Hannah. *The Belle's Stratagem*. 1780. Finberg, *Eighteenth-Century Women Dramatists* 211–80.

———. *The Belle's Stratagem*. Facsim. Link, *Plays*, vol. 1.

———. *The Belle's Stratagem*. Rogers, *Meridian Anthology* 409–88.

———. *A Bold Stroke for a Husband*. Facsim. Link, *Plays*, vol. 1.

———. *A School for Greybeards; or, The Mourning Bride: A Comedy, in Five Acts*. London: G. G. J. and J. Robinson, 1786. Print.

Cowper, William. *The Correspondence, with Annotations by Thomas Wright*. Vol. 3. London: Hodder and Stoughton, 1904. Print. 4 vols.

Cox, Jeffrey N., and Michael Gamer, eds. *The Broadview Anthology of Romantic Drama*. Peterborough: Broadview, 2003. Print.

———. Introduction. Cox and Gamer, *Broadview Anthology* vii–xxiv.

The Crafty Whore; or, The Misery and Iniquity of Bawd-Houses, Laid Open in a Dialogue between Two Subtle Bawds. London, 1658. Print.

Craven, Elizabeth. *The Miniature Picture; A Comedy in Three Acts: Performed at the Theatre-Royal, Drury-Lane*. 1780. London: G. Riley, 1781. Print.

Cribb, T. J. Rev. of *Oroonoko* and *Happy Birthday, Mister Deka D*, by 'Biyi Bandele. *Research in African Literatures* 31.1 (2000): 173–78. Print.

Crochunis, Thomas C., ed. *Joanna Baille, Romantic Dramatist: Critical Essays*. London: Routledge, 2004. Print.

Crochunis, Thomas, and Michael Eberle-Sinatra, eds. *The Broadview Anthology of British Women Playwrights, 1777–1843*. Peterborough: Broadview, 2009. Print.

Cuder-Domínguez, Pilar. "The Islamization of Spain in William Rowley and Mary Pix: The Politics of Gender and Nation." *Comparative Drama* 36.3-4 (2002–03): 321–36. Print.

———. "Of Spain, Moors, and Women: The Tragedies of Aphra Behn and Mary Pix." Luis-Martínez and Figueroa-Dorrego 157–73.

Cumberland, Richard. "Critique on the *Bold Stroke for a Wife*." Centlivre, *Bold Stroke* [Copeland] 151.

———. "Life of Susannah Centlivre." Centlivre, *Bold Stroke* [Copeland] 150.

Damrosch, David, and Kevin J. H. Dettmar, gen. eds. *The Longman Anthology of British Literature*. 4th ed. New York: Longman, 2010. Print.

Daniels, Sarah. *Masterpieces*. London: Methuen, 1994. Print.

Darby, Barbara. *Frances Burney Dramatist: Gender, Performance, and the Late Eighteenth-Century Stage*. Lexington: UP of Kentucky, 1997. Print.

Davenant, William. *The Siege of Rhodes*. Ed. Ann-Mari Hedbäck. Uppsala: U of Uppsala, 1973. Print.

Davies, Thomas. *Memoirs of the Life of David Garrick*. Vol. 2. London, 1780. Print. 2 vols.

Davis, Tracy C. "The Sociable Playwright and Representative Citizen." *Women and Playwriting in Nineteenth-Century Britain*. Ed. Davis and Ellen Donkin. Cambridge: Cambridge UP, 1999. 15–34. Print.

Dawson, Mark S. *Gentility and the Comic Theatre of Late Stuart London*. Cambridge: Cambridge UP, 2005. Print.

Defoe, Daniel. *Roxana, the Fortunate Mistress; or, A History of the Life and Vast Variety of Fortunes of Mademoiselle de Beleau*. Ed. John Mullan. Oxford: Oxford UP, 2008. Print.

———. "Stockjobbing." Centlivre, *Bold Stroke* [Copeland] 152–58.

Dekker, Rudolf M., and Lotte C. van de Pol. *The Tradition of Female Transvestism in Early Modern Europe*. New York: St. Martin's, 1989. Print.

de Lauretis, Teresa. *Technologies of Gender: Essays on Theory, Film, and Fiction*. Bloomington: Indiana UP, 1987. Print.

DeMaria, Robert, Jr., ed. *British Literature: 1640–1789: An Anthology*. 3rd ed. Malden: Blackwell, 2008. Print.

Demers, Patricia. *The World of Hannah More*. Lexington: UP of Kentucky, 1996. Print.

Descartes, René. *Les passions de l'âme*. Paris: Michel Bobin and Nicolas Le Gras, 1664. Print.

Desens, Marliss C. *The Bed Trick in English Renaissance Drama: Explorations in Gender, Sexuality, and Power*. Newark: U of Delaware P, 1994. Print.

Dessen, Alan C. *Rescripting Shakespeare: The Text, the Director, and Modern Productions*. Cambridge: Cambridge UP, 2002. Print.

Diamond, Elin. "Gestus and Signature in Aphra Behn's *The Rover*." *English Literary History* 56.3 (1989): 519–41. Print.

———. *Unmaking Mimesis: Essays on Feminism and Theatre*. London: Routledge, 1997. Print.

Dibdin, Charles. *A Complete History of the Stage*. 5 vols. London, 1800. Print.

Digby, George. *Elvira; or, The Worst Not Always True*. London: Henry Broome, 1667. Print.

Dilke, Thomas. "Dedication to Lord Raby." *The Lover's Luck*. London, 1696. *Early English Books Online*. U of Exeter Lib. Web. 1 Oct. 2007.

Donkin, Ellen. *Getting into the Act: Women Playwrights in London, 1776–1829*. London: Routledge, 1995. Print.

Doody, Margaret Anne. *Frances Burney: The Life in the Works*. New Brunswick: Rutgers UP, 1988. Print.

———. "Frances Sheridan: Morality and Annihilated Time." *Fetter'd or Free? British Women Novelists, 1670–1815*. Ed. Mary Anne Schofield and Cecilia Macheski. Athens: Ohio UP, 1986. 324–58. Print.

Downer, Alan S. "Nature to Advantage Dressed: Eighteenth-Century Acting." *PMLA* 58.4 (1943): 1002–37. Print.

Dryden, John. *All for Love*. London: Tho. Newcomb, 1678. Print.

———. *Aureng-Zebe, A Tragedy*. London, 1692. Print.

———. *The Conquest of Granada by the Spaniards*. London, 1673. Print.

———. *An Essay of Dramatic Poesy. Selected Poetry and Prose of John Dryden*. Ed. Earl Miner. New York: Mod. Lib., 1985. 27–104. Print.

———. *The Indian Queen*. London: Henry Herringman, 1665. Print.

———. *Marriage à la Mode: A Comedy*. London: Henry Herringman, 1673. Print.

Duncan-Jones, Katherine. "Sidney's Urania." *RES* ns 17 (1966): 123–33. Print.

Duncombe, John. "The Feminead: A Poem." 1754. *Spenser and the Tradition: English Poetry, 1579–1800*. Ed. David Hill Radcliffe. Virginia Tech, n.d. Web. 26 Apr. 2010.

Durang, Christopher. *The Actor's Nightmare. Christopher Durang Explains It All for You: Six Plays by Christopher Durang*. New York: Grove, 1983. 137–66. Print.

D'Urfey, Thomas. *The Virtuous Wife; or, Good Luck at Last.* London: R. Bentley, and M. Magnes, 1680. *Early English Books Online.* Swarthmore Coll. Web. 1 Nov. 2007.

Eger, Elizabeth. "Spectacle, Intellect, and Authority: The Actress in the Eighteenth Century." *The Cambridge Companion to the Actress.* Ed. Maggie B. Gale and John Stokes. Cambridge: Cambridge UP, 2007. 33–51. Print.

Eigen, Joel Peter. *Witnessing Insanity: Madness and Mad-Doctors in the English Court.* Fwd. Nigel Walker. New Haven: Yale UP, 1995. Print.

Elam, Keir. *The Semiotics of Theatre and Drama.* 2nd ed. London: Routledge, 2002. Print.

Emeljanow, Victor. "Repertoire, Taste and Audiences." *Romantic and Revolutionary Theatre, 1789–1860.* Ed. Donald Roy. Comp. and introd. Emeljanow et al. Cambridge: Cambridge UP, 2003. 110–62. Print.

Ennis, Daniel J., and Judith Bailey Slagle, eds. *Prologues, Epilogues, Curtain-Raisers, and Afterpieces: The Rest of the Eighteenth-Century London Stage.* Newark: U of Delaware P, 2007. Print.

Erickson, Amy Louise. *Women and Property in Early Modern England.* London: Routledge, 1993. Print.

Etherege, George. *The Man of Mode.* Fisk, *Four Restoration Libertine Plays* 85–172.

Faderman, Lillian. *Surpassing the Love of Man: Romantic Friendship and Love between Women, from the Renaissance to the Present.* New York: Morrow, 1981. Print.

Farquhar, George. *The Beaux' Stratagem: A Comedy.* London: B. Lintott, 1707. Print.

———. *The Constant Couple; or, A Trip to the Jubilee.* London: Ralph Smith and Bennet Banbury, 1700. Print.

The Female Wits; or, The Triumvirate of Poets at Rehearsal. London: W. Turner, 1704. Print.

Ferguson, Oliver W. "Kate's Stratagem and the Naming of *She Stoops to Conquer.*" *Restoration and Eighteenth-Century Theatre Research* 6.2 (1991): 26–29. Print.

Fielding, Henry. *Eurydice Hiss'd; or, A Word to the Wise: A Farce.* New York: D. Longworth, 1817. Print.

———. *The Historical Register, for the Year 1736: As It Is Acted at the New Theatre in the Hay-Market.* 2nd ed. London: J. Roberts, 1737. Print.

———. *The Tragedy of Tragedies; or, The Life and Death of Tom Thumb the Great, with the Annotations of H. Scriblerus Secundus.* Ed. James T. Hillhouse. New Haven: Yale UP, 1918. Print.

Finberg, Melinda C., ed. *Eighteenth-Century Women Dramatists.* Oxford: Oxford UP, 2001. Print.

———. Introduction. Finberg, *Eighteenth-Century Women Dramatists* ix–xlvii.

———. Select bibliography. Finberg, *Eighteenth-Century Women Dramatists* lvii–lix.

Finding Nemo. Dir. Andrew Stanton. Disney, 2003. Film.

Findlay, Alison, and Stephanie Hodgson-Wright, with Gweno Williams. *Women and Dramatic Production, 1550–1700.* London: Longman, 2000. Print.

Finney, Gail, ed. *Look Who's Laughing: Gender and Comedy.* Vol. 1. Langhorne: Gordon, 1994. Print.

———. "Unity in Difference? An Introduction." Finney, *Look* 1–14.

Fisk, Deborah Payne, ed. (*see also* Payne, Deborah C.). *Four Restoration Libertine Plays.* Oxford: Oxford UP, 2005. Print.

———. "The Restoration Actress." *A Companion to Restoration Drama.* Ed. Susan J. Owen. Oxford: Blackwell, 2001. 69–91. Print.

Foote, Samuel. *The Minor: A Comedy.* 7th ed. London: J. Coote, 1767. Print.

———. *A Treatise on the Passions, So Far As They Regard the Stage.* London: C. Corbett, n.d. Print.

The 40-Year-Old Virgin. Dir. Judd Apatow. Universal Pictures, 2005. Film.

Foucault, Michel. *The History of Sexuality.* Trans. Robert Hurley. 3 vols. New York: Pantheon, 1978. Print.

Four Weddings and a Funeral. Dir. Mike Newell. PolyGram Filmed Entertainment, 1994. Film.

Franceschina, John. "Shadow and Substance in Aphra Behn's *The Rover*: The Semiotics of Restoration Performance." *Restoration* 19.1 (1995): 29–42. Print.

Frank, Marcie. *Gender, Theatre, and the Origins of Criticism, from Dryden to Manley.* Cambridge: Cambridge UP, 2002. Print.

Franklin, Nancy. "Bawdy Night." *New Yorker* 1 Aug. 1994: 73. Print.

Freeman, Lisa. *Character's Theater: Genre and Identity on the Eighteenth-Century English Stage.* Philadelphia: U of Pennsylvania P, 2002. Print.

———. "The Social Life of Eighteenth-Century Comedy." Moody and O'Quinn 73–86.

Friedland, Paul. *Political Actors: Representative Bodies and Theatricality in the Age of the French Revolution.* Ithaca: Cornell UP, 2002. Print.

Frushell, Richard C., ed. *The Plays of Susanna Centlivre.* 2 vols. New York: Garland, 1982. Print.

Frye, Northrop. *Anatomy of Criticism: Four Essays.* Princeton: Princeton UP, 1957. Print.

Gale, Maggie B., and Viv Gardner, eds. *Women, Theatre and Performance: New Histories, New Historiographies.* Manchester: Manchester UP, 2000. Print.

Gallagher, Catherine. "Who Was That Masked Woman? The Prostitute and the Playwright in the Comedies of Aphra Behn." *Women's Studies* 15.1–3 (1988): 23–42. Print.

Garfield, John. *The Wandring Whore.* London, 1660. Print.

Garnai, Amy. "Radicalism, Caution, and Censorship in Elizabeth Inchbald's *Every One Has His Fault.*" *Studies in English Literature, 1500–1900* 47.3 (2007): 703–22. Print.

Garrett, Jane. *The Triumphs of Providence: The Assassination Plot, 1696.* Cambridge: Cambridge UP, 1980. Print.

Garrick, David. *Miss in Her Teens.* [London]: n.p., 1747. Print.

Gay, John. *Trivia; or, The Art of Walking the Streets of London.* London: B. Lintott, 1716. Print.

Gay, John, Alexander Pope, and John Arbuthnot. *Three Hours after Marriage.* London, 1717. *Eighteenth Century Collections Online.* U of Exeter Lib. Web. 1 Oct. 2007.

Genest, John. *Some Account of the English Stage, from the Restoration in 1660 to 1830.* 10 vols. Bath: H. E. Carrington, 1832. Print.

Genette, Gérard. *Palimpsests: Literature in the Second Degree.* Lincoln: U of Nebraska P, 1997. Print.

Gilbert, Sandra M., and Susan Gubar, eds. *The Norton Anthology of Literature by Women: The Traditions in English.* 3rd ed. New York: Norton, 2007. Print.

Gill, Pat. "Gender, Sexuality, and Marriage." *The Cambridge Companion to English Restoration Theatre.* Ed. Deborah Payne Fisk. Cambridge: Cambridge UP, 2000. 191–208. Print.

Gilman, Rebecca. *Boy Gets Girl.* New York: Faber, 2000. Print.

Gilpin, John. *The Quaker Shaken.* Kendal: n.p., 1653. Print.

Glaspell, Susan. *The Outside. Plays by Susan Glaspell.* Ed. C. W. E. Bigsby. Cambridge: Cambridge UP, 1991. 47–55. Print.

Godwin, William. *Caleb Williams.* Ed. Pamela Clemit. Oxford: Oxford UP, 2009. Print.

Goldoni, Carlo. *Le bourru bienfaisant, comédie en trois actes et en prose.* Paris: Duchesne, 1771. Print.

Goldsmith, Oliver. "An Essay on the Theatre; or, A Comparison between Laughing and Sentimental Comedy." *British Dramatists from Dryden to Sheridan.* Ed. George H. Nettleton and Arthur E. Case. Boston: Houghton, 1939. 761–63. Print.

———. *The Novel; or, Mistakes of a Night.* Larpent MS 349. Huntington Lib., San Marino.

———. *She Stoops to Conquer.* The Beggar's Opera *and Other Eighteenth-Century Plays.* Ed. David Lindsay. London: Everyman, 1993. 328–99. Print.

———. *She Stoops to Conquer; or, Mistakes of a Night.* 1st ed. London: F. Newberry, 1773. Print.

Gómez, Carlos J. "Witty Women Masking Gender and Identity: The Comedies of Mary Pix in Context." Luis-Martínez and Figueroa-Dorrengo 123–56.

Goodman, Lizbeth. "*The Rover* in Performance." *Shakespeare, Aphra Behn and the Canon.* Ed. W. R. Owens and Goodman. London: Routledge, 1996. 175–90. Print.

Gould, Robert. "The Playhouse." *Poems, Chiefly Consisting of Satyrs and Satyrical Epistles.* London, 1689. *Early English Books Online.* U of Exeter Lib. Web. 1 Oct. 2007.

Grapko, Andy Garrett. "Re: The Massacre." Message to Thomas C. Crochunis. 23 Nov. 2004. E-mail.

Gravois, John. "Academic Group Meets in Mount Vernon to Contemplate Remaking the Modern University." *Chronicle of Higher Education.* Chronicle of Higher Educ., 8 Oct. 2007. Web. 8 Oct. 2007.

Gray, John. *Men Are from Mars, Women Are from Venus: A Practical Guide for Communication and Getting What You Want from Your Relationships.* New York: Harper, 1992. Print.

Green, Katherine S. "Mr. Harmony and the Events of January 1793: Elizabeth Inchbald's *Every One Has His Fault.*" *Theatre Journal* 56.1 (2004): 47–62. Print.

———. " 'You Should Be My Master': Imperial Recognition Politics in Elizabeth Inchbald's *Such Things Are.*" *Clio* 27.3 (1998): 387–414. Print.

Greenblatt, Stephen, gen. ed. *The Norton Anthology of English Literature*. 8th ed. New York: Norton, 2006. Print.

Greenblatt, Stephen, et al., eds. *The Norton Shakespeare*. New York: Norton, 1997. Print.

Gregg, Edward. *Queen Anne*. Rev. ed. New Haven: Yale UP, 2001. Print.

Griffin, Dustin. *Literary Patronage in England, 1650–1800*. Cambridge: Cambridge UP, 1996. Print.

Griffith, Elizabeth. *The Delicate Distress*. Ed. Cynthia Booth Ricciardi and Susan Staves. Lexington: UP of Kentucky, 1997. Print.

———. *The Double Mistake*. Rizzo, *Elizabeth Griffith* 71–130.

———. *Essays, Addressed to Young Married Women*. London: T. Cadell and J. Robson, 1782. Print.

———. Letter to David Garrick. 17 Aug. 1766. *The Private Correspondence of David Garrick with the Most Celebrated Persons of His Times*. Ed. James Boaden. London: H. Colburn and R. Bentley, 1821. 1: 234–35. Print. 2 vols.

———. *The Morality of Shakespeare's Drama Illustrated*. London: T. Cadell, 1775. Print.

———. *The Platonic Wife*. Rizzo, *Elizabeth Griffith* 1–62.

———. *The School for Rakes*. Rizzo, *Elizabeth Griffith* 137–202.

———. *Theodorick, King of Denmark: A Tragedy: Never before Published: By a Young Gentlewoman*. Dublin: James Esdall, 1752. Print.

———. *The Times*. 1779. Finberg, *Eighteenth-Century Women Dramatists* 145–210.

———. *A Wife in the Right*. Rizzo, *Elizabeth Griffith* 207–64.

Griffith, Elizabeth, and Richard Griffith. *A Series of Genuine Letters between Henry and Frances*. 6 vols. London: W. Johnston (vols. 1–4); W. Richardson and L. Urquhart (vols. 5–6), 1757–70. Print.

Griffith, Richard. *The Triumvirate; or, The Authentic Memoirs of Andrews, Beville, and Carewe*. 2 vols. Dublin: J. Hoey et al., 1765. Print.

Griffiths, Malcolm. "Past Polemics, Present Problematics: Complexities in Reclaiming Aphra Behn's Plays for Contemporary Production." *European Legacy* 2.1 (1997): 22–27. Print.

The Guardians Over-reached in Their Own Humour; or, The Lover Metamorphosed. The Stroler's Paquet Open'd. London, 1742. 124–67. Print.

Habermas, Jürgen. *The Structural Transformation of the Public Sphere: An Inquiry into a Category of Bourgeois Society*. Trans. Thomas Burger. Cambridge: MIT P, 1991. Print.

Haggerty, George E. *Men in Love: Masculinity and Sexuality in the Eighteenth Century*. New York: Columbia UP, 1999. Print.

———. "'The Queen Was Not Shav'd Yet': Edward Kynaston and the Regendering of the Restoration Stage." *The Eighteenth Century: Theory and Interpretation* 50.4 (2009): 309–26. Print.

Hamlet. Dir. Michael Almereyda. Perf. Ethan Hawke. Miramax, 2000. DVD.

———. Dir. Franco Zeffirelli. Perf. Mel Gibson. Warner Bros., 1990. DVD.

Harman, Claire. *Fanny Burney: A Biography*. New York: Knopf, 2001. Print.

Harris, Barbara J. *English Aristocratic Women, 1450–1550*. Oxford: Oxford UP, 2002. Print.

Harris, Frances. *A Passion for Government: The Life of Sarah, Duchess of Marlborough.* Oxford: Oxford UP, 1991. Print.

Harvey, Karen. "Spaces of Erotic Delight." *Georgian Geographies: Essays on Space, Place and Landscape in the Eighteenth Century.* Ed. Miles Ogborn and Charles W. J. Withers. Manchester: Manchester UP, 2004. 130–50. Print.

Hatton, Ranghild Marie. *George I, Elector and King.* 1978. New Haven: Yale UP, 2001. Print.

Hawkesworth, John. *Adventurer* 72-73 (1759): n. pag. Print.

Hayley, William. *The Triumphs of Temper.* London: Cadell, 1781. Print.

Haywood, Eliza. "Advertisement to the Reader." *The Fair Captive.* London, 1721. a2. *Eighteenth Century Collections Online.* U of Exeter Lib. Web. 1 Oct. 2007.

———. *Anti-Pamela; or, Feign'd Innocence Detected.* Ed. Catherine Ingrassia. Peterborough: Broadview, 2004. Print.

———. *The Dramatic Historiographer. Selected Works of Eliza Haywood.* Vol. 1. Ed. Christine Blouch, Alexander Pettit, and Rebecca Sayers Hanson. London: Pickering, 2001. 1–174. Print. Rpt. as *A Companion to the Theatre.*

———. *Fantomina; or, Love in a Maze.* Ed. Jack Lynch. Rutgers U, n.d. Web. 3 Feb. 2010.

———. *Fantomina; or, Love in a Maze. A Celebration of Women Writers.* Ed. Mary Mark Ockerbloom. Ockerbloom, 2010. Web. 13 July 2010.

———. *Fantomina; or, Love in a Maze.* Fantomina *and Other Works.* Ed. Alexander Pettit, Margaret Case Croskey, and Anna C. Patchias. Peterborough: Broadview, 2004. 41–71. Print.

———. *Fantomina; or, Love in a Maze. Popular Fiction by Women, 1660–1730: An Anthology.* Ed. Paula R. Backscheider and John J. Richetti. Oxford: Oxford UP, 1996. 226–48. Print.

———. *Female Spectator* 1–4 (1745–46). *Eighteenth Century Collections Online.* Yeshiva U, n.d. Web. 12 Apr. 2010.

———. *The History of Miss Betsy Thoughtless.* Ed. Beth Fowkes Tobin. Oxford: Oxford UP, 1997. Print.

———. *A Wife to Be Lett: A Comedy. Selected Fiction and Drama of Eliza Haywood.* Ed. Paula R. Backscheider. Oxford: Oxford UP, 1999. 1–83. Print.

Hazlitt, William. "On the Comic Writers of the Last Century." Centlivre, *Wonder* [O'Brien] 142–43.

Head, Richard. *Miss Display'd for All Her Wheedling Arts.* London, 1675. Print.

Hendricks, Margo. "Civility, Barbarism, and Aphra Behn's *The Widow Ranter.*" *Women, "Race" and Writing in the Early Modern Period.* Ed. Hendricks and Patricia Parker. London: Routledge, 1994. 225–39. Print.

Herman, Peter. "We All Smoke Here: Behn's *The Widow Ranter* and the Invention of American Identity." *Envisioning an English Empire: Jamestown and the Making of the North Atlantic World.* Ed. Robert Appelbaum and John Sweet. Philadelphia: U of Pennsylvania P, 2005. 254–74. Print.

Herman, Ruth. *The Business of a Woman: The Political Writings of Delarivier Manley.* Newark: U of Delaware P, 2003. Print.

Highfill, Philip H., Kalman A. Burnim, and Edward A. Langhans. *A Biographical Dictionary of Actors, Actresses, Musicians, Dancers, Managers and Other Stage*

Personnel in London, 1660–1800. 16 vols. Carbondale: Southern Illinois UP, 1973–93. Print.

Hill, Aaron. "The Art of Acting." *The Works of the Late Aaron Hill, Esq.* 2nd ed. London: n.p., 1753–54. n. pag. Print.

———. *An Essay on the Art of Acting, in Which the Dramatic Passions Are Properly Defined and Described.* London: J. Dixwell, 1779. Print.

Hill, John. *The Actor; or, A Treatise on the Art of Playing.* London: R. Griffiths, 1755. Print.

Hobby, Elaine, and Bill Overton. "'There Is Not Space for Margaret Cavendish and Dryden': Higher Education Teaching, 1640–1700." *Women's Writing* 1.3 (1994): 257–75. Print.

Hogan, Charles Beecher, ed. *The London Stage, 1660–1800: Part 5, 1776–1800.* 3 vols. Carbondale: Southern Illinois UP, 1968. Print.

Hogan, Robert, and Jerry C. Beasley. Introduction. Hogan and Beasley, *Plays* 13–35.

Hogan, Robert, and Jerry C. Beasley, eds. *The Plays of Frances Sheridan.* Newark: U of Delaware P, 1984. Print.

Holland, Peter. *The Ornament of Action: Text and Performance in Restoration Comedy.* Cambridge: Cambridge UP, 1979. Print.

Honeymoon in Las Vegas. Dir. Andrew Bergman. Castle Rock Entertainment, 1992. Film.

Hook, Harriet Horncastle. *The Double Disguise.* London: J. Bell, 1784. Print.

Hopkins, Lisa. "Judith Shakespeare's Reading: Teaching *The Concealed Fancies.*" *Shakespeare Quarterly* 47.4 (1996): 396–406. Print.

Hornby, Richard. "Suit the Action to the Word." *Hudson Review* 53.4 (2001): 624–30. Print.

Howe, Elizabeth. *The First English Actresses: Women and Drama, 1660–1700.* Cambridge: Cambridge UP, 1992. Print.

Hughes, Derek. "Aphra Behn and the Restoration Theatre." Hughes and Todd 29–45.

———, gen. ed. *Eighteenth-Century Women Playwrights.* 6 vols. London: Pickering, 2001. Print.

———. *English Drama, 1660–1700.* Oxford: Clarendon, 1996. Print.

———. *The Theatre of Aphra Behn.* Houndmills: Palgrave, 2001. Print.

Hughes, Derek, and Janet Todd, eds. *The Cambridge Companion to Aphra Behn.* Cambridge: Cambridge UP, 2004. Print.

Hume, David. *A Treatise of Human Nature.* Ed. L. A. Selby-Bigge. 2nd ed. rev. P. H. Nidditch. Oxford: Clarendon, 1978. Print.

Hume, Robert D. "Goldsmith and Sheridan and the Supposed Revolution of 'Laughing' against 'Sentimental' Comedy." *Studies in Change and Revolution: Aspects of English Intellectual History, 1640–1800.* Ed. Paul J. Korshin. Menston: Scholar, 1972. 237–76. Print.

———. *Henry Fielding and the London Theatre, 1728–1737.* Oxford: Clarendon, 1988. Print.

———. "The Myth of the Rake in 'Restoration' Comedy." *Studies in the Literary Imagination* 10.1 (1977): 25–55. Print.

———. *The Rakish Stage: Studies in English Drama, 1660–1800.* Carbondale: Southern Illinois UP, 1983. Print.

Hunt, Alan. *Governing Morals: A Social History of Moral Regulation.* Cambridge: Cambridge UP, 1999. Print.

Hunt, Lynn. *The Family Romance of the French Revolution.* Berkeley: U of California P, 1992. Print.

———. *Inventing Human Rights: A History.* New York: Norton, 2007. Print.

Hutcheon, Linda. *A Theory of Adaptation.* London: Routledge, 2006. Print.

———. *A Theory of Parody: The Teaching of Twentieth-Century Art Forms.* New York: Methuen, 1985. Print.

Hutner, Heidi. *Colonial Women: Race and Culture in Stuart Drama.* Oxford: Oxford UP, 2001. Print.

Ikegami, Robin. "Teaching Aphra Behn's *The Rover.*" Woods and Hannay 308–11.

Inchbald, Elizabeth. *A Case of Conscience.* 1800. Boaden, *Memoirs* 2: 297–352.

———. "Criticism." Centlivre, *Bold Stroke* [Copeland] 148–51.

———. *The Diaries of Elizabeth Inchbald.* Ed. Ben P. Robertson. 3 vols. London: Pickering, 2007. Print.

———. *Every One Has His Fault.* Cox and Gamer 39–74.

———. *I'll Tell You What: A Comedy, in Five Acts, as It Is Performed at the Theatre Royal, Haymarket.* London: G. G. J. and J. Robinson, 1786. Print.

———. Letter. *Artist* 14: 13 June 1807. Rpt. in Inchbald, *Simple Story* 343–48.

———. Letter to Frances Phillips. *The British Letter Writers: A Comprehensive Collection of the Best English Letters from the Fifteenth Century to the Present Time Comprising Letters Familiar and Domestic, Historical, Political, Literary, and Descriptive.* Ed. Robert Cochrane. Edinburgh: William P. Nimmo, 1892. 194. Print.

———. Letter to George Colman the Younger. *British Theatre* 21: n. pag.

———. *Lovers' Vows: A Play, in Five Acts.* London: J. Cumberland, 1798. Print. Adapt. of *Das Kind der Liebe*, by August von Kotzebue.

———. *The Massacre.* 1792. Boaden, *Memoirs* 1: 359–80.

———. *The Massacre.* 1792. *British Women Playwrights around 1800.* Ed. Thomas C. Crochunis and Michael Eberle-Sinatra. U de Montréal, 15 Apr. 1999. Web. 1 Nov. 2007.

———. *A Mogul Tale: A Farce in Two Acts.* New York: E. M. Murden, 1827. Print.

———. *Nature and Art.* Ed. and introd. Shawn Lisa Maurer. Peterborough: Broadview, 2005. Print.

———. *Remarks for* The British Theatre*, 1806–1809.* Facsim. Delmar: Scholars' Facsims. and Rpts., 1990. Print.

———. " 'Remarks' on *The Wonder, British Theatre.*" Centlivre, *Wonder* [O'Brien] 140.

———. *A Simple Story.* Ed. and introd. Anna Lott. Peterborough: Broadview, 2007. Print.

———. *Such Things Are.* Rogers, *Meridian Anthology* 489–558.

———. *Wives as They Were, and Maids as They Are.* 1797. Facsim. Backscheider, *Plays* vol. 2.

Indecent Proposal. Dir. Adrian Lyne. Paramount Pictures, 1993. Film.

Index to The London Stage, 1660–1800. Comp. Ben Ross Schneider, Jr. Carbondale: Southern Illinois UP, 1979. Print.

"*The Inflexible Captive; a Tragedy.* By Miss Hannah More." *Monthly Review* 4 (1774): 243–51. Print.

Isikoff, Erin. "Masquerade, Modesty, and Comedy in Hannah Cowley's *The Belle's Stratagem.*" Finney, *Look* 99–117.

Jacob, Giles. "Mrs. Susanna Cent Livre." Centlivre, *Bold Stroke* [Copeland] 144.

James, Susan, ed. *Margaret Cavendish: Political Writings.* Cambridge: Cambridge UP, 2003. Print.

Jameson, Fredric. *The Political Unconscious: Narrative as a Socially Symbolic Act.* Ithaca: Cornell UP, 1981. Print.

Jankowski, Theordora A. "Good Enough to Eat: The Domestic Economy of Woman—Eroticism in Margaret Cavendish and Andrew Marvell." *Privacy, Domesticity, and Women in Early Modern England.* Ed. Corinne S. Abate. Aldershot: Ashgate, 2003. 83–110. Print.

Jenkins, Annibel. *I'll Tell You What: The Life of Elizabeth Inchbald.* Lexington: UP of Kentucky, 2003. Print.

Johnson, Samuel. *The Rambler.* Ed. W. J. Bate and Albrecht B. Strauss. Vol. 2. New Haven: Yale UP, 1969. Print. 3 vols.

Jones, Darryl. "Radical Ambivalence: Frances Burney, Jacobinism, and the Politics of Romantic Fiction." *Women's Writing* 10.1 (2003): 3–25. Print.

Jones, Kathleen. *A Glorious Fame: The Life of Margaret Cavendish, Duchess of Newcastle, 1623–1673.* London: Bloomsbury, 1988. Print.

Jones, Vivien. Introduction. V. Jones, *Women and Literature* 1–19.

———, ed. *Women and Literature in Britain, 1700–1800.* Cambridge: Cambridge UP, 2000. Print.

———, ed. *Women in the Eighteenth Century: Constructions of Femininity.* London: Routledge, 1990. Print.

Juggernaut Theatre Company. "First 100 Years: The Professional Female Playwright." *Juggernaut Theatre Company.* Juggernaut Theatre, 26 Apr. 2006. Web. 15 Sept. 2009.

Kasser, Tim. *The High Price of Materialism.* Cambridge: MIT P, 2002. Print.

Kavenik, Frances M. *British Drama, 1660–1779: A Critical History.* New York: Twayne, 1995. Print.

Kelley, Anne. *Catharine Trotter: An Early Modern Writer in the Vanguard of Feminism.* Aldershot: Ashgate, 2002. Print.

———, ed. *Mary Pix and Catharine Trotter.* Vol. 2 of Hughes, *Eighteenth-Century Women Playwrights.*

Kendall. "Finding the Good Parts: Sexuality in Women's Tragedies in the Time of Queen Anne." Schofield and Macheski 165–76.

———. *Love and Thunder: Plays by Women in the Age of Queen Anne.* London: Methuen, 1988. Print.

Kennedy, Adrienne. *The Ohio State Murders. The Alexander Plays.* Minneapolis: U of Minnesota P, 1992. 25–63. Print.

Kenny, Shirley Strum. "Humane Comedy." *Modern Philology* 75.1 (1977): 29–43. Print.

Kewes, Paulina. *Authorship and Appropriation: Writing for the Stage in England, 1660–1710.* Oxford: Clarendon, 1998. Print.

Kinney, Suz-Anne. "Confinement Sharpens the Invention: Aphra Behn's *The Rover* and Susanna Centlivre's *The Busie Body.*" Finney, *Look* 81–98.

Kinservik, Matthew J. *Disciplining Satire: The Censorship of Satiric Comedy on the Eighteenth-Century London Stage.* Lewisburg: Bucknell UP, 2002. Print.

Klein, Lawrence E. "Gender and the Public/Private Distinction in the Eighteenth Century: Some Questions about Evidence and Analytic Procedure." *Eighteenth-Century Studies* 29.1 (1996): 97–109. Print.

Knight, John. *A Sermon Preached at the Funeral of the Rt Hon the Lady Guilford.* London, 1699. Print.

Knipe, Charles. *A City Ramble; or, The Humours of the Compter: As It Is Acted at the Theatre in Lincoln's-Inn-Fields.* London: E. Curll, 1715. Print.

Kowaleski-Wallace, Elizabeth. "Theatricality and Cosmopolitanism in Hannah Cowley's *Belle's Stratagem.*" *Comparative Drama* 35.3 (2001): 415–33. Print.

———. "Transnationalism and Performance in 'Biyi Bandele's *Oroonoko.*" *PMLA* 119.2 (2004): 265–81. Print.

———. "Women, China, and Consumer Culture in Eighteenth-Century England." *Eighteenth-Century Studies* 29.2 (1995–96): 153–67. Print.

Kronman, Anthony. "Why Are We Here? Colleges Ignore Life's Biggest Questions, and We All Pay the Price." *Boston Globe.* Boston Globe, 16 Sept. 2007. Web. 16 Sept. 2007.

Kubek, Elizabeth. "Iphis among the Goddesses: Hybridity, Progressive Ideology, and the Visual Image." *Word and Image in the Eighteenth Century: An Interdisciplinary Dialogue.* Ed. Renata Schellenberg and Christina Ionescu. Cambridge: Cambridge Scholars', 2007. 103–32. Print.

———. "'Night Mares of the Commonwealth': Royalist Passion and Female Ambition in Aphra Behn's *The Roundheads.*" *Restoration* 17.1 (1993): 88–103. Print.

Langhans, Edward A. "The Post-1660 Theatres as Performance Spaces." Owen, *Companion* 3–18.

The Laws Respecting Women. 1777. Dobbs Ferry: Oceana, 1974. Print.

Le Brun, Charles. *A Method to Learn to Design the Passions: Proposed in a Conference on Their General and Particular Expression.* Trans. John Williams. London: J. Huggonson, 1734. Print.

Lee, Sophia. *The Chapter of Accidents: A Comedy, in Five Acts, as It Is Performed at the Theatre-Royal in the Hay-Market.* London: T. Cadell, 1780. Print.

Lennox, Charlotte. *Shakespear Illustrated; or, The Novels and Histories, on Which the Plays of Shakespear Are Founded, Collected, and Tr. from the Original Authors.* London: A. Millar, 1753–54. Print.

Le Noble de Tennelière, Eustache. *Histoire d'Ildegerte, reign de Danemark et de Norwege, ou L'amour magnanime.* Amsterdam: Jean Louis de Lorme, 1695. Print.

———. *Ildegerte, Queen of Norway; or, Heroick Love: A Novel. Written Originally in French, by the Author of* The Happy Slave, *and Translated into English by a Gentleman of Oxford: In Two Parts.* London: W. Chetwood, 1721. Print.

Lesage, Alain-René. "The History of the Count de Belflor and Leonora de Cespedes." *Le diable boiteux.* Paris, 1707. N. pag. Print.

Lewcock, Dawn. "Computer Analysis of Restoration Staging, II: 1671–1682." *Theatre Notebook* 47 (1993): 141–56. Print.

———. "More for Seeing than Hearing: Behn and the Use of Theatre." Todd, *Aphra Behn Studies* 66–83.

The Libertine. Dir. Laurence Dunmore. Weinstein, 2004. Film.

Liesenfeld, Vincent J. *The Licensing Act of 1737.* Madison: U of Wisconsin P, 1984. Print.

Lillo, George. *The London Merchant.* London: T. Lowndes, 1770. Print.

Link, Frederick. Introduction. Link, *Plays* 1: v–xlvi.

———, ed. *The Plays of Hannah Cowley.* 2 vols. New York: Garland, 1979. Print.

Lock, F. P. *Susanna Centlivre.* Boston: Twayne, 1979. Print.

Locke, John. *An Essay concerning Human Understanding.* 1689. Ed. Peter Nidditch. Oxford: Clarendon, 1975. Print.

———. *The Second Treatise of Government.* 1689. *Political Writings of John Locke.* Ed. David Wooten. New York: Penguin, 1993. Print.

———. *Some Thoughts concerning Education.* Ed. John W. Yolton. and Jean S. Yolton. Oxford: Clarendon, 1989. Print.

The London Stage, 1660–1800. Pt. 1: 1660–1700. Ed. William Van Lennep, Emmett L. Avery, and Arthur H. Scouten. Pt. 2: 1700–1729. Ed. Avery. 2 vols. 1960. Pt. 3: 1729–1747. Ed. Scouten. 2 vols. 1961. Pt. 4: 1747–1776. Ed. George Winchester Stone, Jr. 3 vols. 1962. Pt. 5: 1776–1800. Ed. Charles Beecher Hogan. 3 vols. 1968. 11 vols. Carbondale: Southern Illinois UP, 1960–68. Print.

Lott, Anna. Introduction. Inchbald, *Simple Story* 13–46.

———. "Sexual Politics in Elizabeth Inchbald." *Studies in English Literature, 1500–1900* 34.3 (1994): 635–48. Print.

Lowenthal, Cynthia J. *Performing Identities on the Restoration Stage.* Carbondale: Southern Illinois UP, 2003. Print.

———. "Sticks and Rags, Bodies and Brocade: Essentializing Discourses and the Late Restoration Playhouse." *Broken Boundaries: Women and Feminism in Restoration Drama.* Ed. Katherine M. Quinsey. Lexington: UP of Kentucky, 1996. 219–33. Print.

Luis-Martínez, Zenón, and Jorge Figueroa-Dorrengo, eds. *Re-shaping the Genres: Restoration Women Writers.* Bern: Lang, 2003. Print.

Lumley, Jane, trans. *Iphigenia at Aulis.* By Euripides. Facsim. London: Chiswick, 1909. Print.

Lust's Dominion; or, The Lascivious Queen. London: F. Kirkman, 1661. Print.

Lyons, Paddy, and Fidelis Morgan, eds. *Female Playwrights of the Restoration: Five Comedies.* Rutland: Dent, 1991. Print.

Macheski, Cecilia. Introduction. Inchbald, *Remarks* 7–12.

MacVey, Carol Elliott. "Directing *The Rover.*" *Types of Drama.* Ed. Sylvan Barnet et al. 7th ed. New York: Longman, 1997. 393–94. Print.

Mamet, David. *Glengarry Glen Ross.* New York: Grove, 1982. Print.

Manley, Delarivier. *The Adventures of Rivella.* London, 1714. *Eighteenth Century Collections Online.* U of Exeter Lib. Web. 1 Oct. 2007.

———. *Almyna; or, The Arabian Vow.* London: William Turner, 1707. Print.

———. *Letters Written by Mrs. Manley*. London, 1696. *Early English Books Online*. U of Exeter Lib. Web. 1 Oct. 2007.

———. *The Lost Lover*. London, 1696. *Early English Books Online*. U of Exeter Lib. Web. 1 Oct. 2007.

———. *Lucius, the First Christian King of Britain*. 1717. Ed. and introd. Melinda A. Rabb. Canfield, *Broadview Anthology* 76–102.

———. *The Royal Mischief*. London, 1696. *Early English Books Online*. U of Exeter Lib. Web. 1 Oct. 2007.

———. "To the Author of Agnes de Castro." *Agnes de Castro*. London, 1696. *Early English Books Online*. U of Exeter Lib. Web. Oct. 2007.

Mann, David D., and Susan Garland Mann, with Camille Garnier. *Women Playwrights in England, Ireland, and Scotland, 1660–1823*. Bloomington: Indiana UP, 1996. Print.

Markley, Robert. "'Be Impudent, Be Saucy, Forward, Bold, Touzing, and Leud': The Politics of Masculine Sexuality and Feminine Desire in Behn's Tory Comedies." Canfield and Payne 114–40.

Marmontel, Jean François. *Moral Tales by M. Marmontel*. London: T. Becket and P. A. De Hondt, 1764. Print.

Marsden, Jean I. *Fatal Desire: Women, Sexuality, and the English Stage, 1660–1720*. Ithaca: Cornell UP, 2006. Print.

———. "Rape, Voyeurism, and the Restoration Stage." Quinsey 185–200.

———. *The Re-imagined Text: Shakespeare, Adaptation, and Eighteenth-Century Literary Theory*. Lexington: UP of Kentucky, 1995. Print.

———. "Tragedy and Varieties of Serious Drama." Owen, *Companion* 228–42.

Maslin, Janet. "A Very Different Oscars Broadcast." *New York Times*. New York Times, 1 Apr. 1992. Web. 24 Sept. 2007.

Maurer, Shawn Lisa. Introduction. Inchbald, *Nature* 11–32.

McConachie, Bruce. "Theatre and the State, 1600–1900." Gary Jay Williams 199–234.

———. "Theatres for Knowledge through Feeling, 1700–1900." Gary Jay Williams 235–69.

McCormick, Ian. Introduction. *Secret Sexualities: A Sourcebook of Seventeenth- and Eighteenth-Century Writing*. Ed. McCormick. London: Routledge, 1997. 117–21. Print.

McDowell, Paula. *The Women of Grub Street: Press, Politics, and Gender in the London Literary Marketplace, 1678–1730*. Oxford: Clarendon, 1998. Print.

McKeon, Michael. *The Origins of the English Novel, 1600–1740*. Baltimore: Johns Hopkins UP, 1987. Print.

McLaren, Juliet. "Presumptuous Poetess, Pen-Feathered Muse: The Comedies of Mary Pix." *Gender at Work: Four Women Writers of the Eighteenth Century*. Ed. Ann Messenger. Detroit: Wayne State UP, 1990. 77–113. Print.

McMillin, Scott, ed. *Restoration and Eighteenth-Century Comedy*. New York: Norton, 1997. Print.

McMullen, Lorraine. *An Odd Attempt in a Woman: The Literary Life of Frances Brooke*. Vancouver: U of British Columbia P, 1983. Print.

McNulty, Charles. "Sightlines." Rev. of *The London Cuckolds*, by Edward Ravenscroft, and *The Rover*, by Aphra Behn. *Village Voice* 21–27 Mar. 2001: 115. Print.

Meet the Parents. Dir. Jay Roach. Universal Pictures, 2002. Film.

Mellor, Anne K. “Embodied Cosmopolitanism and the British Romantic Woman Writer.” *European Romantic Review* 17.3 (2006): 289–300. Print.

———. *Mothers of the Nation: Women’s Political Writing in England, 1780–1830.* Bloomington: Indiana UP, 2000. Print.

Mendelson, Sara. “Playing Games with Gender and Genre: The Dramatic Self-Fashioning of Margaret Cavendish.” Cottegnies and Weitz 195–212.

Mendelson, Sara, and Patricia Crawford. *Women in Early Modern England.* Oxford: Clarendon, 1998. Print.

Merrens, Rebecca. “ ‘Unmanned with Thy Words’: Regendering Tragedy in Manley and Trotter.” Quinsey 31–53.

Merritt, Juliette. *Beyond Spectacle: Eliza Haywood’s Female Spectators.* Toronto: U of Toronto P, 2004. Print.

Messenger, Ann. “Frances Sheridan.” *Restoration and Eighteenth-Century Dramatists.* Ed. Paula Backscheider. Detroit: Gale, 1989. 289–300. Print. Second Ser.

Milhous, Judith. “Smith, William (d. 1695).” *Oxford Dictionary of National Biography.* Ed. H. C. G. Matthew and Brian Harrison. Oxford: Oxford UP, 2004. *Oxford Dictionary of National Biography.* Web. 23 Nov. 2007.

———. *Thomas Betterton and the Management of Lincoln’s Inn Fields, 1698–1708.* Carbondale: Southern Illinois UP, 1979. Print.

Milhous, Judith, and Robert D. Hume, eds. *The Frolicks.* By Elizabeth Polwhele. Ithaca: Cornell UP, 1977. Print.

———. *The London Stage, 1660–1800.* Pt. 2. 2001. TS. *Penn State University.* Web. 15 Jan. 2008.

———. *Producible Interpretation: Eight English Plays, 1675–1707.* Carbondale: Southern Illinois UP, 1985. Print.

Milling, Jane. “*A Gotham Election*: Women and Performance Politics.” *Restoration and Eighteenth-Century Theatre Research* 21.2 (2007): 72–87. Print.

Mirabeau, Honoré Gabriel de Riquetti, comte de. *Des lettres de cachet et des prison d’état.* Hamburg, 1782. Print.

———. *Enquiries concerning Lettres de Cachet: The Consequences of Arbitrary Imprisonment, and a History of the Inconveniences, Distresses, and Sufferings of State Prisoners: Written in the Dungeon of the Castle of Vincennes.* London: G. J. and J. Robinson, 1787. Print.

The Modern Theatre: A Collection of Successful Modern Plays, as Acted at the Theatres Royal, London . . . Selected by Mrs. Inchbald. 10 vols. London: Longman, Hurst, Rees, Orme, and Brown, 1811. Print.

Molière. *School for Wives.* Trans. Richard Wilbur. New York: Harcourt, 1971. Print.

Montagu, Elizabeth. *Essay upon the Writings and Genius of Shakespear, Compared with the Greek and French Dramatic Poets: With Some Remarks upon the Misrepresentations of Mons. de Voltaire.* 2nd ed. London: J. and H. Hughs, 1770. Print.

Moody, Jane. *Illegitimate Theatre in London, 1770–1840.* Cambridge: Cambridge UP, 2000. Print.

———. “Suicide and Translation in the Dramaturgy of Elizabeth Inchbald and Anne Plumptre.” Burroughs, *Women* 257–84.

Moody, Jane, and Daniel O’Quinn, eds. *The Cambridge Companion to British Theatre, 1730–1830.* Cambridge: Cambridge UP, 2007. Print.

More, Hannah. *Cœlebs in Search of a Wife: Comprehending Observations on Domestic Habits and Manners, Religion and Morals.* Ed. Patricia Demers. Peterborough: Broadview, 2007. Print.

———. *The Fatal Falsehood.* More, *Works* 2: 231–306.

———. *The Inflexible Captive: A Tragedy.* More, *Works* 2: 307–84.

———. *Percy: A Tragedy.* 1777–78. More, *Works* 2: 159–230.

———. "Preface to the Tragedies." More, *Works* 2: 125–58.

———. *Sacred Dramas, Chiefly Intended for Young Persons: The Subjects Taken from the Bible, to Which Are Added, Reflections of King Hezekiah, Sensibility, a Poem, and Essays on Various Subjects, Principally Designed for Young Ladies.* More, *Works* 1: xxv–162.

———. *The Search after Happiness: A Pastoral Drama for Young Ladies.* 1773. More, *Works* 1: 249–88.

———. *Strictures on the Modern System of Female Education; With a View of the Principles and Conduct Prevalent among Women of Rank and Fortune.* More, *Works* 5: 1–440.

———. *The Works.* 11 vols. London: T. Cadell, 1830. Print.

Morgan, Fidelis. *The Female Wits: Female Playwrights of the Restoration.* London: Virago, 1981. Print.

Morgan, Paul. "Frances Wolfreston and 'Hor Bouks': A Seventeenth-Century Woman Book-Collector." *Library* ser. 6, 11.3 (1989): 197–219. Print.

Mottley, John. *Scanderbeg; or, Love and Liberty: A Tragedy: Written by the Late Thomas Whincop, Esq. to Which Are Added a List of All the Dramatic Authors.* London, 1747. *Eighteenth Century Collections Online.* U of Exeter Lib. Web. 1 Oct. 2007.

Mucklow, William. *The Spirit of the Hat.* London: F. Smith, 1673. Print.

Mulvey, Laura. "Visual Pleasure and Narrative Cinema." *Screen* 16.3 (1975): 6–18. Rpt. in *The Sexual Subject: A Screen Reader in Sexuality.* London: Routledge, 1992. 22–34. Print.

Mulvihill, Maureen E. "A Feminist Link in the Old Boys' Network: The Cosseting of Katherine Philips." Schofield and Macheski 71–104.

Munns, Jessica. "Barton and Behn's *The Rover*; or, The Text Transpos'd." *Restoration and Eighteenth-Century Theatre Research* ser. 2, 3.2 (1988): 11–22. Print.

———. "Reviving *Oroonoko* 'in the Scene': From Thomas Southerne to 'Biyi Bandele." *Troping* Oroonoko *from Behn to Bandele.* Ed. Susan B. Iwanisziw. Aldershot: Ashgate, 2004. 174–97. Print.

Myers, Mitzi. "'A Peculiar Protection': Hannah More and the Cultural Politics of the Blagdon Controversy." *History, Gender, and Eighteenth-Century Literature.* Ed. Beth Fowkes Tobin. Athens: U of Georgia P, 1994. 227–57. Print.

Myers, Victoria. "Joanna Baillie and the Emergence of Medico-Legal Discourse." *European Romantic Review* 18.3 (2007): 339–59. Print.

———. "Joanna Baillie: Speculations on Legal Cruelty." *Wordsworth Circle* 35.3 (2004): 123–27. Print.

———. "Joanna Baillie's Theatre of Cruelty." Crochunis 87–107.

Neill, Michael. "Heroic Heads and Humble Tails: Sex, Politics, and the Restoration Comic Rake." *Eighteenth Century: Theory and Interpretation* 24.2 (1983): 115–39. Print.

Nelson, Alfred R., et al. *The London Stage, 1800–1900: A Documentary Record and Calendar of Performances.* Pts. 1–2. Westport: Greenwood, 1990–93. Print.

Nelson, Bonnie A. *Serious Drama and the London Stage: 1729–1739.* Salzburg: Inst. fur Anglistik und Amerikanistik, U Salzburg, 1981. Print.

Newey, Katherine. "Women and History on the Romantic Stage: More, Yearsley, Burney, and Mitford." Burroughs, *Women* 79–101.

Newton, Judith Lowder. *Women, Power, and Subversion: Social Strategies in British Fiction, 1778–1860.* New York: Methuen, 1985. Print.

Nicoll, Allardyce. *The Garrick Stage: Theatres and Audience in the Eighteenth Century.* Athens: U of Georgia P, 1980. Print.

Nielsen, Wendy C. "A Tragic Farce: Revolutionary Women in Elizabeth Inchbald's *The Massacre* and European Drama." *European Romantic Review* 17.3 (2006): 275–88. Print.

Nussbaum, Felicity A. "Eighteenth-Century Women's Autobiographical Commonplaces." *The Private Self: The Theory and Practice of Women's Autobiographical Writings.* Ed. Shari Benstock. Chapel Hill: U of North Carolina P, 1989. 147–72. Print.

O'Brien, John. "Busy Bodies: The Plots of Susanna Centlivre." *Eighteenth-Century Genre and Culture: Serious Reflections on Occasional Forms: Essays in Honor of J. Paul Hunter.* Ed. Dennis Todd and Cynthia Wall. Newark: U of Delaware P, 2001. 165–89. Print.

———. *Harlequin Britain: Pantomime and Entertainment, 1690–1760.* Baltimore: Johns Hopkins UP, 2004. Print.

———. Introduction. Centlivre, *Wonder* [O'Brien] 9–28.

O'Donnell, Mary Ann. "Recent Productions of Behn's Plays and Reviews of Those Productions." App. 9. *Aphra Behn: An Annotated Bibliography of Primary and Secondary Sources.* 2nd ed. Aldershot: Ashgate, 2004. 647–57. Print.

O'Donnell, Mary Ann, Bernard Dhuicq, and Guyonne Leduc, eds. *Aphra Behn, 1640–1689: Identity, Alterity, Ambiguity.* Paris: Harmattan, 2000. Print.

Ogg, David. *England in the Reigns of James II and William III.* Oxford: Clarendon, 1955. Print.

O'Quinn, Daniel. "Bread: The Eruption and Interruption of Politics in Elizabeth Inchbald's *Every One Has His Fault.*" *European Romantic Review* 18.2 (2007): 149–57. Print.

———. *Staging Governance: Theatrical Imperialism in London, 1770–1800.* Baltimore: Johns Hopkins UP, 2005. Print.

Orel, Gwen. "*The Feigned Courtesans.*" *TheaterScene.net.* Theater Scene, 26 Aug. 2004. Web. 30 May 2007.

Orr, Bridget. *Empire on the English Stage, 1660–1714.* Cambridge: Cambridge UP, 2001. Print.

Otway, Thomas. *The Atheist; or, The Second Part* of The Souldiers Fortune. London: R. Bentley and I. Tonson, 1684. *Early English Books Online.* Swarthmore Coll. Web. 1 Nov. 2007.

———. *Friendship in Fashion.* Fisk, *Four Restoration Libertine Plays* 247–330.

———. *The Souldiers Fortune.* London: R. Bentley and M. Magnes, 1681. Print.

———. *Venice Preserv'd. The Complete Works of Thomas Otway.* Ed. Montague Summers. 1926. Vol. 3. New York: AMS, 1967. 1–83. Print.

Owen, Susan J., ed. *A Companion to Restoration Drama.* Oxford: Blackwell, 2001. Print.

———. *Restoration Theatre and Crisis.* Oxford: Clarendon, 1996. Print.

———. "Sexual Politics and Party Politics in Behn's Drama, 1678–83." Todd, *Aphra Behn Studies* 15–29.

Pacheco, Anita. "Rape and the Female Subject in Aphra Behn's *The Rover.*" *English Literary History* 65.2 (1998): 323–45. Print.

Parks, Suzan-Lori. *Top Dog/Underdog.* New York: Theatre Communications, 1999. Print.

Pascoe, Judith. "Romantic Drama." *Romanticism: An Oxford Guide.* Ed. Nicholas Roe. Oxford: Oxford UP, 2005. 409–25. Print.

———. *Romantic Theatricality: Gender, Poetry, and Spectatorship.* Ithaca: Cornell UP, 1997. Print.

Pasquin, Anthony. *The Children of Thespis: A Poem.* 13th ed. London, 1792. Print.

Pasupathi, Vimala. "Old Playwrights, Old Soldiers, New Martial Subjects: The Cavendishes and the Drama of Soldiery." Romack and Fitzmaurice 121–46.

Paulson, Ronald. *Hogarth: His Art, Life, and Times.* Vol. 1. New Haven: Yale UP, 1971. Print.

———. *Hogarth's Harlot: Sacred Parody in Enlightenment England.* Baltimore: Johns Hopkins UP, 2003. Print.

Payne, Deborah C. (*see also* Fisk, Deborah Payne). "Patronage and the Dramatic Marketplace under Charles I and II." *Yearbook of English Studies* 21 (1991): 137–52. Print.

———. "Reified Object or Emergent Professional? Retheorizing the Restoration Actress." Canfield and Payne 13–38.

Pearson, Jacqueline. "Blacker Than Hell Creates: Pix Rewrites *Othello.*" Quinsey 13–30.

———. Introduction. J. Pearson, *Susanna Centlivre* ix–xx.

———. "List of Actors." J. Pearson, *Susanna Centlivre* xxiii–xxix.

———. *The Prostituted Muse: Images of Women and Women Dramatists, 1642–1737.* New York: Harvester, 1988. Print.

———, ed. *Susanna Centlivre.* Vol. 3 of Hughes, *Eighteenth-Century Women Playwrights.*

———. "Textual Variants and Inconsistencies in Susanna Centlivre's *The Basset-Table* (1705)." *Restoration and Eighteenth-Century Theatre Research* 15.2 (2002): 40–59. Print.

———. *Women's Reading in Britain, 1750–1835: A Dangerous Reaction.* Cambridge: Cambridge UP, 1999. Print.

Pearson, Norman. "The Lighter Side of Hannah More." *Nineteenth Century* 59 (1906): 842–58. Print.

Pedicord, Harry William. *The Theatrical Public in the Time of Garrick.* Carbondale: Southern Illinois UP, 1954. Print.

Pedley, Colin. "'Terrific and Unprincipled Compositions': The Reception of *Lovers' Vows* and *Mansfield Park.*" *Philological Quarterly* 74.3 (1995): 297–316. Print.

Pepys, Samuel. *The Diary of Samuel Pepys.* Ed. Robert Latham and William Matthews. 11 vols. Berkeley: U of California P, 1970. Print.

Perry, Ruth. *The Celebrated Mary Astell: An Early English Feminist*. Chicago: U of Chicago P, 1986. Print.

Philips, Katherine, trans. *Pompey*. By Pierre Corneille. Dublin, 1663. Print.

Pix, Mary. *The Beau Defeated; or, The Lucky Younger Brother: A Comedy*. 1700. Facsim. Steeves.

———. *The Conquest of Spain*. Facsim. Steeves.

———. *The Different Widows; or, Intrigue All-A-Mode: A Comedy*. Facsim. Steeves.

———. *The Double Distress*. London: R. Wellington and Bernard Lintott, 1701. Print.

———. *The False Friend; or, the Fate of Disobedience*. London: Richard Basset, 1699. Print.

———. *Ibrahim, the Thirteenth Emperour of the Turks*. 1696. Facsim. Steeves.

———. *The Innocent Mistress: A Comedy*. 1697. Facsim. Steeves.

———. *Queen Catharine; or, the Ruines of Love*. 1698. Kelley, *Mary Pix* 67–128.

———. *The Spanish Wives*. 1696. Rogers, *Meridian Anthology* 131–84.

Pocahontas. Dir. Mike Gabriel and Eric Goldberg. Disney, 1995. Film.

Pocock, J[ohn] G[reville] A[gard]. *The Ancient Constitution and the Feudal Law: A Study of English Historical Thought in the Seventeenth Century: A Reissue with a Retrospect*. Cambridge: Cambridge UP, 1987. Print.

Poovey, Mary. *The Proper Lady and the Woman Writer: Ideology as Style in the Works of Mary Wollstonecraft, Mary Shelley, and Jane Austen*. Chicago: U of Chicago P, 1984. Print.

Pope, Alexander. *The Rape of the Lock: An Heroi-Comical Poem*. 5th ed. London: B. Lintot, 1718. Print.

Porter, Joseph A. "Mercutio's Brother." *South Atlantic Review* 19.4 (1984): 31–41. *JSTOR*. Web. 2 Nov. 2007.

Poullain, François de La Barre. *De l'egalité des deux sexes, discourse physique et moral, où l'on voit l'importance de se défaire des préjugez*. Paris: Jean Dupuis, 1673. Print.

The Princess Bride. Dir. Rob Reiner. Act III Communications, 1987. Film.

Purinton, Marjean D. "Gender, Nationalism, and Science in Hannah More's Pedagogical Plays for Children." *Culturing the Child, 1690–1914: Essays in Memory of Mitzi Myers*. Ed. Donelle Ruwe. Lanham: Scarecrow, 2005. 113–36. Print.

———. *Romantic Ideology Unmasked: The Mentally Constructed Tyrannies in Dramas of William Wordsworth, Lord Byron, Percy Shelley, and Joanna Baillie*. Newark: U of Delaware P, 1994. Print.

Queen's Company. "Who We Are." *Queen's Company*. Queen's Company, n.d. Web. 30 Apr. 2007.

Quinsey, Katherine M., ed. *Broken Boundaries: Women and Feminism in Restoration Drama*. Lexington: UP of Kentucky, 1996. Print.

Rabb, Melinda A. Introduction. Canfield, *Broadview Anthology* 75.

Raby, Gyllian, adapt. *The Rover*. By Aphra Behn. Toronto: PUC, 1996. Print.

Ranger, Paul. *"Terror and Pity Reign in Every Breast": Gothic Drama, 1750–1820*. London: Soc. for Theatre Research, 1991. Print.

"Ranter." *Oxford English Dictionary Online*. Oxford UP, 2009. Web. 22 Feb. 2010.

Rauchway, Eric. "The Lessons of the History of State Universities: The State Game." *New Republic*. New Republic, 4 Oct. 2007. Web. 8 Oct. 2007.

Ravenscroft, Edward. *The London Cuckolds: A Comedy, as It Is Acted at the Theatre Royal*. London: Jos. Hindmarsh, 1688. Print.

Ready, Kathryn. "Damaris Cudworth Masham, Catharine Trotter Cockburn, and the Feminist Legacy of Locke's Theory of Personal Identity." *Eighteenth-Century Studies* 35.4 (2002): 563–76. Print.

———. "From the Stage to the Closet: Hannah More's Abandonment of Theater." *Eighteenth-Century Women: Studies in Their Lives, Work, and Culture* 4 (2006): 185–214. Print.

Rees, Emma. *Margaret Cavendish: Gender, Genre, Exile*. Manchester: Manchester UP, 2003. Print.

Remarques on the Humours and Conversations of the Town: Written in a Letter to Sir T. L. London: Allen Banks, 1673. Print.

Restoration Theatre. Ed. Rupert Spiers. U of St. Andrews, 2002. Web. 22 Nov. 2007.

Rev. of *Every One Has His Fault*, by Elizabeth Inchbald. *Morning Chronicle* 31 Jan. 1793. *Early English Newspapers: 1622–1820*. Woodbridge: Research, 1978. Microfilm.

Rev. of *Every One Has His Fault*, by Elizabeth Inchbald. *Morning Chronicle* 1 Feb. 1793. *Early English Newspapers: 1622–1820*. Woodbridge: Research, 1978. Microfilm.

Rev. of *Every One Has His Fault*, by Elizabeth Inchbald. *True Briton* 30 Jan. 1793. *Early English Newspapers: 1622–1820*. Woodbridge: Research, 1978. Microfilm.

Richardson, Alan. *British Romanticism and the Science of the Mind*. Cambridge: Cambridge UP, 2001. Print.

———. *A Mental Theater: Poetic Drama and Consciousness in the Romantic Age*. University Park: Penn State UP, 1988. Print.

———. "A Neural Theatre: Joanna Baillie's 'Plays on the Passions.'" Crochunis 130–45.

Richardson, Samuel. *Clarissa; or, The History of a Young Lady*. Ed. and introd. Angus Ross. Harmondsworth: Penguin, 1985. Print.

———. *Pamela; or, Virtue Rewarded*. Ed. Thomas Keymer and Alice Wakely. Oxford: Oxford UP, 2001. Print.

Riviere, Joan. "Womanliness as a Masquerade." *International Journal of Psychoanalysis* 10 (1929): n. pag. Rpt. in *Formations of Fantasy*. Ed. Victor Burgin, James Donald, and Cora Kaplan. London: Methuen, 1986. 35–44. Print.

Rizzo, Betty. "'Depressa Resurgam': Elizabeth Griffith's Playwriting Career." Schofield and Macheski 120–42.

———, ed. *Elizabeth Griffith*. Vol. 4 of Hughes, *Eighteenth-Century Women Playwrights*.

———. Introduction to *Double Mistake*. By Elizabeth Griffith. Rizzo, *Elizabeth Griffith* 66–69.

Roach, Joseph A. *Cities of the Dead: Circum-Atlantic Performance*. New York: Columbia UP, 1996. Print.

Robe, Jane. *The Fatal Legacy*. London: E. Symon, J. Roberts, and A. Dodd, 1723. Print.

———. *The Fatal Legacy.* London, 1723. *Eighteenth Century Collections Online.* U of Exeter Lib. Web. 1 Oct. 2007.

Roberts, David. *The Ladies: Female Patronage of Restoration Drama, 1660–1700.* Oxford: Clarendon, 1989. Print.

Roberts, William. *Memoirs of the Life and Correspondence of Mrs. Hannah More.* 4 vols. London: R. B. Seeley and W. Burnside, 1834. Print.

Robinson, Alan. *Imagining London, 1770–1900.* Houndmills: Palgrave, 2004. Print.

Robinson, Mary. *A Letter to the Women of England.* A Letter to the Women of England *and* The Natural Daughter. Ed. Sharon S. Setzer. Peterborough: Broadview, 2003. 39–88. Print.

———. "The Present State of the Manners, Society, &c. &c. of the Metropolis of England." *Monthly Magazine* Aug. 1800: 35–38; Sept. 1800: 138–40; Oct. 1800: 218–22; Nov. 1800: 305–06. Print.

Rogers, Katharine M. "Britain's First Woman Drama Critic: Elizabeth Inchbald." Schofield and Macheski 277–90.

———. *Feminism in Eighteenth-Century England.* Urbana: U of Illinois P, 1982. Print.

———. Introduction. Rogers, *Meridian Anthology* vii–xviii.

———, ed. *The Meridian Anthology of Restoration and Eighteenth-Century Plays by Women.* New York: Penguin, 1994. Print.

———. "Sensibility and Feminism: The Novels of Frances Brooke." *Genre* 11.1 (1978): 159–71. Print.

Romack, Katherine, and James Fitzmaurice, eds. *Cavendish and Shakespeare, Interconnections.* Aldershot: Ashgate, 2006. Print.

———. Introduction. Romack and Fitzmaurice, *Cavendish* 1–7.

Rosenthal, Laura J. *Infamous Commerce: Prostitution in Eighteenth-Century British Literature and Culture.* Ithaca: Cornell UP, 2006. Print.

———. *Playwrights and Plagiarists in Early Modern England: Gender, Authorship, Literary Property.* Ithaca: Cornell UP, 1996. Print.

Ross, Shannon. "*The Widdow Ranter*: Old World, New World: Exploring an Era's Authority Paradigm." O'Donnell, Dhuicq, and Leduc 81–90.

The Rover. By Aphra Behn. Dir. Jules Wright. Routledge–Open U, 1996. Videocassette.

Rowley, William. *All's Lost by Lust.* London: Thomas Harper, 1633. Print.

Rubik, Margarete. *Early Women Dramatists, 1550–1800.* Basingstoke: Macmillan; New York: St. Martin's, 1998. Print.

———. "Estranging the Familiar, Familiarizing the Strange: Self and Other in *Oroonoko* and *The Widdow Ranter.*" O'Donnell, Dhuicq, and Leduc 33–41.

Russell, Anne. Introduction. *The Rover; or, The Banished Cavaliers.* By Aphra Behn. 1677. Peterborough: Broadview, 1999. 9–42. Print.

Russell, Gillian. "Theatre." *Oxford Companion to the Romantic Age: British Culture, 1776–1832.* Ed. Iain McCalman. Oxford: Oxford UP, 1999. 223–31. Print.

———. *Women, Sociability, and Theatre in Georgian London.* Cambridge: Cambridge UP, 2007. Print.

Sabor, Peter, ed. *The Cambridge Companion to Frances Burney.* Cambridge: Cambridge UP, 2007. Print.

———, ed. *The Complete Plays of Frances Burney.* 2 vols. London: Pickering, 1995. Print.

Sabor, Peter, and Geoffrey Sill, eds. *Frances Burney:* The Witlings *and* The Woman-Hater. Peterborough: Broadview, 2002. Print.

———. Introduction. Sabor and Sills, *Frances Burney* 9–35.

Satrapi, Marjane. *Persepolis: The Story of a Childhood.* New York: Pantheon, 2003. Print.

Savage, Richard. *Authors of the Town.* London: J. Roberts, 1725. Print.

Schofield, Mary Anne. *Masking and Unmasking the Female Mind: Disguising Romances in Feminine Fiction, 1713–1799.* Newark: U of Delaware P, 1990. Print.

Schofield, Mary Anne, and Cecilia Macheski, eds. *Curtain Calls: British and American Women and the Theater, 1660–1820.* Athens: Ohio UP, 1991. Print.

The School for Scandal. Designed and prod. Hal Burton. Perf. Felix Aylmer and Joan Plowright. 1965. Video Images, 1983. Videocassette.

Scott-Douglass, Amy. "Enlarging Margaret: Cavendish, Shakespeare, and French Women Warriors and Writers." Romack and Fitzmaurice 147–78.

Scouten, A. H. *The London Stage, 1729–1747: A Critical Introduction.* Carbondale: Southern Illinois UP, 1968. Print.

Scouten, Arthur H., and Robert D. Hume. "'Restoration Comedy' and Its Audiences, 1660–1776." *The Rakish Stage: Studies in English Drama, 1660–1800.* Ed. Hume. Carbondale: Southern Illinois UP, 1983. 46–81. Print.

———. "'Restoration Comedy' and Its Audiences, 1660–1776." *Yearbook of English Studies* 10 (1980): 45–69. Print.

"*The Search after Happiness. A Pastoral Drama.* By Miss Hannah More." *Gentleman's Magazine* 44 (1774): 225. Print.

Senelick, Laurence. "Mollies or Men of Mode? Sodomy and the Eighteenth-Century London Stage." *Journal of the History of Sexuality* 1.1 (1990): 33–67. Print.

Settle, Elkanah. *The Empress of Morocco: A Tragedy.* London: William Cademan, 1673. Print.

Shadwell, Charles. *The Fair Quaker of Deal; or, The Humours of the Navy: A Comedy: As It Is Acted at the Theatre-Royal, in Drury-Lane.* London: J. and P. Knapton, 1737. Print.

Shadwell, Thomas. *The Libertine.* Fisk, *Four Restoration Libertine Plays* 1–84.

Shakespeare, William. *Hamlet.* Greenblatt et al. 1668–759.

———. *Henry V. The Riverside Shakespeare.* Ed. G. Blakemore Evans et al. 2nd ed. Boston: Houghton, 1997. 1: 930–75. Print.

———. *Macbeth.* Greenblatt et al. 2564–618.

———. *The Taming of the Shrew.* Greenblatt et al. 133–202.

Shakespeare in Love. Dir. John Madden. Universal, 1998. Film.

Shaver, Anne, ed. The Convent of Pleasure *and Other Plays.* By Margaret Cavendish. Baltimore: Johns Hopkins UP, 1999. Print.

———. Introduction. Shaver, Convent 1–17.

———. "Margaret Cavendish, Duchess of Newcastle." Woods and Hannay 195–203.

Shepard, Alexandra. *Meanings of Manhood in Early Modern England.* Oxford: Oxford UP, 2003. Print.

Sheridan, Frances. *The Discovery*. Hogan and Beasley, *Plays* 41–102.

———. *The Dupe*. Hogan and Beasley, *Plays* 105–57.

———. *The History of Nourjahad*. London: C. Cooke, [1798?]. Print.

———. *A Journey to Bath*. Hogan and Beasley, *Plays* 161–201.

———. *Memoirs of Miss Sidney Bidulph*. 1761. London: Harrison, 1786. Print.

Sheridan, Patricia. "Locke's Ethics and the British Moralists: The Lockean Legacy in Eighteenth Century Moral Philosophy." Diss. U of Toronto, 2001. Print.

———. "Reflection, Nature, and Moral Law: The Extent of Catharine Cockburn's Lockeanism in Her *Defence of Mr. Locke's Essay*." *Hypatia* 22.3 (2007): 134–51. Print.

Sheridan, R. B. *The Rivals, a Comedy: As It Is Acted at the Theatre-Royal in Covent-Garden*. London: John Wilkie, 1775. Print.

———. *The School for Scandal, a Comedy, as It Is Performed at the Theatre Royal Drury-Lane*. London: E. Powell, 1798. Print.

Sherman, Sandra. "'Does Your Ladyship Mean an Extempore?': Wit, Leisure, and the Mode of Production in Frances Burney's *The Witlings*." *Centennial Review* 40 (1996): 401–28. Print.

Shevelow, Kathryn. *Charlotte: Being a True Account of an Actress's Flamboyant Adventures*. New York: Henry Holt, 2005. Print.

Shield, William. Libretto. *Rosina: A Comic Opera, in Two Acts*. By Frances Brooke. London: T. Cadell, 1783. Print.

Shore, Robert. Rev. of *The Rover*, by Aphra Behn. Centurion Theatre Company. Courtyard Theatre, London. *Theatre Record* 12–15 Mar. 2005: 398. Print.

Sidney, Mary, trans. *The Tragedie of Antonie*. By Robert Garnier. London: William Ponsonby, 1595. Print.

Simons, Tad. "Sisters across the Centuries." *American Theatre* 11.7 (1994): 10–11. Print.

Slagle, Judith Bailey. *Joanna Baillie: A Literary Life*. Cranbury: Assoc. UP, 2002. Print.

Smallwood, Angela J. "Women and the Theatre." V. Jones, *Women and Literature* 238–62.

Smith, Adam. *The Theory of Moral Sentiments*. Ed. D. D. Raphael and A. L. Macfie. Indianapolis: Liberty Fund, 1984. Print.

Smith, John Harrington. "Shadwell, the Ladies, and the Change in Comedy." *Modern Philology* 46.1 (1948): 22–33. Print.

Smith, Nicholas D. "An Unidentified Translation by Hannah More in *The London Magazine* (1773)." *Notes and Queries* 51.4 (2004): 414–15. Print.

———. "Unpublished Poems by Hannah More in Osborn Shelves C. 341 and Folger MS M.A. 179." *Review of English Studies* ns 57 (2005): 581–606. Print.

Snook, Edith. *Women, Reading, and the Cultural Politics of Early Modern England*. Aldershot: Ashgate, 2005. Print.

Snyder, Henry Leonard, ed. *Marlborough-Godolphin Correspondence*. Oxford: Clarendon, 1975. Print.

Southern, Richard. *Changeable Scenery: Its Origin and Development in the British Theatre*. London: Faber, 1952. Print.

Southerne, Thomas. *The Fatal Marriage*. London, 1694. Print.

———. *Sir Anthony Love*. London: Joseph Fox and Abel Roper, 1691. Print.

Spacks, Patricia Meyer. "Oscillations of Sensibility." *New Literary History* 25.3 (1994): 505–20. Print.

Spedding, Patrick. *A Bibliography of Eliza Haywood.* London: Pickering, 2004. Print.

Spencer, Jane. *Behn's Afterlife.* Oxford: Oxford UP, 2000. Print.

———. Introduction. Spencer, Rover vii–xxii.

———, ed. The Rover *and Other Plays.* By Aphra Behn. Oxford: Oxford UP, 1995. Print. Oxford World's Classics.

Stage Beauty. Dir. Richard Eyre. Qwerty, 2004. Film.

Starke, Mariana. *The Widow of Malabar: A Tragedy, in Three Acts.* London: W. Lane, 1791. Print.

Stathas, Thalia. Introduction. *A Bold Stroke for a Wife.* By Susanna Centlivre. Lincoln: U of Nebraska P, 1968. xi–xxvi. Print.

Staves, Susan. "A Few Kind Words for the Fop." *Studies in English Literature* 22.3 (1982): 413–28. Print.

———. *A Literary History of Women's Writing in Britain, 1660–1789.* Cambridge: Cambridge UP, 2006. Print.

———. *Married Women's Separate Property in England, 1660–1833.* Cambridge: Harvard UP, 1990. Print.

Steele, Richard. *The Conscious Lovers: A Comedy.* London: J. Tonson, 1723. Print.

———. Revs. of *The Wonder*, by Susanna Centlivre. Centlivre, *Wonder* [O'Brien] 121.

Steeves, Edna L., ed. *The Plays of Mary Pix and Catharine Trotter.* Vol. 1. New York: Garland, 1982. Print.

"Stoop." Def. 6a. *Oxford English Dictionary Online.* Oxford UP, 2009. Web. 5 Feb. 2010.

Stott, Anne. *Hannah More: The First Victorian.* Oxford: Oxford UP, 2003. Print.

Straub, Kristina. *Sexual Suspects: Eighteenth-Century Players and Sexual Ideology.* Princeton: Princeton UP, 1992. Print.

Straznicky, Marta. "Restoration Women Playwrights and the Limits of Professionalism." *English Literary History* 64.3 (1997): 703–26. Print.

Styan, J. L. *Restoration Comedy in Performance.* Cambridge: Cambridge UP, 1986. Print.

Szilagyi, Stephen. "The Sexual Politics of Behn's *The Rover*: After Patriarchy." *Studies in Philology* 95.4 (1998): 435–55. Print.

Taylor, George. *The French Revolution and the London Stage, 1789–1805.* Cambridge: Cambridge UP, 2000. Print.

Thaddeus, Janice Farrar. *Frances Burney: A Literary Life.* Houndmills: Macmillan, 2000. Print.

Thelma and Louise. Dir. Ridley Scott. Writ. Callie Khouri. Metro-Goldwyn-Mayer, 1991. MGM Home Entertainment LLC, 2004. DVD.

Thomas, Susie. "'This Thing of Darkness I Acknowledge Mine': Aphra Behn's *Abdelazer; or, The Moor's Revenge.*" *Restoration* 22.1 (1998): 18–39. Print.

Thomson, James. *The Seasons.* London: J. Murray, 1794. Print.

Todd, Janet, ed. *Aphra Behn Studies.* Cambridge: Cambridge UP, 1996. Print.

———. *The Secret Life of Aphra Behn.* London: Deutsch, 1996. Print.

———. "A Spectacular Death: History and Story in *The Widow Ranter.*" *Aphra Behn: New Casebooks.* Ed. Todd. New York: St. Martin's, 1999. 73–84. Print.

———, ed. *The Works of Aphra Behn.* 7 vols. London: Pickering; Columbus: Ohio State UP, 1992–96. Print.

Tollet, Elizabeth. *Susanna. Poems on Several Occasions.* London: J. Clarke, 1775. Print.

Tomlinson, Sophie B. "'My Brain the Stage': Margaret Cavendish and the Fantasy of Female Performance." *Readings in Renaissance Women's Drama: Criticism, History, and Performance, 1594–1998.* Ed. S. P. Cerasano and Marion Wynne-Davies. New York: Routledge, 1998. 272–92. Print.

Trotter, Catharine (*see also* Cockburn, Catharine Trotter). *Agnes de Castro.* London, 1696. *Early English Books Online.* U of Exeter Lib. Web. 1 Oct. 2007.

———. *Agnes de Castro.* 1696. *Catharine Trotter's* The Adventures of a Young Lady *and Other Works.* Ed. Anne Kelley. Burlington: Ashgate, 2006. 153–207. Print.

———. *Fatal Friendship.* London: n.p., 1698. Print.

———. Letter to Thomas Burnet. 7 July 1705. Birch, *Works* 2: 187.

———. *Love at a Loss; or, Most Votes Carry It.* 1701. Ed. Roxanne Kent-Drury. Canfield, *Broadview Anthology* 857–902.

———. *Olinda's Adventures; or, The Amours of a Young Lady.* 1718. Los Angeles: Augustan Rpt. Soc. 138, 1969. Print.

———. *The Revolution of Sweden.* 1706. Kelley, *Mary Pix* 193–276.

———. *The Unhappy Penitent.* London: n.p., 1701. Print.

A True Narrative of the Late Rebellion in Virginia, by the Royal Commissioners, 1677. Narratives of the Insurrections, 1675–1690. Ed. Charles Andrews. New York: Scribner, 1915. 105–41. Print.

Trumbach, Randolph. "London's Sapphists: From Three Sexes to Four Genders in the Making of Modern Culture." *Body Guards: The Cultural Politics of Gender Ambiguity.* Ed. Julia Epstein and Kristina Straub. New York: Routledge, 1991. 112–41. Print.

———. "Sex, Gender, and Sexual Identity in Modern Culture: Male Sodomy and Female Prostitution in Enlightenment London." *Journal of the History of Sexuality* 2.2 (1991): 186–203. Print.

Turner, Cheryl. *Living by the Pen: Women Writers in the Eighteenth Century.* New York: Routledge, 1992. Print.

Turner, James Grantham. *Libertines and Radicals in Early Modern London: Sexuality, Politics, and Literary Culture, 1630–1685.* Cambridge: Cambridge UP, 2002. Print.

Ty, Eleanor. *Unsex'd Revolutionaries: Five Women Novelists of the 1790s.* Toronto: U of Toronto P, 1993. Print.

Uphaus, Robert W., and Gretchen M. Foster, eds. *The Other Eighteenth Century: English Women of Letters, 1660–1800.* East Lansing: Colleagues, 1991. Print.

Vanbrugh, John. *The Provok'd Wife: A Comedy, as It Is Acted at the New Theatre, in Little Lincolns-Inn-Fields.* London: R. Wellington, 1697. Print.

Van Lennep, William, et al. eds. *The London Stage, 1660–1800: Part 1, 1660–1700.* Carbondale: Southern Illinois UP, 1961. Print.

Vaughan, Virginia Mason. *Performing Blackness on English Stages, 1500–1800.* Cambridge: Cambridge UP, 2005. Print.

Vicinus, Martha. "'They Wonder to Which Sex I Belong': The Historical Roots of the Modern Lesbian Identity." *Homosexuality, Which Homosexuality? Proceedings, International Conference on Gay and Lesbian Studies.* London: GMP, 1989. 171–98. Print.

Visconsi, Elliott. "A Degenerate Race: English Barbarism in Aphra Behn's *Oroonoko* and *The Widow Ranter.*" *English Literary History* 69.3 (2002): 673–701. Print.

Vitkus, Daniel. *Turning Turk: English Theater and the Multicultural Mediterranean, 1570–1630.* London: Palgrave, 2003. Print.

Vogel, Paula. *How I Learned to Drive. The Mammary Plays.* New York: Theatre Communications, 1998. 1–92. Print.

Wahrman, Dror. *The Making of the Modern Self: Identity and Culture in Eighteenth-Century England.* New Haven: Yale UP, 2004. Print.

Waithe, Mary Ellen. "Catharine Trotter Cockburn." *A History of Women Philosophers.* Vol. 3. Ed. Waithe. Dordrecht: Kluwer Acad., 1991. 101–25. Print.

Wall, Cynthia. "A Geography of Georgian Narrative Space." *Georgian Geographies: Essays on Space, Place and Landscape in the Eighteenth Century.* Ed. Miles Ogborn and Charles W. J. Withers. Manchester: Manchester UP, 2004. 114–29. Print.

Wallace, Tara Ghoshal. "Burney as Dramatist." Sabor, *Cambridge Companion* 55–73.

Ward, A. W. *A History of English Dramatic Literature to the Death of Queen Anne.* Vol. 3. London: Macmillan, 1899. Print. 3 vols.

Ward, Edward. *The Coffeehouse Mob.* Frontispiece to pt. 4. *Vulgus Britannicus; or, The British Hudibras.* London: Sam Briscoe, 1710. Print.

———. *The Libertines Choice; or, The Mistaken Happiness of the Fool in Fashion.* London: H. Hills, 1709. Print.

Warren, Victoria. "Gender and Genre in Susanna Centlivre's *The Gamester* and *The Basset Table.*" *Studies in English Literature* 43.3 (2003): 605–24. Print.

Waters, Mary. *British Women Writers and the Profession of Literary Criticism, 1789–1832.* New York: Palgrave, 2004. Print.

Watkins, Daniel. *A Materialist Critique of Romantic Drama.* Gainesville: U of Florida P, 1993. Print.

Webster, Jeremy W. *Performing Libertinism in Charles II's Court: Politics, Drama, Sexuality.* New York: Palgrave, 2005. Print.

Weiner, Dora B. "Mind and Body in the Clinic: Philippe Pinel, Alexander Crichton, Dominique Esquirol, and the Birth of Psychiatry." *The Language of Psyche: Mind and Body in Enlightenment Thought.* Ed. G. S. Rousseau. Berkeley: U of California P, 1990. 331–401. Print. Clark Library Lectures 1985–86.

West, Shearer. "Siddons, Celebrity and Regality: Portraiture and the Body of the Aging Actress." *Theatre and Celebrity in Britain, 1660–2000.* Ed. Mary Luckhurst and Jane Moody. New York: Palgrave, 2005. 191–214. Print.

When Harry Met Sally. Dir. Rob Reiner. Castle Rock Entertainment, 1989. Film.

Whitaker, Katie. *Mad Madge: Margaret Cavendish, Duchess of Newcastle, Royalist, Writer, and Romantic.* London: Chatto, 2002. Print.

The Whore's Rhetorick. London, 1683. Print.

Whyte, Samuel. *Miscellanea Nova*. 1800. New York: Garland, 1974. Print.

Widmayer, Anne F. "The Politics of Adapting Behn's *Oroonoko*." *Comparative Drama* 37.2 (2003): 189–223. Print.

Wiley, Autrey Nell. *Rare Prologues and Epilogues, 1642–1700*. London: Allen, 1940. Print.

Williams, Gary Jay, ed. *Theatre Histories: An Introduction*. 2nd ed. New York: Routledge, 2010. Print.

Williams, Gordon. *Dictionary of Sexual Language and Imagery in Shakespearean and Stuart Literature*. London: Athlone, 1994. Print.

Wilmot, John. *The Complete Poems of John Wilmot, Earl of Rochester*. Ed. and introd. David M. Veith. New Haven: Yale UP, 1968. Print.

Wolcot, John. *The Works of Peter Pindar, Esq.* 5 vols. London: J. Walker, 1794–1801. Print.

Wollstonecraft, Mary. "To William Godwin." 2 Aug. 1796. Letter 224 of *The Collected Letters of Mary Wollstonecraft*. Ed. Janet Todd. New York: Columbia UP, 2003. 345. Print.

Womersley, David. Introduction. *The Busie Body*. Womersley, *Restoration Drama* 778.

———, ed. *Restoration Drama: An Anthology*. Malden: Blackwell, 2000. Print.

Woods, Susanne, and Margaret P. Hannay, eds. *Teaching Tudor and Stuart Women Writers*. New York: MLA, 2000. Print.

Woodward, Josiah. *Account of the Societies for Reformation of Manners, in England and Ireland*. London: J. Downing, 1701. Print.

Woolf, Virginia. *A Room of One's Own*. 1929. New York: Harcourt, 1957. Print.

Worrall, David. *Theatric Revolution: Drama, Censorship, and Romantic Period Subcultures, 1773–1832*. Oxford: Oxford UP, 2006. Print.

Wray, Ramona. *Women Writers of the Seventeenth Century*. Tavistock: Northcote, 2004. Print.

Wycherley, William. *The Country Wife*. Ed. Thomas H. Fujimura. Lincoln: U of Nebraska P, 1965. Print.

———. *The Country Wife*. Womersley, *Restoration Drama* 173–222.

———. *The Plain Dealer*. Ed. Leo Hughes. London: Arnold, 1968. Print.

Wyett, Jodi. "Of Innocence and Experience: Fame, Fortune, and Women's Intellectual Labor in Frances Brooke's *The Excursion*." *The Eighteenth-Century Novel*. Ed. Albert J. Rivero and George Justice. Vol. 3. New York: AMS, 2003. 129–56. Print.

Ziegler, Georgianna. "Lost in the Archives? Searching for Records of Early Modern Women." Woods and Hannay 315–47.

Zozaya, Pilar. "Representing Women in Restoration England: A Reassessment of Aphra Behn's *The Rover*." Luis-Martínez and Figueroa-Dorrengo 99–122.

Index

Modern Language Association of America
Options for Teaching

Teaching British Women Playwrights of the Restoration and Eighteenth Century. Ed. Bonnie Nelson and Catherine Burroughs. 2010.

Teaching Narrative Theory. Ed. David Herman, Brian McHale, and James Phelan. 2010.

Teaching Early Modern English Prose. Ed. Susannah Brietz Monta and Margaret W. Ferguson. 2010.

Teaching Italian American Literature, Film, and Popular Culture. Ed. Edvige Giunta and Kathleen Zamboni McCormick. 2010.

Teaching the Graphic Novel. Ed. Stephen E. Tabachnick. 2009.

Teaching Literature and Language Online. Ed. Ian Lancashire. 2009.

Teaching the African Novel. Ed. Gaurav Desai. 2009.

Teaching World Literature. Ed. David Damrosch. 2009.

Teaching North American Environmental Literature. Ed. Laird Christensen, Mark C. Long, and Fred Waage. 2008.

Teaching Life Writing Texts. Ed. Miriam Fuchs and Craig Howes. 2007.

Teaching Nineteenth-Century American Poetry. Ed. Paula Bernat Bennett, Karen L. Kilcup, and Philipp Schweighauser. 2007.

Teaching Representations of the Spanish Civil War. Ed. Noël Valis. 2006.

Teaching the Representation of the Holocaust. Ed. Marianne Hirsch and Irene Kacandes. 2004.

Teaching Tudor and Stuart Women Writers. Ed. Susanne Woods and Margaret P. Hannay. 2000.

Teaching Literature and Medicine. Ed. Anne Hunsaker Hawkins and Marilyn Chandler McEntyre. 1999.

Teaching the Literatures of Early America. Ed. Carla Mulford. 1999.

Teaching Shakespeare through Performance. Ed. Milla C. Riggio. 1999.

Teaching Oral Traditions. Ed. John Miles Foley. 1998.

Teaching Contemporary Theory to Undergraduates. Ed. Dianne F. Sadoff and William E. Cain. 1994.

Teaching Children's Literature: Issues, Pedagogy, Resources. Ed. Glenn Edward Sadler. 1992.

Teaching Literature and Other Arts. Ed. Jean-Pierre Barricelli, Joseph Gibaldi, and Estella Lauter. 1990.

New Methods in College Writing Programs: Theories in Practice. Ed. Paul Connolly and Teresa Vilardi. 1986.

School-College Collaborative Programs in English. Ed. Ron Fortune. 1986.

Teaching Environmental Literature: Materials, Methods, Resources. Ed. Frederick O. Waage. 1985.

Part-Time Academic Employment in the Humanities: A Sourcebook for Just Policy. Ed. Elizabeth M. Wallace. 1984.

Film Study in the Undergraduate Curriculum. Ed. Barry K. Grant. 1983.

The Teaching Apprentice Program in Language and Literature. Ed. Joseph Gibaldi and James V. Mirollo. 1981.

Options for Undergraduate Foreign Language Programs: Four-Year and Two-Year Colleges. Ed. Renate A. Schulz. 1979.

Options for the Teaching of English: Freshman Composition. Ed. Jasper P. Neel. 1978.

Options for the Teaching of English: The Undergraduate Curriculum. Ed. Elizabeth Wooten Cowan. 1975.